ASCENT

CENTER FOR TECHNICAL KNOWLEDGE

Autodesk® Revit® 2025 Fundamentals for MEP

Part 2

Learning Guide

Imperial Units - Edition 1.0

ASCENT - Center for Technical Knowledge®
Autodesk® Revit® 2025
Fundamentals for MEP - Part 2
Imperial Units - Edition 1.0

Prepared and produced by:

ASCENT Center for Technical Knowledge
630 Peter Jefferson Parkway, Suite 175
Charlottesville, VA 22911

866-527-2368
www.ASCENTed.com

Lead Contributor: Cherisse Biddulph

ASCENT - Center for Technical Knowledge (a division of Rand Worldwide Inc.) is a leading developer of professional learning materials and knowledge products for engineering software applications. ASCENT specializes in designing targeted content that facilitates application-based learning with hands-on software experience. For over 25 years, ASCENT has helped users become more productive through tailored custom learning solutions.

We welcome any comments you may have regarding this guide, or any of our products. To contact us please email: feedback@ASCENTed.com.

Contents

Construction Documentation

Chapter 14: Working with Annotations   14-1

Preface

To take full advantage of Building Information Modeling, the *Autodesk® Revit® 2025: Fundamentals for MEP* guide (Part 1 and Part 2) has been designed to teach the concepts and principles of creating 3D parametric models of MEP systems from engineering design through construction documentation.

This guide is intended to introduce you to the user interface and the basic HVAC, electrical, and piping/plumbing components that make Autodesk Revit a powerful and flexible engineering modeling tool. The guide will also familiarize users with the tools required to create, document, and print the parametric model. The examples and practices are designed to take users through the basics of a full MEP project from linking in an architectural model to construction documents.

Topics Covered in Chapters 1 to 7 (Part 1)

- Introduction to the Autodesk Revit software, including navigating the Revit interface.
- Starting an MEP project based on a linked architectural model and creating levels and grids as datum elements for the model.
- Understanding the project browser and working with views.
- Understanding Revit families and components.
- Working with the basic sketching and modifying tools.
- Copying and monitoring elements and coordinating linked models.
- Creating spaces so that you can analyze heating and cooling loads.

Topics Covered in Chapters 8 to 16 (Part 2)

- Connecting and testing basic systems.
- Creating pipe systems with plumbing fixtures and pipes.
- Creating duct systems with air terminals, mechanical equipment, and ducts.
- Creating advanced HVAC and plumbing systems with automatic duct and piping layouts.
- Creating electrical circuits with electrical equipment, devices, and light fixtures and adding cable trays and conduits.
- Setting up sheets, and placing and modifying views on sheets.
- Working with dimensions, text, annotations, and legends.

- Adding tags and working with schedules.

- Setting up detail views and adding detail components.

Prerequisites

- Access to the 2025.0 version of the software, to ensure compatibility with this guide. Future software updates that are released by Autodesk may include changes that are not reflected in this guide. The practices and files included with this guide might not be compatible with prior versions (e.g., 2024).

- This guide introduces the fundamental skills you need to learn the Autodesk Revit MEP software. It is highly recommended that users have experience and knowledge in MEP engineering and its terminology.

- It is recommended that users have a standard three-button mouse to successfully complete the practices in this guide.

Note on Learning Guide Content

ASCENT's learning guides are intended to teach the technical aspects of using the software and do not focus on professional design principles and standards. The practices aim to demonstrate the capabilities and flexibility of the software rather than following specific design codes or standards.

Note on Software Setup

This guide assumes a standard installation of the software using the default preferences during installation. This includes the Revit templates and Revit Content (Families) that can be found on the Autodesk website at https://knowledge.autodesk.com/ by searching *How to download Revit Content*. Lectures and practices use the standard software templates and default options.

Lead Contributor: Cherisse Biddulph

Cherisse is an Autodesk Certified Professional for Revit as well as an Autodesk Certified Instructor. She brings over 19 years of industry, teaching, and technical support experience to her role as a Learning Content Developer with ASCENT. With a passion for design and architecture, she has worked in the industry assisting firms with their Building Information Modeling (BIM) management and software implementation needs as they modernize to a BIM design environment. Although her main devotion is the Revit design product, she is also proficient in AutoCAD, Autodesk BIM 360, and Autodesk Navisworks. Today, Cherisse continues to expand her knowledge in the ever-evolving AEC industry and the software used to support it.

Cherisse Biddulph has been the Lead Contributor for *Autodesk Revit: Fundamentals for MEP* since 2020.

In This Guide

The following highlights the key features of this guide.

Feature	Description
Practice Files	The Practice Files page includes a link to the practice files and instructions on how to download and install them. The practice files are required to complete the practices in this guide.
Chapters	A chapter consists of the following: Learning Objectives, Instructional Content, Practices, Chapter Review Questions, and Command Summary.
	• **Learning Objectives** define the skills you can acquire by learning the content provided in the chapter.
	• **Instructional Content**, which begins right after Learning Objectives, refers to the descriptive and procedural information related to various topics. Each main topic introduces a product feature, discusses various aspects of that feature, and provides step-by-step procedures on how to use that feature. Where relevant, examples, figures, helpful hints, and notes are provided.
	• **Practice** for a topic follows the instructional content. Practices enable you to use the software to perform a hands-on review of a topic. It is required that you download the practice files (using the link found on the Practice Files page) prior to starting the first practice.
	• **Chapter Review Questions**, located close to the end of a chapter, enable you to test your knowledge of the key concepts discussed in the chapter.
	• **Command Summary** concludes a chapter. It contains a list of the software commands that are used throughout the chapter and provides information on where the command can be found in the software.
Appendices	Appendices provide additional information to the main course content. It could be in the form of instructional content, practices, tables, projects, or skills assessment.

Practice Files

To download the practice files for this guide, use the following steps:

1. Type the URL *exactly as shown below* into the address bar of your Internet browser to access the Course File Download page.

   Note: If you are using the ebook, you do not have to type the URL. Instead, you can access the page simply by clicking the URL below.

   ## https://www.ascented.com/getfile/id/dioecusPF

   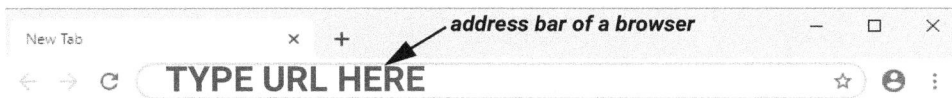

2. On the Course File Download page, click the **DOWNLOAD NOW** button, as shown below, to download the .ZIP file that contains the practice files.

3. Once the download is complete, unzip the file and extract its contents.

   The recommended practice files folder location is:
   C:\Revit 2025 Fundamentals for MEP Practice Files

   Note: It is recommended that you do not change the location of the practice files folder. Doing so may cause errors when completing the practices.

   Stay Informed!

   To receive information about upcoming events, promotional offers, and complimentary webcasts, visit:

   www.ASCENTed.com/updates

Basic Systems Tools

Systems can be created by connecting elements such as air terminals, plumbing fixtures, and light fixtures using ducts, pipes, and panels. You can then use the System Browser to review the systems.

Learning Objectives

- Connect components using ducts, pipes, cable trays, and conduits.
- Create MEP systems.
- Review MEP systems in the System Browser.

8.1 Connecting Components

The process of creating MEP systems in Autodesk Revit is simple. All you need to do is insert components such as air terminals, plumbing fixtures, or light fixtures and then connect them using ducts (as shown in Figure 8–1), pipes, cable trays, and conduits. For electrical systems, wiring can also be generated, but these elements are only symbolic and annotative.

Note: In-depth steps for creating these connections are covered later in this guide.

Figure 8–1

* When you draw the connecting elements, the Autodesk® Revit® software calculates the height and size of the opening and applies the appropriate fittings.

There are several ways of drawing connections between components:

* Select a component and click on the connector icon, shown in Figure 8–2.

* Select a component and right-click on a connector to select one of the options, as shown for a plumbing fixture in Figure 8–2.

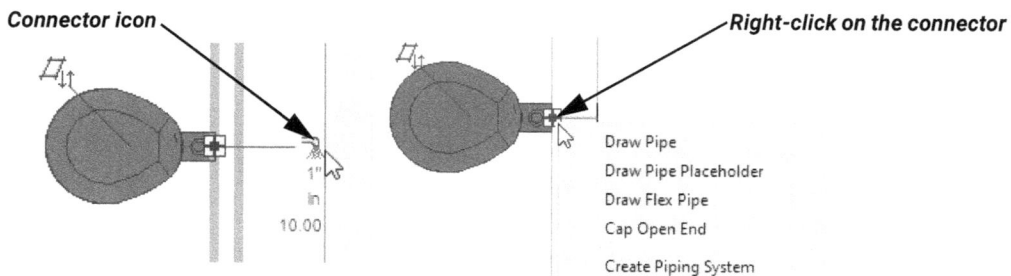

Figure 8–2

* You can also type in the associated shortcut key that displays when you hover over the tool in the ribbon, as shown in Figure 8–3.

Note: Cable trays and conduits are typically placed separately from the components.

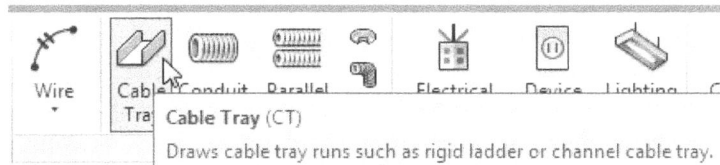

Figure 8–3

- Start the commands from the *Systems* tab>HVAC, Plumbing & Piping, and Electrical panels. Primary tools include:

 HVAC: Duct (**DT**) and Flex Duct (**FD**)

 Plumbing, Hydronic Piping, and Fire Suppression: Pipe (**PI**) and Flex Pipe (**FP**)

 Electrical: Wire (**EW**), Cable Tray (**CT**), and Conduit (**CN**)

Drawing Vertically

> **Note:** *You can draw ducts and pipes vertically.*

When in plan view, in order to draw segments vertically, you can use **Middle Elevation** from the Options Bar. For the example shown in Figure 8–4, the pipe from the lavatory is drawn to the middle of the wall. Then, from the Options Bar, **Middle Elevation** is set to **9'-0"**, which draws the pipe **9'-0"** up, then the pipe is continued down the wall.

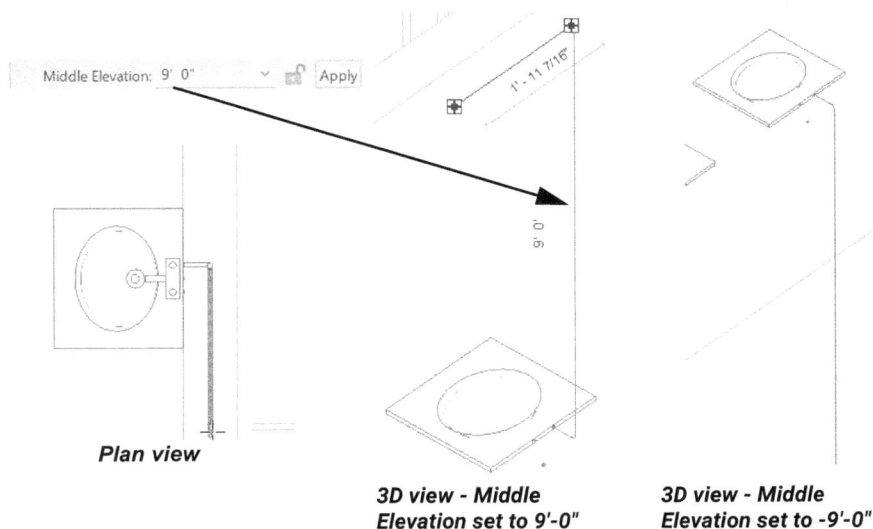

Plan view

*3D view - Middle
Elevation set to 9'-0"*

*3D view - Middle
Elevation set to -9'-0"*

Figure 8–4

How To: Connect Components

1. Select a component and click on the connector icon.

2. In the Type Selector, select the type, as shown in Figure 8–5. For example, you would select a pipe that matches the kind of system you are creating.

Figure 8–5

3. In the contextual tab, Options Bar, and Properties, specify the required options, as shown in Figure 8–6. The options that are available depend on the type of elements you are using.

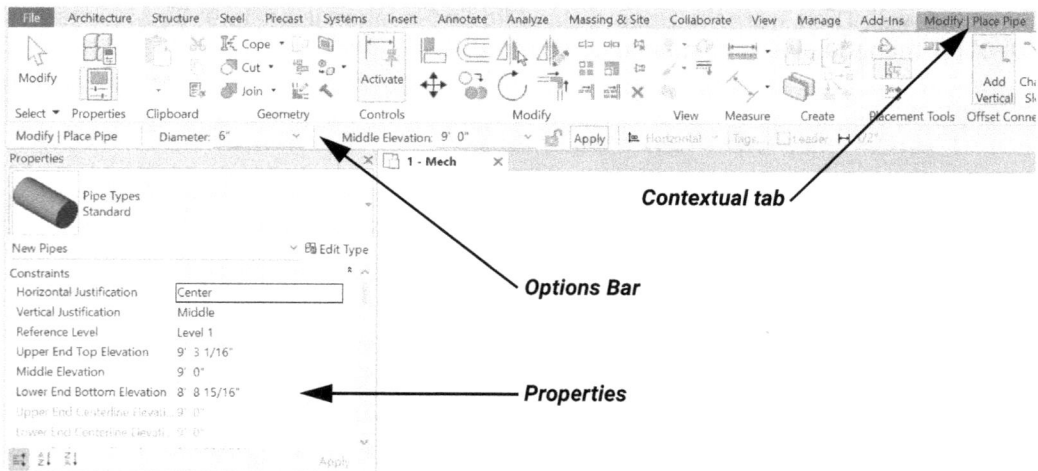

Figure 8–6

4. Draw the objects using temporary dimensions and snaps, as shown in Figure 8–7. Ensure that you are selecting the correct connector or related element. Fittings are automatically applied.

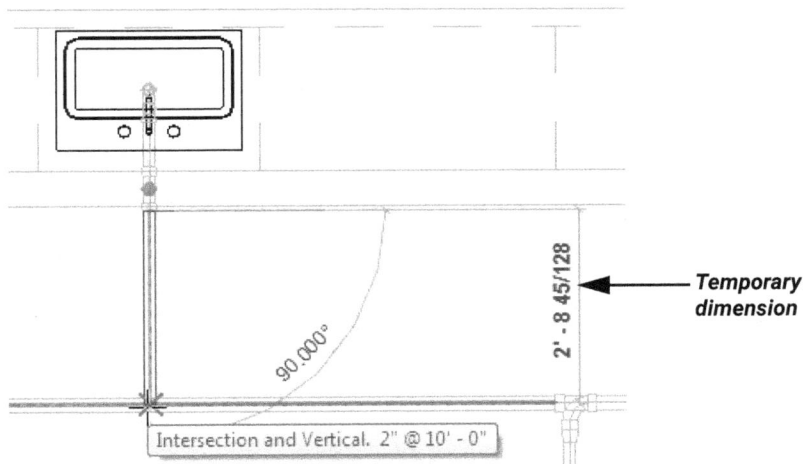

Figure 8–7

💡 Hint: Placeholders

Placeholders can be used in the early stage of design to give approximate locations of duct or pipe layouts. These are represented as single-line layouts without fittings. Later in the design phase, you can convert the placeholders to two-line duct or pipe layouts with fittings.

- To place placeholders, from the *System* tab>*HVAC* panel, click ⬚ (Duct Placeholder) or from the *System* tab>*Plumbing & Piping* panel, click ⬚ (Pipe Placeholder).
  - Specify a type and size for the duct or pipe, then specify other settings as needed.
- To convert a placeholder, select the pipe or duct system, and from the *Modify | Pipe Placeholders* or *Modify | Duct Placeholders* tabs, select ⬚ (Convert Placeholder).
  - Once converted, you cannot return a system back to a placeholder.

Connecting Into

A quick way to generate connections is to use the **Connect Into** tool. To use this tool, you must already have some duct, pipe, conduit, or cable trays in the project, as well as have the components you need to connect. When you select a component, the **Connect Into** option is available in the contextual tab.

- Check your project in a 3D view to ensure that the path is acceptable.

How To: Connect a Component to Existing Connectors

1. Select the component that you want to connect to an existing connector.

2. In the *Modify* contextual tab>*Layout* panel, click ⊩⧉ (Connect Into).

3. If the fixture has more than one connector, in the *Select Connector* dialog box, click on the system type (as shown in Figure 8–8) and click **OK**.

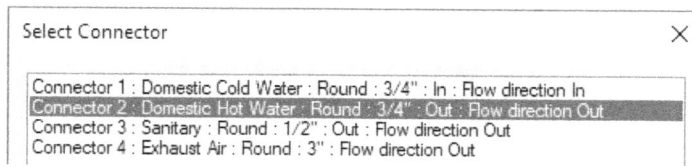

Figure 8–8

4. Select the connector, such as the pipe shown in Figure 8–9.

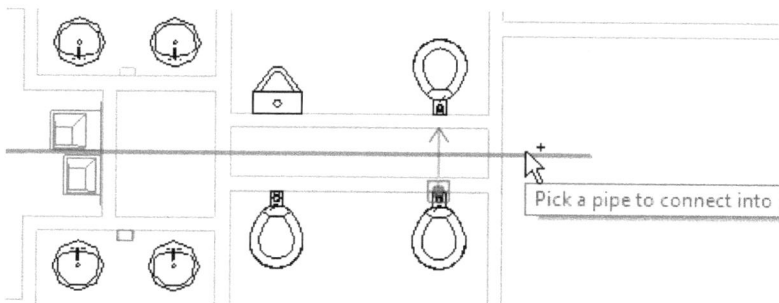

Figure 8–9

- This process automatically connects the component into a system.

- If you select a connector that cannot work with the component, an error is displayed, as shown in Figure 8–10. Click **Cancel** and then try a different connector, or add the connectors separately.

  - This error most often occurs because the offset between two elements is too close for the software to create the connection based on the default fittings.

  - Another cause of this error is that the connector is the wrong system type. The *System Type* can be changed in the Properties of the element, as required.

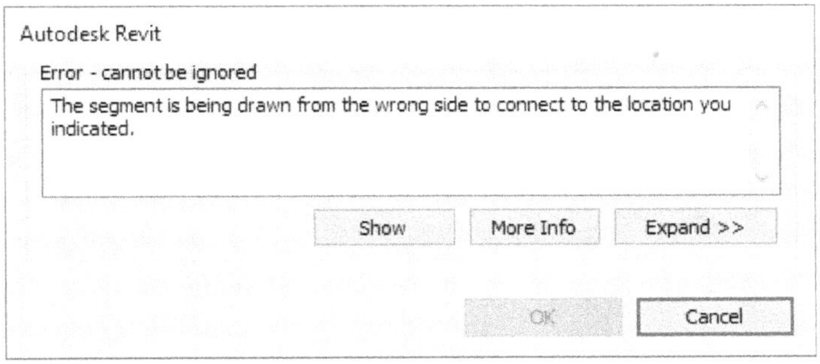

Figure 8–10

Modifying Fittings

Fittings are added automatically when connectors touch each other, turn, or change size. Fittings can be modified using the Type Selector, Properties, Options Bar, or a variety of connectors and controls. For example, when using ducts, an elbow can be changed to a tee connection by clicking a control, as shown in Figure 8–11. You can then add another duct to the newly-opened connector.

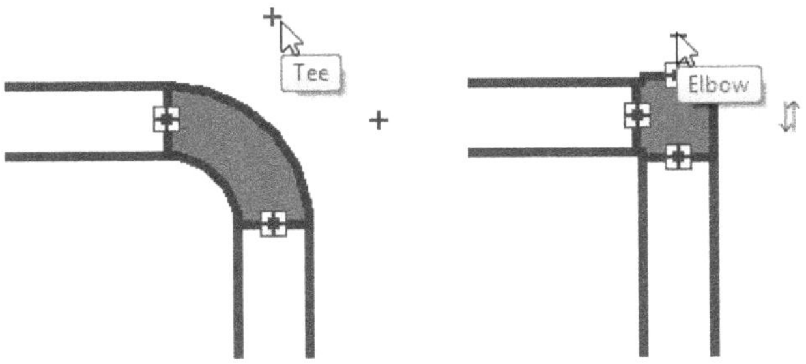

Figure 8–11

Testing Connections

A quick way to test the continuity of connectors is to hover the cursor over a linear connection and press <Tab> until the entire system is highlighted. For example, one of the ducts shown in Figure 8–12 is not highlighted because it is not attached to the fitting.

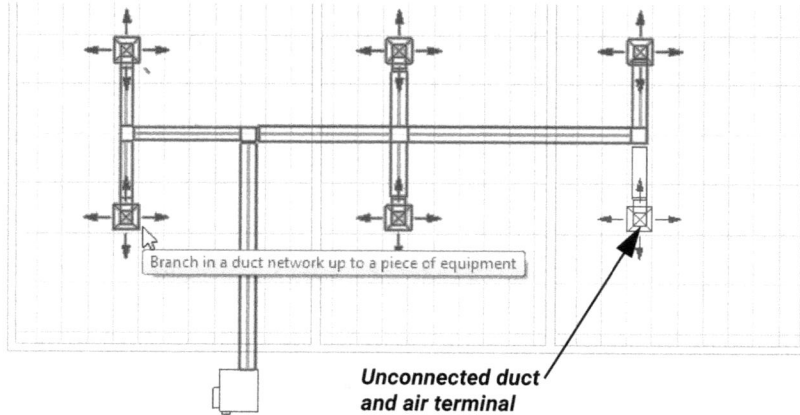

Branch in a duct network up to a piece of equipment

Unconnected duct and air terminal

Figure 8–12

Alternatively, you can also display the disconnects using the **Show Disconnects** tool.

How To: Show Disconnects

1. In the *Analyze* tab>*Check Systems* panel, click ⚠ (Show Disconnects).

2. In the *Show Disconnects Options* dialog box, select the types of systems you want to display (as shown in Figure 8–13) and click **OK.**

Figure 8–13

3. Any disconnects display ⚠ (Warning), as shown in Figure 8–14.

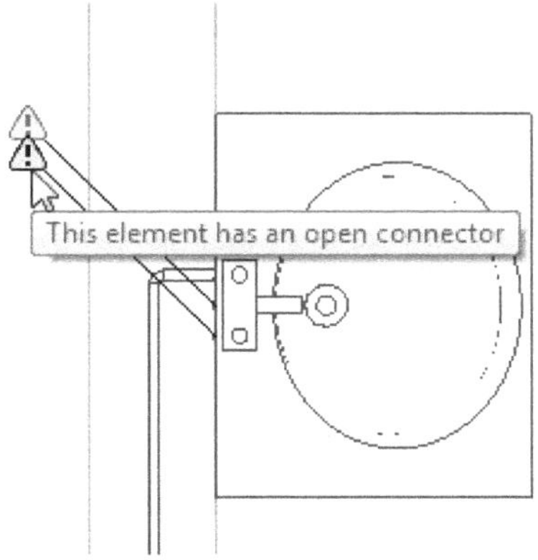

Figure 8–14

- The disconnects continue to display until you either correct the situation or run **Show Disconnects** again and clear all of the selections.
- Hover the cursor over the warning icon to display a tooltip with the warning. You can also click on the icon to open the warning dialog box.

Practice 8a
Connect Components – Mechanical

Practice Objectives

- Draw a duct.
- Connect fixtures to the duct.

In this practice, you will create a duct using controls and commands. You will also use the **Connect Into** command to connect air terminals.

1. In the practice files *Working Models>Mechanical* folder, open **Mech-Connect.rvt**.

2. Open the Mechanical>HVAC>Floor Plans>**1 - Mech** view and the 3D Views>**3D - Mech** view. Close the SP - Starting Page.

3. Activate the **1 - Mech** view and tile the two views by typing **WT**. Type **ZA** or **ZF** to zoom both views.

4. In the Quick Access Toolbar, verify ▧ (Thin Lines) is on.

5. In the **Mech/Elec 106** room, select the air handling unit (AHU). Note that it has connectors for electrical and pipes, and in and out connectors for ducts, as shown in Figure 8–15.

6. Select the return air (In) **Create Duct** icon to create the duct.

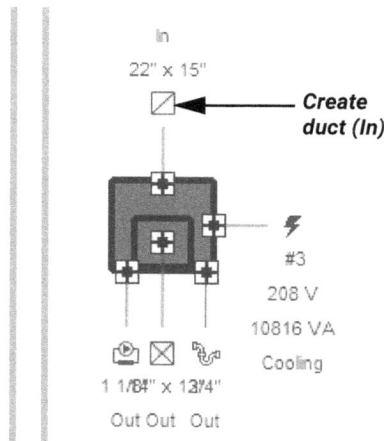

Figure 8–15

7. Move the cursor towards the hall away from the AHU and note that the duct is connected to the cursor. Using the temporary dimensions, type **2** and press <Enter>.

8. You now need to draw the duct up in the vertical direction. In the Options Bar, set the *Middle Elevation* to **10'-0"** and press <Enter>, then click **Apply**. This draws the duct in the vertical direction. Move the cursor into the view to complete the action. The vertical duct now displays in the 3D view, as shown in Figure 8−16.

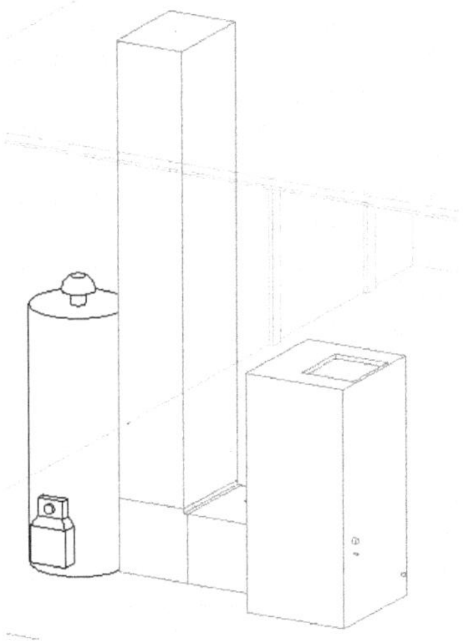

Figure 8−16

9. You are still in the **Duct** command. Hover your cursor over the duct you just created. When the connect icon displays, as shown in Figure 8−17, click to continue drawing the duct.

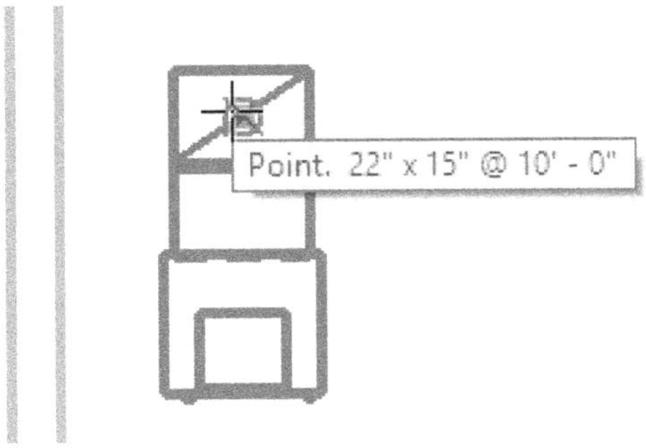

Figure 8−17

10. Click a point straight up into the hall approximately in the middle of the hall, then down the hall to the right past **Lab 104**'s door, as shown in Figure 8−18.

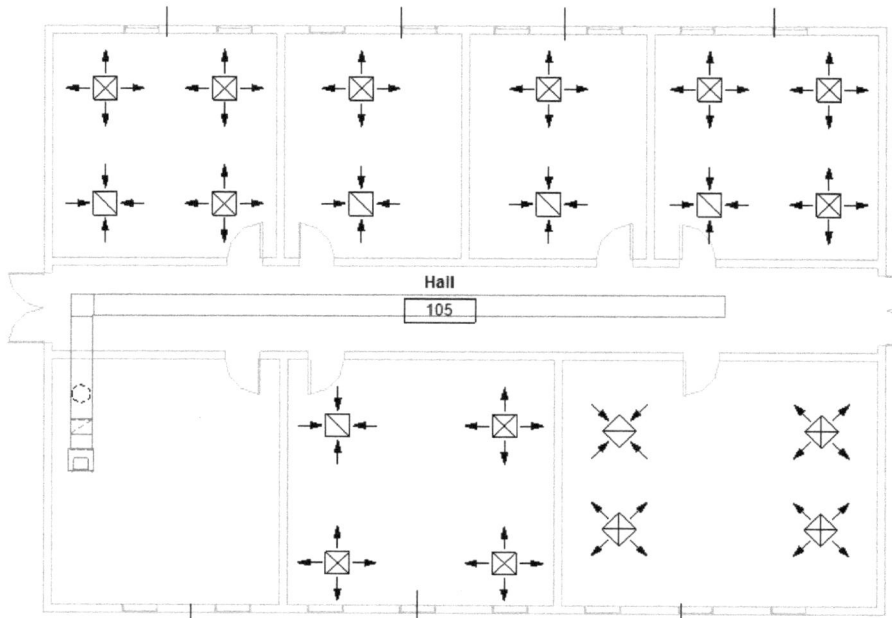

Figure 8−18

11. Click ⬚ (Modify).

12. In **Lab 107**, select the return diffuser.

13. In the *Modify | Air Terminals* tab>*Layout* panel, click ⬚ (Connect Into) and select the duct running down the hall. Your model should look similar to that shown in Figure 8−19.

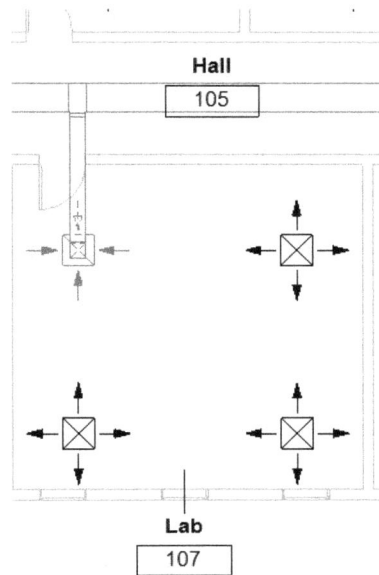

Figure 8–19

14. Repeat the process with the other Return diffusers except for in **Office 108**, as shown in Figure 8–20.

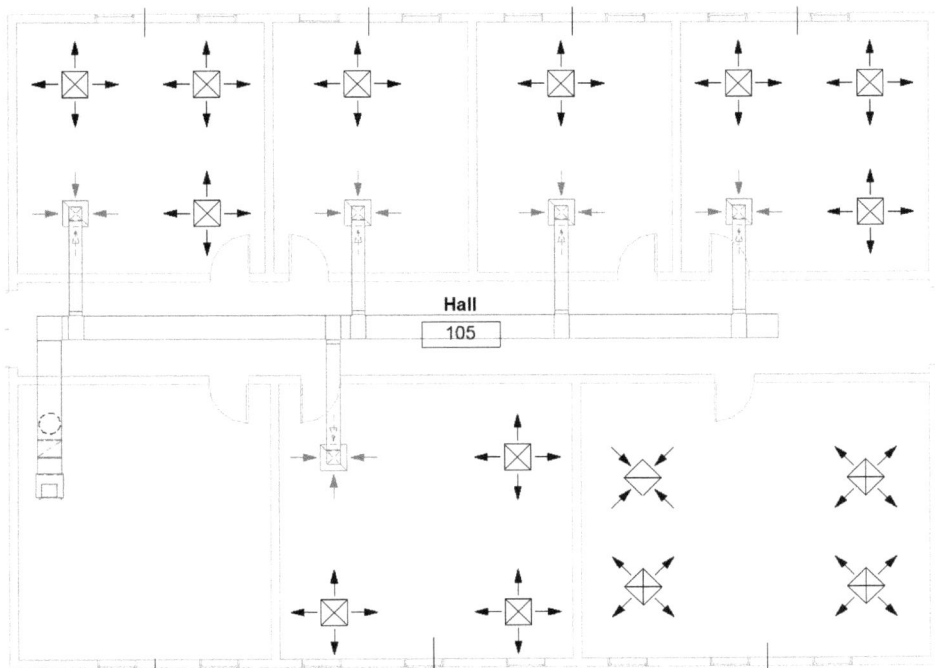

Figure 8–20

15. Zoom into **Office 108** and select the return diffuser.

16. Click on the **Create Duct** icon. In the Options Bar, set the *Middle Elevation* to **10'-0"** and press <Enter>.

17. Draw a duct approximately **4'-0"** on a 45-degree angle away from the return diffuser, as shown on the left in Figure 8–21. Continue drawing the duct to connect into the duct in the hall, as shown on the right in Figure 8–21.

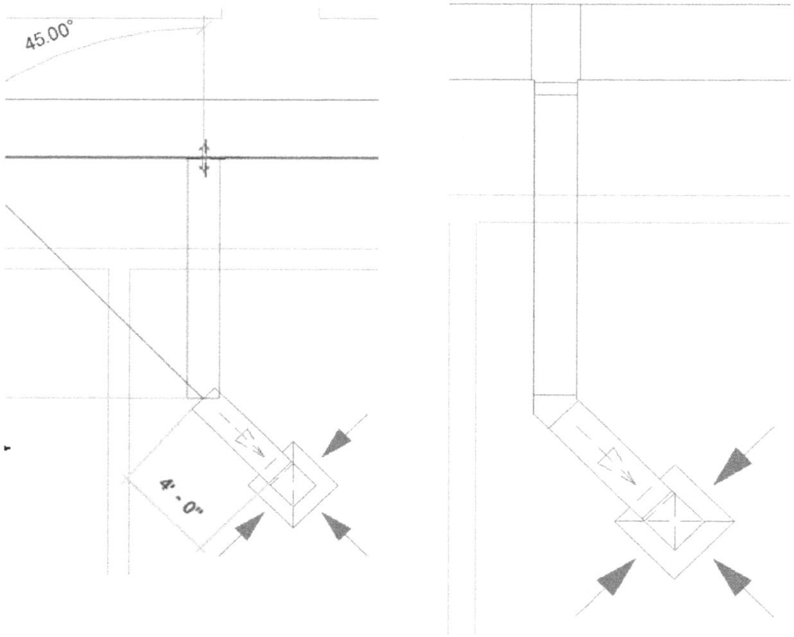

Figure 8–21

18. All of the elements connect, as shown in Figure 8–22, and display in magenta, which indicates that they are all part of a return air system.

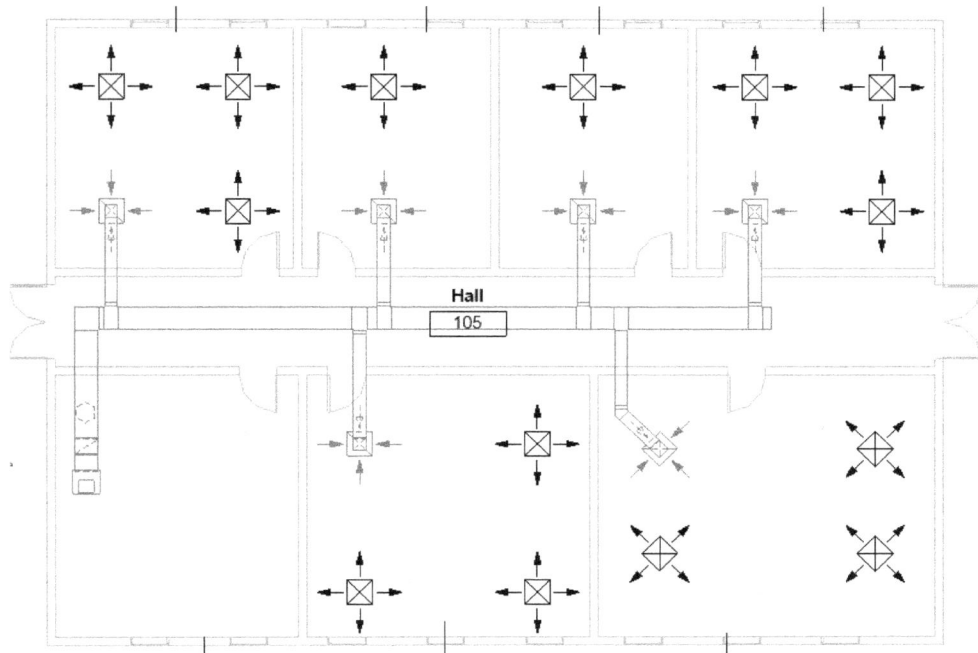

Figure 8–22

19. Click ⌕ (Modify), then save and close the project.

End of practice

Practice 8b
Connect Components – Plumbing

Practice Objectives

- Draw piping.
- Connect equipment to the piping.

In this practice, you will create piping using controls and commands. You will also use the **Connect Into** command.

1. In the practice files *Working Models>Plumbing* folder, open **Plumb-Connect.rvt**.

2. Open the Plumbing>Plumbing>Floor Plans>**1 - Plumbing** view and the 3D Views>**3D Plumbing** view. Close the SP - Starting Page.

3. Activate the **1 - Plumbing** view and tile the views by typing **WT**. Type **ZA** to zoom both views.

4. In the Quick Access Toolbar, verify ▓ (Thin Lines) is on.

5. Pan and zoom in on the **RR 2** room.

6. Select the lavatory (sink) closest to the window. Zoom in so that the three connectors display and click on the Hot Water connector.

    - In the Options Bar, note that *Diameter* and *Middle Elevation* are automatically set to the height of the fixture connector.

7. In the Type Selector, select **Pipe Types: Standard**.

8. Draw the pipe horizontally into the wall. Note that the sink turns red, indicating that it is now part of the Domestic Hot Water system.

9. You need to draw the pipe going up the wall in the vertical direction. In the Options Bar, change the *Middle Elevation* to **9'-0"** and press <Enter>, then click **Apply**. This draws the pipe vertically in the wall. Move the cursor into the view to complete the action. The vertical pipe now displays in the 3D view, as shown in Figure 8–23.

   Note: Make sure you click Apply to draw the pipe in the vertical direction.

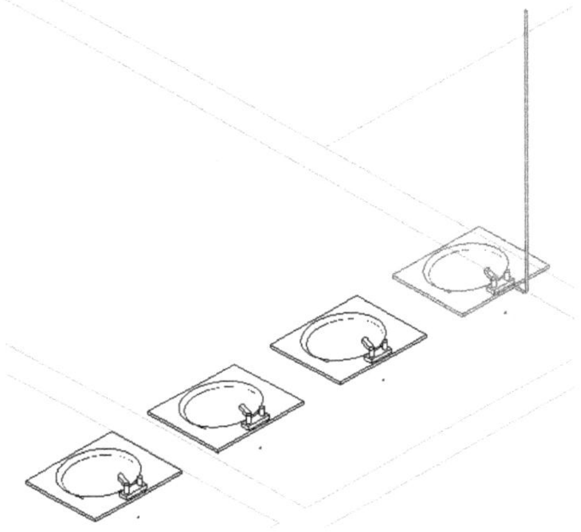

Figure 8–23

10. The *Detail Level* of the 1 - Plumbing view is set to **Medium**. In the View Control Bar set the *Detail Level* to ▨ (Fine). The pipe now displays full scale rather than in schematic.

11. Still in the **Pipe** command, hover your cursor over the pipe you just created. When you see the connect icon, as shown in Figure 8–24, click to continue drawing the pipe.

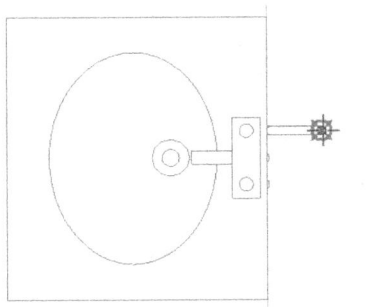

Figure 8–24

12. Draw the pipe down the wall, into the hall, and then towards the west side of the building past the water heater, as shown in Figure 8–25 (the pipe line has been enhanced in the image for clarity).

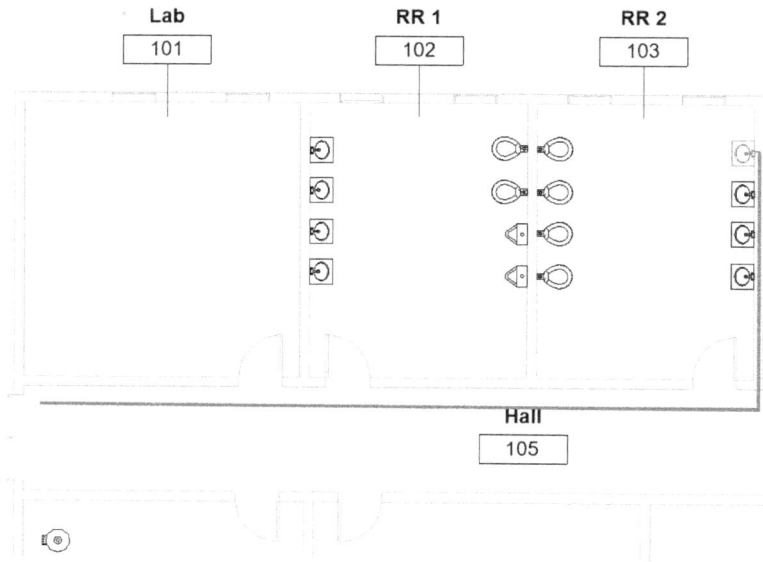

Figure 8–25

13. Click ↳ (Modify) and select the water heater.

14. In the *Modify | Plumbing Equipment* tab>*Layout* panel, click 🖳 (Connect Into).

15. In the *Select Connector* dialog box, select **Connector 2: Domestic Hot Water** and click **OK**.

16. Select the pipe in the hall. The correct pipe and connections are automatically added.

17. Zoom in to the pipe connection in the hall. Delete the extra pipe and transition fitting on the left of the tee pipe fitting, then select the tee pipe fitting and select the **Elbow** control, as shown on the left in Figure 8–26. (You may need to zoom out to view the controls.) The elbow is automatically added, as shown on the right.

Figure 8–26

18. Activate the **3D Plumbing** view.

19. Pan to room RR 2 and select one of the other lavatories.

20. In the *Modify | Plumbing Fixtures* tab>*Layout* panel, click (Connect Into).

21. In the *Select Connector* dialog box, select the **Domestic Hot Water** connector and click **OK**. Select the pipe above the lavatory.

22. Repeat with the other two lavatories. They are added to the hot water system and a pipe and the correct fittings are added, as shown in Figure 8−27.

Figure 8−27

23. Save and close the project.

End of practice

8.2 Creating Systems – Overview

When you connect components, such as air terminals with ducts or plumbing fixtures with pipes, systems are automatically created. These systems frequently overlap. For example, as part of an HVAC installation, an air handling unit is connected to supply and return duct systems, as well as hydronic supply and return systems. It is also connected to an electrical system (circuit), as shown in Figure 8–28.

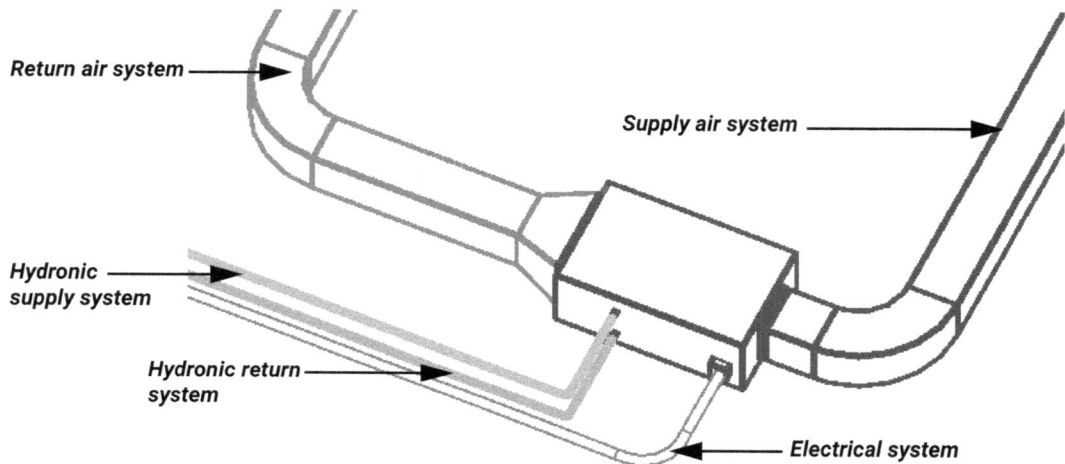

Figure 8–28

- Creating systems correctly is critical for Revit to understand and calculate flow, pressure, etc.

- While most systems are created automatically as you connect components with duct or pipe, you can create the system first and then connect the components later.

- Electrical systems (such as switches and data) do not have connecting elements and therefore need to be created.

How To: Create a System

Note: The images in this How To are showing pipe systems as the example, but will differ depending on the component(s) selected.

1. Select one or more related components. Do not select source equipment at this point.

2. In the *Modify* contextual tab>*Create Systems* panel, click ▣ (Duct), ⬚ (Power), ▣ (Piping), ▤ (Data), ◈ (Fire Alarm), ⊘ (Controls), or other system types.

3. For duct and piping systems, you are prompted to select the *System type* and assign a *System name*, as shown in Figure 8–29. Click **OK**.

   - If you know you want to add the source equipment or more components to the system at this time, select **Open in System Editor**.

   Create Piping System   ?   ✕

   System type: Sanitary ⌄

   System name: Sanitary 1

   ☐ Open in System Editor

   [OK]   [Cancel]

   Figure 8–29

4. In the *Modify* contextual tab>*System Tools* panel, click 📷 (Select Equipment) as shown in Figure 8–30, or for electrical circuits, click ⚡ (Select Panel). Select the equipment or panel.

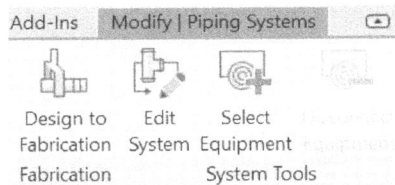

   Add-Ins   Modify | Piping Systems

   Design to Fabrication   Edit System   Select Equipment

   Fabrication   System Tools

   Figure 8–30

   - The number of options that display in the *Modify* tab depends on where you are in the system creation.

5. To add additional end components, in the *Modify* contextual tab>*System Tools* panel, click the **Edit Systems/Circuit** tool. The related contextual tab displays, as shown in Figure 8–31.

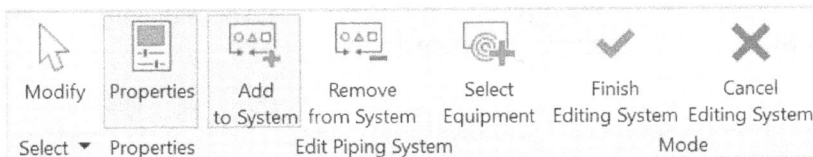

   Modify   Properties   Add to System   Remove from System   Select Equipment   Finish Editing System   Cancel Editing System

   Select ▾   Properties   Edit Piping System   Mode

   Figure 8–31

   - While the icon and name for each system type is different, the processes and locations are still the same.

6. The related **Add to System/Circuit** tool is automatically selected. Click on other components in the model to add them to the system. Remove components from the system using the **Remove from System/Circuit** tool.

7. To add mechanical equipment or an electrical panel to a system, you can use the related **Select Equipment/Select Panel** tool and select the equipment from a view.

8. When you have completed your selection, click ✔ (Finish Editing System/Circuit).

Selecting Systems

You can select systems by hovering over one component and pressing <Tab> until the system displays, as shown in Figure 8–32. If duct and pipe are in place, the system outline follows the linear elements. If not, there is a bounding box around all of the system elements.

Pay attention to the Status Bar located in the lower right corner. This will display which components, branches, networks, and systems are being highlighted as you press <Tab>.

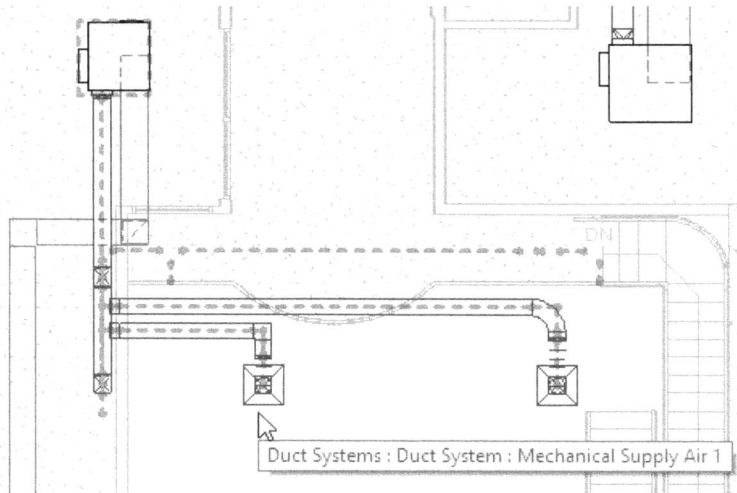

Duct Systems : Duct System : Mechanical Supply Air 1

Figure 8–32

- Whenever you select a component that is assigned to a system, you can return to editing the system by clicking on the contextual tabs, as shown for an air handling unit, then selecting on the *Duct Systems* tab, as shown in Figure 8–33.

Figure 8–33

Using the System Browser with Systems

The System Browser, as shown in Figure 8–34, is an important part of determining the relationships between components and the systems they are a part of. It also enables you to identify and select the components, especially those not assigned to a system.

Note: *Switch systems do not display in the System Browser as they only denote which fixtures are connected to the switch.*

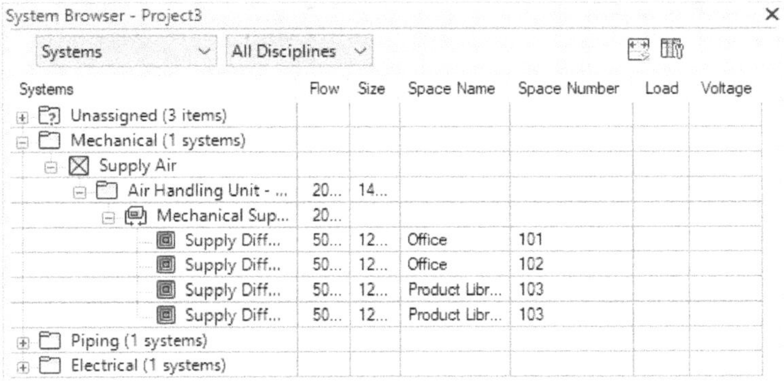

Figure 8–34

How To: Open the System Browser

1. In the *View* tab>*Window* panel, expand (User Interface), or press <F9>.

2. Expand *Systems* and select what you want to display: **Systems**, **Zones**, **Analytical Systems**, or **Electrical Analytical Systems**. You can leave it as **Systems** (as shown in Figure 8–35) to display all the system types.

3. Expand *All Disciplines* and select the discipline you would like to display, as shown in Figure 8–35, or leave it on **All Disciplines**. Selecting a discipline limits the display of elements to that specific discipline.

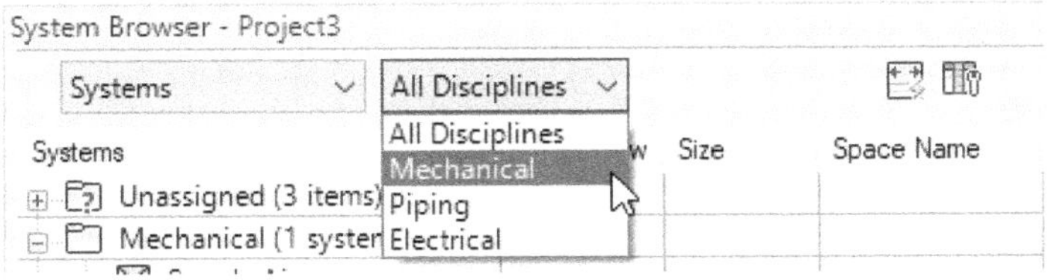

Figure 8–35

- The two buttons at the top right of the System Browser help display what you need to see.

  - Click ⬚ (Autofit all Columns) to change the width of the columns so that the contents fit exactly in the column.

  - Click ⬚ (Column Settings) to open the *Column Settings* dialog box, in which you can select the parameters to display for the various system types.

- Components that are not in a system display in the **Unassigned** list.

- In the System Browser, when you hover the cursor over the system name or select it, or select an individual component, it gets selected in the model, as shown in Figure 8–36. It also works the other way when you select the element in the model.

⊞ 🗀 Indoor AHU - Horiz...	12...	12...	COF
⊟ 🗀 Indoor AHU - Horiz...	13...	12...	COF
⊟ 🔲 01 - SA12	13...		
🔲 Indoor AHU ...	75...	12...	COF
🔲 Supply Diffu...	15...	6"	CLA
🔲 Supply Diffu...	15...	6"	CLA
🔲 Supply Diffu...	15...	6"	CLA
🔲 Supply Diffu...	15...	6"	CLA
🔲 Supply Diffu...	10...	6"	OFF
🔲 Supply Diffu...	10...	6"	COF
🔲 Supply Diffu...	10...	6"	OFF
🔲 Supply Diffu...	10...	6"	OFF
🔲 Supply Diffu...	10...	6"	OFF
🔲 Supply Diffu...	12...	6"	REC
🔲 Supply Diffu...	12...	6"	REC
⊞ 🔲 SA 1	12...		
⊞ 🔲 SA 2	12...		
⊞ 🔲 SA 3	12...		

Figure 8–36

- Properties also updates to match the selection, enabling you to modify parameters associated with the elements.

- Hold <Ctrl> or <Shift> to select multiple items in the System Browser.

- If you select a component that is referenced to multiple systems, it is highlighted in each of those systems as shown in Figure 8–37.

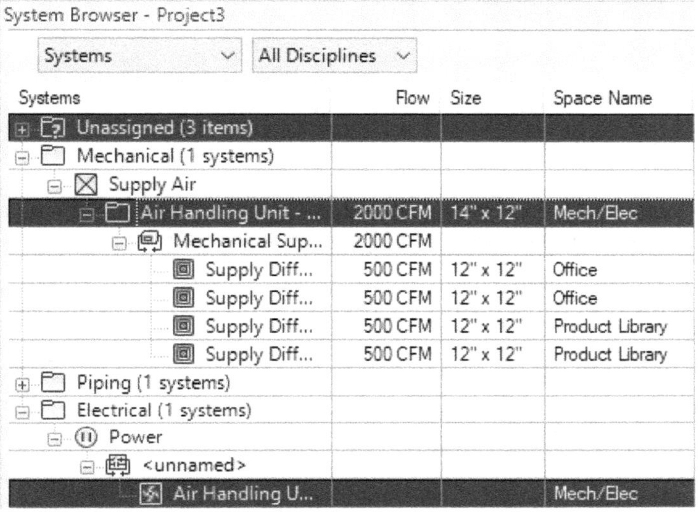
System Browser - Project3
Systems
All Disciplines
Systems
Flow
Size
Space Name
Unassigned (3 items)
Mechanical (1 systems)
Supply Air
Air Handling Unit - ...
2000 CFM
14" x 12"
Mech/Elec
Mechanical Sup...
2000 CFM
Supply Diff...
500 CFM
12" x 12"
Office
Supply Diff...
500 CFM
12" x 12"
Office
Supply Diff...
500 CFM
12" x 12"
Product Library
Supply Diff...
500 CFM
12" x 12"
Product Library
Piping (1 systems)
Electrical (1 systems)
Power
<unnamed>
Air Handling U...
Mech/Elec

Figure 8–37

- To get a close-up view of a component, select it in the System Browser, right-click, and select **Show**. If a view with the component is already open, it zooms into that view. In the *Show Element(s) In View* dialog box, as shown in Figure 8–38, click **Show** to search for other views.

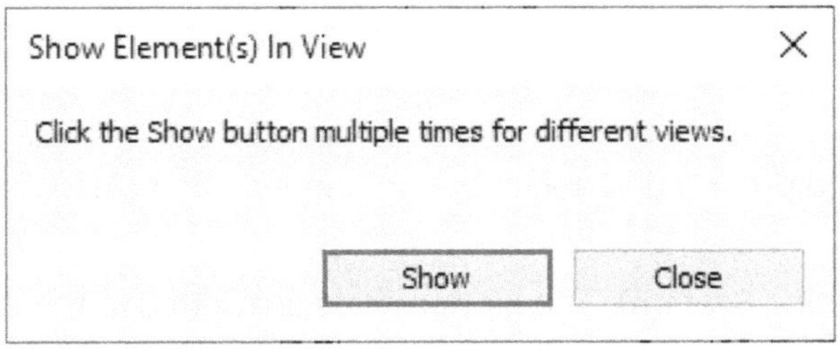
Show Element(s) In View
Click the Show button multiple times for different views.
Show
Close

Figure 8–38

- To delete a component through the System Browser, right-click on it and select **Delete**. This deletes it from the project.

Practice 8c
View and Create Systems – Mechanical

Practice Objectives

- Create systems.
- Review and update systems.

In this practice, you will create systems and use the System Browser to find elements in the system. You will then change the name of the system within Properties.

Task 1: Create a system.

1. In the practice files *Working Models>Mechanical* folder, open **Mech-Systems.rvt**.

2. Open the Mechanical>HVAC>Floor Plans> **1 - Mech** view.

3. In the **Lab 101** room, select one of the supply diffusers.

4. In the *Modify | Air Terminals* tab>*Create Systems* panel, click 📠 (Duct).

5. In the *Create Duct System* dialog box, verify that the *System* type is set to **Supply Air**. Accept the default system name and check the checkbox next to **Open in System Editor**, then click **OK**.

6. The *Edit Duct System* tab displays with **Add to System** already selected.

7. Select the other supply air terminals in the rooms on the same side of the hall (rooms **RR 1**, **RR 2**, and **Lab 104**). As you select them, they change from grayed out to a black line.

   - If you select the return air terminal, a warning displays that you cannot connect to this system.

8. Click 📠 (Select Equipment) and select the air handling unit (AHU) in the **Mech/Elec 106** room.

9. Click ✔ (Finish Editing System). The air terminals are added to the system and turn blue to indicate that it is a supply air system, and the AHU turns black because there are now two systems connected to it.

10. Save the project.

Task 2: Review systems in the System Browser.

1. Open the Mechanical>HVAC>3D views>**3D - Mech** view.

2. Open the System Browser by pressing <F9>. Verify that the System Browser has the **Systems** options selected and that the discipline is set to **Mechanical**, as shown at the top of Figure 8–39.

3. In the System Browser, click 📠 (AutoFit All Columns) to widen the columns.

4. Expand the **Mechanical (2 systems)>Return Air> Mechanical Return Air 1** nodes to display the systems, as shown in Figure 8–39. (Click **AutoFit All Columns** as needed.)

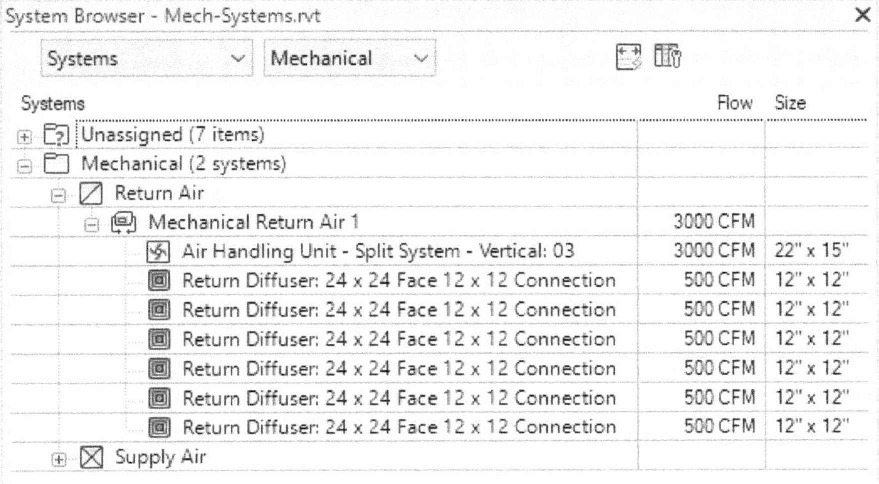

Figure 8–39

5. In the view, select one of the return diffusers and note how it relates to the system in the System Browser.

6. Click ⬚ (Modify).

7. In the System Browser, hover your cursor over the system name, as shown in Figure 8–40. In the view, the system displays a dashed line showing all that is connected.

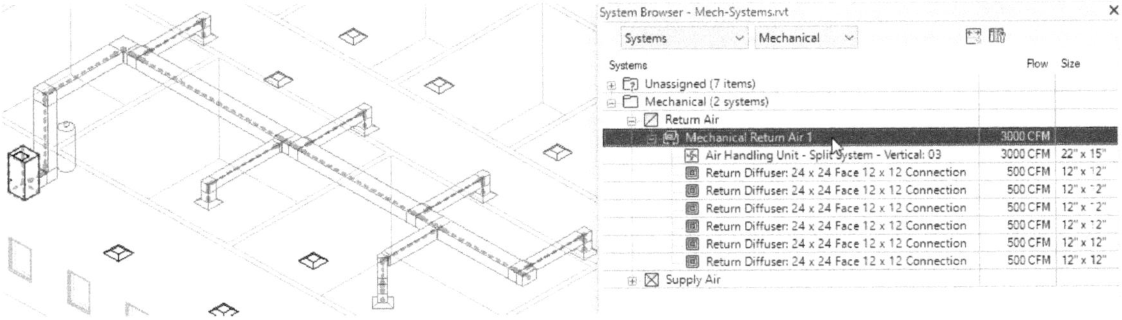

Figure 8–40

8. Select the system name and note that the *Modify | Duct System* contextual tab displays in the ribbon. Keep the system selected.

9. In Properties, change the *System Name* to **Return Air**.

10. Click **Apply** or move the cursor over in the view. The name updates in the System Browser.

11. Save and close the project.

End of practice

Practice 8d
View and Create Systems – Electrical

Practice Objectives

- Create systems.
- Review and update systems.

In this practice, you will create systems and use the System Browser to find elements in the system. You will then modify the system by selecting the system and modifying it within the ribbon.

Task 1: Create a system.

1. In the practice files *Working Models>Electrical* folder, open **Elec-Systems.rvt**.

2. Open the Electrical>Lighting>Floor Plans>**1 - Lighting** view.

3. In **Office 108** (with the rotated lights), select the top left light fixture.

4. In the *Modify | Lighting Fixtures* tab>*Create Systems* panel, click ⬜ (Switch).

5. In the *Modify | Switch Systems* tab>*System Tools* panel, click ⬜₊ (Select Switch).

6. Select the switch near the door in the same room. A dashed line connecting the light fixture to the switch displays, as shown in Figure 8–41.

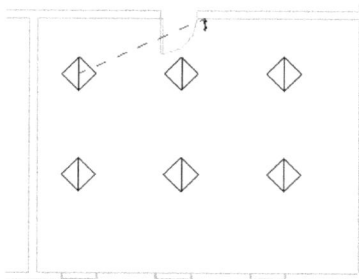

Figure 8–41

7. The new switch system is still selected. In the *Modify | Switch System* tab>*System Tools* panel, click ⬜ (Edit Switch System). ⬛ (Add to System) is automatically selected.

8. Click on the other light fixtures in the same room and click ✓ (Finish Editing System).

9. Hover over one of the light fixtures and press <Tab> until the Switch System displays, as shown in Figure 8–42.

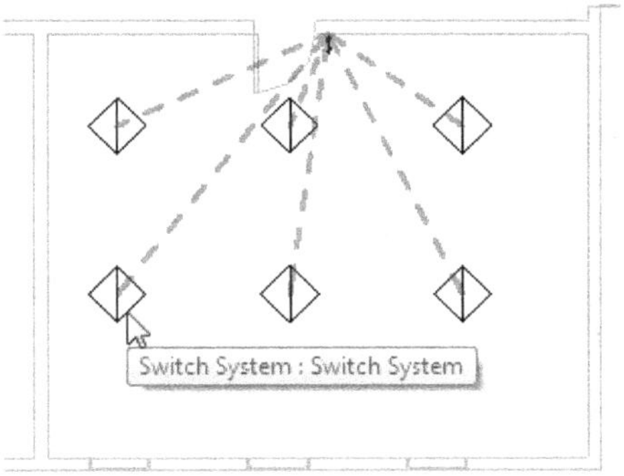

Figure 8–42

10. Move the cursor away from the selection.

11. Select all the light fixtures in room 108. In the *Modify | Lighting Fixtures* tab>*Create Systems* panel, select ⓘ (Power).

12. In the *Modify | Electrical Circuits* tab>*System Tools* panel, select 🔲 (Select Panel) and select one of the panels in the **Mech/Elec 106** room. The circuit displays with a blue dashed line, as shown in Figure 8–43.

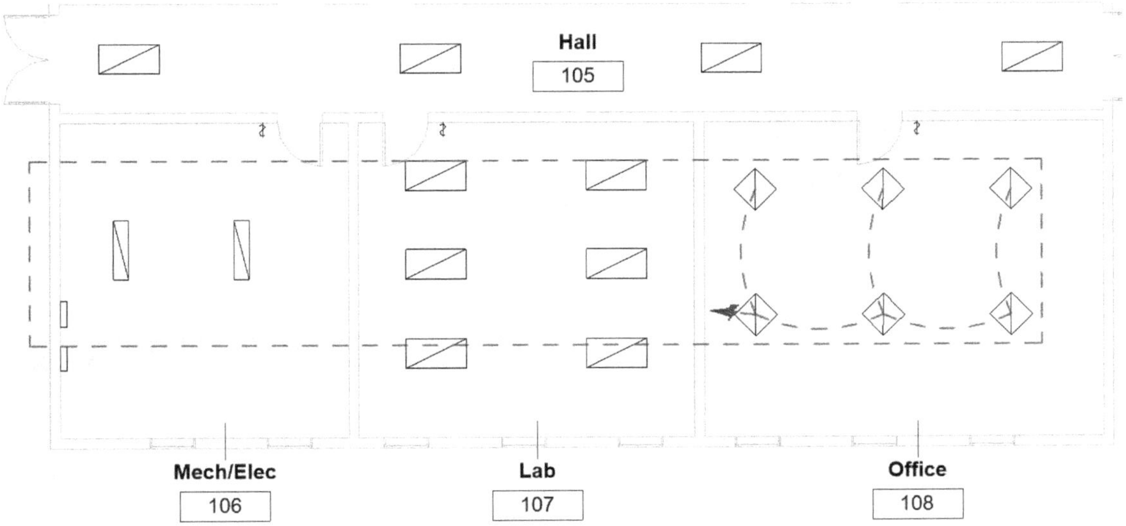

Figure 8–43

13. Click ⌖ (Modify).

14. Save the project.

Task 2: Review systems in the System Browser.

1. Open the System Browser by pressing <F9>. Verify that the System Browser has the **Systems** options selected and that the discipline is set to **Electrical**, as shown on the top of Figure 8–44.

2. In the System Browser, click 🖾 (AutoFit All Columns) to widen the columns.

   Note: Switch systems are not included in the System Browser.

3. Expand the **Electrical (1 systems)** nodes to display the systems, as shown in Figure 8–44. (Click AutoFit All Columns as needed.)

Figure 8–44

4. In the view, select one of the light fixtures in **Office 108** and note how the related information displays in the System Browser.

5. Hover your cursor over the circuit number, as shown in Figure 8–45.

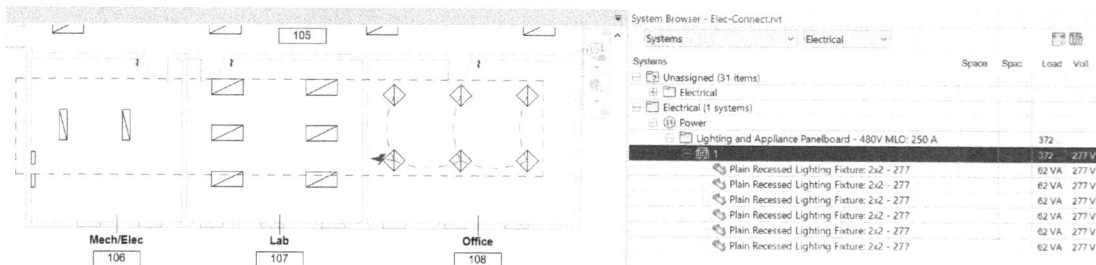

Figure 8–45

6. Select the panel or circuit number. The related *Modify | Electrical* contextual tab displays in the ribbon.

7. Save and close the project.

End of practice

Practice 8e
View and Create Systems – Plumbing

Practice Objectives

- Create systems.
- Review and update systems.

In this practice, you will create a system and use the System Browser to find elements in the system. You will modify the system by selecting the system in the view and editing the system from the ribbon.

Task 1: Create a system.

1. In the practice files *Working Models>Plumbing* folder, open **Plumb-Systems.rvt**.

2. Open the Plumbing>Plumbing>Floor Plans>**1 - Plumbing** view.

3. Select the lavatory (sink) closest to the window in room **RR 1**.

4. In the *Modify | Plumbing Fixtures* tab>*Create Systems* panel, click 🔲 (Piping).

5. In the *Create Piping System* dialog box, expand the *System type* drop-down list, select **Sanitary**, and keep the default system name, then click **OK**.

6. In the *Modify | Piping Systems* tab>*System Tools* panel, select 🔲 (Edit System). Note that 🔲 (Add to System) is automatically selected.

7. Click on the other lavatories in the same room and click ✓ (Finish Editing System). Note that the fixtures all turn green to indicate a sanitary system.

8. Save the project.

Task 2: Review systems in the System Browser.

1. Open the System Browser by pressing <F9>. Verify that the System Browser has the **Systems** option selected and that the discipline is set to **Piping**.

2. Expand the following System Browser nodes:
   - Unassigned>Piping>Domestic Cold Water
   - Piping (2 Systems)>Sanitary>Sanitary 1

3. In the System Browser, click 🔲 (AutoFit All Columns) to widen the columns.

4. In the view, select the lavatory in room RR 1 closest to the window. Note that in the System Browser, it is highlighted under the *Unassigned - Domestic Cold Water*, *Piping - Domestic Hot Water*, and *Piping - Sanitary* sections.

5. Open the **3D - Plumbing** view and click in an empty area in the view to clear the selection.

6. In the System Browser, select **Sanitary 1**. The group of lavatories highlights in the view, as shown in Figure 8–46.

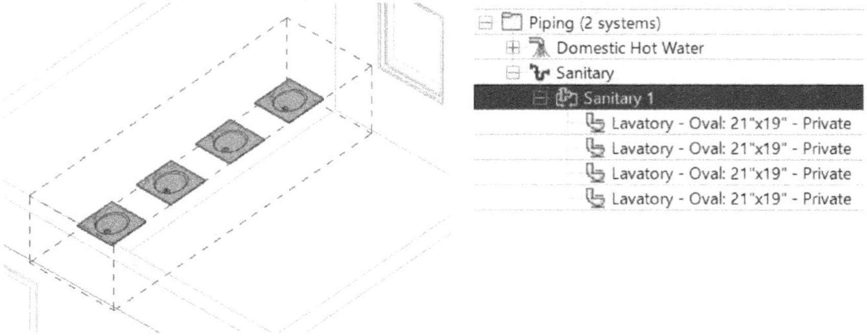

Figure 8–46

7. In the *Modify | Piping Systems* tab>*System Tools* panel, click ⬚ (Edit System).

8. Select the lavatories in the other restroom, then click ✔ (Finish Editing System).

9. Save and close the project.

End of practice

Chapter Review Questions

1. When you select a Mechanical Equipment component, several icons display. What is the purpose of these icons?

   a. They are where ducts, pipes, or electrical circuits connect to the equipment.

   b. You can draw ducts, pipes, or circuits from them.

   c. They establish the size or power of the connection.

   d. All the above.

2. When you draw connecting elements (such as duct or pipe) directly from a component, the connector you select controls the size and elevation.

   a. True

   b. False

3. Which of the following happens when you select components in the System Browser?

   a. The components highlight in the current view.

   b. The component changes to a different system.

   c. You are put into edit mode.

   d. Nothing happens.

4. To create a system, you need to select the components and the source equipment.

   a. True

   b. False

Command Summary

Button	Command	Location
Connectors		
	Cable Tray	• **Ribbon:** *Systems* tab>*Electrical* panel • **Shortcut:** CT • Right-click on a control: **Draw Cable Tray**
	Conduit	• **Ribbon:** *Systems* tab>*Electrical* panel • **Shortcut:** CN • Right-click on a control: **Draw Conduit**
	Connect Into	• **Ribbon:** *Modify* contextual tab>*Layout* panel
	Duct	• **Ribbon:** *Systems* tab>*HVAC* panel • **Shortcut:** DT • Right-click on a control: **Draw Duct**
	Flex Duct	• **Ribbon:** *Systems* tab>*HVAC* panel • **Shortcut:** FD • Right-click on a control: **Draw Flex Duct**
	Flex Pipe	• **Ribbon:** *Systems* tab>*Plumbing & Piping* panel • **Shortcut:** FP • Right-click on a control: **Draw Flex Pipe**
	Pipe	• **Ribbon:** *Systems* tab>*Plumbing & Piping* panel • **Shortcut:** PI • Right-click on a control: **Draw Pipe**
	Show Disconnects	• **Ribbon:** *Analyze* tab>*Check Systems* panel
	Wire (Arc)	• **Ribbon:** *Systems* tab>*Electrical* panel • **Shortcut:** EW
Systems		
(varies)	**Add to System**	• **Ribbon:** *Edit System/Circuit* tab>*Edit System/Circuit* panel
	Data	• **Ribbon:** *Modify* contextual tab>*Create Systems* panel • Right-click on a control: **Create Data Circuit**
	Duct	• **Ribbon:** *Modify* contextual tab>*Create Systems* panel • Right-click on a control: **Create Duct System**

Button	Command	Location
	Fire Alarm	• **Ribbon:** *Modify* contextual tab>*Create Systems* panel • Right-click on a control: **Create Fire Alarm Circuit**
	Piping	• **Ribbon:** *Modify* contextual tab>*Create Systems* panel • Right-click on a control: **Create Piping System**
	Power	• **Ribbon:** *Modify* contextual tab>*Create Systems* panel • Right-click on a control: **Create Power Circuit**
	Switch	• **Ribbon:** *Modify* contextual tab>*Create Systems* panel • Right-click on a control: **Create Switch Circuit**
	Select Equipment	• **Ribbon:** *Modify* contextual tab>*System Tools* panel • **Ribbon:** *Edit <contextual> System* tab>*Edit <contextual> System* panel
	Select Panel	• **Ribbon:** *Modify* contextual tab>*System Tools* panel • **Ribbon:** *Edit Circuit* tab>*Edit Circuit* panel
N/A	**System Browser**	• **Ribbon:** *View* tab>*Window* panel, expand 🗔 (User Interface) • **Shortcut:** <F9>

Pipe Systems

Pipe systems consist of pipes that connect plumbing or mechanical fixtures and equipment to their respective systems. The process of putting these together and ensuring they work correctly is a significant part of developing any piping project.

Learning Objectives

- Understand pipe settings.
- Learn about pipe placement tools.
- Add pipes to connect plumbing fixtures and equipment.
- Modify pipes and fittings.
- Add hydronic supply and returns to equipment.
- Add sprinklers and piping for fire protection systems.

9.1 Connecting Pipes

Pipes connect mechanical equipment to a hydronic supply (as shown on the left in Figure 9–1), as well as plumbing systems that include sanitary, domestic hot water, and domestic cold water (as shown on the right). The pipes in a system connect fixtures together and indicate how the network is configured. You can draw the pipes independently or using connectors in the fixtures and equipment. Fire protection networks include wet and dry sprinklers with the associated piping.

Hydronic system *Plumbing system*

Figure 9–1

- Pipes can be drawn horizontally and vertically in plan, elevation/section, and 3D views.

- To get the pipes at the right height, it is recommended to start from the connectors in the mechanical equipment or plumbing fixtures.

- Fittings between changes of height or size are automatically applied as you model the elements, as shown in Figure 9–2. When you place parts, Revit will try to match the orientation of the connectors.

- Plumbing, hydronic, sanitary, fire protection, and vent piping design layouts can be created using the same tools located in the *Systems* tab>*Plumbing & Piping* panel.

  Note: Check sanitary pipe fittings in particular to ensure that they are pointing the right way.

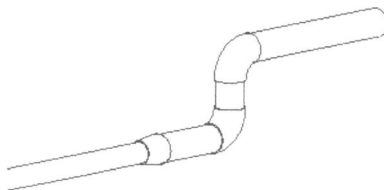

Figure 9–2

- If you need to sketch out the path, use either a pipe placeholder or a Standard type, which will be converted to the system and type when connected.

Mechanical Settings for Pipes

Before you add pipes, review and modify the Mechanical Settings to suit your project or office standards. These settings control the angles at which the pipes can be drawn, the default types, offsets, sizes, slopes, and the Pressure Drop calculation method.

- In the *Systems* tab>*Mechanical* panel, click ⅏ (Mechanical Settings), or type **MS** to open the *Mechanical Settings* dialog box (shown in Figure 9–3).

Figure 9–3

Hidden Line	Specify the size and type of hidden lines that show when pipes cross over each other.
Pipe Settings	Displays all parameters common to piping, plumbing, and fire protection systems.
Angles	Specify at what angles fittings are applied for pipe runs.
Conversion	Specify how the pipes work when using the Generate Layout tool. (These are also available in that command.)
Segments and Sizes	Specify the sizes and other properties for piping by material type.
Fluids	Specify the temperature, viscosity, and density of fluids by fluid type.
Slopes	Specify slope values for piping runs.
Calculation	Specify the pipe pressure drop for straight sections. You can select from a variety of calculation methods.

- Mechanical Settings are set by project and can be included in templates or imported into a project from another one using **Transfer Project Standards**.

Connecting Pipes

You can connect pipes by first starting the **Pipe** command and hovering your cursor over the end of another pipe, fixture, or equipment. When you see the connector highlight, click on it to start drawing pipe. Alternatively, you can select an element then right-click on a connector and, from the sub-menu, select to draw **Pipe**, **Pipe Placeholder**, **Flex Pipe**, or **Cap Open End**.

To initiate the **Pipe** command from a fixture or equipment, select the element first so the connection icons display, as shown in Figure 9−4. Select the desired connection icon to start the **Pipe** command with the correct system type, such as hot water, sanitary or cold water shown in Figure 9−4.

Figure 9−4

- Drawing from existing connectors automatically applies the *System Type*.

- If you start from a connector, the default diameter and middle elelvation in the Options Bar will match the parameters of the selected connector.

Pipe Placement Tools

When placing pipes, there are various placement tools in the *Placement Tools* panel in the ribbon, such as ⊞ (Automatically Connect) (on/off), ◁ (Justification), ⊞ (Inherit Elevation) (on/off), and ▦ (Inherit Size) (on/off). Figure 9–5 shows how pipes can be affected by using these tools.

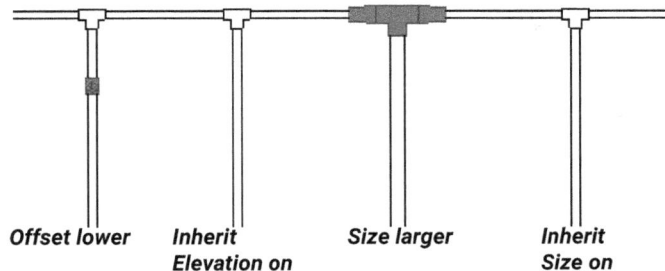

Offset lower   *Inherit Elevation on*   *Size larger*   *Inherit Size on*

Figure 9–5

- If you already have some pipes in the project, you can select on a fixture or equipment and use ⊞ (Connect Into). This option displays in the contextual tab when you select a component. If your pipe and fixtures/equipment are too close to each other, you will get a message that cannot be ignored that an auto-route was not found, as shown in Figure 9–6. Click **Cancel** and try to manually draw the pipes if possible.

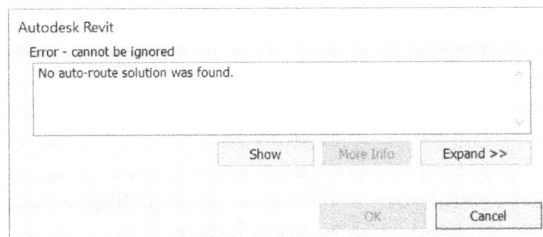

Figure 9–6

- To display centerlines for pipe, in the *Visibility/Graphic Overrides* dialog box, toggle on the *Center Line* subcategory for pipes and pipe fittings. Centerlines display in plan and elevation views set to the **Wireframe** or **Hidden Line** visual style.

Sloped Piping

When drawing pipes with a slope, it helps to identify the direction that *drains to daylight* (the point in the system where it attaches to the exterior sanitary pipes). Then, start drawing the pipes from the top most fixture in the system as shown in Figure 9–7.

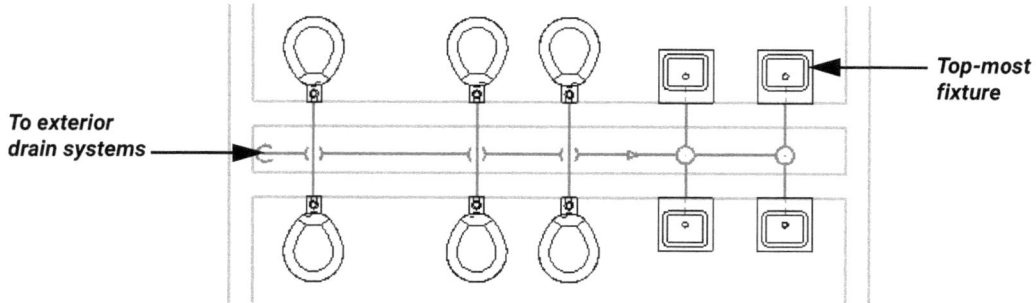

Figure 9–7

- As you are drawing pipes with slopes, you can set the information in the *Modify | Place Pipe* tab>*Sloped Piping* panel, as shown in Figure 9–8. You can change the direction of the slope, the slope value, and toggle the slope off or specify that it be ignored when connecting.

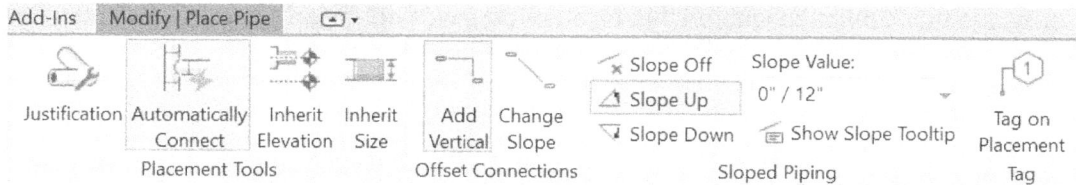

Figure 9–8

- In the *Sloped Piping* panel, toggle on (Show Slope Tooltip) to see the exact information of the offsets and slope as you draw, as shown in Figure 9–9.

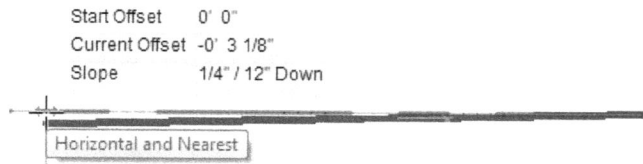

Figure 9–9

Creating Parallel Pipes

The **Parallel Pipes** tool helps you create piping runs that are parallel to an existing run, as shown in Figure 9–10. This can save time because only one run needs to be laid out, and the tool generates the parallel runs for you.

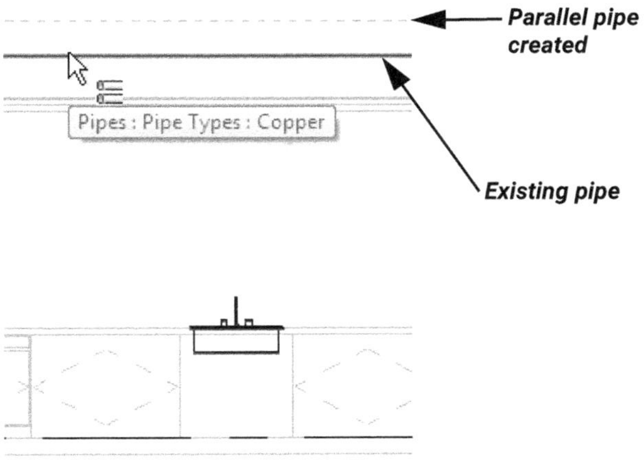

Figure 9–10

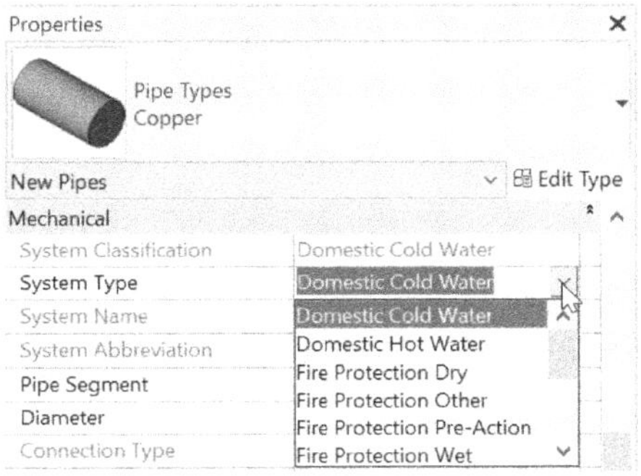

Figure 9–11

- The **Parallel Pipes** tool creates an exact duplicate of the selected pipe, including the system type. You can change the *System Type* in Properties (as shown above in Figure 9–11) before connecting other pipes into it.

- It might be easier to draw the parallel pipes directly from the fixtures so that the pipe takes on the correct system type. Also, you might have to modify connectors to get the pipe in the correct place.

- Parallel pipes can be created in plan, section, elevation, and 3D views.

How To: Create Parallel Pipe Runs

1. Create an initial pipe run, or use an existing pipe run.

2. In the *Systems* tab>*Plumbing & Piping* panel, click (Parallel Pipes).

3. In the *Modify | Place Parallel Pipes* tab>*Parallel Pipes* panel, set the required options, as shown in Figure 9–12.

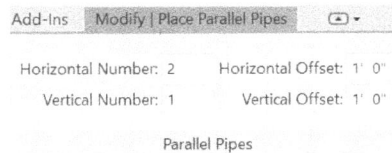

Figure 9–12

4. Hover the cursor over the existing piping (as shown in Figure 9-13) and press <Tab> to select the existing run.

    Note: If you do not press <Tab>, parallel pipes are only created for the single piece of existing pipe.

The side the parallel pipe will be placed on

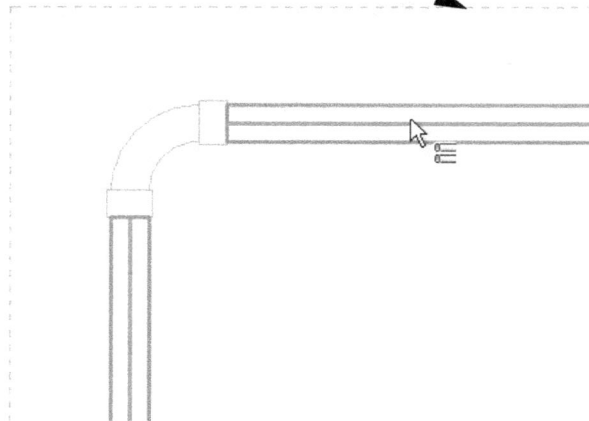

Figure 9-13

5. When the preview displays, click to create the parallel runs. The preview varies depending on which side of the existing run you hover the cursor.

Parallel Pipe Creation Options

Horizontal Number	The total number of parallel pipe runs, in the horizontal direction.
Horizontal Offset	The distance between parallel pipe runs, in the horizontal direction.
Vertical Number	The total number of parallel pipe runs, in the vertical direction.
Vertical Offset	The distance between parallel pipe runs, in the vertical direction.

*   In section and elevation views, horizontal refers to parallel to the view (visually up, down, left, or right from the original conduit). Vertical creates parallel pipe runs perpendicular to the view, in the direction of the user.

Practice 9a
Add Plumbing Pipes

Practice Objectives

- Set mechanical settings.
- Add pipes.
- Change the size and height of the pipes as you draw them.
- Create sloped pipes.

In this practice, you will draw cold water mains from the origin point to the classroom wing, changing the diameter and offset of the pipes as you draw them. You will connect water heaters into the mains and then draw hot water pipes from the water heater to the classroom wing. Finally, you will draw sloped sanitary piping from floor drains, as shown in Figure 9–14.

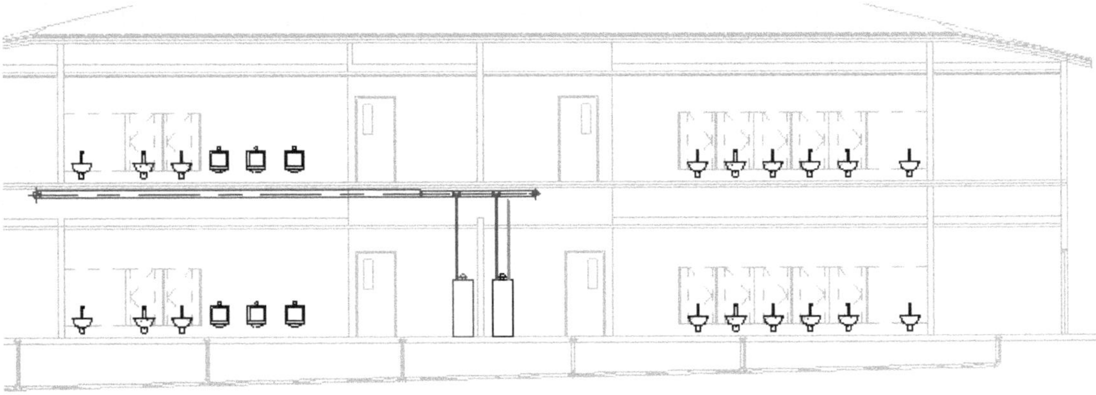

Figure 9–14

Task 1: Set mechanical settings.

1. In the practice files *Working Models>Plumbing* folder, open the project **Plumb-Piping.rvt**.

2. Open the Plumbing>Plumbing>Floor Plans>**01 Plumbing Plan** view.

3. In the *Systems* tab>*Plumbing & Piping* panel title bar, click ⌄ (Mechanical Settings).

4. In the *Mechanical Settings* dialog box, in *Pipe Settings,* select **Angles**.

5. In the right pane, select **Use specific angles** and clear the checkmarks for 22.50° and 11.25°, as shown in Figure 9–15. Then, click **OK.** This limits the angles you can use to draw the piping to industry specific fittings.

Figure 9–15

Task 2: Run cold water mains.

In this task, you will model cold water pipes starting from the building's water main and following the path shown in Figure 9–16. You will change the diameter and offset of the pipes as you progress.

> *Note: The piping lines in this image are enhanced for clarity.*

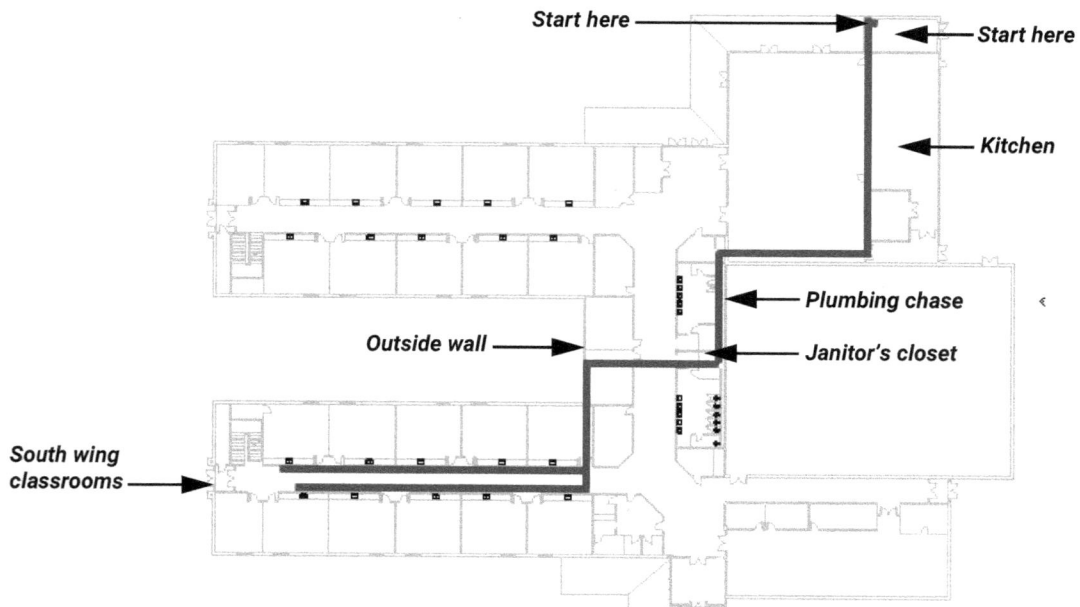

Figure 9–16

1. In the **01 Plumbing Plan** view, review the path of the piping shown in Figure 9–16.

2. Turn off **Select Links** (there should be a red x over the icon) from the Status Bar so you do not accidentally select the linked model while working.

3. In Properties, in the *Underlay* area, set the following:

   - *Range: Base Level:* **Level 2**
   - *Range: Top Level:* **Unbounded**
   - *Underlay Orientation:* **Look down**

   Click in an empty area in the view. These settings will display the piping as it is being drawn above the first level.

4. Zoom in on the utility area outside the kitchen. There is a water main connector available, as shown in Figure 9–17.

(Found in the upper-right side of the building)

Figure 9–17

5. Select the pipe connector that is hosted to the wall and click on the cold water connector (shown in Figure 9–18) to start the **Create Pipe** command.

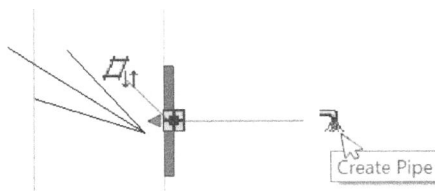

Figure 9–18

6. In the Type Selector, select **Pipe Types: Copper**.

7. Verify that the following is set based on the information stored in the connector:

   - In Properties, the *System Type* is set to **Domestic Cold Water**.
   - In the Options Bar, the *Diameter* is set to **4"** and the *Middle Elevation* is set to **2'-6"**.

8. Draw the pipe to the right approximately **12"**. Hint: Use the temporary dimensions to guide you.

9. In the Options Bar, change the *Middle Elevation* to **12'-0"** and press <Enter>, then click **Apply**.

10. You are still in the **Pipe** command. Hover your cursor over the pipe. When the connector highlights (as shown in Figure 9–19), click to continue drawing pipe.

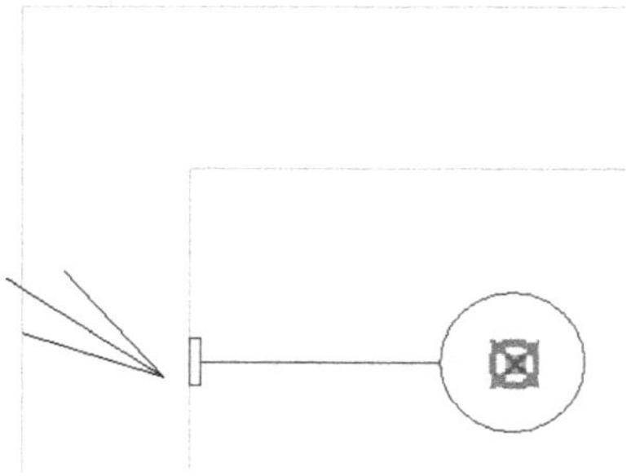

Figure 9–19

11. Continue drawing the pipe down the side of the kitchen, as shown in Figure 9–20.

Figure 9–20

12. Draw the pipe close to the gym wall and then turn left to draw towards the restrooms.

13. Refer to the image in Figure 9–21. Draw the pipe around the restrooms in the plumbing chase, and then across the hall to the exterior wall of the building. In the Options Bar, change the *Diameter* and *Middle Elevation* at the points shown in Figure 9–21.

- Note: When you change elevation, make sure you press <Enter> then click **Apply** (in the Options Bar) for the pipe to draw vertically up the wall. To continue drawing pipe, click on the vertical pipe's connector.

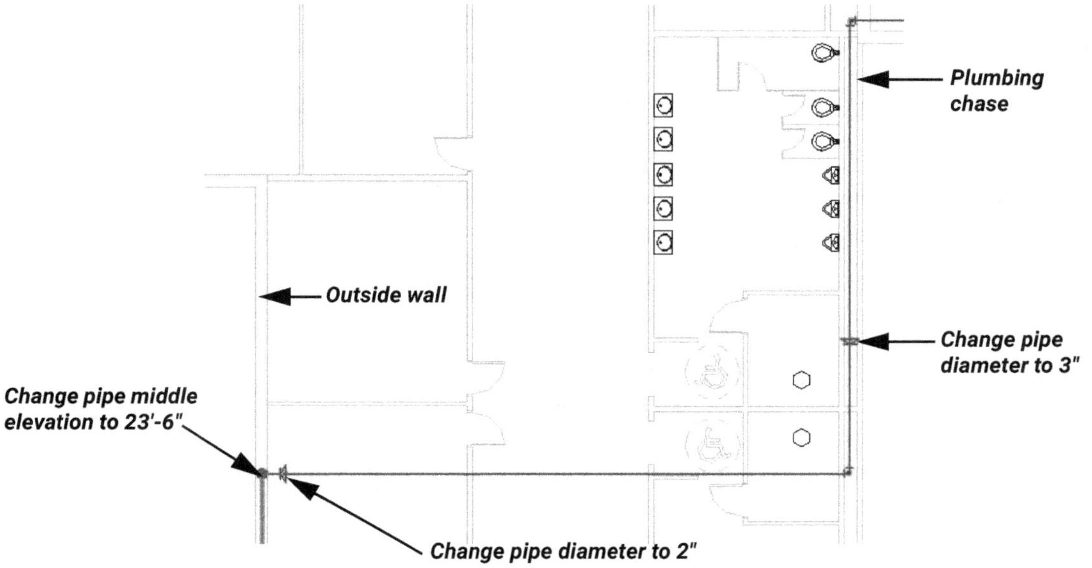

Plumbing chase

Outside wall

Change pipe diameter to 3"

Change pipe middle elevation to 23'-6"

Change pipe diameter to 2"

Figure 9–21

14. Continue drawing the pipe down to the south wing hall so that it is close to the south wing – south classrooms' wall, then down the hall to the left until it is past the last sink.

15. Press <Esc> once to stop the pipe run but stay in the command.

16. Draw a pipe run starting from the last sink on the other side of the hall until it ties into the vertical pipe, as shown in Figure 9–22.

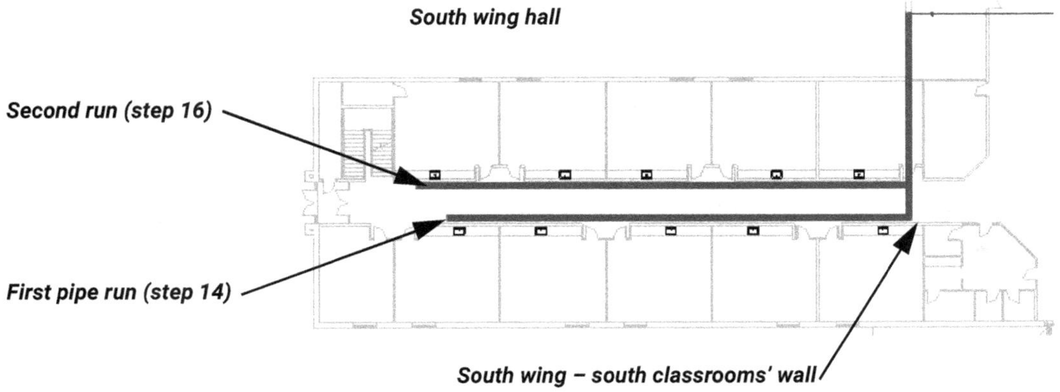

South wing hall

Second run (step 16)

First pipe run (step 14)

South wing – south classrooms' wall

Figure 9–22

17. Click ⬐ (Modify).

18. Switch to the **South Wing - South Classrooms** section to see that the pipe is at the second level. (More work will be done later on.)

19. Switch back to the **01 Plumbing Plan** view.

20. Zoom in on the water heaters in the Janitor's closets in the restrooms.

21. Select one of the water heaters. In the *Modify | Plumbing Equipment* tab>*Layout* panel, click

    (Connect Into).

22. In the *Select Connector* dialog box, select **Domestic Cold Water** and click **OK**.

23. Select the cold water pipe in the plumbing chase.

24. Repeat the process with the other water heater. The pipes are connected as shown in Figure 9−23.

Figure 9−23

25. Save the project.

Task 3: Add hot water lines.

1. Continue working zoomed in to the water heaters.

2. Select the water heater closest to the south wing of the building.

3. Click on the hot water connector to start the **Create Pipe** command.

4. In the Options Bar, change *Middle Elevation* to **11'-6"** and press <Enter>, then click **Apply**.

5. Verify in the Type Selector that **Pipe Types: Copper** is selected.

6. Continue drawing the pipe following the path of the cold water pipes, changing the *Middle Elevation* to **24'-0"** at the point shown in Figure 9–24.

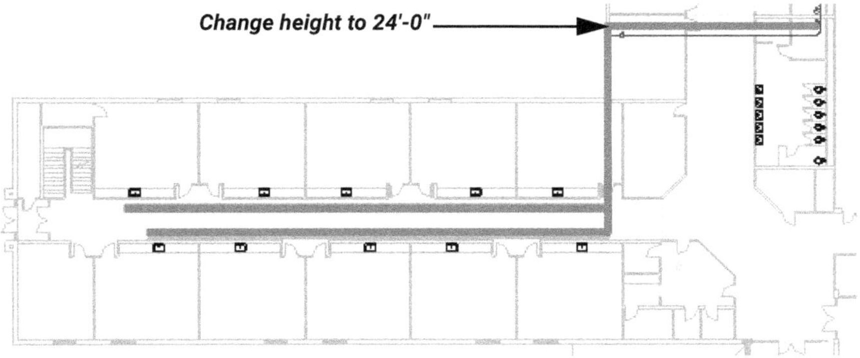

Change height to 24'-0"

Figure 9–24

*   When you draw the second horizontal pipe, ensure that the extra pipe connects to the hot water pipe and not the cold water pipe. Press <Tab> to cycle through the options. In the Status Bar, you want to see **Pipe Type Copper 3/4" @24'-0"**.
*   If you need to make changes to the pipe on the second floor, open the **02 Plumbing Plan** view.

7. Save the project.

Task 4: Draw sloped pipes for drains.

1. Open the Plumbing>Plumbing>Sections (Building Section)> **Restroom Section** view. Note that the floor drains display.
2. Select the floor drain on the far right and click the Sanitary connector to start the **Create Pipe** command.
3. In the Type Selector, select **Pipe Types: Standard**. (This type acts as a placeholder until a later practice.)
4. In the *Modify | Place Pipe* tab>*Sloped Piping* panel, select (Slope Down) and set the *Slope Value* to **1/4" / 12"**.

5. Draw the pipe down and then over to the left, as shown in Figure 9–25.

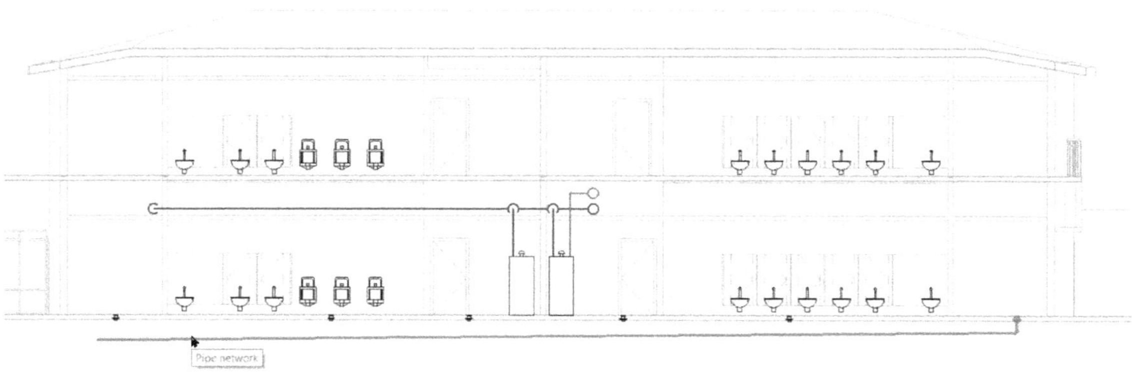

Figure 9–25

6. Click ⌖ (Modify).
7. Draw a pipe from each of the other floor drains into the sloped pipe.
8. Save and close the project.

End of practice

9.2 Modifying Pipes

Pipes can be modified using a variety of standard and specialty tools, such as converting placeholders, changing rigid pipes to flexible ones, adding insulation, and modifying the justification of pipes.

For the example shown in Figure 9–26, the fittings are incorrect for sanitary systems. In Figure 9–27, these have been changed to create the appropriate layout.

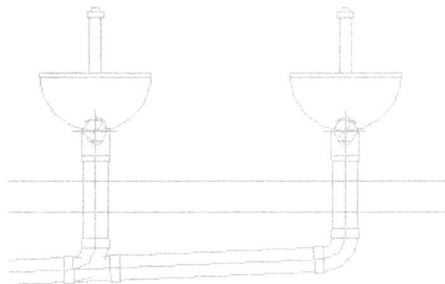

Figure 9–26   **Figure 9–27**

* You can modify pipes using universal methods by making changes in Properties or the Options Bar or by using temporary dimensions, controls, and connectors. You can also use modify tools, such as **Move**, **Rotate**, **Split Trim/Extend**, and **Align**, to help you place the pipes at the required locations.

Pipe Fittings and Accessories

One of the challenges about working with plumbing is specifying the correct pipe fitting or accessory and verifying that it is working as expected. For example, if a fitting is facing the wrong direction, you can use ⇔ (Flip) to switch it, as shown in Figure 9–28.

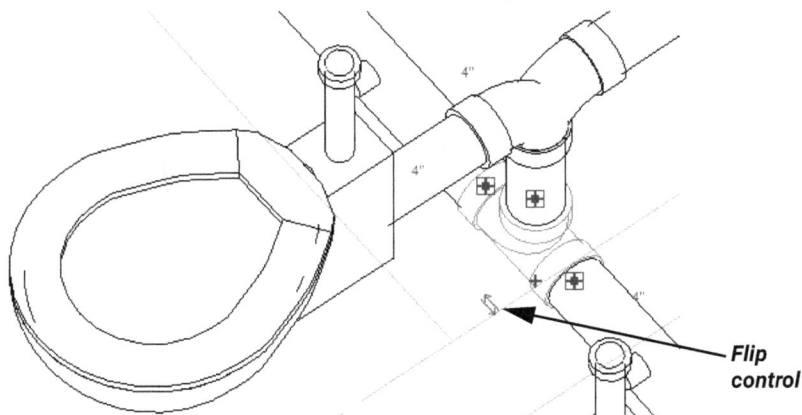

Flip control

Figure 9–28

Many fittings are automatically applied as you draw pipes. However, you might want to modify or add new fittings or accessories, such as a butterfly valve (shown in Figure 9–29) or temperature gauge, and place it at an appropriate connector.

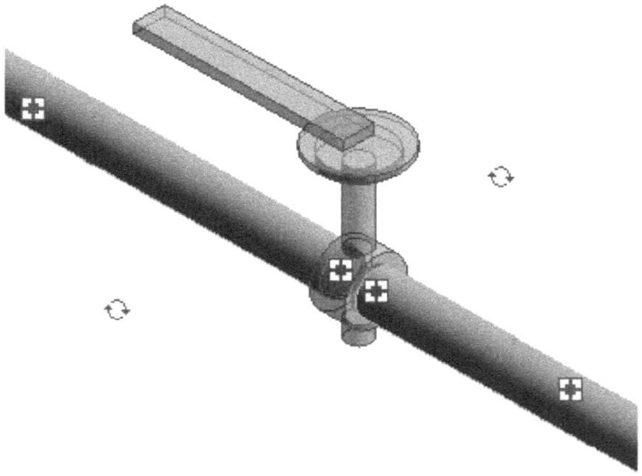

Figure 9–29

- Check various views to verify that you have correctly attached the pipe fittings to the pipes.

- Some pipe fittings are specified in the Routing Preferences in the type properties of the pipe but others have to be added separately. Accessories are always added later.

- Pipe fittings and accessories can be loaded from the Revit Library in the *Pipe>Fittings* and *Pipe>Accessories* subfolders. Select the folder for the type of pipe you are using, such as **PVC**. You can load fittings when you have started the **Pipe Accessory** command.

How To: Add a Pipe Fitting or Accessory

1. In the *Systems* tab>*Plumbing & Piping* panel, select the appropriate command: (Pipe Fitting) (**PF**) or (Pipe Accessory) (**PA**).

2. In the Type Selector, select the fitting or accessory you want to use.

3. Click on the pipe where you want the fitting or accessory. The fitting or accessory resizes to fit the element on which it is placed.

4. In some cases, the fitting or accessory might be pointing in the wrong direction, as shown on the left in Figure 9–30. Click ⟳ (Rotate) until it points in the required direction.

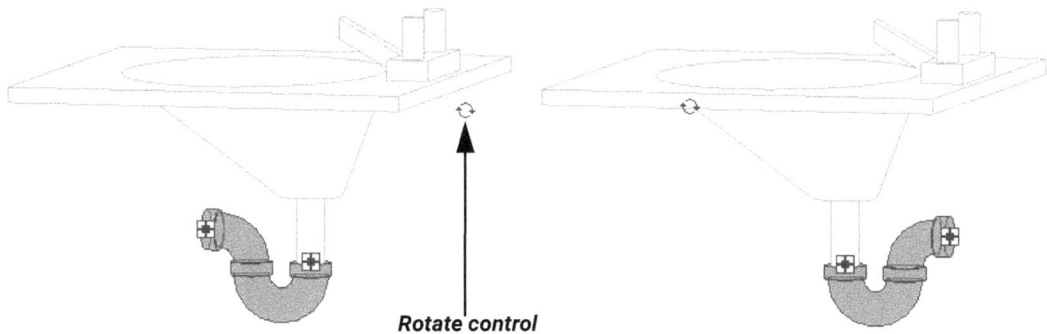

Rotate control

Figure 9–30

Modifying Pipe Fittings

Whether added automatically or manually, fittings can be modified using the Type Selector, Properties, Options Bar, and a variety of connectors and controls. For example, an elbow can be changed to a tee by clicking a control, as shown in Figure 9–31.

Figure 9–31

Capping Open Pipe Ends

You can cap the open end of a pipe by right-clicking on the end control and selecting **Cap Open End**. Alternatively, if you have more than one opening on the ends of a run, in the *Modify* contextual tab>*Edit* panel, click ⫧ (Cap Open Ends) to apply the caps.

Changing the Slope

To change the slope of a pipe, select it and modify the **Edit Slope** control, as shown in

Figure 9−32. You can also click ✏ (Slope) to open the Slope Editor. The controls are available in plan or section/elevation views.

Figure 9−32

*   You can change the diameter of the pipe in the Options Bar or Properties. The offset of the pipe ends can be changed using Properties or the *Edit Start/End Offset* controls.

Pipe Sizing

It is easiest to draw pipes using the default sizes provided by the opening sizes of the equipment and fittings, or as preset in the Mechanical Settings. However, these sizes are often incorrect for the system being used. The **Duct/Pipe Sizing** tool uses a specified sizing method and constraints to determine how to correctly size the pipes.

*   If you select only one pipe, it analyzes just that one set of connections. Select the entire system to ensure that all of the connections are analyzed.

How To: Size Pipes

1. Select all of the components in a pipe system.

2. In the *Modify | Multi-Select* tab>*Analysis* panel, click 🖼 (Duct/Pipe Sizing).

3. In the *Pipe Sizing* dialog box, set the *Sizing Method* and *Constraints* as required, as shown in Figure 9–33.

   Note: Pipes should be sized according to company design standards.

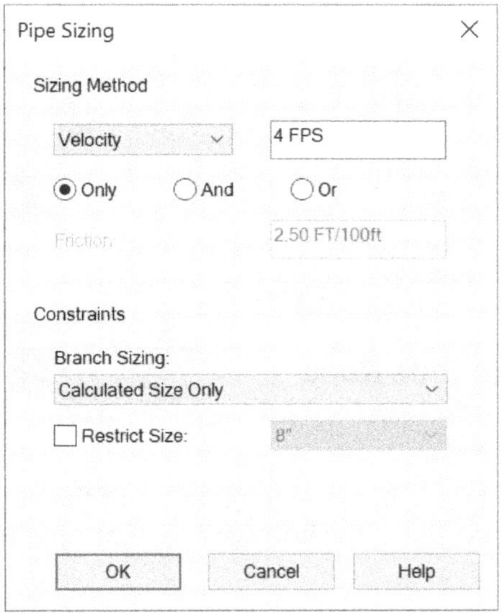

Figure 9–33

4. Click **OK**.

- Once you make a change to the system, you need to run the tool again.

- You can also modify pipe sizes on your own to create the most appropriate layout for your methodology. A helpful tool to separate lengths of pipe before you change the size is

  ⊏⊐ (Split Element).

Converting Pipe Types

After placing pipes, you can change the type of the entire run (including fittings). If the definition of a type has been changed, you can reapply the type to existing runs. You can also convert placeholders to standard pipes.

How To: Change the Type of Pipe Runs

1. Select the pipe run and filter out everything except the related pipe, accessories, and fittings.

2. In the *Modify | Multi-Select* tab>*Edit* panel, click ⊞ (Change Type).

3. In the Type Selector, select a new type of run. For the example shown in Figure 9–34, the type **Standard** was changed to **PVC - DWV**.

Figure 9–34

How To: Reapply a Type to Pipe Runs

1. Select a single pipe run.

    *   You can select different runs, but they must all be of the same type and system. If you select runs in different systems, the software prompts you to select one system to which to reapply the type.

2. Filter out everything except pipes, fittings, and accessories.

3. In the *Modify | Multi-Select* tab>*Edit* panel, click (Reapply Type).

How To: Convert Placeholders to Pipe

1. Select the pipe placeholder(s).

2. In the *Modify* contextual tab>*Edit* panel, click (Convert Placeholder).

3. The placeholders are changed into the pipe type and includes the appropriate fittings, as shown in Figure 9–35.

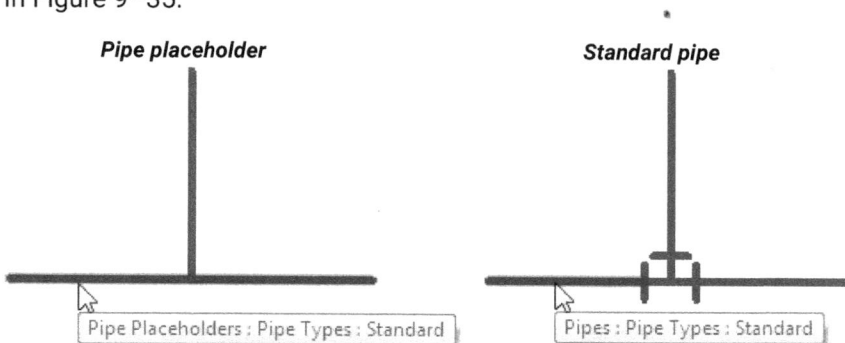

Pipe placeholder   *Standard pipe*

Pipe Placeholders : Pipe Types : Standard   Pipes : Pipe Types : Standard

Figure 9–35

Adding Insulation

You can add insulation to pipes which displays in plan as a thin line outside of the pipe. Accessories can also be insulated, as shown in Figure 9-36.

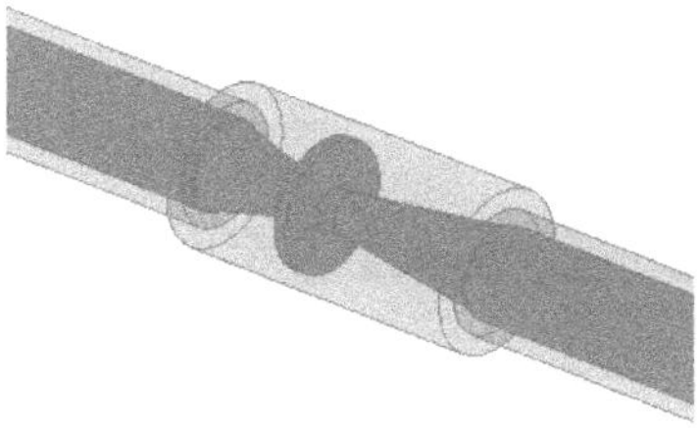

Figure 9-36

How To: Add Insulation

1. Select the pipe run that you want to insulate. You can select more than one system at a time for this command.

2. Use ⵛ (Filter) to select only the pipes, pipe fittings, and pipe accessories.

3. In the *Modify* contextual tab>*Pipe Insulation* panel, click ⬤ (Add Insulation).

4. In the *Add Pipe Insulation* dialog box, select a *Insulation Type* and set the *Thickness*, as shown in Figure 9-37. Click **OK**.

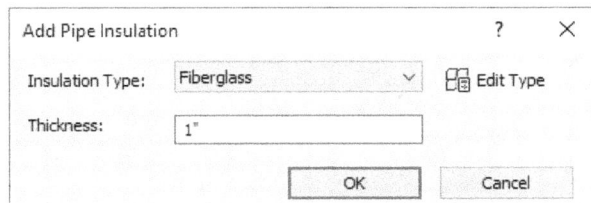

Figure 9-37

- To modify the insulation, select the insulated pipe and in the contextual ribbon, select either

  ⬤ (Edit Insulation) or ⬤ (Remove Insulation). When editing, change the type in the Type Selector and/or change the thickness in Properties.

Modifying the Justification

If a pipe run has different sized pipe, you can modify the justification, as shown in Figure 9–38.

Figure 9–38

How To: Modify Justifications

1. Select the pipe run.
2. In the *Modify | Multi-Select* tab>*Edit* panel, click ▥ (Justify).
3. To specify the point on the pipe that you want to justify around, in the *Justification Editor* tab>*Justify* panel, click ↖ (Control Point) to cycle between the end point references.

   • The alignment location displays as an arrow, as shown in Figure 9–39.

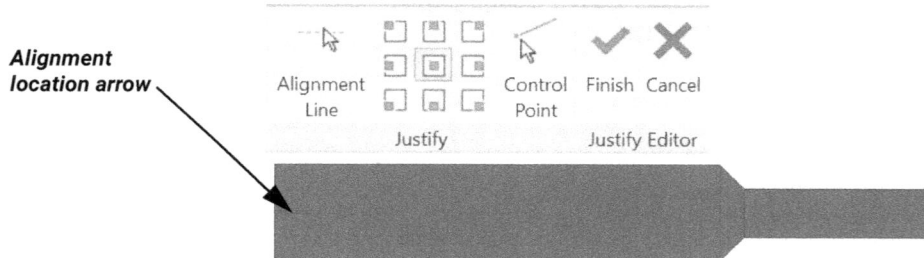

Figure 9–39

4. To indicate the required alignment, either click one of the nine alignment buttons in the *Justify* panel, or in a 3D view, use (Alignment Line) to select the required dashed line, as shown in Figure 9–40.

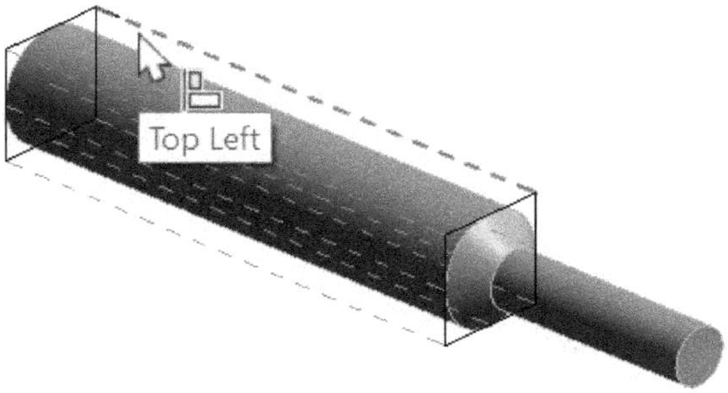

Figure 9–40

Hint: Using Thin Lines

Line thickness can negatively impact the display of elements, such as insulation or lining. To toggle lineweight on or off, in the Quick Access Toolbar, click (Thin Lines), or type **TL**.

Practice 9b
Modify Plumbing Pipes

Practice Objectives

- Change the type of pipe runs.
- Modify locations and sizes of pipes.
- Connect fixtures to pipes.
- Modify pipe fittings.

In this practice, you will change the type of a piping run to the correct sanitary type. You will modify the size and location of pipes. You will connect two classroom sinks to the cold and hot water mains and then copy the sinks and piping along the hall. Finally, you will modify connections where the copies did not clean up automatically, as shown in Figure 9–41.

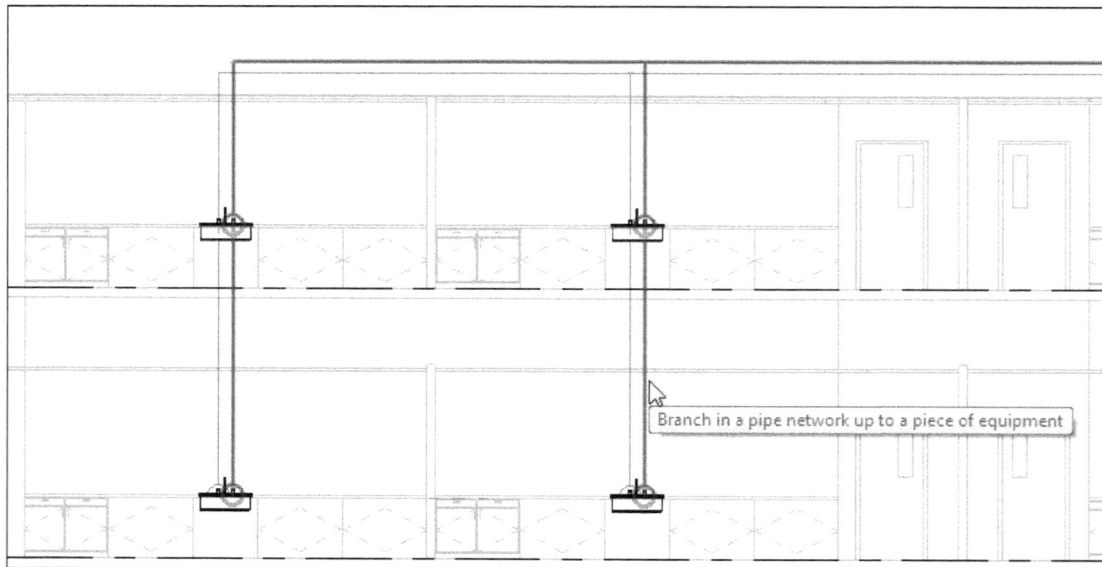

Figure 9–41

Task 1: Change the type of pipe and pipe slope.

1. In the practice files *Working Models>Plumbing* folder, open **Plumb-Modify-Piping.rvt**.

2. Open the Plumbing>Plumbing>Sections (Building Section)>**Restrooms Section** view.

3. Zoom in to the second piping intersection to the right and highlight the fitting. As shown in Figure 9–42, this is not the correct type of fitting for a sanitary system.

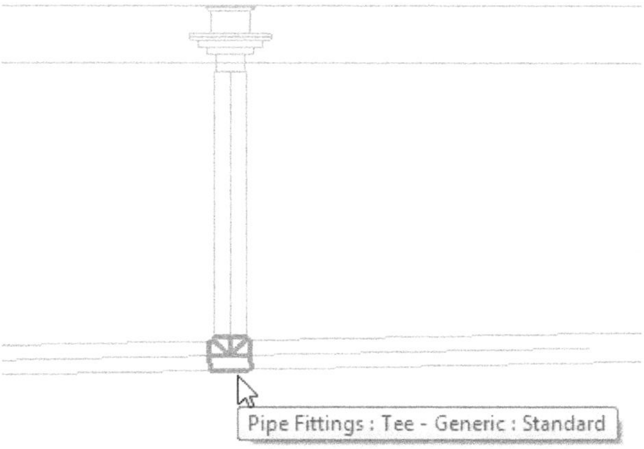

Pipe Fittings : Tee - Generic : Standard

Figure 9–42

4. Zoom out to see the full view.

5. Hover the cursor over one of the sanitary sloped pipes and press <Tab> until everything in the pipe network highlights (watch the Status Bar to know when the network is selected so you do not select the system).

6. Click to select the pipe network.

7. In the *Modify | Multi-Select* tab>*Selection* panel, click ▽ (Filter).

8. In the *Filter* dialog box, clear the checkmark beside **Plumbing Fixtures** and then click **OK**. Note that:

   • The ribbon tabs have now changed because only pipes and pipe fittings are selected.

   • The Type Selector is grayed out. You cannot make changes to the pipe type here.

9. In the *Modify | Multi-Select tab>Edit* panel, click ▦ (Change Type).

10. In the Type Selector, select **Pipe Types: PVC - DWV**.

11. Zoom back in and check the fitting. It is now the correct type, as shown in Figure 9–43.

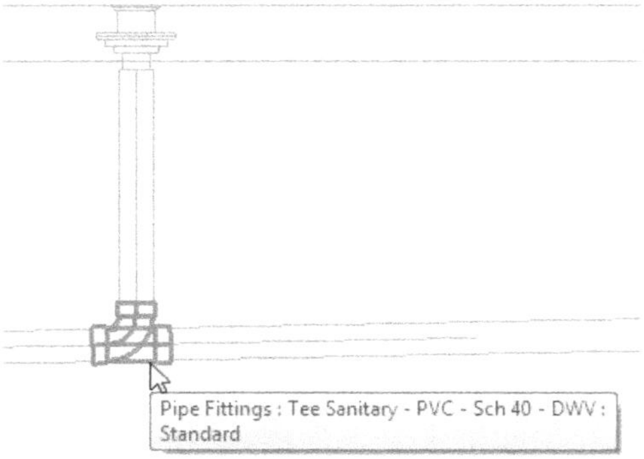

Figure 9–43

12. Select the two floor drains and related piping near the water heaters. (Hint: You may have to select a bit more to get the visual that matches the one shown in Figure 9–44.)

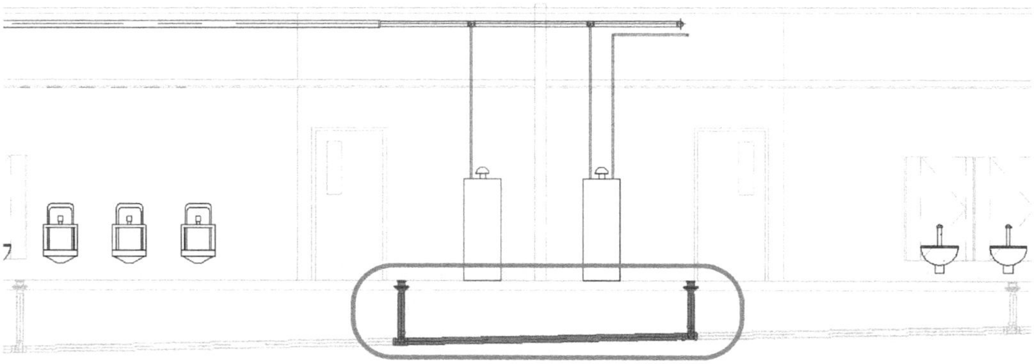

Figure 9–44

13. In the *Modify | Multi-Select* tab>*View* panel, click (Selection Box). A 3D view opens with the selected elements displaying. The *Detail Level* should be set to **Fine** so you can see the pipe, as shown in Figure 9–45.

- Use the ViewCube to rotate the view around to see the pipe at different angles.

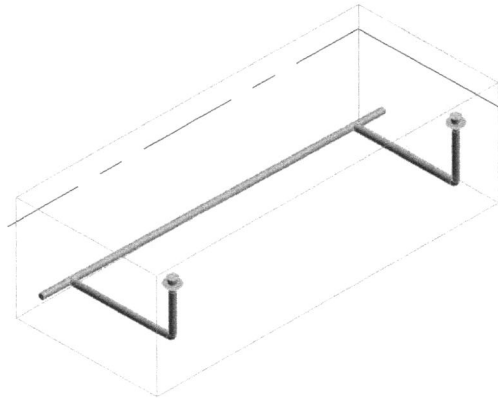

Figure 9–45

14. Still in the 3D view, select one of the lateral pipes and in the *Modify | Pipes* tab>*Edit* panel, click ✐ (Slope).

15. In the Slope Editor, change the *Slope Value* to **1/4" / 12"** and click ✓ (Finish). The pipe is now sloped. Repeat with the other pipe.

16. Save the project.

Task 2: Modify location and size of piping.

1. Open the Plumbing>Plumbing>Floor Plans>**02 Plumbing Plan** view.

2. Zoom in on the sinks at the far right of the hall in the south classroom wing, as shown in Figure 9–46.

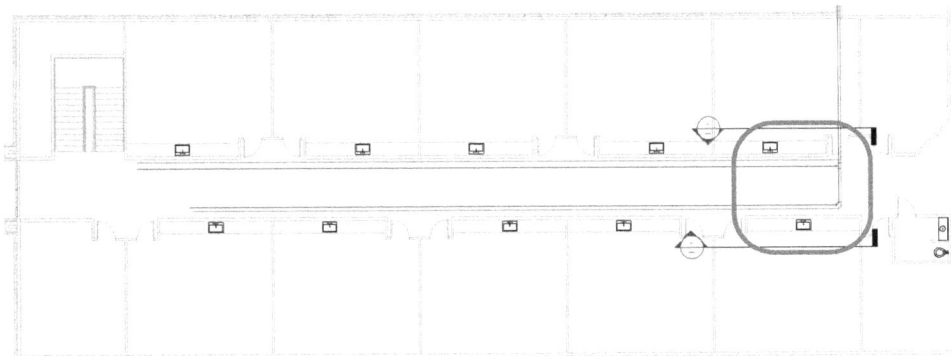

Figure 9–46

3. Change the *Detail Level* to **Fine** to display the pipe sizes clearly and hide the two sections in the view.

---

4. The hot and cold water pipes show as stacked. Select one of the hot water pipes (zoom in) and drag slightly to the right, as shown in Figure 9–47.

5. Select the two cold water pipes running down the hall in the south wing. Note that they are larger in diameter than they need to be, as shown in Figure 9–47.

6. In the Options Bar, change the *Diameter* to **1"**. New step down fittings are applied, as shown in Figure 9–48.

Figure 9–47   **Figure 9–48**

7. Change the *Detail Level* to **Coarse**.

8. The piping needs to be moved out of the hall. Select one of the cold water pipes and drag it into the wall. Repeat with the other cold and hot water pipes, as shown in Figure 9−49.

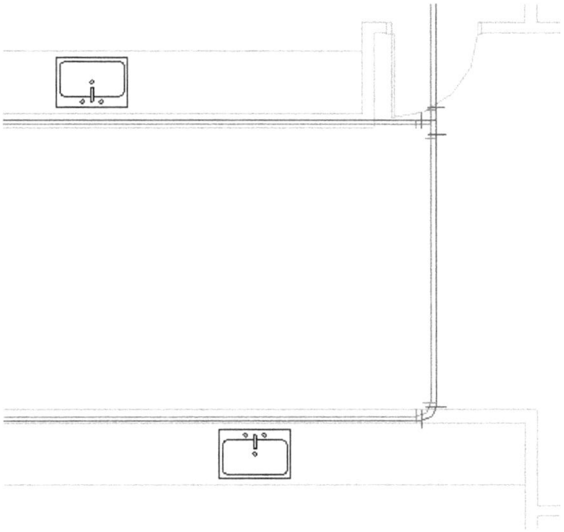

Figure 9−49

• Zoom in as needed to place the pipes inside the wall.

9. Save the project.

Task 3: Connect the sinks into the piping.

At this point there are only four sinks in the classroom wing: two on the first floor and two directly above on the second floor. In this task, you will attach piping to the sinks. In the next task, you will copy the entire set of four sinks and related piping to the rest of the locations.

1. Open the Plumbing>Plumbing>Sections (Building Section)> **South Wing - North Classrooms** view.

2. Turn on **Crop View** in the View Control Bar and zoom in to the sinks.

3. Use the **Connect Into** command to connect the sink on the first floor to the hot and cold water pipes running above the second floor, as shown in Figure 9–50.

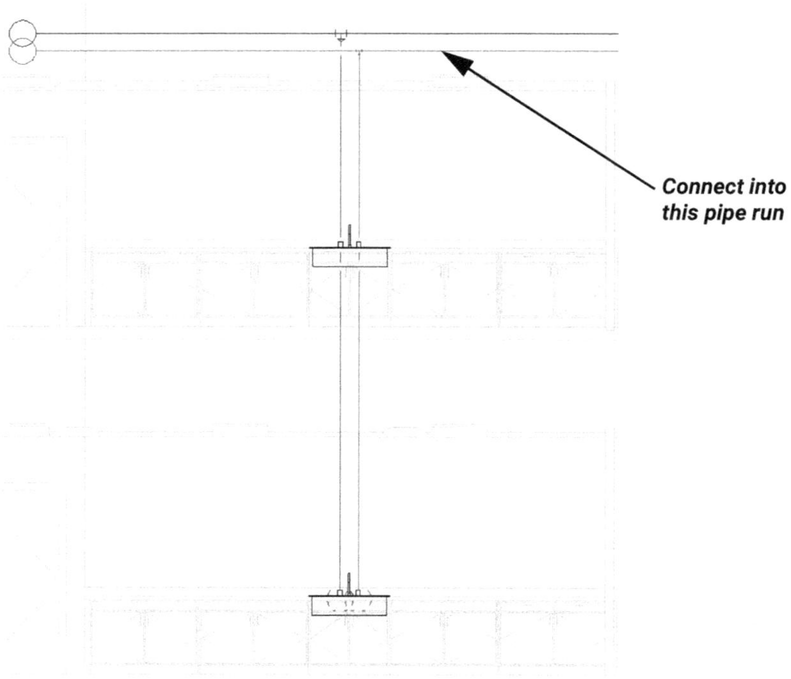

*Connect into
this pipe run*

Figure 9–50

4. Select the second-floor sink and use the **Connect Into** command to tie into the pipes that are running up from the first floor, as shown in Figure 9–51.

   • Note: You must connect the first floor before connecting the second floor. If you try to connect them in the reverse order, it will not work.

   • Hint: To verify the connections are correct, draw a selection window around the two sinks and pipes and click **Selection Box**, which will open a 3D view of the sinks and pipes.

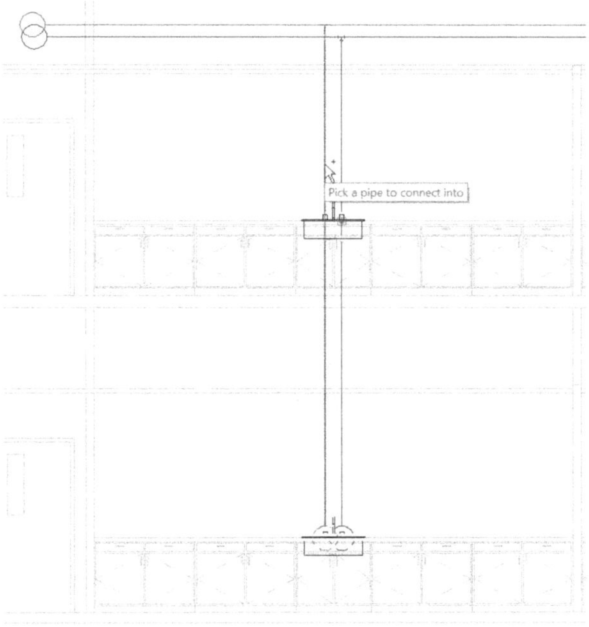

Figure 9–51

5. Open the **South Wing - South Classrooms** view. Repeat the **Connect Into** command to connect and tie the pipes from the first floor and second floor sinks to the appropriate pipes.

6. Save the project.

Task 4: Copy the sinks and piping to other locations.

1. Continue working in the **South Wing - South Classrooms** view.

2. In the View Control Bar, turn off **Crop View** so that you can see the rest of the sinks along the same side of the hall.

3. Select the sinks, vertical pipes, and associated connectors (use a window selection - left to right).

4. In the *Modify | Multi-Select* tab>*Modify* panel, click ⚬⃕ (Copy).

    Note: Constrain forces the copied elements to stay in the same positioning vertically as the original.

5. In the Options Bar, select **Constrain** and **Multiple**. (Yours may already be checked if you have changed them for another practice.)

6. As the start point of the copy, select the top corner of one of the sinks.

7. Copy the elements to the same top corner on the next sink, as shown in Figure 9–52.

   Note: You can select other points as the start point, just ensure that they are ones that you can place directly on the sinks in the linked architectural model.

Figure 9–52

8. Continue copying the elements down the hall until there is a sink and piping in each of the classrooms, as shown in Figure 9–53.

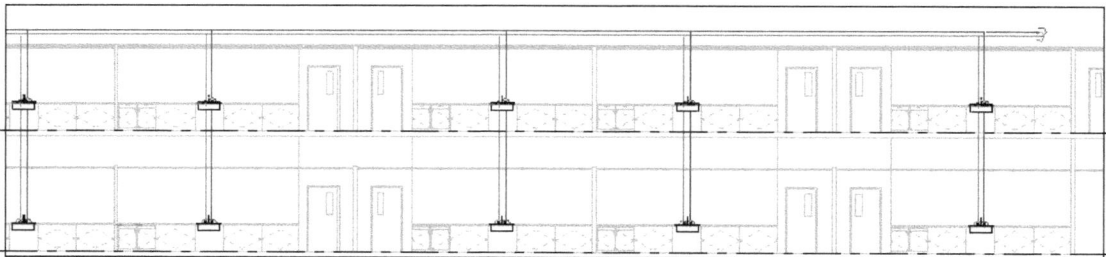

Figure 9–53

9. Click ⌖ (Modify). Open the **South Wing - North Classrooms** view and repeat copying the sinks and connecting pipes and fittings to all of the classrooms.

10. Save the project.

Task 5: Modify fittings.

1. Return to the **South Wing - South Classrooms** section view.

2. Hover the cursor over one of the vertical pipes coming from the first sink and press <Tab>. The full length of the connected pipe should highlight, as shown in Figure 9–54. (The pipe that is selected in the image below has been enhanced for clarity.)

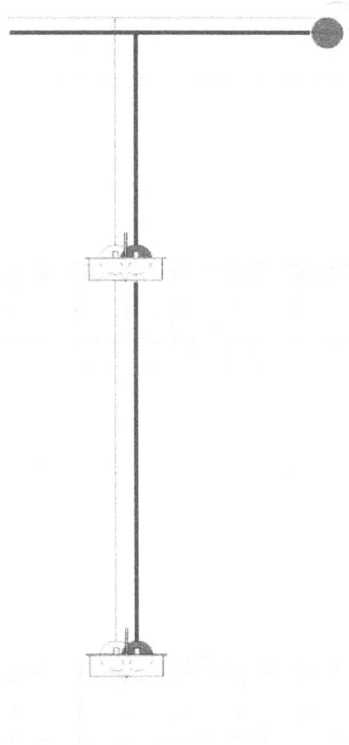

Figure 9–54

3. Hover the cursor over one of the vertical pipes from another sink and press <Tab> until the pipes highlight.

4. If you continue pressing tab you will see that the two sinks are connected in a Piping System, as shown in Figure 9–55. (The pipe that is selected in the image below has been enhanced for clarity.)

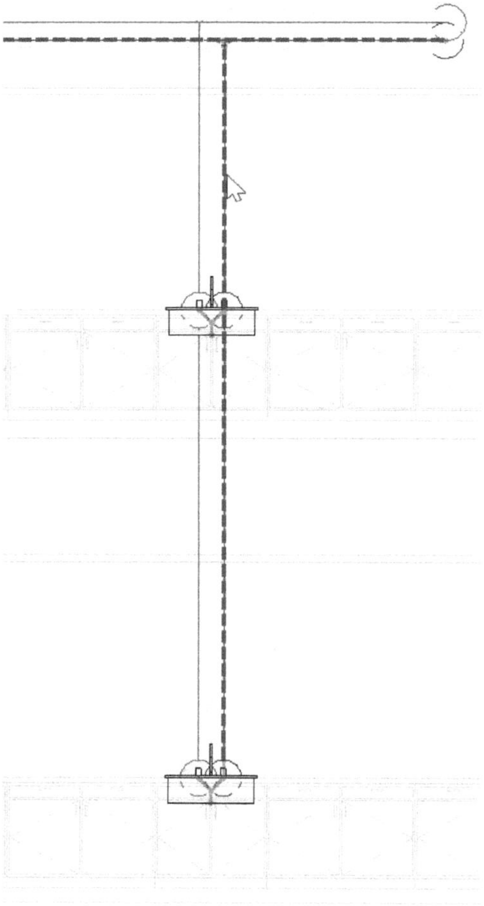

Figure 9–55

5. Zoom out to see the entire section view and then zoom in on the fittings at the end of the hall to the far left side.

6. Delete the tee and transition fittings. Use the **Trim /Extend to Corner** command to clean up the pipe fittings to an elbow fitting, as shown in Figure 9–56. (The pipes that are selected in the image below have been enhanced for clarity.)

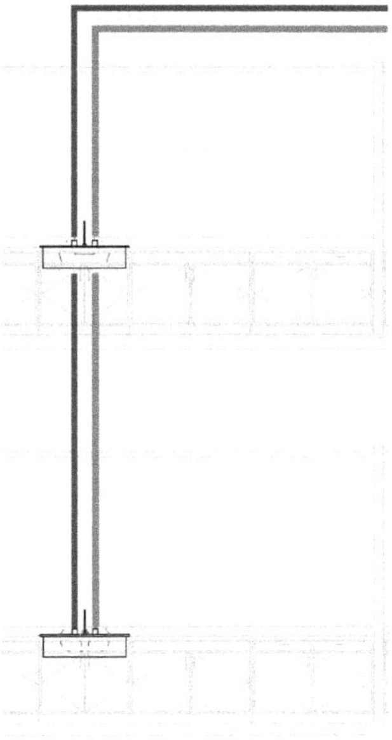

Figure 9–56

7. Repeat cleaning up the pipes in the **South Wing - North Classrooms** section view, as shown in Figure 9–57.

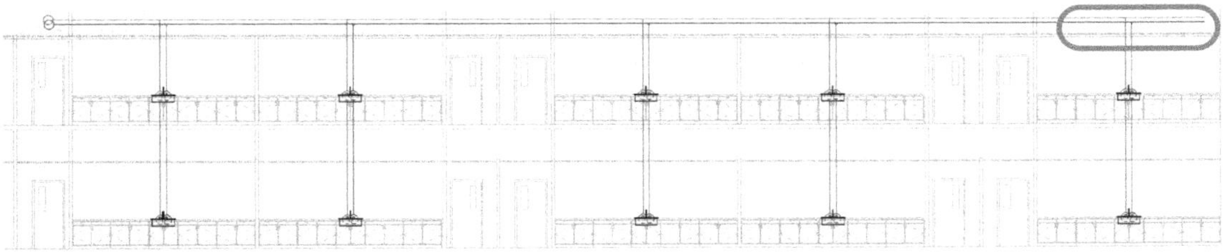

Figure 9–57

8. Save and close the project.

End of practice

9.3 Adding Hydronic Systems

If you are working with hydronic piping, you need to set up the analysis process in **Mechanical Settings** on the *Pipe Settings>Calculation>Hydronic Networks* tab. Select **Enable analysis for closed loop hydronic piping networks**.

In the early stages of a project, you might not want to create all of the exact connections between hydronic piping and mechanical equipment, but you still want to be able to calculate flow and pressure drop. To do this, you can add analytical connections, as shown in Figure 9-58.

Select mechanical equipment or hydronic piping, then in the *Modify | Pipe* contextual tab>

Create panel, click ⊐ (Analytical Connections) and select the pipe or equipment you want to connect into.

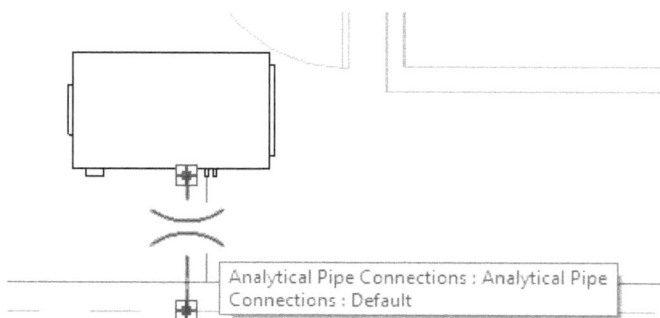

Analytical Pipe Connections : Analytical Pipe Connections : Default

Figure 9-58

After the element is placed, you can assign the **Pressure Drop** (which is 0 by default) in the type properties of the analytical connection element.

* It is best to draw hydronic pipe starting from equipment.

Practice 9c
Add Hydronic Pipes

Practice Objective

- Add hydronic piping.

In this practice, you will add hydronic piping from the mechanical equipment using connectors and the **Connect Into** tool. The completed project is shown in Figure 9–59.

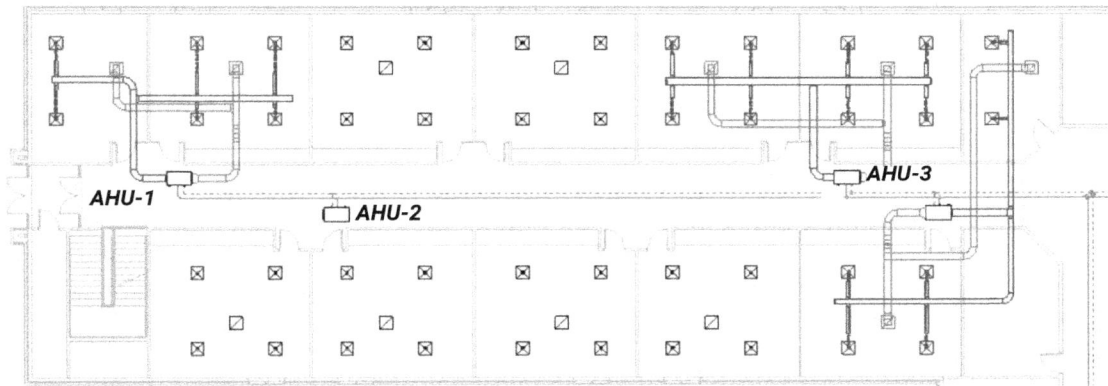

Figure 9–59

Keep in mind the air handling units (AHUs) and their numbers as this will come in handy while doing the practices.

Task 1: Draw pipe.

1. In the practice files *Working Models>Mechanical* folder, open the project **Mech-Hydronic.rvt**.

2. Open the Mechanical>HVAC>Floor Plans>**01 Mechanical Plan** view and zoom in on the upper northwest rooms of the north wing.

3. Select the AHU-1 unit to the far left of the north wing and zoom in so that the three pipe outlets clearly display, as shown in Figure 9–60.

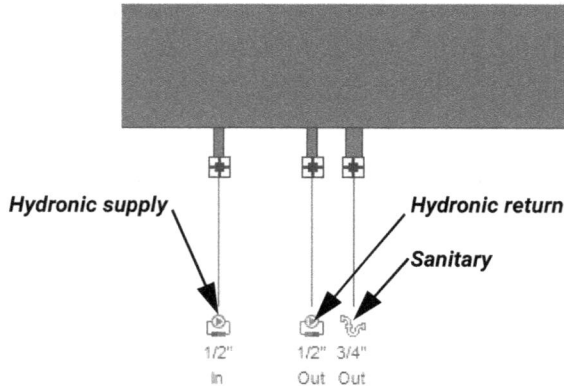

Figure 9–60

4. Select the **Hydronic Supply** icon to start the **Draw Pipe** command.

5. In the Type Selector, select **Pipe Types: Standard**.

6. Draw the pipe down and away from the AHU, then continue drawing the pipe down the hall to the right until it is near but not touching the existing pipe (as shown in Figure 9–61), zooming out as needed.

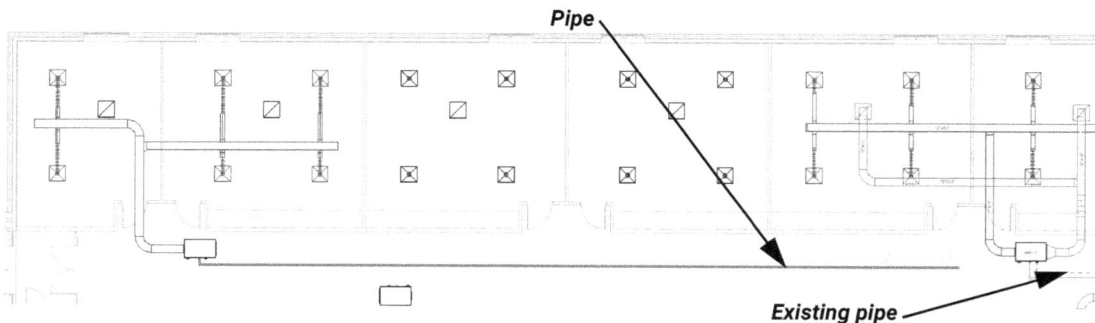

Figure 9–61

7. Click ⬚ (Modify).

8. In the *Modify* tab>*Modify* panel, click ⬚ (Align), or type **AL**.

9. In the *Modify | Align* tab>*Align* panel, uncheck **Multiple Alignment** and **Lock** if checked.

10. Select the existing hydronic supply pipe as the reference alignment line.

11. Select the new hydronic supply pipe as the entity to align.

12. Click ⬚ (Modify).

13. Repeat the drawing and aligning process with the hydronic return pipe using the **Pipe Types: Standard**. The hydronic return pipe displays with a dashed line style.

14. Zoom in on and select the other AHU in the hall that has no pipes connected to it, as shown in Figure 9–62.

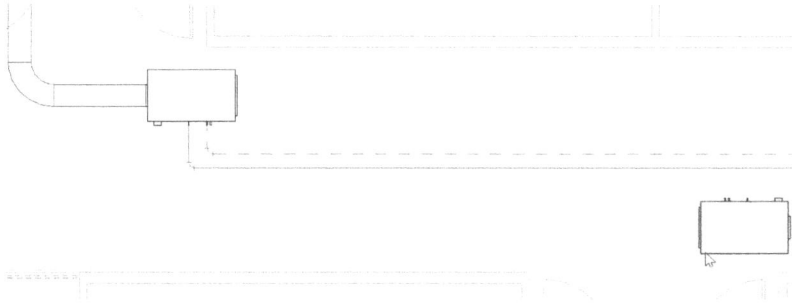

Figure 9–62

15. In the *Modify | Mechanical Equipment* tab>*Layout* panel, click ▯▯▢ (Connect Into).

16. In the *Select Connector* dialog box, select the **Hydronic Return** connector and click **OK**.

17. Select the hydronic return pipe (the dashed line). Repeat the process with the hydronic supply connector and pipe (the solid line). The AHU is now connected with the pipe, as shown in Figure 9–63.

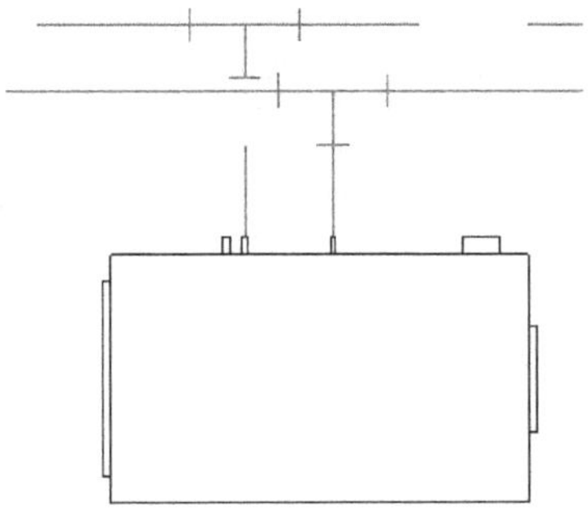

Figure 9–63

18. Zoom out to fit the model in the view.

19. Save and close the project.

End of practice

9.4 Adding Fire Protection Systems

Fire protection systems work in much the same way as plumbing and hydronic piping systems. You place sprinkler heads where they are required and add piping to connect them, as shown in Figure 9–64. The systems are created automatically based on the sprinkler type.

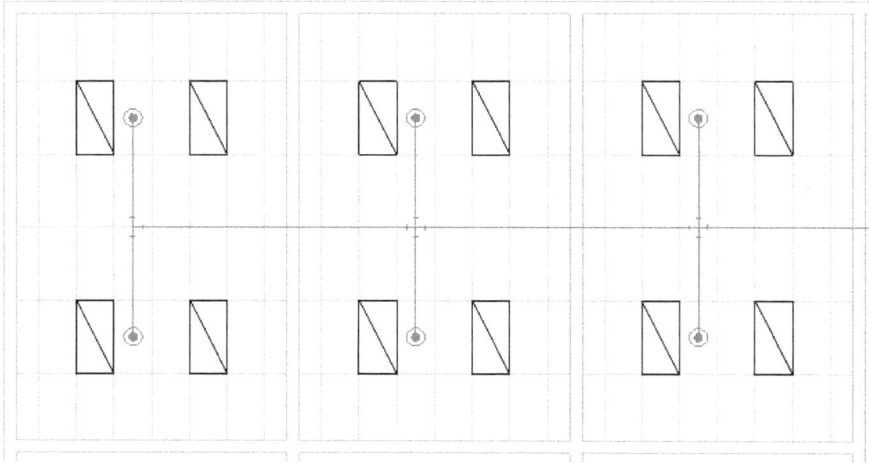

Figure 9–64

- Sprinkler types include wet and dry. All sprinklers in a system must be of the same type.

- To insert sprinklers, in the *Systems* tab>*Plumbing & Piping* panel, click 🗲 (Sprinkler), or type **SK**.

- You can load sprinklers from the *Fire Protection>Sprinklers* folder of the Revit Library.

- Hosted sprinklers need to be placed on ceilings. Therefore, it is best to use a reflected ceiling plan when adding them.

Practice 9d
Add Fire Protection Systems

Practice Objectives

- Add two different types of sprinklers.
- Add piping.

In this practice, you will add both wet and dry sprinklers. You will also add piping that connects the sprinklers, as shown in Figure 9–65.

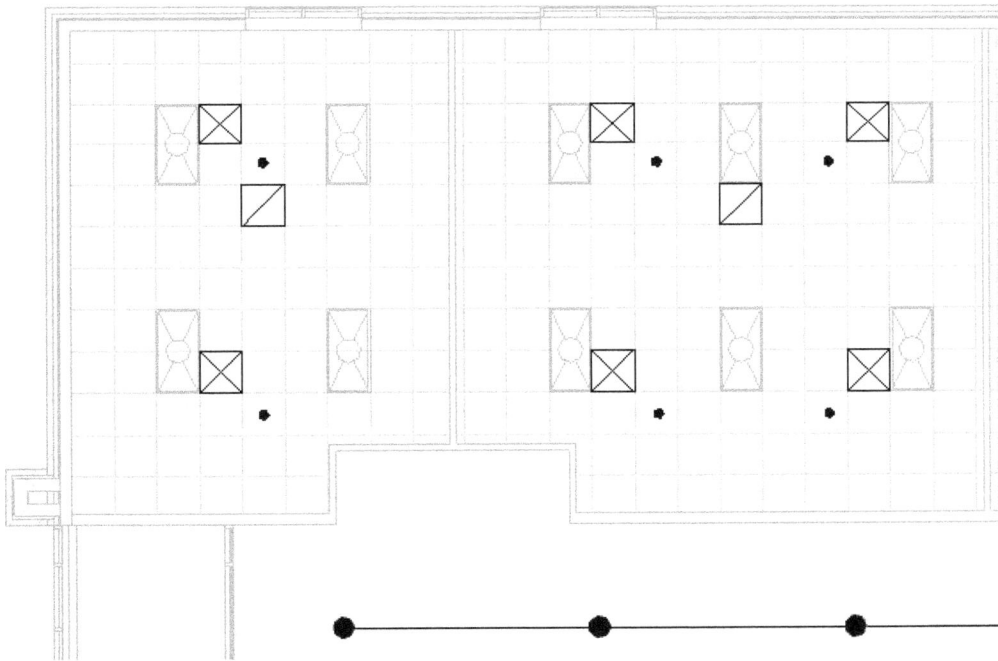

Figure 9–65

Task 1: Add sprinklers.

1. In the practice files *Working Models>Plumbing* folder, open **Plumb-Fire Protection.rvt**.
2. Open the Plumbing>Fire>Ceiling Plans>**01 Fire RCP** view and close the SP - Starting Page.
3. Zoom in on the north wing.
4. In the *Systems* tab>*Plumbing & Piping* panel, click 🚿 (Sprinkler), or type **SK**.
5. A warning displays noting that no sprinklers are loaded in the project yet. Click **Yes** to load them.

6. Navigate to the practice files *Working Models>Plumbing> Families* folder and select the following families:

- **Sprinkler - Dry - Pendent - Hosted.rfa**
- **Sprinkler - Pendent.rfa**

7. Click **Open**.

8. In the Type Selector, select **Sprinkler - Dry - Pendent - Hosted: 1/2" Dry Pendent**.

9. In the *Modify | Place Sprinkler* tab>*Placement* panel, click ⬚ (Place on Face).

10. Move the cursor over the hall. A ⊘ symbol displays because it does not recognize anything to host to in this area.

11. Move the cursor into the top leftmost classroom where there is a ceiling. Place one of the sprinklers on a grid intersection and then move it so it is in the center of one of the ceiling tiles.

12. Copy the sprinkler to additional locations in the two classrooms, similar to that shown in Figure 9-66.

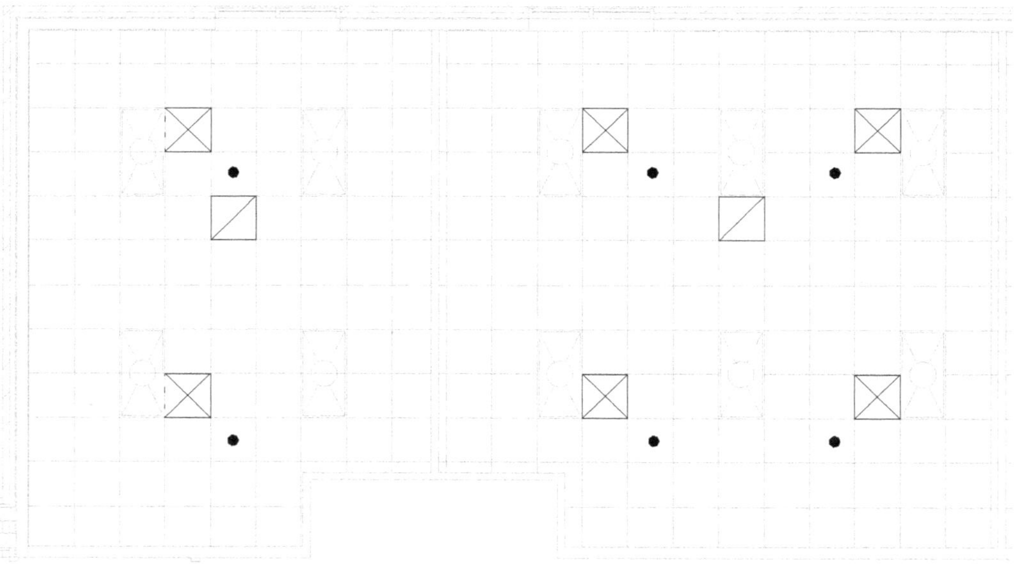

Figure 9-66

13. Start the **Sprinkler** command again. In the Type Selector, select **Sprinkler - Pendent: 1/2" Pendent**. This is a non-hosted sprinkler so you can place it anywhere without a qualifying host.

14. In Properties, set the *Offset from Host* to **9'-0"**.

15. Place sprinklers down the hall. Place the first one approximately **6'-0"** off the vestibule door and then **12'-0"** on center down the hall, as shown in Figure 9–67. You can place the first one and then array or copy the rest.

  * If you array the sprinklers, toggle off **Group and Associate** or ungroup the sprinklers after you finish.

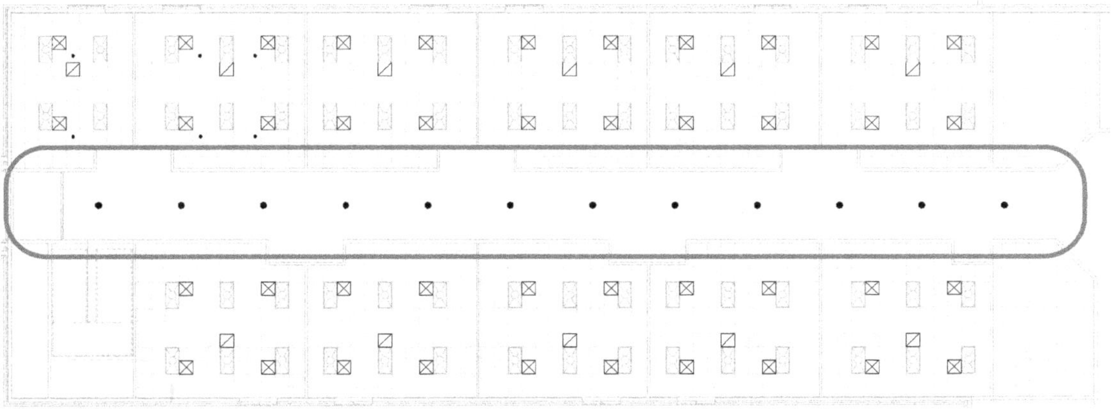

Figure 9–67

16. Save the project.

Task 2: Add piping for fire protection systems.

1. Select the left most sprinkler in the hall. Right-click on the connector and select **Draw Pipe**.

2. In the *Modify | Place Pipe* tab>*Sloped Piping* panel, select ✕ (Slope: Off) to make sure this piping is not sloped.

3. In the Type Selector, select **Pipe Types: Copper.**

4. In the Options Bar, the *Diameter* and *Middle Elevation* match the location of the connector. Change the *Middle Elevation* to **10'-0"** and press <Enter>. This moves the first segment of the pipe directly up from the sprinkler.

5. Draw the pipe down the hall and past the last sprinkler, as shown in Figure 9-68.

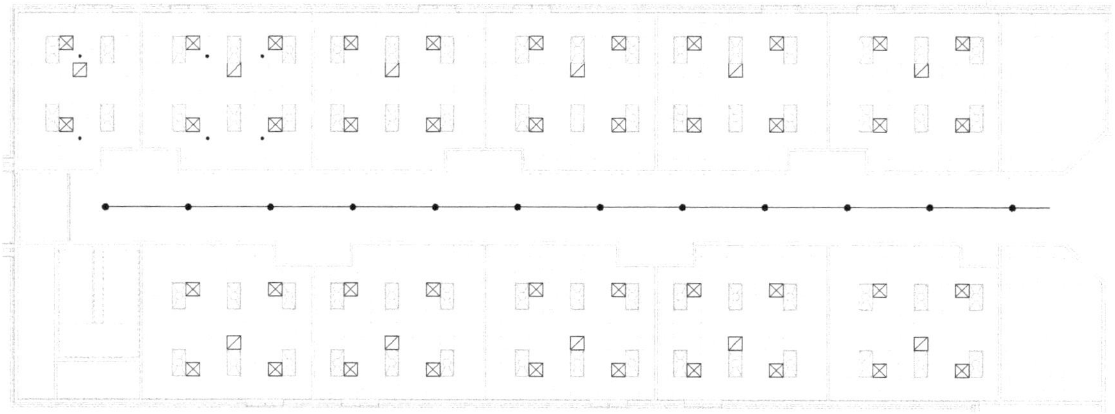

Figure 9-68

6. Open the Plumbing>Fire>Sections (Building Section)>**North Wing - Hall Section** view.

    Note: Toggle on ▤ *(Thin Lines), if required, to see the pipes and fittings clearly.*

7. Zoom in so that one of the sprinklers is displayed. Note that some of the sprinklers are not connected.

8. Select the first unconnected sprinkler, as shown in Figure 9-69. In the *Modify | Sprinklers* tab>*Layout* panel, click ⊪ (Connect Into).

9. Select the pipe to connect into. The new connection is created with appropriate fittings, as shown in Figure 9–70.

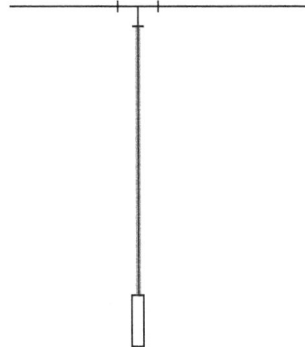

Figure 9–69   **Figure 9–70**

10. Continue connecting the sprinklers in the hall to the main pipe.

11. Save and close the project.

End of practice

Chapter Review Questions

1. After tying in piping to a sloped sanitary pipe, the automatically placed fittings are facing the wrong direction, as shown in Figure 9–71. How would you fix this?

Figure 9–71

a. Use **Rotate**.

b. Place its opposite type.

c. Click the **Flip** arrow.

d. Click **AutoSlope** in the ribbon.

2. Which placement option can be used for placing a face based plumbing fixture on the wall, as shown in Figure 9–72?

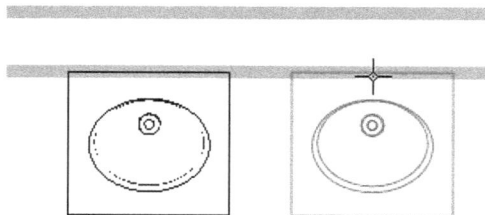

Figure 9–72

a. Place on Vertical Face

b. Place on Face

c. Place on Work Plane

3. How do you specify the direction in which a pipe slopes as you are creating it, as shown in Figure 9–73?

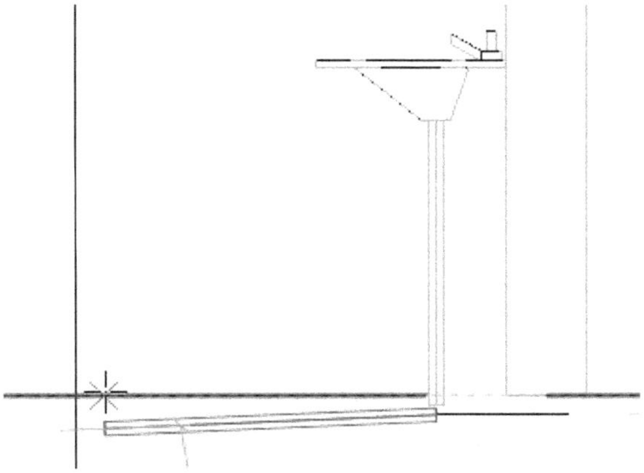

Figure 9–73

a. Set the *Slope Value* in the Options Bar.

b. Draw the pipe in a section view to ensure that it slopes correctly.

c. Create it flat and slope it later.

d. Set the *Slope Value* in the ribbon.

4. You can copy pipe, pipe fittings, and pipe accessories.

a. True

b. False

5. Parallel pipe runs are created automatically at the correct distance from equipment, as shown in Figure 9–74.

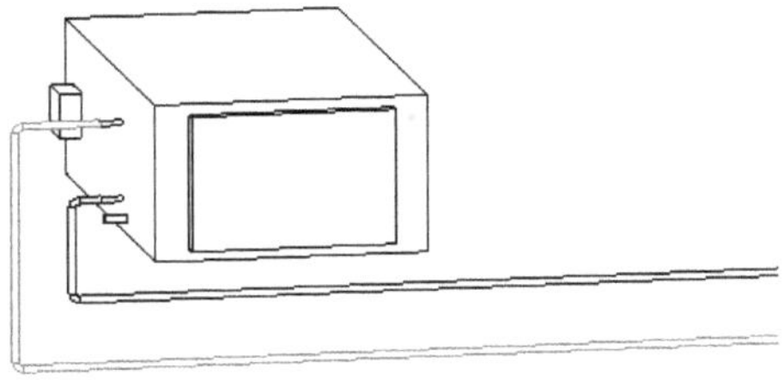

Figure 9–74

a. True

b. False

6. When adding pipe accessories, such as the butterfly valve, what are you first required to do?

    a. Split the pipe using ⊹ (Split Element).

    b. Split the pipe using ⊶ (Split with Gap).

    c. Place the accessory near the pipe and then move it in place.

    d. Do nothing extra, just place the accessory on the pipe.

7. How do you change an elbow fitting to a tee fitting?

    a. Delete the elbow and place a tee instead.

    b. Select the elbow and use the Type Selector to select a tee fitting instead.

    c. Select the elbow and click **+** (Plus).

    d. Select the elbow and click **Convert to Tee** in the ribbon.

8. Which of the following commands can be used when modifying pipe? (Select all that apply.)

    a. Change Type

    b. Reapply Type

    c. Add Insulation

    d. Edit Lining

    e. Modify Justification

    f. Modify Material

    g. Change Offset

Command Summary

Button	Command	Location
Plumbing & Piping Tools		
	Flex Pipe	• **Ribbon:** *Systems* tab>*Plumbing & Piping* panel • **Shortcut:** FP
	Mechanical Equipment	• **Ribbon:** *Systems* tab>*Mechanical* panel • **Shortcut:** ME
	Mechanical Settings	• **Ribbon:** *Systems* tab>*Mechanical* panel title • **Shortcut:** MS
	Parallel Pipes	• **Ribbon:** *Systems* tab>*Plumbing & Piping* panel
	Pipe	• **Ribbon:** *Systems* tab>*Plumbing & Piping* panel • **Shortcut:** PI
	Pipe Accessory	• **Ribbon:** *Systems* tab>*Plumbing & Piping* panel • **Shortcut:** PA
	Pipe Fitting	• **Ribbon:** *Systems* tab>*Plumbing & Piping* panel • **Shortcut:** PF
	Pipe Placeholder	• **Ribbon:** *Systems* tab>*Plumbing & Piping* panel
	Plumbing Fixture	• **Ribbon:** *Systems* tab>*Plumbing & Piping* panel • **Shortcut:** PX
	Sprinkler	• **Ribbon:** *Systems* tab>*Plumbing & Piping* panel
Pipe Modification		
	Add Insulation	*With one or more Pipes selected*: • **Ribbon:** *Modify | Pipe* tab>*Edit* panel *With Pipes and Pipe Fittings selected*: • **Ribbon:** *Modify | Multi-Select* tab>*Edit* panel
	Automatically Connect	• **Ribbon:** *Modify | Place Pipe* tab>*Placement Tools* panel

Button	Command	Location
	Cap Open Ends	• **Ribbon:** *(with one or more pipes selected) Modify* contextual tab>*Edit* panel
	Change Type	*With one or more Pipes selected:* • **Ribbon:** *Modify	Pipe* tab>*Edit* panel *With Pipes and Pipe Fittings selected:* • **Ribbon:** *Modify	Multi-Select* tab>*Edit* panel
	Convert Placeholder	• **Ribbon:** *Modify	Pipe Placeholders* tab>*Edit* panel
	Edit Insulation	*With one or more Pipes selected:* • **Ribbon:** *Modify	Pipe* tab>*Edit* panel *With Pipes and Pipe Fittings selected:* • **Ribbon:** *Modify	Multi-Select* tab>*Edit* panel
	Inherit Elevation	• **Ribbon:** *Modify	Place Pipe* tab>*Placement Tools* panel
	Inherit Size	• **Ribbon:** *Modify	Place Pipe* tab>*Placement Tools* panel
	Justification (Settings)	• **Ribbon:** *Modify	Place Pipe* tab>*Placement Tools* panel
	Justify	• **Ribbon:** *(with one or more Pipes selected) Modify	Pipe* tab>*Edit* panel or *(with Pipes and Pipe Fittings selected) Modify	Multi-Select* tab>*Edit* panel
	Reapply Type	*With one or more Pipes selected:* • **Ribbon:** *Modify	Pipe* tab>*Edit* panel *With Pipes and Pipe Fittings selected:* • **Ribbon:** *Modify	Multi-Select* tab>*Edit* panel
	Remove Insulation	*With one or more Pipes selected:* • **Ribbon:** *Modify	Pipe* tab>*Edit* panel *With Pipes and Pipe Fittings selected:* • **Ribbon:** *Modify	Multi-Select* tab>*Edit* panel
	Slope	• **Ribbon**: *(when piping in a system is selected) Modify	Multi-Select* tab>*Edit* panel

Duct Systems

HVAC systems consist of components that include mechanical equipment, air terminals, ducts, and pipes. The process of combining these components and ensuring they work correctly is a significant part of developing an HVAC project.

Learning Objectives

- Add ducts to connect HVAC components.
- Modify ducts.

10.1 Connecting Ducts

Ducts connect mechanical equipment to air terminals, as shown in Figure 10–1. There are various shapes and sizes that can be used both for regular and flex duct. By using connectors on the equipment and the air terminals, you can quickly attach the ducts and have the software automatically calculate any differences in height.

Figure 10–1

- Ducts can be drawn horizontally and vertically in plan, elevation/section, and 3D views.

- To get the ducts at the right height, it is recommended to start from the mechanical equipment.

- Fittings are added between changes of height or size as you model the elements, as shown in Figure 10–2.

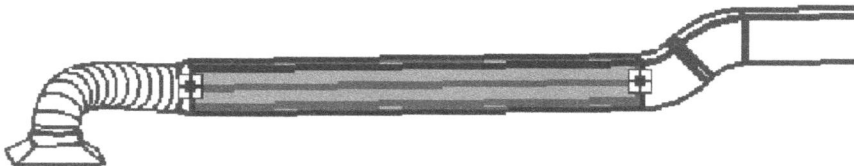

Figure 10–2

- If you need to lay the runs, but the type and size has not yet been determined, create Duct Placeholders and convert them to standard ducts at a later stage.

Mechanical Settings for Ducts

Before you add ducts, review and modify the Mechanical Settings to suit your project or office standards. These settings control the angles at which the ducts can be drawn and the default types, offsets, sizes, and Pressure Drop calculation method.

- In the *Systems* tab>*Mechanical* panel, click ⌐ (Mechanical Settings), or type **MS** to open the *Mechanical Settings* dialog box (shown in Figure 10–3).

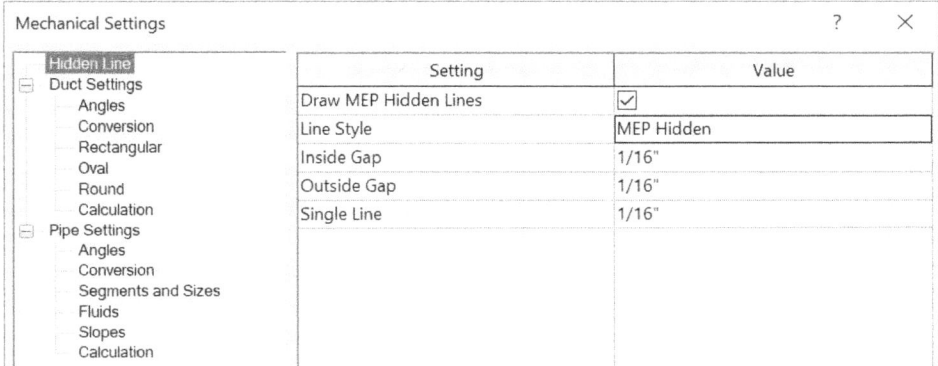

Mechanical Settings	? ✕

	Setting	Value
	Draw MEP Hidden Lines	☑
	Line Style	MEP Hidden
	Inside Gap	1/16"
	Outside Gap	1/16"
	Single Line	1/16"

Tree items: Hidden Line, Duct Settings (Angles, Conversion, Rectangular, Oval, Round, Calculation), Pipe Settings (Angles, Conversion, Segments and Sizes, Fluids, Slopes, Calculation)

Figure 10–3

Hidden Line	Specify the size and type of hidden lines that show when ducts or pipe cross over each other.
Duct Settings	Specifies a set of common duct system parameters.
Angles	Specify at what angles fittings are applied for both duct and pipe.
Conversion	Specify how the ducts or pipe work when using the Generate Layout tool. (These are also available in that command.)
Rectangular, Oval, and Round	Specify the sizes that can be used when placing ducts. (Duct only.)
Calculation	Specify the duct or pipe pressure drop for straight sections. You can select from a variety of calculation methods.

- Duct Settings are set by project and can be included in templates or imported into a project from another project using **Transfer Project Standards**.

Connecting Ducts

You can connect ducts by first starting the **Duct** command and hovering your cursor over the end of another duct, fixture, or equipment. When you see the connector highlight, click on it to start drawing duct. Alternatively, you can right-click on a connector and, from the sub-menu, select to draw **Duct**, **Duct Placeholder**, **Flex Duct**, or **Cap Open End**. When snapping to another element with connectors, ensure that you select the point snap on the end of the other element to create the connection, as shown in Figure 10–4.

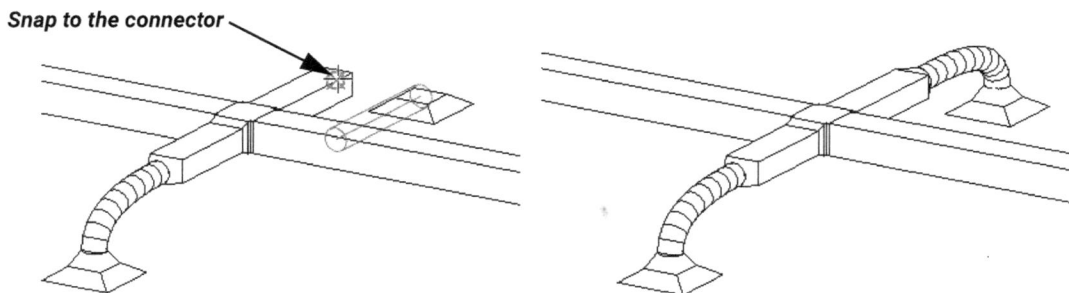

Figure 10–4

Duct Placement Tools

	Automatically Connect (on/off)	On by default. Ducts connect to other ones and automatically place all of the required fittings. To draw a duct that remains at the original elevation, toggle this option off.
		• Even if **Automatically Connect** is not toggled on, when you snap to a connector any changes in height and size are applied with the appropriate fittings.
	Justification	Opens the *Justification Setting* dialog box, which enables you to set the default settings for the *Horizontal Justification, Horizontal Offset,* and *Vertical Justification.*
	Inherit Elevation (on/off)	If the tool is toggled on and you start modeling a duct by snapping to an existing one, the new duct takes on the elevation of the existing one regardless of what is specified, as shown in Figure 10–5.
	Inherit Size (on/off)	If the tool is toggled on and you start modeling a duct by snapping to an existing one, the new duct takes on the size of the existing one regardless of what is specified, as shown in Figure 10–5.

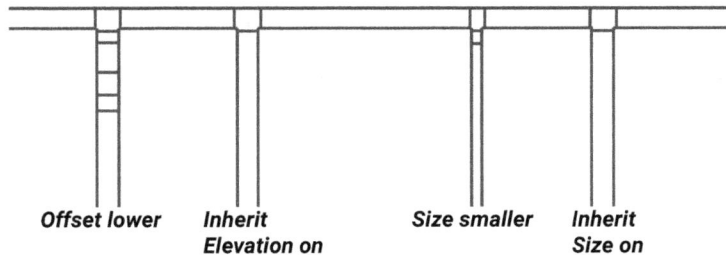

Offset lower   **Inherit Elevation on**   **Size smaller**   **Inherit Size on**

Figure 10–5

- If you already have some ducts in the project, you can select on a fixture or equipment and use ⬛ (Connect Into). This option displays in the contextual tab when you select a component. If your duct and fixtures/equipment are too close to each other, you will get a message that cannot be ignored that an auto-route was not found, as shown in Figure 10–6. Click **Cancel** and try to manually draw the ducts, if possible.

Figure 10–6

- To display centerlines for round ducts, in the *Visibility/Graphic Overrides* dialog box, toggle on the *Center line* subcategory for duct and duct fittings. Centerlines display in plan and elevation views set to the **Wireframe** or **Hidden Line** visual style.

Practice 10a
Add and Connect Ducts

Practice Objective

- Add ductwork.

In this practice, you will draw ducts from mechanical equipment connectors and from air terminals using flex duct. The completed project is shown in Figure 10–7.

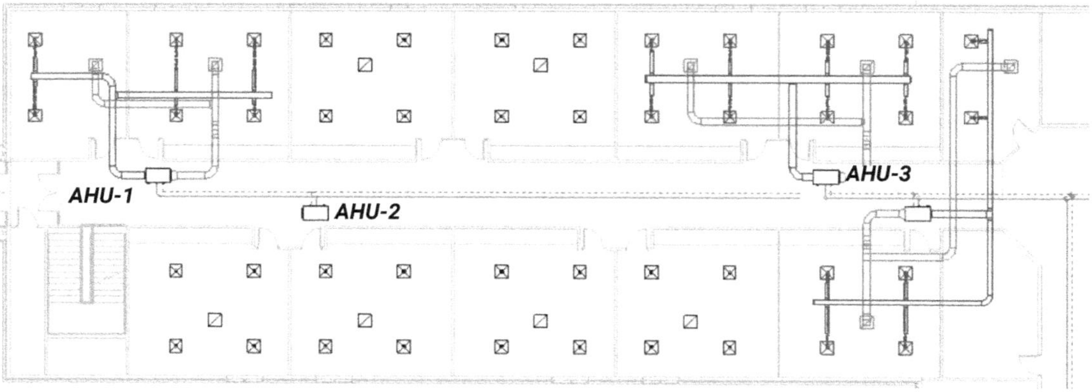

Figure 10–7

Note: Keep in mind the air handling units (AHUs) and their numbers as this will come in handy while doing the practices. These are not tags but annotative notes for reference purposes only.

Task 1: Add ducts.

1. In the practice files *Working Models>Mechanical* folder, open the project **Mech-Ducts.rvt**.
2. Open the Mechanical>HVAC>Floor Plans>**01 Mechanical Plan** view and zoom in on the upper northwest rooms of the north wing.

3. Select the AHU in the hall. From the Out duct connector, click the **Create Duct** icon, as shown in Figure 10−8.

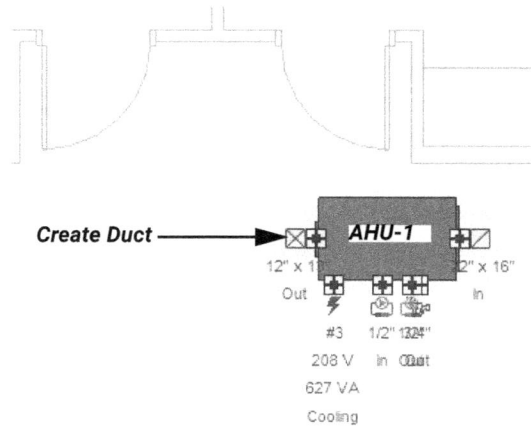

Figure 10−8

4. In the Type Selector, select **Rectangular Duct: Radius Elbow / Taps**.

5. Draw the duct into the first room past the two air terminals, as shown in Figure 10−9. Press <Esc> once and then draw a duct from the main duct over into the other room, as shown in Figure 10−9.

   Note: If the tap is reversed, select on the tap and click ⇕ (Flip the instance facing) arrow control to change the orientation of the tap.

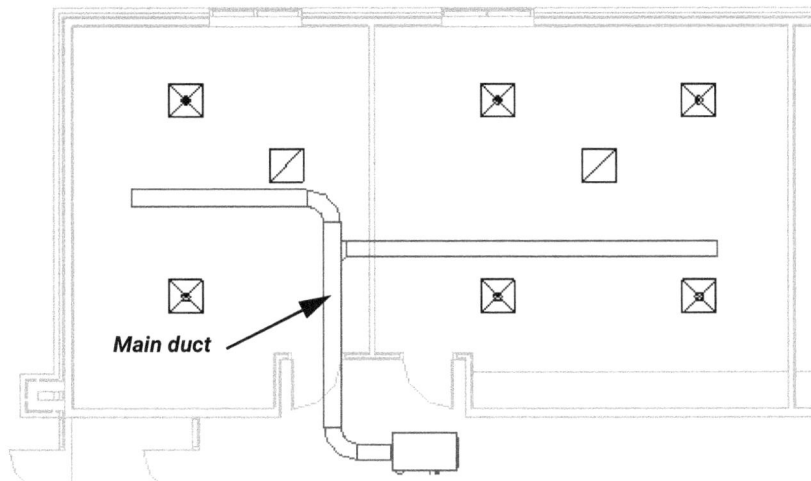

Figure 10−9

6. In the Status Bar, click ⬚ (Select Link). This turns off the ability to select the linked architectural model. (A red X will appear on the icon.)

7. In the *Systems* tab>*HVAC* panel, click ⬚ (Duct).

8. In the Type Selector, select **Round Duct: Taps / Long Radius**.

9. In the *Modify | Place Duct* tab>*Placement Tools* panel, click ⬚ (Inherit Elevation).

10. In the Options Bar, set *Diameter* to **6"** and click **Apply**.

11. In the top leftmost classroom, select a point on the duct where it is aligned to the air terminal (as shown in Figure 10–10), and draw it about halfway to the air terminal (as shown in Figure 10–11). Hint: To display the alignment line, hover your cursor over the air terminal and move your cursor towards the duct (the alignment line in Figure 10–10 has been enhanced for clarity).

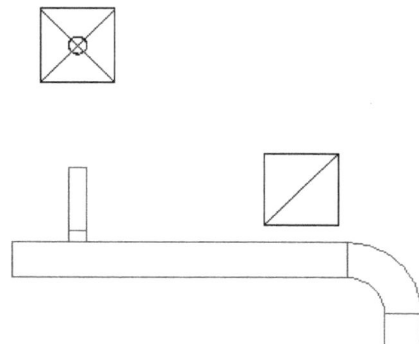

Figure 10–10   **Figure 10–11**

12. Click ⬚ (Modify).

13. Select the air terminal, right-click on the connector, and select **Draw Flex Duct**, as shown in Figure 10–12.

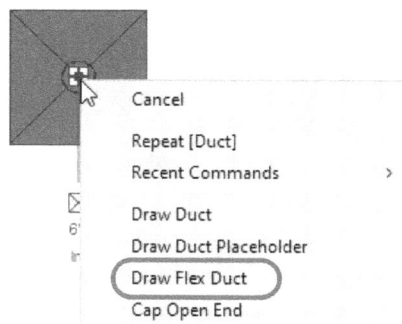

Figure 10–12

14. Draw the flex duct from the air terminal to the new duct, ensuring that you select the point connector shown in Figure 10-13. As soon as you connect the duct, the air terminal turns blue. It is now attached to the supply air system.

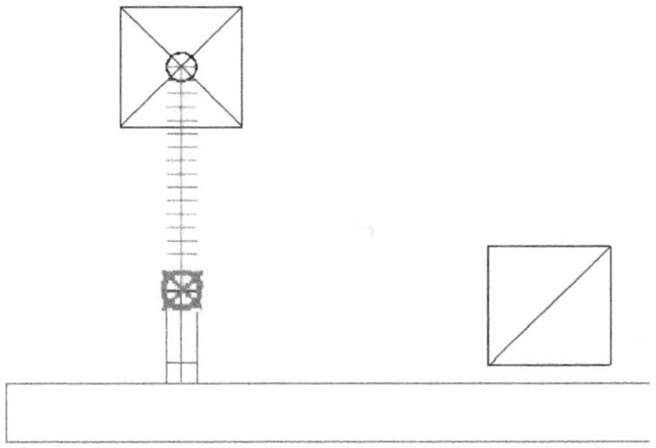

Figure 10-13

15. Repeat the process to connect the other air terminals to the ducts. The final system should look similar to Figure 10-14. Make sure to click ⟶ (Inherit Elevation) before drawing the duct. For the shorter distances, you will get a warning if there is not enough room to create the duct. Make sure the round ducts are drawn long enough.

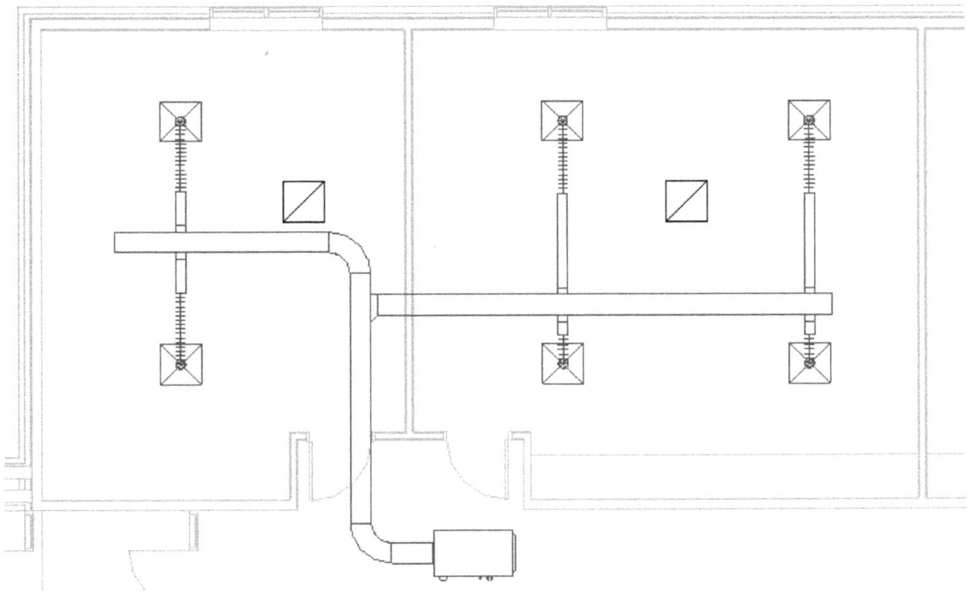

Figure 10-14

16. Save the project.

Task 2: (Optional) Add return air ducts.

1. Add return air ducts to the same area where you added the supply air ducts. You will need to start the duct from the AHU and in the Options Bar, set the *Width* to **12"** and the *Height* to **12"** You will need to bring the middle elevation of the duct run to **11'-6"** to avoid the supply duct, as shown in a section view in Figure 10–15. Hint: Use the return ducts at the end of the hall as guidance.

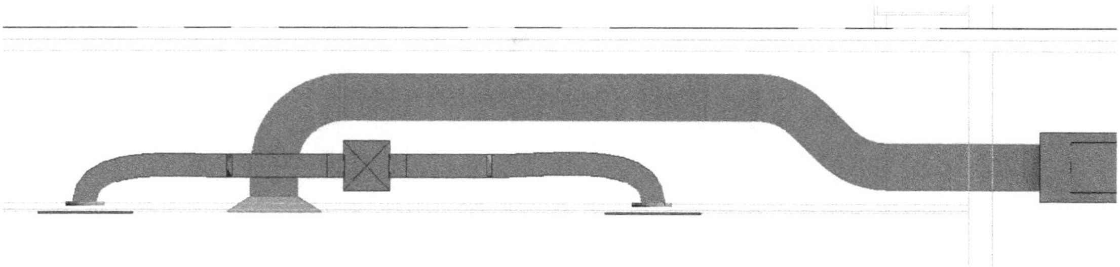

Figure 10–15

You can also add ducts to the air terminals across the hall.

End of practice

10.2 Modifying Ducts

Ducts, similarly to pipes, can be modified using a variety of standard modifying tools and other specialty tools, such as duct sizing, converting placeholders, changing rigid ducts to flexible ones, adding insulation and lining, and modifying the justification of ducts.

For example, the elbow fitting in Figure 10-16 is too large. In Figure 10-17, the size has changed, a fitting automatically applied, and another fitting added to create the appropriate layout.

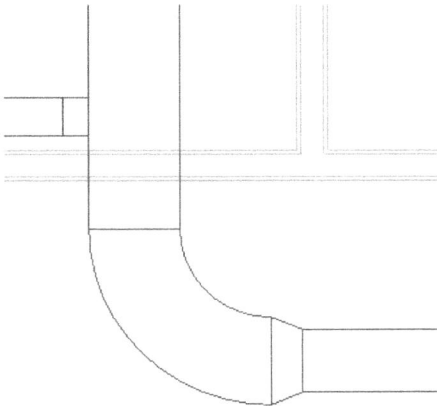 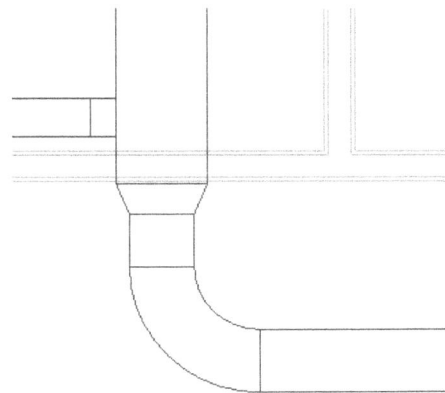

Figure 10-16   **Figure 10-17**

* You can modify ducts using universal methods by making changes in Properties and the Options Bar and using temporary dimensions, controls, and connectors.You can also use modify tools (e.g., **Move**, **Rotate**, **Split**, **Trim/Extend**, and **Align**) to help you place the ducts at the correct locations.

Duct Fittings and Accessories

Duct fittings can be loaded from the Revit Library in the *Duct>Fittings* subfolder. Select the folder for the type of duct you are using, such as **Round**. Duct accessories, like fire dampers or filters, are in the *Duct>Accessories* subfolder. You can load fittings when you have started the **Duct Accessory** command.

How To: Add Duct Fittings or Accessories

1. In the *Systems* tab>*HVAC* panel, select the appropriate command: 👓 (Duct Fitting) (**DF**) or 🖺 (Duct Accessory) (**DA**).

2. In the Type Selector, select the type of fitting or accessory you want to use.

3. Hover the cursor over the duct. Only usable locations are highlighted.

4. Click on the required location. The fitting or accessory resizes to fit the element on which it is placed.

Modifying Duct Fittings

Whether added automatically or manually, fittings can be modified using the Type Selector, Properties, the Options Bar, and a variety of connectors and controls. For example, an elbow can be changed to a tee by clicking a control, as shown in Figure 10–18.

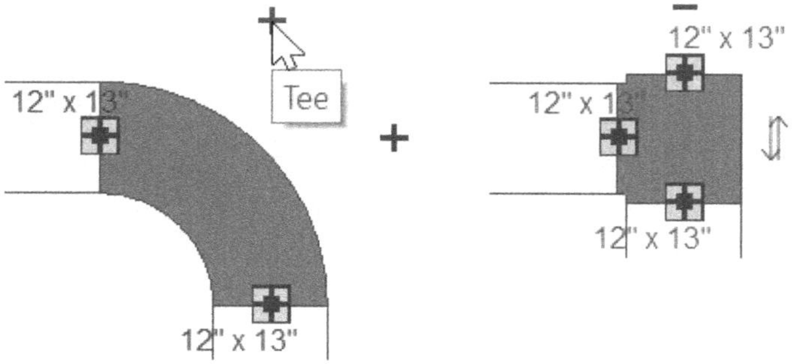

Figure 10–18

Capping Open Duct Ends

You can cap the open end of a duct by right-clicking on the end control and selecting **Cap Open End**, as shown in Figure 10–19.

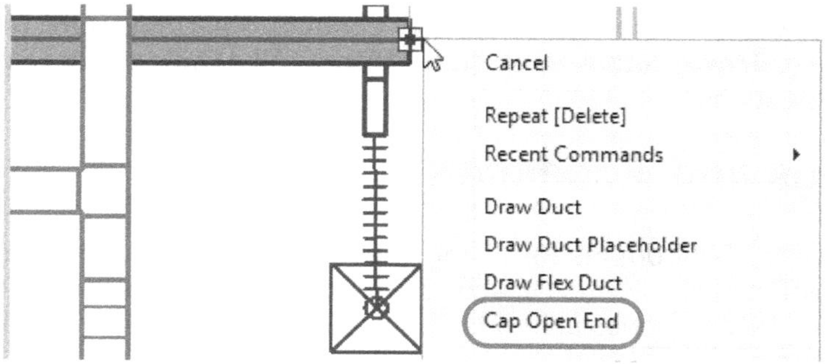

Figure 10–19

Alternatively, if you have more than one opening on the ends of a run, in the *Modify* contextual tab>*Edit* panel, click ⊤⊤ (Cap Open Ends) to apply the caps.

Duct Sizing

It is easiest to draw ducts using the default sizes provided by the opening sizes of the equipment, or as preset in the Mechanical Settings. However, these sizes are often incorrect for the system being used. The **Duct/Pipe Sizing** tool uses a specified sizing method and constraints to determine how to correctly size the ducts, as shown in Figure 10-20.

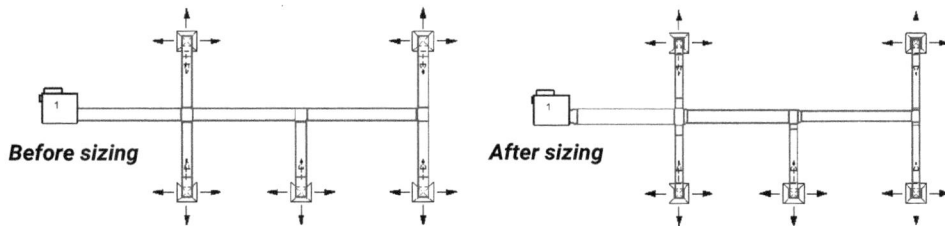

Before sizing   *After sizing*

Figure 10-20

- If you select only one duct, it analyzes just that one set of connections. Select the entire system to ensure that all of the connections are analyzed.

How To: Size Ducts

1. Select all of the components in a duct system.
2. In the *Modify | Multi-Select* tab>*Analysis* panel, click ▦ (Duct/Pipe Sizing).
3. In the *Duct Sizing* dialog box, set the *Sizing Method* and *Constraints* according to company design standards, as shown in Figure 10-21.

Figure 10-21

4. Click **OK**.

- Once you make a change to the system, you need to run the **Duct/Pipe Sizing** tool again.

- You can also modify duct sizes on your own to create the most appropriate layout for your methodology. A helpful tool to separate lengths of duct before you change the size is ⊏⊐ (Split Element).

Converting Ducts

After placing ducts, you can change the type of the entire run (including fittings). If the definition of a type has been changed, you can reapply the type to existing runs. You can also convert placeholders to standard ducts and rigid duct to flex duct when connected to an air terminal.

How To: Change the Type of Duct Runs

1. Select the duct run and filter out everything except the related duct, accessories, and fittings.
2. In the *Modify | Multi-Select* tab>*Edit* panel, click ▦ (Change Type).
3. In the Type Selector, select a new type of run. For the example shown in Figure 10–22, the type **Rectangular Duct: Radius Elbows / Tees** was changed to the type **Round Duct: Taps**.

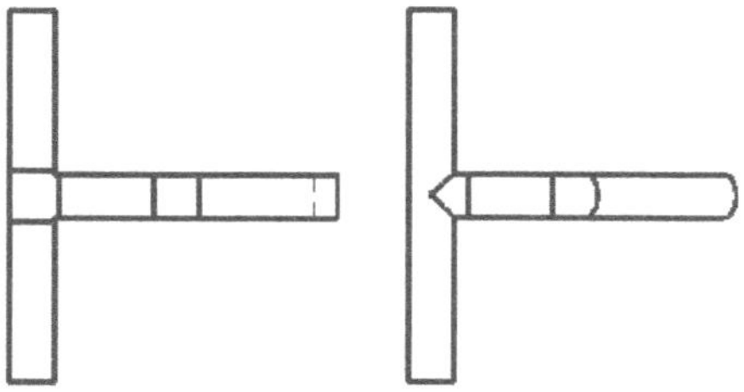

Figure 10–22

How To: Reapply the Type to Runs

1. Select a single duct run. You can select different runs, but they must be all of the same type and same system. If you select runs in different systems, the software prompts you to select one system to which to reapply the type.
2. Filter out everything except ducts, fittings, and accessories.
3. In the *Modify | Multi-Select* tab>*Edit* panel, click ▦ (Reapply Type).

How To: Convert Placeholders to Duct

1. Select the duct placeholder(s).
2. In the *Modify* contextual tab>*Edit* panel, click ⤴ (Convert Placeholder).
3. The placeholders are changed into the duct type, including the appropriate fittings, as shown in Figure 10–23.

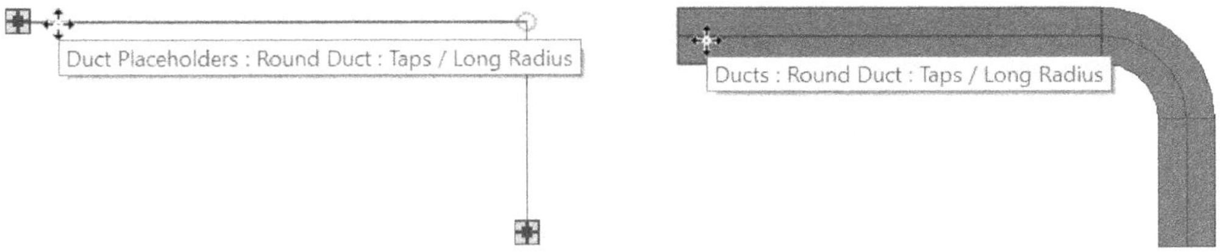

Duct Placeholders : Round Duct : Taps / Long Radius

Ducts : Round Duct : Taps / Long Radius

Figure 10–23

How To: Convert Rigid Duct to Flex Duct

1. In the *Systems* tab>*HVAC* panel, click ▯ (Convert to Flex Duct), or type **CV**.
2. In the Options Bar, set the *Max Length*. The default is **6'-0"**, a standard code requirement.
3. Select the air terminal connected to the rigid duct. The duct is converted as shown in Figure 10–24.

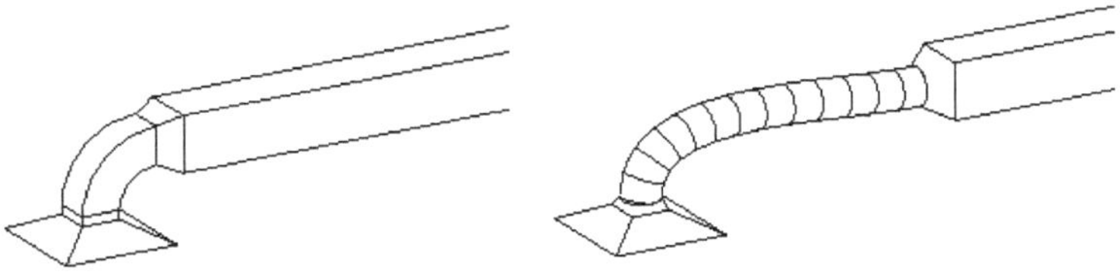

Figure 10–24

• This command only works if the rigid duct is connected to an air terminal.

Adding Insulation and Lining

You can add insulation and lining to ducts. This information displays as a thin line outside of the duct for insulation and a dashed line inside the duct for lining, as shown in Figure 10-25.

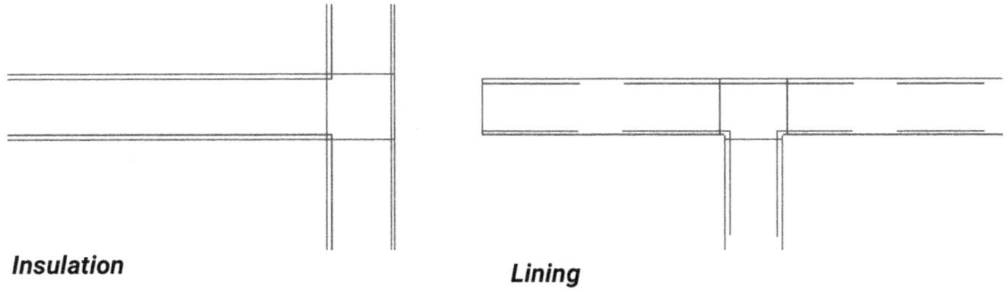

Insulation   *Lining*

Figure 10-25

- Accessories can also be insulated.

How To: Add Insulation or Lining

1. Select the duct run that you want to insulate or line. You can select more than one system at a time for these commands.

2. Use ▽ (Filter) to select only the ducts, fittings, and accessories.

3. In the *Modify* contextual tab>*Duct Insulation* panel or *Duct Lining* panel, select either ▤ (Add Insulation) or ▤ (Add Lining).

4. In the associated dialog box, select a *Insulation Type* and set the *Thickness,* as shown for Duct Insulation in Figure 10-26. Click **OK**.

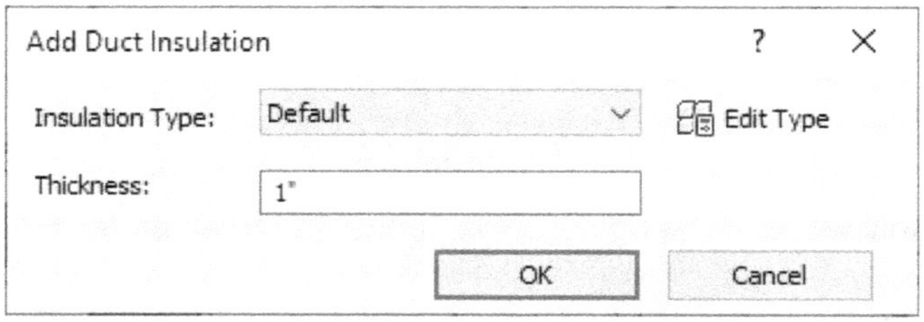

Figure 10-26

- To modify the insulation, select the insulated duct and in the contextual ribbon, select the appropriate command: ▤ (Edit Insulation), ▤ (Edit Lining), ▤ (Remove Insulation), or ▤ (Remove Lining). When editing, change the *Type* in the Type Selector and/or change the *Thickness* in Properties.

Modifying the Justification

If a duct run has different sized duct, you can modify the justification, as shown in Figure 10–27.

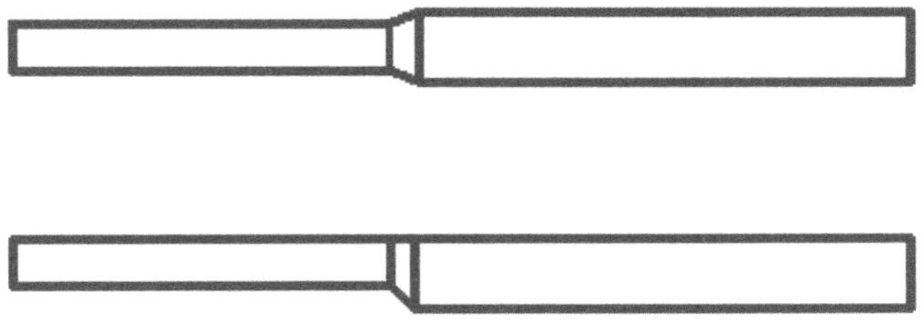

Figure 10–27

How To: Modify Justifications

1. Select the duct run.

2. In the *Modify | Multi-Select* tab>*Edit* panel, click ⏛ (Justify).

3. To specify the point on the duct that you want to justify around, in the *Justification Editor* tab>*Justify* panel, click ⬉ (Control Point) to cycle between the end point references.

   * The alignment location displays as an arrow, as shown in Figure 10–28.

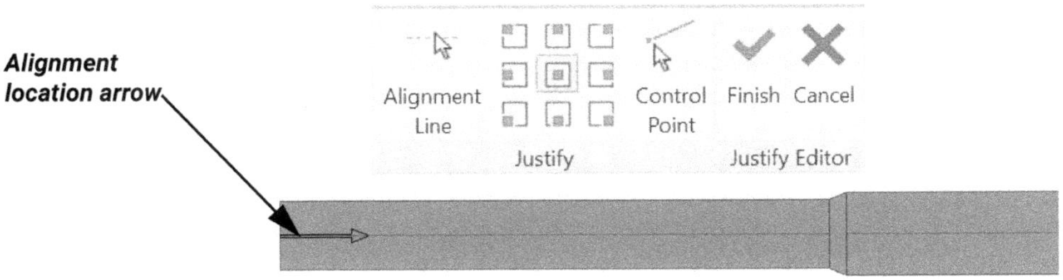

Figure 10–28

4. To indicate the required alignment, either click one of the nine alignment buttons in the *Justify* panel, or in a 3D view, use ⬐ (Alignment Line) to select the required dashed line, as shown in Figure 10–29.

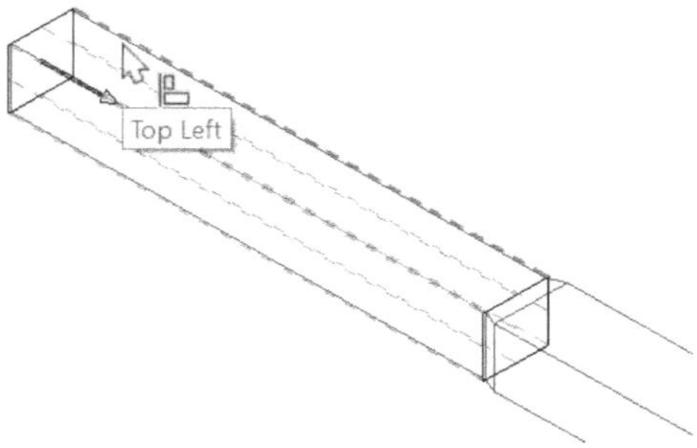

Figure 10–29

💡 Hint: Using Thin Lines

Line thickness can negatively impact the display of elements, such as insulation or lining. To toggle lineweight on or off, in the Quick Access Toolbar, click 🗏 (Thin Lines), or type **TL**.

Practice 10b
Modify Ducts and Pipes

Practice Objectives

- Change pipe types.
- Modify pipe fittings.
- Cap open duct ends.
- Use the Duct/Pipe Sizing tool.
- Add lining to ducts.

In this practice, you will change a run of pipes from one type to another. You will view the pipes in 3D, modify fittings, and make revisions to the pipes to match existing pipes. You will also modify ducts by capping open ends, using the **Duct/Pipe Sizing** tool, and modifying the duct fittings, as shown in Figure 10–30. Finally, you will add lining to all of the duct networks in the project.

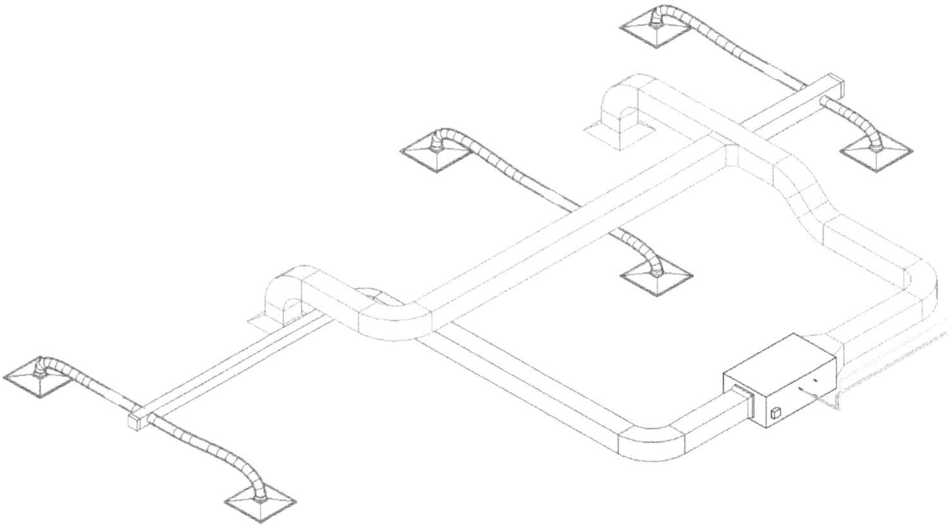

Figure 10–30

Task 1: Modify the type of pipes.

1. In the practice files *Working Models>Mechanical* folder, open **Mech-Modify-Ducts.rvt**.

2. Open the Mechancial>HVAC>**01 Mechanical Plan** view and zoom in on the area near **AHU-3**, as shown in Figure 10–31. Note that the pipes are not connected. (The model's AHU units have been labeled in the figures and practice files for clarity.)

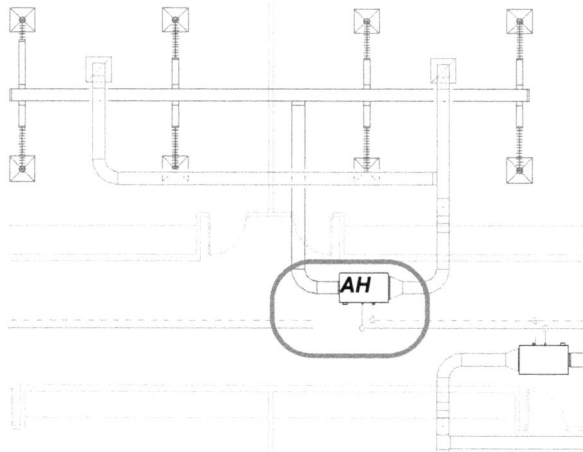

Figure 10–31

3. Hover the cursor over one of the pipes on the left and then over one of the pipes on the right. Note that they are two different types, as shown in Figure 10–32.

Pipe Types: Standard   *Pipe Types: Copper*

Figure 10–32

4. Zoom out to see the entire piping layout.

5. Hover the cursor over the hydronic supply pipe (solid line) of the pipes on the left and press <Tab> until the entire branch pipe run is highlighted, then select it.

6. In the *Modify | Multi-Select* tab>*Edit* panel, click ⊞ (Change Type).

7. In the Type Selector, change the type to **Pipe Types: Copper**.

8. Click (Modify).

9. Repeat the process with the hydronic return (dashed line) standard pipes.

10. Save the project.

Task 2: Modify fittings.

1. Open the Mechancial>HVAC>**3D Views: 3D Mechanical** view.

   - The hydronic return system color has been changed to a green hidden line for clarity in the model.
   - If you still have **Select Links** turned off, turn it back on by clicking the icon.

2. Tile the **01 Mechanical Plan** and **3D Mechanical** views by typing **WT**, and then type **ZA** to zoom all.

3. In the 3D view, select the linked model. In the View Control Bar, click (Temporary Hide/ Isolate) and select **Hide Element**.

4. Hold <Shift> and the mouse wheel to rotate the 3D view so you can see the pipes clearly.

5. Zoom in on **AHU-3**. Note that the pipes are not connected and are at different heights, as shown in Figure 10–33.

6. Delete the pipes shown in Figure 10–33.

   Note: *If you tried to move or align the pipes while they are connected to the mechanical equipment, the AHUs will also move.*

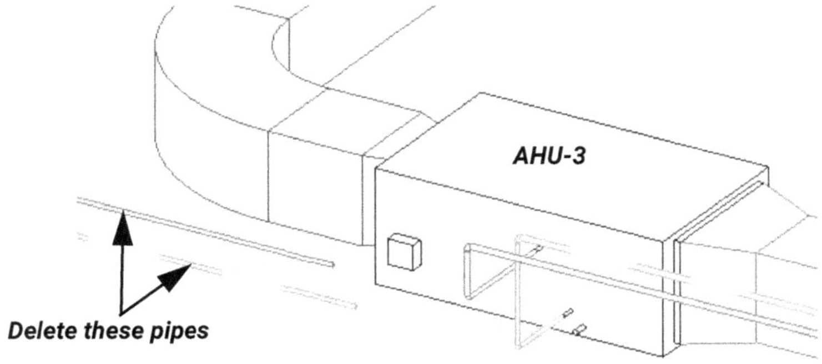

Figure 10–33

7. Select the elbow fitting for the hydronic supply and click the **Tee** icon, as shown on the left in Figure 10–34. Repeat with the green hydronic return fitting. The fittings should now be tee fittings, as shown on the right in Figure 10–34.

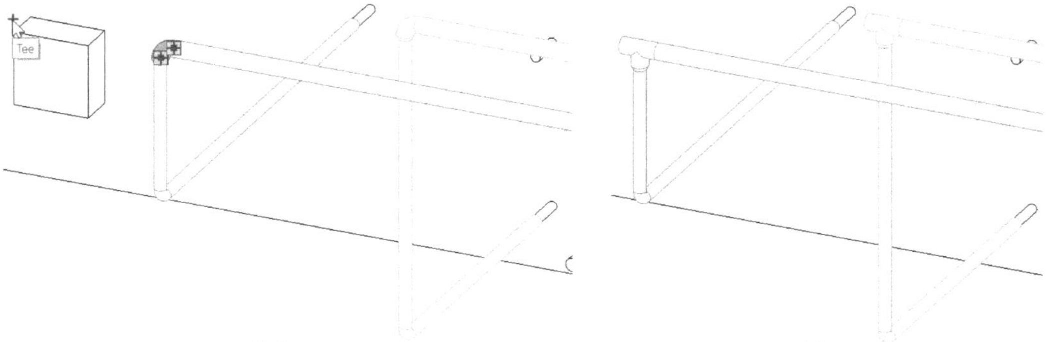

Before   *After*

Figure 10–34

8. Click in the plan view to make it active.

9. Zoom and pan over to the far left side of the north wing. Delete the pipes running down the hall and keep the pipes coming out of the AHUs. Zoom in on **AHU-1** and **AHU-2** at the far left end of the north wing and delete the fittings as indicated in Figure 10–35.

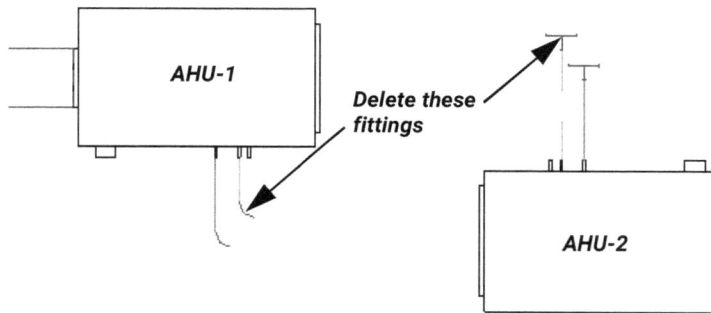

Figure 10–35

10. Click in the 3D view to activate it, and zoom or pan back over to **AHU-3**.

11. Select the Tee fitting, right-click on the open connector, and then select **Draw Pipe**.

12. Draw the pipe down the hall past **AHU-1**. You can pan and zoom using your mouse while in the Draw Pipe command. Hint: When you are in the location that you want to end the pipe run, hold down <Shift> to force the pipe straight, then click to end the pipe run.

13. Click ⬚ (Modify).

14. Repeat the process with the other pipe. Keep the 3D view on the AHU-1 element; this way, you will see the next steps in action.

15. Activate the plan view and zoom in on **AHU-1**. Select the pipe coming out of the AHU-1 element and use the control to drag it closer to the AHU-1 element. Repeat for the other pipe coming out of the AHU-1 element.

16. In the *Modify* tab>*Modify* panel, click ⃗║ (Trim/Extend to Corner). Select the pipe coming from the **AHU-1** and then the horizontal pipe. Repeat with the second pipe, as shown in Figure 10–36.

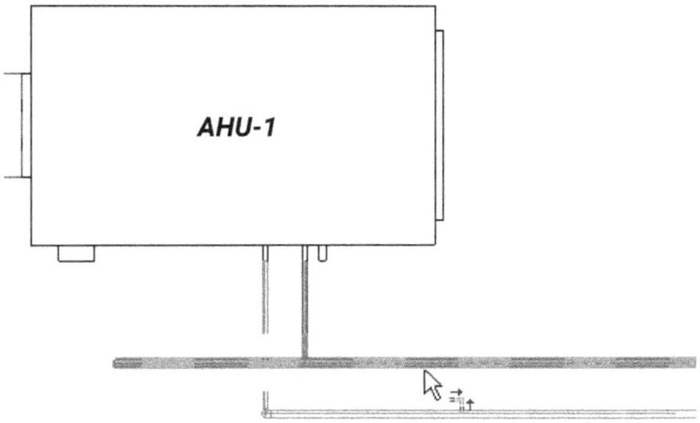

Figure 10–36

17. In both the plan and 3D views, pan over to **AHU-2**.

18. Activate the plan view. Select the pipe coming out of the AHU-2 element and use the control to drag it closer to the AHU-2 element. Repeat for the other pipe coming out of the AHU-2 element.

19. Use the ⃗║ (Trim/Extend Single Element) command to clean up the intersection between the pipes coming from the AHU (line to extend) and the new run of pipe (reference extend boundary). Follow the prompts in the Status Bar in the lower-left corner.

20. Click ⃗ (Modify).

21. Return to the 3D Mechanical view to see the revised pipe layout.

22. Use the ViewCube to rotate the model and zoom in on the supply duct system connected to **AHU-1**, as shown in Figure 10–37.

Figure 10–37

23. Save the project.

Task 3: Cap open duct ends.

1. Still in the **3D Mechanical** view, in the *Analyze* tab>*Check Systems* panel, click ⚠ (Show Disconnects).

2. In the *Show Disconnects Options* dialog box, select **Duct** and click **OK**.

* Warning icons display at each end of the supply ducts. Hover your cursor over the warning icon to see a brief description, indicating there is an open connector, as shown in Figure 10–38. The warning icons will also display if there are elements not connected to anything.

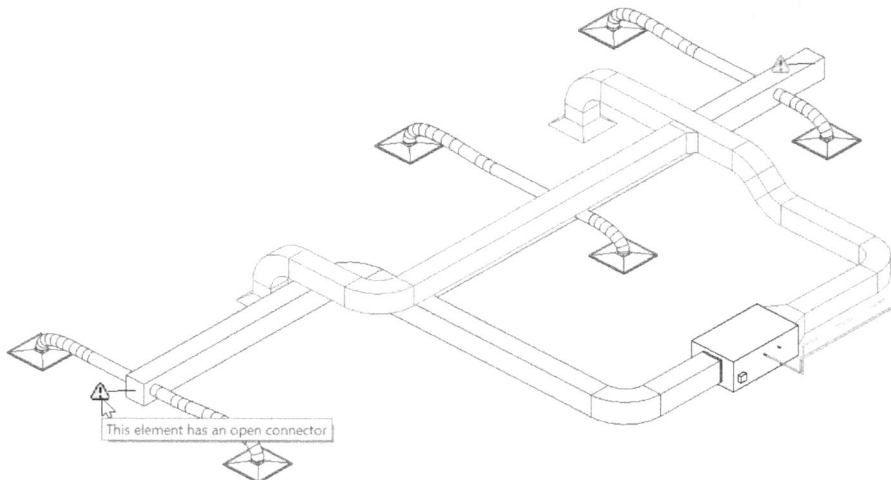

This element has an open connector

Figure 10–38

3. Select the duct, then right-click on the end connector and select **Cap Open End**, as shown in Figure 10–39.

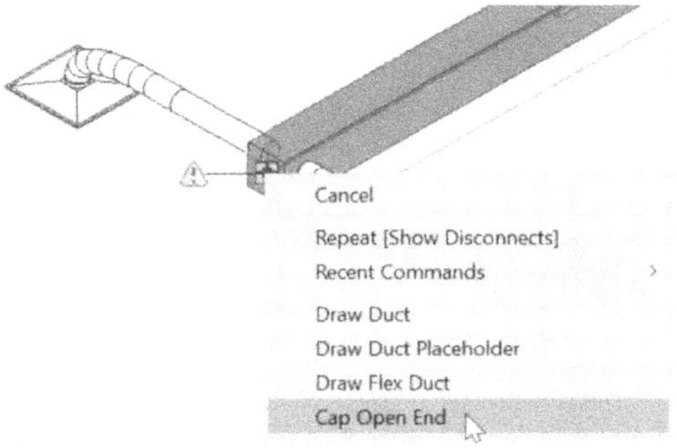

Figure 10–39

The duct is capped and the warning icon no longer displays.

4. Repeat the process on the end of the other open duct.

5. In the *Analyze* tab>*Check Systems* panel, click ⚐ (Show Disconnects).

6. In the *Show Disconnects Options* dialog box, uncheck **Duct** and click **OK**.

7. Save the project.

Task 4: Resize the ducts.

1. Continue working in the **3D Mechanical** view.

2. Rotate the view using the ViewCube so you can see the supply duct under the return duct.

    Note: For smoother rotation, select a duct and rotate the model.

3. Hover the cursor over one supply duct and press <Tab> until the full supply network displays, then select it.

4. In the *Modify | Multi-Select* tab>*Analysis* panel, click 🖿 (Duct/Pipe Sizing).

5. In the *Duct Sizing* dialog box, accept the defaults and click **OK**. The ducts resize, as shown in Figure 10–40.

Figure 10–40

6. One of the connections needs to be revised, as shown above in Figure 10–40.

7. In the **01 Mechanical Plan** view, zoom in on the supply duct network in the top-left classroom.

8. Delete the transition fitting shown in Figure 10–41.

9. Select the open end of the duct and drag it closer to the intersection on the right.

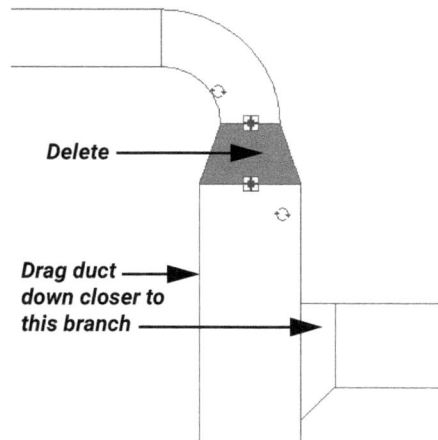

Figure 10–41

10. Click ⊾ (Modify) and select the elbow duct.

11. Right-click on the open end of the elbow and select **Draw Duct**. Draw the duct until it connects to the vertical duct. The appropriate fitting is reapplied, as shown in Figure 10–42.

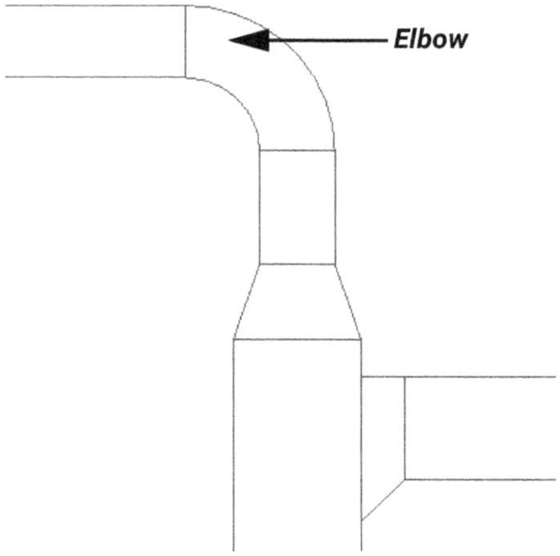

— Elbow

Figure 10–42

12. (Optional) Make additional adjustments to the ducts, including shortening the ducts past the final air terminals.

13. Zoom to fit everything in the view.

14. Save the project.

Task 5: Add duct lining.

1. Continue working in the **01 Mechanical Plan** view.

2. Type **ZA** to zoom all in the view.

3. Draw a window around all of the elements in the view.

4. In the Status Bar or in the *Modify | Multi-Select* tab>*Selection* panel, click ▽ (Filter).

5. In the *Filter* dialog box, clear everything except **Ducts**, **Duct Fittings**, and **Flex Ducts**. Click **OK**.

6. In the *Modify | Multi-Select* tab>*Duct Lining* panel, click 🗖 (Add Lining).

7. In the *Add Duct Lining* dialog box, set the *Insulation Type* to **Fiberglass Board** and set the *Thickness* to **1/2"**, then click **OK**.

8. Click ⬚ (Modify).

9. Zoom in and see the lining applied to the ducts, as shown in Figure 10–43.

    Note: If required, in the Quick Access Toolbar, click ▦ *(Thin Lines).*

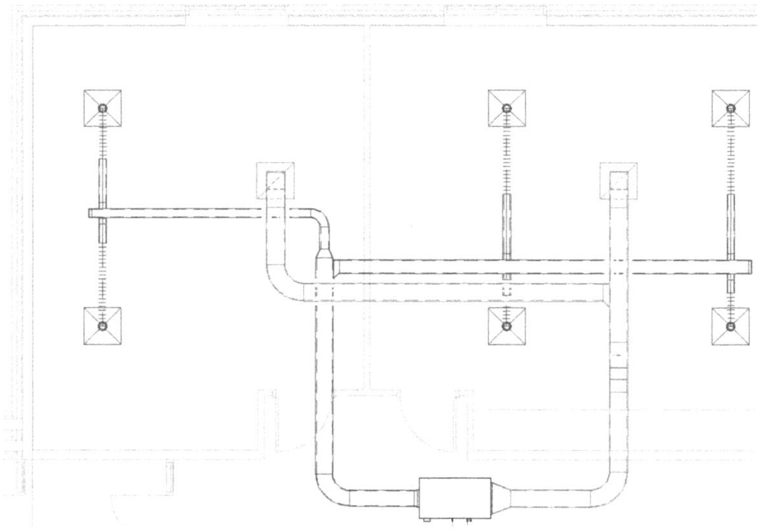

Figure 10–43

10. Zoom out.

11. Save and close the project.

End of practice

Chapter Review Questions

1. Which method enables you to move an air terminal hosted by a ceiling that has been copied, as shown in Figure 10–44, up to a different ceiling height?

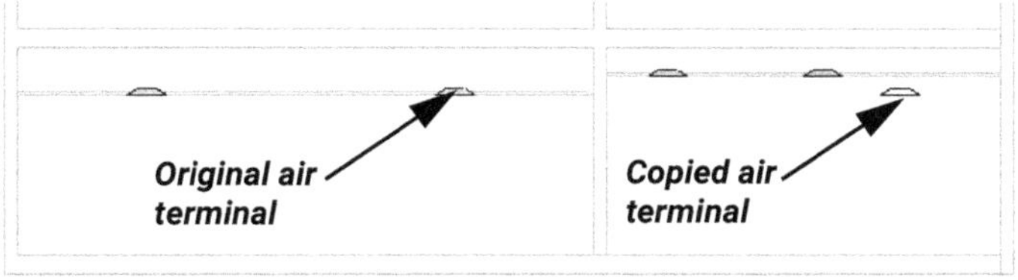

Original air terminal

Copied air terminal

Figure 10–44

   a. Move the air terminal.

   b. Pick New Host.

   c. Change the elevation in Properties.

   d. Copied air terminals cannot be moved off the original plane.

2. The size of the duct drawn from a control on mechanical equipment must remain the same size as the opening on the equipment until it intersects with another duct.

   a. True

   b. False

3. When can you convert a rigid duct to a flexible duct?

   a. When the rigid duct is round.

   b. When the air terminal is already connected by a rigid duct.

   c. When creating a system and sizing the ducting.

   d. When the **Allow Conversion** parameter is selected in the rigid duct's instance properties.

4. Which of the following commands can be used when modifying ducts? (Select all that apply.)

   a. Change Type

   b. Reapply Type

   c. Add Insulation

   d. Edit Lining

   e. Modify Justification

   f. Modify Material

   g. Change Offset

5. You can use the **Transfer Project Standards** tool to copy mechanical settings from another project.

   a. True

   b. False

6. You cannot transition from rectangular duct to a round duct while remaining in the Duct command by changing the duct type in Properties.

   a. True

   b. False

Command Summary

Button	Command	Location
HVAC Tools		
	Air Terminal	• **Ribbon:** *Systems* tab>*HVAC* panel • **Shortcut:** AT
	Air Terminal on Duct	• **Ribbon:** *Modify	Place Air Terminal* tab>*Layout* panel
	Analytical Connections	• **Ribbon:** *Modify	Mechanical Equipment* (or *Modify | Pipes*) tab>*Create* panel
	Cap Open Ends	• **Ribbon:** *Modify* contextual tab>*Edit* panel
	Duct	• **Ribbon:** *Systems* tab>*HVAC* panel • **Shortcut:** DT
	Duct Accessory	• **Ribbon:** *Systems* tab>*HVAC* panel • **Shortcut:** DA
	Duct Fitting	• **Ribbon:** *Systems* tab>*HVAC* panel • **Shortcut:** DF
	Duct Placeholder	• **Ribbon:** *Systems* tab>*HVAC* panel
	Flex Duct	• **Ribbon:** *Systems* tab>*HVAC* panel • **Shortcut:** FD
	Mechanical Equipment	• **Ribbon:** *Systems* tab>*Mechanical* panel • **Shortcut:** ME
	Mechanical Settings	• **Ribbon:** *Systems* tab>*HVAC* or *Mechanical* panel title • **Shortcut:** MS
Duct Modification		
	Add Insulation	• **Ribbon:** (*with Ducts and Duct Fittings selected*) *Modify	Multi-Select* tab>*Duct Insulation* panel
	Add Lining	• **Ribbon:** (*with Ducts and Duct Fittings selected*) *Modify	Multi-Select* tab>*Duct Lining* panel

Button	Command	Location
	Change Type	• **Ribbon:** (*with Ducts and Duct Fittings selected*) *Modify | Multi-Select* tab>*Edit* panel
	Convert to Flex Duct	• **Ribbon:** *Systems* tab>*HVAC* panel • **Shortcut:** CV
	Edit Insulation	• **Ribbon:** (*with Ducts and Duct Fittings that have Insulation selected*) *Modify | Multi-Select* tab>*Duct Insulation* panel
	Edit Lining	• **Ribbon:** (*with Ducts and Duct Fittings that have Lining selected*) *Modify | Multi-Select* tab>*Duct Lining* panel
	Inherit Elevation	• **Ribbon:** *Modify | Place Duct* tab>*Placement Tools* panel
	Inherit Size	• **Ribbon:** *Modify | Place Duct* tab>*Placement Tools* panel
	Justification (Settings)	• **Ribbon:** *Modify | Place Duct* tab>*Placement Tools* panel
	Justify	• **Ribbon:** (*with Ducts and Duct Fittings selected*) *Modify | Multi-Select* tab>*Edit* panel
	Remove Insulation	• **Ribbon:** (*with Ducts and Duct Fittings that have Insulation selected*) *Modify | Multi-Select* tab>*Duct Insulation* panel
	Remove Lining	• **Ribbon:** (*with Ducts and Duct Fittings that have Lining selected*) *Modify | Multi-Select* tab>*Duct Lining* panel

Advanced Systems for HVAC and Plumbing

HVAC and plumbing networks are automatically placed in systems as you connect the elements. However, there are times when you want to create a system first, and then use automatic layouts to connect everything together with ducts or pipes. It is also important to test the systems to ensure that they are completely connected and they have the correct flow and sizes.

Learning Objectives

- Create duct and piping systems without first connecting the components.
- Modify duct and piping systems by adding or removing elements, renaming them, and dividing them.
- Create automatic duct and piping layouts that connect elements in systems.
- Test systems by showing disconnects, checking systems, and using the System Inspector.

11.1 Creating and Modifying Systems

When you place components and connect them using ducts or pipes, systems are automatically created, as shown for several duct systems in Figure 11–1. You can also create systems before you connect components, which is especially helpful if you want to use the automatic layout tools that connect components for you.

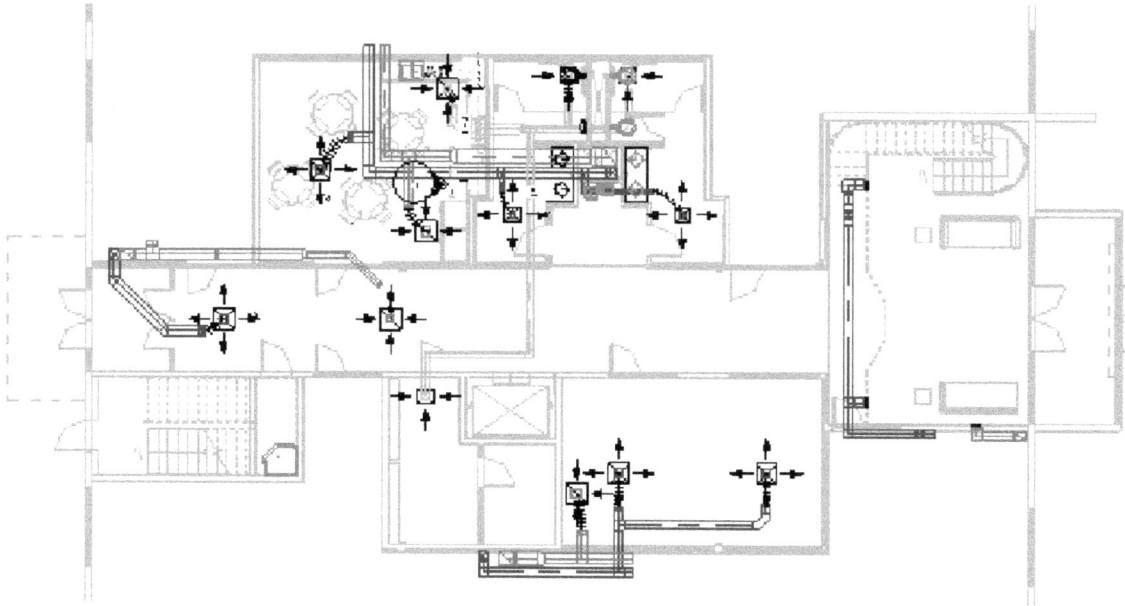

Figure 11–1

How To: Create a Duct or Piping System

1. Select at least one of the components that is to be part of the system, such as air terminals or plumbing fixtures.

    *   The elements must all be the same system type.
    *   Do not select the source equipment at this time.

2. In the *Modify contextual* tab>*Create Systems* panel, click the related systems button, such as ▦ (Duct) or ▦ (Piping).

    *   You can also right-click on an air terminal or plumbing fixture connector and select **Create Duct/Piping System**.

3. Proceed as follows:

If you started the command...	Then...
By right-clicking on a connector	In the *Create System* dialog box, the *System type* is preset.
Using a button	There are multiple options. Select the type of system you want to create from the drop-down list, as shown in Figure 11-2.

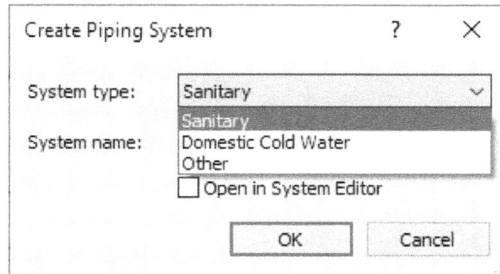

Create Piping System ? X

System type: Sanitary

Sanitary
System name: Domestic Cold Water
Other
☐ Open in System Editor

OK   Cancel

Figure 11-2

- If you want to continue working in the system, select **Open in the System Editor**.

*Note: For information about creating system types and applying color information, see **A.6 Work with System Graphics** in **Appendix A Additional Tools for Design Development**.*

4. In the *System name* field, enter a name and click **OK**.

5. If you did not open the System Editor in the previous step, in the *Modify | Duct Systems* or *Modify | Piping Systems* tab>*System Tools* panel, click (Edit System).

6. In the *Edit Duct System* or *Edit Piping System* tab (shown in Figure 11-3), you can:

   - Add and remove elements from the system.
   - Select the equipment connected to the system.

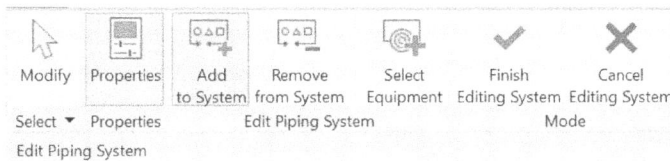

Modify Properties Add Remove Select Finish Cancel
                  to System from System Equipment Editing System Editing System
Select ▼ Properties Edit Piping System Mode
Edit Piping System

Figure 11-3

7. Click (Finish Editing System).

   Note: If multiple systems are applied to an element, the color returns to the neutral black.

- The elements take on the color of the system (if specified), as shown for a sanitary system in Figure 11–4.

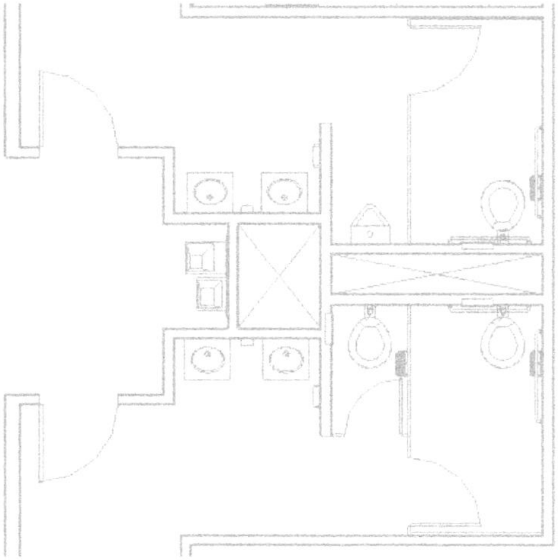

Figure 11–4

Hint: Using the System Browser While Creating Systems

It is helpful to have the System Browser open when you are creating systems because it can help you to identify which elements have been assigned to a system and which still need assignment, as shown in Figure 11–5.

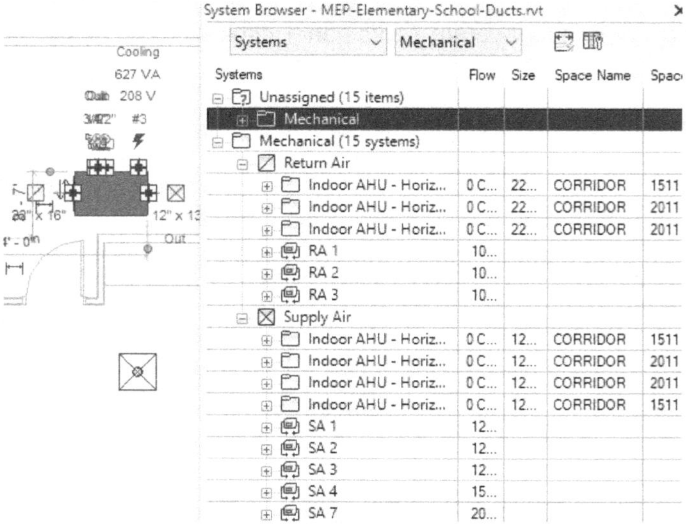

Figure 11–5

Modifying Systems

You can modify a system at any time. Hover the cursor over one of the elements and press <Tab> until you see the system border highlighted (as shown in Figure 11–6), then select it. The tools you use to modify systems display in the related *Modify | Duct Systems* or *Modify | Piping Systems* tab.

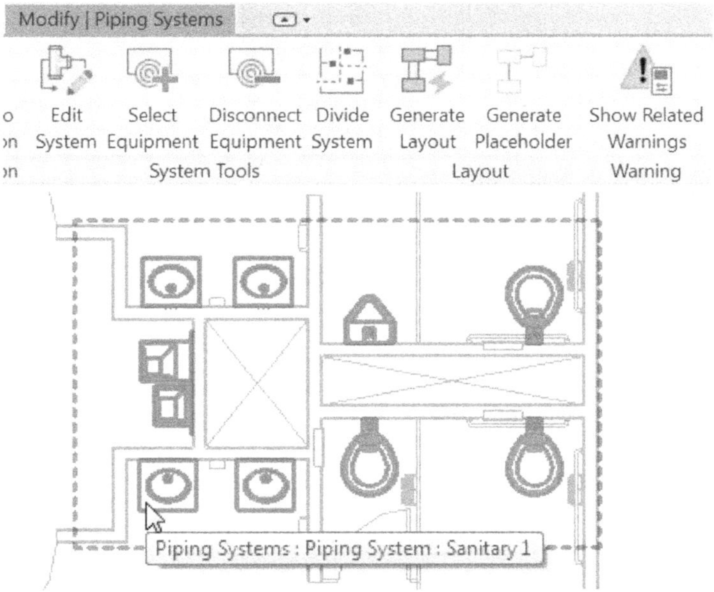

Figure 11–6

- You can change the *System Name* in Properties.

- (Edit System) (Duct) or (Edit System) (Pipe) takes you to the *Edit Duct System* or *Edit Piping System* tab, which enables you to add and remove elements from the system and select equipment.

- (Select Equipment) prompts you to select a mechanical or plumbing equipment component in the project.

- (Generate Layout) displays various placeholder layout solutions. Specify slope and routing parameters for ductwork and piping.

Dividing Systems

Systems can be divided if they have more than one network of ducts or pipes. In the example shown in Figure 11–7, there are three networks of ducts, each of which are connected to a different air handling unit.

Figure 11–7

- If you need to divide a system even further, add another piece of equipment and connect some of the existing components to it.

How To: Divide Systems

1. Select the system you want to divide.
2. In the *Modify | Duct Systems* or *Modify | Piping Systems* tab>*System Tools* panel, click (Divide System).
3. An alert box displays indicating the number of networks that are to be converted into individual systems.
4. Click **OK**. The systems are separated as shown in Figure 11–8.

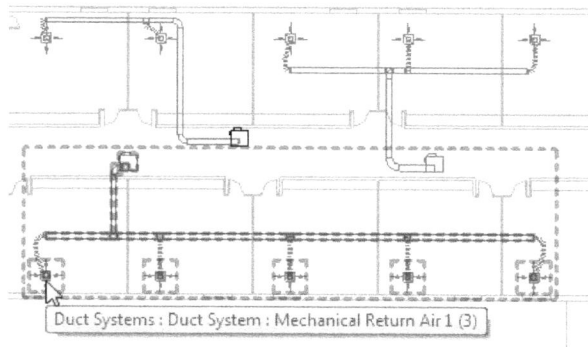

Figure 11–8

Practice 11a
Create and Modify HVAC Systems

Practice Objectives

- Review elements in the System Browser.
- Create duct systems.

In this practice, you will view unassigned elements in the System Browser and then add them to a new supply air duct system, as shown in Figure 11−9. You will repeat the process with the return air duct system.

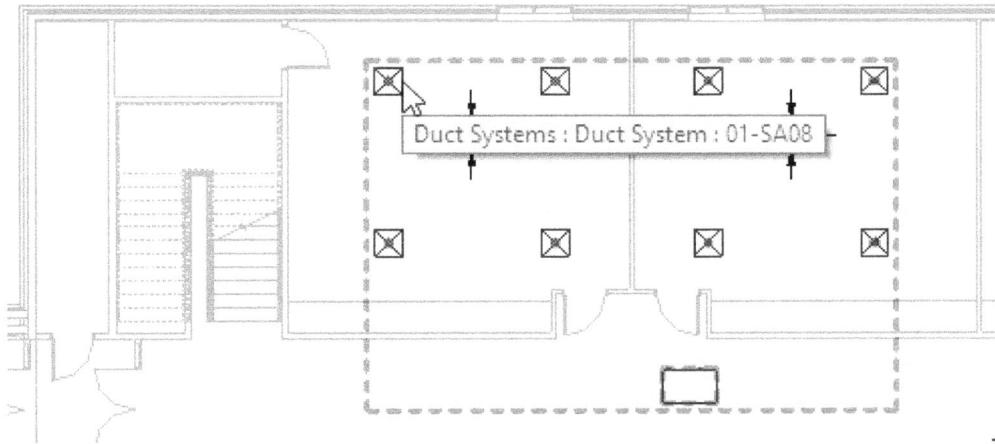

Figure 11−9

1. In the practice files *Working Models>Mechanical* folder, open **Mech-Modify-HVAC.rvt**.

2. Open the Mechanical>HVAC>Floor Plans>**01 Mechanical Plan** view.

3. Open the System Browser by pressing <F9>.

4. In the System Browser, verify that the **Systems** option is selected and set the *Discipline* to **Mechanical**.

5. In the System Browser, expand **Unassigned>Mechanical> Supply Air**. Note that there are several air terminals and an air handling unit (AHU) listed.

6. Select one of the unassigned Supply Diffusers. It highlights in the view. Right-click and select **Show** to automatically zoom in on the selected diffuser. Click **Close** in the *Show Element(s) in View* dialog box.

7. Zoom out enough so that you can see the classroom the diffuser is in.

8. In the *Modify | Air Terminals* tab>*Create Systems* panel, click 📷 (Duct).

9. In the *Create Duct System* dialog box, type **01 - SA08** for the *System name*. Select **Open in System Editor** and click **OK**.

10. In the *Edit Duct Systems* tab>*Edit Duct System* panel, click ⬚ (Select Equipment) and select the nearby AHU.

11. Click ⬚ (Add to System) and select the other supply air terminals in the classroom and in the classroom next to the current one, as shown in Figure 11−10. The selected air terminals will turn black and the air terminals that are not selected will remain in halftone.

Figure 11−10

12. Click ✔ (Finish Editing System).

13. In the view, select one of the air terminals in the new system. In the System Browser, expand the highlighted levels until the new system displays.

14. In the same classrooms, select the two return air terminals.

15. In the *Modify | Air Terminals* tab>*Create Systems* panel, click 🗔 (Duct).

16. In the *Create Duct System* dialog box, type the *System Name* **01 - RA08**. Do not select **Open in System Editor**. Click **OK**.

Note: You do not need to open the System Editor because you have already selected all of the elements you want in the system.

17. In the *Modify | Duct Systems* tab>*System Tools* panel, click ⬚ (Select Equipment) and select the same AHU.

18. The new system displays, as shown in Figure 11–11.

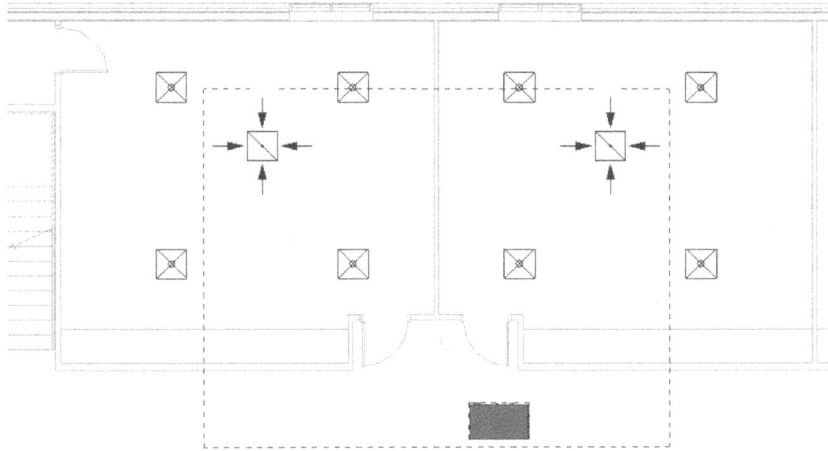

Figure 11–11

19. In the System Browser, the *Unassigned* category should now display **0 items**.

20. Save and close the project.

End of practice

Practice 11b
Create and Modify Plumbing Systems

Practice Objective

- Create plumbing and fire protection systems.

In this practice, you will create sanitary and domestic cold water systems for a series of water closets. You will then investigate an existing fire protection system and create an additional one, as shown in Figure 11–12.

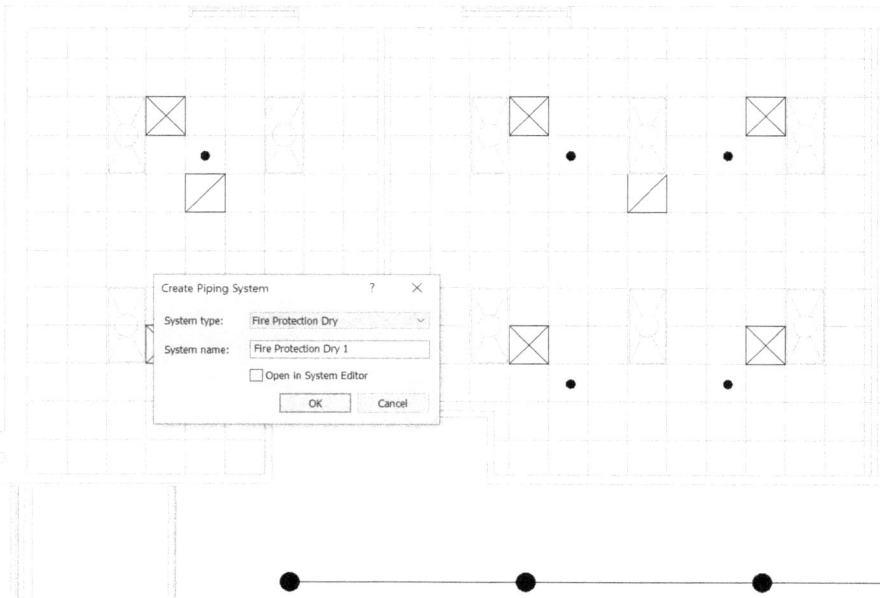

Figure 11–12

Task 1: Create systems for the water closets.

1. In the practice files *Working Models>Plumbing* folder, open the project **Plumb-Modify-Systems.rvt**.

2. Open the Plumbing>Plumbing>Floor Plans>**01 Plumbing Plan** view.

3. Zoom in on the **southernmost** restroom closest to the main entrance and select one of the water closets.

4. In the *Modify | Plumbing Fixtures* tab>*Create Systems* panel, click ⬚ (Piping).

5. In the *Create Piping System* dialog box, ensure that the *System type* is set to **Sanitary**. Accept the default name and select **Open in System Editor**, as shown in Figure 11–13. Click **OK**.

Figure 11–13

6. The *Edit Piping System* tab displays with ⊞ (Add to System) selected.

7. Select the other water closets in the room.

8. Click ✔ (Finish Editing Systems). The new system is created and all of the water closets display in green to indicate that they are part of the sanitary system.

9. Hover your cursor over a water closet and press <Tab> to select the system, as shown in Figure 11–14.

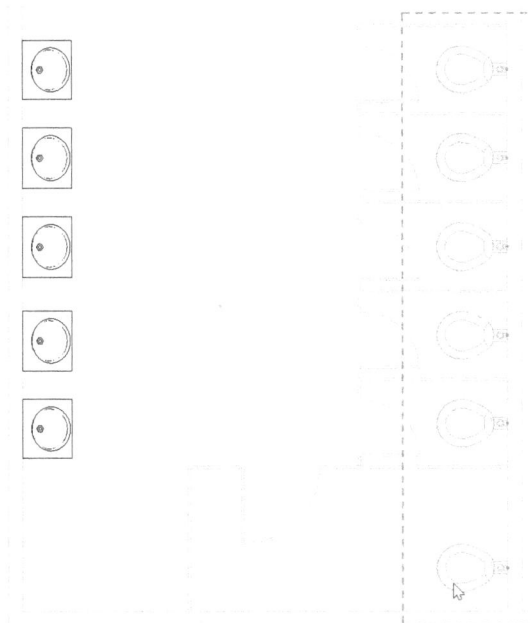

Figure 11–14

10. In the *Modify | Plumbing Fixtures* tab>*Create Systems* panel, click ⬚ (Piping). This option is available because there is another system that the water closets can be assigned to.

11. In the *Create Piping System* dialog box, set the *System type* to **Domestic Cold Water**. Accept the default name, ensure that the **Open in System Editor** option is not selected, and then click **OK**.

    • You do not need to open the System Editor because you have already selected all of the elements you want in the system.

    • All of the water closets are now part of the Domestic Cold Water and Sanitary systems and display black because they are connected to more than one system.

12. Click ⬚ (Modify).

13. Save the project.

Task 2: Create a fire protection system.

1. Open the Plumbing>Fire>Ceiling Plans>**01 Fire RCP** view.

2. In the **north wing**, select one of the sprinklers in the hall. Note that the option to create a system is not available because the system was automatically created when the piping was added.

3. Select the *Piping Systems* tab. The *System Tools* panel displays.

4. Click ⬚ (Edit System).

5. With ⬚ (Add to System) selected, select one of the classroom sprinklers. A warning displays (as shown in Figure 11–15) noting that you cannot add this sprinkler to the wet system because it belongs in a dry system. Close the warning dialog box.

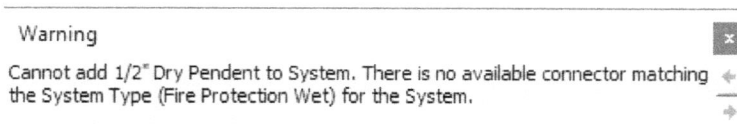

> Warning   [×]
>
> Cannot add 1/2" Dry Pendent to System. There is no available connector matching ←
> the System Type (Fire Protection Wet) for the System.   →

Figure 11–15

6. Click ✕ (Cancel Editing System).

7. Select all of the classroom sprinklers in the two rooms at the far left end of the hall.

8. In the *Modify | Sprinklers* tab>*Create Systems* panel, click ⬚ (Piping).

9. In the *Create Piping System* dialog box, leave the default system type and system name and ensure that the **Open in System Editor** option is not selected, then click **OK**. The software knows that this sprinkler needs to be part of a dry system, as shown in Figure 11–16.

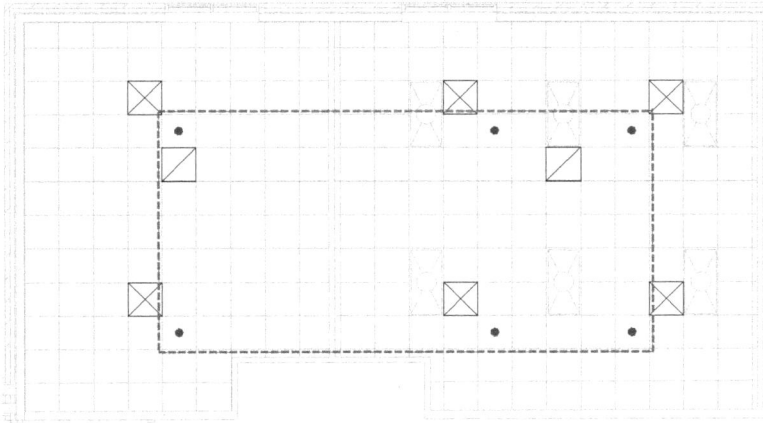

Figure 11–16

10. Save and close the project.

End of practice

11.2 Generating Layouts

After selecting a system in a plan or 3D view, you can utilize the **Generate Layout** tool to create piping or duct layouts that connect system components. This tool allows you to specify slope and routing parameters for the ductwork and piping. Additionally, it provides the ability to explore different layout solutions (shown in Figure 11–17 for ducts), as well as enabling you to manually modify the layout as needed.

Figure 11–17

* The workflow for creating both single-level and multiple-level layouts is identical.

How To: Generate a Layout

1. Hover the cursor over one of the elements and press <Tab> until you see the outline of the system, as shown with a duct system in Figure 11–18. Click to select the system.

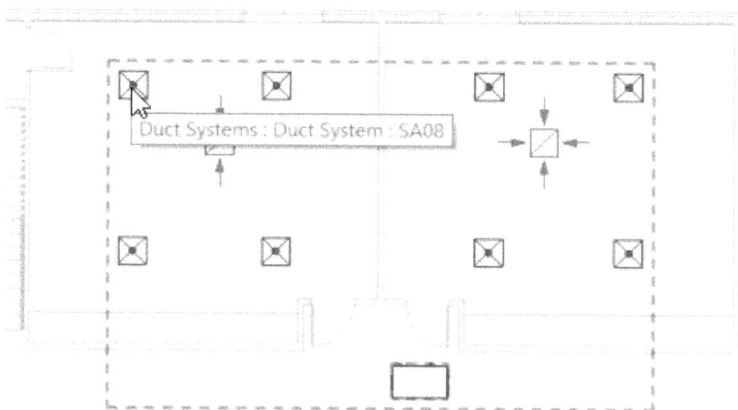

Figure 11–18

2. In the *Modify | Duct Systems* or *Modify | Pipe Systems* tab>*Layout* panel, click ⛭ (Generate Layout).

3. In the *Generate Layout* tab>*Modify Layout* panel, click ⚙ (Place Base). This is used if a system is not connected to equipment (such as the sanitary system shown in Figure 11–19) or in the early stages of setting up the layouts.

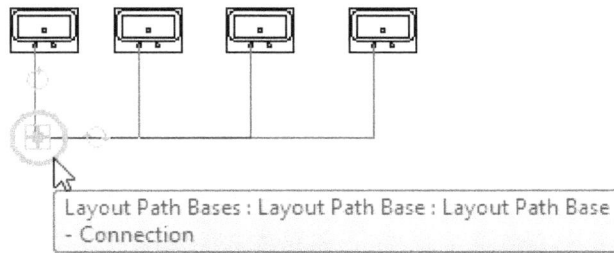

Figure 11–19

- When you place the base, ⚙ (Modify Base) automatically starts. Make changes to the base including the offset from the level and size.
- Use the rotate controls on the base to ensure that it is pointing in the correct direction
- If you no longer want the base, click ⚙ (Remove Base).

4. For pipes, if you need them to slope, use the *Slope* panel to specify the slope for piping systems before selecting a layout or placing a base.

5. In the Options Bar, click **Solutions**. Select a *Solution Type,* as shown in Figure 11–20, and click ⇨ (Next Solution) or ⇦ (Previous Solution) to cycle through the possible options. Click **Settings** to set the types and offsets that apply to this layout.

Generate Layout	Solution Type	Network		1 of 5 ⇦ ⇨	Settings ...
Properties		**Network**		× ☐	*SP - Starti
		Perimeter			
▲		Intersections			

Figure 11–20

Network	Creates a layout with the main segment through the center of a bounding box around the entire system and the branches at 90 degrees from the main branch.
Perimeter	Creates a layout with segments being placed on three of the four sides, and one with segments being placed on all four sides. (The **Inset** value is the offset between the bounding box and components.)
Intersections	Creates a layout with segments extending from each connector of the components. Where they intersect perpendicularly, proposed intersection junctions are created.

- Blue-colored lines identify the main trunk, while green-colored lines identify branches off of the trunk.

- Gold-colored lines indicate a potential open connection that might cause problems when the ducts or pipes are added (as shown in Figure 11–21), or other issues related to adequate space to place the required fittings.

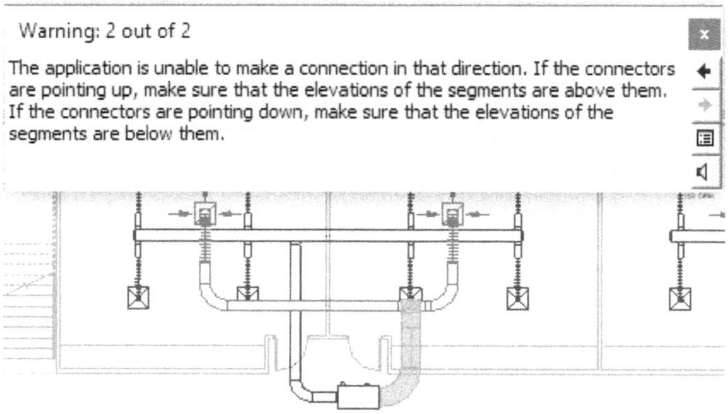

Figure 11–21

- In the Options Bar, click **Settings...**. The *Conversion Settings* dialog box (shown for ducts in Figure 11–22) displays and enables you to set the type of duct or pipe and the offset from the level where you are working.

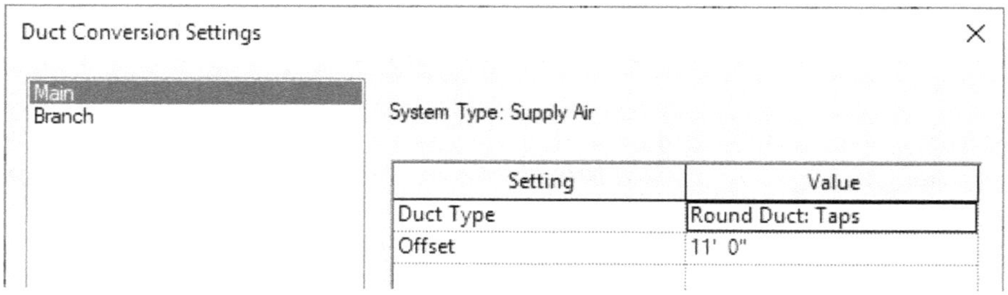

Figure 11–22

- These settings are specific to this system only. Global settings are defined in Mechanical Settings.

- For duct branches, you can also specify a *Flex Duct Type* and *Maximum Flex Duct Length* if you want air terminals automatically connected that way.

6. In the *Generate Layout* tab>*Generate Layout* panel, click ✔ (Finish Layout) when you have a solution that looks best.

How To: Customize the Layout

1. Using ▦ (Solutions), select a layout design similar to what you want to use.

2. In the *Generate Layout* tab>*Modify Layout* panel, click ▦ (Edit Layout).

3. Select one of the layout lines. You can use the move control to change the location of the line, as shown in Figure 11–23. You can also change the height of the offset by clicking on the number control.

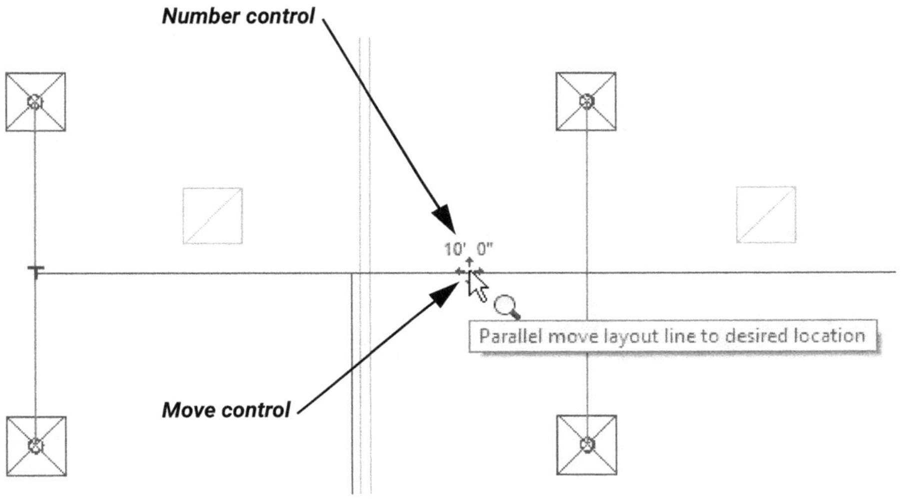

Figure 11–23

4. Click ▦ (Solutions) to finish customizing the layout. In the Options Bar, the *Solution Type* list now has **Custom** as an additional option to the standard three solution types.

    *   The software only permits one custom option at a time.

5. In the *Generate Layout* tab>*Generate Layout* panel, click ✔ (Finish Layout).

*   When the automatic/custom layout is completed, it is important to check the entire system to ensure that the layout is correct. Ensure that you check slopes and fitting directions.

Practice 11c
Create Automatic HVAC Layouts

Practice Objectives

- Create ducts using the **Generate Layout** tool with both standard and custom layouts.
- Modify ductwork after it has been placed.

In this practice, you will create supply ducts using the **Generate Layout** tool and modify the ductwork in the layout after it has been placed. You will also create a custom layout for the return ducts and modify the ductwork. The final systems are shown in Figure 11−24.

Figure 11−24

Task 1: Create an automatic ductwork layout.

1. In the practice files *Working Models>Mechanical* folder, open the project **Mech-Layouts.rvt**.
2. Close any other open projects.
3. Open the Mechanical>HVAC>Floor Plans>01 Mechanical Plan>**01 Mechanical - Area B** view. Close the SP - Starting Page and any other open views.
4. Open the Mechanical>HVAC>3D Views>**01 Mechanical - Area B 3D** view. Rotate the 3D view using the ViewCube.
5. Click on the **01 Mechanical - Area B** view to make it the active view. Type **WT** to tile the views and **ZA** to zoom all.

6. In the plan, hover the cursor over one of the supply air terminals and press <Tab> until the system displays. Click to select it, as shown in Figure 11–25.

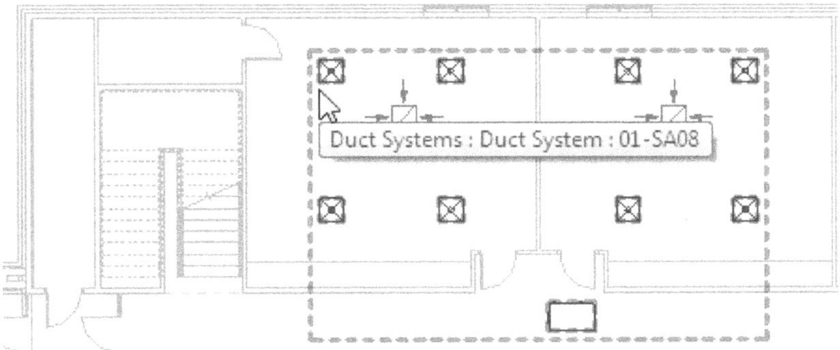

Figure 11–25

7. In the *Modify | Duct Systems* tab>*Layout* panel, click ▦ (Generate Layout).

8. In the *Generate Layout* tab>*Modify Layout* panel, verify ▦ (Solutions) is selected.

9. In the Options Bar, verify the *Solution Type* is set to **Network** and click **Settings...**.

10. In the *Duct Conversion Settings* dialog box, set the following parameters and then click **OK**.
    Main:
    *   *Duct Type:* **Rectangular Duct: Radius Elbows/Taps**
    *   *Offset*: **10'-0"**

    Branch (shown in Figure 11–26):
    *   *Duct Type*: **Round Duct: Taps / Short Radius**
    *   *Offset*: **10'-0"**
    *   *Flex Duct Type*: **Flex Duct Round: Flex - Round**
    *   *Maximum Flex Duct Length*: **6'-0"**

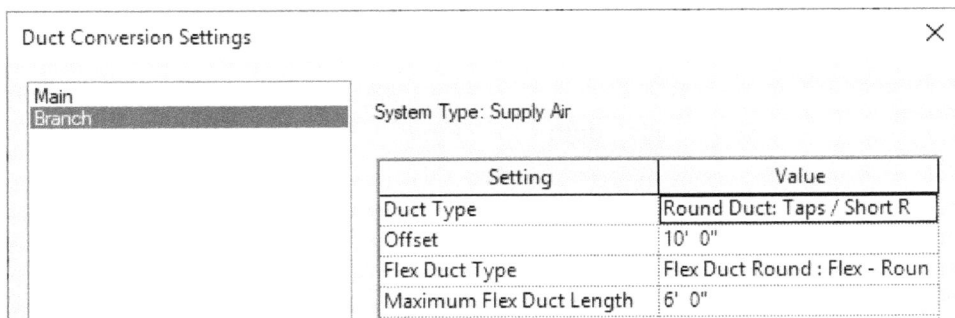

Figure 11–26

11. In the Options Bar, use the arrow buttons and Solution Types to try out several different solutions. End with the solution Network **1 of 6** (which is the layout shown in Figure 11–27) and click ✔ (Finish Layout).

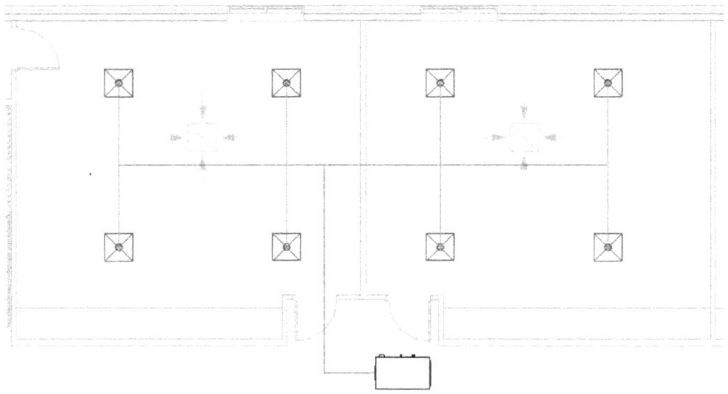

Figure 11–27

12. A warning displays prompting you that there is an open connection, and the horizontal duct is highlighted, as shown in Figure 11–28. You can see in the 3D view that it is missing an endcap. Close the warning.

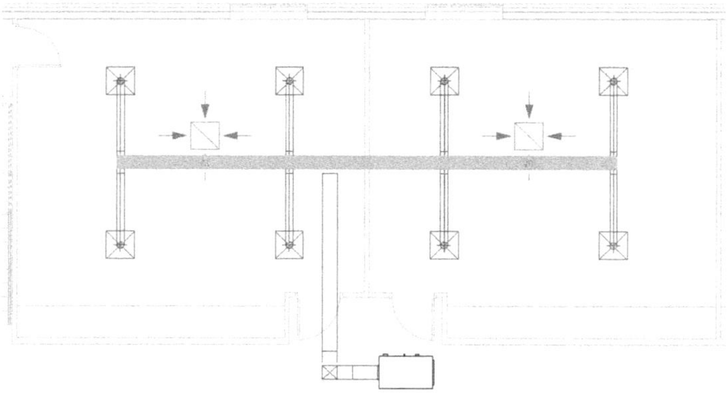

Figure 11–28

13. On both ends of the main duct, add a cap. Select the duct and in the *Modify | Ducts* tab>*Edit* panel, click ⊤ (Cap Open Ends). Both ends of the main duct have cap ends now.

14. Click in an empty area in the view to clear the selection.

15. Save the project.

Task 2: Create a custom ductwork layout.

1. Continue working with the same two views.

2. In the plan view, select the Return Air System.

3. In the *Modify | Duct Systems* tab>*Layout* panel, click ⬚ (Generate Layout).

4. In the *Generate Layout* tab>*Modify Layout* panel, verify ⬚ (Solutions) is selected.

5. View the various solutions. Most of them have some problem with the layout. When the gold lines display it is a warning that the layout could fail in those areas.

6. In the Options Bar, click **Settings...**.

7. In the *Duct Conversion Settings* dialog box, set the following parameters and then click **OK**.

   Main:

   - *Duct Type*: **Rectangular Duct: Radius Elbow and Taps**
   - *Offset*: **11'-6"**

   Branch:

   - *Duct Type*: **Rectangular Duct: Radius Elbow and Taps**
   - *Offset*: **11'-6"**
   - *Flex Duct Type*: **None** (ignore the offset)

8. This still did not correct all of the problems, but it solved some by changing the heights of the ducts.

9. Cycle through the solutions to review the options.

10. Stay on Network 3 of 5. In the *Generate Layout* tab>*Modify Layout* panel, click ⬚ (Edit Layout).

11. In the plan view, select the vertical line shown in Figure 11–29 and move it approximately **6"** to the left (you can use the move icon to move the duct and use the bottom temporary dimension to see how far you are moving it).

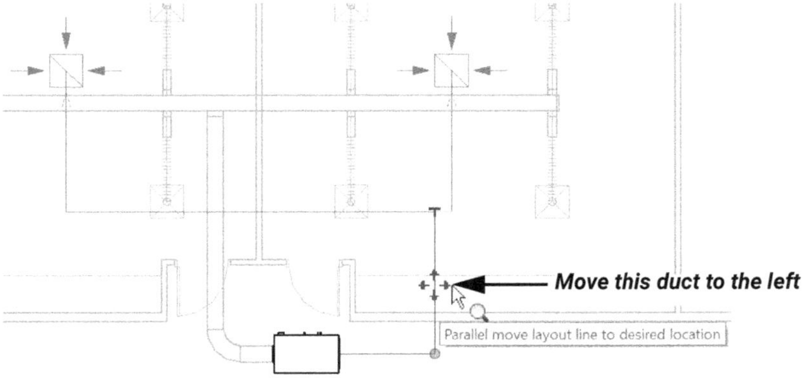

Figure 11–29

Note: Your model may differ from the image shown. You will need to delete any ducts that are incorrect and redraw them.

12. Click ✔ (Finish Layout). There are still some problems that need to be corrected and are highlighted in orange.

13. In the warning dialog box, click through the various warnings to see the other issues. The corresponding ducts are also highlighted. You can see that the issues are all related to the ducts coming from the air handling unit.

- If you selected a different layout, there will be different issues but the principles of fixing them are still the same.

14. Close the warning dialog box. Figure 11–30 shows how the system displays in the 3D view.

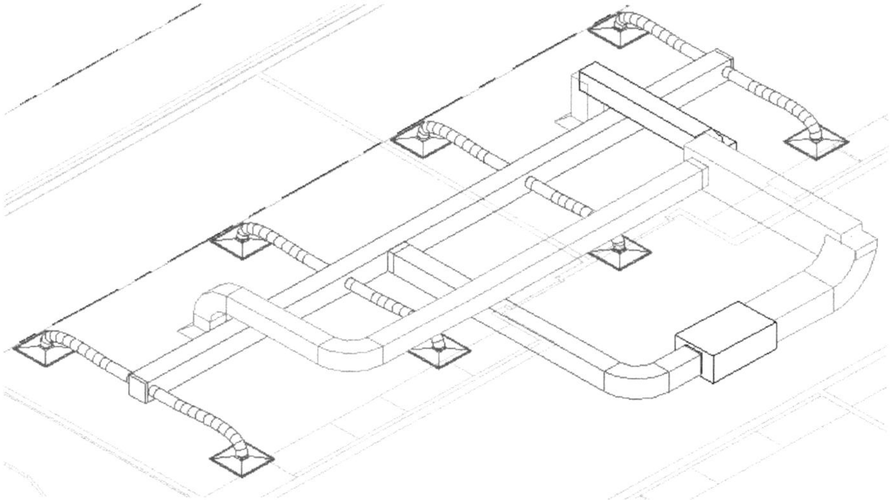

Figure 11–30

15. Save the project.

Task 3: Correct issues with the layout.

1. In the 3D view, select the ducts and related duct fittings coming out of the air handling unit and delete them up to the main duct. The remaining return air ducts (which are highlighted) should look similar to what is shown in Figure 11–31.

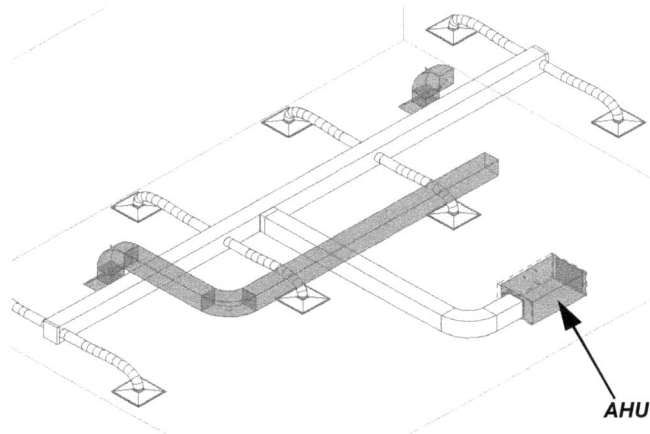

Figure 11–31

2. In plan view, select the duct coming out of the return air terminal and draw a duct downward toward the main duct, as shown in Figure 11–32.

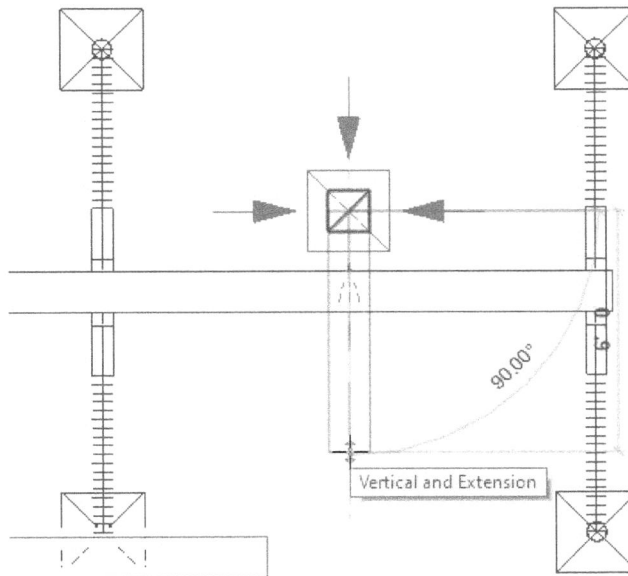

Figure 11–32

3. Click ⌖ (Modify).

4. Use ⫟ (Trim/Extend to Corner) to trim the main duct and the duct running to the return diffuser, as shown in Figure 11–33.

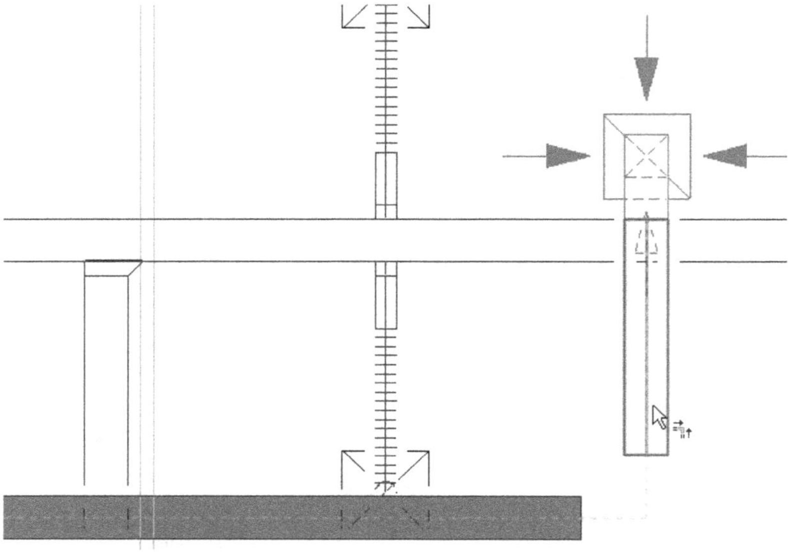

Figure 11–33

5. Click ⌖ (Modify).

6. Select the AHU Mechanical Equipment unit, right-click on the Return Air control, and select **Draw Duct**.

7. In the Type Selector, verify that the type is set to **Rectangular Duct: Radius Elbows/Taps**.

8. In the Options Bar, set the *Width* and *Height* to **12"** and the *Middle Elevation* to **10'-0"**.

9. Draw the duct out approximately **3'-6"**.

10. In the Options Bar, set *Middle Elevation* to **11'-6"** and continue drawing the duct until it connects with the main horizontal duct. The appropriate fittings are added to resize the duct coming from the AHU and changing the height going to the other duct, as shown in Figure 11–34.

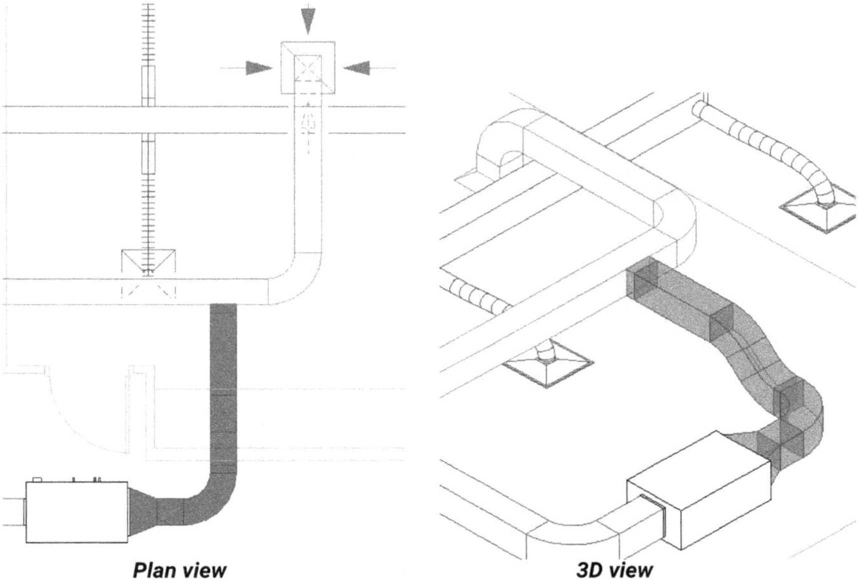

Plan view   *3D view*

Figure 11–34

11. Save and close the project.

End of practice

Practice 11d
Create Automatic Plumbing Layouts

Practice Objectives

- Create pipes using the **Generate Layout** tool with both standard and custom layouts.
- Modify pipes after they have been placed.

In this practice, you will create a piping layout for a sprinkler system. You will then create a sanitary system and use the layout tools, including **Place Base**, to add sloped piping, as shown in Figure 11–35.

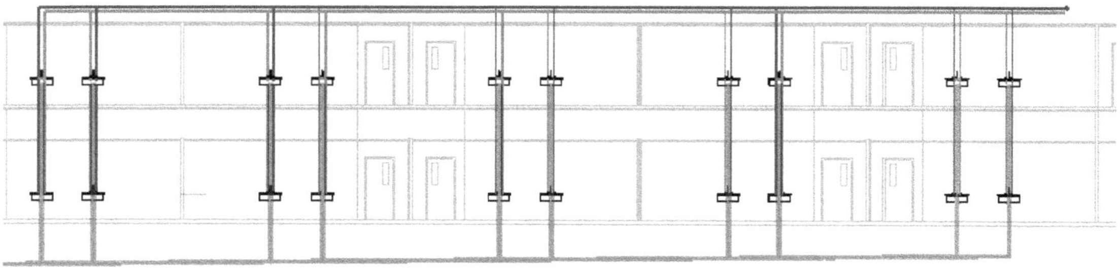

Figure 11–35

Task 1: Create a piping layout for a sprinkler system.

1. In the practice files *Working Models>Plumbing* folder, open the project **Plumb-Layouts.rvt**.
2. Open the Plumbing>Fire>Ceiling Plans>**01 Fire RCP** view and close the SP* - Starting Page and any other open views.
3. Open the Plumbing>Fire>3D Views>**01 Fire 3D** view.
4. Return to the **01 Fire RCP** view and type **WT** to tile the two windows so that both the 3D view and the north wing of the RCP display.

5. In plan view, zoom in to the north wing's upper classrooms. Hover the cursor over one of the sprinklers in the classroom and press <Tab> until the piping system displays, as shown in Figure 11–36. Click to select the system.

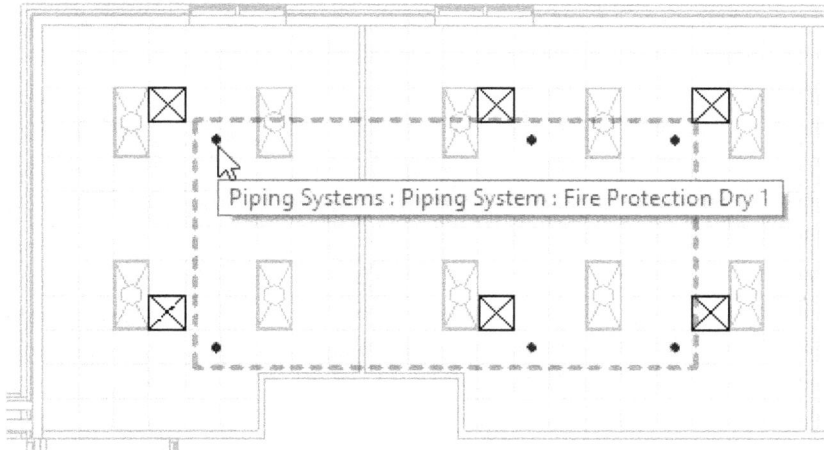

Figure 11–36

6. In the *Modify | Piping Systems* tab>*Layout* panel, click ⬚ (Generate Layout).

7. In the *Generate Layout* tab>*Modify Layout* panel, verify ⬚ (Solutions) is selected.

8. In the *Slope* panel, set the *Slope Value* to **0" / 12"**.

9. In the Options Bar, click **Settings....**

10. In the *Pipe Conversion Settings* dialog box, verify that the following parameters are set and click **OK**.

    Main:

    - *Pipe Type:* **Pipe Types: Copper**
    - *Offset:* **9'-6"**

    Branch:

    - *Pipe Type:* **Pipe Types: Copper**
    - *Offset:* **9'-0"**

11. In the Options Bar, work through the *Solution Types* and try out different solutions. Most of them have some problem with the layout. When the gold lines display, it is a warning that the layout could fail in those areas. Figure 11–37 shows a layout and indicates what the colors mean.

Figure 11–37

12. In this case, the *Offset* specified in the settings does not work. In the Options Bar, click **Settings...**.

13. Change the branch so that it is *Offset* to **9'-6"** and click **OK**.

14. This time the options work. Select one that you like and click ✔ (Finish Layout).

15. Save the project.

Task 2: Create a sanitary system.

1. Open the Plumbing>Plumbing>3D views>**3D Plumbing** view and maximize it. (The linked model is hidden in this view for clarity.)

2. Close any other open views.

3. Hover the cursor over one of the sinks in the classroom wing and press <Tab> to highlight the various elements. Note that there are piping networks and domestic hot and cold water systems, but there is no sanitary system.

4. In the 3D view, select one sink, right-click, and select **Select All Instances>Visible in View**.

5. In the *Modify | Plumbing Fixtures* tab>*Create Systems* panel, select ⬚ (Piping).

Note: You do not need to open the System Editor because you have already selected all of the elements you want in the system.

6. In the *Create Piping System* dialog box, verify the *System type* is set to **Sanitary**, accept the default name, and click **OK**. The sanitary system is created, as shown in Figure 11−38.

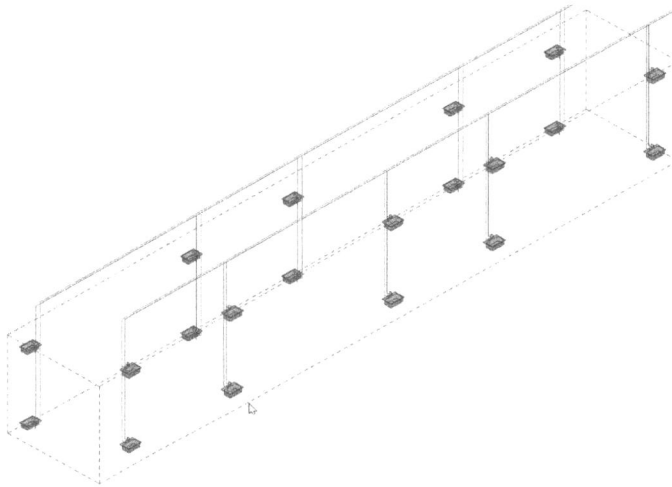

Figure 11−38

7. Click ⌖ (Modify).

8. Open the Plumbing>Sanitary>Sections (Building Section)> **South Wing - Sanitary Section** view.

9. Type **WT** to tile the two views and arrange them so that the sinks display in each view.

10. In the section view, hover your cursor over a sink and press <Tab> until the Sanitary pipe system displays. Click to select the system.

   • Hint: As you press <Tab>, watch the Status Bar in the lower left corner to understand what systems you are cycling through.

11. In the *Modify | Piping Systems* tab>*Layout* panel, click 🔧 (Generate Layout).

12. In the *Slope* panel, ensure the *Slope Value* is set to **1/8" / 12"**.

13. In the *Generate Layout* tab>*Modify Layout* panel, verify 🔧 (Solutions) is selected.

14. View the various solutions and select a solution type similar to the one shown in Figure 11−39.

15. In the Options Bar, click **Settings...**.

16. In the *Pipe Conversion Settings* dialog box, set the following parameters and click **OK**.

    Main:

    - *Pipe Type:* **Pipe Types: PVC - DWV**
    - *Offset:* (negative) **-4'-0"**

    Branch:

    - *Pipe Type:* **Pipe Types: PVC - DWV**
    - *Offset:* (negative) **-4'-0"**

17. Verify that the 3D Plumbing view is active, then in the *Slope* panel, click 🔘 (Place Base).

18. Select a point outside and to the left of the building, as shown in Figure 11–39.

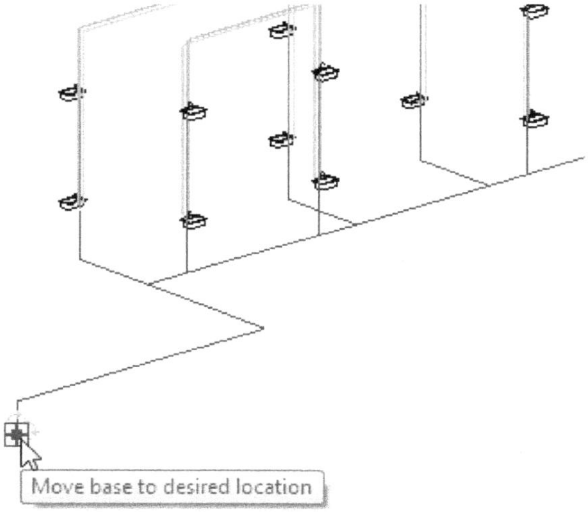

Figure 11–39

19. The **Modify Base** command is automatically selected. In the Options Bar, change the *Offset* to (negative) **-8'-0"** and the *Diameter* to **1"**.

    - If the Base pipe is too large, it causes problems with the connections to the sinks. You can change the main trunk pipe sizes after the layout is finished.

20. In the *Modify Layout* panel, click 🔘 (Solutions).

21. In the Options Bar, work through the *Solution Types* and try out several different solutions. Select the one you like.

22. Click ✔ (Finish Layout).

23. If a warning displays, read it and close the dialog box.

24. Save and close the project.

End of practice

11.3 Testing Systems

As you start working with connectors and systems, it is important to check how the system is working. For a quick way to test the continuity of a system, hover the cursor over one of the linear connections and press <Tab> until the system highlights. For the example shown in Figure 11–40, one of the ducts is not attached to the fitting and therefore is not highlighted.

Figure 11–40

If there are issues with a selected system, the *Warning* panel displays in the related *Modify* toolbar, as shown in Figure 11–41. Click (Show Related Warnings) to open the dialog box and review the issues.

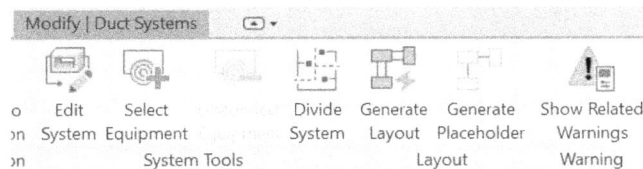

Figure 11–41

Often, these warnings are corrected as you continue working in a system and complete the full connection. However, some errors need to be corrected before the system works as required.

Showing Disconnects

Duct and piping systems can be analyzed and reviewed for issues. This includes searching for disconnects and checking the various systems. For the example shown in Figure 11−42, there are open connectors at three different places. Once the tee fitting is changed to an elbow fitting, and the flex duct connects the end of the existing duct to the air terminal, the warnings are removed.

Figure 11−42

How To: Show Disconnects

1. In the *Analyze* tab>*Check Systems* panel, click ⚠ (Show Disconnects).

2. In the *Show Disconnects Options* dialog box, select the types of systems you want to display and click **OK**.

3. The disconnects displays ⚠ (Warning).

   • The disconnects continue to display until you either correct the situation or run **Show Disconnects** again and clear all of the selections.

4. Hover the cursor over the warning icon to display a tooltip with the warning, or click on the icon to open the warning dialog box, as shown in Figure 11−43.

Figure 11−43

How To: Use the Check Systems Tools

1. In the *Analyze* tab>*Check Systems* panel, click 🖭 (Check Duct Systems) or 🖭 (Check Pipe Systems) to toggle them on.

2. The ⚠ (Warning) icon displays where there are problems. Click one of the icons to open the warning dialog box, as shown in Figure 11–44.

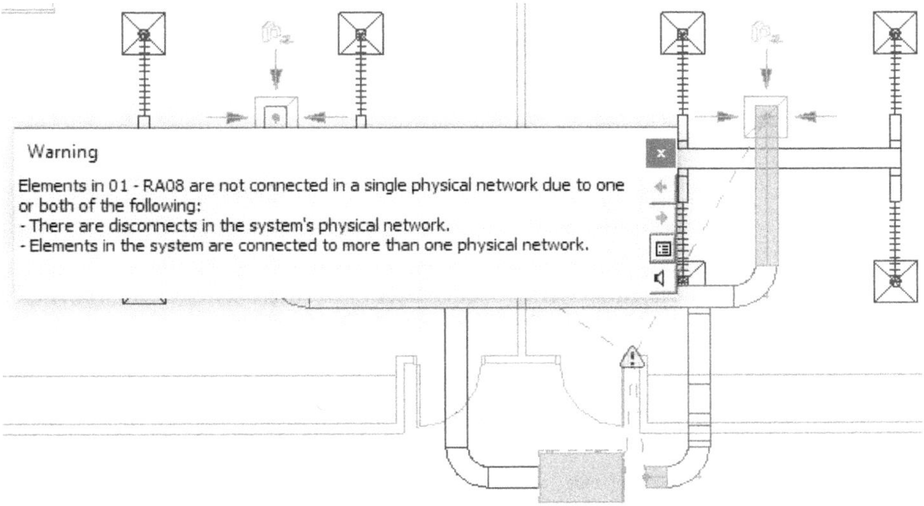

Figure 11–44

*   For icons that have more than one warning, in the warning dialog box, click ➕ (Next Warning) and ➕ (Previous Warning) to search through the list.

3. Click ⊞ (Expand Warning Dialog) to open the dialog box, as shown in Figure 11–45. You can expand each node in the box and select elements to display or delete.

    *Note: If there are a lot of warnings to review, click **Export...** and save the HTML report to review separately.*

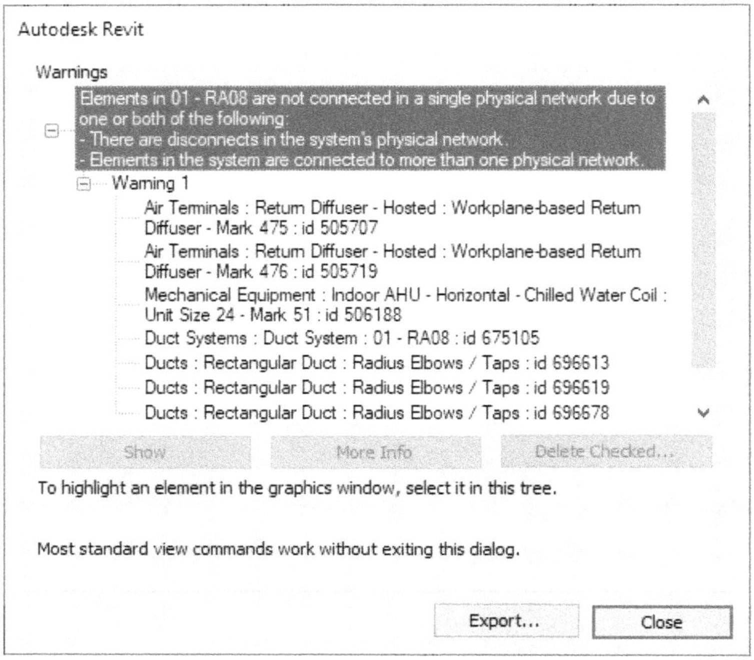

Figure 11–45

System Inspector

The System Inspector provides information such as flow rate, static pressure, and pressure loss at every point in a system, as shown in Figure 11–46 for a domestic cold water system. The System Inspector also enables you to make changes to components of a system as you complete an inspection.

Note: The System Inspector works with all duct and piping systems except fire suppression systems.

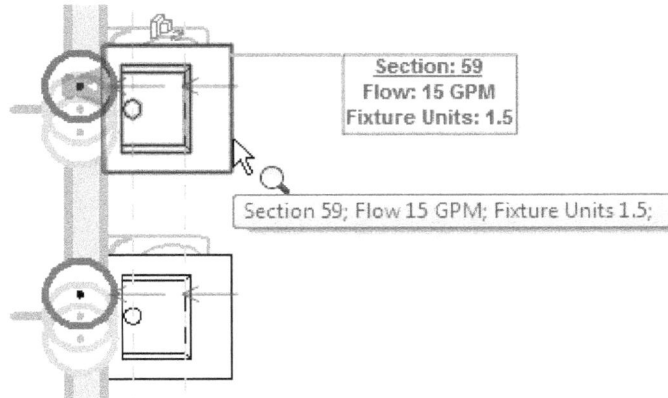

Figure 11–46

- The System Inspector does not display in the ribbon if an open system is selected.

- The pressure loss method settings for duct and pipe fittings and accessories can be set up in Properties.

*Note: For information about pressure loss reporting, see **B.1 Pressure Loss Reports** in **Appendix B Additional Tools for Construction Documents**.*

How To: Use the System Inspector

1. Select any part of a system (e.g., air terminals, ductwork, piping, mechanical or plumbing equipment, or plumbing fixtures, etc.).

   *Note: In the System Browser, right-click on the top level of a system and select **System Inspector**.*

2. In the *Modify* contextual tab>*Analysis* panel, click ⚙ (System Inspector). The floating *System Inspector* panel displays as shown in Figure 11–47.

3. Click ⚙ (Inspect). The air flow displays in the system, as shown in Figure 11–47. Move the cursor over a section of system to display information, such as the Flow, Static Pressure, and Pressure Loss for duct systems.

    *   The red path displays the greatest static pressure.

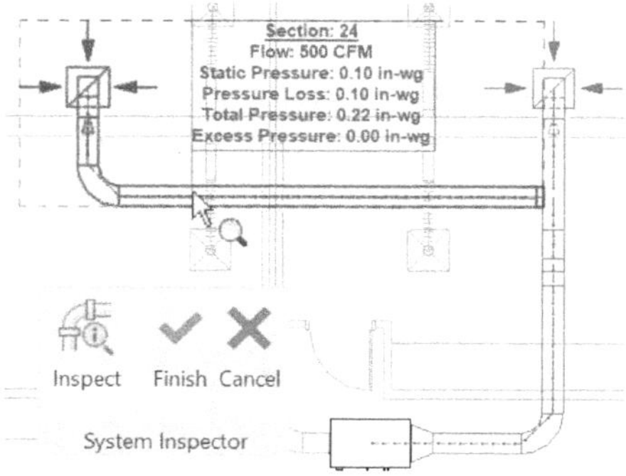

Figure 11–47

4. If you need to change a component of the system, remain in the System Inspector:

    a. In the *Select* panel, click ⬦ (Modify).
    b. Select the component.
    c. Make changes to the component on the screen using the controls or in the Properties.

5. Click ⚙ (Inspect) to return to the flow pattern.

6. Click ✔ (Finish).

*   If you select a piece of mechanical or plumbing equipment that is attached to more than one duct-based or pipe-based system, the *Select a System* dialog box displays, as shown in Figure 11–48. Select the system you want to inspect and click **OK**.

Figure 11–48

*   The System Inspector displays in a floating panel by default. You can move it or make it a part of the ribbon by clicking **Return Panels to Ribbon**.

Duct and Pipe Color Fill Legends

An additional way to view information about ducts and pipes is to create a color fill legend, as shown in Figure 11–49 for friction in ducts.

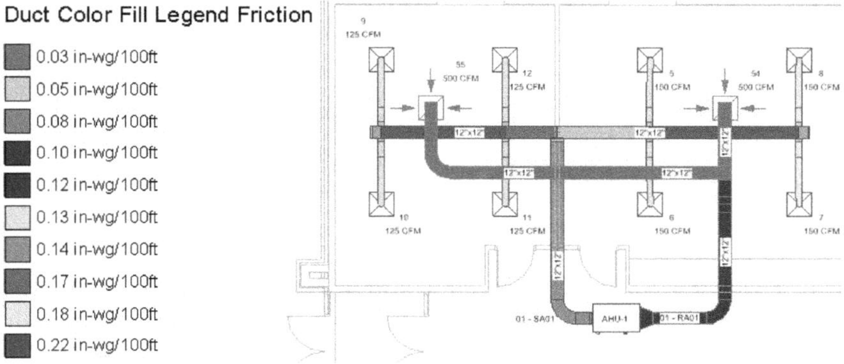

Figure 11–49

* These color fill schemes and legends are similar to those created for spaces and zones.

How To: Create a Color Fill Legend

1. In the *Annotate* tab>*Color Fill* panel, click ⬛ (Duct Legend) or ⬛ (Pipe Legend) and place the legend.

2. If a color scheme is not assigned to the view, the *Choose Color Scheme* dialog box displays. Choose a scheme from the list, as shown in Figure 11–50. When you click **OK**, the view is filled to match the legend.

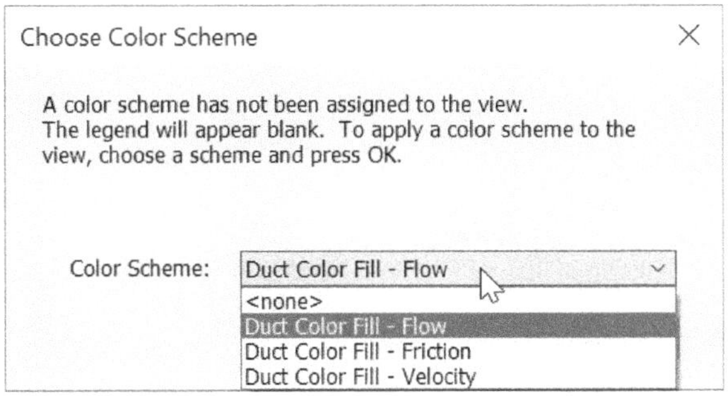

Figure 11–50

3. To make changes to the color fill scheme, select the legend and in the *Modify | Duct/Pipe Color Fill Legends* tab>*Scheme* panel, click ⬛ (Edit Scheme).

4. The *Edit Color Scheme* dialog box opens where you select the color scheme you want to use, as shown in Figure 11–51.

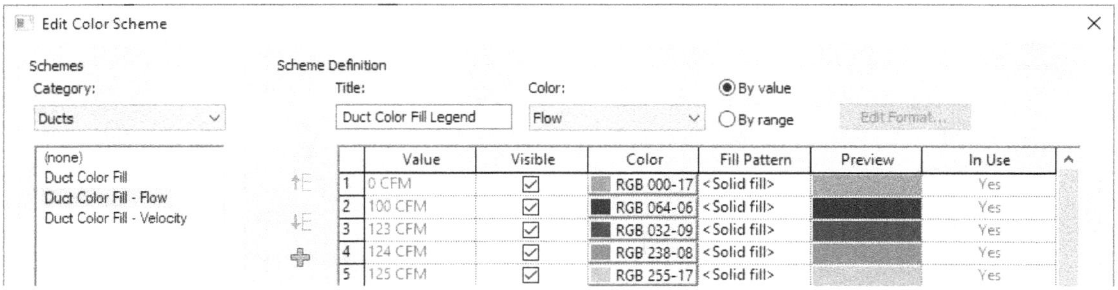

Figure 11–51

*   You can also reach the *Edit Color Scheme* dialog box through the view properties. With nothing selected, in Properties beside *System Color Schemes,* click **Edit...**. In the *Color Schemes* dialog box, click the color scheme button for either **Pipes** or **Ducts**. The *Edit Color Scheme* dialog box displays.

*   To create new color schemes or modify existing ones, see *A.4 Defining Color Schemes* in *Appendix A Additional Tools for Design Development*.

Practice 11e
Review HVAC Systems

Practice Objectives

- Investigate warnings and use Check Duct Systems.
- Review disconnects.
- Add a duct color fill legend.
- Review a schedule setup to show the airflow in spaces.
- Correct issues discovered by the testing tools.

In this practice, you will review warnings, run **Check Duct Systems**, and **Show Disconnects**. You will then correct any problems and run the **System Inspector**. You will add a color fill legend to test the velocity and make corrections. Figure 11–52 shows the corrections made and the Duct Velocity Legend after the practice has been completed.

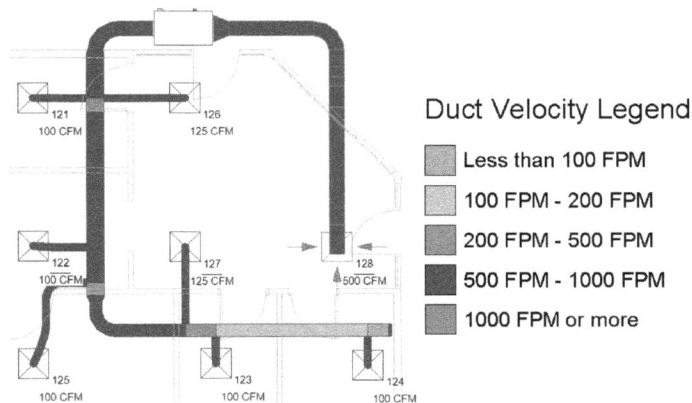

Figure 11–52

Task 1: Review warnings and check duct systems.

1. In the practice files *Working Models>Mechanical* folder, open **Mech-Analyze.rvt**.

2. Open the Mechanical>HVAC>Floor Plans>01 Mechanical Plan>**01 Mechanical Plan- Area C (SOUTH)** view. This displays the office area near the front entrance of the building.

3. Hover over a supply duct and press <Tab> until you see the duct system highlight, as shown in Figure 11–53. Click to select it.

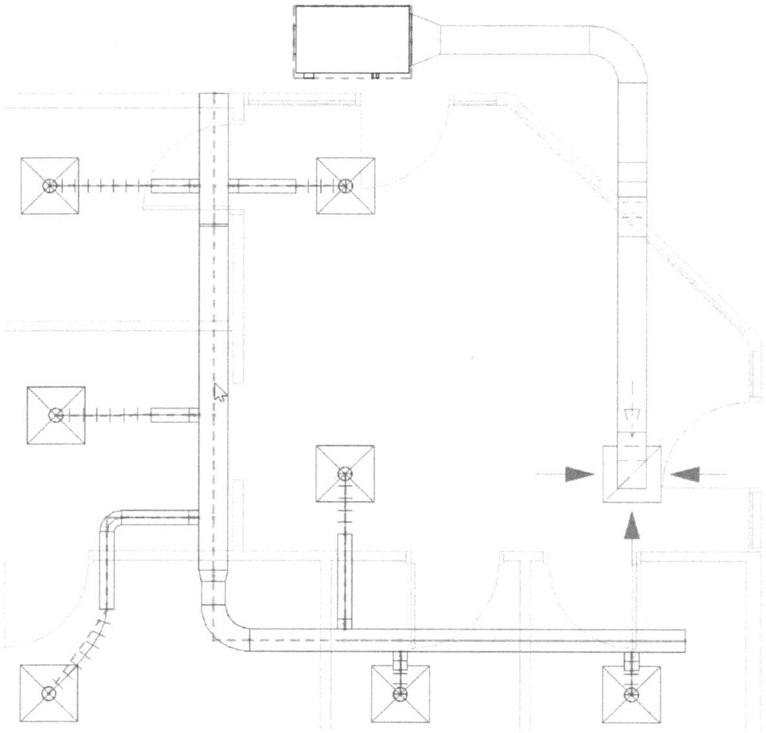

Figure 11–53

4. In the *Modify | Duct Systems* tab>*Warning* panel, click ⚠️🖳 (Show Related Warnings).

5. Review the contents of the dialog box, then close it.

6. In the *Analyze* tab>*Check Systems* panel, click 🖳 (Check Duct Systems).

7. The duct system is not working, as shown in Figure 11–54. On the supply system, note that there is a duct missing, which should be coming out of the AHU.

Missing ducts

Figure 11–54

8. Use the **Draw Duct** tool and set the type to **Rectangular Duct: Radius Elbows / Taps**. Then, draw a duct coming from the AHU (as shown in Figure 11–55).

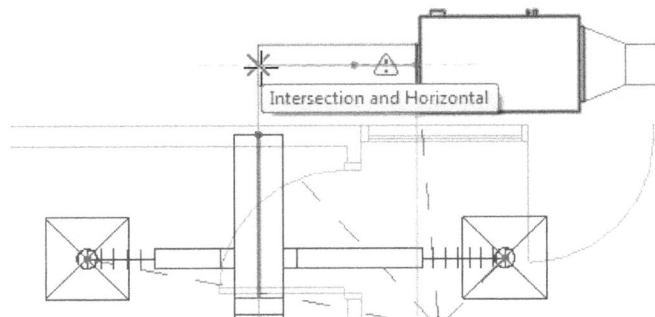

Intersection and Horizontal

Figure 11–55

9. Click ⌖ (Modify).

10. Use ⌐̄┬̄ (Trim/Extend to Corner) to clean up the intersection and automatically apply the required elbow fitting.

11. Click ⌖ (Modify).

12. Now that the duct system is working as expected, toggle off **Check Duct Systems**.

13. Save the project.

Task 2: Check and correct duct disconnects.

1. In the *Analyze* tab>*Check Systems* panel, click ⌐̄⅄ (Show Disconnects).

2. In the *Show Disconnects Options* dialog box, select **Duct** (as shown in Figure 11–56) and click **OK**. While the system is now connected correctly, there is still a disconnect at the end of the system.

3. Select the duct, right-click on the open connector, and select **Cap Open End**. This solves the problem on this end of the system.

4. Hover over a supply air duct and press <Tab> until you see the duct system highlight, then click to select it. Alternatively, you can select a duct within the run you want to inspect.

5. In the *Modify | Duct Systems* tab>*Analysis* panel, click ⚙ (System Inspector).

6. In the *System Inspector* panel, click ⚙ (Inspect).

7. Hover the cursor over parts of the system to view the information, as shown in Figure 11–56. (The information that displays depends on how you drew your duct and the section you are hovering over.)

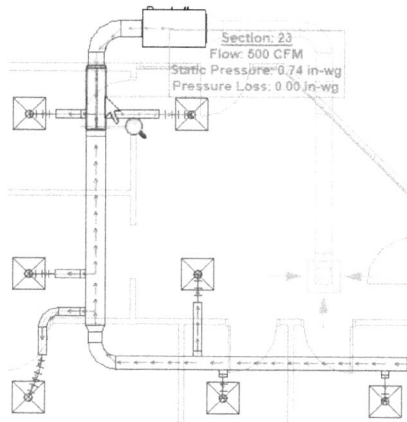

Figure 11–56

8. When you are finished inspecting the system, click ✔ (Finish).

9. Now that the issues have been fixed, in the *Analyze* tab>*Check Systems* panel, click ⚓ (Show Disconnects). Clear the checkmark from **Duct** and click **OK**.

10. Save the project.

Task 3: Add a duct color fill scheme and legend.

1. In the *Analyze* tab>*Color Fill* panel, click ▦ (Duct Legend).

2. Place the legend near the office area.

3. In the *Choose Color Scheme* dialog box, select **Duct Color Fill - Velocity** and click **OK**. The legend and color scheme display as shown in Figure 11–57.

   • If the legend's title does not display, select the legend and click **Edit Type** in Properties. Select **Show Title** from the *Graphics* section.

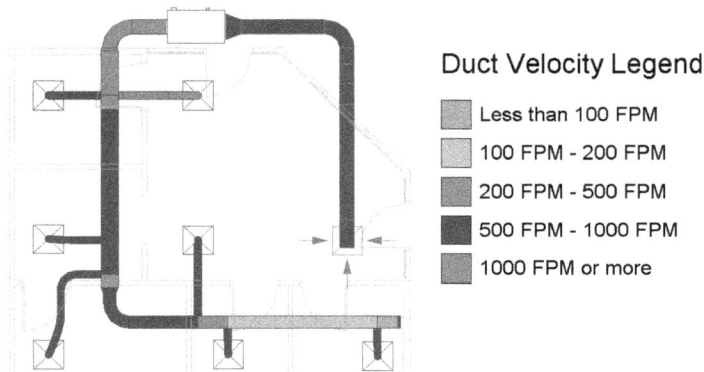

Figure 11–57

4. You can see from the colors that some of the velocity is set too high.

5. Open the *Visibility/Graphic Overrides* dialog box and in the *Annotation Categories* tab, toggle on **Air Terminal Tags**. Click **OK**.

6. The tags display the Flow associated with the diffusers. Select the tag of the diffuser with too large of a flow, as shown in Figure 11–58, and change it to **125**.

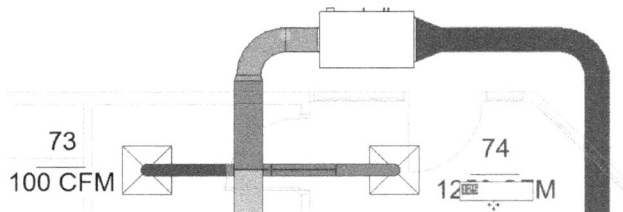

Figure 11–58

7. The colors change to the expected amounts, as shown in Figure 11–59.

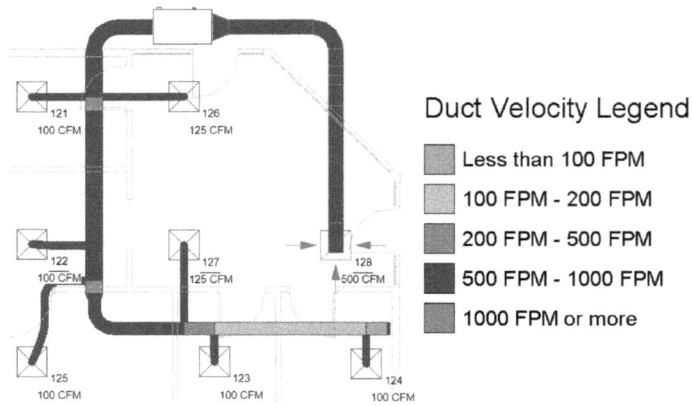

Figure 11–59

8. Save and close the project.

End of practice

Practice 11f
Test Plumbing Systems

Practice Objectives

- Investigate warnings and use Check Pipe Systems.
- Review disconnects.
- Correct issues discovered by the testing tools.
- Add a piping color fill legend.

In this practice, you will review warnings, run **Check Pipe Systems**, and use **Show Disconnects**. You will then correct some of the problems in the south wing, as shown in Figure 11–60. You will also add a piping color fill legend that shows the sizes of pipes in the view.

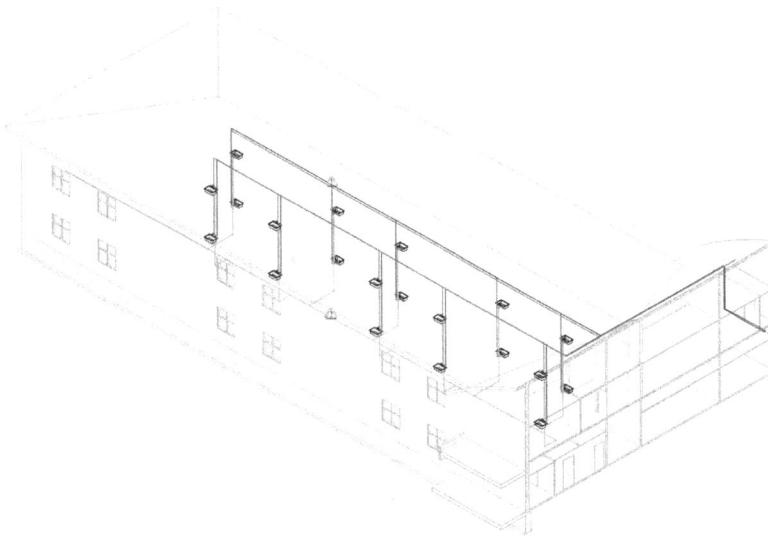

Figure 11–60

Task 1: Review warnings and check pipe systems.

1. In the practice files *Working Models>Plumbing* folder, open **Plumb-Analyze.rvt**.
2. Open the Plumbing>Plumbing>3D Views>**3D Plumbing Area B** view.

3. Hover over one of the domestic cold water system pipes in the south wing of the building and press <Tab> until you see the system highlight, as shown in Figure 11-61. Click to select it.

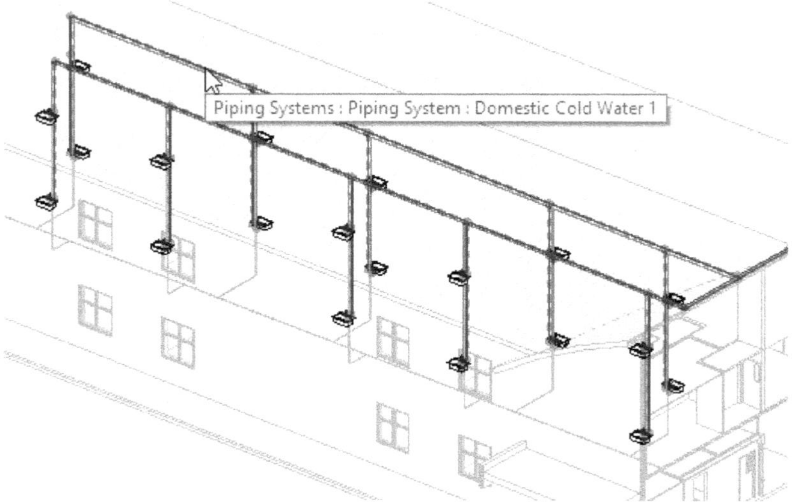

Piping Systems : Piping System : Domestic Cold Water 1

Figure 11-61

4. In the *Modify | Pipe Systems* tab>*Warning* panel, click 🔺 (Show Related Warnings).

5. Review the contents of the dialog box, as shown in Figure 11-62.

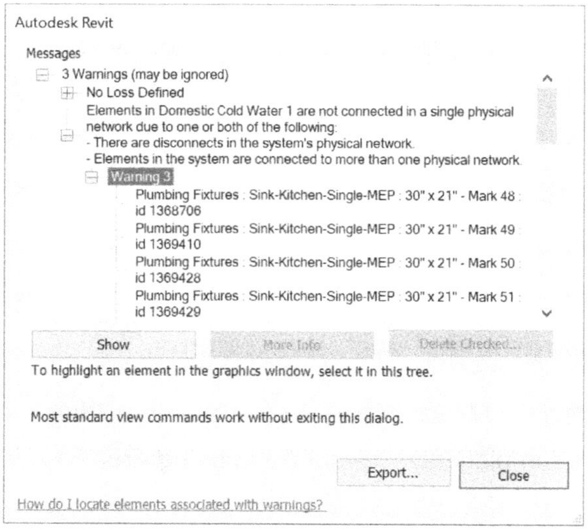

Autodesk Revit

Messages

- 3 Warnings (may be ignored)
  - No Loss Defined
  - Elements in Domestic Cold Water 1 are not connected in a single physical network due to one or both of the following:
    - There are disconnects in the system's physical network.
    - Elements in the system are connected to more than one physical network.
    - Warning 3
      - Plumbing Fixtures : Sink-Kitchen-Single-MEP : 30" x 21" - Mark 48 : id 1368706
      - Plumbing Fixtures : Sink-Kitchen-Single-MEP : 30" x 21" - Mark 49 : id 1369410
      - Plumbing Fixtures : Sink-Kitchen-Single-MEP : 30" x 21" - Mark 50 : id 1369428
      - Plumbing Fixtures : Sink-Kitchen-Single-MEP : 30" x 21" - Mark 51 : id 1369429

Show   More Info   Delete Checked...

To highlight an element in the graphics window, select it in this tree.

Most standard view commands work without exiting this dialog.

Export...   Close

How do I locate elements associated with warnings?

Figure 11-62

6. Close the dialog box.

7. In the *Analyze* tab>*Check Systems* panel, click ✎ (Check Pipe Systems). The pipe system has some issues with it, as shown in Figure 11–63.

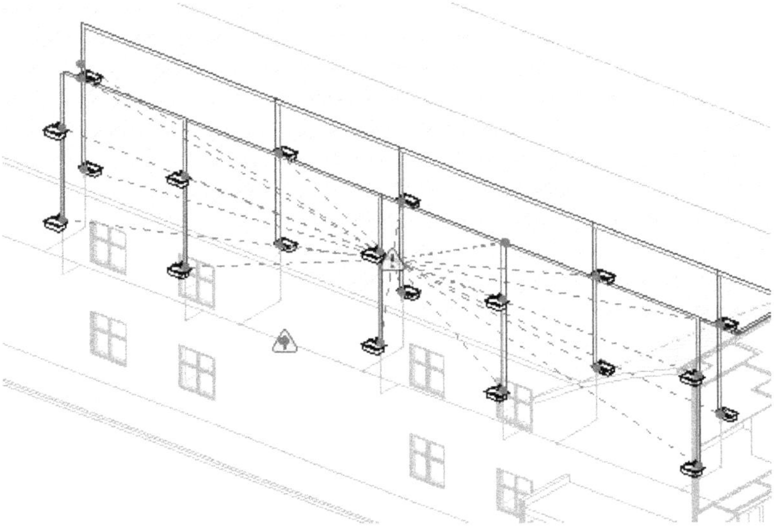

Figure 11–63

8. Toggle off **Check Pipe Systems**.
9. Save the project.

Task 2: Check and correct pipe disconnects.

1. Continue working in the 3D view.
2. In the *Analyze* tab>*Check Systems* panel, click ⚠ (Show Disconnects).
3. In the *Show Disconnects Options* dialog box, select **Pipe** and click **OK**.

4. Zoom in on the cold water pipes with a warning sign above them, as shown in Figure 11–64, to discover the issues. Correct the places where there are extra fittings or the pipes are not connected correctly. For example, the cold water pipes in Figure 11–64 need a connector.

Transition fitting

Figure 11–64

5. Delete the transition fitting, connect the two pipes by dragging one connector to connect with the other, then drag and connect the pipe coming from the first floor into the main pipe. The correct fitting is applied, as shown in Figure 11–65.

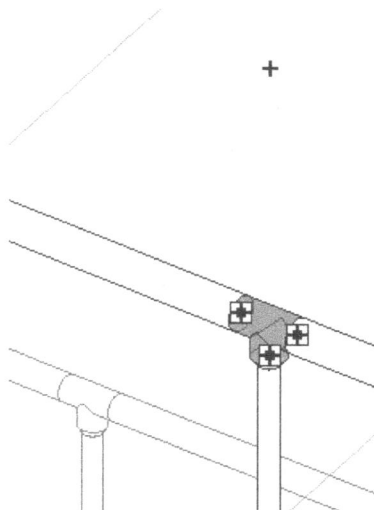

Figure 11–65

6. Zoom and pan down to the sanitary pipe that has a warning sign and zoom in to the warning sign.

7. There is an extra fitting. Delete the fitting and the warning sign is removed.

8. Now that the issues have been fixed, in the *Analyze* tab>*Check Systems* panel, click

   ⚒ (Show Disconnects). Clear the checkmark from **Pipe** and click **OK**.

9. Save the project.

Task 3: Add a pipe color fill scheme and legend.

1. Open the Plumbing>Sanitary>Floor Plans>**01 Sanitary Plan** view.

2. In the *Analyze* tab>*Color Fill* panel, click 📐 (Pipe Legend).

3. Place the legend where the sanitary line exits the building.

4. In the *Choose Color Scheme* dialog box, select **Pipe Color Fill Size** and click **OK**. The legend and color scheme displays, as shown in Figure 11–66.

   • If the legend's title does not display, select the legend and click **Edit Type** in Properties. Select **Show Title** from the *Graphics* section.

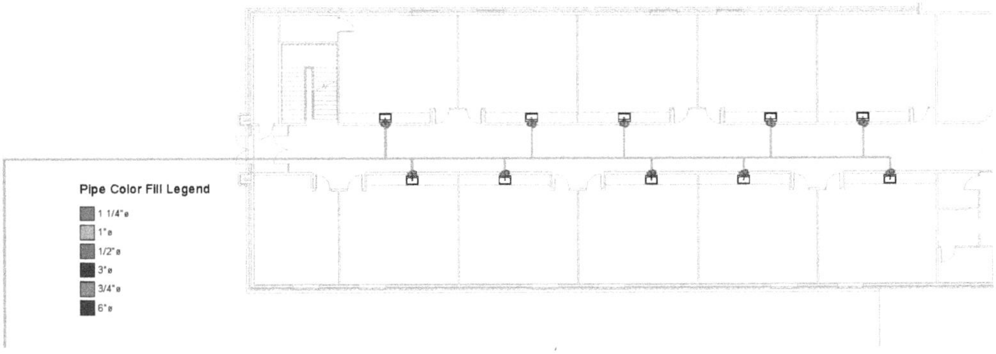

Figure 11–66

5. Change the main pipe and fittings diameter to **3"**.

6. Continue selecting pipes and fittings and adding to the size incrementally down the line. The colors change to match the legend.

7. Zoom out to see the entire building.

8. Save and close the project.

End of practice

Chapter Review Questions

1. How many elements must be selected before you can create a duct or piping system?

    a. One

    b. Two

    c. Three

    d. None need to be selected first

2. How do you specify which type of system you want to create when the element has multiple options, such as the lavatory shown in Figure 11−67?

Figure 11−67

    a. Select the appropriate connector to start the system.

    b. In the contextual tab, select the appropriate system button.

    c. In the Options Bar, select the system type from the drop-down list.

    d. Select the system type from the drop-down list in the dialog box that opens when you click **Create System**.

3. The purpose of a Base is to serve as a placeholder equipment connection point when generating an automatic layout.

    a. True

    b. False

4. Match the color of a line when generating a layout with what the color indicates.

Color	Indicates
a. Gold	_____ Branch
b. Blue	_____ Modeling Error
c. Green	_____ Main

5. Flex duct can be placed automatically on which of the following components of a layout?

   a. Main lines

   b. Branch lines

   c. Both main and branch lines

6. What is a common problem when generating layouts?

   a. Unable to edit standard solutions into custom layouts.

   b. The direction of the connector does not match how the automatic layout wants to connect to it.

   c. Cannot specify which family/type for the main and branch lines to use separately.

7. What is required before you can create an automatic ductwork layout?

   a. Duct System

   b. Air Terminals only

   c. Duct placeholders

   d. All air terminals and equipment placed for the entire project

8. Where do you specify the *Flow* of an air terminal, such as that shown in Figure 11−68? (Select all that apply.)

$$\frac{3}{500 \text{ CFM}}$$

Figure 11−68

a. In the ribbon

b. In the Options Bar

c. In the *Air Flow* dialog box

d. In Properties

e. In the Air Terminal tag

Command Summary

Button	Command	Location
System Tools		
	Add to System	• **Ribbon:** *Edit Duct* or *Piping System* tab>*Edit Duct* or *Piping System* panel
	Disconnect Equipment	• **Ribbon:** *Edit Duct* or *Piping System* tab>*System Tools* panel
	Divide Systems	• **Ribbon:** *Modify	Duct* or *Piping Systems* tab>*System Tools* panel
	Duct (System)	• **Ribbon:** *Modify* contextual tab>*Create Systems* panel • Right-click: **Create Duct System**
	Edit System	• **Ribbon:** *Modify	Duct* or *Piping Systems* tab>*System Tools* panel
	Remove from System	• **Ribbon:** *Edit Duct* or *Piping System* tab>*Edit Duct* or *Piping System* panel and *Generate Layout* tab>*Modify Layout* panel
	Select Equipment	• **Ribbon:** *Modify	Duct* or *Piping Systems* tab>*System Tools* panel and *Edit Duct* or *Piping System* tab>*Edit Duct* or *Piping System* panel
N/A	**System Browser**	• **Ribbon:** *View* tab>*Windows* panel, expand User Interface • **Shortcut:** <F9>
Automatic Duct or Piping Layout		
	Edit Layout	• **Ribbon:** *Generate Layout* tab>*Modify Layout* panel
	Generate Layout	• **Ribbon:** *Modify	Duct* or *Piping Systems* tab>*Layout* panel
	Modify Base	• **Ribbon:** *Generate Layout* tab>*Modify Layout* panel
	Place Base	• **Ribbon:** *Generate Layout* tab>*Modify Layout* panel
	Remove Base	• **Ribbon:** *Generate Layout* tab>*Modify Layout* panel

Button	Command	Location
	Solutions	• **Ribbon:** *Generate Layout* tab>*Modify Layout* panel

Testing Systems

Button	Command	Location
	Check Duct Systems	• **Ribbon**: *Analyze* tab>*Check Systems* panel
	Check Pipe Systems	• **Ribbon**: *Analyze* tab>*Check Systems* panel
	Show Disconnects	• **Ribbon:** *Analyze* tab>*Check Systems* panel
	Show Related Warnings	• **Ribbon:** *Modify* contextual tab>*Warning* panel
	System Inspector	• **Ribbon:** (When an element in a system is selected) *Modify* contextual tab>*Analysis* panel

Electrical Systems

Electrical systems consist of components such as light fixtures, electrical fixtures, fire alarms, security systems, telephone devices, and power equipment. Frequently, the various elements are connected via a power circuit or related systems. Cable trays or conduits can be added to a project, but these do not create system connections between elements.

Learning Objectives

- Establish electrical settings.
- Create power circuits, switch systems, and other circuit systems.
- Create and modify electrical panel schedules.
- Add cable trays and conduits, including parallel conduit runs and fittings.

12.1 About Electrical Systems

Electrical systems in Autodesk® Revit® are circuits consisting of devices, light fixtures, and other electrical equipment. They are elements in a project and are added to the model using the tools in the ribbon. There can be different types of electrical plan views based on the type of information required. A typical electrical view plan might display power, systems, or lighting layouts as shown in Figure 12–1.

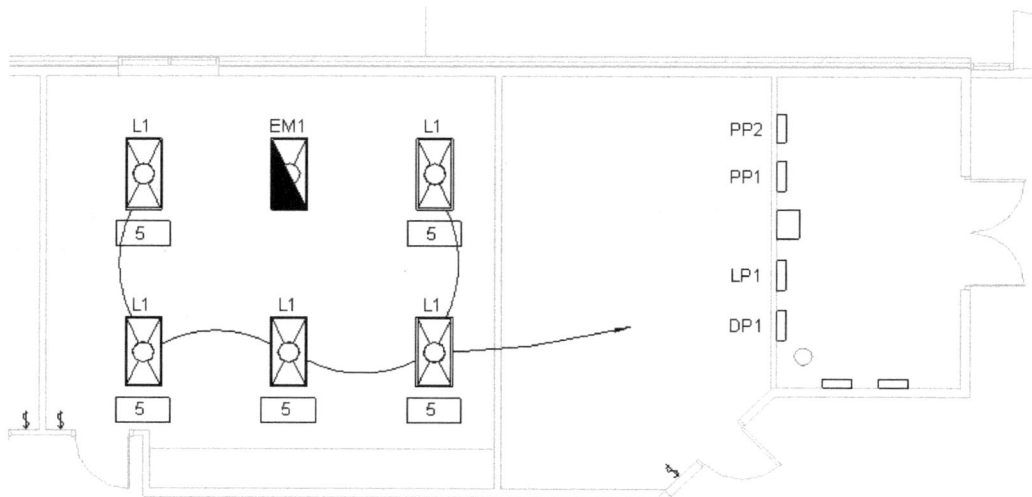

Figure 12–1

There are several steps in the process of creating an electrical system:

1. Place electrical equipment such as distribution panels.

2. Define the *Distribution System* in the Properties of the electrical equipment.

3. Place electrical devices, such as receptacles and light fixtures. Each device represents an electrical load in the system.

4. Select an electrical device or light fixture, and create a power circuit for it and similar devices in the same room or area of the building.

5. Assign circuits to electrical equipment (e.g., panel).

The tools for creating and placing electrical components and circuits are located in the *Systems* tab>*Electrical* panel, as shown in Figure 12–2.

> *Note: If needed, to make room for the electrical tools or to only see electrical tools, in the File tab, click **Options**. In the Options dialog box, on the User Interface pane, clear the checks from **Systems tab: mechanical tools** and **Systems tab: piping tools**.*

Figure 12–2

Electrical Settings

Electrical settings contain many parameters used for various electrical component placement and system/circuit creation. They include wiring parameters, voltage definitions, distribution systems, cable tray and conduit settings, load calculation settings, and circuit naming settings.

In the *Manage* tab>*Settings* panel, expand (MEP Settings) and click (Electrical Settings), or type **ES**. Alternatively, in the *Systems* tab>*Electrical* panel, click (Electrical Settings) to open the *Electrical Settings* dialog box (shown in Figure 12–3).

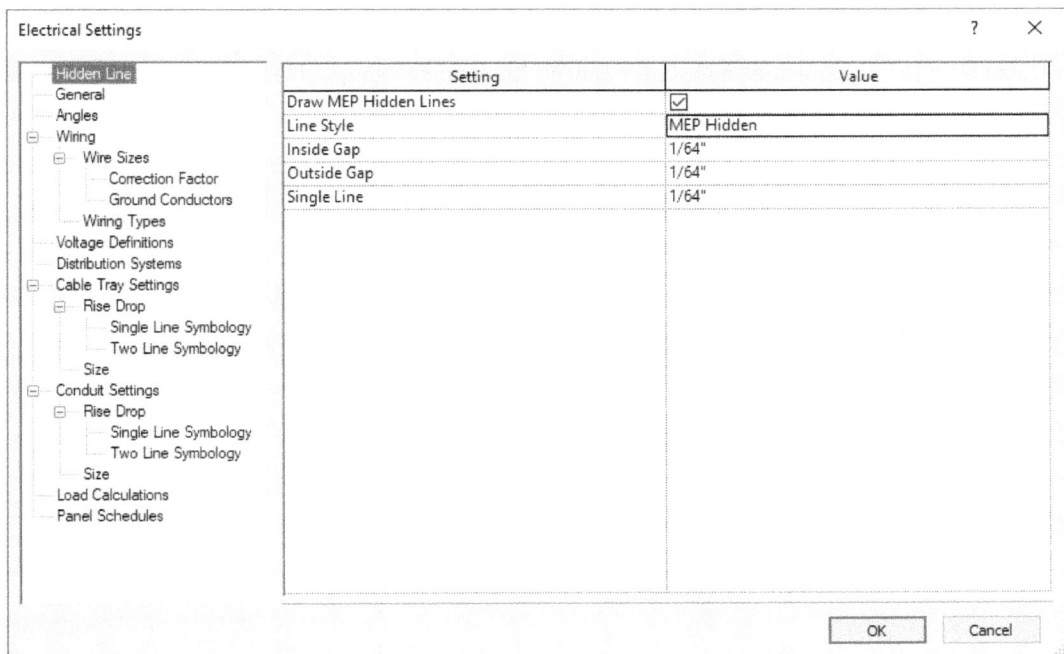

Figure 12–3

The different categories in the left pane have their own specific settings that are available when the category is selected.

Hidden Line	Settings for cable tray and conduit hidden line styles and gaps.
General	Parameters and formats for symbols and styles for various electrical component values, including phase naming. Enables you to specify the sequence in which power circuits are generated (**Numerical**, **Group by Phase**, or **Odd then Even**). You can also set the default Circuit Rating to match the country for which you are designing. Some engineers like to set this to **0** so they know which circuits they have not yet reviewed.
Angles	Enables to set angle increments or specify the use of specific angles for drawing cable trays and conduit. This is typically used to match industry standards for factory fittings.
Wiring	Determines how wires and wire sizes are displayed and calculated.
	Includes type of wires available based on material, temperature, and insulation ratings.
	Specifies which wire types can be used in a project.
Voltage Definitions	Lists the ranges of voltages that can be assigned to the Distribution Systems.
Distributions Systems	Defines available distribution systems. You can add and delete systems, as required. The System includes the Phase, Configuration (Wye or Delta), number of wires, and the **L-L Voltage** and **L-G Voltage** options.
Cable Tray Settings	Specifies annotative scaling for cable tray fittings and rise/drop symbology.
	Specifies cable tray sizes available in a project.
Conduit Settings	Specifies annotative scaling for conduit fittings, size prefix and suffix, and rise/drop symbology.
	Specifies conduit sizes available in a project.
Load Calculations	Specifies whether to enable load calculations for loads in spaces, and defines Load Classifications and Demand Factors. Available methods include Sum true load and reactive load, as well as Sum apparent load.
Panel Schedules	Specifies settings for spares and spaces, and for merging multi-poled circuits

• Load Classifications are assigned to Device Connectors, and Demand Factors are assigned to Load Classifications.

12.2 Creating Electrical Circuits

Once you have placed the electrical equipment, devices, and light fixtures into the model, you need to create the electrical system (circuit) from these components. Circuits connect the similar electrical components to form the electrical system, as shown in Figure 12–4. Once the electrical system is created, you can then add, remove, or modify any of the components. You can also edit the circuit path to establish the accurate length used in voltage drop calculations and wire sizing.

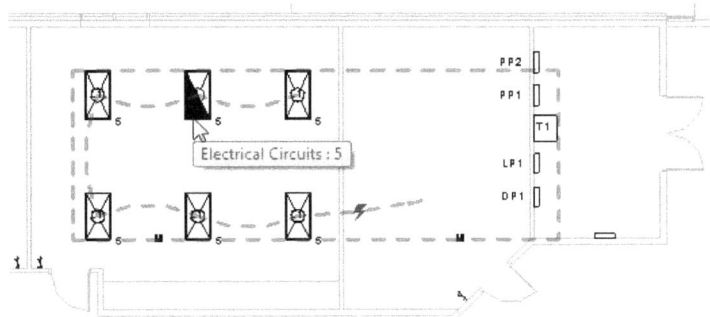

Figure 12–4

- Circuits can be created for power, lighting, switches, data, telephones, fire alarms, nurse call or security systems, and controls. The process is similar no matter which type of circuit you are creating.

- Power systems connect compatible electrical devices and light fixtures in a circuit to an electrical equipment panel, as shown in Figure 12–5.

   Note: *Components that are to be connected in a circuit must be of compatible voltage and distribution system.*

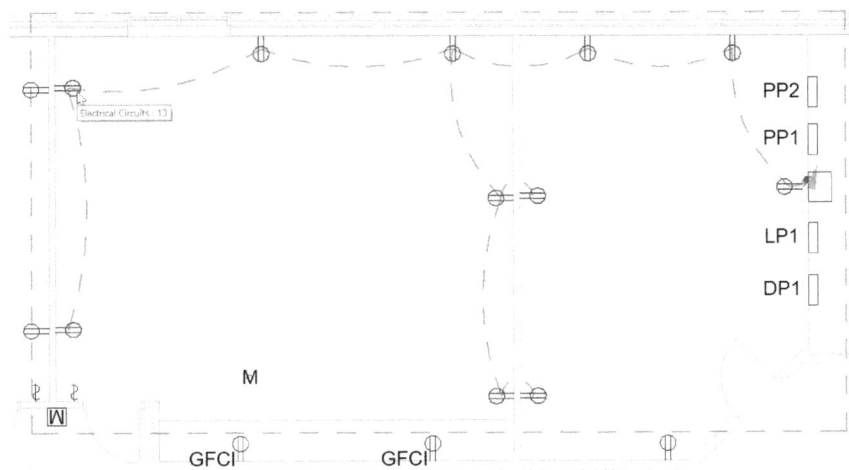

Figure 12–5

- Switch systems enable you to indicate which lights and switches are linked, as shown in Figure 12–6. Note: Linking lines are for reference only and do not plot. This is especially useful for those cases where there are multiple lights on the same circuit that are controlled by different switches.

  Note: You can only place one switch at a time on a switch system.

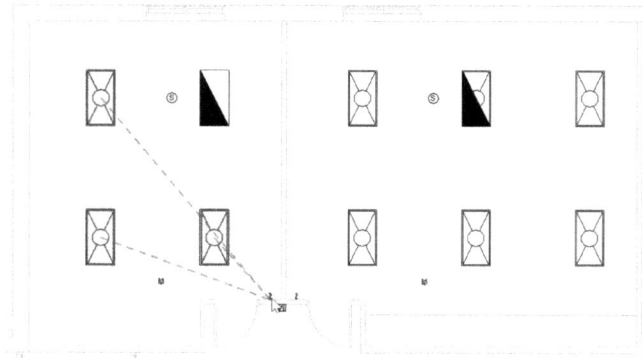

Figure 12–6

How To: Create a Circuit

1. Select at least one of the components that is to be part of the circuit.

2. In the *Modify* contextual tab>*Create Systems* panel, click the related system button:

   (Power), (Switch), or (Data).

3. In the *Electrical Circuits* tab>*System Tools* panel, either:

   - Accept the existing panel.

   - Select a panel from the *Panel* drop-down list (as shown in Figure 12–7) or select a panel in the project and click (Select Panel).

   Note: When you create a circuit, the program automatically connects to the most recently used panel in the current session.

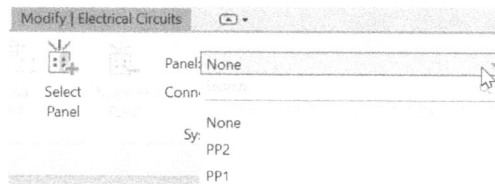

Figure 12–7

- Switch systems are not connected to a panel.

4. In the *Modify | Electrical Circuits* tab>*System Tools* panel, click ⬚ (Edit Circuit).

5. In the *Edit Circuit* tab>*Edit Circuit* panel, click ⬚ (Add to Circuit) and select the other components for that circuit.

   • To remove components from a circuit, click ⬚ (Remove from Circuit) and select the component.

6. Click ✓ (Finish Editing Circuit).

• If a component has more than one electrical connector, a *Select Connector* dialog box opens, as shown in Figure 12-8. Select the connector for which you want to make a circuit and click **OK**.

Select Connector: Emergency Recessed Lighting Fixture ✕

Connector 1 : Power
Connector 2 : Power

Figure 12-8

Editing Circuit Paths

When you add a circuit, an automatic route is processed and the length information (used to calculate the voltage drop and wire sizing) is automatically available. Note that the results might not be what you are expecting (as shown in Figure 12-9) and you can edit the path of the circuit to ensure that it runs in the direction and height you expect, as shown in Figure 12-10. Then the length automatically updates to provide you with the correct information.

Note: You can edit circuit paths in plan or 3D views.

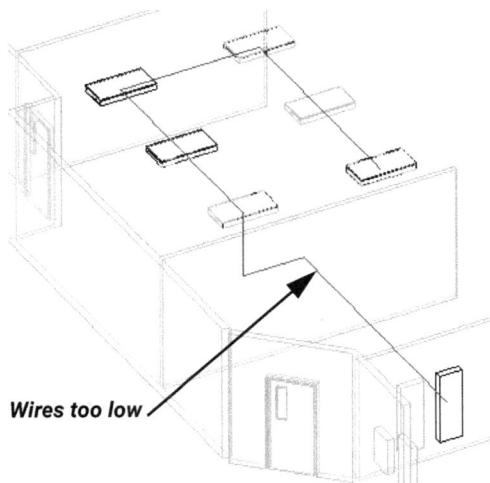

Wires too low

Figure 12-9

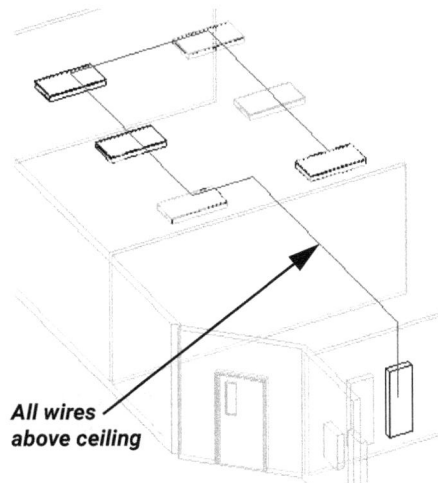

All wires above ceiling

Figure 12-10

How To: Edit the Path of a Circuit

1. Hover the cursor over a circuit component and press <Tab> until you can select the circuit.

2. Select the *Electrical Circuits* tab in the ribbon.

3. In the *System Tools* panel, click ⌧ (Edit Path). The *Edit Path* tab displays, as shown in Figure 12–11.

   - The *Length* automatically updates as you make changes.
   - The *Number of Elements* in the circuit displays in the Options Bar.

Figure 12–11

4. In the *Edit Path* panel, set the *Path Mode* to **All Devices, Farthest Device** (as shown in Figure 12–12), or **Custom** (if you have already edited the path).

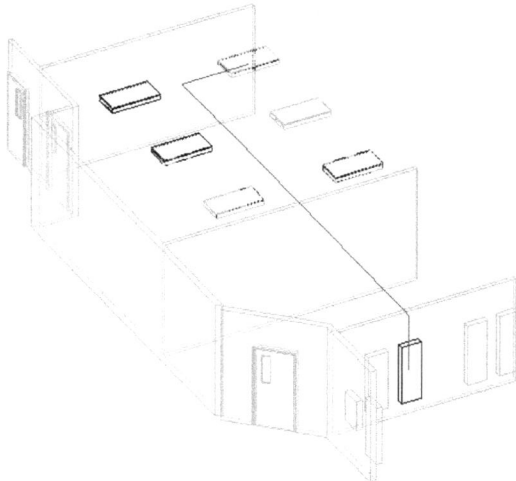

Figure 12–12

5. Change the *Path Offset* in the ribbon to modify the entire circuit path. This is especially useful to get the entire path above the ceiling.

6. Select individual circuit paths to modify the route. You can drag the path line or control points or change the path offset, as shown in Figure 12–13.

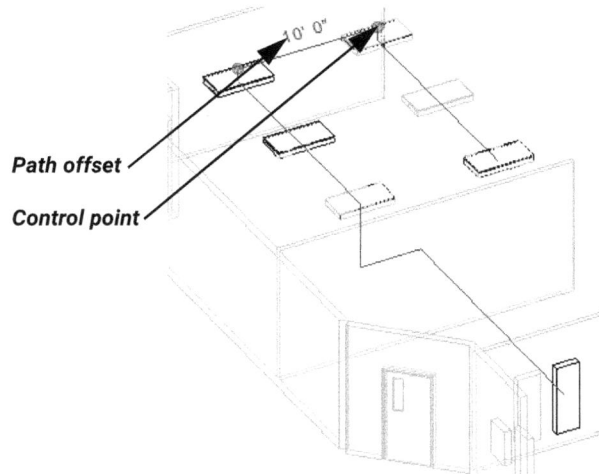

Figure 12–13

7. To remove control points, right-click on a control point and select **Delete Control Point**. To add control points, right-click on a path line and select **Insert Control Point**.

8. When you have finished adjusting the path, in the *Edit Path* tab>*Mode* panel, click ✔ (Finish Editing Path).

Adding Wires

Wiring is typically schematic, frequently used in wiring plans such as that shown in Figure 12–14. You can create wires once you have added circuits.

Note: When wiring a switch system you have to connect the elements manually. Then, the switch can be placed on a power circuit and acts as sort of an outlet going back to the panel.

Figure 12–14

- Wires stay connected if you move a fixture, adjusting to the new location.

- Wires are view specific.

- Add conduits or cable trays to show the exact location where the wires will run.

How To: Add Wires to a View

1. Create the circuits that connect the fixtures and panel.

2. Create a duplicated view in which you want to display the wires.

3. Hover the cursor over one of the elements in the circuit. Press < Tab> to highlight the circuit and then click to select it.

4. In the *Modify | Electrical Circuits* tab>*Convert to Wire* panel, click ⌇ (Arc Wire) or ⌇ (Chamfered Wire). Alternatively, you can click on the **Generate arc** (or **chamfered**) **type wiring** control in the drawing area, as shown in Figure 12–15.

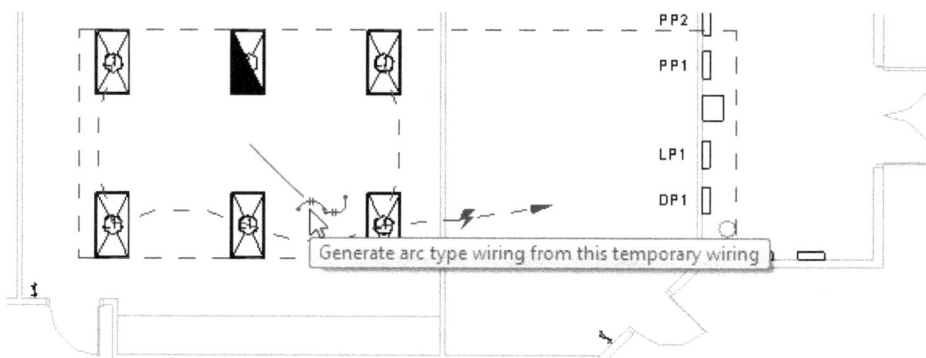

Figure 12–15

5. Click ⌖ (Modify) and select the wiring. Use the controls to add, remove, and move vertices as required, as shown in Figure 12–16.

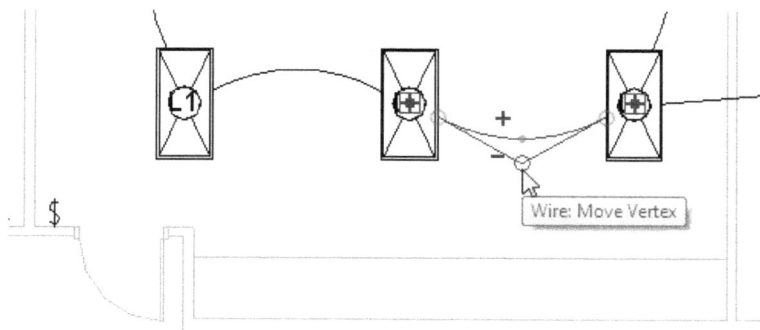

Figure 12–16

Wiring Settings

You can set up how the wires display in the *Electrical Settings* dialog box under the **Wiring** node. This includes the styles of tick marks for various wires, as shown in Figure 12–17.

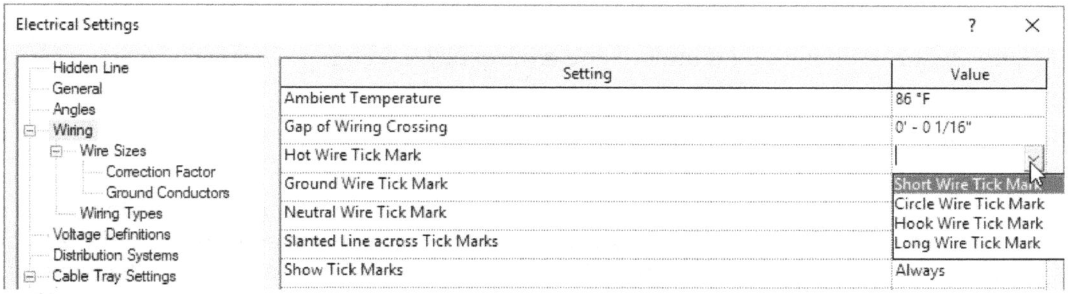

Figure 12–17

- Tick marks can be loaded from the Revit Library's *Annotations>Electrical>TickMarks* folder.

Practice 12a
Create Electrical Circuits

Practice Objectives

- Create electrical circuits for standard and emergency lighting.
- Edit the circuit path.
- Display wire connections for a wiring plan.

In this practice, you will connect light fixtures together in a power circuit. You will also create an emergency power circuit and add light fixtures to the circuit. You will edit the path of the circuit and view the changes to the length. You will also add a transformer and connect panels to it. Finally, you will display wire connections to create a wiring plan, as shown in Figure 12–18.

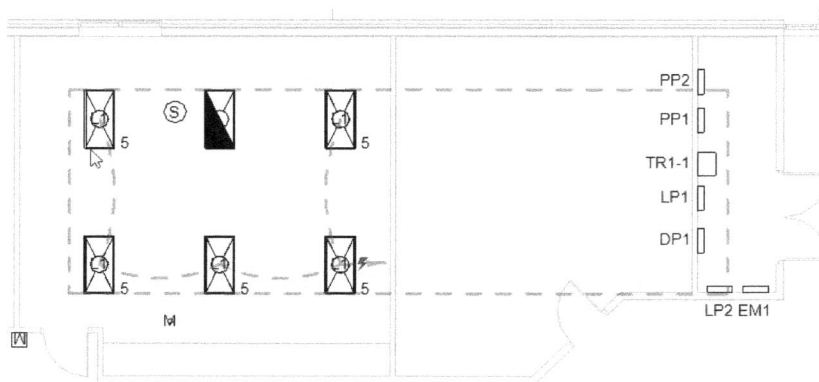

Figure 12–18

Task 1: Create an electrical circuit system.

1. In the practice files *Working Models>Electrical* folder, open **Elec-Circuits.rvt**.

2. Open the Electrical>Lighting>Floor Plans>**01 Lighting Plan** view and zoom to the north wing.

3. From the north wing, zoom in to the upper leftmost class room. Select the upper-left light and in the *Modify | Lighting Fixtures* tab>*Create Systems* panel, click ⏸ (Power).

4. In the *Modify | Electrical Circuits* tab>*System Tools* panel, expand the *Panel* list and select **LP1**.

5. In the *System Tools* panel, click 🖼 (Edit Circuit).

6. In the *Edit Circuit* tab>*Edit Circuit* panel, ensure that ⬚ (Add to Circuit) is selected. Select the other two standard lights in the room but not the emergency light, as shown in Figure 12–19.

Note: Do not select the emergency light fixture until the next step.

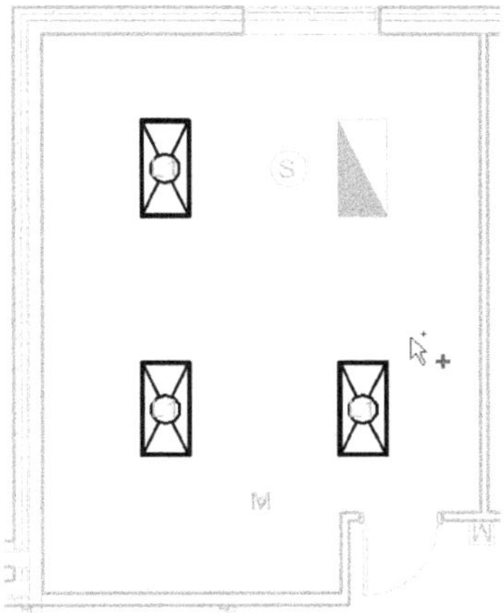

Figure 12–19

7. While still in the same circuit, select the emergency light. In the *Select Connector* dialog box, select **Connector 2: Power**, as shown in Figure 12–20, and click **OK**.

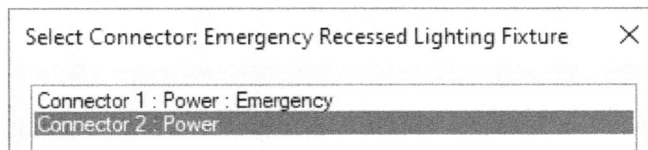

Figure 12–20

8. Click ✓ (Finish Editing Circuit).

9. Open the System Browser. (Hint: Press <F9>.)

10. In the System Browser, verify that the **Systems** and **Electrical** options are selected, as shown at the top in Figure 12–21. Click ▧ (AutoFit All Columns) to widen the columns.

11. In the view, select one of the Troffer light fixtures which you just circuited.

12. In the System Browser, expand the **Electrical>Power>LP1>1** nodes to display the selected light fixtures, as shown in Figure 12–21. Only one light is highlighted in the project.

Figure 12–21

13. In the System Browser, select the related circuit **1**. The selection in the view changes to display the circuit outline, as shown in Figure 12–22.

Note: The extents box surrounds the system and the panel with connecting arcs to each fixture in this circuit.

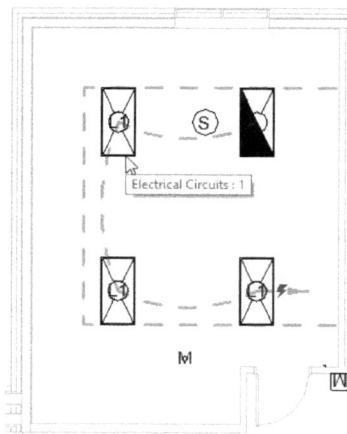

Figure 12–22

14. In Properties, review the circuit properties. In the *Electrical - Loads* area, the *Circuit Number* should be set to **1** as it is a circuit that has not been used yet. This field is editable in the related panel schedule.

15. Scroll down to note the *Length* of the circuit. This is read only, but updates when you edit the circuit path.

16. Click in an empty area in the view to clear the selection.

17. Select the **Emergency Recessed Lighting Fixture**. In the System Browser, note that the **Unassigned** node highlights as well. This is because the fixture has two connectors, and you have only circuited one of them. This will be resolved in the next task.

18. Save the project.

Task 2: Add and move emergency light fixtures to an emergency circuit and panel.

1. Continue working in the **01 Lighting Plan** view.

   Note: Because there is now only one uncircuited connector on this fixture, the Select Connector dialog box does not open.

2. Select the emergency light fixture added earlier.

3. In the *Modify | Lighting Fixtures* tab>*Create Systems* panel, click ⓘ (Power).

4. In the *Modify | Electrical Circuits* tab>*Systems Tools* panel, expand the *Panel* list and select **EM1**.

5. With the same light selected, in the *Systems Tools* panel, click 🖫 (Edit Circuit).

6. In the *Edit Circuit* tab>*Edit Circuit* panel, verify that 🖳 (Add to Circuit) is selected.

7. Select the emergency fixture in the room directly to the right of the room that you are working in.

8. In the *Select Connector* dialog box, select **Connection 1: Power : Emergency** and click **OK**.

   • Many emergency light fixtures have a battery backup. This is the method used when the fixtures are connected to an emergency circuit.

9. Click ✔ (Finish Editing Circuit).

10. Save the project.

Task 3: Edit the circuit path.

1. Hover the cursor over one of the standard light fixtures in the far left room and press <Tab> to select the circuit.

   • Hint: As you press <Tab>, watch the Status Bar in the lower left corner to understand what you are cycling through.

2. In the *Modify | Electrical Circuits* tab>*System Tools* panel, click 🖼 (Edit Path).

3. In the *Edit Path* panel, note the *Length*, *Path Mode*, and *Path Offset*, as shown in Figure 12−23.

Length:	Path Mode:	Path Offset:		
164' 1 19/64"	Farthest Device ▾	9' 0"	✔ Finish Editing Path	✖ Cancel Editing Path
	Edit Path		Mode	

Figure 12−23

4. Change the *Path Mode* to **All Devices** and the *Path Offset* to **10'-0"**. The *Length* also changes, as shown in Figure 12−24.

Length:	Path Mode:	Path Offset:		
182' 1 5/64"	All Devices ▾	10' 0"	✔ Finish Editing Path	✖ Cancel Editing Path
	Edit Path		Mode	

Figure 12−24

5. Click ✔ (Finish Editing Path).

6. Save the project.

Task 4: Add a step down transformer.

1. Open the Electrical>Power>Floor Plans>**01 Electrical Room** view.

2. In the *Systems* tab>*Electrical* panel, click ⛿ (Electrical Equipment).

3. In the Type Selector, select **Dry Type Transformer - 480-208Y120 - NEMA Type 3R: 15 kVA**.

4. In the *Modify | Place Equipment* tab>*Placement* panel, click ⬚ (Place on Vertical Face).

5. Place the transformer between PP1 and LP1, as shown in Figure 12–25.

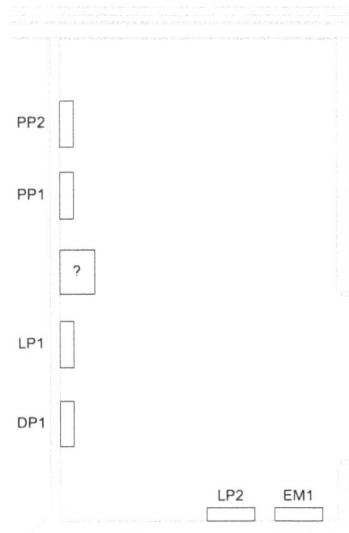

Figure 12–25

6. Click ⬚ (Modify) and select the new transformer.

7. In Properties, do the following and click **Apply**:

   * In the *Electrical - Loads* section, set the *Secondary Distribution System* to **120/208 Wye**.

   * In the *General* section, verify the *Panel Name* is **TR1-1**.

   * In the *Electrical - Circuiting* section, verify that the *Distribution System* is set to **480/277 Wye**.

   Note: The transformer has a primary and secondary distribution system; both are set as properties of the transformer.

8. Click ⬚ (Modify) and select the panel **PP1**.

9. In the *Modify | Electrical Equipment* tab>*Create Systems* panel, click ⊕ (Power).

10. In the *Modify | Electrical Circuits* tab>*System Tools* panel, click ⬚ (Select Panel).

11. Select the new TR1-1 panel. The load from panel PP1 is now assigned to the transformer TR1-1.

12. Click ⬚ (Modify) and select **TR1-1**.

13. Right-click on the **Power** connector and select **Create Power Circuit**, as shown in Figure 12–26.

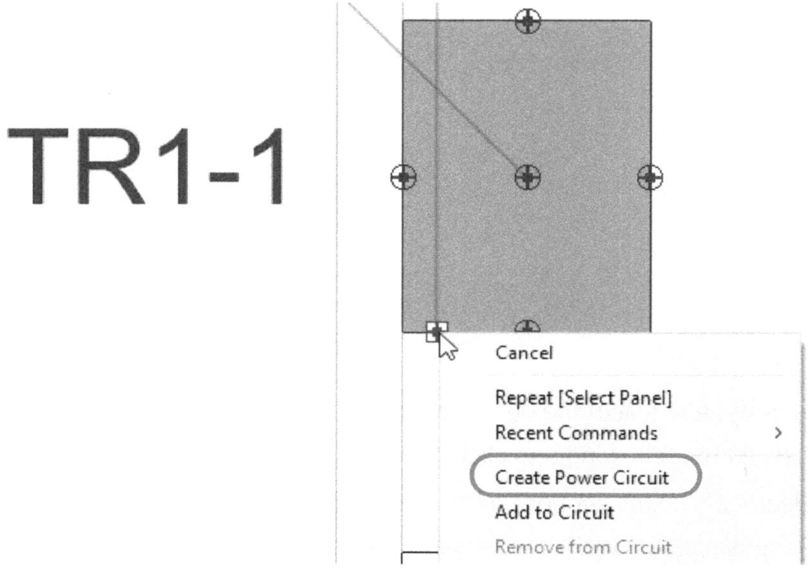

Figure 12–26

14. In the *System Tools* panel, in the *Panel* list, select **DP1**. The system displays as shown in Figure 12–27.

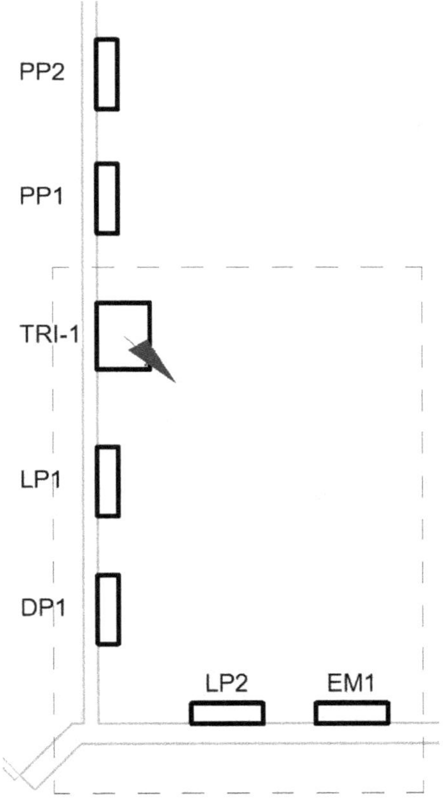

Figure 12–27

15. Click in an empty space in the view to clear the selection.

16. Save the project.

Task 5: Create a wiring plan.

1. Duplicate (with Detailing) the Electrical>Lighting>Floor Plans>**01 Lighting Plan** view and name it **01 Wiring Plan**.

2. Zoom in to the area near the electrical room with the nearby classroom with light fixtures displaying as well.

3. Hover the cursor over one of the lights in the classroom and press <Tab> to highlight the circuit, as shown in Figure 12–28. Click to select it.

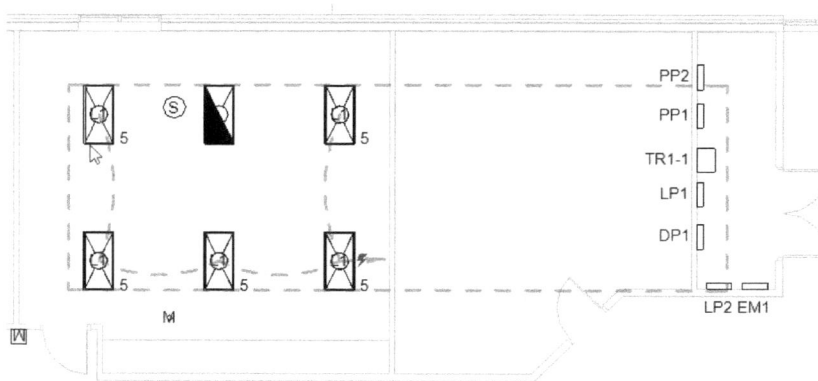

Figure 12–28

4. In the *Modify | Electrical Circuits* tab>*Convert to Wire* panel, click (Arc Wire). Alternatively, click on the Generate arc type wiring control in the drawing.

5. Wire displaying schematic routing of the circuit is automatically drawn. Adjust the wire arcs manually by pulling the add, remove, and move vertex controls, as shown in Figure 12–29.

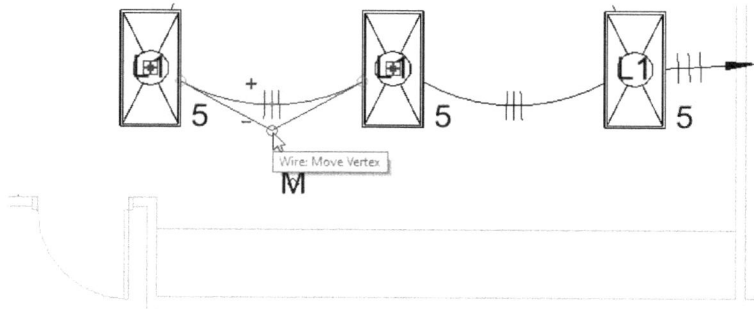

Figure 12–29

6. Move a fixture and observe that the wire stays connected adjusting to the new fixture location. Wires are view specific.

   Note: The fixture that remains in place is in the linked file.

7. Undo the move.

8. Continue adding the schematic wiring throughout the north wing of the building. Add additional circuits, if required.

9. Save and close the project. If you have time, you can also create switch systems for the same wing in the next task.

Task 6: Add switches and connect them to the lighting system.

If time permits, add switches and connect them to the light fixtures within their associated rooms.

1. Pan and zoom to the far left classroom.
2. In the *Systems* tab>*Electrical* panel, in the *Devices* drop-down list, select ▣ (Lighting).
3. In the Type Selector, change the type to **Lighting Switch: Single Pole**.
4. In the *Placement* panel, verify **Place on Vertical Face** is selected.
5. Place a light switch in each room's entrance, as shown in Figure 12–30.

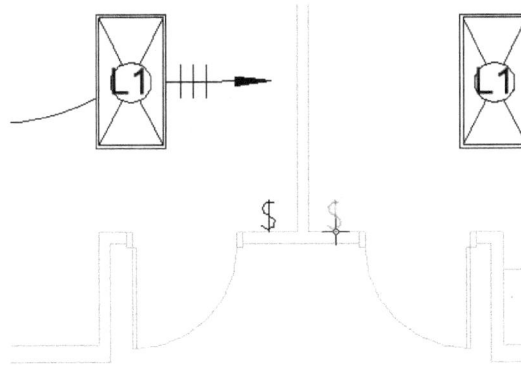

Figure 12–30

6. In the far left classroom, select the three light fixtures excluding the emergency light fixture.

7. In the *Modify | Lighting Fixtures* tab>*Create Systems* panel, select ▣ (Switch).

8. In the *Modify | Switch System* tab, select ⬛ (Select Switch) and select the switch you placed in the room. The switch shows which light fixtures it is connected to, as shown in Figure 12–31. (Your classroom may differ if you have not added wire to the light fixtures.)

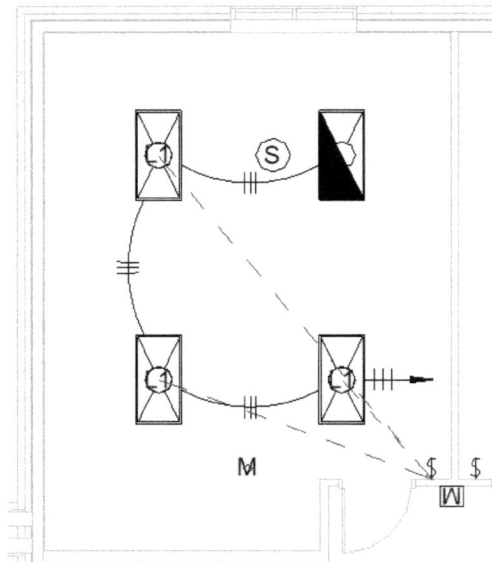

Figure 12–31

9. Click ⬚ (Modify).

10. Save and close the project.

End of practice

12.3 Setting Up Panel Schedules

Panel schedules are used to concisely present information about panels and the components connected to them through their corresponding circuits. They also list the load values of these circuits, as shown in Figure 12–32. The Autodesk Revit software creates panel schedules and automatically update them as the panel's circuits change.

Branch Panel: LP1

Location: ELECTRICAL 2500A	Volts: 480/277 Wye	A.I.C. Rating:
Supply From:	Phases: 3	Mains Type:
Mounting: Surface	Wires: 4	Mains Rating: 100 A
Enclosure: Type 3R		MCB Rating: 400 A

Notes:

CKT	Circuit Description	Trip	Poles	A		B		C		Poles	Trip	Circuit Description	CKT
1	Lighting - Dwelling Unit CLASSROOM 1509	20 A	1	496 VA	496 VA					1	20 A	Lighting - Dwelling Unit CLASSROOM 1507	2
3	Lighting - Dwelling Unit CLASSROOM 1505	20 A	1			496 VA	496 VA			1	20 A	Lighting - Dwelling Unit CLASSROOM 1503	4
5	Lighting - Dwelling Unit CLASSROOM 1501	20 A	1					496 VA	496 VA	1	20 A	Lighting - Dwelling Unit CLASSROOM 1508	6
7	Lighting - Dwelling Unit CLASSROOM 1506	20 A	1	496 VA	496 VA					1	20 A	Lighting - Dwelling Unit CLASSROOM 1504	8
9	Lighting - Dwelling Unit CLASSROOM 1502	20 A	1			496 VA	496 VA			1	20 A	Lighting - Dwelling Unit CLASSROOM 1500	10
11	Lighting - Dwelling Unit CLASSROOM 2009	20 A	1					496 VA	496 VA	1	20 A	Lighting - Dwelling Unit CLASSROOM 2007	12
13	Lighting - Dwelling Unit CLASSROOM 2005	20 A	1	496 VA	496 VA					1	20 A	Lighting - Dwelling Unit CLASSROOM 2003	14
15	Lighting - Dwelling Unit CLASSROOM 2001	20 A	1			496 VA	496 VA			1	20 A	Lighting - Dwelling Unit CLASSROOM 2008	16
17	Lighting - Dwelling Unit CLASSROOM 2006	20 A	1					496 VA	496 VA	1	20 A	Lighting - Dwelling Unit CLASSROOM 2004	18
19	Lighting - Dwelling Unit CLASSROOM 2002	20 A	1	496 VA	496 VA					1	20 A	Lighting - Dwelling Unit CLASSROOM 2000	20
21	Lighting - Dwelling Unit CLASSROOM 5009	20 A	1			496 VA	496 VA			1	20 A	Lighting - Dwelling Unit CLASSROOM 5008	22
23	Lighting - Dwelling Unit CLASSROOM 5004	20 A	1					496 VA	496 VA	1	20 A	Lighting - Dwelling Unit CLASSROOM 5003	24
25	Lighting - Dwelling Unit CLASSROOM 5000	20 A	1	496 VA	496 VA					1	20 A	Lighting - Dwelling Unit CLASSROOM 5010	26
27	Lighting - Dwelling Unit CLASSROOM 5007	20 A	1			496 VA	496 VA			1	20 A	Lighting - Dwelling Unit CLASSROOM 5006	28
29	Lighting - Dwelling Unit CLASSROOM 5002	20 A	1					496 VA	496 VA	1	20 A	Lighting - Dwelling Unit CLASSROOM 5001	30
31	Lighting - Dwelling Unit CLASSROOM 4509	20 A	1	496 VA	496 VA					1	20 A	Lighting - Dwelling Unit CLASSROOM 4508	32
33	Lighting - Dwelling Unit CLASSROOM 4504	20 A	1			496 VA	496 VA			1	20 A	Lighting - Dwelling Unit CLASSROOM 4503	34
35	Lighting - Dwelling Unit CLASSROOM 4500	20 A	1					496 VA	496 VA	1	20 A	Lighting - Dwelling Unit CLASSROOM 4510	36
37	Lighting - Dwelling Unit CLASSROOM 4507	20 A	1	496 VA	496 VA					1	20 A	Lighting - Dwelling Unit CLASSROOM 4506	38
39	Lighting - Dwelling Unit CLASSROOM 4502	20 A	1			496 VA	496 VA			1	20 A	Lighting - Dwelling Unit CLASSROOM 4501	40
41	Spare	0 A	1					0 VA					42
	Total Load:			6944 VA		6944 VA		5952 VA					
	Total Amps:			25 A		25 A		21 A					

Legend:

Load Classification	Connected Load	Demand Factor	Estimated Demand	Panel Totals	
Lighting	3840 VA	100.00%	3840 VA		
Lighting - Dwelling Unit	16000 VA	47.19%	7550 VA	Total Conn. Load:	19840 VA
				Total Est. Demand:	11390 VA
				Total Conn.:	24 A
				Total Est. Demand:	14 A

Figure 12–32

Creating Panel Schedules

Panel schedules can be created for each panel in the model, and it can be created anytime before or after circuits are created for the panel. Once created, panel schedules are listed in the Project Browser, in the **Panel Schedule** node.

How To: Create a Panel Schedule

1. Select the panel for which you want to create the panel schedule.

2. In the *Modify | Electrical Equipment* tab>*Electrical* panel, expand ⊞ (Create Panel Schedule) and click either ⊞ (Use Default Template or ⊞ (Choose a Template).

   Note: *If a panel schedule has already been created for the selected equipment, the command is grayed out.*

   A new panel schedule is created. Its view opens, and is listed in the Project Browser.

- Panel schedules can be placed on sheets for construction documentation.

- Panel Schedule Templates specify the formating and information displayed in the schedule. They can be created and edited. In the *Manage* tab>*Settings* panel, expand ⊞ (Panel Schedules Templates) and click ⊞ (Manage Templates) or ⊞ (Edit at Template).

Modifying Panel Schedules

Circuits in a panel schedule can be rearranged, locked, grouped, or renamed. You can also balance loads across phases and add spares to the panel. While viewing, you can edit circuits, electrical equipment, and project information from the properties.

How To: Modify a Panel Schedule

1. In the panel schedule view, select the particular circuit(s) or empty slot(s) that you want to modify.

2. In the *Modify | Panel Schedule* tab, click the particular command that you want to conduct:

Icon	Command	Function
	Change Template	Opens a dialog box where you can choose from a list of available templates.
	Rebalance Loads	Rearranges the panels circuits to redistribute the loads evenly across each phase.
	Renumber Indexes	In the current panel, renumber the circuit naming index.
	Move Up, Down, Across, To	Moves the selected circuit up, down, across, or to a new slot on the circuit panel without disturbing the other circuit locations.
	Assign/Remove Spare/Space	Assigns a slot as either a spare or a space (and are automatically locked), or removes a spare or space from a slot.
	Lock/Unlock	Locks or unlocks circuits, spares, or spaces in a specific slot location.
	Group/Ungroup	Groups single-pole circuits/spares together to act as a multi-pole circuit (or ungroups them).
	Update Names	Updates the names of the circuits on panel schedules.
	Edit Font	Opens the *Edit Font* dialog box where you can select a font and modify the font size, style, and color.
	Horizontally Align and Vertically Align	Select the alignment of the text in the selected cells

Practice 12b
Set Up Panel Schedules

Practice Objective

*   View and create panel schedules.

In this practice, you will view an existing electrical panel schedule, shown in Figure 12–33. You will also create a new panel schedule and add a power system that connects to that panel.

Branch Panel: LP1

Location: ELECTRICAL 2500A   Volts: 480/277 Wye
Supply From: Phases: 3
Mounting: Surface   Wires: 4
Enclosure: Type 3R

Notes:

CKT	Circuit Description	Trip	Poles	A		B		C		Pole
1	Lighting - Dwelling Unit CLASSROOM 1509	20 A	1	400 VA	400 VA					1
3	Lighting - Dwelling Unit CLASSROOM 1505	20 A	1			400 VA	400 VA			1
5	Lighting - Dwelling Unit CLASSROOM 1501	20 A	1					400 VA	400 VA	1
7	Lighting - Dwelling Unit CLASSROOM 1506	20 A	1	400 VA	400 VA					1
9	Lighting - Dwelling Unit CLASSROOM 1502	20 A	1			400 VA	400 VA			1
11	Lighting - Dwelling Unit CLASSROOM 2009	20 A	1					400 VA	496 VA	1
13	Lighting - Dwelling Unit CLASSROOM 2005	20 A	1	496 VA	496 VA					1
15	Lighting - Dwelling Unit CLASSROOM 2001	20 A	1			496 VA	496 VA			1
17	Lighting - Dwelling Unit CLASSROOM 2006	20 A	1					496 VA	496 VA	1

Figure 12–33

Task 1: Viewing and creating panel schedules.

1. In the practice files *Working Models>Electrical* folder, open **Elec-Panel.rvt**.

2. In the Project Browser, expand the **Panel Schedules** node and double-click on the **LP1** schedule to open it.

3. Select circuit number **37**, and note its description **Lighting - Dwelling Unit CLASSROOM 4502**.

4. In the *Modify Panel Schedule* tab>*Circuits* panel, click 🔳 (Move Across). The circuit switches places with circuit number **38** on the right (**Lighting - Dwelling Unit CLASSROOM 4506**).

5. Continue to move the circuit up, down, or across, and then in the *Circuits* panel, click ⬚ (Lock/Unlock) to lock it. Try to move others near it. The locked circuit will not move.

6. Select an empty circuit in the panel schedule.

7. In the *Circuits* panel, click ⬚ (Assign Spare) and a spare is inserted into that circuit. Note that in the ribbon, it is automatically locked, but you can unlock it and move it if required.

8. Close Panel Schedule **LP1**.

Task 2: Create a panel schedule.

1. Open the Electrical>Power>**01 Electrical Room** view.

2. Select electrical panel **LP2**.

3. In the *Modify | Electrical Equipment* tab>*Electrical* panel, expand ⬚ (Create Panel Schedules) and click ⬚ (Use Default Template).

4. The Panel Schedule **LP2** is created and automatically opened, as shown in Figure 12–34. It is also listed in the *Panel Schedules* node in the Project Browser. There are no values assigned to the schedule. Close any open views other than the LP2 schedule.

Branch Panel: LP2

Location: ELECTRICAL 2500				Volts: 480/277 Wye				A.I.C. Rating:			
Supply From:				Phases: 3				Mains Type:			
Mounting: Surface				Wires: 4				Mains Rating: 100 A			
Enclosure: Type 1								MCB Rating: 125 A			

Notes:

CKT	Circuit Description	Trip	Poles	A	B	C	Poles	Trip	Circuit Description	CKT
1										2
3										4
5										6
7										8
9										10
11										12
13										14
15										16
17										18
19										20

Figure 12–34

5. Open the Electrical>Power>**01 Power Plan** view. Type **WT** to tile the view and the LP2 schedule.

6. Zoom in to the top leftmost classroom in the north wing. Select one of the Ceiling Occupancy Sensors, as shown in Figure 12–35.

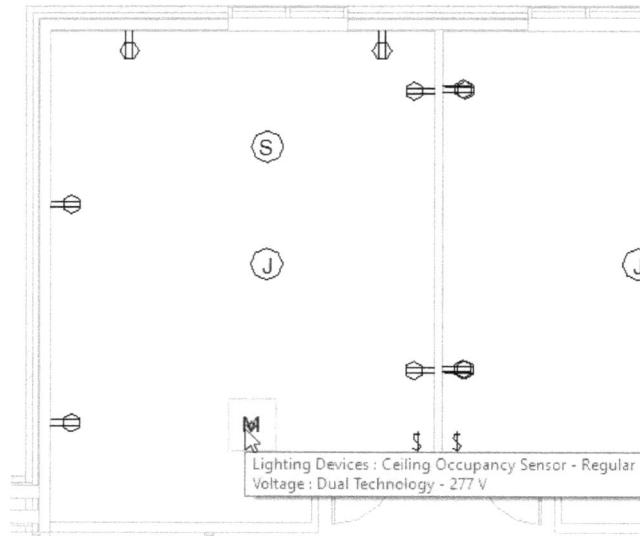

Figure 12–35

7. Right-click and select **Select All Instances>Visible in View**.

8. In the *Modify | Lighting Devices* tab>*Create Systems* panel, click ⊕ (Power).

9. In the *Modify | Electrical Circuits* tab>*System Tools* panel, expand the *Panel* list and select **LP2**.

10. Open the Panel Schedule **LP2**. Note that the items are added to the *Circuit Description* column, as shown in Figure 12–36.

CKT	Circuit Description	Trip	Poles	A	
1	Other Room 1510, 1509, 1507, 1505, 1503, 1501, ...	20 A	1	0 VA	
3					
5					
7					
9					
11					

Figure 12–36

11. Save and close the project.

End of practice

Practice 12c
Modify Electrical Circuits

Practice Objectives

- Modify electrical circuits, including changing the circuit naming.
- Add a switchboard and set phases for circuits.

In this practice, you will change circuit naming and use the **Switch Phases** tool to assign a phase to a circuit in a switchboard panel.

Task 1: Modify electrical circuits and change circuit naming.

1. Open **Elec-Switchboard.rvt** from the practice files *Working Models>Electrical* folder.
2. In the *Manage* tab>*Settings* panel, expand the *MEP Settings* drop-down list and select ⬛ (Electrical Settings).
3. In the *Electrical Settings* dialog box>*General* tab, change the values for the three *Circuit Naming by Phase* labels, as shown in Figure 12–37.

Setting	Value
Electrical Connector Separator	-
Electrical Data Style	Connector Description Voltage / Number of Poles – ...
Circuit Description	480V-3P/30A
Circuit Naming by Phase - Phase A Label	L1
Circuit Naming by Phase - Phase B Label	L2
Circuit Naming by Phase - Phase C Label	L3

Figure 12–37

4. In the *Electrical Settings* dialog box, select the *Circuit Naming* tab, and then click 📄 (New Scheme).
5. In the *Circuit Naming Scheme* dialog box, type **By Way By Phase** for the *Circuit Naming Scheme Name*.

6. Add the *Circuit Parameters* **Ways** and **Phase Label** to the *Circuit Naming Parameters* list, as shown in Figure 12–38, by selecting the parameter and clicking the green arrow or by double-clicking the parameter. Click **OK** twice to close the dialog box.

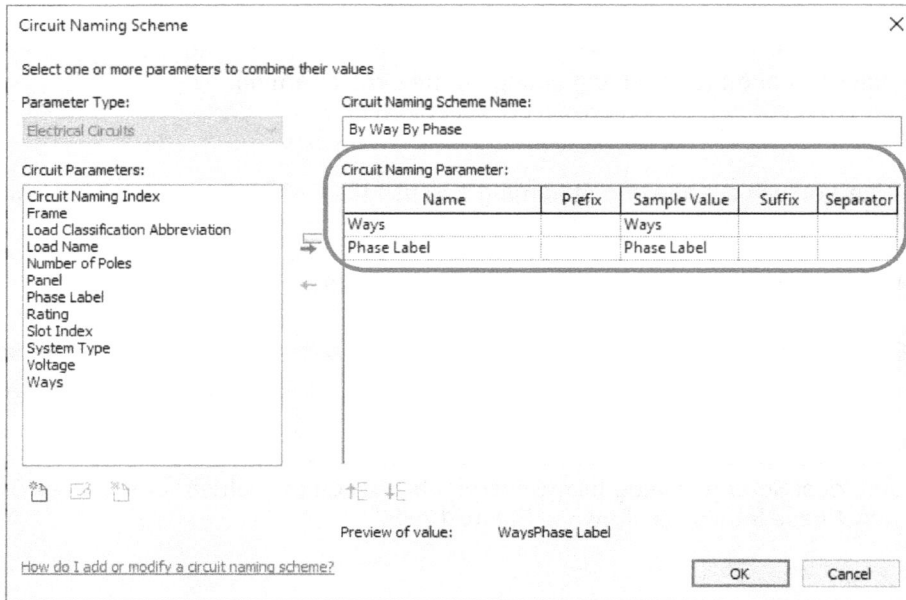

Figure 12–38

7. From the Project Browser, open the **LP2** schedule.

8. At the top of the schedule, click on **Branch Panel: LP2**.

9. In Properties, in the *Electrical - Circuiting* section, set the value for *Circuit Naming* to **By Way By Phase**, as shown in Figure 12–39. Click **Apply**.

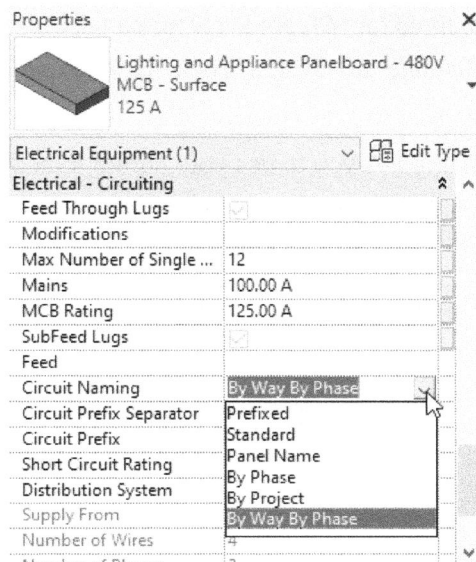

Figure 12–39

10. Click 📭 (Close Inactive Views).

11. In the Project Browser, open the Electrical>Lighting>Floor Plans>**01 Lighting Plan** view. Type **WT** to tile the plan and the panel schedule.

12. Zoom and pan to the north wing and select a light in the lower classroom that is next to the stairs, as shown in Figure 12–40.

Figure 12–40

13. In the *Modify | Lighting Fixtures* tab>*Create Systems* panel, click ⓘ (Power).

14. In the *Modify | Electrical Circuits* tab>*System Tools* panel, expand the *Panel* drop-down list to select **Panel (LP2)**.

- Hint: ▦ (Select Panel) enables you to use your cursor to select the panel in the view.

15. Repeat this process with another light fixture in the next room. Each room with lights should be on its own circuit, as shown in Figure 12–41.

Branch Panel: LP2

Location: ELECTRICAL 2500A
Supply From: SW1
Mounting: Surface
Enclosure: Type 1

Notes:

CKT	Circuit Description	Trip	Poles
1L1	Lighting - Dwelling Unit CLASSROOM 1508	20 A	1
1L2	Lighting - Dwelling Unit CLASSROOM 1504	20 A	1
1L3	Lighting - Dwelling Unit CLASSROOM 1500	20 A	1

Figure 12–41

- Note that the circuit naming is using the new circuit naming scheme: **By Way By Phase**.

16. Type **TW** to return the views to tab mode.

17. Save the project.

Task 2: Create switchboard schedule.

1. In the Project Browser, open the **01 Electrical Room** floor plan view. Close any other open view.

2. Select the **SW2 SB** switchboard.

3. In the *Modify | Electrical Equipment* tab>*Electrical* panel, expand the *Create Panel Schedules* drop-down list and select **Choose a Template**.

4. In the *Change Template* dialog box, **Switchboard** is the default template. Click **Cancel** to close the dialog box.

5. Click ⌕ (Modify).

6. In the *Manage* tab>*Settings* panel, expand the *Panel Schedule Templates* drop-down list and select **Manage Templates**.

7. In the *Manage Panel Schedule Templates* dialog box, in the *Manage Templates* tab, expand the Template type drop-down list and select **Switchboard**, as shown in Figure 12–42.

Figure 12–42

8. Click ⬚ (Duplicate) at the bottom of the dialog box. In the *Duplicate Panel Schedule Template* dialog box, enter the name **Circuit Switchboard** and click **OK**.

9. In the *Manage Panel Schedule Templates* dialog box, select **Circuit Switchboard** (the new template you created), then click ✎ (Edit) at the bottom of the dialog box.

10. In the *Modify Panel Schedule Template* tab>*Template* panel, click ▦ (Set Template Options).

11. In the *Set Template Options* dialog box, click **Circuit Table** in the left-hand pane and select **Separate Phase Loads per Circuit** in the *Choose format for displaying loads* area, as shown in Figure 12–43. Click **OK**.

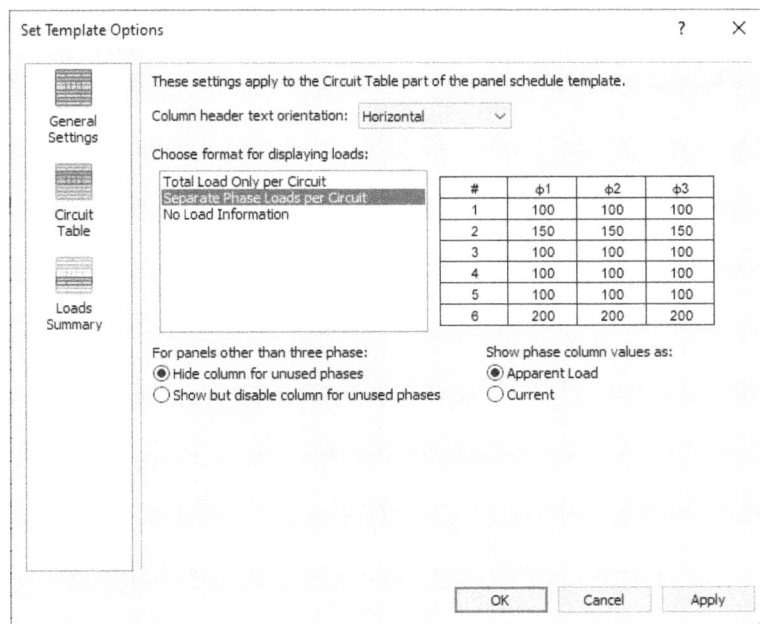

Figure 12–43

12. In the Switchboard schedule, click on the Remarks column and in the *Modify Panel Schedule Template* tab>*Columns and Rows* panel, click ▣ (Delete Column). Resize columns *A*, *B*, and *C* by dragging the column width, as shown in Figure 12–44, so that the three columns are equal sizes.

Figure 12–44

13. In the *Modify Panel Schedule Template* tab>*Template Editor* panel, click ✔ (Finish Template).

14. In the **01 Electrical Room** plan view, select the **SW2 SB** switchboard. In the *Modify | Electrical Equipment* tab>*Electrical* panel, expand the *Create Panel Schedules* drop-down list and select **Choose a Template**.

15. In the *Change Template* dialog box, select the **Circuit Switchboard** template and click **OK**. Note that the Switchboard panel schedule opens.

16. Return to the **01 Electrical Room** plan view. Tile the Circuit Switchboard schedule and 01 Electrical Room view.

17. Click on one of the duplex receptacles in the room, as shown in Figure 12–45.

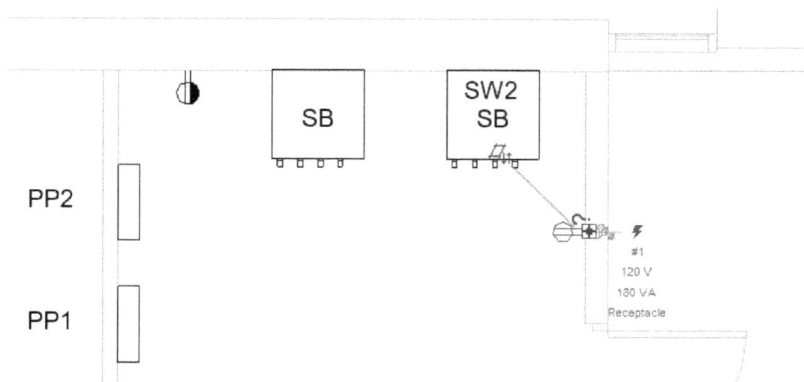

Figure 12–45

18. In the *Modify | Electrical Fixtures* tab>*Create Systems* panel, click ⓘ (Power).

19. In the *Modify | Electrical Circuits* tab>*System Tools* panel, expand the *Panel* drop-down list and select **SW2**.

20. In the **SW2** panel schedule, note that the receptacle has been added to *CKT 1* and the load is on phase *A*.

21. Click on the receptacle's name in the *Circuit Description* column. In the *Modify Panel Schedule* tab>*Circuits* panel, click ⊞ (Switch Phases) and move the load to phase **B**, as shown in Figure 12–46. Note that the load can be moved to any of the three phases (A, B, or C).

	Switchboard: SW2							
	Location: ELECTRICAL 2500A		Volts: 120/240 Wye		A.I.C. Rating:			
	Supply From:		Phases: 3		Mains Type:			
	Mounting:		Wires: 4		Mains Rating:			
	Enclosure:				MCB Rating: 400 A			
Notes:								
CKT	Circuit Description	# of Poles	Frame Size	Trip Rating	A	B	C	
1	Receptacle ELECTRICAL 2500A	1	400 A	20 A		180 VA		
2								
3								

Figure 12–46

22. Return to the **01 Electrical Room** plan view. Connect the remainder of the receptacles. Note that the loads can be moved using the **Switch Phases** command for 1, 2, or 3-pole devices.

23. Save and close the project.

End of practice

12.4 Working with Cable Trays and Conduits

Cable trays and conduits, as shown in Figure 12–47, hold electrical wiring either for power or data.The wiring that connects electrical equipment, devices, and light fixtures is schematic. Cable trays and conduits are not directly connected to the components in the same way that ducts and pipes are.

Figure 12–47

- The commands to create conduits and their appropriate fittings are located in the *Systems* tab>*Electrical* panel, as shown above in Figure 12–47.

- Conduits and fittings can be placed in any view, including plan, elevation, and 3D.

Creating Cable Trays and Conduits With and Without Fittings

The process of placing cable trays and conduits is the same whether you select a type with fittings (separate elbows and tees) or a type without fittings (in the field the elements are bent to create curves and bends). In both cases, the software adds fitting components, but the one with fittings includes options to create tees and crosses, as shown on the left in Figure 12–48. The type without fittings does not, as shown on the right in Figure 12–48.

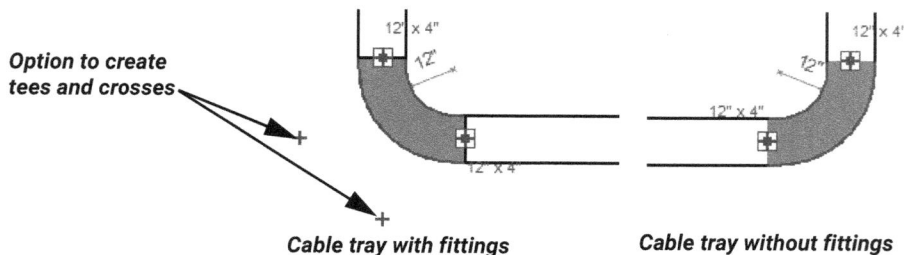

Cable tray with fittings   Cable tray without fittings

Figure 12–48

- The without fittings type also displays as a continuous element without lines between the straight segments and the fittings. It can use the special Conduit Runs or Cable Tray Runs schedules to schedule each run for a real-life length of conduit that is going to be used at the site.

Cable Tray and Conduit Placement Options

	Justification Settings	Opens the *Justification Setting* dialog box where you can specify the default settings for the **Horizontal Justification**, **Horizontal Offset**, and **Vertical Justification**.
	Inherit Elevation	An on/off toggle. If the tool is toggled on and you start drawing a cable tray/conduit by snapping to an existing element, the new cable tray/conduit takes on the elevation of the existing one regardless of what is specified, as shown in Figure 12–49.
	Inherit Size	An on/off toggle. If the tool is toggled on and you start drawing a cable tray/conduit by snapping to an existing element, the new cable tray/conduit takes on the size of the existing one regardless of what is specified, as shown in Figure 12–49.

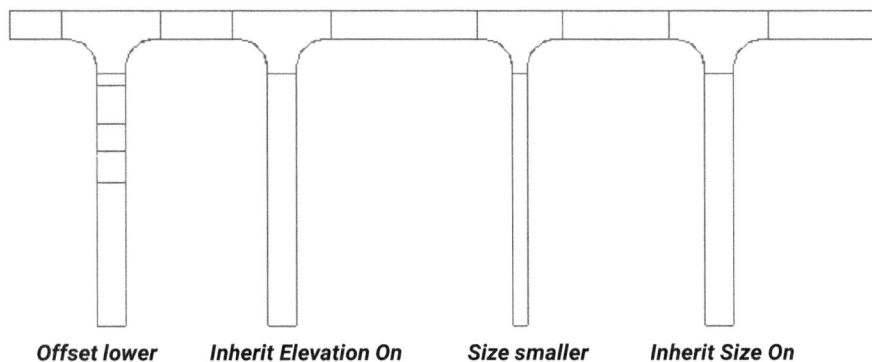

Offset lower   *Inherit Elevation On*   *Size smaller*   *Inherit Size On*

Figure 12–49

Creating Parallel Conduit Runs

The **Parallel Conduits** tool facilitates the creation of conduit runs parallel to an existing run, as shown in Figure 12–50. This saves time because only one run needs to be laid out, and the tool generates the parallel runs for you.

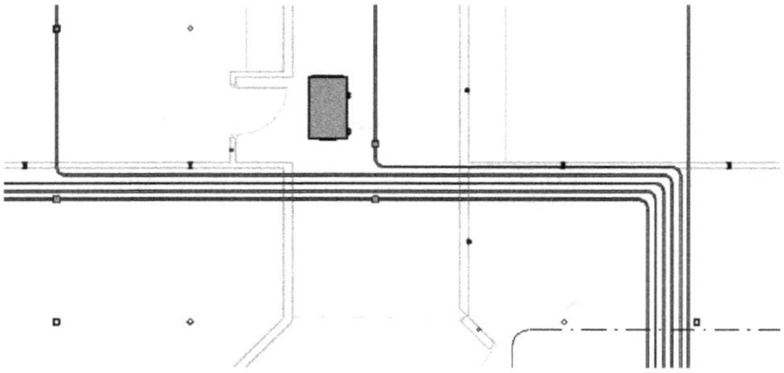

Figure 12–50

- Parallel conduit can be created in plan, section, elevation, and 3D views.

How To: Create Parallel Conduit Runs

1. Create the initial single run of conduit as required.
2. In the *Systems* tab>*Electrical* panel, click ▒ (Parallel Conduits).
3. In the *Modify | Place Parallel Conduits* tab>*Parallel Conduits* panel, set the options as required (see below).
4. Hover the cursor over the existing conduit and press <Tab> to select the existing run.
   - If you do not press <Tab>, the parallel conduit is only created for the single piece of existing conduit.
5. When the preview displays as required, click to create the parallel runs.
   - The preview and resulting parallel conduit varies depending on which side of the existing run you hover the cursor.

Parallel Conduit Creation Options

▧	**Bend Radius**	Parallel runs use the same bend radius as the original.
▧	**Concentric Bend Radius**	The bend radius of the parallel runs varies in order to remain concentric to the original run.
		This option results in concentric bend radii only when used with parallel conduit types without fittings. For conduit types with fittings, it gives the same result as the Same Bend Radius option.

N/A	Horizontal Number	The total number of parallel conduit runs in the horizontal direction.
N/A	Horizontal Offset	The distance between parallel conduit runs in the horizontal direction.
N/A	Vertical Number	The total number of parallel conduit runs in the vertical direction.
N/A	Vertical Offset	The distance between parallel conduit runs in the vertical direction.

- In section and elevation views, horizontal refers to parallel to the view (visually up, down, left or right from the original conduit). Vertical creates parallel conduit runs perpendicular to the view, in the direction of the user.

Connecting Cable Trays and Conduit

How To: Automatically Connect Cable Trays and Conduits

1. Select the cable tray or conduit you want to modify.

2. In the *Modify | Place Cable Tray* tab or *Modify | Place Conduit* tab>*Placement Tools* panel, click (Automatically Connect) if you want a cable tray or conduit to connect to a lower segment and put in all of the right fittings as shown in the background in Figure 12-51. Toggle it off if you want to draw a tray that remains at the original elevation, as shown in the foreground in Figure 12-51.

   *Note: When you snap to a connector, if **Automatically Connect** is not on, any changes in height and size are applied with the appropriate fittings.*

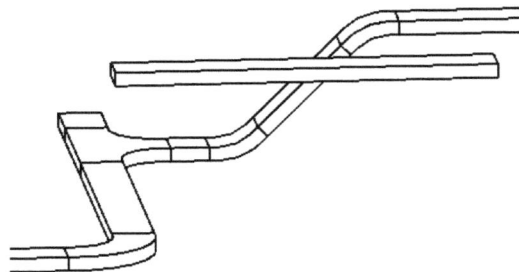

Figure 12-51

- To connect a conduit to a cable tray, start the conduit segment on a cable tray, regardless of elevation.

- The **Placement Tools** option ⌐ (Ignore Slope to Connect) draws conduit directly from a higher point to a lower point without any fittings, as shown on the right in Figure 12–52. If the option is off, then the conduit does not slope but bends down at the point of connection, as shown on the left in Figure 12–52.

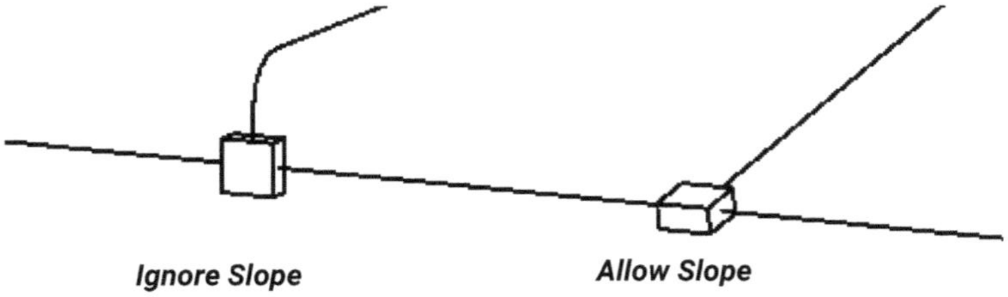

Ignore Slope   *Allow Slope*

Figure 12–52

Modifying Cable Tray and Conduit

Cable tray and conduit can be modified using a variety of standard modifying tools. You can also change type, modify the justification, and (in the case of conduits) ignore slope to connect.

You can modify cable tray and conduit using universal methods by making changes in Properties, in the Options Bar, and by using temporary dimensions, controls, and connectors. Modify tools such as **Move**, **Rotate**, **Trim/Extend**, and **Align** enable you to place the elements in the correct locations.

Often a change using these tools automatically applies the correct fittings. For example, in Figure 12–53, the *Edit End Offset* control is changed from **12'-0"** on the left to **10'-0"** on the right and the appropriate cable tray fittings are automatically placed to facilitate the change in elevation.

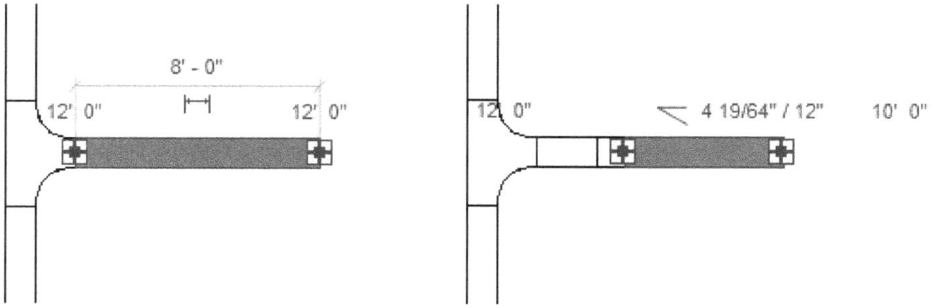

Figure 12–53

How To: Change the Type of Cable Tray and Conduit Runs

1. Select the cable tray or conduit run. Ensure that you filter out everything except related elements and fittings.

2. In the *Modify | Multi-Select* tab>*Edit* panel, click ⊞ (Change Type).

3. In the Type Selector, select a new type of conduit or cable tray. This changes the cable tray or conduit and also any related fittings. For example, as shown in Figure 12–54, a solid bottom cable tray is changed to a ladder cable tray.

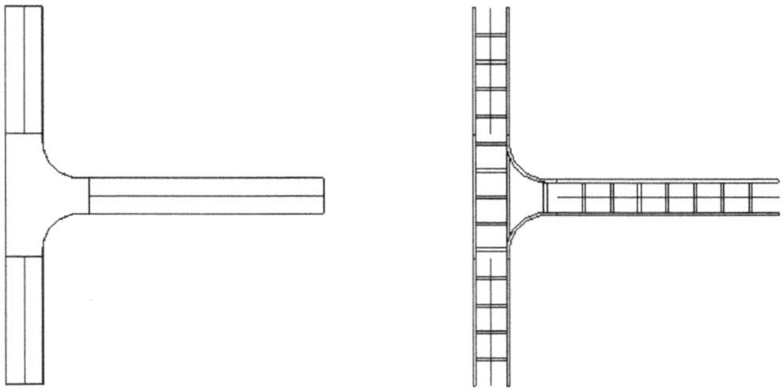

Figure 12–54

Modifying the Justification

If a cable tray or conduit run has different sizes along its run, you can modify the justification of the cable tray or conduit, as shown in Figure 12–55.

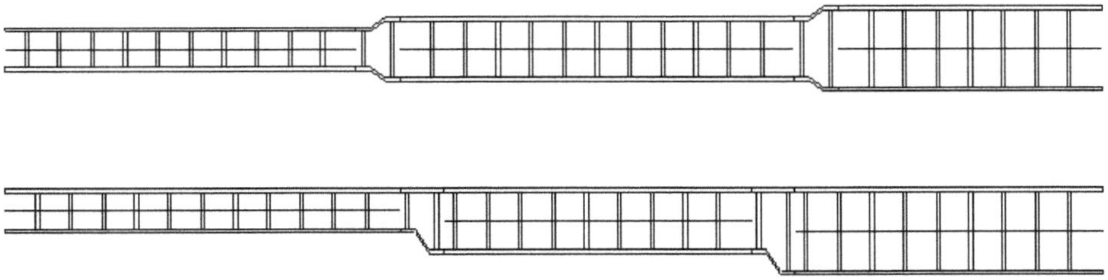

Figure 12–55

- While you can justify conduit, it is not typically required.

How To: Modify Cable Tray Justifications

1. Select the cable tray run.

2. In the *Modify | Multi-Select* tab>*Edit* panel, click ▥ (Justify).

3. To specify the point on the cable tray you want to justify around, in the *Justification Editor* tab>*Justify* panel, click ⬈ (Control Point) to cycle between the end point references. The alignment location displays as an arrow, as shown in Figure 12–56.

Figure 12–56

4. To indicate the required alignment, either click one of the nine alignment buttons in the *Justify* panel, or in a 3D view, use ⬈ (Alignment Line) to select the required dashed line, as shown in Figure 12–57.

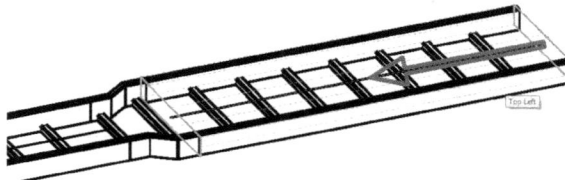

Figure 12–57

5. In the Justification Editor, click ✔ (Finish).

Adding Fittings

Revit MEP software automatically adds fittings to cable tray and conduit segments during their creation. It is also possible to manually add cable tray and conduit fittings to any existing segment or segment run. You can also use the controls on the fittings to modify the type, as shown in Figure 12–58.

Figure 12–58

- Only Cable Tray and Conduit types with fittings display **+** to turn elbows into tees and tees into crosses.

How To: Manually Add a Cable Tray or Conduit Fitting to a Plan View

1. Open the view in which you are going to place the fitting.

2. In the *Systems* tab>*Electrical* panel, click either 📷 (Cable Tray Fitting) or 🍥 (Conduit Fitting).

3. In the Type Selector, select the appropriate type you want to place.

4. In Properties, verify that the *Level* and *Offset* values are set as required.

5. Click in the view where you want to place the fitting.

6. Click 🡒 (Modify) to end and exit the command.

12.5 Testing Electrical Layouts

As you are working with electrical circuits, cable trays, and conduits, the **Show Disconnects** (shown in Figure 12–59) and **Check Circuits** tools can help you find areas that might need to be corrected.

Note: These tools along with schedules based on spaces and light fixture properties can be used to help you perform lighting analysis.

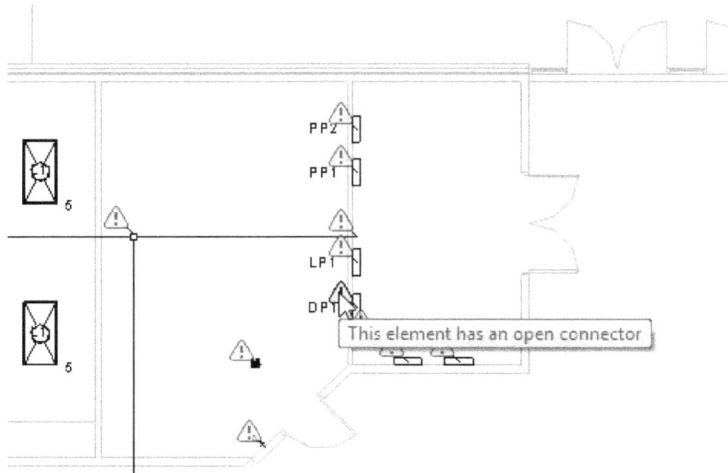

Figure 12–59

Often, these warnings are corrected as you continue working in a circuit and complete the full connection. However, some need to be corrected before the circuit works as required.

How To: Use the Show Disconnects Tool

1. In the *Analyze* tab>*Check Systems* panel, click (Show Disconnects).

2. In the *Show Disconnects Options* dialog box, select the types of systems you want to display, as shown in Figure 12–60. Click **OK**.

Figure 12-60

3. The disconnects display ⚠ (Warning).

   • The disconnects continue to display until you either correct the situation or run **Show Disconnects** again and clear all of the selections.

4. Hover the cursor over the warning icon to display a tooltip with the warning. You can also click on the icon to open the warning dialog box, shown in Figure 12-61.

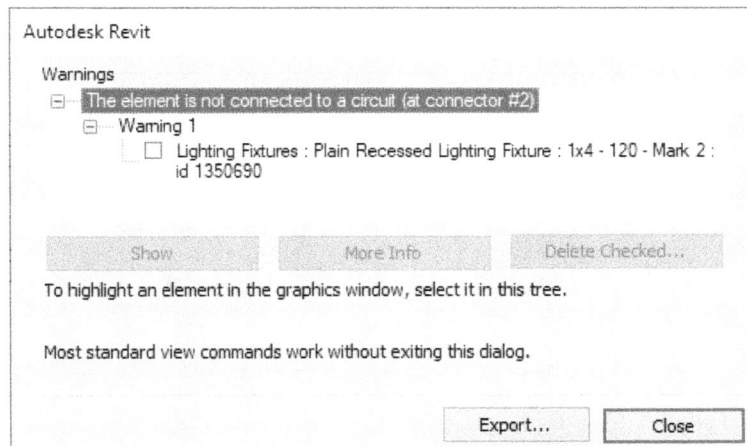

Figure 12-61

How To: Use the Check Circuits Tool

1. In the *Analyze* tab>*Check Systems* panel, click ⊞ (Check Circuits) to toggle it on.

2. The ⚠ (Warning) icon displays wherever there is an issue. Click on one of the icons to open the warning dialog box, shown in Figure 12–62.

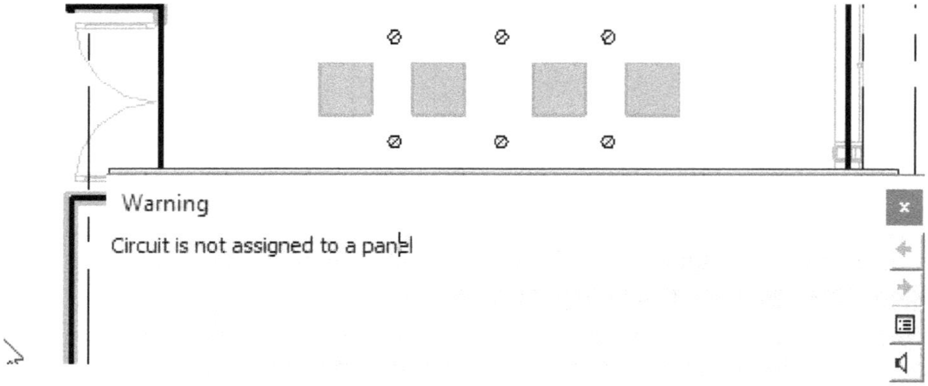

Figure 12–62

* For icons that have more than one warning, in the warning dialog box, click ✚ (Next Warning) and ✚ (Previous Warning) to search through the list.

* Click 🔲 (Expand Warning Dialog) to open the dialog box, shown in Figure 12–63. You can expand each node in the box and select elements to display or delete.

   Note: *If there are a lot of warnings to review, you can click* **Export...** *and save an HTML report.*

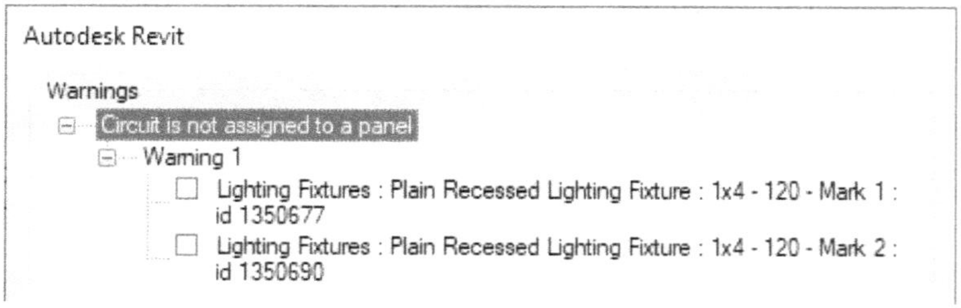

Figure 12–63

Practice 12d
Add Conduit

Practice Objective

- Add conduit to a lighting plan.

In this practice, you will add conduit and fittings to a project.

1. In the practice files *Working Models>Electrical* folder, open **Elec-Conduit.rvt**.

2. In the *Systems* tab>*Electrical* panel title bar, click ⌐ (Electrical Settings).

3. In the *Electrical Settings* dialog box, select **Angles**.

4. In the **Angles** pane, select **Use specific angles** and clear the **22.50** and **11.25** checkmarks, as shown in Figure 12-64.

   Note: This limits the angles that you can draw, which is typically used to match factory fittings.

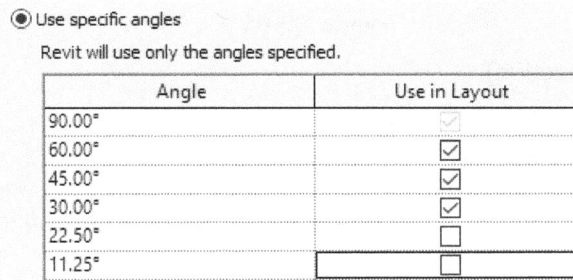

◉ Use specific angles
Revit will use only the angles specified.

Angle	Use in Layout
90.00°	☑
60.00°	☑
45.00°	☑
30.00°	☑
22.50°	☐
11.25°	☐

Figure 12-64

5. Click **OK** to close the dialog box.

6. Open the Electrical>Lighting>Floor Plans>**01 Lighting Plan** view.

7. Zoom in to the electrical room area so that a portion of the north wing classrooms is also displayed.

8. In the *Systems* tab>*Electrical* panel, click ▥ (Conduit).

9. In the Type Selector, select **Conduit with Fittings - Rigid Nonmetallic Conduit (RNC Sch 40)**.

10. In the Options Bar, verify that the *Diameter* is set to **2"** and the *Middle Elevation* is set to **9'-6"**, then press <Enter>.

11. In the Electrical Room, select the panel **LP1**. The program zooms in on the connector and the *Surface Connection* tab displays in the ribbon, as shown in Figure 12–65.

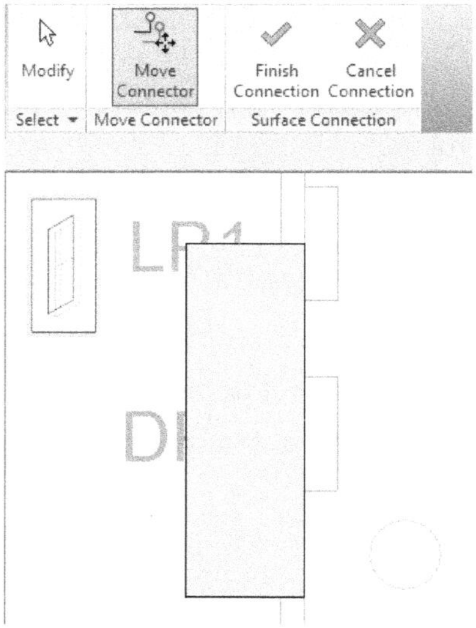

Figure 12–65

12. Click ✓ (Finish Connection).

13. Draw the conduit down the length of the north wing.

14. Press <Esc> once to release the end of the conduit, but remain in the **Conduit** command. Draw another line of conduit vertically and then horizontally across the bottom of the other classroom in the south wing, as shown in Figure 12–66. (The conduit in the image has been enhanced for clarity.)

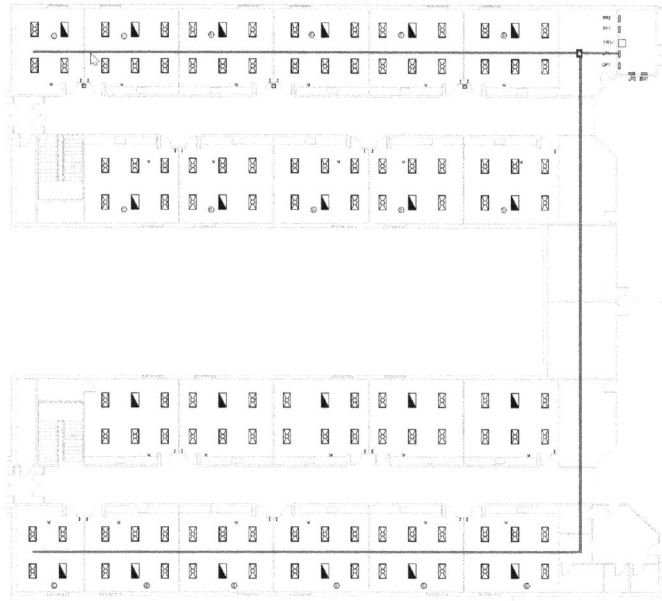

Figure 12–66

15. Draw additional lines of conduit from the vertical line down each of the halls and the other classrooms.

16. Click ⬉ (Modify).

17. Zoom in so that you can see where the junction boxes are automatically placed, as shown in Figure 12–67.

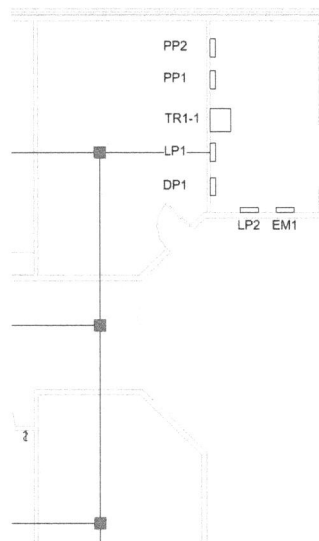

Figure 12–67

18. Pan over to the end of one of the conduit to the far left of the building.

19. In the View Control Bar, set the *Detail Level* to **Fine**.

20. In the *Systems* tab>*Electrical* panel, click 🔧 (Conduit Fitting).

21. In the Type Selector, select **Conduit Junction Box - Cross - Aluminum - Standard**.

22. Place the junction box at the end of the conduit segment you just created. Selecting the endpoint of the conduit so that the junction box takes on the height and size of the conduit.

   *Note: You can hover over the conduit and type **SN** to snap to the nearest location along the conduit.*

23. Add other junction boxes as required along the lines of conduit. Snap to the conduit's centerline (Nearest), as shown in Figure 12–68, to place it correctly. If you did not snap to the correct location, you will see the conduit running through the junction box, as shown in Figure 12–68.

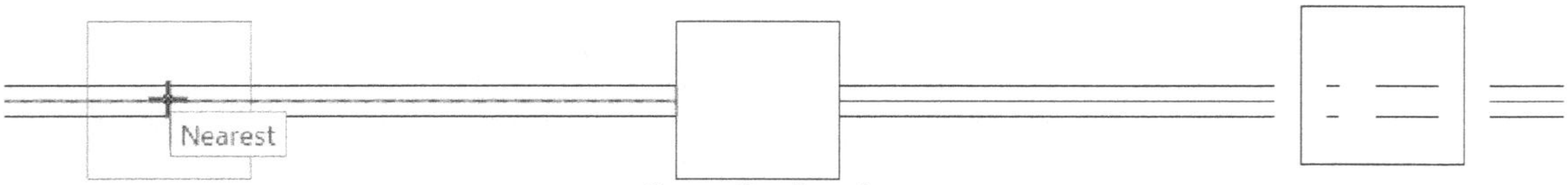

Snap to conduit   **Correctly placed junction box**   **Incorrectly placed junction box**

Figure 12–68

24. Save and close the project.

End of practice

Chapter Review Questions

1. Which of the following is NOT a type of system that can be created in the Autodesk Revit MEP software?

    a. Power

    b. Communications

    c. Low Voltage

    d. Lighting

2. Which of the following are electrical devices that can be added to a project? (Select all that apply.)

    a. Lighting switches

    b. Communication

    c. Electrical panels

    d. Data

3. What happens to hosted, face-based light fixtures in an Autodesk Revit MEP project if the ceiling (as shown in Figure 12–69) is deleted and then a new one is added at a different height in the architectural linked model?

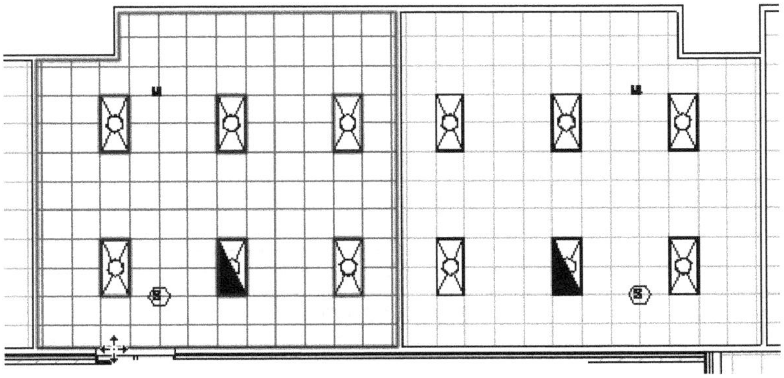

    Figure 12–69

    a. The hosted light fixtures are deleted.

    b. A warning displays that you need a coordination review.

    c. A warning displays that the hosting element no longer exists in the linked model.

    d. Nothing happens, but in the 3D view, the light fixtures are not connected to the ceiling.

4. What must you do to change the type of a cable tray or conduit run, as shown in Figure 12–70?

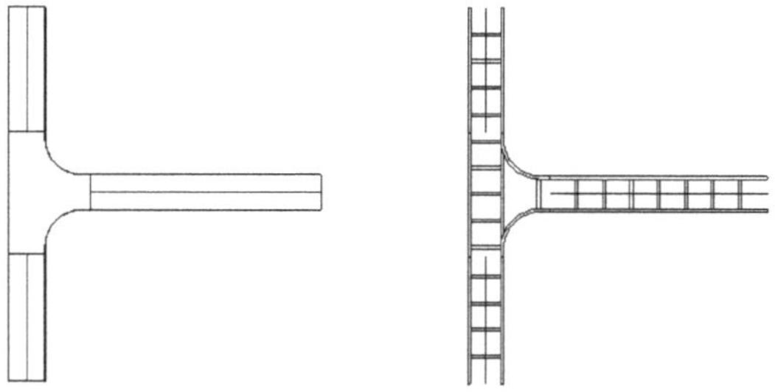

Figure 12–70

a. Redraw the run using the correct type.

b. Select one element in the run and change it in the Type Selector.

c. Select all of the elements in the run and change it in the Type Selector.

d. Select all the elements in the run and use **Change Type**.

5. Can a panel schedule, such as that shown in Figure 12–71, be modified once a circuit has been added to it?

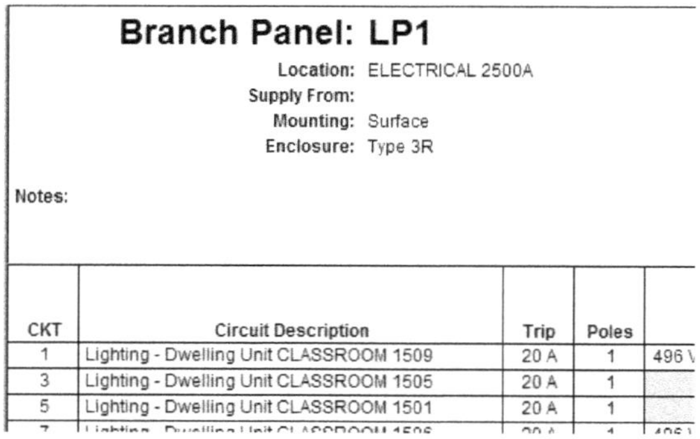

Branch Panel: LP1

Location: ELECTRICAL 2500A
Supply From:
Mounting: Surface
Enclosure: Type 3R

Notes:

CKT	Circuit Description	Trip	Poles	
1	Lighting - Dwelling Unit CLASSROOM 1509	20 A	1	496 \
3	Lighting - Dwelling Unit CLASSROOM 1505	20 A	1	
5	Lighting - Dwelling Unit CLASSROOM 1501	20 A	1	

Figure 12–71

a. Yes

b. No

6. How do you move a spare circuit in a panel schedule?

    a. Select it and use the **Move** tool in the *Modify* tab.

    b. Select it and use **Move Up**, **Move Down**, or **Move Across**.

    c. Unlock it and use the **Move** tools in the *Circuits* panel.

    d. Move the circuit in the plan view. The panel schedule updates accordingly.

Command Summary

Button	Command	Location
Electrical Devices and Components		
	Communication	• **Ribbon:** *Systems* tab>*Electrical* panel, expand Device
	Data	• **Ribbon:** *Systems* tab>*Electrical* panel, expand Device
	Electrical Equipment	• **Ribbon:** *Systems* tab>*Electrical* panel
	Electrical Fixture	• **Ribbon:** *Systems* tab>*Electrical* panel, expand Device
	Fire Alarm	• **Ribbon:** *Systems* tab>*Electrical* panel, expand Device
	Lighting (switch)	• **Ribbon:** *Systems* tab>*Electrical* panel, expand Device
	Lighting Fixture	• **Ribbon:** *Systems* tab>*Electrical* panel
	Nurse Call	• **Ribbon:** *Systems* tab>*Electrical* panel, expand Device
	Security	• **Ribbon:** *Systems* tab>*Electrical* panel, expand Device
	Telephone	• **Ribbon:** *Systems* tab>*Electrical* panel, expand Device
Electrical Circuits		
	Add to Circuit	• **Ribbon:** *Edit Circuit* tab>*Edit Circuit* panel
	Create Panel Schedule	• **Ribbon:** *Modify	Electrical Equipment* tab>*Electrical* panel
	Edit Circuit	• **Ribbon:** *Modify	Electrical Circuits* tab>*System Tools* panel
	Edit Path (Circuits)	• **Ribbon:** *Modify	Electrical Circuits* tab>*System Tools* panel

Button	Command	Location
	Edit a Template	• **Ribbon:** *Manage* tab>*Settings* panel, expand Panel Schedule Templates
	Manage Templates	• **Ribbon:** *Manage* tab>*Settings* panel, expand Panel Schedule Templates
	Power	• **Ribbon:** *Modify	Lighting Fixtures* tab or *Modify Electrical Equipment* tab>*Create Systems* panel
	Remove from Circuit	• **Ribbon:** *Edit Circuit* tab>*Edit Circuit* panel
	Select Panel	• **Ribbon:** *Modify	Electrical Circuits* tab>*System Tools* panel

Cable Tray and Conduit

Button	Command	Location
	Automatically Connect	• **Ribbon:** *Modify	Place Cable Tray* or *Place Conduit* tab> *Placement Tools* panel
	Cable Tray	• **Ribbon:** *Systems* tab>*Electrical* panel
	Cable Tray Fitting	• **Ribbon:** *Systems* tab>*Electrical* panel
	Conduit	• **Ribbon:** *Systems* tab>*Electrical* panel
	Conduit Fitting	• **Ribbon:** *Systems* tab>*Electrical* panel
	Ignore Slope to Connect (Conduit only)	• **Ribbon:** *Modify	Place Conduit* tab>*Placement Tools* panel
	Inherit Elevation	• **Ribbon:** *Modify	Place Cable Tray* or *Place Conduit* tab> *Placement Tools* panel
	Inherit Size	• **Ribbon:** *Modify	Place Cable Tray* or *Place Conduit* tab> *Placement Tools* panel
	Justification	• **Ribbon:** *Modify	Place Cable Tray* or *Place Conduit* tab> *Placement Tools* panel
	Parallel Conduits	• **Ribbon:** *Systems* tab>*Electrical* panel

Construction Documentation

The third section of this guide continues to teach the Autodesk® Revit® tools, focusing on tools that help you to create accurate construction documents for a design.

This section includes the following chapters:

- Chapter 13: Creating Construction Documents
- Chapter 14: Working with Annotations
- Chapter 15: Adding Tags and Schedules
- Chapter 16: Creating Details

Creating Construction Documents

The accurate creation of construction documents in Revit® ensures that the design is correctly communicated to downstream users and other stakeholders. Construction documents are created primarily in special views call sheets. Selecting title blocks, assigning title block information, placing views, and printing the sheets are essential steps in the construction documentation process.

Learning Objectives

- Add sheets with title blocks and views of a project.
- Enter the title block information for individual sheets and for an entire project.
- Place and organize views on sheets.
- Print sheets using the default *Print* dialog box.

13.1 Setting Up Sheets

While you are modeling a project, the foundations of the working drawings are already in progress. Any view (such as a floor plan, section, callout, or schedule) can be placed on a sheet, as shown in Figure 13–1.

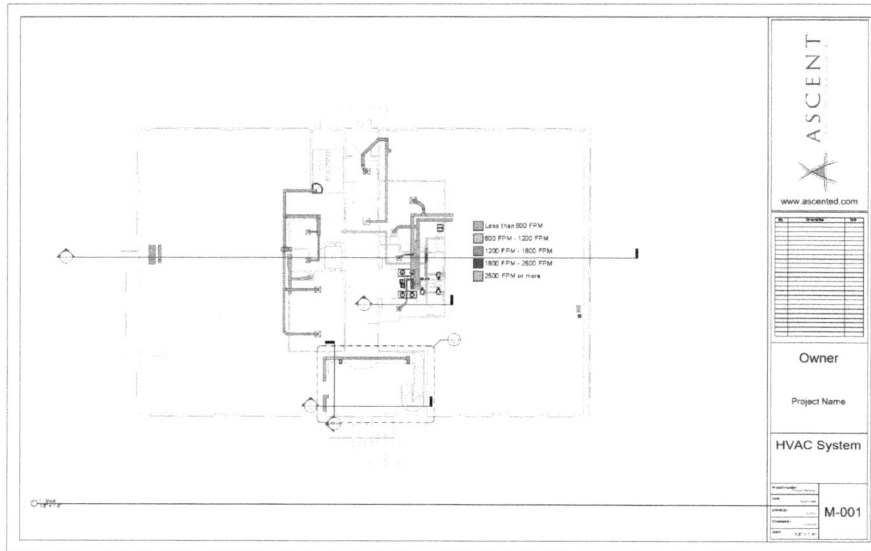

Figure 13–1

- Company templates can be created with standard sheets using the company (or project) title block and related views already placed on the sheet.

- The sheet size is based on the selected title block family.

- Sheets are listed in the *Sheets* node in the Project Browser.

- Most information on sheets is included in the views. You can add general notes and other non-model elements directly to the sheet, though it is better to add them using drafting views or legends, as these can be placed on multiple sheets.

How To: Set Up Sheets

1. In the Project Browser, right-click on the *Sheets* area header and select **New Sheet...**, or in the *View* tab>*Sheet Composition* panel, click ⬚ (Sheet).

    - Alternatively, in the Project Browser, right-click on **Sheets (all)** and select **New Sheet...**.

2. In the *New Sheet* dialog box, select a title block from the list, as shown in Figure 13–2.

   Note: *Click* **Load...** *to load a sheet from the Revit Library or your company's custom sheet.*

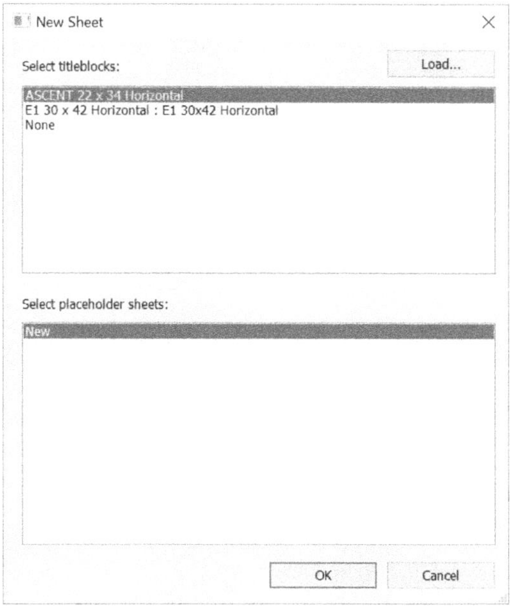

Figure 13–2

3. Click **OK**. A new sheet is created using the selected title block.
4. Fill out the information in the title block as needed.
5. Add views to the sheet.

- When you create sheets, the next sheet is incremented numerically.
- Double-click on the sheet name to change the name and number in the *Sheet Title* dialog box.
- When you change the *Sheet Name* and/or *Number* in the title block, it automatically changes the name and number of the sheet in the Project Browser.
- The plot stamp on the side of the sheet automatically updates according to the current date and time. The format of the display uses the regional settings of your computer.
- The Scale is automatically entered when a view is inserted onto a sheet. If a sheet has multiple views with different scales, the scale displays **As Indicated**.

Sheet (Title Block) Properties

Each new sheet includes a title block. You can change the title block information in Properties, as shown on the left in Figure 13-3, or by selecting any blue label you want to edit (Sheet Name, Sheet Number, Drawn by, etc.), as shown on the right.

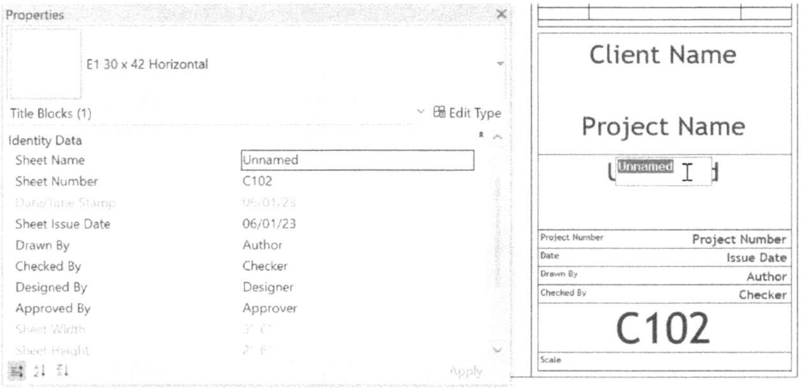

Figure 13-3

Properties that apply to all sheets can be entered in the *Project Information* dialog box (shown in Figure 13-4). In the *Manage* tab>*Settings* panel, click (Project Information).

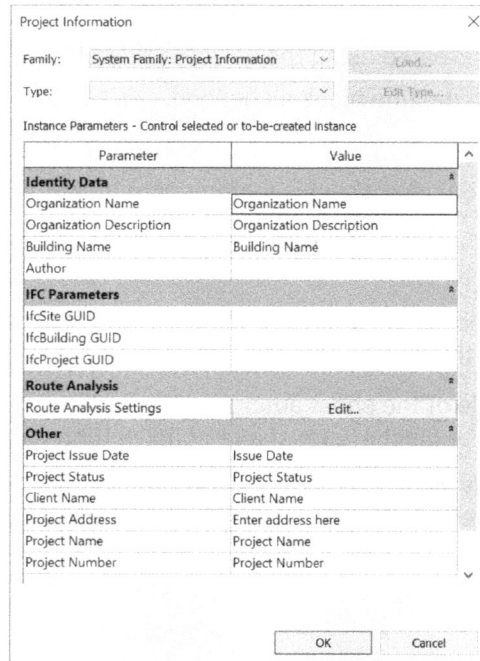

Figure 13-4

13.2 Placing and Modifying Views on Sheets

The process of adding views to a sheet is simple. Drag and drop a view from the Project Browser onto the sheet, as shown in Figure 13–5. The new view on the sheet is displayed at the scale specified in the original view. The view title displays the name, number, and scale of the view, as shown in Figure 13–5. Once the view has been placed on a sheet, the icon next to the view name in the Project Browser is filled in.

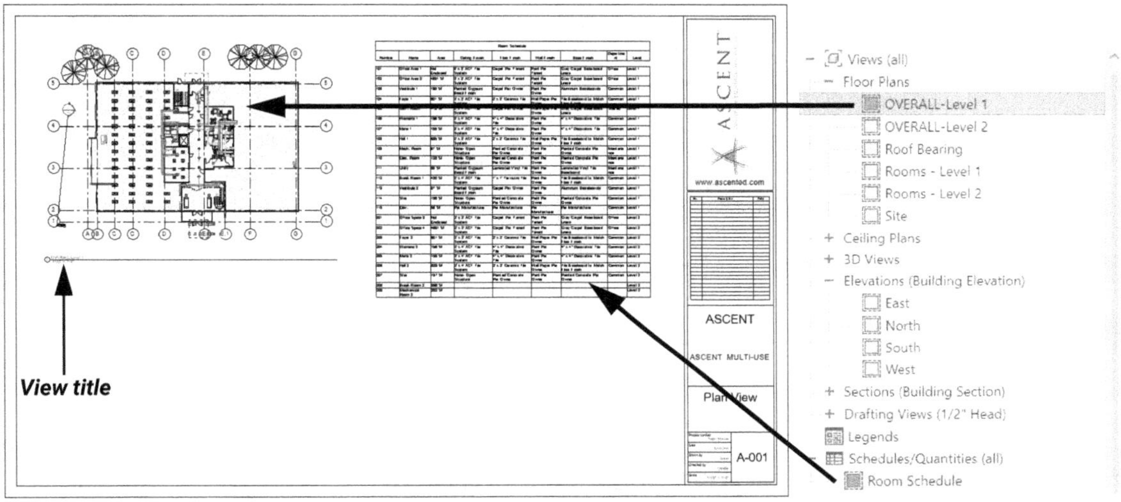

Figure 13–5

How To: Place Views on Sheets

1. Set up the view as you want it to display on the sheet, including the scale and visibility of elements.

2. Create or open the sheet where you want to place the view.

3. Select the view in the Project Browser and drag and drop it onto the sheet.

   Note: Alignment lines from existing views display to help you place additional views.

4. The center of the view is attached to the cursor. Click to place it on the sheet.

- Views can only be placed on a sheet once. However, you can duplicate the view and place that copy on a sheet.

- Views on a sheet are associative. They automatically update to reflect changes to the project.

- Each view on a sheet is listed under the sheet name in the Project Browser, as shown in Figure 13–6.

Figure 13–6

How To: Add Multiple Views and Schedules to a Sheet

1. Open a sheet that you want to place views on.

   - In the *View* tab>*Sheet Composition* panel, click ⬚ (Place View). Alternatively, in the Project Browser, right-click on the sheet name and select **Add View...**.

2. In the *Select View* dialog box (shown in Figure 13–7), you can use the search at the top of the dialog box to narrow down the views in the list, then use <Shift> or <Ctrl> to select multiple views you want to use and click **OK**.

   Note: This method lists only those views which have not yet been placed on a sheet.

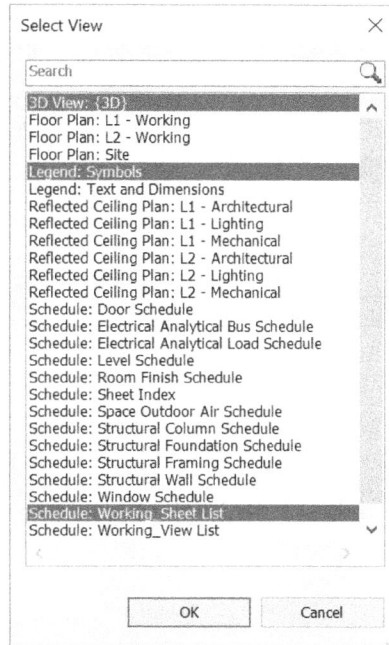

Figure 13-7

3. The views will be attached to your cursor, as shown in Figure 13-8. Click to place the views on the sheet.

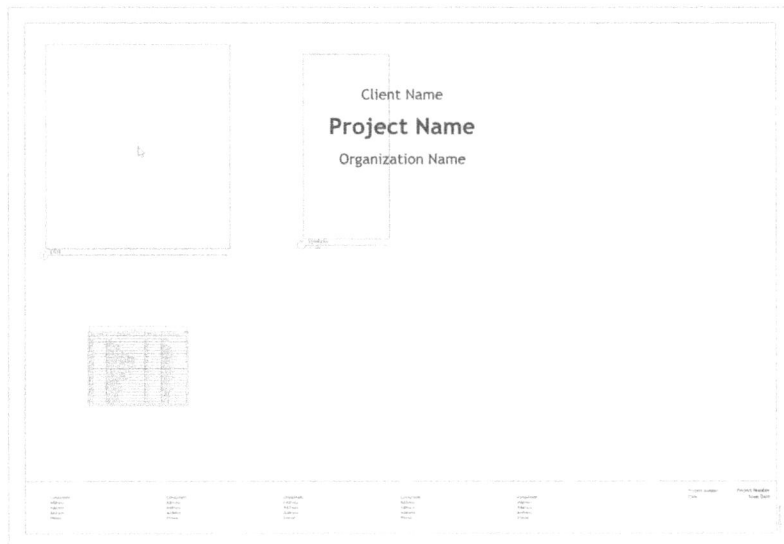

Figure 13-8

- Alternatively, you can open a sheet that you want to place views on. In the Project Browser, use <Shift> or <Ctrl> to select multiple views, then drag them to the sheet.

- To remove a view from a sheet, select it and press <Delete>. Alternatively, in the Project Browser, expand the individual sheet information to show the views, right-click on the view name, and select **Remove From Sheet**.

Open Sheet

To open sheets from the Project Browser, you can double-click on a sheet from the *Sheets (all)* section. As the project gets larger, you can easily open multiple views, schedules, legends, and 3D views directly from the drawing area or from the Project Browser.

- In an open view with nothing selected, right-click and select **Open Sheet**, as shown in Figure 13-9.

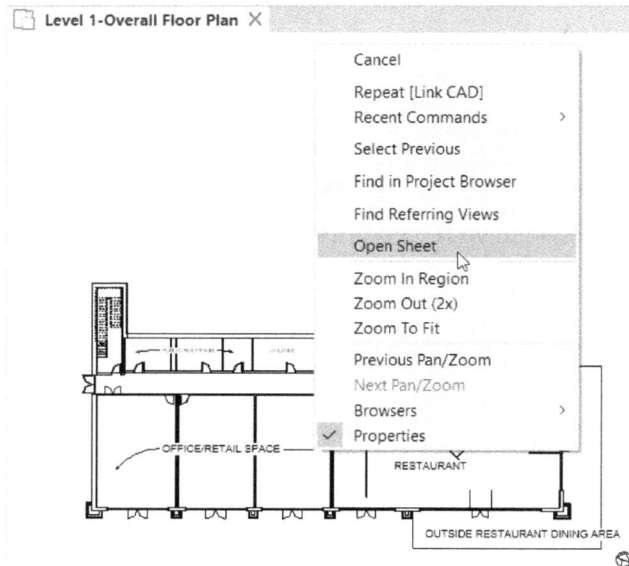

Figure 13-9

- Select multiple views (e.g., plan views, 3D views, schedules, and legends) that have the placed on sheet indicator next to them, as shown in Figure 13–10. Right-click and select **Open Sheet**. Click **OK** in the *Open View* dialog box to open all the sheets.

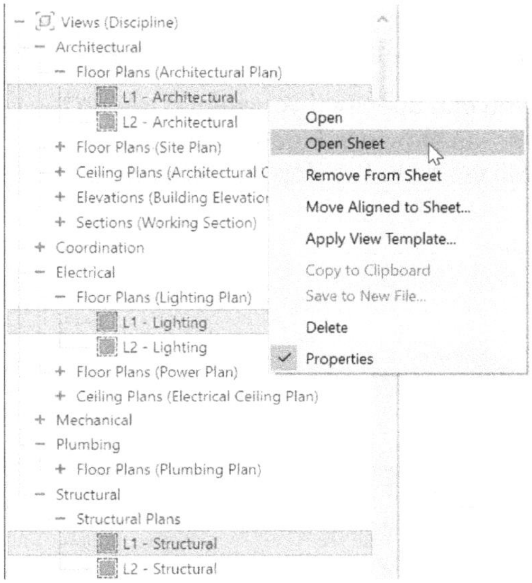

Figure 13–10

13.3 Swapping Views on a Sheet

You can reduce the time it takes to modify the views that are placed on a sheet by quickly swapping out a view with another view from the ribbon or Properties.

- You can swap a view on a sheet with a view that is already on another sheet.

- When swapping views, you can specify if you want to retain the view title's position from a viewport's type properties, as shown in Figure 13–11. When **Preserve Title Position** is checked, the view title will resize to the viewport when a different size view is swapped.

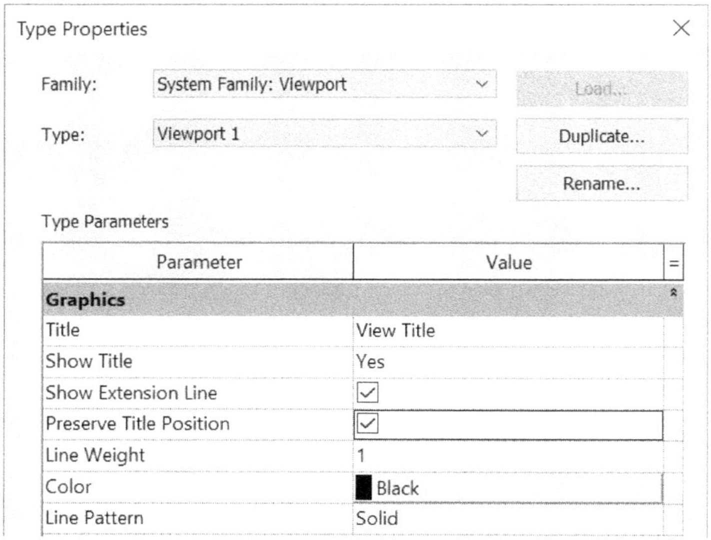

Figure 13–11

How To: Swap a View on a Sheet

1. From the Project Browser>*Sheets* node, open the sheet view.
2. Select the view that is on the sheet.

3. In the *Modify | Viewports* tab>*Positioning & View* panel, expand the views, as shown in Figure 13–12, and select one from the list. You can use the search bar to filter the list.

- Views already on sheets will have suffixes at the end of their names with the sheet number.

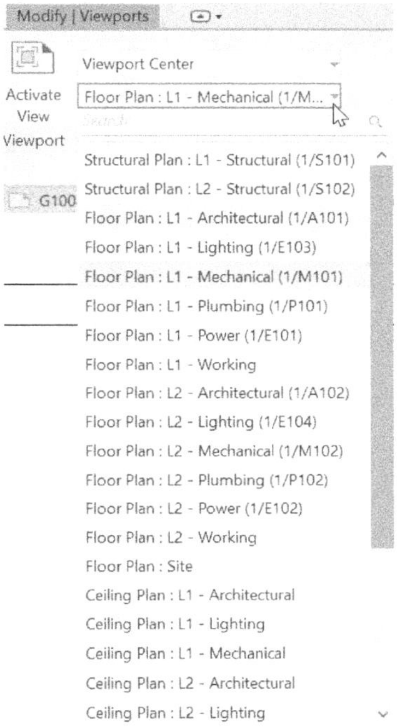

Figure 13–12

4. If you select a view that is already on a sheet, the *View Already Placed* dialog box will display, as shown in Figure 13–13.

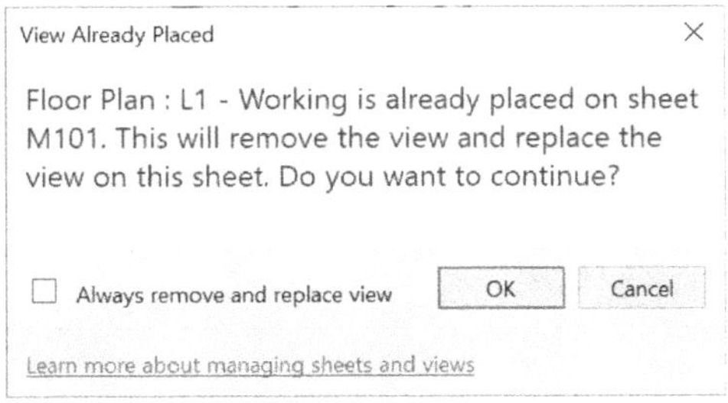

Figure 13–13

5. Select **OK** to swap the view.

- Alternatively, with the viewport selected, in Properties, in the *Identity Data* section, change the *View* on the sheet by expanding the parameter's drop-down list and selecting a different view, as shown in Figure 13–14. If you select a view that is already on another sheet, the *View Already Placed* dialog box will display.

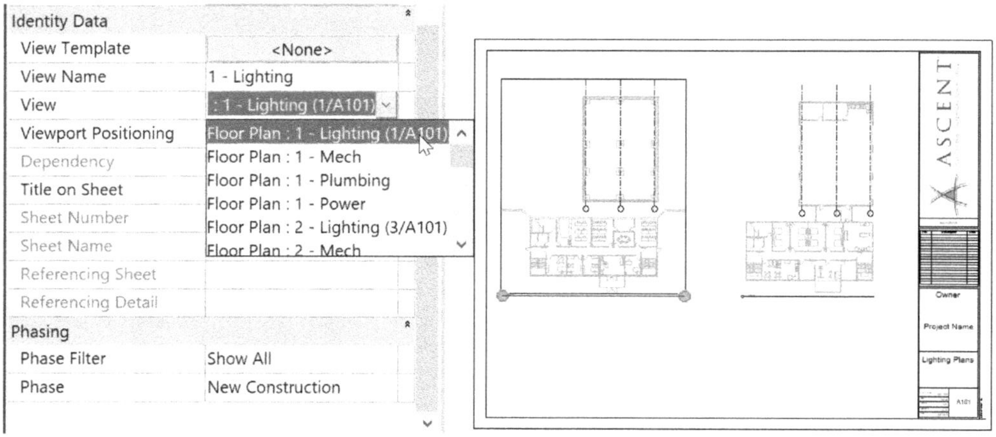

Figure 13–14

How To: Drag a View Aligned to Another Sheet

1. In the Project Browser, *Sheet* section, expand a sheet and select one or multiple views, right-click, and select **Move View Aligned to Sheet...**, as shown in Figure 13–15.

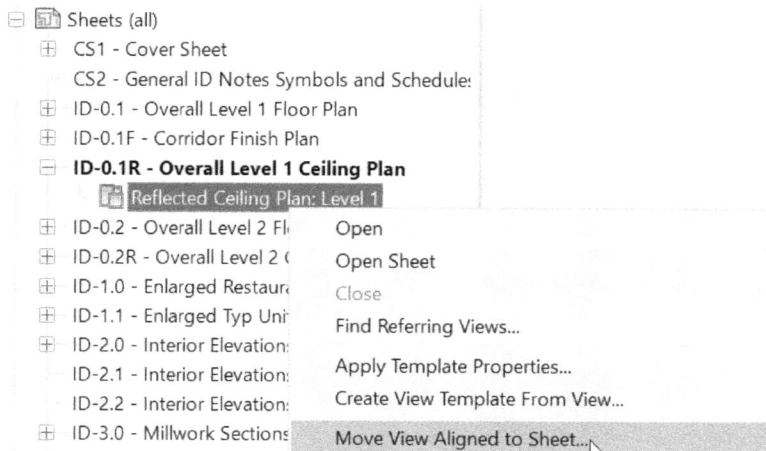

Figure 13–15

2. In the *Select Sheet* dialog box, select a sheet, as shown in Figure 13–16, and click **OK**. The view moves to the sheet, keeping its original alignment.

- To quickly find a sheet from the list, use the search bar at the top of the dialog box.

Figure 13–16

- Alternatively, under the *Sheet* section, expand a sheet and manually drag a view to another sheet. The view is moved and keeps its original alignment.

Removing Views from Sheets

There are three ways to remove a view from a sheet:

- In the Project Browser, select one or multiple views, right-click, and select **Remove From Sheet**, as shown in Figure 13–17.

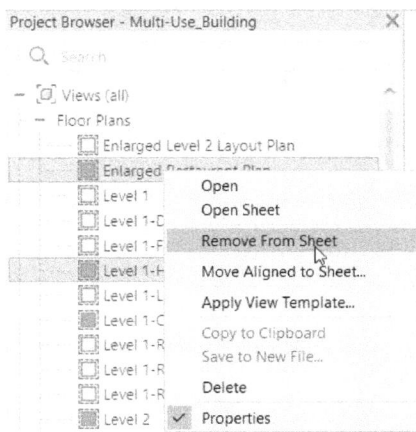

Figure 13–17

- If multiple views are selected, click **OK** in the *Remove From Sheet* dialog box, as shown in Figure 13–18.

Figure 13–18

- In the Project Browser under the *Sheets* node, you can expand the sheet, select the views, right-click, and select **Remove From Sheet**, as shown in Figure 13–19. If multiple views are selected, click **OK** in the *Remove From Sheet* dialog box.

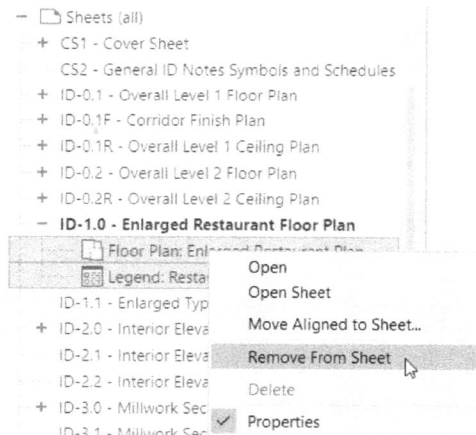

Figure 13–19

- You can remove a view directly from a sheet by selecting the view and pressing <Delete>.

Duplicating Sheets

Duplicating a sheet will add a suffix of *Copy 1* after the sheet name, as shown in Figure 13–20. It will also automatically generate with the next available sheet title number, like G101 shown in Figure 13–20.

- You can duplicate a sheet number but this duplication will remain on your project's warning list.

Figure 13–20

How To: Duplicate Sheets

1. In the Project Browser>*Sheets* node, right-click on a sheet and select **Duplicate Sheet**.
2. Select one of the following options:
   - **Duplicate Empty Sheet:** Creates a new sheet with the same titleblock and project information.
     - No model or annotation elements on the sheet are duplicated.
   - **Duplicate with Sheet Detailing:** Creates a new sheet with the same titleblock, project information, and any legends, keynotes, schedules, and annotations.

- **Duplicate with Views:** Before a sheet gets created, you are prompted to specify how you would like the views on the sheet to be duplicated, as shown in Figure 13–21.

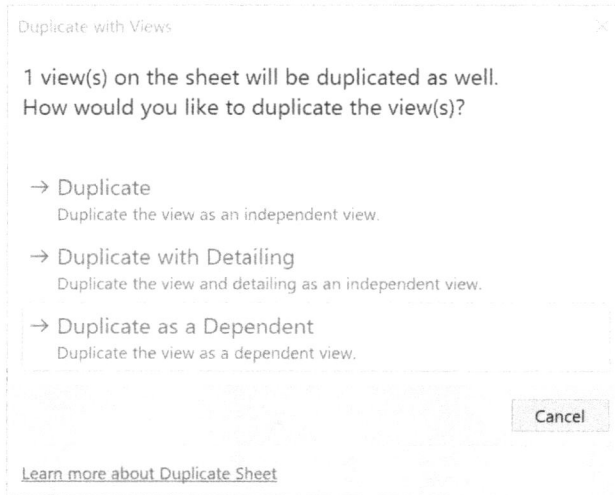

Duplicate with Views ⊗

1 view(s) on the sheet will be duplicated as well.
How would you like to duplicate the view(s)?

→ Duplicate
   Duplicate the view as an independent view.

→ Duplicate with Detailing
   Duplicate the view and detailing as an independent view.

→ Duplicate as a Dependent
   Duplicate the view as a dependent view.

Cancel

Learn more about Duplicate Sheet

Figure 13–21

Note: *To review duplicating view types, refer to* ***Chapter 3 Working with Views****.*

- In the *Duplicate with Views* dialog box, select **Duplicate**, **Duplicate with Detailing**, or **Duplicate as a Dependent**.
- If you are duplicating a sheet that has drafting views and want to duplicate the view with the model and annotation elements, you need to use the **Duplicate with Detailing** option.

Sheet Collections

A sheet collection is a way to create various construction document submission sets or groupings, for example construction document submittals, within the *Sheet* node in the Project Browser. After sheets have been created, you can create sheet collections and add desired sheets to the collection by dragging and dropping the sheet into the collection or by selecting the sheet and setting the *Sheet Collection* in Properties.

How To: Create a Sheet Collection

1. In the Project Browser>*Sheets* node, right-click on a sheet and select **New Sheet Collection**.

2. Name the new sheet collection using one of the following methods:

    - In Properties, click in the *Name* value and type the desired name.

    - In the Project Browser, click on the newly created sheet collection and type the desired name.

    - Right-click on the newly created sheet collection and select **Rename...**.

3. Drag the sheet to the new collection. Alternatively, select the sheet and in Properties next to *Sheet Collection*, expand the drop-down list and select the sheet collection you would like to add the sheet to.

    - It may be necessary to duplicate the sheet. You can keep the same sheet number to create the various sheet collections.

13.4 Modifying Views and View Titles

After you have the desired views on a sheet, you can modify their locations and titles. You can use some of the modify tools, like **Move** and **Rotate**, as well as the arrow keys.

- You cannot use any tools that utilize the copy feature, like **Copy**, **Mirror**, and **Offset**.

How To: Move a View on a Sheet

1. Open a sheet view.
2. Select and drag a view to another location on the sheet. When selecting the view, the view title moves with the view.

How To: Modify the Viewport's View Title

1. Open a sheet view.
2. Select only the view title and drag it to the new location.

- To modify the length of the line under the title name, select the viewport and drag the controls, as shown in Figure 13–22.

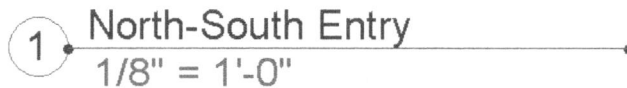

$$\textbf{1} \quad \text{North-South Entry}$$
$$\text{1/8" = 1'-0"}$$

Figure 13–22

- To change the title of a view on a sheet without changing its name in the Project Browser, select either the viewport or the view title, then in Properties, in the *Identity Data* section, type a new title for the *Title on Sheet* parameter, as shown in Figure 13–23.

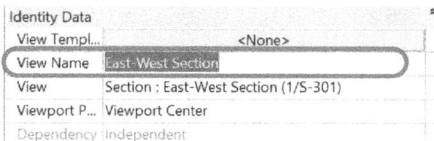

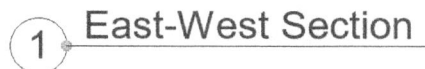

Identity Data	
View Templ...	<None>
View Name	East-West Section
View	Section : East-West Section (1/S-301)
Viewport P...	Viewport Center
Dependency	Independent

1 East-West Section

Figure 13–23

Rotating Views

When creating a vertical sheet, you can rotate the view on the sheet by 90° counterclockwise or clockwise. Select the view on the sheet and set the direction of rotation in the *Rotation on Sheet:* drop-down list in Properties, as shown in Figure 13–24.

Figure 13–24

Note: *For more information about rotating the project or individual views to angles other than 90°, refer to the ASCENT guide Autodesk Revit: Site Planning and Design.*

Working Inside Views

To make small changes to a view while working on a sheet:

- Double-click *inside* the view to activate it.
- Double-click *outside* the view to deactivate it.

Only elements in the viewport are available for modification. The rest of the sheet is grayed out, as shown in Figure 13–25. Use this method only for small changes. Significant changes should be made directly in the view.

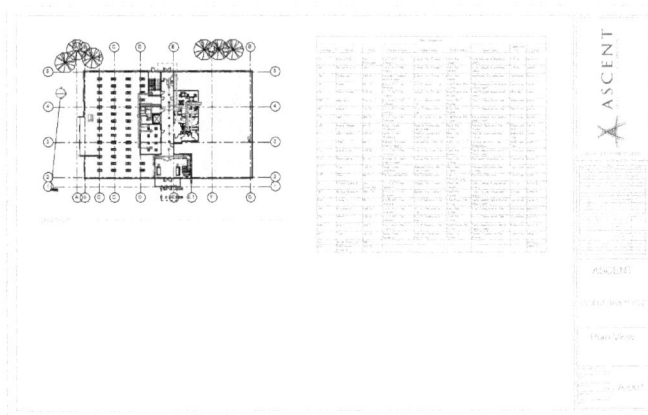

Figure 13–25

- You can activate and deactivate views by selecting the viewport, right-clicking, and selecting from the menu, or by using the tools found in the *Modify | Viewports* or *Views* tab>*Sheet Composition* panel.

- Changes you make to elements when a view is activated also display in the original view.

- If you are unsure which sheet a view is on, right-click on the view in the Project Browser and select **Open Sheet**. This is not available for schedules and legends, which can be placed on more than one sheet.

Resizing Views on Sheets

Each view displays the extents of the model or the elements contained in the crop region. If the view does not fit on a sheet (as shown in Figure 13–26), you might need to crop the view or move the elevation markers closer to the building.

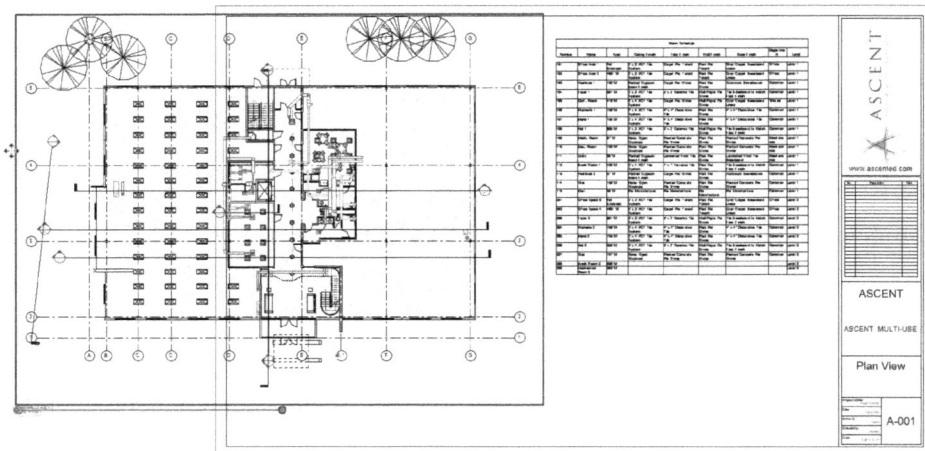

Figure 13–26

Note: If the extents of the view change dramatically based on a scale change or a crop region, it is easier to delete the view on the sheet and drag it over again.

- For information about laying out views on sheets using guide grids, see *B.2 Working with Guide Grids on Sheets* in *Appendix B Additional Tools for Construction Documents*.

- For information about working with revisions in views and on sheets, see *B.3 Revision Tracking* in *Appendix B Additional Tools for Construction Documents*.

How To: Add an Image to a Sheet

Company logos and renderings saved to image files (such as .JPG and .PNG) can be added directly on a sheet or in a view.

1. In the *Insert* tab>*Import* panel, click ▨ (Image).
2. In the *Import Image* dialog box, select and open the image file. The extents of the image display, as shown in Figure 13-27.

Figure 13-27

3. Place the image where you want it.
4. The image is displayed. Pick one of the grips and extend it to modify the size of the image.

• In Properties, you can adjust the height and width and also set the *Draw Layer* to either **Background** or **Foreground**, as shown in Figure 13-28.

Dimensions	
Width	1' 0"
Height	1' 0 19/128"
Horizontal Scale	1.774127
Vertical Scale	1.774127
Lock Proportions	☑
Other	
Draw Layer	Background

Figure 13-28

• You can select more than one image at a time and move them as a group to the background or foreground.

• In the *Modify | Raster Images* tab (shown in Figure 13-29), you can access the Arrange options and the **Manage Images** command.

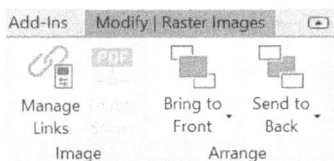

Figure 13-29

Practice 13a
Set Up Sheets – All Disciplines

Practice Objectives

- Set up project properties.
- Create sheets individually.
- Move a view aligned to another sheet.
- Modify views to prepare them to be placed on sheets.
- Place views on sheets.

In this practice, you will complete the project information, add new sheets and use existing sheets. You will fill in title block information and then add views to sheets, such as the Lighting Plan sheet shown in Figure 13–30. Complete as many sheets as you have time for.

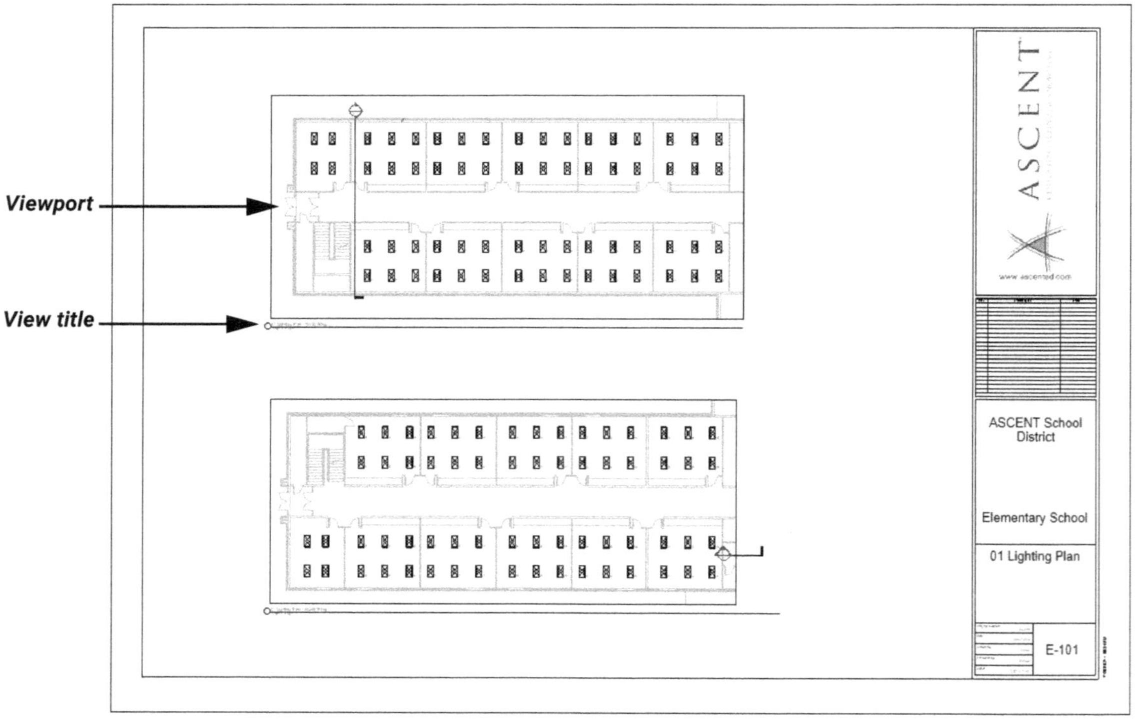

Figure 13–30

Task 1: Complete the project information.

1. In the practice files *Working Models>General* folder, open **Gen-Sheets.rvt**.

2. In the *Manage* tab>*Settings* panel, click 📷 (Project Information).

3. In the *Project Properties* dialog box, add the following values:

   - *Project Issue Date:* **Today's date**
   - *Project Status:* **Design Development**
   - *Client Name:* **ASCENT School District**
   - *Project Name:* **Elementary School**
   - *Project Number:* **1234.56**

   Note: These values are added automatically to any sheet you create.

4. Click **OK** and save the project.

Task 2: Create a cover sheet, import an image, and modify the title block.

1. In the *View* tab>*Sheet Composition* panel, click 🗋 (Sheet).

2. In the *New Sheet* dialog box, select the **ASCENT 22 x 34 Horizontal** title block.

3. Click **OK.**

4. Zoom in on the lower-right corner of the title block. The Project Properties filled out earlier are automatically added to the sheet (e.g., Project number, Project Status, etc.).

5. Continue filling out the title block by changing *unnamed* to **Cover Sheet** and the sheet number to **CS-000**, as shown in Figure 13–31.

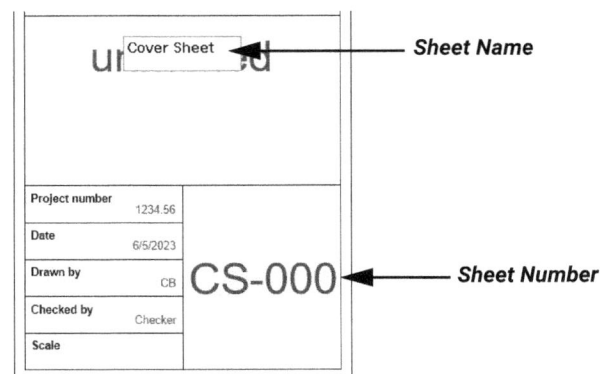

Figure 13–31

6. Set *Drawn by* to your initials. Leave the *Checked by* and *Date* parameters as is.

   *Note: The Scale is empty because this will be automatically entered when a view is inserted onto a sheet. If a sheet has multiple scales, the scale reads **As Indicated**.*

7. In the Project Browser, expand the *Sheets (all)* node. Note that the sheet you created is now in the list of sheets.

8. Open another sheet. The project parameter values are repeated but note that the *Drawn By* value is not added because it is a parameter that is set per sheet.

9. Go back to the **CS-000 - Cover Sheet** and type **ZA** to zoom out and display the whole sheet.

10. In the *Insert* tab>*Import* panel, click 🖼 (Import Image).

    • Note: If the image is one that might change, you would use the **Link Image** command so it can be updated through the *Manage Links* dialog box when required.

11. In the *Import Image* dialog box, navigate to the practice files *Images* folder and select **School Perspective.jpg**.

12. Click **Open**.

13. Your cursor will have an X shape (indicating the size of your image). Click to place the image on the sheet.

14. Click ⌖ (Modify).

15. Use the grips to adjust the size of the image so it is smaller and move it into the upper left corner of the sheet, as shown in Figure 13–32, to make room for notes.

Figure 13–32

16. In the Project Browser, right-click on *Sheets (all)* and select **New Sheet...**.

17. In the *New Sheet* dialog box, select the title block **ASCENT 30x42 Horizontal** and click **OK**.

18. Select the titleblock and in the Type Selector, select **ASCENT 22 x 34 Horizontal**. Note that the title block changes.

19. With the title block still selected, in Properties, in the *Identity Data* section, change the *Sheet Name* to **Electrical Details** and *Sheet Number* to **E-002**.

20. Click in an empty area in the view. Note that the title block information updates on the sheet.

21. Save the project.

Task 3: Duplicate a sheet, and add and modify views.

1. In the Project Browser, right-click on **CS-000 - Cover Sheet** and select **Duplicate Sheet>Duplicate Empty Sheet**.

2. In the Project Browser, right-click on the new sheet and select **Rename...**.

3. In the *Sheet Title* dialog box, set the *Number* to **G-001** and the *Name* to **School Perspective View**.

4. Click **OK**. The sheet updates with the information.

5. In the Project Browser, from the *Coordination>MEP>3D Views* section, drag and drop the **3D - School Perspective View** view onto the upper right side of the sheet, as shown in Figure 13–33.

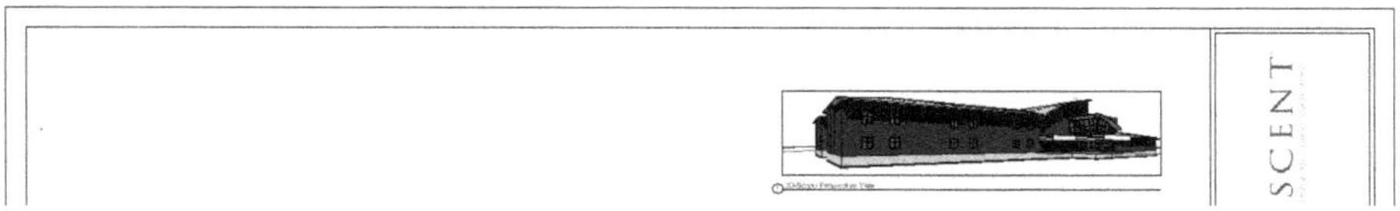

Figure 13–33

6. Select the edge of the viewport. In the Type Selector, select **Viewport: NoTitle**.

7. Double-click inside the viewport; the titleblock grays out and you can modify the actual view.

8. In Properties, in the *Extents* section, clear the check from **Crop Region Visible**. (This could also be done in the View Control Bar.)

9. Double-click outside the viewport to deactivate the view and return to the sheet.

10. Select the perspective view, right-click, and select **Move Aligned to Sheet...**, as shown in Figure 13–34.

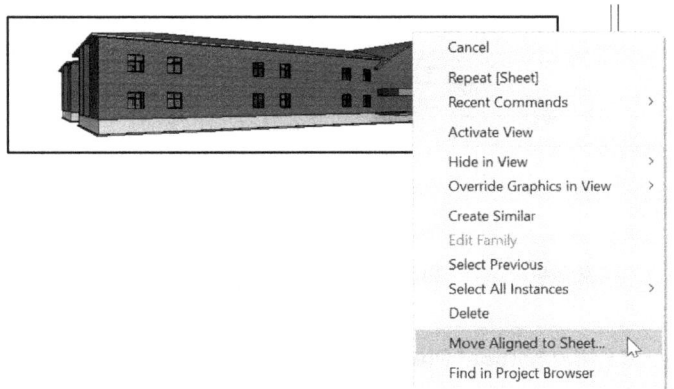

Figure 13–34

11. In the *Select Sheet* dialog box, select **Sheet: CS-000 - Cover Sheet** and click **OK**. The persecutive view is no longer displayed on the sheet.

12. Open the **CS-000 Cover Sheet** and note that the 3D perspective view is now on the sheet in the upper right corner or in the location you placed it on the original sheet.

13. In the Project Browser, right-click on **M-102 - 01 Mechanical Schematic** and select **Duplicate Sheet>Duplicate with Views**, as shown in Figure 13–35.

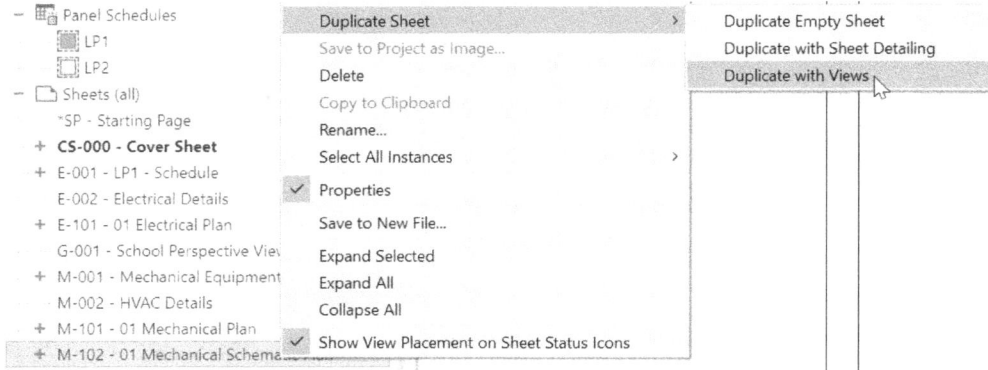

Figure 13–35

14. In the *Duplicate with Views* dialog box, select **Duplicate**.

15. The sheet opens. Note that the new sheet number (in this example **M-103**, as shown in Figure 13–36) follows the sequence from the duplicated sheet (M-102). The sheet name will have **Copy** and a number added after the name, as shown in Figure 13–36.

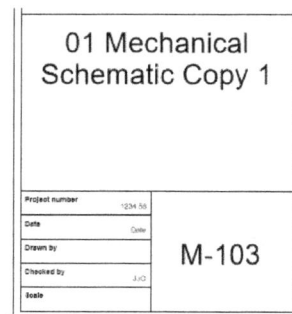

Figure 13–36

Note: You can change the sheet number and name in the title block or by renaming it in the Project Browser.

16. Rename the sheet **01 Mechanical Plan - Area A**.

17. In the Project Browser, in the *Mechanical>HVAC>Floor Plans* section, note that there is now a **01 Mechanical Schematic Copy 1.** This was created when selecting **Duplicate with Views**. Note: This is useful if you need to modify the view but do not want to modify the original view.

18. With sheet **M-103 - 01 Mechanical - Area A** the active view, select the view on the sheet.

19. In the *Modify | Viewports* tab>*Positioning & View* panel, expand the floor plan, as shown in Figure 13–37, and select **Floor Plan : 01 Mechanical Plan - Area A**. The view updates.

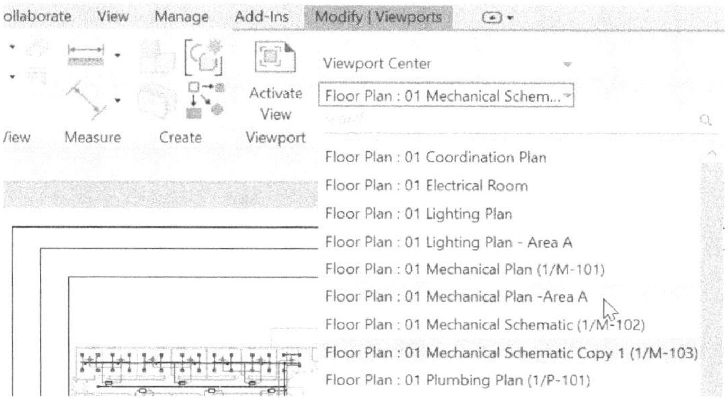

Figure 13–37

20. In the Project Browser, right-click on sheet **E-101 - 01 Electrical Plan** and select **Duplicate Sheet>Duplicate with Views**.

21. In the *Duplicate with Views* dialog box, select **Duplicate as a dependent**.

22. A copy of the 01 Electrical plan sheet opens with a copy of the 01 Electrical Plan view as **01 Lighting Plan - Dependent 1** view.

23. Rename just the sheet name to **01 Electrical North/South Wing Plan**.

24. In the Project Browser, expand **Electrical>Lighting>Floor Plans>01 Lighting Plan** and note that there is a dependent copy of the view. Rename the dependent view to **01 Lighting Plan - North Wing**.

25. Right-click on the **01 Lighting Plan** view and select **Duplicate Views>Duplicate as Dependent**. Create another dependent view of the 01 Lighting Plan view.

26. Name the dependent view **01 Lighting Plan - South Wing**.

27. Open the **01 Lighting Plan - North Wing** view, zoom out to see the crop region (toggle it on, if needed), and resize it to fit the north classroom wing, as shown in Figure 13–38.

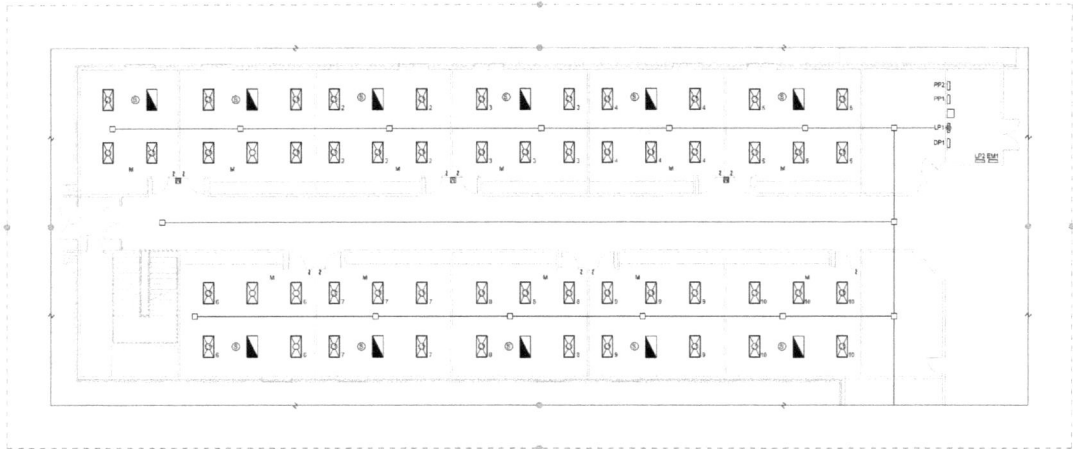

Figure 13–38

28. Toggle the crop region off.

29. Repeat the steps with the **01 Lighting Plan - South Wing** view.

30. Open the **E-102 - 01 Electrical North/South Wing Plan** sheet.

31. Because the view's crop region was adjusted, you now need to adjust the view title. Select just the view title and move the view title closer to the north wing view. Click in an empty area in the view.

32. Select the view. Using the view title grip, drag the view title's extension line in to align with the view.

33. From the Project Browser, drag and drop the **1st Floor Lighting Plan South Wing** view you just created onto the sheet.

34. Save and close the project.

End of practice

13.5 Printing Sheets

With the **Print** command, you can print individual sheets or a list of selected sheets. You can also print an individual view or a portion of a view for check prints or presentations. To open the

Print dialog box (shown in Figure 13–39), in the *File* tab, click ⎙ (Print), or press <Ctrl>+<P>.

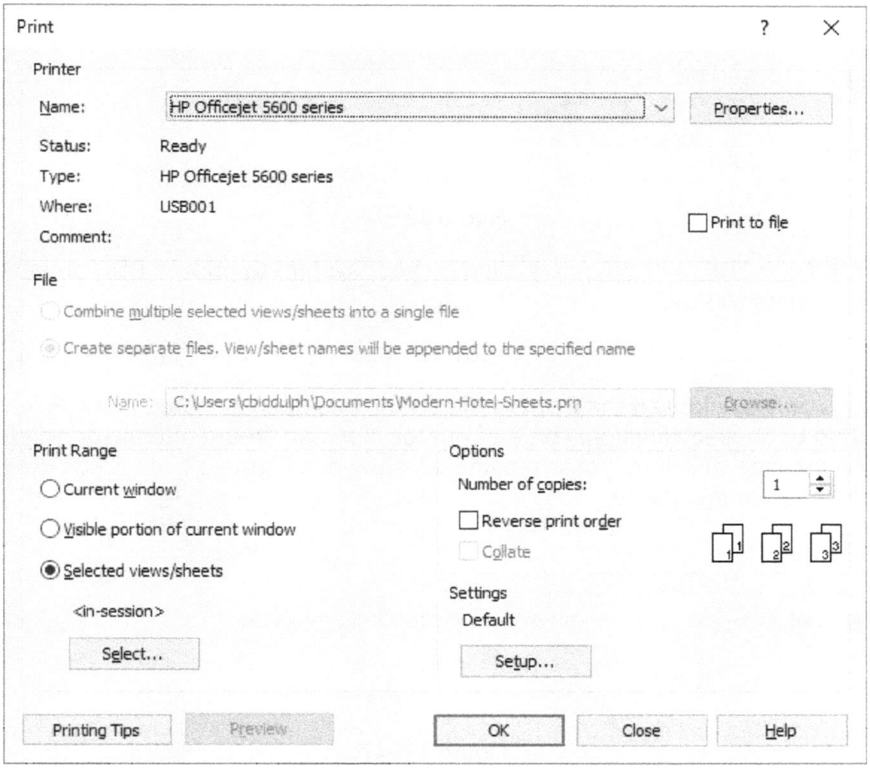

Figure 13–39

Printing Options

The *Print* dialog box is divided into the following areas: *Printer, File, Print Range, Options,* and *Settings.* Modify them as needed to produce the plot you want.

- **Printing Tips:** Opens Autodesk WikiHelp online, in which you can find help with troubleshooting printing issues.

- **Preview:** Opens a preview of the print output so that you can see what is going to be printed.

Printer

Select from the list of available printers, as shown in Figure 13–40. Click **Properties...** to adjust the properties of the selected printer. The options vary according to the printer. Select the **Print to file** option to print to a file rather than directly to a printer. You can create .PLT or .PRN files.

Figure 13–40

- You must have a PDF print driver installed on your system to print to PDF, or you can export views and sheets to PDF.

File

The *File* area is only available if the **Print to file** option has been selected in the *Printer* area or if you are printing to an electronic-only type of printer. You can create one file or multiple files depending on the type of printer you are using, as shown in Figure 13–41. Click **Browse...** to select the file location and name.

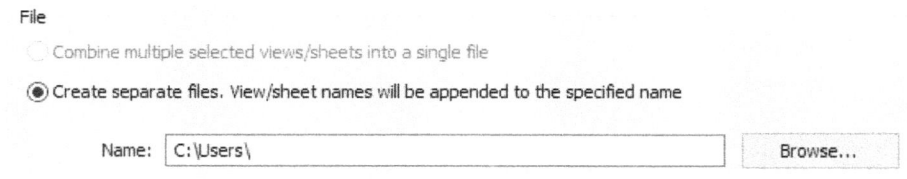

Figure 13–41

Print Range

The *Print Range* area enables you to print individual views/sheets or sets of views/sheets, as shown in Figure 13–42.

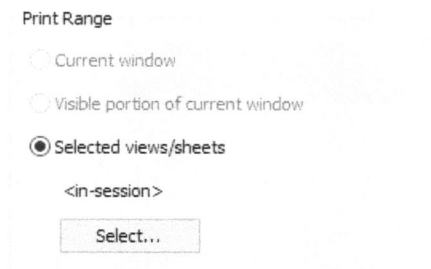

Figure 13–42

- **Current window:** Prints the entire current sheet or view you have open.

- **Visible portion of current window:** Prints only what is displayed in the current sheet or view.

- **Selected views/sheets:** Prints multiple views or sheets. Click **Select...** to open the *Select Views/Sheets* dialog box (shown in Figure 13–43) to choose what to include in the print set. You can save these sets by name so that you can more easily print the same group again.

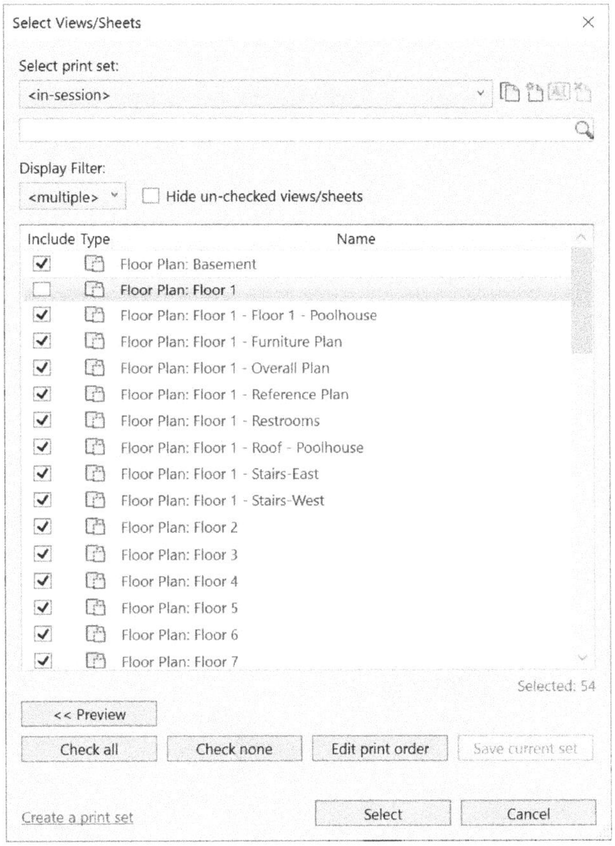

Figure 13–43

- You can edit the selected views and sheets by **Browser organization**, **Sheet Number (Ascending)**, or **Manual order**. If you select **Manual order**, you can drag the views and sheets to put them in a custom order, as shown in Figure 13–44.

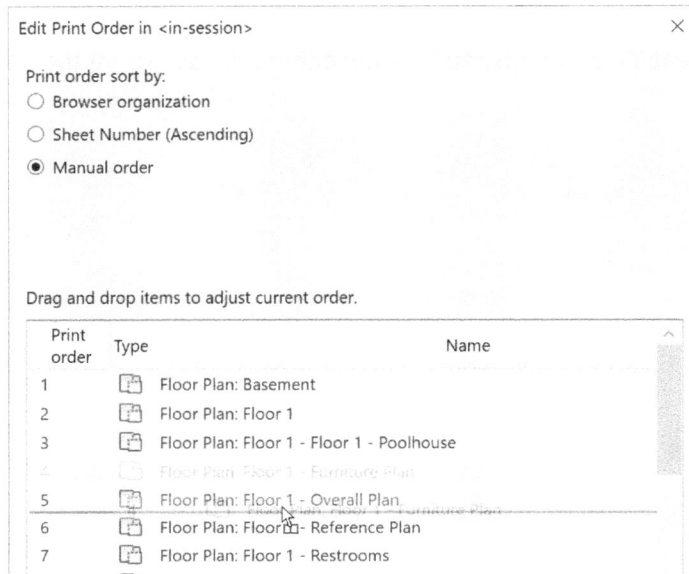

Figure 13–44

Options

If your printer supports multiple copies, you can specify the number in the *Options* area, as shown in Figure 13–45. You can also reverse the print order or collate your prints. These options are also available in the printer properties.

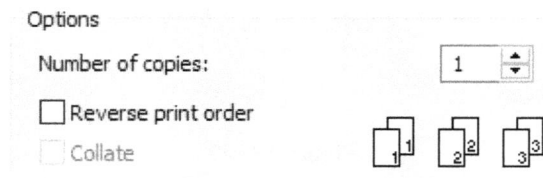

Figure 13–45

Settings

Click **Setup...** to open the *Print Setup* dialog box, as shown in Figure 13–46. Here, you can specify the *Orientation* and *Zoom* settings, among others. You can also save these settings by name.

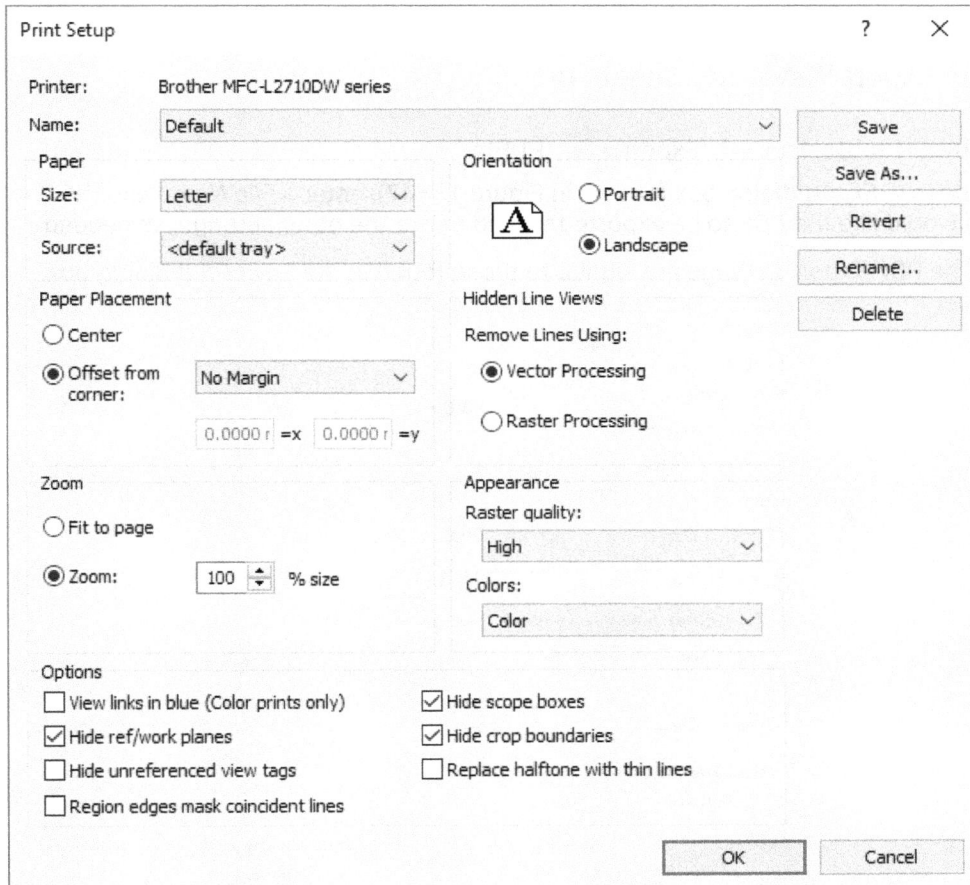

Figure 13–46

- In the *Options* area, specify the types of elements you want to print or not print. Unless specified, all of the elements in a view or sheet print.

- Sheets should always be printed at **Zoom** set to **100%** size unless you are creating a quick markup set that does not need to be exact.

Export Views and Sheets to PDF

If you do not have a PDF driver to utilize in the *Print* dialog box, you can export your views or sheets to PDF. If you set the *Export Range* to **Selected views/sheets**, you have the ability to edit the print order of the views/sheets by **Browser organization**, **Sheet Number (Ascending)**, or **Manual order**.

How To: Export Views and Sheets to PDF

1. In the *File* tab, select ⬆️ (Export)> 📑 (PDF).

2. In the *PDF Export* dialog box (shown in Figure 13–47), enter a *File Name* and the *Location* you would like the PDF to be exported to, and select the other settings, as needed.

   - The PDF Export settings are similar to those found in the Revit *Print* dialog box.

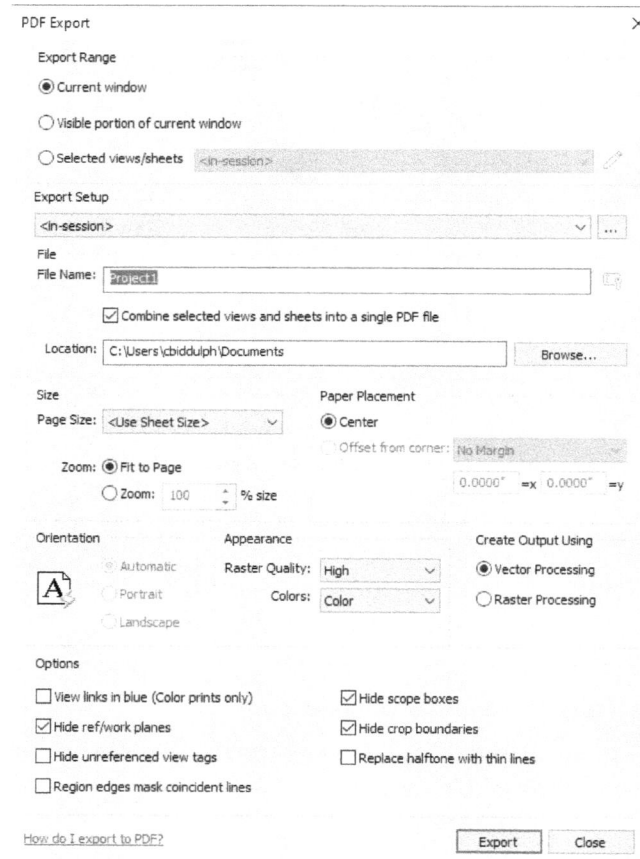

Figure 13–47

3. Click **Export**.

Chapter Review Questions

1. How do you specify the size of a sheet?

    a. In the Sheet Properties, specify the **Sheet Size**.

    b. In the Options Bar, specify the **Sheet Size**.

    c. In the *New Sheet* dialog box, select a title block to control the Sheet Size.

    d. In the Sheet view, right-click and select **Sheet Size**.

2. How is the title block information filled in, as shown in Figure 13–48? (Select all that apply.)

| ASCENT Properties |
| Office Building |

Cover Sheet

Project Number	1234.56
Date	Issue Date
Drawn By	Author
Checked By	Checker

CS000

| Scale | |

Figure 13–48

    a. Select the title block and select the label that you want to change.

    b. Select the title block and modify it in Properties.

    c. Right-click on the sheet in the Project Browser and select **Information**.

    d. Some of the information is filled in automatically from the Project Information.

3. On how many sheets can a floor plan view be placed?

    a. 1

    b. 2-5

    c. 6+

    d. As many as you want

4. Which of the following is the best method to use if the size of a view is too large for a sheet, as shown in Figure 13–49?

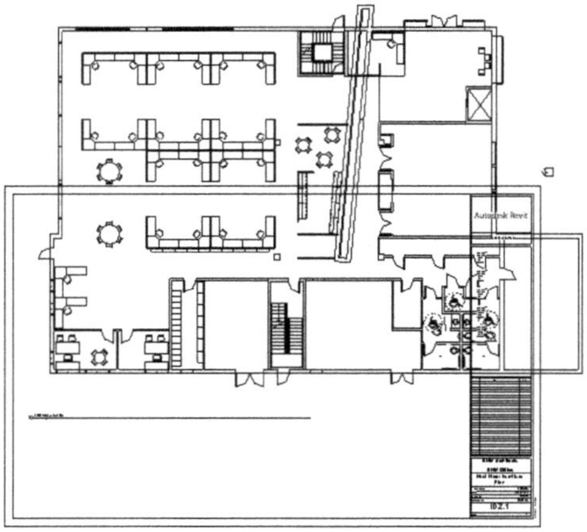

Figure 13–49

   a. Delete the view, change the scale, and place the view back on the sheet.

   b. Change the scale of the sheet.

5. How do you set up a view on a sheet that only displays part of a floor plan?

   a. Drag and drop the view to the sheet and use the crop region to modify it.

   b. Activate the view and rescale it.

   c. Create a callout view displaying the part that you want to use and place the callout view on the sheet.

   d. Open the view in the Project Browser and change the *View Scale*.

6. Images can be placed on sheets.

   a. True

   b. False

7. You can only export sheets to PDF.

   a. True

   b. False

Command Summary

Button	Command	Location
	Activate View	• **Ribbon:** (*select the view*) *Modify	Viewports* tab> *Viewport* panel • **Double-click:** (*in viewport*) • **Right-click:** (*on view*) Activate View
	Deactivate View	• **Ribbon:** *View* tab>*Sheet Composition* panel, expand Viewports • **Double-click:** (*on sheet*) • **Right-click:** (*on view*) Deactivate View
	PDF	• *File* **tab**>Export
	Place View	• **Ribbon:** *View* tab>*Sheet Composition* panel
	Print	• *File* **tab**
	Sheet	• **Ribbon:** *View* tab>*Sheet Composition* panel

Working with Annotations

When you create construction documents, annotations are essential for showing the design intent. Annotations such as dimensions and text can be added to views at any time during the creation of a project. Detail lines and symbols can also be added to views as you create the working drawing, while legends can be created to provide a place to document any symbols that are used in a project.

Learning Objectives

- Add dimensions to the model as a part of the working drawings.
- Add text to a view and use leaders to create notes pointing to a specific part of the model.
- Create text types using different fonts and sizes to suit your company standards.
- Draw detail lines to further enhance the documentation view.
- Add view-specific annotation symbols for added clarity.
- Create legend views and populate them with symbols of elements in the project.

14.1 Working with Dimensions

You can create permanent dimensions using aligned, linear, angular, radial, diameter, and arc length dimensions. These can be individual or a string of dimensions, as shown in Figure 14–1. With aligned dimensions, you can also dimension entire walls with openings, grid lines, and/or intersecting walls.

Figure 14–1

• Dimensions referencing model elements must be added to the model in a view. You can dimension on sheets, but only to items added directly on the sheets.

• Dimensions are available in the *Annotate* tab>*Dimension* panel (shown in Figure 14–2) and in the *Modify* tab>*Measure* panel.

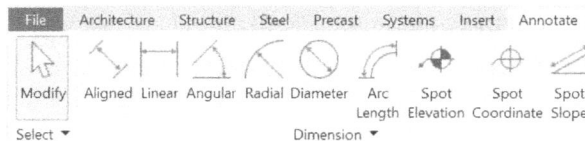

Figure 14–2

> **Note:** ↖ *(Aligned) is also located in the Quick Access Toolbar.*

• Dimensions can be added to isometric 3D views whether they are locked or not. Proceed with caution when selecting the items to dimension. You can set the work plane or use <Tab> to cycle through elements.

• Ensure that the witness lines and text orientation is snapping to and extending in the correct direction as intended.

How To: Add Aligned Dimensions with Options

1. Start the ⟋ (Aligned) command or type **DI**.

2. In the Type Selector, select a dimension style.

3. In the Options Bar, select the location line of the wall to dimension from, as shown in Figure 14–3. This option can be changed as you add dimensions.

Figure 14–3

*   Most MEP fixtures have alignment lines along their centerline. You can also dimension to individual parts of components, as shown in Figure 14–4.

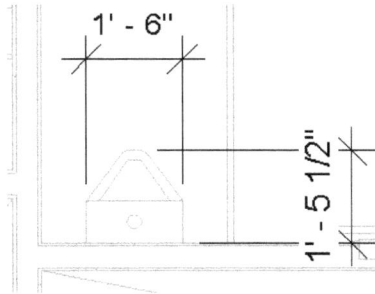

Figure 14–4

4. In the Options Bar, select your preference from the *Pick:* drop-down list:

*   **Individual References:** Select the elements in order (as shown in Figure 14–5) and then click in an empty space in the view to position the dimension string.

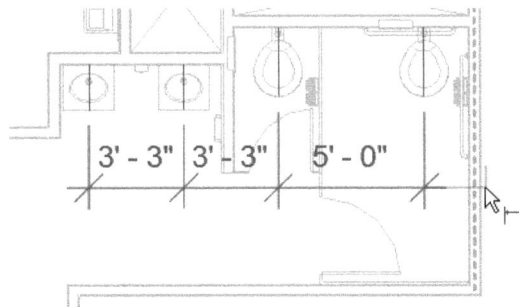

Figure 14–5

How To: Add Other Types of Dimensions

1. In the *Annotate* tab>*Dimension* panel, select one of the following dimension methods:

	Aligned	Most commonly used dimension type. Select individual elements or entire walls to dimension.
	Linear	Used when you need to specify certain points on elements.
	Angular	Used to dimension the angle between two elements.
	Radial	Used to dimension the radius of circular elements.
	Diameter	Used to dimension the diameter of circular elements.
	Arc Length	Used to dimension the length of the arc of circular elements.

    Note: The dimension methods are also accessible in the Modify | Place Dimensions tab>Dimension panel when any of the dimension commands are active.

2. In the Type Selector, select the dimension type.

3. Follow the prompts for the selected method.

Modifying Dimensions

When you move elements that are dimensioned (e.g., a wall), the dimensions automatically update. You can also modify dimensions by selecting a dimension or dimension string and making changes. Figure 14–6 shows the various parts of dimensions that aid in modifying.

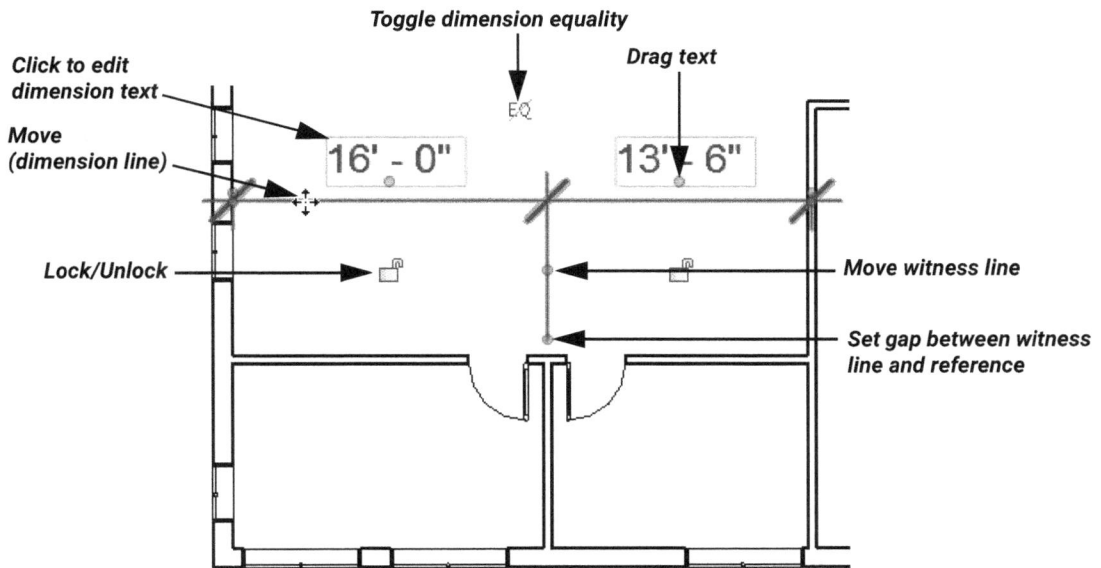

Figure 14-6

- To move the dimension text, select the **Drag text** control under the text and drag it to a new location. It automatically creates a leader from the dimension line if you drag it away. The style of the leader (arc or line) depends on the dimension style.

- To move the dimension line (the line parallel to the element being dimensioned), simply drag the line to a new location, or select the dimension and drag the ⊹ (Drag to new position) control.

- To change the gap between the witness line and the element being dimensioned, drag the control at the end of the witness line.

- To move the witness line (the line perpendicular to the element being dimensioned) to a different element or face of a wall, use the **Move Witness Line** control in the middle of the witness line. While moving the witness line, you can hover your cursor over a element or component and press <Tab> repeatedly to cycle through the various options. You can also drag this control to move the witness line to a different element, or right-click on the control and select **Move Witness Line**.

Adding and Deleting Dimensions in a String

* To add a witness line to a string of dimensions, select the dimension and, in the *Modify |*

  Dimensions tab>*Witness Lines* panel, click ⊢⊦ (Edit Witness Lines). Select the element(s) you want to add to the dimension, as shown in Figure 14–7. Click in an empty space in the view to finish.

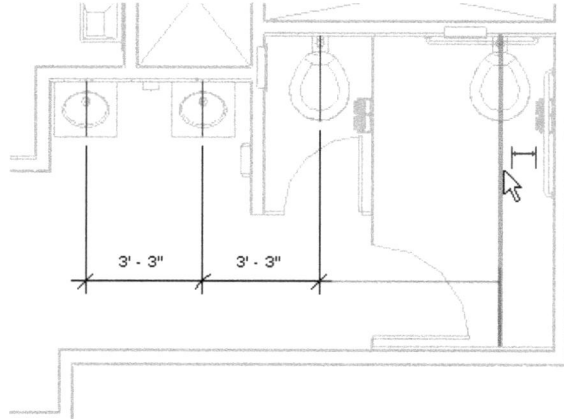

Figure 14–7

* To delete a witness line, drag the **Move Witness Line** control to a nearby witness line's element. Alternatively, you can hover the cursor over the control, right-click, and select **Delete Witness Line**.

* To delete one dimension in a string and break the string into two separate dimensions, select the string, hover your cursor over the dimension that you want to delete, and press <Tab>. When it highlights (as shown on the left in Figure 14–8), pick it and press <Delete>. The selected dimension is deleted and the dimension string is separated into two elements, as shown on the right in Figure 14–8.

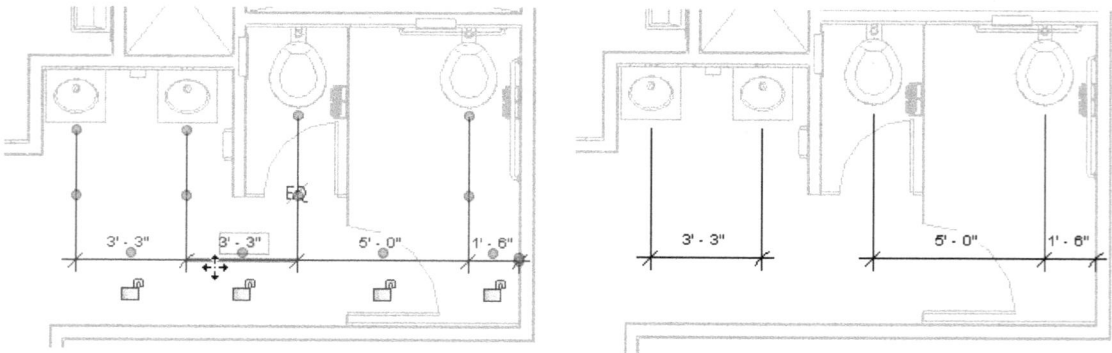

Figure 14–8

Modifying the Dimension Text

Because Revit is parametric, changing the dimension text without changing the elements dimensioned would cause problems throughout the project. These issues could cause problems beyond the model if you use the project model to estimate materials or work with other disciplines.

You can append the existing dimension text with prefixes and suffixes (as shown in Figure 14–9), or create a dimension style that has a prefix or suffix preset in the type properties. This can help you in renovation projects.

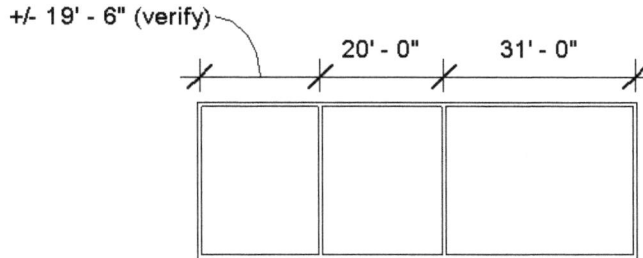

Figure 14–9

Double-click on the dimension text to open the *Dimension Text* dialog box, as shown in Figure 14–10, and make modifications as needed.

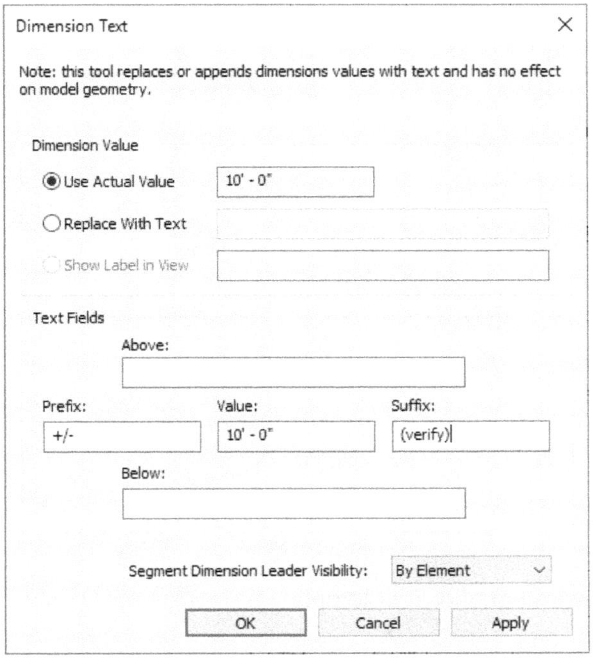

Figure 14–10

💡 Hint: Multiple Dimension Options

If you are creating details that show one element with multiple dimension values, as shown in Figure 14–11, you can easily modify the dimension text.

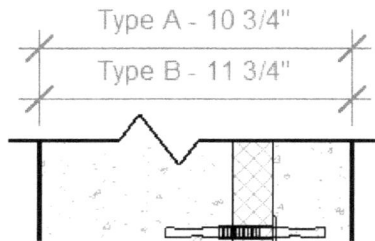

Figure 14–11

Select the dimension and then the dimension text. The *Dimension Text* dialog box opens. You can replace the text, as shown in Figure 14–12, or add text fields above or below, as well as a prefix or suffix.

Figure 14–12

- This also works with Equality Text Labels.

If you find that you are always modifying dimensions manually, you can create a type-driven dimension style by duplicating the dimension style and specifying a set prefix and suffix within the type parameters, as shown in Figure 14–13.

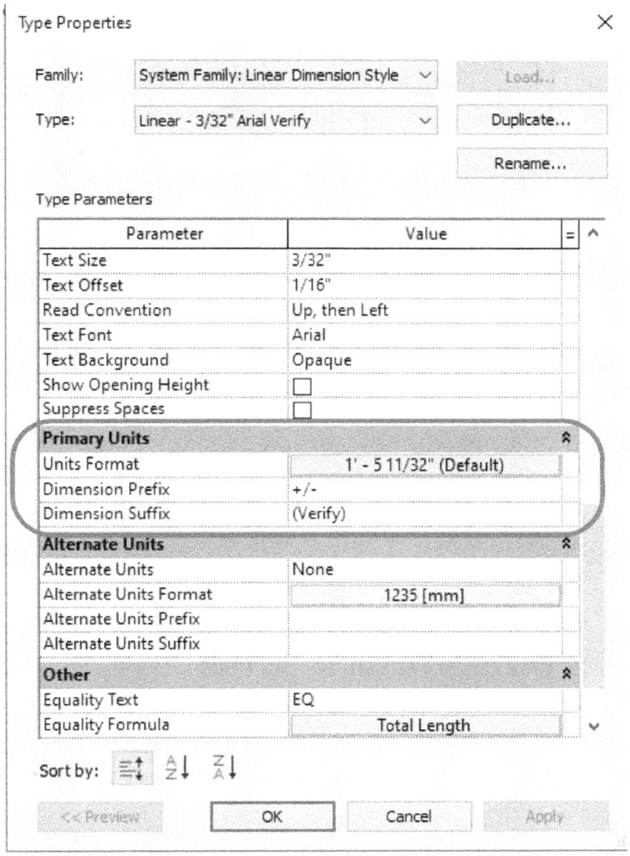

Figure 14–13

This eliminates the need to manually modify the dimension every time you need to add a prefix or suffix.

Setting Constraints

The three types of constraints that work with dimensions are locks and equal settings, as shown in Figure 14–14, as well as labels.

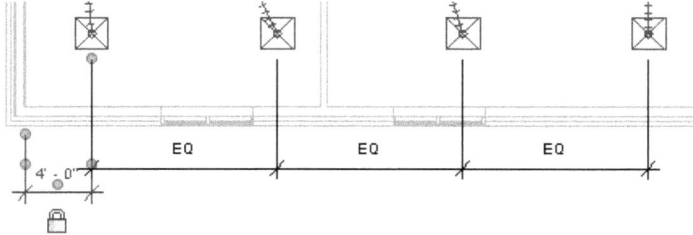

Figure 14–14

Locking Dimensions

When you lock a dimension, the value is set and you cannot make a change between it and the referenced elements. If it is unlocked, you can move it and change its value.

- Note that when you use this and move an element, any elements that are locked to the dimension also move.

Setting Dimensions Equal

For a string of dimensions, select the **EQ** symbol to constrain the elements to be at an equal distance apart. This actually moves the elements that are dimensioned.

- The equality text display can be changed in Properties, as shown in Figure 14–15. The style for each of the display types is set in the dimension type.

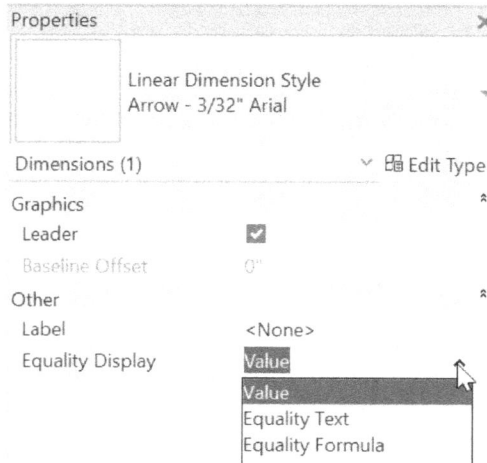

Figure 14–15

Labeling Dimensions

If you have a distance that needs to be repeated multiple times, such as the *Wall to AT* label shown in Figure 14–16, or one where you want to use a formula based on another dimension, you can create and apply a global parameter, also called a label, to the dimension.

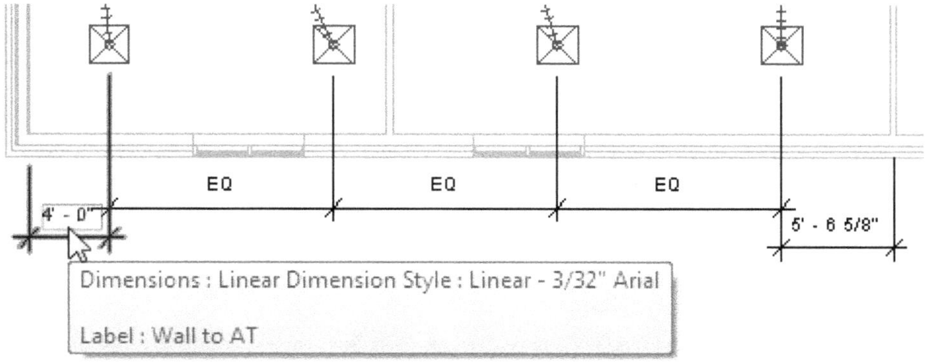

Figure 14–16

- To apply an existing label to a dimension, select the dimension and in the *Modify | Dimensions* tab>*Label Dimension* panel, select the label in the drop-down list, as shown in Figure 14–17.

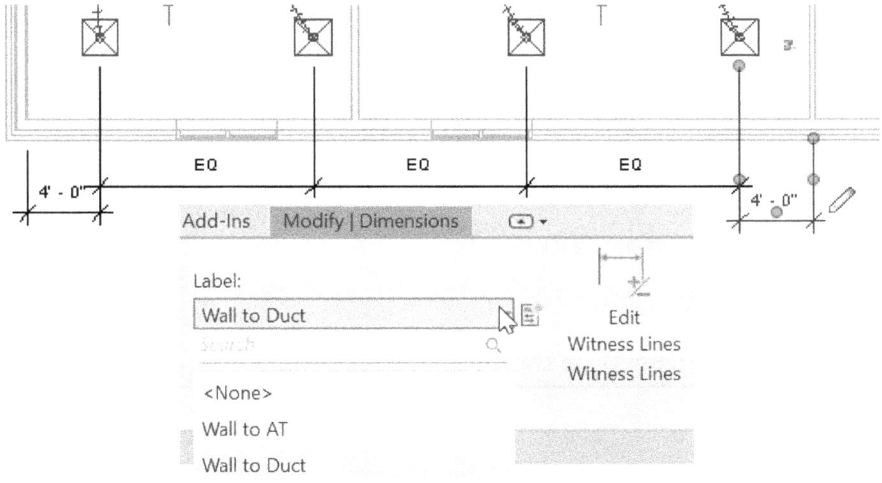

Figure 14–17

How To: Create a Label

1. Select a dimension.
2. In the *Modify | Dimensions* tab>*Label Dimension* panel, click 🖹 (Create Parameter).
3. In the *Global Parameter Properties* dialog box, type in a *Name*, as shown in Figure 14–18, and click **OK**.

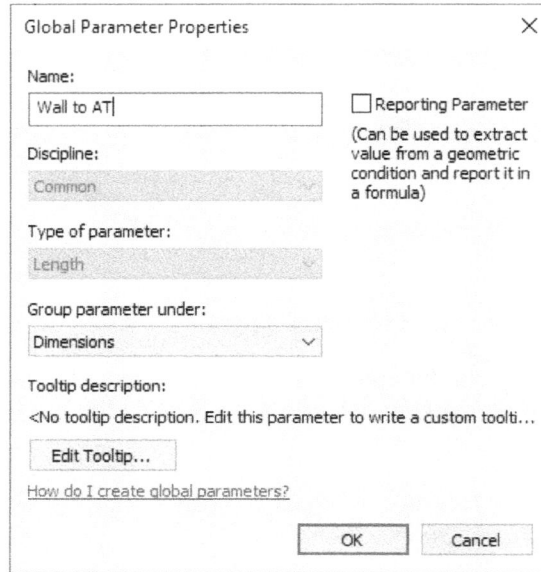

Figure 14–18

4. The label is applied to the dimension.

How To: Edit the Label Information

1. Select a labeled dimension.
2. Click ✐ (Global Parameters), as shown in Figure 14–19.

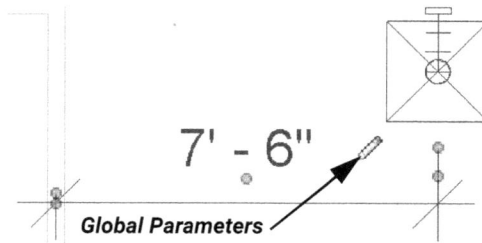

Figure 14–19

3. In the *Global Parameters* dialog box, in the *Value* column, type the new distance, as shown in Figure 14–20.

Figure 14–20

4. Click **OK**. The selected dimension and any other dimensions using the same label are updated.

* You can also edit, create, and delete global parameters in this dialog box.

Working with Constraints

To find out which elements have constraints applied to them, in the View Control Bar, click

(Reveal Constraints). Constraints display as shown in Figure 14–21.

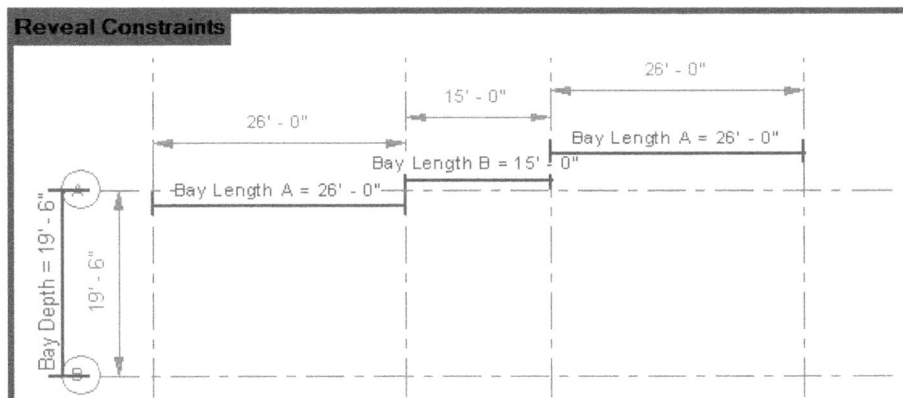

Figure 14–21

- If you try to move the element beyond the appropriate constraints, a warning dialog box displays, as shown in Figure 14–22.

Figure 14–22

- If you delete dimensions that are constrained, a warning dialog box displays, as shown in Figure 14–23. Click **OK** to retain the constraint or click **Unconstrain** to remove the constraint.

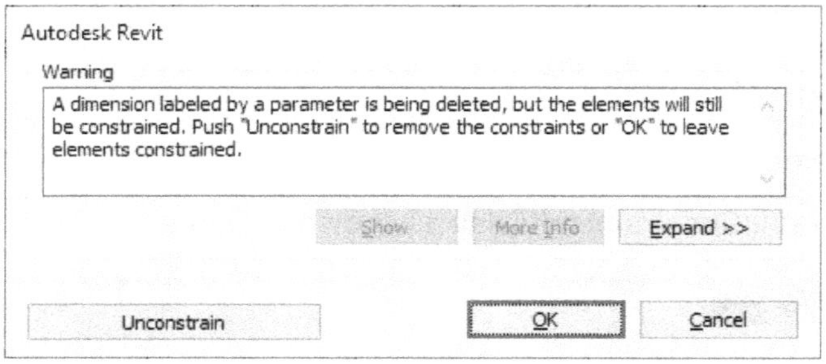

Figure 14–23

Practice 14a
Work with Dimensions – Mechanical

Practice Objectives

- Add a string of dimensions.
- Modify the dimension string.

In this practice, you will add and modify dimensions for a mechanical floor plan view.

1. In the practice files *Working Models>Mechanical* folder, open **Mech-Dimensions.rvt**.
2. Open the Mechanical>HVAC>Floor Plans>**01 Mechanical Plan** view and zoom in on the upper-left corner of the north wing.
3. In the *Annotate* tab>*Dimension* panel, click (Aligned).
4. In the Options Bar, verify that the **Wall centerlines** option is selected.
5. Dimension the first four duct branches (not the diffusers or the flex duct), starting from the left side wall to the rightmost branch in the two rooms, as shown in Figure 14–24.

   - Hint: While dimensioning, press <Tab> to select the center of the duct branches.

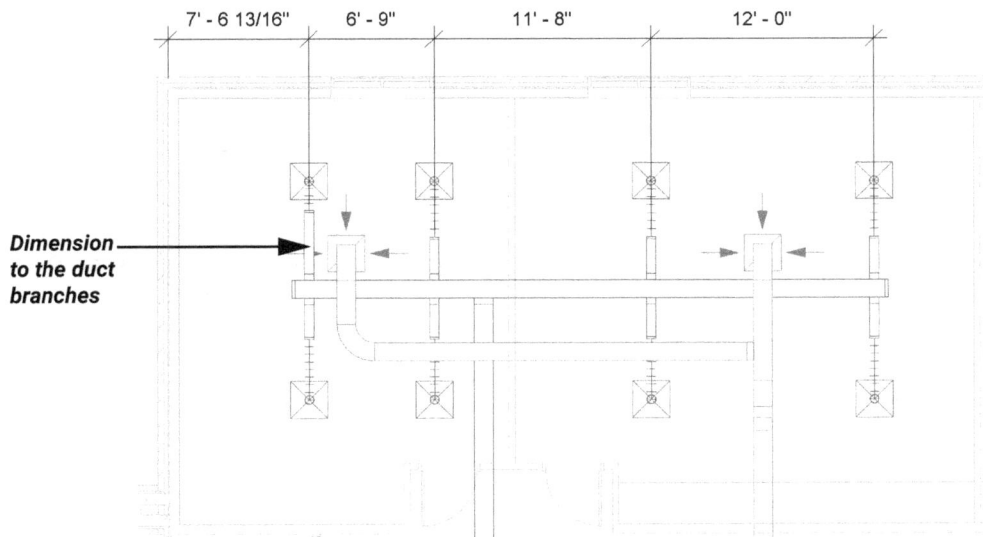

Figure 14–24

6. Click (Modify).

7. Select the dimension, then select the **Move Witness Line** control on the far left, as shown in Figure 14–25.

8. Drag the control towards the interior side of the wall and press <Tab>. When the inside of the wall highlights, release the left mouse button to place the witness line, as shown in Figure 14–26.

Figure 14–25   Figure 14–26

9. Click ⯎ (Modify).

10. Select the far right duct branch, as shown in Figure 14–27.

11. The corresponding dimension text turns blue. Select the dimension and change its value from **12'** to **10'**. The duct branch and the flex ductwork move accordingly, but the air terminal maintains its original position, as shown in Figure 14–27.

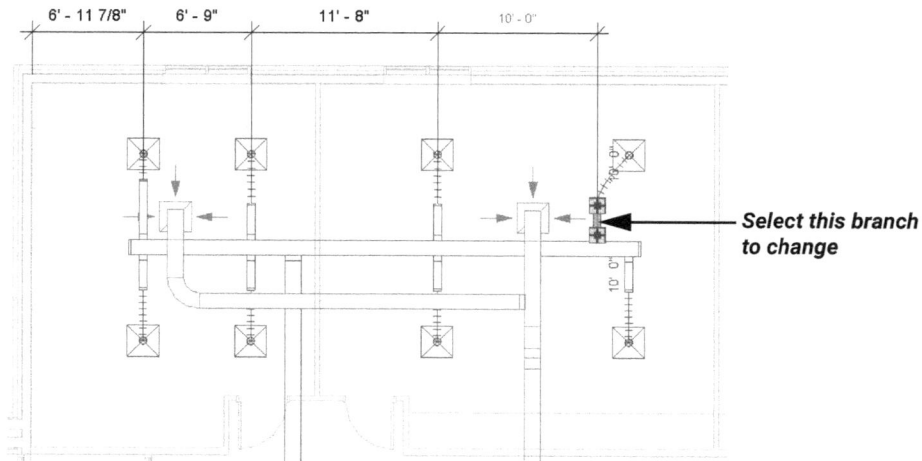

Figure 14–27

12. Click ⯎ (Modify) and select the dimension line.

13. In the *Modify | Dimensions* tab>*Witness Lines* panel, click ⊢₌ (Edit Witness Lines).

14. Select the center of the wall to add a fifth dimension to the string of dimensions. Click in an empty space in the view away from any objects to place the new dimension. Figure 14–28 shows the new dimension added to the dimension string. Add more dimensions, as needed.

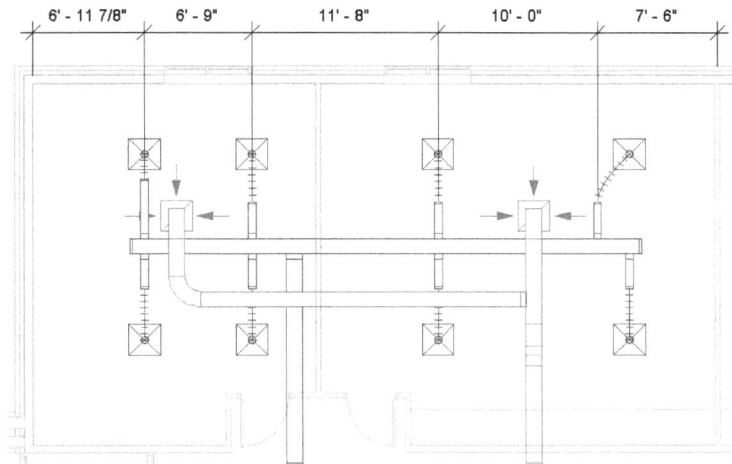

Figure 14–28

15. Click ⌖ (Modify).

16. Save and close the project.

End of practice

Practice 14b
Work with Dimensions – Electrical

Practice Objectives

* Add a string of dimensions.
* Modify the dimension string.

In this practice, you will add and modify dimensions.

1. In the practice files *Working Models>Electrical* folder, open **Elec-Dimensions.rvt**.

2. Open the Electrical>Power>Floor Plans>**01 Power Plan** view and zoom in on the upper-left corner of the north wing.

3. In the *Annotate* tab>*Dimension* panel, click ⟍ (Aligned).

4. In the Options Bar, verify that the **Wall centerlines** option is selected.

5. Dimension the location of the receptacles at their connection points in the first two classrooms, starting from the left side wall and including the other walls, as shown in Figure 14–29.

Figure 14–29

6. Select the **Move Witness Line** control on the far left, as shown in Figure 14–30.

7. Drag the control towards the interior side of the wall and press <Tab>. When the inside of the wall highlights, release the left mouse button to place the witness line, as shown in Figure 14–31.

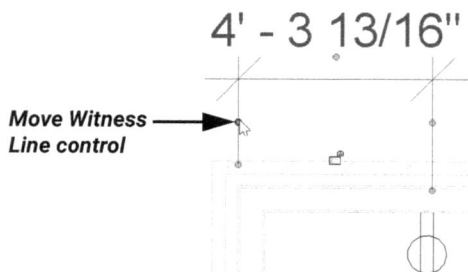

Figure 14–30

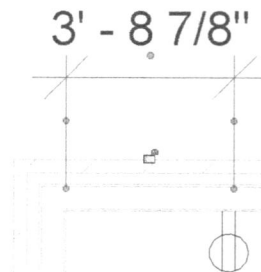

Figure 14–31

8. Repeat the process and move the witness lines at the center of the interior walls to the left side of the walls.

9. In the *Modify | Dimensions* tab>*Witness Lines* panel, click ⊢⊣⁒ (Edit Witness Lines).

10. Add another dimension to the right side of both interior walls (press <Tab> to select the outer edge rather than the default alignment of center), as shown for the second wall in Figure 14–32. Click in an empty space in the view away from any objects to add the new dimension.

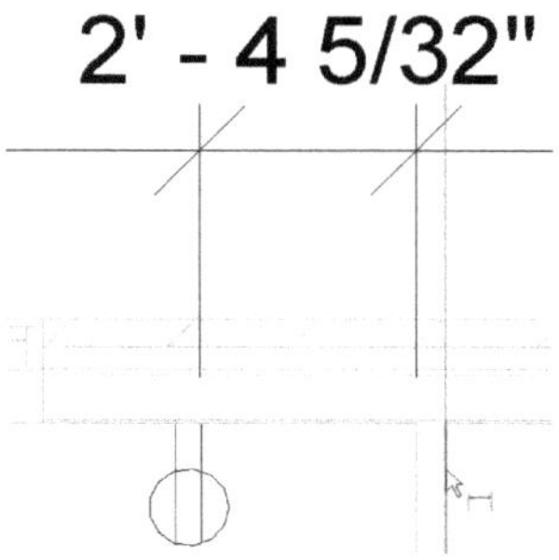

Figure 14–32

11. Select the dimension string and click and drag the **Drag Text** control to move some of the text so you can read each number. Figure 14–33 shows the overlapping dimensions dragged up above the dimension line.

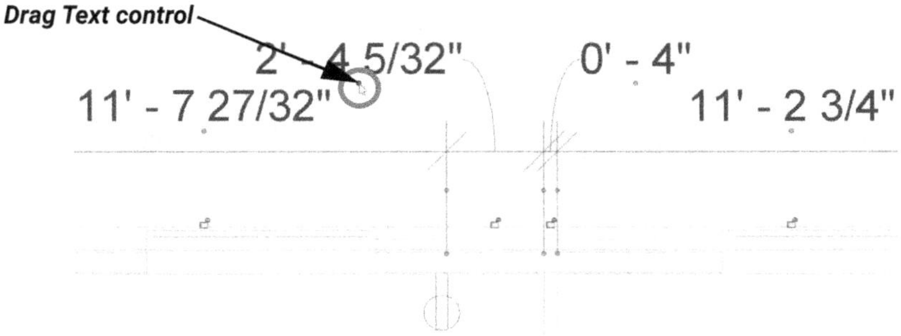

Figure 14–33

12. Click ⬚ (Modify).

13. Select one of the receptacles. The corresponding dimension text turns blue. Select the dimension and change its value to **3'-6"**, as shown in Figure 14–34. The receptacle moves.

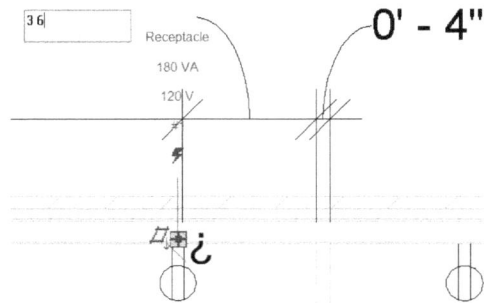

Figure 14–34

14. Click in an empty area in the view to release the selection.

15. Make any other changes to the dimensions that you may want, as shown in Figure 14–35.

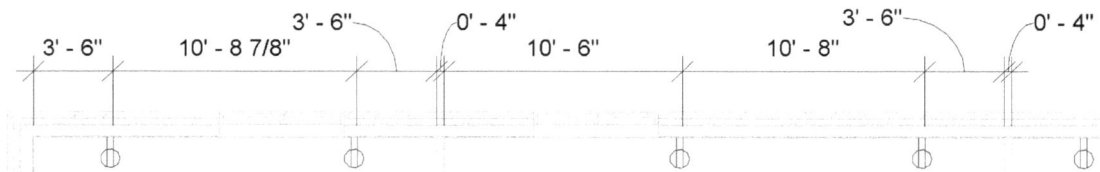

Figure 14–35

16. Save and close the project.

End of practice

Practice 14c
Work with Dimensions – Plumbing

Practice Objectives

- Add a string of dimensions.
- Modify the dimension string.

In this practice, you will add and modify dimensions.

1. In the practice files *Working Models>Plumbing* folder, open **Plumb-Dimensions.rvt**.
2. Open the Plumbing>Plumbing>Floor Plans>**01 Plumbing Plan** view and zoom in on one of the restrooms near the gym.
3. In the *Annotate* tab>*Dimension* panel, click ⟋ (Aligned).
4. In the Options Bar, verify that the **Wall centerlines** is selected.
5. Dimension the location of the center of the lavatories, as shown in Figure 14–36.

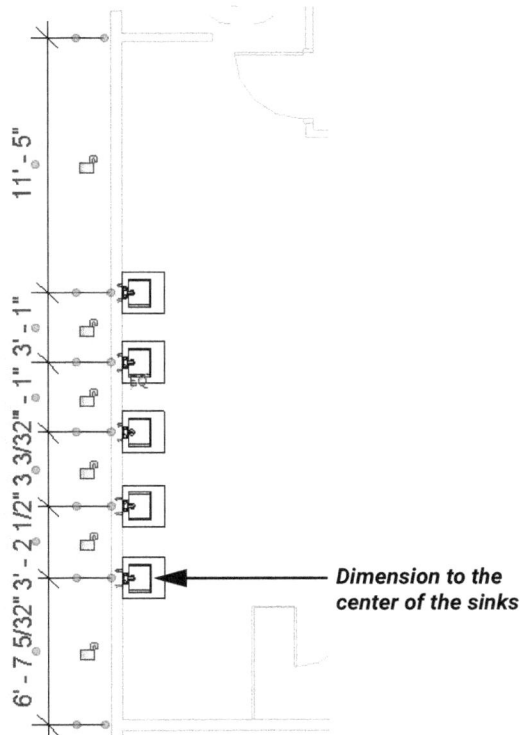

Figure 14–36

6. Select the **Move Witness Line** control (shown in Figure 14–37) on the dimension that is dimensioning to the center of the wall.

7. Drag the control towards the interior side of the wall and press <Tab>. When the inside of the wall highlights, release the left mouse button to place the witness line, as shown in Figure 14–38.

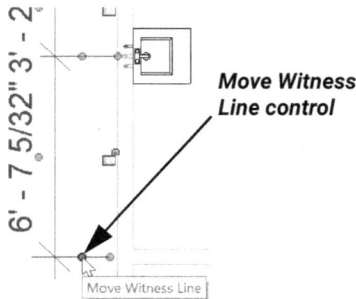

Move Witness Line control

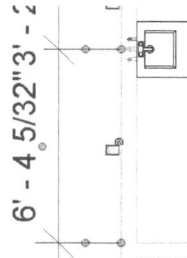

Figure 14–37   **Figure 14–38**

8. Click (Modify) and select the top lavatory closest to the restroom exit.

9. The corresponding dimension text turns blue. Select the dimension text and change its value to **4'-0"**. You get an error that the family is connected to a network, as shown in Figure 14–39. Click **Cancel**.

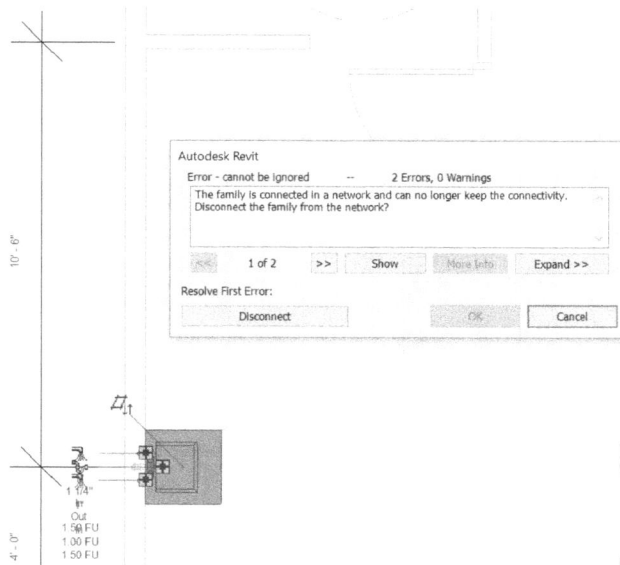

Figure 14–39

• Note that it is not advisable to modify the location of fixtures once you have connected piping to them.

10. Select the dimension string and click and drag the **Drag Text** control to move some of the text so you can read each number. Figure 14–40 shows the overlapping dimensions dragged up above the dimension line.

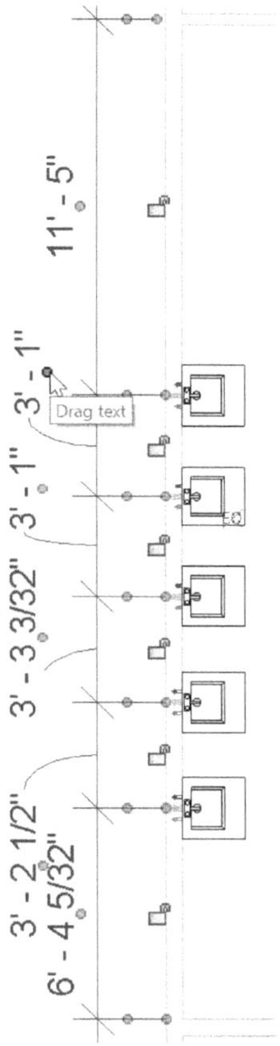

Figure 14–40

11. Save and close the project.

End of practice

14.2 Working with Text

The **Text** command enables you to add notes to views or sheets, such as the detail shown in Figure 14–41. The same command is used to create text with or without leaders.

1. All ductwork shown on plans shall be concealed above ceiling or in walls unless noted otherwise.
2. All duct dimensions are in inches and are inside clear.
3. All branch duct runouts to diffusers shall be full connection size of diffuser, unless noted otherwise.

Figure 14–41

The text height is automatically set by the text type in conjunction with the scale of the view (as shown in Figure 14–42, using the same size text type at two different scales). Text types display at the specified height, both in the views and on the sheet.

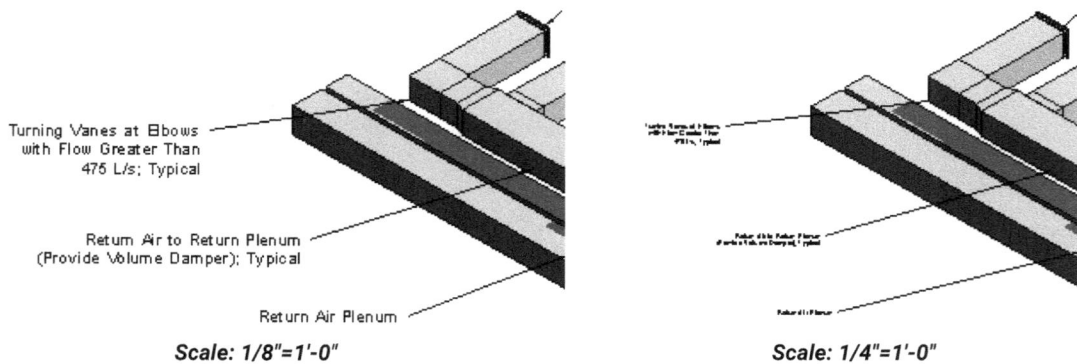

Turning Vanes at Elbows with Flow Greater Than 475 L/s; Typical

Return Air to Return Plenum (Provide Volume Damper); Typical

Return Air Plenum

Scale: 1/8"=1'-0"

Scale: 1/4"=1'-0"

Figure 14–42

How To: Add Text

1. In the *Annotate* tab>*Text* panel, click A (Text).

2. In the Type Selector, set the text type.

   Note: *The text type sets the font and height of the text.*

3. In the *Modify | Place Text* tab>*Leader* panel, select the method you want to use: A (No Leader), $\leftarrow A$ (One Segment), $\llcorner A$ (Two Segments), or $\int A$ (Curved).

4. In the *Alignment* panel, set the overall justification for the text and leader, as shown in Figure 14–43.

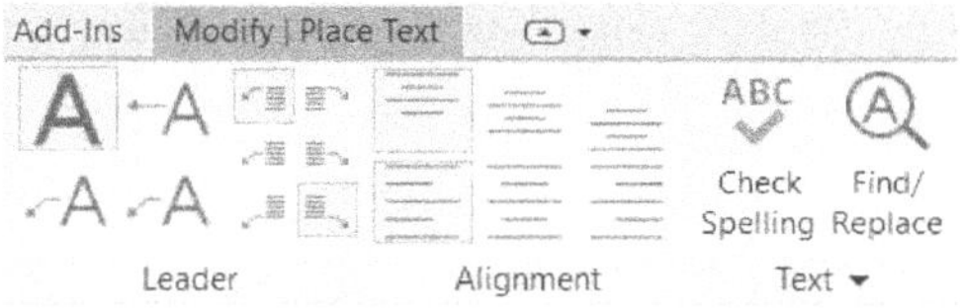

Figure 14–43

5. Select the location for the leader and text.

   - Use alignment lines to help you align the text with other text elements.
   - If **No leader** is selected, select the start point for the text and begin typing.
   - If using a leader, the first point places the arrow and you then select points for the leader. The text starts at the last leader point.
   - To set a word wrapping distance, click and drag the circle grip controls to set the start and end points of the text.

6. Type the needed text. In the *Edit Text* tab, specify additional options for the font and paragraph, as shown in Figure 14–44.

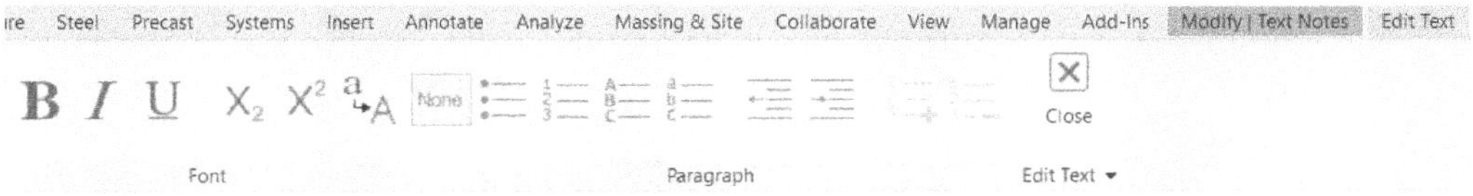

Figure 14–44

7. In the *Edit Text* tab>*Edit Text* panel, click $\boxed{\times}$ (Close) or click outside the text box to complete the text element.

   - Pressing <Enter> after a line of text starts a new line of text in the same text window.

How To: Add Text Symbols

1. Start the **Text** command and click to place the text.

2. As you are typing text and need to insert a symbol, right-click and select **Symbols** from the shortcut menu. Select from the list of commonly used symbols, as shown in Figure 14–45.

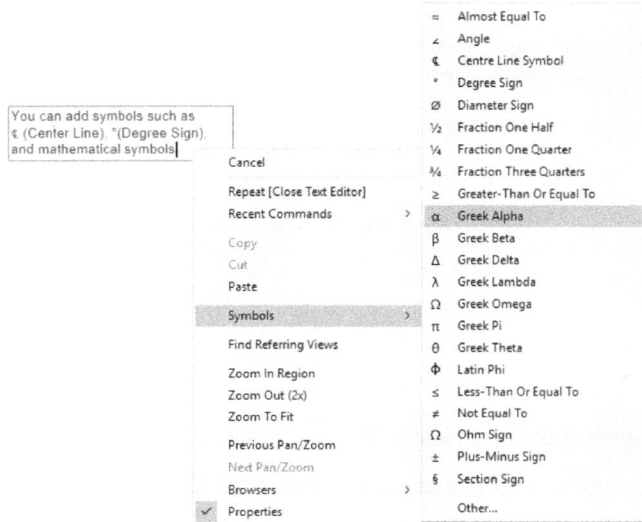

Figure 14–45

3. If the symbol you need is not listed, click **Other...**.

4. In the *Character Map* dialog box, click on a symbol and click **Select**, as shown in Figure 14–46.

Figure 14–46

5. Click **Copy** to copy the character to the clipboard and paste it into the text box.

•   The font in the Character Map should match the font used by the text type. You do not want to use a different font for symbols.

Modifying Text

After you have added text notes, you can begin editing. You can edit text notes to have leaders, change the text style that is being used, and change the positioning.

•   You can modify the text note, including the **Leader** and **Paragraph** styles.

•   You can edit the text, including changes to individual letters, words, and paragraphs in the text note.

•   You can modify all text notes in a view so that they all align either left (as shown on the left in Figure 14–47), right, top, bottom, middle, or center justified within the text note bounding box, as well as distributing the text notes horizontally or vertically between all the text. These tools are also available for aligning tags and keynotes.

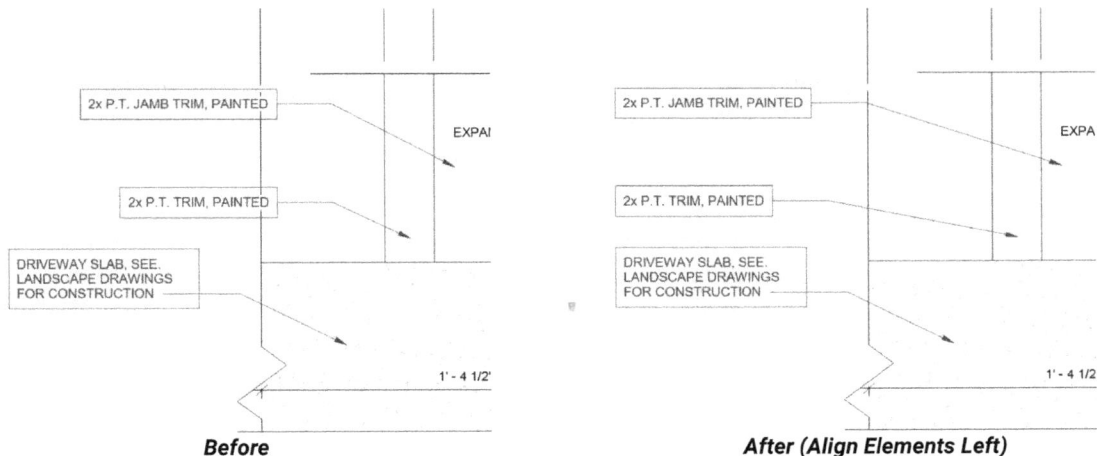

Before   *After (Align Elements Left)*

Figure 14–47

Modifying the Text Note Using Controls

Click once on the text note to modify the text box and leaders using controls, as shown in Figure 14–48, or using the tools in the *Modify | Text Notes* tab.

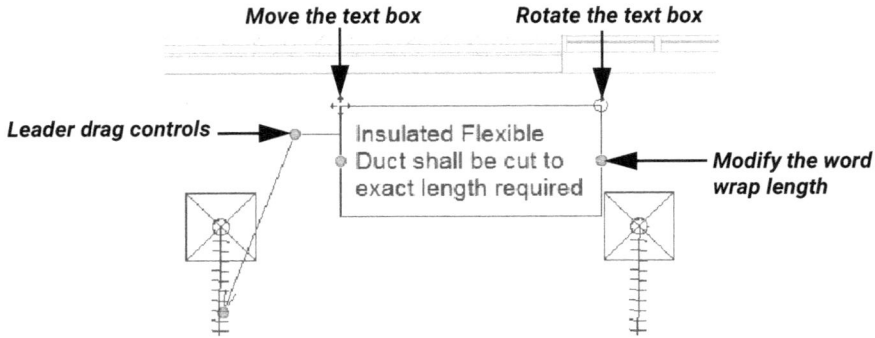

Figure 14–48

How To: Add a Leader to Text Notes

1. Select the text note.

2. In the *Modify | Text Notes* tab>*Leader* panel, select the direction and justification for the new leader, as shown in Figure 14–49.

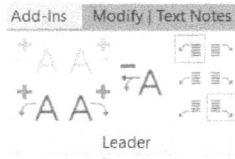

Figure 14–49

3. The leader is applied, as shown in Figure 14–50. Use the drag controls to place the arrow as needed.

Figure 14–50

*   You can remove leaders by clicking ⃠A (Remove Last Leader).

Editing the Text

The *Edit Text* tab enables you to make various customizations. These include modifying the font of selected words as well as creating bulleted and numbered lists, as shown in Figure 14–51.

General Notes
1. Notify designer of intention to start construction at least 10 days prior to start of site work.
2. Installer shall provide the following:
   • 24-hour notice of start of construction
   • Inspection of bottom of bed or covering required by state inspector
   • All environmental management inspection sheets must be emailed to designer's office within 24 hours of inspection.

Figure 14–51

• You can **Cut**, **Copy,** and **Paste** text using the clipboard. For example, you can copy text from a document and then paste it into the text editor in Revit.

• To help you see the text better as you are modifying it, in the *Edit Text* tab, expand the *Edit Text* panel and select one or both of the options, as shown in Figure 14–52.

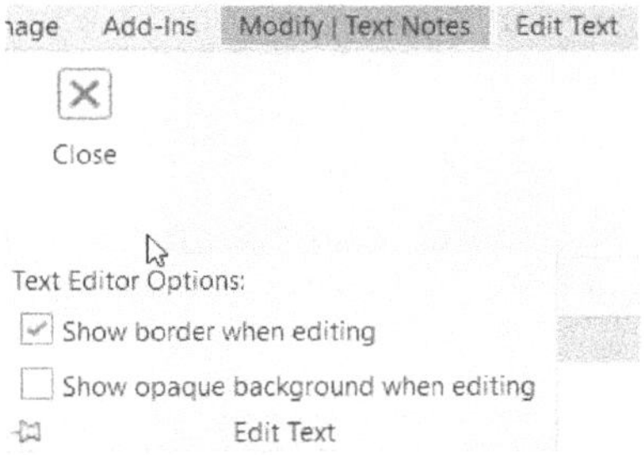

Figure 14–52

How To: Modify the Font

1. Select individual letters or words.

2. Click on the font modification you want to include:

   • **B** (Bold)   • X_2 (Subscript)

   • *I* (Italic)   • X^2 (Superscript)

   • U̲ (Underline)   • $^a_↳A$ (All Caps)

• When pasting text from a document outside of Revit, font modifications (e.g, Bold, Italic, etc.) are retained.

How To: Create Lists

1. In Edit Text mode, place the cursor in the line where you want to add to a list.

2. In the *Edit Text* tab>*Paragraph* panel, click the type of list you want to create:

   - ☰ (Bullets)   - ☰ (Uppercase Letters)

   - ☰ (Numbers)   - ☰ (Lowercase Letters)

3. As you type, press <Enter> and the next line in the list is incremented.

   Note: If you do not want a line to be a part of the list, select the line and click None *(None) on the Paragraph panel.*

4. To include sub-lists, at the beginning of the next line, click ☰ (Increase Indent) or press <Tab>. This indents the line and applies the next level of lists, as shown in Figure 14–53.

> 4. The applicant shall be responsible:
>   A. First Indent
>   a. Second Indent
>   • Third Indent

Figure 14–53

Note: The indent distance is set up by the text type Tab Size.

   - You can change the type of list after you have applied the first increment. For example, you might want to use a list of bullets instead of letters, as shown in Figure 14–54.

5. Click ☰ (Decrease Indent) or press <Shift>+<Tab> to return to the previous list style.

- Press <Shift>+<Enter> to create a blank line in a numbered list.

- To create columns or other separate text boxes that build on a numbering system (as shown in Figure 14–54), create the second text box and list, then place the cursor on one of the lines and in the *Paragraph* panel, click (Increment List Value) until the list matches the next number in the sequence.

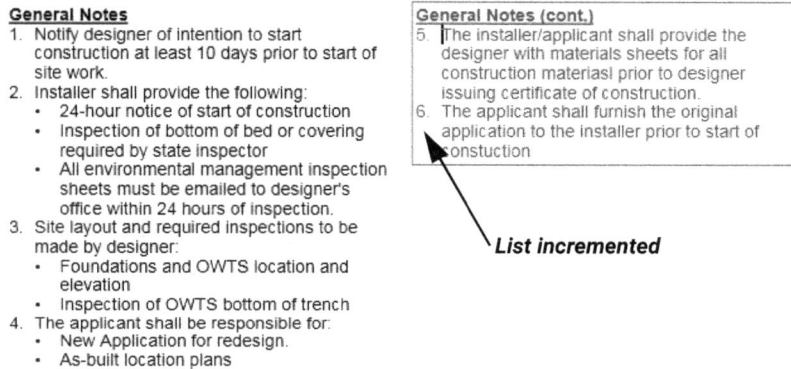

General Notes
1. Notify designer of intention to start construction at least 10 days prior to start of site work.
2. Installer shall provide the following:
   - 24-hour notice of start of construction
   - Inspection of bottom of bed or covering required by state inspector
   - All environmental management inspection sheets must be emailed to designer's office within 24 hours of inspection.
3. Site layout and required inspections to be made by designer:
   - Foundations and OWTS location and elevation
   - Inspection of OWTS bottom of trench
4. The applicant shall be responsible for:
   - New Application for redesign.
   - As-built location plans

General Notes (cont.)
5. The installer/applicant shall provide the designer with materials sheets for all construction materiasl prior to designer issuing certificate of construction.
6. The applicant shall furnish the original application to the installer prior to start of constuction

List incremented

Figure 14–54

6. Click (Decrement List Value) to move back a number.

💡 Hint: Model Text

Model text is different from annotation text. It is designed to create full-size text on the model itself. For example, you would use model text to create a sign on a door, as shown in Figure 14–55. One model text type is included with the default template. You can create other types as needed.

No Entry

Figure 14–55

- Model text can be viewed in all views.
- Model text is added from the *Architecture* tab>*Model* panel by clicking (Model Text).

How To: Align Multiple Text Notes

1. Select all text notes in the view.

2. In the *Modify | Text Notes* tab>*Multiple Align* panel, select one of the following alignment tools:

- ⊓ (Align Elements Top)
- ⊞ (Align Elements Middle)
- ⊟ (Align Elements Bottom)
- ⊟ (Distribute Vertically)

- ⊟ (Align Elements Left)
- ⊞ (Align Elements Center)
- ⊟ (Align Elements Right)
- ⊞ (Distribute Horizontally)

Spell Checking

The *Check Spelling* dialog box displays any misspelled words in context and provides several options for changing them, as shown in Figure 14–56.

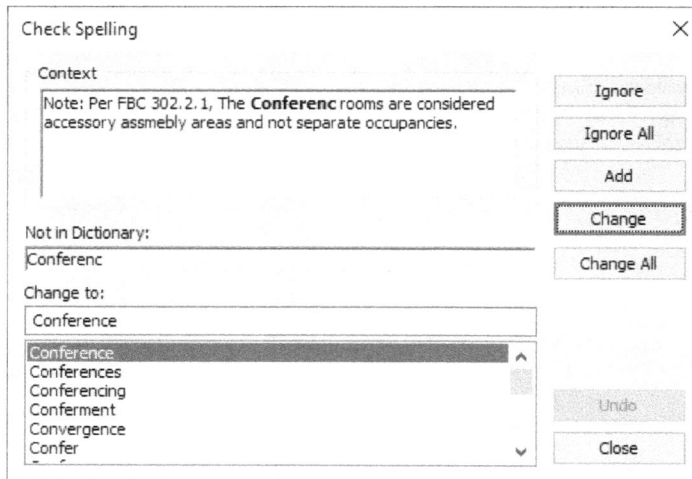

Figure 14–56

- Revit does not have active spell checking. It will only spell check when the command is activated.

- To spell check all text in a view, in the *Annotate* tab>*Text* panel, click ^{ABC}✓ (Spelling), or press <F7>. As with other spell checkers, you can **Ignore**, **Add**, or **Change** the word.

- You can also check the spelling in selected text. With text selected, in the *Modify | Text Notes* tab>*Tools* panel, click ^{ABC}✓ (Check Spelling).

Creating Text Types

If you need new text types with a different text size or font (such as for a title or hand-lettering), you can create new ones, as shown in Figure 14–57. It is recommended that you create these in a project template so they are available in future projects.

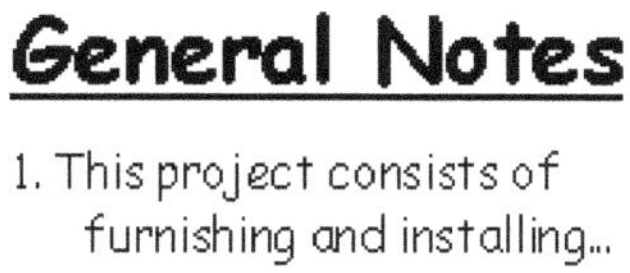

General Notes

1. This project consists of
furnishing and installing...

Figure 14–57

- You can copy and paste text types from one project to another or use **Transfer Project Standards**.

How To: Create Text Types

1. In the *Annotate* tab>*Text* panel, click ⌄ (Text Types).

   - Alternatively, start the **Text** command.

2. In Properties, click **Edit Type**.

3. In the *Type Properties* dialog box, click **Duplicate**.

4. In the *Name* dialog box, type a new name and click **OK**.

5. Modify the text parameters, as needed. The parameters are shown in Figure 14–58.

Type Parameters

Parameter	Value	=
Graphics		⌃
Color	■ Black	
Line Weight	1	
Background	Opaque	
Show Border	☐	
Leader/Border Offset	5/64"	
Leader Arrowhead	Arrow 30 Degree	
Text		⌃
Text Font	Arial	
Text Size	1/4"	
Tab Size	1/2"	
Bold	☐	
Italic	☐	
Underline	☐	
Width Factor	1.000000	

Figure 14–58

- The *Background* parameter can be set to **Opaque** or **Transparent**. An opaque background includes a masking region that hides lines or elements behind the text.
- In the *Text* area, the *Width Factor* parameter controls the width of the lettering, but does not affect the height. A width factor greater than **1** spreads the text out and a width factor less than **1** compresses it.
- The *Show Border* parameter, when selected, includes a rectangle around the text.

6. Click **OK** to close the *Type Properties* dialog box.

Practice 14d
Annotate Construction Documents – All Disciplines

Practice Objective

* Add a bulleted list of general notes to a sheet.

In this practice, you will open a sheet and add general notes to it using the text command.

1. In the practice files *Working Models>General* folder, open **Gen-Text-Note.rvt**.
2. Open the sheet **CS-000 - Cover Sheet**.
3. Open a text editor such as Microsoft Word or Notepad.
4. Within the text editor software, open either **General Notes.docx** or **General Notes.txt** from the practice files *Documents* folder.
5. Copy the entire contents of the file to the clipboard (select all <Ctrl>+<A> and copy <Ctrl>+<C>).
6. In Revit, start the **Text** command. In the Quick Access Toolbar or *Annotate* tab>*Text* panel, click **A** (Text).
7. Verify that no leader is selected, set the text type to **3/32" Arial,** and draw a text box similar to the one shown in Figure 14–59.

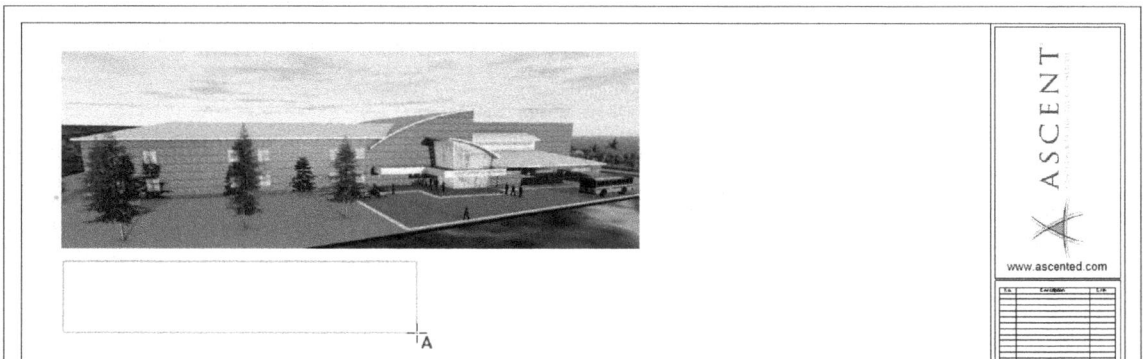

Figure 14–59

8. In the *Edit Text* tab>*Clipboard* panel, click 🗋 (Paste).
9. Remain in Edit Text mode and zoom in on the text box. Note that there are numbered and lettered lists in the text but that they are not quite correct.

10. Select all of the text and in the *Edit Text* tab>*Paragraph* panel, click ≔ (List: Numbers).

    * Depending on which document you opened and copied from, the paragraphs are recognized and numbered. If you copied from the .TXT file, the existing numbers and letters are still there. You will need to delete the existing numbering and modify the indents.

11. Select the paragraphs that were lettered in the original document and in the *Edit Text* tab>*Paragraph* panel, click ≣ (Increase Indent), then click ≔ (List: Lowercase letters) to change to a lettered list.

12. Select the numbered line and in the *Edit Text* tab>*Paragraph* panel, click ≣ (Increase Indent). If your number changes to a letter, click ≔ (List: Numbers).

13. Zoom in and remove the additional numbers and letters. Use **Increase Indent** or **Decrease Indent** to get the desired look, as shown in Figure 14–60.

1. General
   a. Existing ductwork and piping are shown only where necessary to establish relationship or connection points with new work. Not all existing ducts, pipes, and equipment are shown.
   b. For existing services at project site, verify exact size and location. Verify required clearances of equipment to new and existing material and electrical equipment.
   c. Raise, lower, remove, relocate or replace with new and reconnect to existing all piping and ductwork as required to maintain existing areas in operation during construction.
2. HVAC
   a. Examine architectural drawings to ensure that all ducts crossing fire and/or smoke separations are equipped with fire and/or smoke dampers. Notify the architect where additional dampers are required.
   b. Provide reheat coil transitions and transitions to smoke and/or fire dampers as required.
   c. Locate ceiling air outlets according to the architectural reflected ceiling plans. Confirm ceiling types shown on architectural drawings and install ceiling type supply and return or exhaust outlets to suit.
   d. All duct sizes show are inside clear dimensions.
3. Plumbing and Piping
   a. Verify exact invert elevation of points of connection to existing service prior to installation of new branch, mains or service relocation.
   b. Provide a valved drain at the low point in each piping system.
   c. Vent all high points in heating water and chilled water piping as specified.
   d. Provide condensate drip trap assemblies at the ends of steam mains, branches, and at all low points in the steam lines.
4. Electrical
   a. The electrical works shall comply with all the provisions in the Electrical Code and with consideration on the rules and regulations of local power company.
   b. Unless otherwise specified, wiring shall be done with PVC pipe.
   c. Electric meters installed by the power utility company are supplied and installed by the power utility company.
   d. The Electrical Code provides that only professional engineers can sign the electrical plans.
   e. Samples of materials to be used shall be submitted to the construction engineering office for approval before execution of the work.

Figure 14–60

14. At the beginning of the list, add the text **General Notes**. Make it bold and underlined, as shown in Figure 14–61.

15. Place the cursor at the end sentence of the **1. General** section. Hold <Shift> and press <Enter>. A new line is created without disrupting the numbering sequence.

16. Repeat this at the end of the discipline sections, as shown in Figure 14–61.

<u>General Notes</u>
1. General
    a. Existing ductwork and piping are shown only where necessary to establish relationship or connection points with new work. Not all existing ducts, pipes, and equipment are shown.
    b. For existing services at project site, verify exact size and location. Verify required clearances of equipment to new and existing material and electrical equipment.
    c. Raise, lower, remove, relocate or replace with new and reconnect to existing all piping and ductwork as required to maintain existing areas in operation during construction.

2. HVAC
    a. Examine architectural drawings to ensure that all ducts crossing fire and/or smoke separations are equipped with fire and/or smoke dampers. Notify the architect where additional dampers are required.
    b. Provide reheat coil transitions and transitions to smoke and/or fire dampers as required.
    c. Locate ceiling air outlets according to the architectural reflected ceiling plans. Confirm ceiling types shown on architectural drawings and install ceiling type supply and return or exhaust outlets to suit.
    d. All duct sizes show are inside clear dimensions.

3. Plumbing and Piping
    a. Verify exact invert elevation of points of connection to existing

Figure 14–61

17. In the *Edit Text* tab>*Edit Text* panel, click ☒ (Close) or click outside the text box to complete the text element.

18. Use the controls to relocate or resize the text note, if needed.

19. Zoom out to see the full sheet.

20. Save and close the project.

End of practice

Practice 14e
Add Annotations – Mechanical

Practice Objective

- Add text with two segment leaders.

In this practice, you will annotate an HVAC system in a 3D view.

1. In the practice files *Working Models>Mechanical* folder, open **Mech-Annotate.rvt**.

2. Open the Mechanical>HVAC>3D Views>**Typ Classroom 3D HVAC Systems** view.

3. In the *Annotate* tab>*Text* panel, click **A** (Text).

4. In the Type Selector, select **Text: 3/32" Arial**.

5. In the *Modify | Place Text* tab>*Leader* panel, click ⌐A (2 Segments).

6. Select a point touching one of the supply air ducts and then two other points to define the leader. Type **Supply Air Ducts**, as shown in Figure 14–62, and click an empty space in the view to finish the text note.

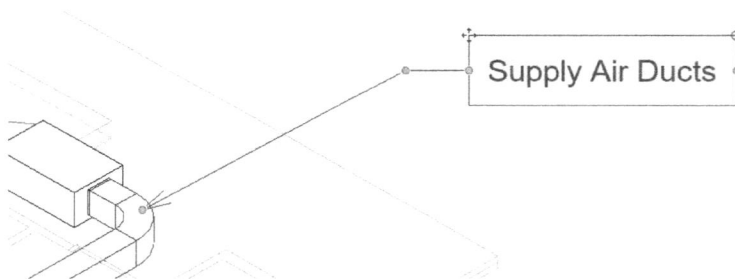

Figure 14–62

7. You are still in the **Text** command. Continue to add the leaders and text shown in Figure 14–63.

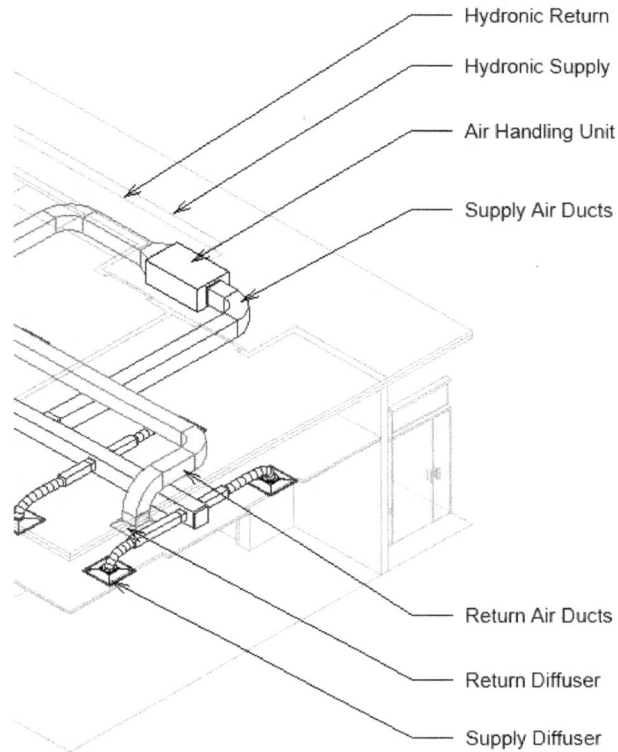

Hydronic Return

Hydronic Supply

Air Handling Unit

Supply Air Ducts

Return Air Ducts

Return Diffuser

Supply Diffuser

Figure 14–63

8. Save and close the project.

End of practice

Practice 14f
Add Annotations – Electrical

Practice Objectives

- Add detail lines.
- Duplicate a text style and add text.

In this practice, you will create an area within the electrical room and add text to denote that the area needs to stay clear.

1. In the practice files *Working Models>Electrical* folder, open **Elec-Annotate.rvt**.
2. Open the Electrical>Power>Floor Plans>**01 Electrical Room** view.
3. In the *Annotate* tab>*Detail* panel, click 🔲 (Detail Line).
4. In the *Modify | Place Detail Lines* tab>*Line Style* panel, set the *Line Style* to **MEP Hidden**.
5. Draw a rectangle from the upper-left corner of the room to the lower-right corner of the room, approximately **15' x 7'-4"**, as shown in Figure 14–64.

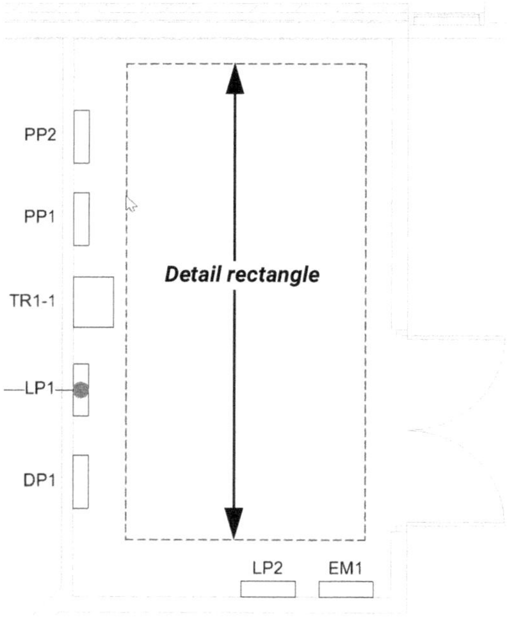

Figure 14–64

6. In the *Annotate* tab>*Text* panel, click **A** (Text).
7. In the Type Selector, select **Text: 3/32" Arial**.

8. In Properties, click **Edit Type**. In the *Type Properties* dialog box, click **Duplicate**. Type **3/64" Arial - Red** for the name and click **OK**.

9. Set the following properties:

   - *Color*: **Red**
   - *Text Font*: **Arial**
   - *Text Size*: **3/64"**
   - Select **Italic**

10. Click **OK** to save and close the *Type Properties* dialog box.

11. Using the **3/64" Arial - Red** text type, add the following text inside the rectangular detail lines without a leader: **Keep this area clear for access to Electrical Panels**, as shown in Figure 14–65.

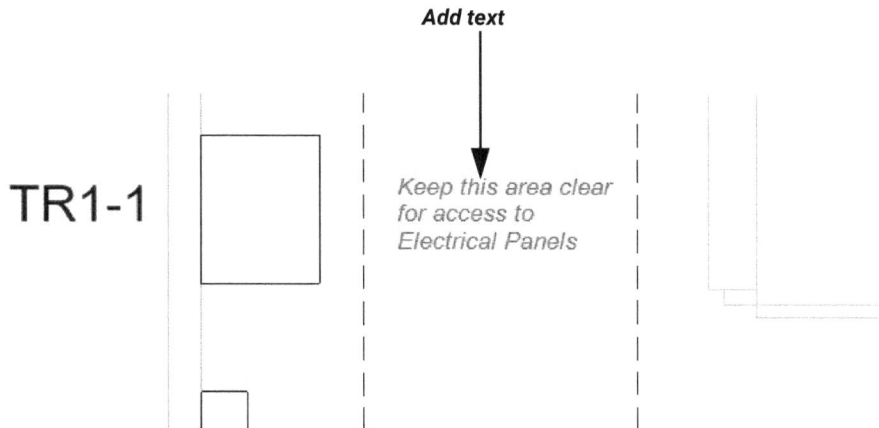

Add text

TR1-1

Keep this area clear for access to Electrical Panels

Figure 14–65

12. Save and close the project.

End of practice

Practice 14g
Add Annotations – Plumbing

Practice Objective

- Add text with two segment leaders.

In this practice, you will annotate plumbing systems in a 3D view.

1. In the practice files *Working Models>Plumbing* folder, open **Plumb-Annotate.rvt**.
2. Open the Mechanical>Plumbing>3D Views>**Typ Classroom 3D Plumb Systems** view.
3. In the *Annotate* tab>*Text* panel, click A (Text).
4. In the Type Selector, select **Text: 3/32" Arial**.
5. In the *Modify | Place Text* tab>*Leader* panel, click ⌐A (2 Segments).
6. Select a point touching one of the hot water lines and then two other points to define the leader. Type **Domestic Hot Water**, as shown in Figure 14–66, and click in an empty space in the view to finish the text note.

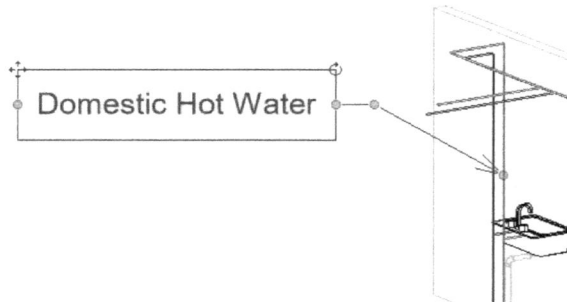

Figure 14–66

7.   You are still in the **Text** command. Add the leaders and text shown in Figure 14–67.

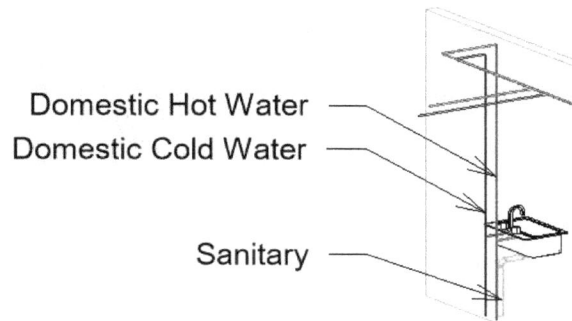

Figure 14–67

8.   Save and close the project.

End of practice

14.3 Creating Legends

A legend is a separate view that can be placed on multiple sheets. Legends can be used to hold installation notes that need to be placed on a sheet with each floor plan, key plans, or any 2D items that need to be repeated. You can also create and list the annotations, line styles, and symbols that are used in your project, and provide explanatory notes next to the symbol, as shown in Figure 14–68. Additionally, legends can provide a list of materials or elevations of equipment used in the project.

> *Note: The elements in this figure are inserted using the **Symbol** command rather that the **Legend Component** or **Detail Component** commands.*

Electrical Legend	
⊟	Dimmer Switch
⊟	3-Way Switch
⊠	Key Operated Switch
⊠⊐	Manual Pull Fire Alarm

Figure 14–68

- You use ⊡ (Detail Line) and A (Text) to create the table and explanatory notes. Once you have a legend view, you can use commands, such as ⊞ (Legend Component), ⊞ (Detail Component), and ⊕ (Symbol), to place elements in the view.

- Unlike other views, legend views can be attached to more than one sheet.

- You can set a legend's scale in the View Control Bar.

- Elements in legends can be dimensioned.

- When creating a legend, you can add legend components, tags, and symbols. You cannot add any room elements.

How To: Create a Legend

1. In the *View* tab>*Create* panel, expand ⊞ (Legends) and click ⊞ (Legend), or in the Project Browser, right-click on the *Legends* area title and select **Legend**.

2. In the *New Legend View* dialog box, enter a name and select a scale for the legend, as shown in Figure 14–69, then click **OK**.

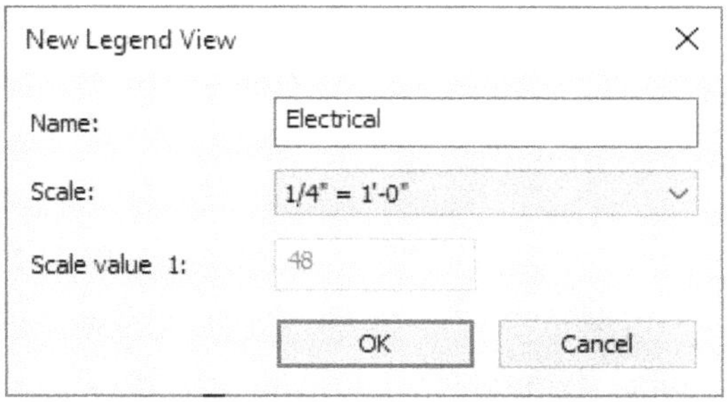

Figure 14–69

3. Place the components in the view first, and then sketch the outline of the table when you know the sizes. Use the **Reference Plane** command to line up the components.

How To: Use Legend Components

1. In a legend view, in the *Annotate* tab>*Detail* panel, expand (Detail Component) and click (Legend Component).

2. In the Options Bar, select the *Family* type that you want to use, as shown in Figure 14–70.

   • This list contains all of the elements in the project that can be used in a legend. For example, you might want to display all air terminals used in the project.

Figure 14–70

3. Select the *View* of the element that you want to place. For example, you might want to display the section or elevation of the floors or roofs, and the front elevation of an electrical, plumbing, or mechanical fixture or equipment.

4. For section elements (such as walls, floors, and roofs), type a distance for the *Host Length*.

   • Elements that are full size, such as planting components or doors, come in at their full size.

   • Legends are views that can be placed on multiple sheets. You can use **Copy to the Clipboard** and **Paste** to copy legends from sheet to sheet.

Practice 14h
Create a Key Plan – All Disciplines

Practice Objective

- Create a key plan, then place it on a sheet.

In this practice, you will create a key plan of the building and add it to the cover sheet.

1. In the practice files *Working Models>General* folder, open **Gen-Key-Plan.rvt**.

2. In the *View* tab>*Create* panel, expand ⬚ (Legends) and click ⬚ (Legend) to create a new legend view.

3. In the *New Legend View* dialog box, change the *Name* to **Key Plan** and verify the *Scale* is set to **1"=100'-0"**, then click **OK**.

4. Open the Coordination>All>Floor Plans>**Site** view.

5. In the *Annotate* tab>*Detail* panel, click ⬚ (Detail Line). In the *Line Style* panel, select **Outline**.

6. In the *Draw* panel, click ⬚ (Line).

7. In the Options Bar, select **Chain**.

8. Trace over the outer edges of the building, following the outline shown in Figure 14–71. It does not have to be exactly on the edges of the building.

Note: Click ⬚ (Thin Lines) so the line width displays.

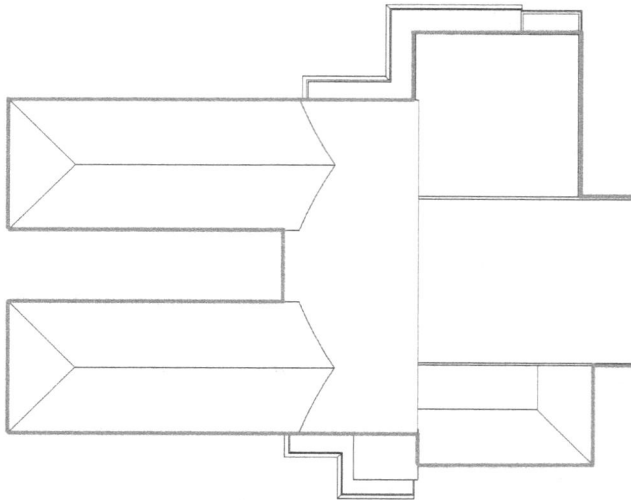

Figure 14–71

9. Click (Modify).
10. Select all of the new detail lines.
11. In the *Modify | Lines* tab>*Clipboard* panel, click (Cut to Clipboard).
12. Return to the Key Plan view and press <Ctrl>+<V> to paste from the clipboard. Click to place the elements and then in the *Modify | Detail Groups* tab>*Edit Pasted* panel, click (Finish).
13. Select all of the lines (they will be very thick if Thin Lines is not on). In the *Modify | Lines* tab>*Line Style* panel, change the *Line Style* to **Wide Lines**.
14. Use the modify tools to clean up the edges and add text, as shown in Figure 14–72.

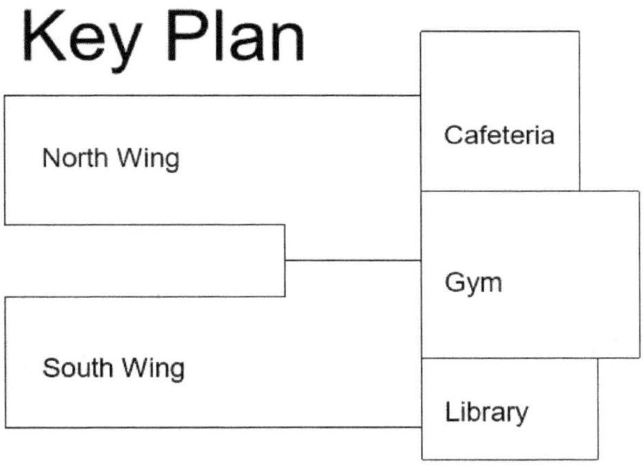

Figure 14–72

15. In the *Annotate* tab>*Symbol* panel, click (Symbol).
16. In the Type Selector search path, start typing **North**. Select **North Arrow 2** and place it near the word Key Plan.
17. Drag and drop the Key Plan legend to sheet **CS-000 - Cover Sheet and place it** next to the school image.

18. With the legend still selected, in the Type Selector, select **Viewport: No Title** so there is no title below the key plan, as shown in Figure 14-73.

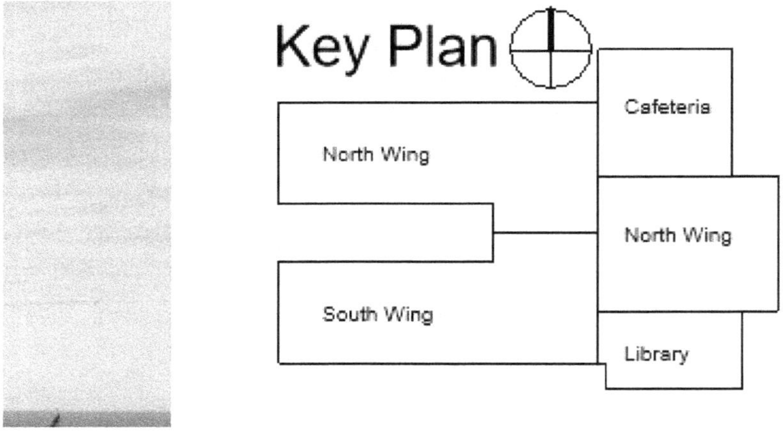

Figure 14-73

19. Zoom out to display the full sheet.

20. Save and close the project.

End of practice

Practice 14i
Create a Legend – Mechanical

Practice Objectives

- Create a legend using legend components and text.
- Add the legend to a sheet.

In this practice, you will create a legend using legend components, text, and detail lines, then add it to the cover sheet.

Task 1: Add a mechanical legend.

1. In the practice files *Working Models>Mechanical* folder, open **Mech-Legend.rvt**.

2. In the *View* tab>*Create* panel, expand ▦ (Legends) and click ▦ (Legend) to create a new legend view.

3. Name the legend **Mechanical Legend**, set the *Scale* to **1/4"=1'-0"**, and click **OK**.

4. In the *Annotate* tab>*Detail* panel, expand ◻ (Component) and click ◻ (Legend Component).

5. In the Options Bar, add the following symbols from the *Family* list with the following views:

Family	View
Air Terminals: Return Diffuser - Hosted: Workplane-based Return Diffuser	• Floor Plan • Elevation: Front
Air Terminals: Supply Diffuser - Perforated - Round Neck - Ceiling Mounted: 24x24x10 In Neck	• Floor Plan • Elevation: Front
Air Terminals: Supply Diffuser - Sidewall: 24 x 12	• Floor Plan • Elevation: Front

6. Remove the front elevation details and add lines, text, and a title, as shown in Figure 14–74.

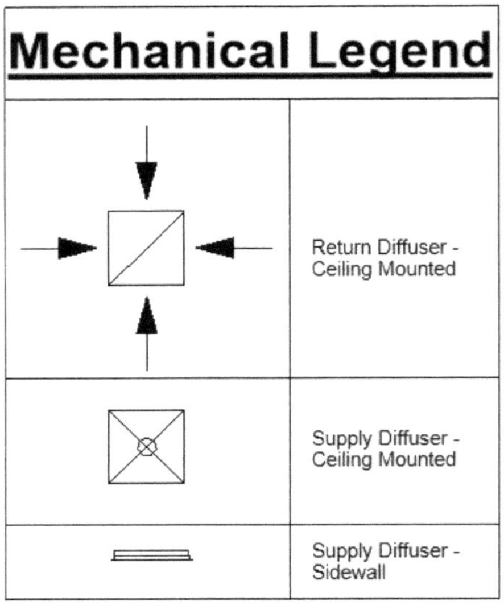

Figure 14–74

Task 2: Add legend to cover sheet.

1. Open the **M-101- 01 Mechanical Plan** sheet.

2. Drag and drop the mechanical legend onto the sheet.

3. With the legend still selected, in the Type Selector, select **Viewport: No Title**.

4. Save and close the project.

End of practice

Practice 14j
Create a Legend – Electrical

Practice Objectives

- Create a legend using legend components and text.
- Add the legend to a sheet.

In this practice, you will create a legend using legend components, text, and detail lines, then add it to the cover sheet.

Task 1: Add an electrical legend.

1. In the practice files *Working Models>Electrical* folder, open **Elec-Legend.rvt**.

2. In the *View* tab>*Create* panel, expand 🔲 (Legends) and click 🔲 (Legend) to create a new legend view.

3. Name the legend **Light Fixtures Legend**, set the *Scale* to **1/4"=1'-0"**, and click **OK**.

4. In the *Annotate* tab>*Detail* panel, expand 🔲 (Component) and click 🔲 (Legend Component).

5. In the Options Bar, set the *View* to **Floor Plan** and *Host Length* to **0'-3"**, and place the following from the *Family* list:

    - **Lighting Fixtures : Emergency Recessed Lighting Fixture : 2x4 - 277**
    - **Lighting Fixtures : Plain Recessed Lighting Fixture : 2x4 - 277**
    - **Lighting Fixtures : Troffer Light - 2x4 Parabolic : 2'x4' (2 Lamp) - 277V**

6. Add the lines and text. Figure 14–75 shows an example of a lighting fixture legend.

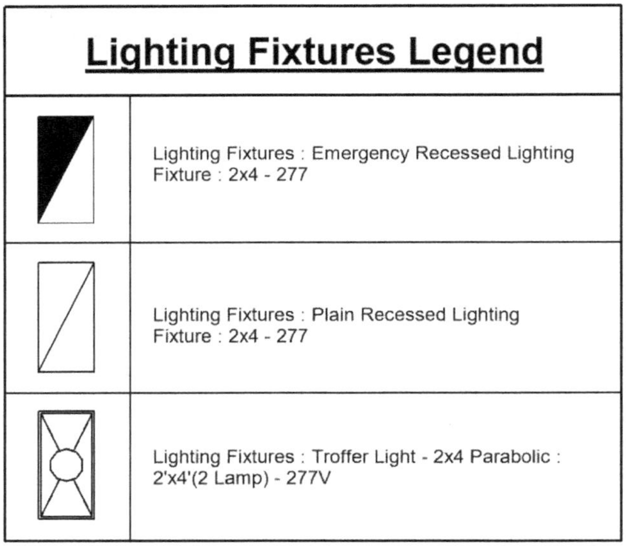

Lighting Fixtures Legend

	Lighting Fixtures : Emergency Recessed Lighting Fixture : 2x4 - 277
	Lighting Fixtures : Plain Recessed Lighting Fixture : 2x4 - 277
	Lighting Fixtures : Troffer Light - 2x4 Parabolic : 2'x4'(2 Lamp) - 277V

Figure 14–75

Task 2: Add legend to cover sheet.

1. Open the **E-101- 01 Lighting Plan sheet**.
2. With the legend still selected, in the Type Selector, select **Viewport: No Title**.
3. Drag and drop the **Light Fixtures** legend onto the sheet.
4. Save and close the project.

End of practice

Practice 14k
Create a Legend – Plumbing

Practice Objectives

* Create a legend using legend components and text.
* Add the legend to a sheet.

In this practice, you will create a legend using legend components, text, and detail lines, then add it to the cover sheet.

Task 1: Add a plumbing legend.

1. In the practice files *Working Models>Plumbing* folder, open **Plumb-Legend.rvt**.

2. In the *View* tab>*Create* panel, expand ▦ (Legends) and click ▦ (Legend) to create a new legend view.

3. Name the legend **Plumbing Fixture - Flush Tank** and set the *Scale* to **1/4"=1'-0"**, then click **OK**.

4. In the *Annotate* tab>*Detail* panel, expand ▱ (Component) and click ▤ (Legend Component).

5. In the Options Bar, set *Family* to **Plumbing Fixtures: Water Closet - Flush Tank: Public - 1.6 gpf** and set *View* to **Elevation - Front**. Add a single instance to the current legend view.

6. In the Options Bar, set *Family* to **Plumbing Fixtures: Water Closet - Quiet Flush Tank: Public - 1.6 gpf** and set *View* to **Elevation - Front**. Add a single instance next to the first one, as shown in Figure 14–76. Click ⬚ (Modify) to finish.

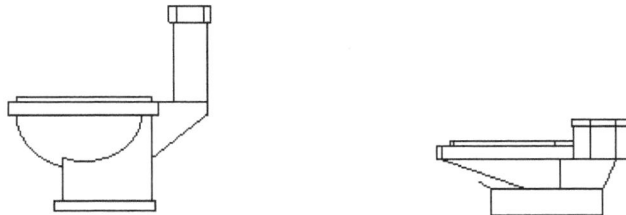

Figure 14–76

7. In the *Annotate* tab>*Text* panel, click **A** (Text) and label the elements, as shown in Figure 14–77.

8. Click 🔲 (Detail Line) in the *Annotate* tab>*Detail* panel. Use the tools on the *Modify | Place Detail Lines* tab>*Draw* panel to add the boxes around the elements and text, as shown in Figure 14–77.

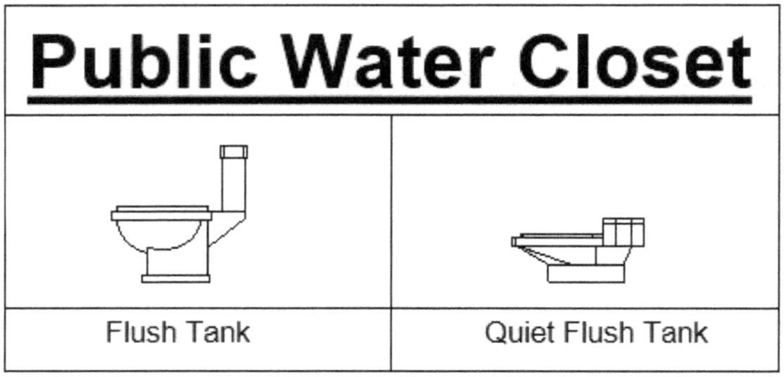

Public Water Closet

Flush Tank	Quiet Flush Tank

Figure 14–77

Task 2: Add legend to cover sheet.

1. Open the **P-101- 01 Plumbing Plan** sheet.

2. Drag and drop the plumbing fixture legend onto the sheet.

3. With the legend still selected, in the Type Selector, select **Viewport: No Title**.

4. Save and close the project.

End of practice

Chapter Review Questions

1. When a fixture is moved, how do you update the dimension?

    a. Edit the dimension and move it over.

    b. Select the dimension and then click **Update** in the Options Bar.

    c. The dimension automatically updates.

    d. Delete the existing dimension and add a new one.

2. How do you create new text styles?

    a. Using the **Text Styles** command.

    b. Duplicate an existing type.

    c. They must be included in a template.

    d. Using the **Format Styles** command.

3. When you edit text, how many leaders can be added using the leader tools shown in Figure 14–78?

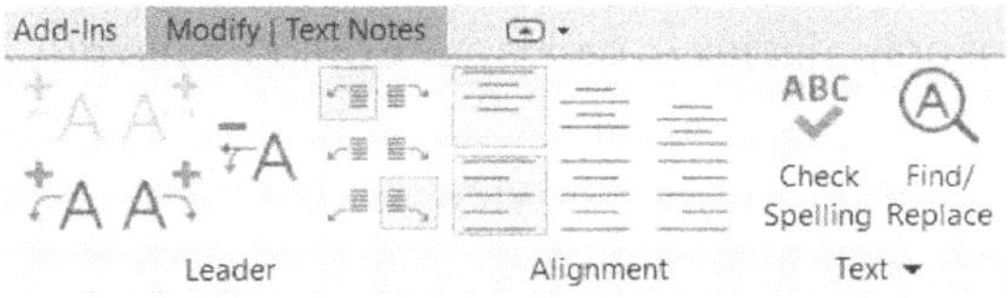

    Figure 14–78

    a. One

    b. One on each end of the text

    c. As many as you want at each end of the text

4. In which type of view (access shown in Figure 14–79) can you NOT add detail lines?

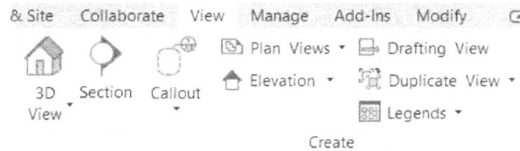

Figure 14–79

a. Plans

b. Elevations

c. 3D views

d. Legends

5. Detail lines created in one view also display in the related view.

a. True

b. False

6. Which of the following describes the difference between a symbol and a component?

a. Symbols are 3D and only display in one view. Components are 2D and display in many views.

b. Symbols are 2D and only display in one view. Components are 3D and display in many views.

c. Symbols are 2D and display in many views. Components are 3D and only display in one view.

d. Symbols are 3D and display in many views. Components are 2D and only display in one view.

7. When creating a legend, which of the following elements cannot be added?

a. Legend components

b. Tags

c. Rooms

d. Symbols

Command Summary

Button	Command	Location
Dimensions and Text		
	Aligned (Dimension)	• **Ribbon:** *Annotate* tab>*Dimension* panel or *Modify* tab>*Measure* panel, expanded drop-down list • **Quick Access Toolbar** • **Shortcut:** DI
	Angular (Dimension)	• **Ribbon:** *Annotate* tab>*Dimension* panel or *Modify* tab>*Measure* panel, expanded drop-down list
	Arc Length (Dimension)	• **Ribbon:** *Annotate* tab>*Dimension* panel or *Modify* tab>*Measure* panel, expanded drop-down list
	Diameter (Dimension)	• **Ribbon:** *Annotate* tab>*Dimension* panel or *Modify* tab>*Measure* panel, expanded drop-down list
	Linear (Dimension)	• **Ribbon:** *Annotate* tab>*Dimension* panel or *Modify* tab>*Measure* panel, expanded drop-down list
	Radial (Dimension)	• **Ribbon:** *Annotate* tab>*Dimension* panel or *Modify* tab>*Measure* panel, expanded drop-down list
A	**Text**	• **Ribbon:** *Annotate* tab>*Text* panel • **Shortcut:** TX
Detail Lines and Symbols		
	Detail Line	• **Ribbon:** *Annotate* tab>*Detail* panel • **Shortcut:** DL
	Symbol	• **Ribbon:** *Annotate* tab>*Symbol* panel
Legends		
	Legend (View)	• **Ribbon:** *View* tab>*Create* panel, expand Legends
	Legend Component	• **Ribbon:** *Annotate* tab>*Detail* panel, expand Component

Adding Tags and Schedules

Adding tags to your views helps you to identify elements such as doors, windows, or walls in the model. Tags are 2D annotation families with labels that extract information about the elements being tagged from their properties. Tags are typically added when you insert an element, but can also be added at any point in the design process.

Schedules are used to gather information stored in the various elements in the project and present them in a table format. In Revit®, you can create schedules specifically for MEP projects, such as building component schedules and material takeoff schedules. These schedules can then be added to sheets to create construction documentation.

Learning Objectives

- Add tags to elements in 2D and 3D views to prepare the views to be placed on sheets.
- Load tags that are required for projects.
- Understand schedules and their use in a project.
- Modify schedule content, including the instance and type properties of related elements.
- Add schedules to sheets as part of the construction documents.

15.1 Adding Tags

Tags are used to identify elements in a project. When placing certain elements, such as air terminals, ducts, mechanical equipment, and piping, you can select **Tag on Placement** from the ribbon and a tag will be placed along with the element. Revit supplies tags for every category in the family library, which can then be placed on elements in the drawing anytime during the design process. Figure 15–1 shows elements that have been tagged.

Note: Additional tags are stored in the Revit Library in the Annotations folder.

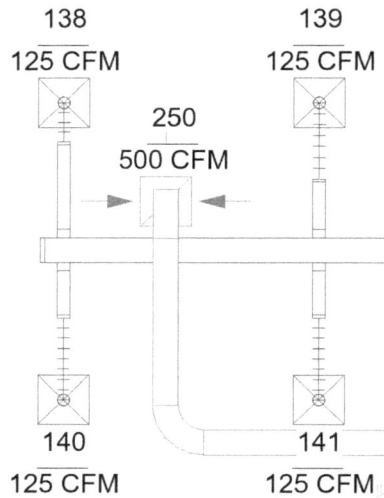

Figure 15–1

- The **Tag by Category** command works for most elements, except for a few that have separate commands.

- Tags can be letters, numbers, or a combination of the two.

You can place three types of tags, as follows:

- (Tag by Category): Tags according to the category of the element. It places door tags on doors and wall tags on walls.

- (Multi-Category Tag): Tags elements belonging to multiple categories. The tags display information from parameters that they have in common.

- (Material Tag): Tags that display the type of material. They are typically used in detailing.

Tag Options

* In Properties, you can set tag options for leaders and tag orientation, as shown in Figure 15–2. You can also press <Spacebar> to toggle the rotation while placing or modifying the tag.

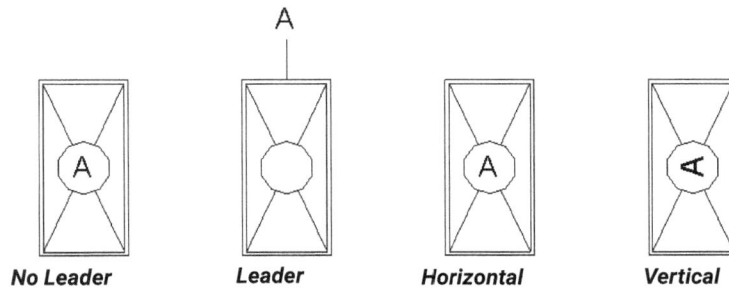

A

| No Leader | Leader | Horizontal | Vertical |

Figure 15–2

* Tag orientation can be set to the following:

  * **Horizontal:** Tag stays horizontal (0°) to the element it is tagging.
  * **Vertical:** Forces the tag to stay vertical (90°) to the element it is tagging no matter what.
  * **Model:** Tag rotates freely from the element, similar to room tags.

* Leaders can have an **Attached End** or a **Free End**, as shown in Figure 15–3. The attached end must be connected to the element being tagged. A free end has an additional drag control where the leader touches the element.

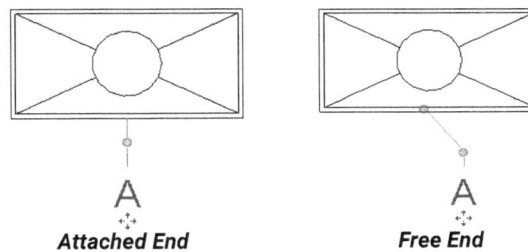

A   A

| Attached End | Free End |

Figure 15–3

* If you change between **Attached End** and **Free End**, the tag does not move and the leader does not change location.

* The **Length** option specifies the length of the leader in plotting units. It is grayed out if **Leader** is not selected or if a **Free End** leader is defined.

- If a tag is not loaded, a *No Tag Loaded* dialog box opens, as shown in Figure 15–4. Click **Yes** to open the *Load Family* dialog box in which you can select the appropriate tag.

Figure 15–4

- Tags can be pinned so they stay in place if you move the element that is tagged. This is primarily used when tags have leaders, as shown in Figure 15–5.

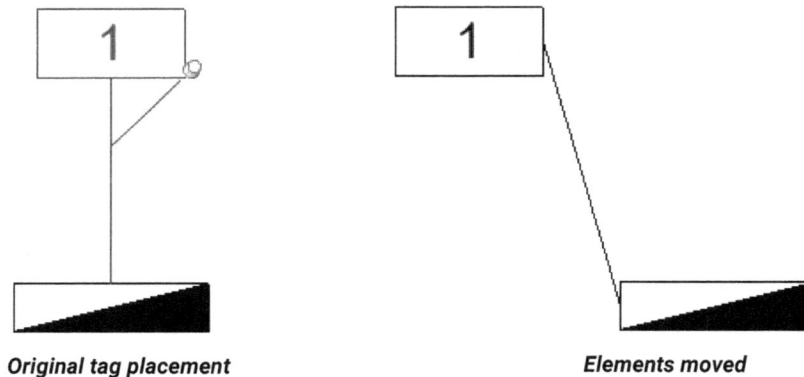

Original tag placement   *Elements moved*

Figure 15–5

How To: Add Tags

1. In the *Annotate* tab>*Tag* panel, click ⬚ (Tag by Category), ⬚ (Multi-Category Tag), or ⬚ (Material Tag) depending on the type of tag you want to place.

2. In Properties, specify the leader options, orientation, and angle, as needed, as shown in Figure 15−6.

Figure 15−6

3. In the *Modify | Tag* tab>*Placement* panel, set the *Leader Length*.

4. Select the element you want to tag. If a tag for the selected element is not loaded, you are prompted to load it from the Revit Library.

Multi-Leader Tags

If you have elements that need to be tagged that are in close proximity to one another, you can tag one element and then select other similar elements. This adds more leader lines from the elements to the tag, as shown with the electrical outlets in Figure 15−7. When selecting the tag, you can see how many host elements it is tagging in Properties (as shown on the left in Figure 15−7).

You cannot select elements that are of different categories, like an air handling unit (AHU) and a panel. You can only select similar elements to share a tag, like all AHUs or all panels.

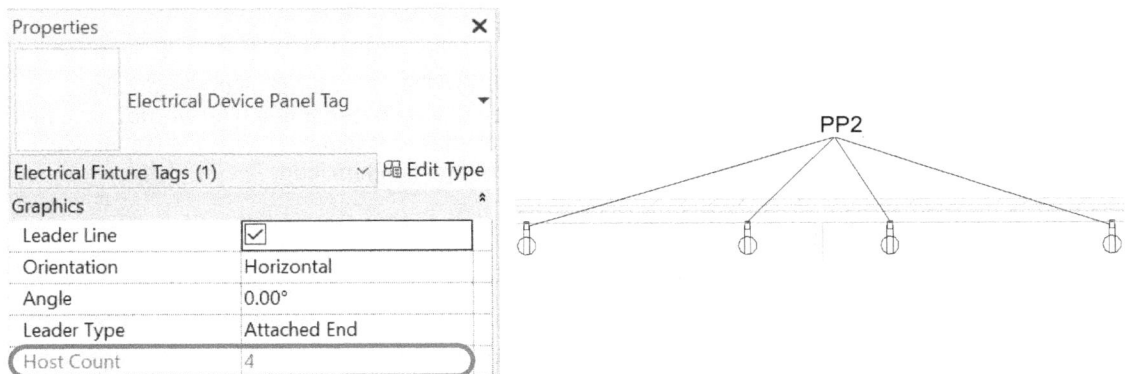

Figure 15−7

If you select, for instance, two air terminal types that are different sizes, you will get a <varies> tag, as shown in Figure 15–8, because they are not the same size.

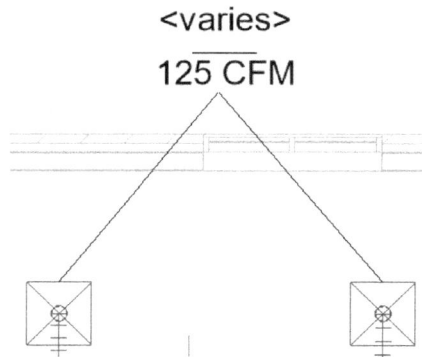

Figure 15–8

You can modify how the leaders are displayed when using the multi-leader tags. You can adjust how they will display in the view by showing all leaders, hiding select leaders, or hiding all leaders.

(Show All Leaders)	This turns on all leaders of any tag that is selected that used Multi-Leader tagging.
(Hide All Leaders)	This turns off all leaders of any tag that is selected that used Multi-Leader tagging.
(Show One Leader)	This turns off all leaders except for one leader of any tag that is selected that used Multi-Leader tagging.
(Select Leaders to Show)	This puts you into edit mode and enables you to select specific leaders to show or hide. When finished, you need to click (Finish).
(Merge Leaders)	Select to turn this feature on. This will merge all the leader line elbows to one location on the main leader line. You will not have the ability to adjust the leader lines individually. To get the leader line elbows back, select the **Merge Leaders** icon.

How To: Add a Multi-Leader Tag

1. Start the **Tag by Category** command.
2. Set the options in Properties.
3. Tag one element in the model.
4. In the *Modify | Tag* tab>*Host* panel, verify **Add/Remove Host** is on, as shown in Figure 15–9.

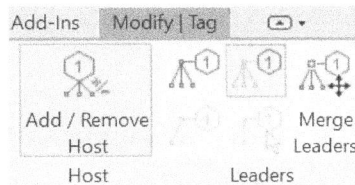

Figure 15–9

5. Select the other similar elements to add to the tag.

* Alternatively, if you have a tag already placed in the model and you want to add elements to the tag, select the tag, and in the contextual tab, click ⬡ (Add/Remove Host), then select the other elements.

6. In Properties, set the leader options as needed.
7. A leader line will be added for each element you select.

How To: Remove Elements from a Multi-Leader Tag

1. To remove an element from the tag, select the tag and in the ribbon, select ⬡ (Add/Remove Host).
2. Select the element in the model. The leader line is removed.

How To: Add Multiple Tags

1. In the *Annotate* tab>*Tag* panel, click ⌐⊚ (Tag All).

2. In the *Tag All Not Tagged* dialog box (shown in Figure 15–10), select the checkbox beside one or more categories to tag. Selecting the checkbox beside the *Category* title selects all of the tags.

    Note: To tag only some elements, select them before starting this command. In the Tag All Not Tagged dialog box, select **Only selected objects in current view**.

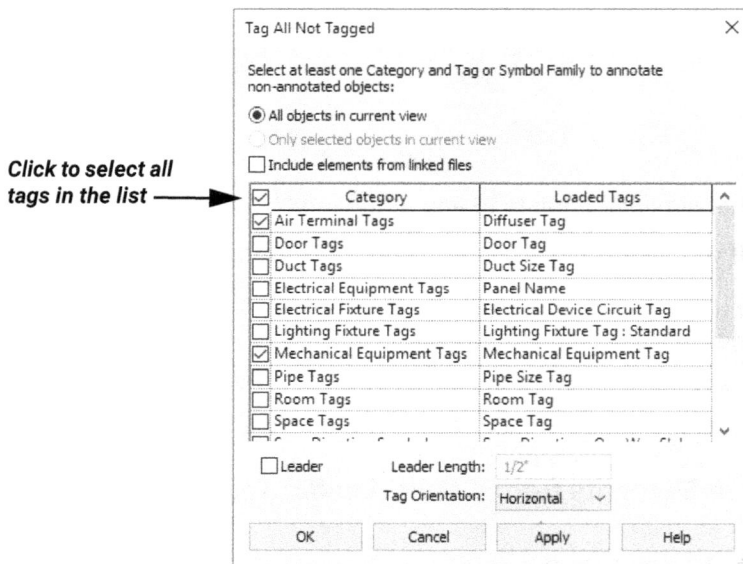

Figure 15–10

3. Set the *Leader* and *Tag Orientation* as needed.

4. Click **Apply** to apply the tags and stay in the dialog box. Click **OK** to apply the tags and close the dialog box.

*   When you select a tag, the properties of that tag display. To display the properties of the tagged element, in the *Modify* contextual tab>*Host* panel, click 🖾 (Select Host).

How To: Load Tags

1. In the *Annotate* tab, expand the *Tag* panel and click 🔾 (Loaded Tags And Symbols) or,

   when a Tag command is active, in the *Modify | Tag* tab>*Tags* panel, click 🔾 (Loaded Tags And Symbols).

2. In the *Loaded Tags And Symbols* dialog box (shown in Figure 15–11), click **Load Family...**.

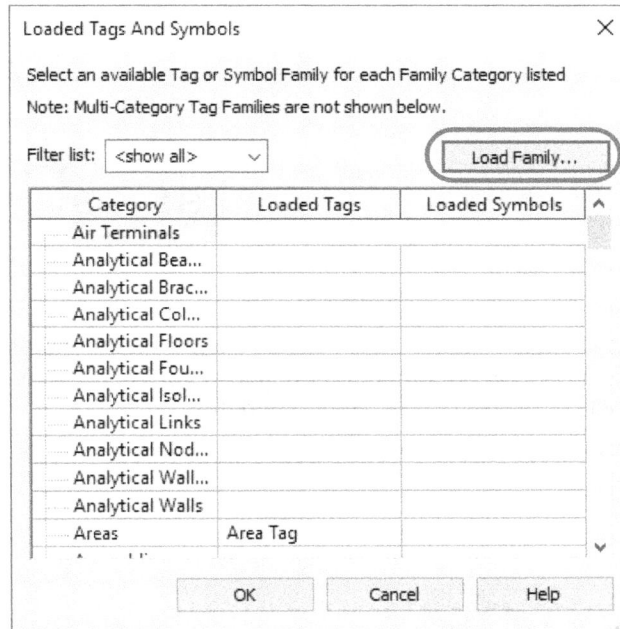

Loaded Tags And Symbols			X
Select an available Tag or Symbol Family for each Family Category listed			
Note: Multi-Category Tag Families are not shown below.			
Filter list: <show all> ⌄		Load Family...	
Category	Loaded Tags	Loaded Symbols	⌃
Air Terminals			
Analytical Bea...			
Analytical Brac...			
Analytical Col...			
Analytical Floors			
Analytical Fou...			
Analytical Isol...			
Analytical Links			
Analytical Nod...			
Analytical Wall...			
Analytical Walls			
Areas	Area Tag		⌄

OK   Cancel   Help

Figure 15–11

3. In the *Load Family* dialog box, navigate to the appropriate *Annotations* folder in the Revit Library, select the tag(s) needed, and click **Open**.

4. The tag is added to the category in the dialog box. Click **OK**.

Instance vs.Type Based Tags

Many elements (such as air terminals) are tagged in a numbered sequence, with each instance of the air terminal having a separate tag number. Other elements (such as lighting and plumbing fixtures) are tagged by type, as shown in Figure 15-12. Changing the information in one tag changes all instances of that element.

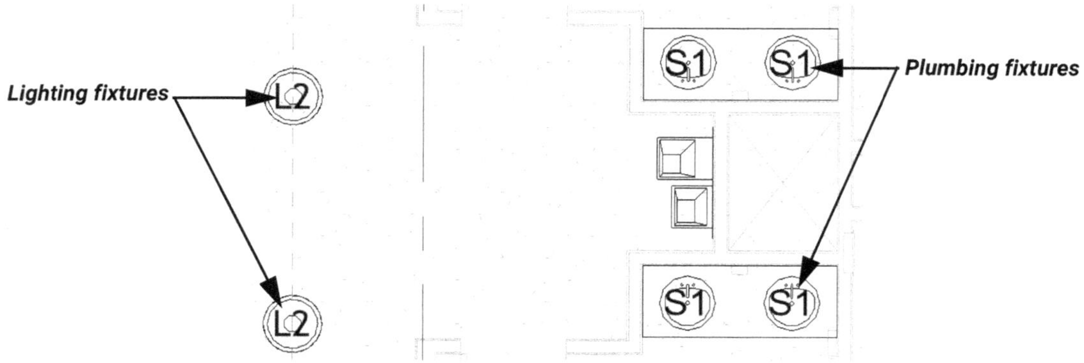

Figure 15-12

- To modify the number of an instance tag (such as a light fixture or air terminal), slowly click twice directly on the number in the tag and modify it, or you can modify the *Mark* property, as shown in Figure 15-13. Only that one instance updates.

Figure 15-13

- To modify the number of a type tag, you can slowly click twice directly on the number or letter in the tag and modify it. Alternatively, you can select the element and in Properties, click ⊞ (Edit Type). In the *Type Properties* dialog box, in the *Identity Data* section, modify the *Type Mark*, as shown in Figure 15–14. All instances of this element then update.

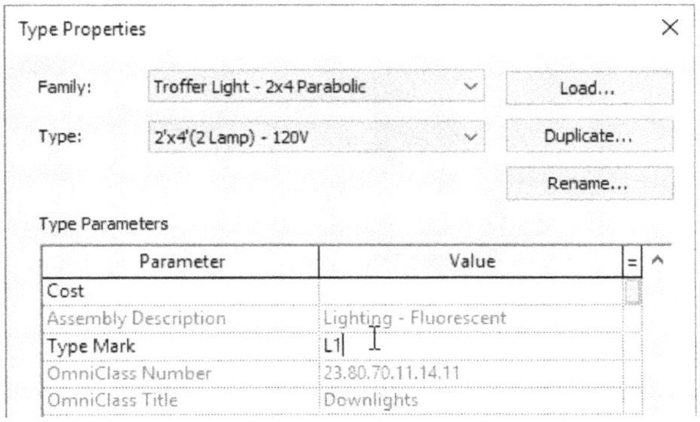

Figure 15–14

- When you change a type tag, an alert box opens to warn you that changing a type parameter affects other elements, as shown in Figure 15–15. If you want this tag to modify all other elements of this type, click **Yes**.

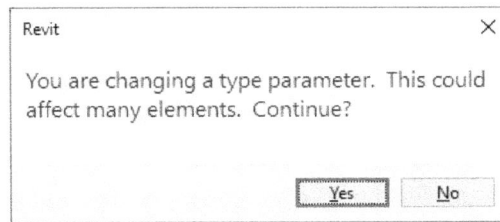

Figure 15–15

- If a tag displays with a question mark, it means that no information has been assigned to that element's parameter yet.

Tagging in 3D Views

You can add tags to isometric 3D views, as shown in Figure 15–16, as long as the views are locked first. Locking a 3D view enables you to create the view as you want it and then save it from being modified.

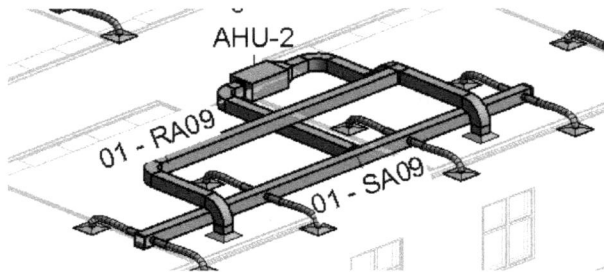

Figure 15–16

- You must lock an isometric 3D view in order to place tags. Dimensions can be added to isometric 3D views whether they are locked or not. Proceed with caution when selecting the items to dimension to ensure that the witness lines and text orient is snapping to and extending in the correct direction as intended.Locked views can be used with perspective views. This enables you to create the view as you want it and then save it from being modified. You cannot tag or add dimensions in a perspective view, as these are views created with the camera tool.

How To: Lock a 3D View

1. Open a 3D view and set it up as you want it to display.

   Note: *When adding text in a 3D view, you do not have to lock the view. When tagging in a 3D view, you have to lock the view.*

2. In the View Control Bar, click 🏠 (Unlocked 3D View), then click 🏠 (Save Orientation and Lock View).

- If you are using the default 3D view and it has not been saved, you are prompted to name and save the view first.

- You can modify the orientation of the view by clicking 🏠 (Locked 3D View), then clicking 🏠 (Unlock View). This also removes any tags you have applied.

- To return to the previous locked view, click 🏠 (Unlocked 3D View), then click 🏠 (Restore Orientation and Lock View).

Practice 15a
Add Tags – Mechanical

Practice Objectives

- Use the *Tag All Not Tagged* dialog box.
- Modify tags.
- Modify tags using the **Add/Remove Host** tool.

In this practice, you will use the **Tag All** tool to add duct, pipe, and air terminal tags to a mechanical floor plan, then you will modify the tags and use the **Add/Remove Host** tool to combined similar tags to reduce confusion.

Task 1: Tag all not tagged.

1. In the practice files *Working Models>Mechanical* folder, open **Mech-Tags.rvt**.
2. Open the Mechanical>HVAC>Floor Plans>**01 Mechanical - North Wing** view. There are tags on the ducting and the air terminals.
3. Open the **01 Mechanical - South Wing** view. This view is missing its tags. (Type **ZF** or **ZA** to fit the model in the view if it is not showing.)
4. In the *Annotate* tab>*Tag* panel, click ⌂ (Tag All).
5. In the *Tag All Not Tagged* dialog box, select the following:

    - *Air Terminal Tags:* **Diffuser Tag**
    - *Mechanical Equipment Tags:* **ASCENT: ME Combination Tag**

6. Verify that the **Leader** is unchecked and click **OK**.

    - If a warning dialog box displays about Elements Have Hidden Tags, click **OK**.

7. All of the air terminals and mechanical equipment are now tagged in this view, as shown in part in Figure 15–17.

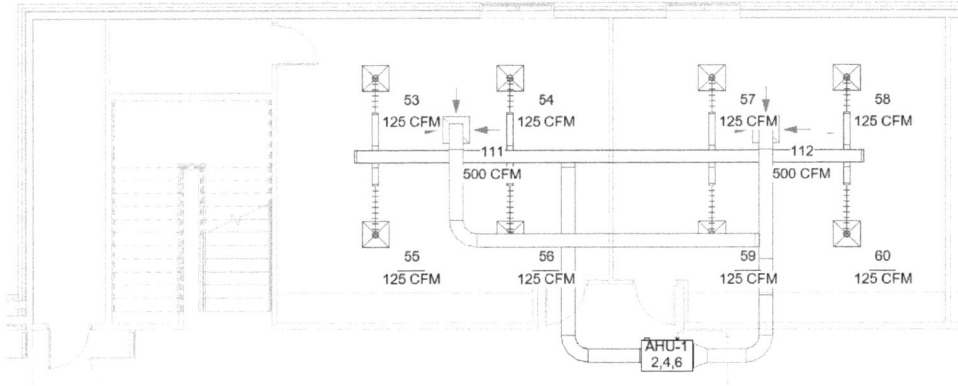

Figure 15–17

8. Save the project.

Task 2: Modify tags.

1. Zoom in to the upper-left classroomsin the south wing (next to the stairwell) and move the air diffuser tags so they are not on top of any other element and are closer to the diffusers. Select the AHU mechanical equipment tag on the mechanical equipment that is the farthest one to the left in the south wing hallway.

2. In the *Modify | Edit Tags* tab>*Host* panel, select ⚒ (Add/Remove Host). In Properties, check the checkbox next to **Leader**.

3. Select the AHU (not the tag) on the other side of the hallway, as shown in Figure 15–18.

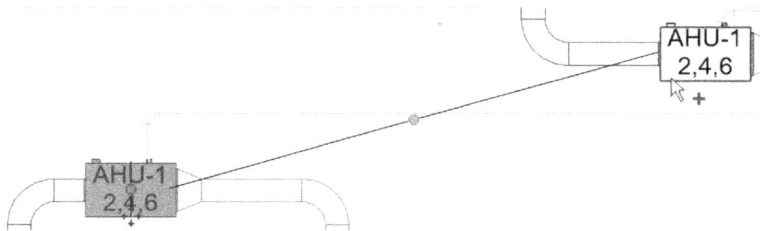

Figure 15–18

4. Click ⬚ (Modify).

Note: While selecting Leader in Properties, you can also change the orientation from Horizontal to Vertical if required.

5. Select the left AHU tag and drag it away from the AHU unit, as shown in Figure 15–19. You will see leaders pointing to both ducts.

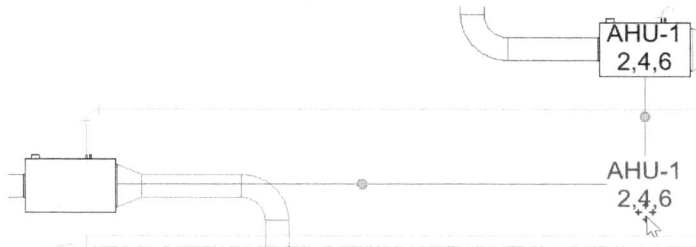

Figure 15–19

6. Click ⬚ (Modify).

7. You can delete the unneeded AHU tag.

8. Repeat the process for any AHU tags that are close to each other.

9. Save and close the project.

End of practice

Practice 15b
Add Tags – Electrical

Practice Objectives

- Add tags to a model.
- Use the *Tag All Not Tagged* dialog box.
- Set the *Type Mark* parameter for tags.
- Modify tags using the **Add/Remove Host** tool.

In this practice, you will add light fixture tags and conduit tags to electrical floor plans and modify the elements' type marks. You will then modify the tags and use the **Add/Remove Host** tool to combine similar tags to reduce confusion.

Task 1: Add tags to a lighting floor plan.

1. In the practice files *Working Models>Electrical* folder, open **Elec-Tags.rvt**.

2. Open the Electrical>Lighting>Floor Plans>**01 Lighting Plan - North Wing** view. There are tags on the light fixtures displaying different ways to use tags.

3. Open the **01 Lighting - South Wing** view. This view is missing its tags. (Type **ZF** or **ZA** to fit the model in the view if it is not showing.)

4. In the *Annotate* tab>*Tag* panel, click 🏷️ (Tag All).

5. In the *Tag All Not Tagged* dialog box, do the following:

   - Select **Lighting Fixture Tags**.
   - Verify the *Loaded Tags* column is set to **Lighting Fixture Tag: Standard**.
   - Select **Leader**.
   - Verify the *Leader Length* is **1/16"**.
   - Verify the *Tag Orientation* is **Horizontal**.

6. Click **OK**. The lights that were not tagged are now tagged, as shown in Figure 15–20. The emergency light fixture tags have a question mark. This means they do not have a type mark assigned to them.

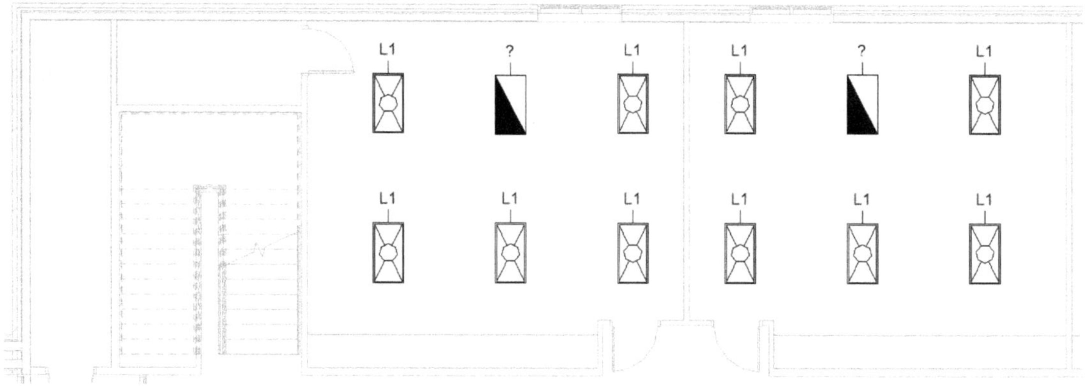

Figure 15–20

7. Click ⌨ (Modify) and select the emergency recessed light fixture. In Properties, click 🗄 (Edit Type).

8. In the *Type Properties* dialog box, in the *Identity Data* area, set the *Type Mark* to **E1** and click **OK**. All of the emergency light fixture tags update to display this information, as shown in two of the classrooms in Figure 15–21.

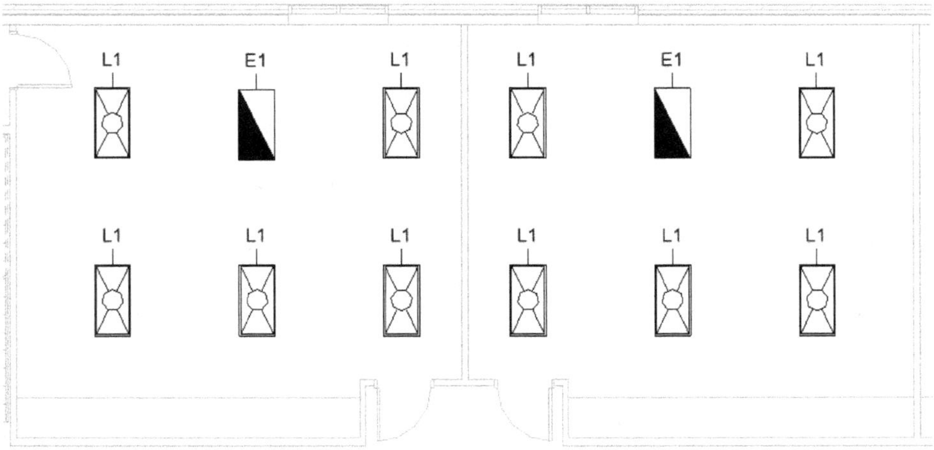

Figure 15–21

9. In the *Annotate* tab>*Tag* panel, click ⌐① (Tag by Category).

10. In Properties, verify that **Horizontal**, **Leader**, and **Attached End** are selected. In the *Modify | Tag* tab>*Placement* panel, set the *Leader Length* to **1/16"**.

11. Click the **Tags...** button.

12. In the *Loaded Tags And Symbols* dialog box, verify that *Lighting Fixtures* shows the default **Lighting Fixture Tag: Standard** tag in the *Loaded Tags* column, as shown in Figure 15–22.

Figure 15–22

13. In the top leftmost classroom in the **01 Lighting - South Wing** view, tag the light fixtures at the bottom, as shown in Figure 15–23. It should appear that you have duplicate tags for each light fixture. Do not tag any other classrooms at this time.

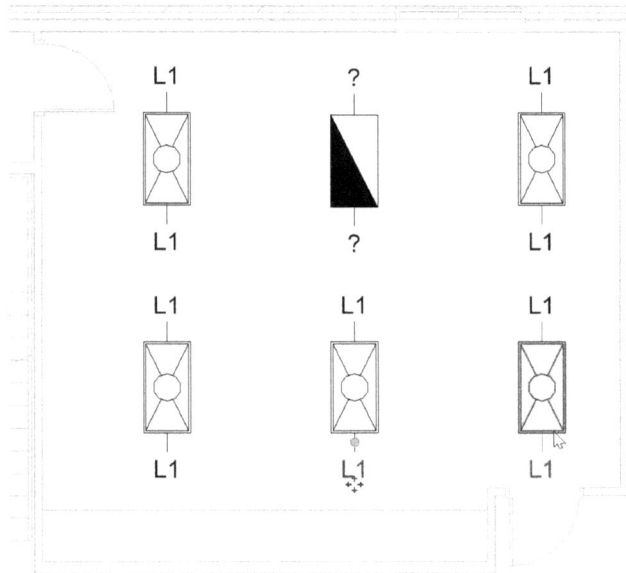

Figure 15-23

14. Click ⌂ (Modify) and select all the tags below the lights.

15. In the Type Selector, select **Lighting Fixture Circuit Tag: Standard**. The tag information changes from displaying the light fixture number to the circuit number, as shown in Figure 15-24.

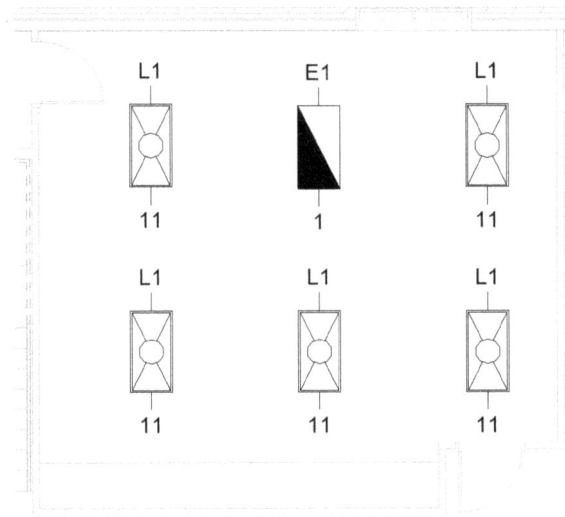

Figure 15-24

• Note that the tags could be combined using the **Add/Remove Host** tool.

16. Select the lower left light fixture circuit **11** tag. In the *Modify | Lighting Fixture Tags* tab>*Host* panel, select 🏠 (Add/Remove Host).

17. Select the light fixture to the right, as shown in Figure 15–25.

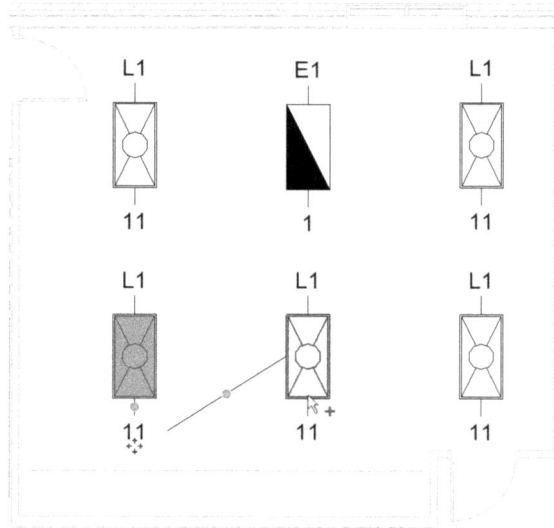

Figure 15–25

18. Select the rest of the light fixtures in the classroom, including the E1 light fixture. Because the light fixture E1 is not on the same circuit, your tag will display **<varies>**, as shown in Figure 15–26. Select the E1 light fixture to remove it from the selection, and the tag will return to 11.

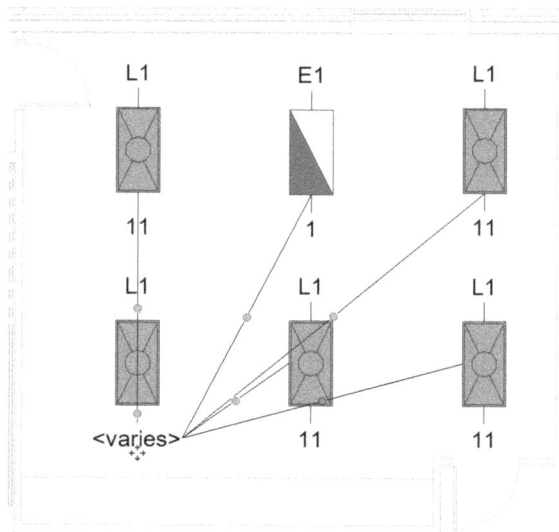

Figure 15–26

19. Click ↖ (Modify).

20. Drag the tag to the center of the classroom and delete the unneeded circuit tags, as shown in Figure 15–27. You will see leaders pointing to the light fixtures. Adjust the leaders using the grips as needed so other tags can be seen as well.

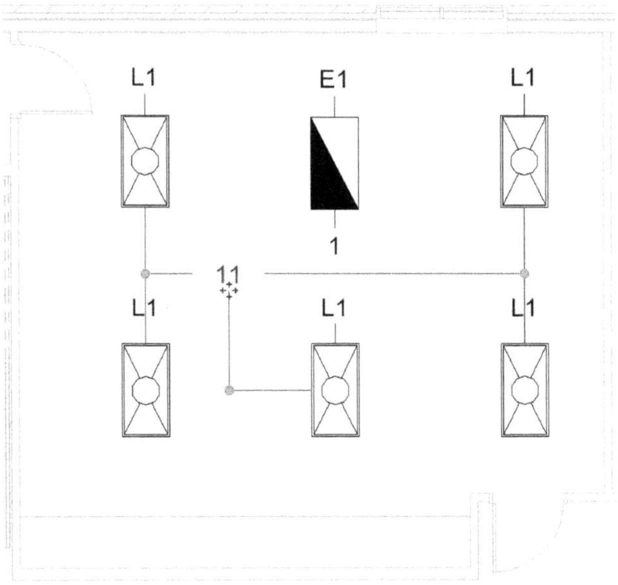

Figure 15–27

21. Click ↖ (Modify).

22. Continue tagging the rest of the classrooms, changing the tag type and merging tags using the **Add/Remove Host** tool.

23. Save the project.

Task 2: Load and use a conduit tag.

1. Open the Electrical>Power>Floor Plans>**01 Power Plan** view.

2. Zoom in on the same rooms you worked in with the light fixtures.

3. In the *Annotate* tab>*Tag* panel, click 🏷 (Tag All).

4. In the *Tag All Not Tagged* dialog box, do the following:

- Select **Conduit Tag**.
- Deselect **Leader**, if applicable.
- Set the *Tag Orientation* to **Horizontal**.

5. Click **OK**. The conduits are now tagged, as shown in Figure 15–28.

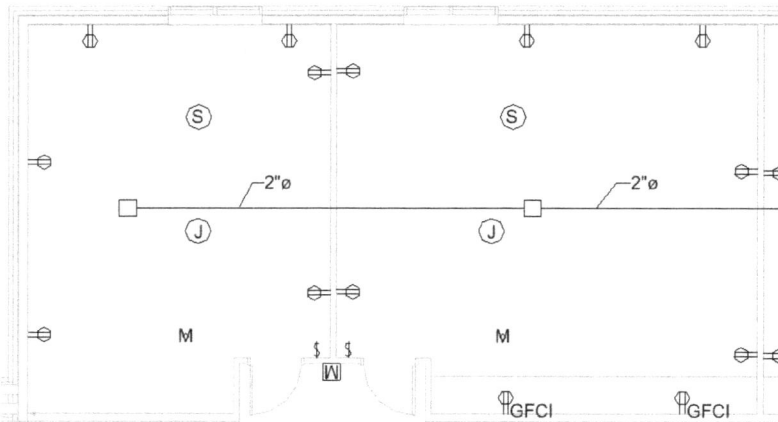

Figure 15–28

6. Click ⌂ (Modify) and select the conduit in the smaller classroom.

7. In the Options Bar, change the *Diameter* to **3/4**". The tag updates automatically, as shown in Figure 15–29.

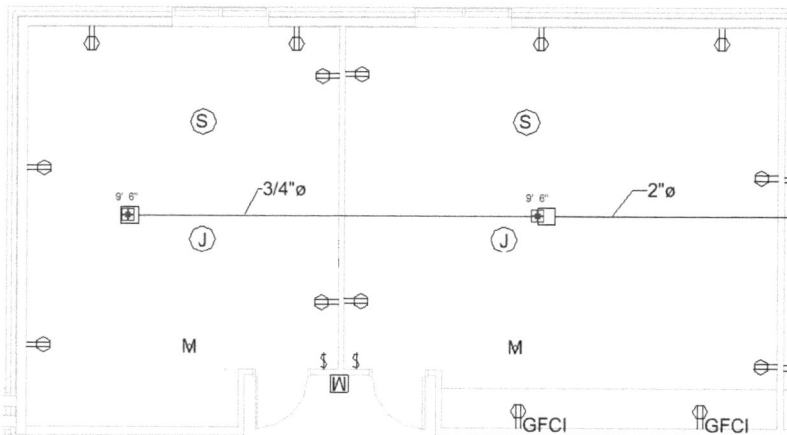

Figure 15–29

8. Type **ZF** to zoom out to fit the view.

9. Save and close the project.

End of practice

Practice 15c
Add Tags – Plumbing

Practice Objectives

- Add tags to a model.
- Lock a 3D view to tag plumbing systems and fixtures.
- Modify the Type Mark parameter for tags.

In this practice, you will add plumbing fixture tags and rotate a 3D view and lock it into place. You will then add tags to plumbing systems and fixtures, then modify the fixtures' type marks to update the tags.

Task 1: Add tags to a floor plan.

1. In the practice files *Working Models>Plumbing* folder, open **Plumb-Tags.rvt**.

2. Duplicate the **3D Plumbing** view and rename it to **3D Plumbing - 2nd Floor Restroom**.

3. Select the linked architectural model and type **VH** to hide it in the view.

   Note: *Alternatively, you can select the restroom items and from the Modify | Multi-Select tab, select* 🔲 *Section Box.*

4. In Properties, turn on **Section Box** and use the control grips to only see the second floor bathroom, as shown in Figure 15–30.

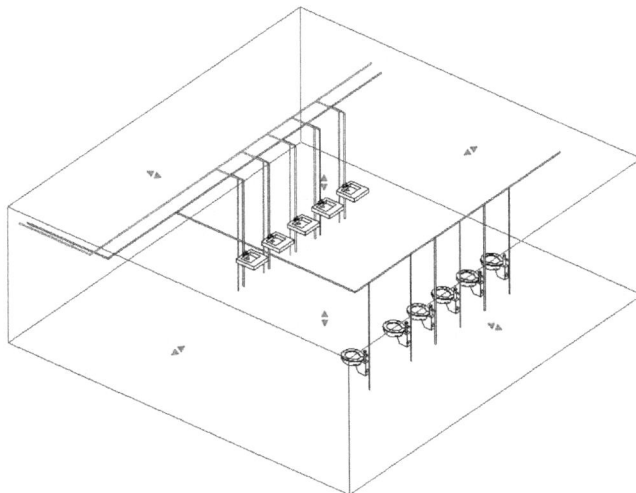

Figure 15–30

5. With the section box still selected, right-click and select **Hide in View>Elements** to hide the section box.

6. In the View Control Bar, click 🏠 (Unlocked 3D View) and select **Save Orientation and Lock View** to lock the view in place.

7. In the *Annotate* tab>*Tag* panel, click ⌐① (Tag by Category). In Properties, set the tag orientation to **Horizontal** and uncheck **Leader**. Tag the pipe.

8. While still in the **Tag by Category** command, in Properties, check **Leader** and **Attached End**.

9. In the *Modify | Tag* tab>*Placement* panel, set the *Leader Length* to **1/8"**.

10. Tag one lavatory and one water closet.

11. Click ⌖ (Modify).

12. The new tags appear empty but when you select them, they both have question marks for their tags.

13. Click ⌖ (Modify).

14. Save the project.

Task 2: Modify plumbing fixtures to update the tags.

1. Select one of the lavatories. In Properties, click ⊞ (Edit Type).

2. In the *Type Properties* dialog box, in the *Identity Data* area, set the *Type Mark* to **LS2** and click **OK**. The tags update in the view.

3. Repeat the process with a water closet and set the *Type Mark* to **WC2**.

4. In the *Annotate* tab>*Tag* panel, click ⌐⌐ (Tag All).

5. In the *Tag All Not Tagged* dialog box, do the following:

   • Check **Plumbing Fixture Tags** and verify the *Loaded Tags* column is set to **Tags Plumbing Fixture Tag : Boxed**.

   • Check **Leader**.

   • Set the *Leader Length* to **1/8"**.

   • Set the *Tag Orientation* to **Horizontal**.

6. Click **OK**. The lavatories and water closets are now tagged.

   • The tags for all the lavatories and water closets will be the same because the tag is pulling parameter information from the elements' type properties.

7. Select the first water closet tag. In the *Modify | Duct Tags* tab>*Host* panel, select ① (Add/Remove Host).

8. Select the other water closets. Drag the tag out from the water closets, as shown in Figure 15–31. Delete the unneeded tags.

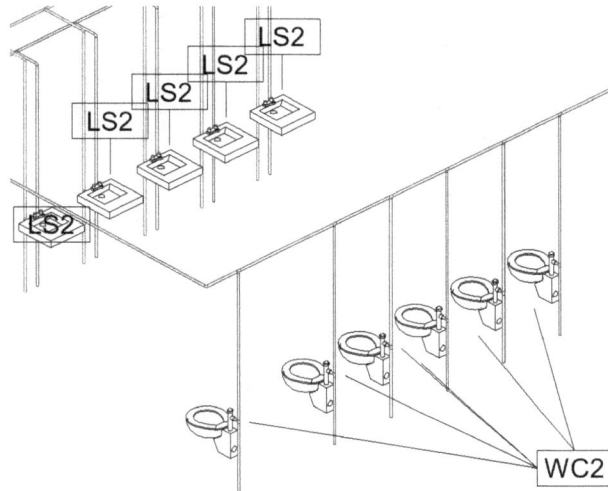

Figure 15–31

9. Click ⬚ (Modify).

10. Repeat **Add/Remove Host** for the lavatory tags.

11. Adjust the view scale if needed.

12. Save and close the project.

End of practice

15.2 Working with Schedules

Revit enables you to quickly create accurate schedules that can otherwise be time-consuming and difficult to maintain accurately throughout the lifecycle of a project. Schedules extract information from a project and display it in table form. Each schedule is stored as a separate view and can be placed on sheets, as shown in Figure 15–32. Any changes you make to the project elements that affect the schedules are automatically updated in both views and sheets.

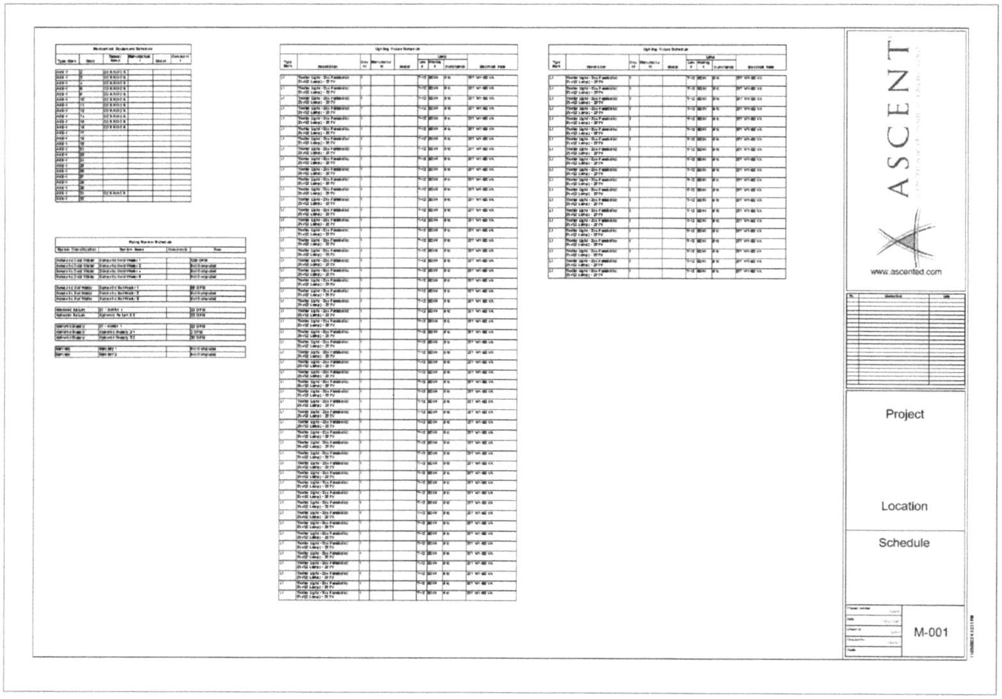

Figure 15–32

- Some of the default Revit templates have schedules included in them. For example the **Imperial Multi-discipline.rte** template file includes useful schedules. If there are no schedules in a project, you can create one of the following types of schedules:

    - (Schedule/Quantities) allows you to create building component schedules of elements in your project.

    - (Graphical Column Schedule) allows you to create a schedule for specific columns or all columns in the project including off-grid columns.

- Schedules can be created in templates so that they can be reused in multiple projects.

- You are not required to have actual elements in the model when you are creating schedules. You can schedule information that model elements contain.

- All properties that are stored in the model elements, as well as those specified by the user, can be added to schedules.

Building Component Schedules

A building component schedule is a table view of the type and instance parameters of a specific element. You can specify the parameters (fields) you want to include in the schedule. All of the parameters found in the type of element you are scheduling are available for use.

- Schedules are automatically filled out with the information stored in the instance and type parameters of related elements that are added to the model. Fill out additional information either in the schedule or in Properties.

- When selecting on a schedule's row, it will highlight in blue.

- You can drag and drop the schedule onto a sheet.

- You can zoom in to read small text in schedule views. Hold down <Ctrl> and scroll using the mouse wheel or press <Ctrl>+<+> to zoom in or <Ctrl>+<-> to zoom out.

How To: Create a Schedule

1. In the *View* tab>*Create* panel, expand ⊞ (Schedules) and click ▦ (Schedule/Quantities), or in the Project Browser, right-click on the **Schedules/Quantities** node and select **New Schedule/Quantities**.

2. In the *New Schedule* dialog box, select the type of schedule you want to create (e.g., Duct Systems) from the *Category* list, as shown in Figure 15–33.

   Note: *In the Filter list: drop-down list, you can specify the discipline(s) to show only the categories that you want to display.*

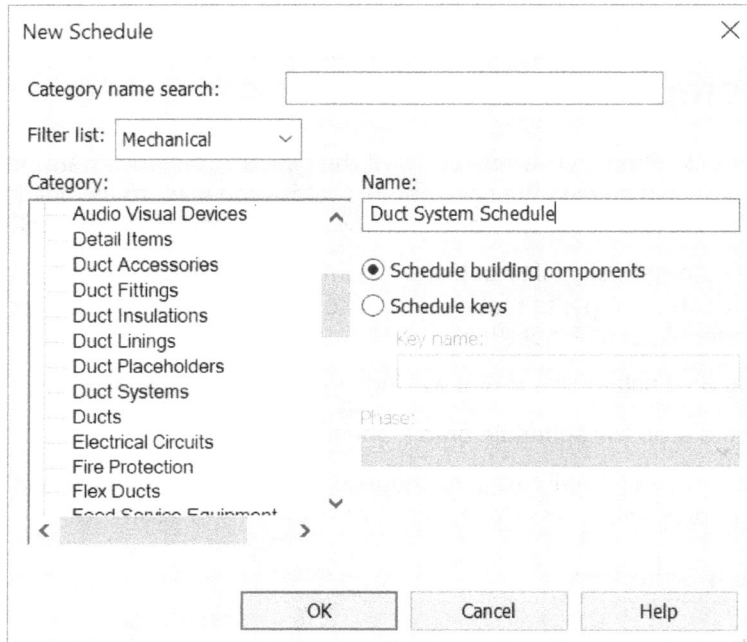

Figure 15–33

3. Revit assigns a name for the schedule. You can also type a new *Name* if the default does not suit.

4. Select **Schedule building components** and specify the *Phase*, as needed.

5. Click **OK**.

6. Fill out the information in the *Schedule Properties* dialog box. This includes the information in the *Fields, Filter, Sorting/Grouping, Formatting,* and *Appearance* tabs.

7. Once you have entered the schedule properties, click **OK**. A schedule view is created, displaying a report of the information configured in the schedule.

• Other elements that can be scheduled include model groups and Revit links.

• If a schedule is long, in the *Modify Schedule/Quantities* tab>*Appearance* panel, you can select 🔲 (Freeze Header) to keep the header row visible while you scroll through the schedule.

Schedule Properties – Fields Tab

In the *Fields* tab, you can select from a list of available fields and organize them in the order in which you want them to display in the schedule, as shown in Figure 15–34. You can also sort the available fields by *Parameter Type* (such as Project Parameters), *Discipline*, or *Value Type*.

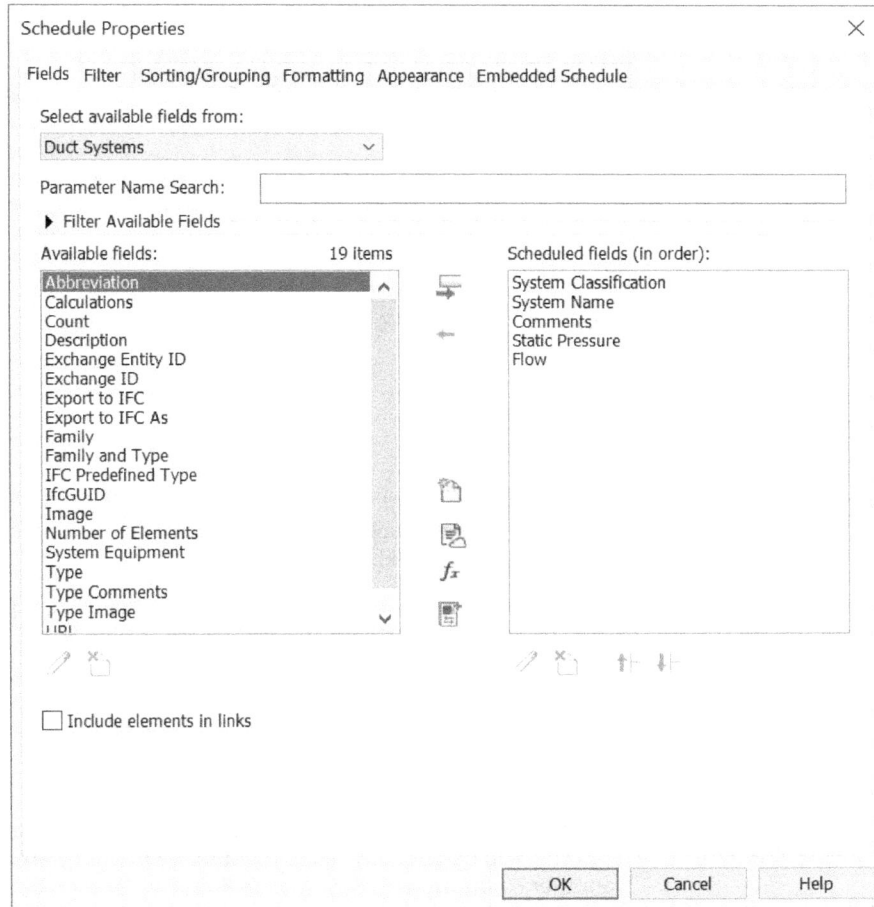

Figure 15–34

How To: Fill Out the Fields Tab

1. In the *Available fields* area, select one or more fields you want to add to the schedule and click ⯮ (Add parameter(s)). The field(s) are placed in the *Scheduled fields (in order)* area.
2. Continue adding fields, as required.

   - Click ⯬ (Remove parameter(s)) to move a field from the *Scheduled fields* area back to the *Available fields* area.

   Note: You can also double-click on a field to move it from the Available fields area to the Scheduled fields area, and double-click on a field to remove it from the Scheduled fields area.

   - Use ⯅E (Move parameter up) and ⯆E (Move parameter down) to change the order of the scheduled fields.

Other Fields Tab Options

Select available fields from	Enables you to select additional category fields for the specified schedule. The available list of fields depends on the original category of the schedule. Typically, they include room information.
Include elements in links	Includes elements that are in files linked to the current project, so that their elements can be included in the schedule.
🗋 **(New parameter)**	Adds a new field according to your specification. New fields can be placed by instance or by type.
f_x **(Add Calculated parameter)**	Enables you to create a field that uses a formula based on other fields.
🗐 **(Combine parameters)**	Enables you to combine two or more parameters in one column. You can put any fields together even if they are used in another column.
🖉 **(Edit parameter)**	Enables you to edit custom fields. This is grayed out if you select a standard field.
🗋 **(Delete parameter)**	Deletes the selected custom fields. This is grayed out if you select a standard field.

Schedule Properties – Filter Tab

In the *Filter* tab, you can set up filters so that only elements meeting specific criteria are included in the schedule. For example, you might only want to show information for one level, as shown in Figure 15–35. You can create filters for up to eight values. All values must be satisfied for the elements to display.

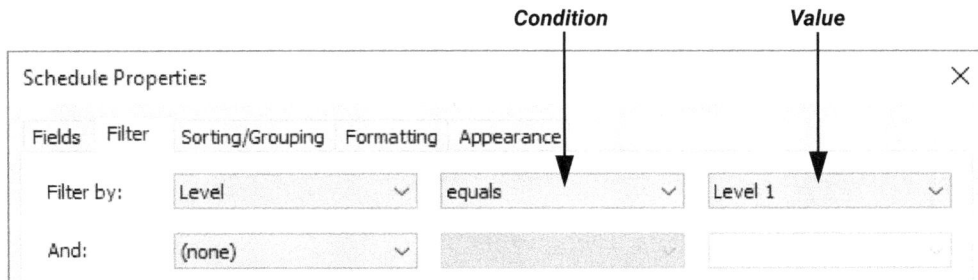

Figure 15–35

- The parameter you want to use as a filter must be included in the schedule. You can hide the parameter once you have completed the schedule, if needed.

Filter by

Field/Parameter	Specifies the field/parameter to filter. Not all fields/parameters are available to be used to filter.
Condition	Specifies the condition that must be met. This includes options such as **equal**, **not equal**, **greater than**, and **less than**.
Value	Specifies the value of the element to be filtered. You can select from a drop-down list of appropriate values. For example, if you set *Filter by* to **Level**, it displays the list of levels in the project.

Schedule Properties – Sorting/Grouping Tab

In the *Sorting/Grouping* tab, you can set how you want the information to be sorted, as shown in Figure 15–36. For example, you can sort by **Mark** (number) and then **Type**.

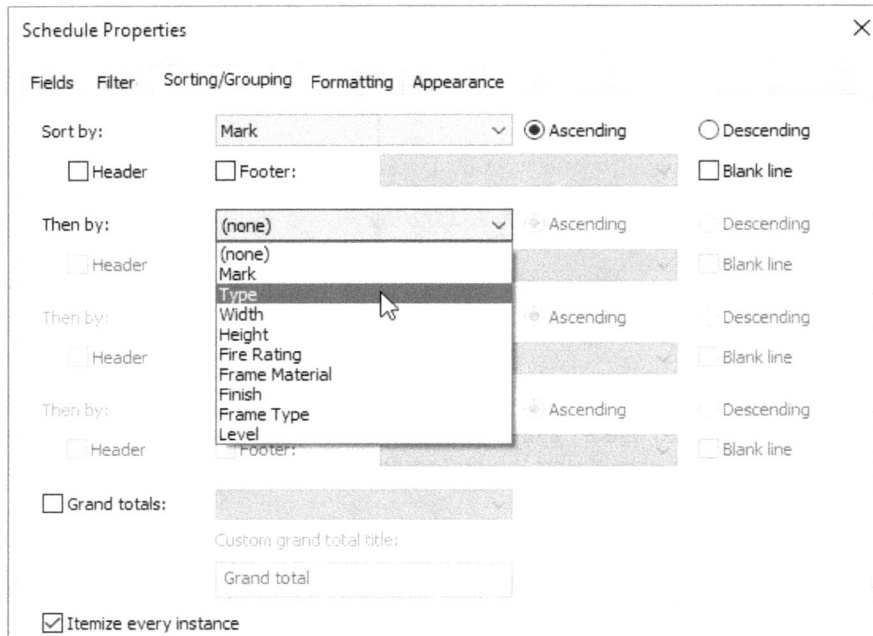

Figure 15–36

Sort by	Enables you to select the field(s) you want to sort by. You can select up to four levels of sorting.
Ascending/ Descending	Sorts fields in **Ascending** or **Descending** order based on an alphanumeric system.
Header/Footer	Enables you to group similar information and separate it by a **Header** with a title and/or a **Footer** with quantity information.
Blank line	Adds a blank line between groups.
Grand totals	Selects which totals to display for the entire schedule. You can specify a name to display in the schedule for the grand total.
Itemize every instance	If selected, displays each instance of the element in the schedule. If not selected, displays only one instance of each type based on the sorting/ grouping categories, as shown in Figure 15–37.

<Duct System Schedule>				
A	B	C	D	E
System Classificatio	System Name	Comments	Static Pressure	Flow
Return Air	<varies>		0.00 in-wg	0 CFM
Return Air	<varies>		0.06 in-wg	500 CFM
Return Air	01 - RA08		0.11 in-wg	500 CFM
Return Air	RA 1		0.15 in-wg	1000 CFM
Return Air	<varies>		0.20 in-wg	<varies>
Return Air	<varies>		0.21 in-wg	<varies>

Figure 15–37

Schedule Properties – Formatting Tab

In the *Formatting* tab, you can control how the headers of each field display, as shown in Figure 15–38. The *Multiple values indication* options enable you to control how fields with multiple values display.

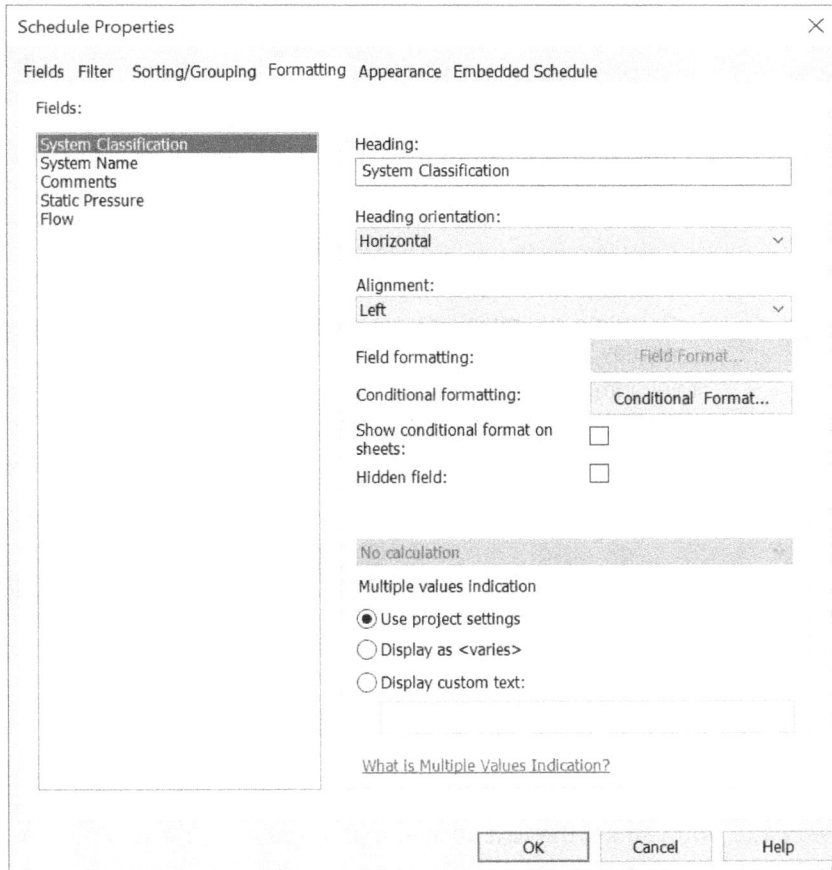

Figure 15–38

Fields	Enables you to select the field for which you want to modify the formatting.
Heading	Enables you to change the heading of the field if you want it to be different from the field name. For example, you might want to replace **Mark** (a generic name) with the more specific **Door Number** in a door schedule.
Heading orientation	Enables you to set the heading on sheets to **Horizontal** or **Vertical**. This does not impact the schedule view.
Alignment	Aligns the text in rows under the heading to be **Left**, **Right**, or **Center** justified.
Field Format...	Sets the units format for numerical fields, e.g., length, area, HVAC air flow, pipe flow, etc. By default, this is set to use the project settings.
Conditional Format...	Sets up the schedule to display visual feedback based on the conditions listed.
Hidden field	Enables you to hide a field. For example, you might want to use a field for sorting purposes, but not have it display in the schedule. You can also modify this option in the schedule view later.
Show conditional format on sheets	Select if you want the color code set up in the *Conditional Format* dialog box to display on sheets.
Calculation options	Select the type of calculation you want to use. • **No Calculation:** All values in a field are calculated separately. • **Calculate totals:** All values in a field are added together. This enables a field to calculate and display in the Grand Totals or Footers. • **Calculate minimum:** Only the smallest amount displays. • **Calculate maximum:** Only the largest amount displays. • **Calculate minimum and maximum:** Both the smallest and largest amounts display. Minimum and maximum calculations only show when **Itemize every instance** is unchecked in the *Sorting/Grouping* tab.
Multiple values indication	When a schedule is not set to itemize every instance, select how the value will display.

💡 Hint: Hiding Columns

If you want to use the field to filter or sort, but do not want it to display in the schedule, select **Hidden field**. Alternatively, once the schedule is completed, select the column header, right-click on it, and select **Hide Columns**.

Schedule Properties – Appearance Tab

In the *Appearance* tab, you can set the text style and grid options for a schedule, as shown in Figure 15–39.

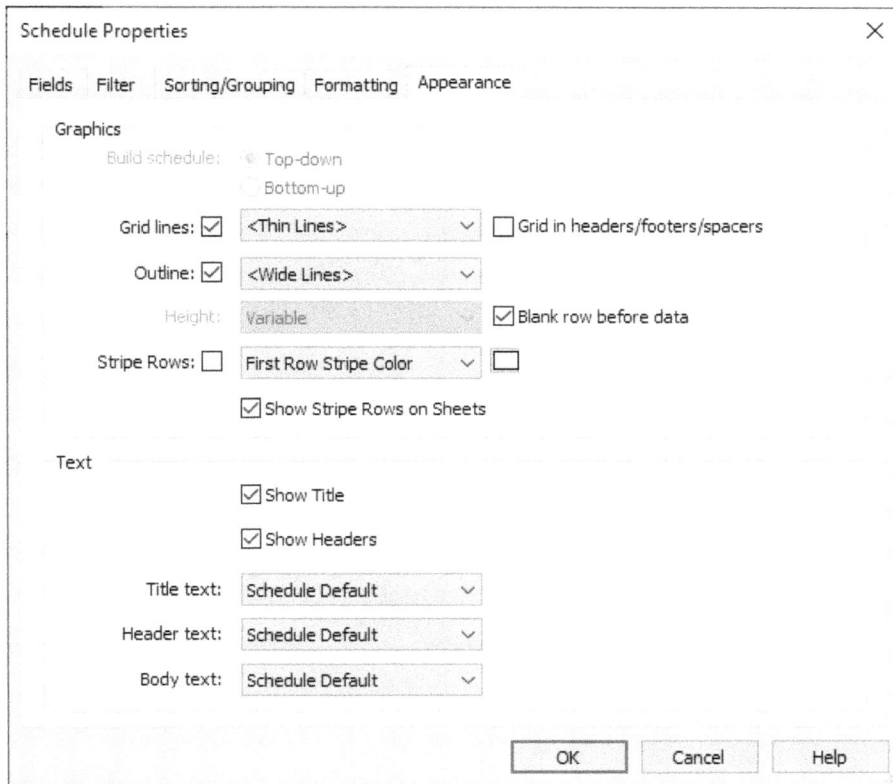

Figure 15–39

Grid lines	Displays lines between each instance listed and around the outside of the schedule. Select the style of lines from the drop-down list; this controls all lines for the schedule, unless modified.
Grid in headers/footers/ spacers	Extends the vertical grid lines between the columns.
Outline	Specify a different line type for the outline of the schedule.
Blank row before data	Select this option if you want a blank row to be displayed before the data begins in the schedule.
Stripe Rows	Select this option if you want to highlight alternating rows within the schedule to help differentiate the rows in large schedules.
Show Title/Show Headers	Select these options to include the text in the schedule.
Title text/Header text/ Body text	Select the text style for the title, header, and body text.

Schedule View Properties

Schedule views have properties, including the *View Template, View Name, Phases*, and methods of returning to the *Schedule Properties* dialog box (as shown in Figure 15–40). In the *Other* section, click the button next to the tab name that you want to open in the *Schedule Properties* dialog box. In the dialog box, you can switch from tab to tab and make any required changes to the overall schedule.

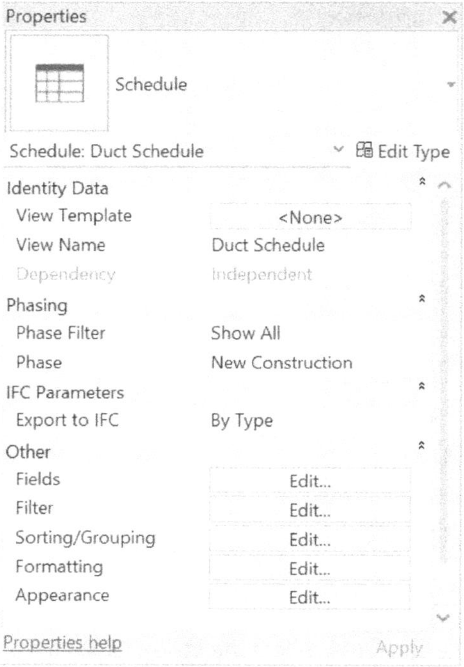

Properties		
Schedule		
Schedule: Duct Schedule	∨	⊞ Edit Type
Identity Data		
View Template	<None>	
View Name	Duct Schedule	
Dependency	Independent	
Phasing		
Phase Filter	Show All	
Phase	New Construction	
IFC Parameters		
Export to IFC	By Type	
Other		
Fields	Edit...	
Filter	Edit...	
Sorting/Grouping	Edit...	
Formatting	Edit...	
Appearance	Edit...	
Properties help	Apply	

Figure 15–40

Just like other views, schedules can have view templates applied. When you specify a view template directly in the view, none of the schedule properties can be modified, as shown in Figure 15–41.

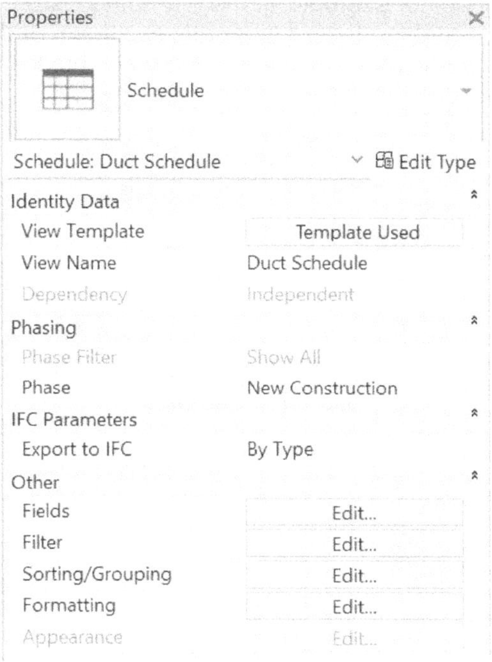

Figure 15–41

- Schedule view templates are type-specific. If you apply one to a different type of element, only the *Appearance* information is applied.

- If you apply a schedule view template to a schedule of the same type, it overrides everything in the existing schedule, including the fields.

- If you have a complicated schedule, you might want to create a view template for it to avoid losing that organization.

- To create schedule view templates, you need to create at least one from an existing view, then you can modify it and duplicate it in the *View Templates* dialog box.

Filtering Elements from Schedules

When you create schedules based on a category, you might need to filter out some of the element types in that category. For example, in the Plumbing Fixture Schedule, it shows all components that are in the plumbing fixture category, as shown at the top in Figure 15–42. To remove drains from the schedule, as shown at the bottom in Figure 15–42, assign a parameter that identifies them and then use that parameter to filter them out of the schedule.

All plumbing fixtures displayed

<Plumbing Fixture Schedule>			
A	B	C	D
Family	Type	Count	System Name
Floor Drain - Round	5" Strainer - 3" Drain	7	
Lavatory - Rectangular	22"x22" - Public	20	Domestic Cold Water 1,Domestic Hot Water 1,Sanitary 1
Sink - Island - Single	30"x21" - Public	40	Domestic Cold Water 1,Domestic Hot Water 1,Sanitary 1
Urinal - Wall Hung	1" Flush Valve	6	Domestic Cold Water 1,Sanitary 1
Water Closet - Flush Valve - Wall Mounted	Public - Flushing Greater than 1.6 gpf	20	Domestic Cold Water 1,Sanitary 1

Floor drains filtered out

<Plumbing Fixture Schedule>			
A	B	C	D
Family	Type	Count	System Name
Lavatory - Rectangular	22"x22" - Public	20	Domestic Cold Water 1,Domestic Hot Water 1,Sanitary 1
Sink - Island - Single	30"x21" - Public	40	Domestic Cold Water 1,Domestic Hot Water 1,Sanitary 1
Urinal - Wall Hung	1" Flush Valve	6	Domestic Cold Water 1,Sanitary 1
Water Closet - Flush Valve - Wall Mounted	Public - Flushing Greater than 1.6 gpf	20	Domestic Cold Water 1,Sanitary 1

Figure 15–42

- This type of filtering can be used for any schedule in any discipline.

How To: Filter Elements in a Schedule

1. Select an element (such as a sink) and modify the Type Parameters. Add a value to one of the parameters that you are not otherwise using in your schedule. For example, you could set *Type Mark* to **S01**, as shown Figure 15–43.

Type Parameters

Parameter	Value	=	^
Identity Data			^
Assembly Description			
Type Mark	S01		

Figure 15–43

2. Create a schedule and include the field for the parameter you used (such as *Type Mark* in the above example).

3. Modify the *Filter* of the schedule so that the parameter does not equal the specified value. In the example shown in Figure 15–44, the filter is set so **Type Mark > does not equal > S01**. Any types that match this filter are excluded from the schedule.

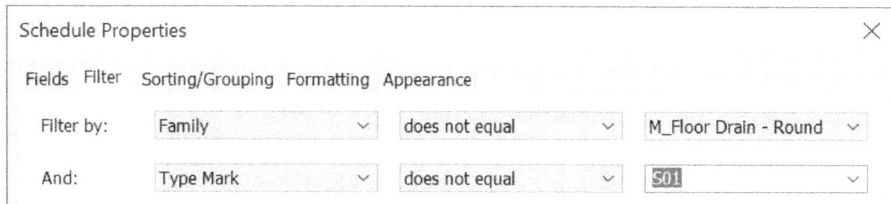

Schedule Properties   ✕

Fields   Filter   Sorting/Grouping   Formatting   Appearance

Filter by: Family   ⌄   does not equal   ⌄   M_Floor Drain - Round ⌄

And: Type Mark   ⌄   does not equal   ⌄   S01   ⌄

Figure 15–44

4. In the final schedule, the elements display with the specified value. Right-click on the column header for the parameter you used to filter the schedule and select **Hide Columns**. It is just used as a filter and does not need to be part of the final schedule.

Note: Hiding a parameter/field in a schedule enables you to use it as a filter, but not have it visible in the schedule.

Modifying Schedules

Information in schedules is bi-directional:

• Make changes to elements and the schedule automatically updates.

• Make changes to information in the schedule cells and the elements automatically update.

How To: Modify Schedule Cells

1. Open the schedule view.

2. Select the cell you want to change. Some cells have drop-down lists, as shown in Figure 15–45. Others have edit fields.

A	B	C
SPACE NO.	NAME	Condition Type
DIFFUSER ID	DIFFUSER TYPE	DIFFUSER AIRFLOW
100	PLUMBING CHASE	Unconditioned
101	PLUMBING CHASE	Unconditioned
200	RECEPTION	Unconditioned
201	RESOURCE	Unconditioned
1500	SPECIAL ED	Heated and cooled
49	STORAGE	150 CFM
	TOILET	

Figure 15–45

3. Add the new information. The change is reflected in the schedule, on the sheet, and in the elements of the project.

- If you change a type property, an alert box opens, as shown in Figure 15-46.

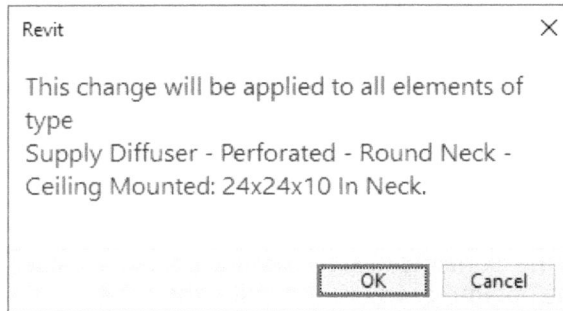

Figure 15-46

Note: If you change a type property in the schedule, it applies to all elements of that type. If you change an instance property, it only applies to that one element.

- When you select an element in a schedule, in the *Modify Schedule/Quantities* tab>*Element* panel, you can click (Highlight in Model). This opens a close-up view of the element with the *Show Element(s) in View* dialog box, as shown in Figure 15-47. Click **Show** to display more views of the element. Click **Close** to finish the command.

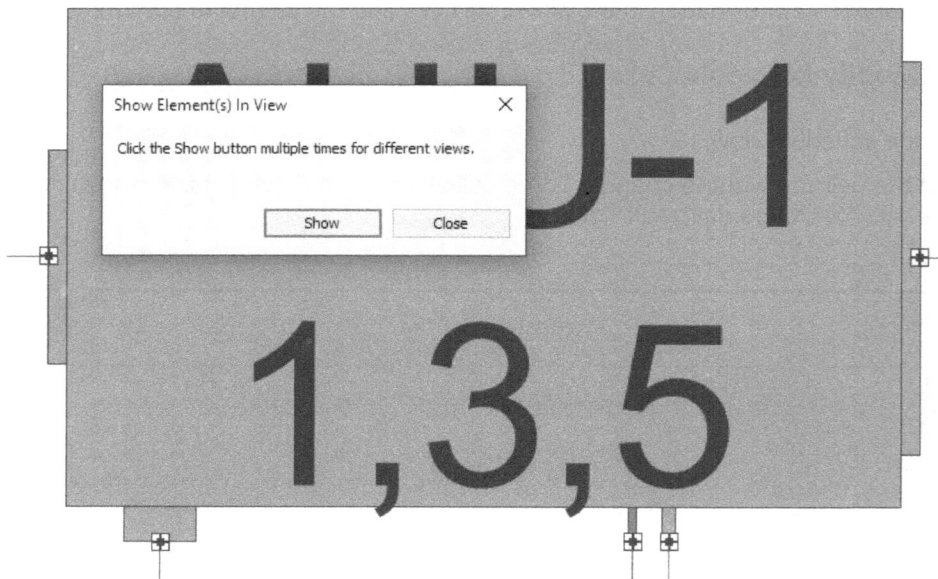

Figure 15-47

Hint: Customizing Schedules

Schedules are typically included in project templates, which are set up by the BIM manager or other advanced users. They can be complex to create as there are many options.

- For information on using schedule data outside of Revit, see ***B.5 Importing and Exporting Schedules*** in ***Appendix B Additional Tools for Construction Documents***.
- For more information about creating schedules, refer to the ASCENT guide *Autodesk Revit BIM Management: Template and Family Creation*.

Modifying a Schedule on a Sheet

Once you have placed a schedule on a sheet, you can manipulate it to fit the information into the available space. Select the schedule to display the controls that enable you to modify it, as shown in Figure 15–48.

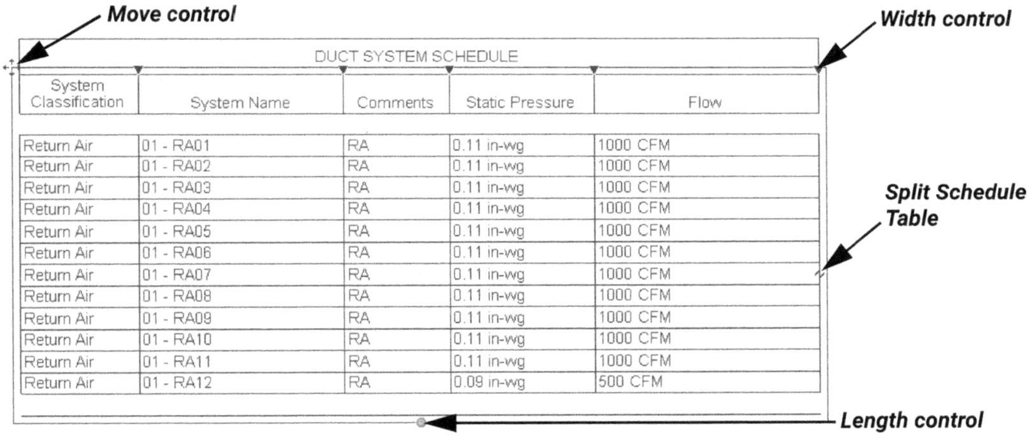

System Classification	System Name	Comments	Static Pressure	Flow
Return Air	01 - RA01	RA	0.11 in-wg	1000 CFM
Return Air	01 - RA02	RA	0.11 in-wg	1000 CFM
Return Air	01 - RA03	RA	0.11 in-wg	1000 CFM
Return Air	01 - RA04	RA	0.11 in-wg	1000 CFM
Return Air	01 - RA05	RA	0.11 in-wg	1000 CFM
Return Air	01 - RA06	RA	0.11 in-wg	1000 CFM
Return Air	01 - RA07	RA	0.11 in-wg	1000 CFM
Return Air	01 - RA08	RA	0.11 in-wg	1000 CFM
Return Air	01 - RA09	RA	0.11 in-wg	1000 CFM
Return Air	01 - RA10	RA	0.11 in-wg	1000 CFM
Return Air	01 - RA11	RA	0.11 in-wg	1000 CFM
Return Air	01 - RA12	RA	0.09 in-wg	500 CFM

Figure 15–48

- The blue triangles modify the width of each column.
- The break mark splits the schedule into two parts.

- In a split schedule, you can use the arrows in the upper-left corner to move that portion of the schedule table. The control at the bottom of the first table changes the length of the table and impacts any connected splits, as shown in Figure 15–49.

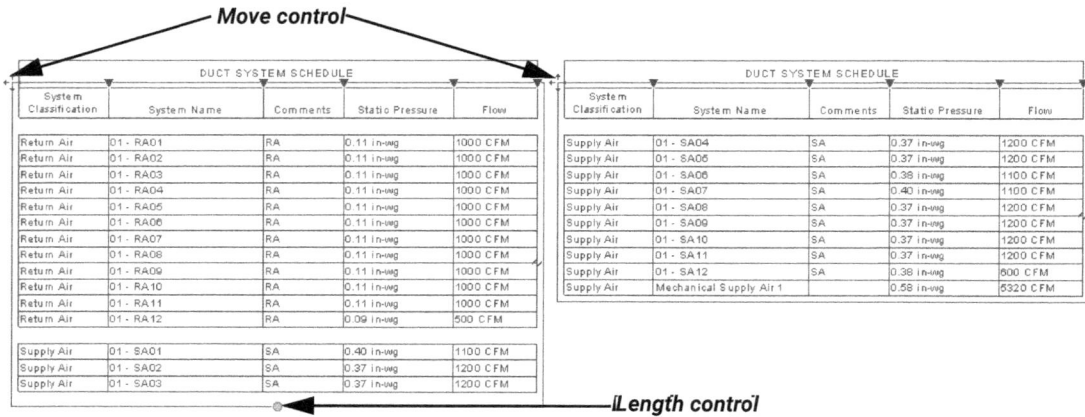

Figure 15–49

- To unsplit a schedule, drag the Move control from the side of the schedule that you want to unsplit back to the original column.

Split a Schedule Across Multiple Sheets

When a schedule becomes too long, you need to be able to split it and place it on multiple sheets. You can split a schedule evenly or by setting a custom height. When a schedule has been split, you can expand **Schedules/Quantities (all)** in the Project Browser to see the segments of the schedule, as shown in Figure 15–50.

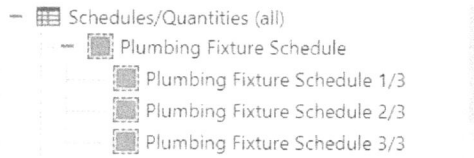

Figure 15–50

If the split is not what you wanted, you can delete the segmented schedules from the Project Browser. Do not delete the main schedule.

How To: Split a Schedule and Place It on Multiple Sheets

1. Make additional sheets, if needed. In a schedule view, in the *Modify Schedule/Quantities* tab>*Split* panel, click 🖼 (Split & Place).

2. In the *Split Schedule and Place on Sheets* dialog box, select the sheets that you want to distribute the split schedule to, as shown in Figure 15–51.

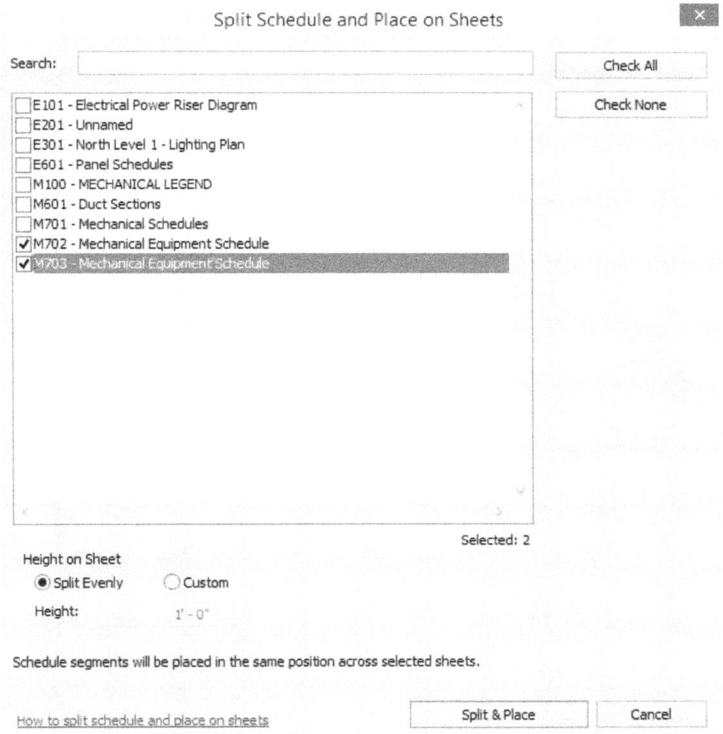

Figure 15–51

3. In the *Height on Sheet* section, select **Split Evenly** or **Custom**. If custom is selected, specify a *Height*.

4. Click **Split & Place**.

5. The first sheet selected in the list opens and the first segment of the split schedule is attached to your cursor. Place it on the sheet.

6. If you had selected multiple sheets in the *Split Schedule and Place on Sheets* dialog box, the rest of the segment schedule will automatically be placed exactly where you had initially placed the first segment of the schedule.

7. Open each sheet and use the control grips to adjust the columns and stretch the schedule to fit the sheet, as needed.

How To: Remove Split Schedules

1. In the Project Browser, expand the schedule.

2. Select the segmented schedules and press <Delete>, or right-click and select **Delete**.

Filter by Sheet

If you place your schedule on a sheet that has a view on it, you can filter the schedule to only display the elements that are in that viewport. In Figure 15–52, the door schedule is only showing Floor 1 doors because the sheet contains the Floor 1 - Plan view and the **Filter by sheet** option has been selected.

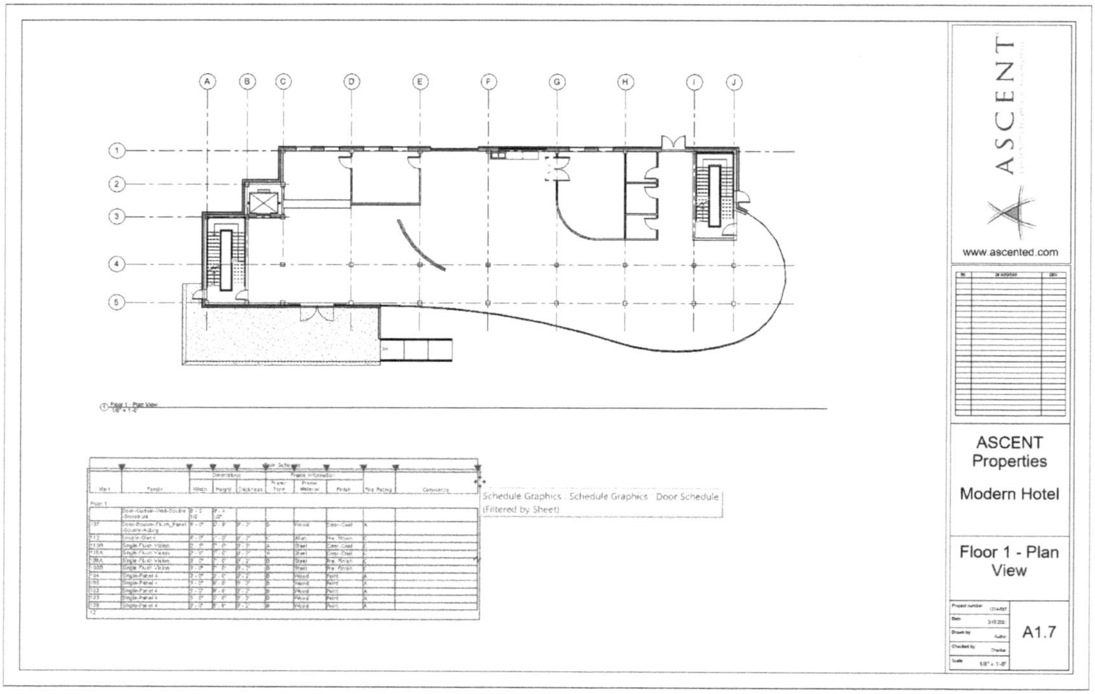

Figure 15–52

- If a view is changed or modified, the schedule and the same sheet will update accordingly.

- Schedules that are split across multiple sheets cannot use the **Filter by sheet** option.

- Panel and revision schedules cannot use the **Filter by sheet** option.

How To: Filter a Schedule by Sheets

1. Open a schedule view.
2. In Properties, click **Edit...** next to *Filter*.

3. In the *Schedule Properties* dialog box, check the checkbox for **Filter by sheet**, as shown in Figure 15–53.

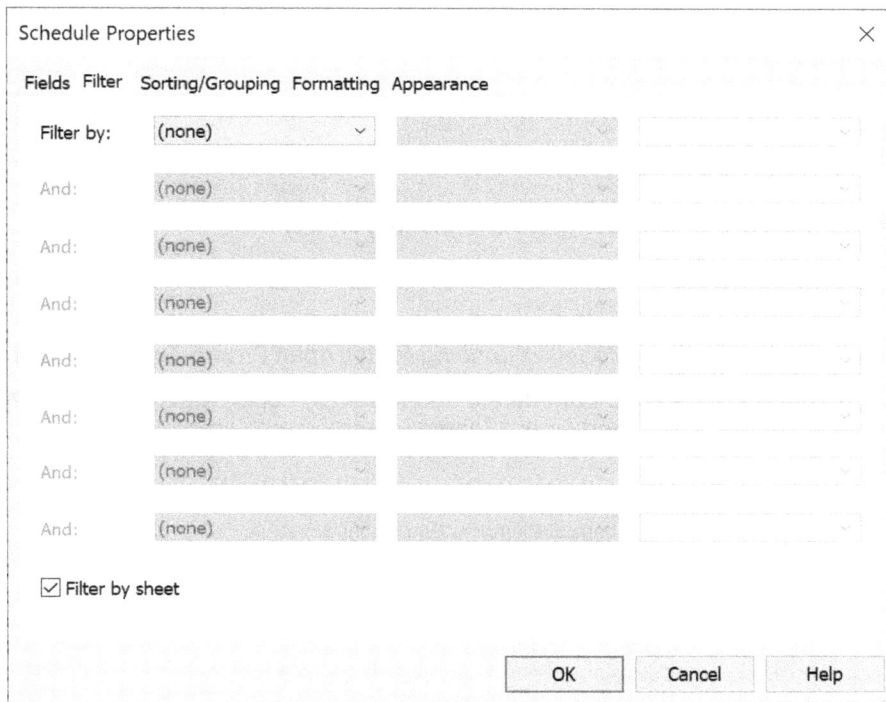

Figure 15–53

4. Click **OK**.

- You cannot use this feature if you have split the schedule.

Practice 15d
Work with Schedules – Mechanical/Plumbing

Practice Objectives

- Update schedule information.
- Add a schedule to a sheet.

In this practice, you will update a schedule and place it on a sheet.

Task 1: Fill in schedules.

1. In the practice files *Working Models>Plumbing* folder, open **Plumb-Schedules.rvt**.

2. In the Project Browser, expand **Schedules/Quantities** and open **Mechanical/Plumbing Equipment Schedule**. The schedule is already populated with some information, as shown in Figure 15–54.

\<Mechanical/Plumbing Equipment Schedule\>					
A	B	C	D	E	F
Type Mark	Mark	Space: Name	Manufacturer	Model	Comments
AHU-1	1	CORRIDOR			
AHU-1	2	CORRIDOR			
AHU-1	3	CORRIDOR			
AHU-1	4	CORRIDOR			
AHU-1	5	CORRIDOR			
AHU-1	6	CORRIDOR			
AHU-1	7	CORRIDOR			
AHU-1	8	CORRIDOR			
AHU-1	9	CORRIDOR			
AHU-1	10	CORRIDOR			
AHU-1	11	CORRIDOR			
	49	JNTR.			
	50	JNTR.			
AHU-1	51	CORRIDOR			
AHU-1	52	CORRIDOR			

Figure 15–54

3. Two *Type Mark* cells are empty. Click in one of the empty *Type Mark* cells. In the *Modify Schedules/Quantities* tab>*Element* panel, click (Highlight in Model).

4. In the dialog box that opens, stating there is no open view that shows any of the highlighted elements (as shown in Figure 15–55), click **OK** to search through closed views.

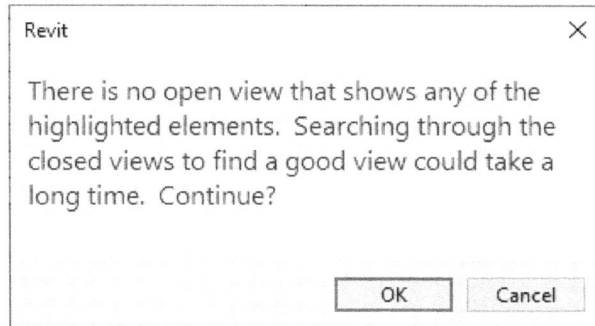

Revit ✕

There is no open view that shows any of the highlighted elements. Searching through the closed views to find a good view could take a long time. Continue?

[OK]   [Cancel]

Figure 15–55

5. In the view that comes up, if it is not showing the water heater element you need to see, click **Show**. If you can see the element, click **Close** in the *Show Element(s) In View* dialog box (shown in Figure 15–56).

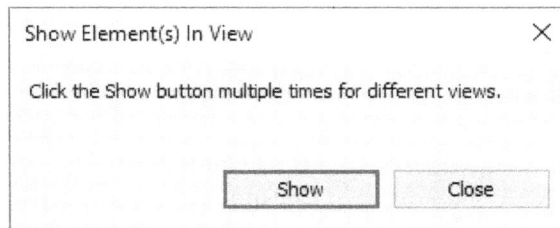

Show Element(s) In View ✕

Click the Show button multiple times for different views.

[Show]   [Close]

Figure 15–56

6. Zoom out so that you can see the element (e.g., a water heater) in context.

7. In Properties, click ⊞ (Edit Type).

8. In the *Type Properties* dialog box, in the *Identity Data* area, set the *Type Mark* to **HW-1**.

9. Click **OK** to finish.

10. Return to the Mechanical/Plumbing Equipment Schedule (select the tab or press <Ctrl>+<Tab> to switch between open windows).

11. The water heaters in the project now have a *Type Mark* set, as shown in Figure 15–57.

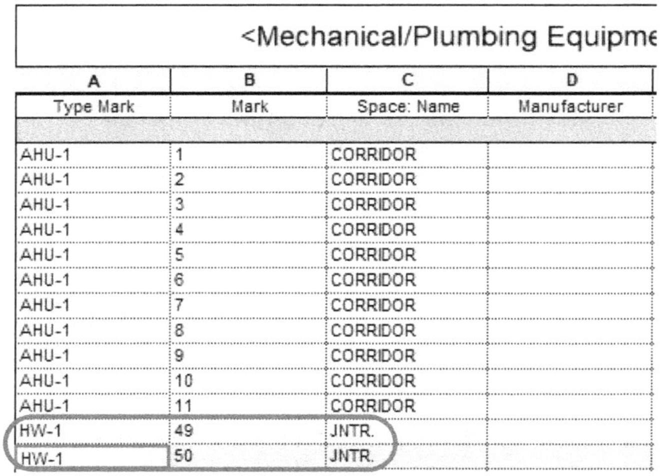

	A	B	C	D
		<Mechanical/Plumbing Equipme		
	Type Mark	Mark	Space: Name	Manufacturer
	AHU-1	1	CORRIDOR	
	AHU-1	2	CORRIDOR	
	AHU-1	3	CORRIDOR	
	AHU-1	4	CORRIDOR	
	AHU-1	5	CORRIDOR	
	AHU-1	6	CORRIDOR	
	AHU-1	7	CORRIDOR	
	AHU-1	8	CORRIDOR	
	AHU-1	9	CORRIDOR	
	AHU-1	10	CORRIDOR	
	AHU-1	11	CORRIDOR	
	HW-1	49	JNTR.	
	HW-1	50	JNTR.	

Figure 15–57

12. In the *Mark* column, you can see that the numbers are out of sequence. The numbering of the water heaters and two air handling units (AHU-1) starts at 49 and is incorrect.

13. Change the *Mark* of the incorrectly numbered AHU-1s from **51** and **52** to **12** and **13**, respectively.

14. In the schedule view, change the name of the *Manufacturer* of one of the AHUs by clicking in the cell and typing **ME Unlimited**, then clicking in another cell. An alert displays warning that changing this changes all of the elements of this type, as shown in Figure 15–58. Click **OK**.

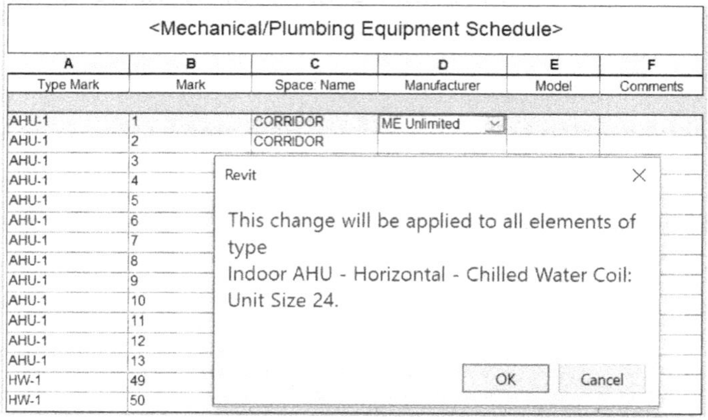

Figure 15–58

15. Open the Mechanical>HVAC>Floor Plans>**01 Mechanical Plan - South Wing** view.

16. Select the AHU that is connected to the Office duct system. In the Type Selector, change it to **Indoor AHU - Horizontal - Chilled Water Coil: Unit Size 12**.

    • Ignore any warnings that display.

17. While it is still selected, click **Edit Type** and set the *Type Mark* to **AHU-2**.

18. Switch back to the schedule view to see the change.

19. In the *Manufacturer* column, use the drop-down list to select the same manufacturer for the modified AHU, as shown in Figure 15–59. Click **OK** in the dialog box notifying you of the change to any other elements of that type.

<Mechanical/Plumbing Equipmen			
A	B	C	D
Type Mark	Mark	Space: Name	Manufacturer
AHU-1	1	CORRIDOR	ME Unlimited
AHU-1	2	CORRIDOR	ME Unlimited
AHU-1	3	CORRIDOR	ME Unlimited
AHU-1	4	CORRIDOR	ME Unlimited
AHU-2	5	CORRIDOR	
AHU-1	6	CORRIDOR	ME Unlimited
AHU-1	7	CORRIDOR	ME Unlimited

Figure 15–59

20. Fill in the other information.

21. Save the project.

Task 2: Modify the plumbing fixture schedule.

1. From the Project Browser, open the **Plumbing Fixture Schedule**. The schedule is already populated with some information.

2. Review the schedule's title and headers. Scroll down using your mouse wheel, and note that the schedule's title and headers no longer display.

3. In the *Modify Schedule/Quantities* tab>*Appearance* panel, select ⊞ (Freeze Header). Scroll down the schedule and note that the schedule's title and headers stay at the top.

4. In Properties, in the *Other* section, click **Edit...** next to *Sorting/Grouping*.

5. In the *Schedule Properties* dialog box>*Sorting/Grouping* tab, select **Type** from the *Sort by:* drop-down list, as shown in Figure 15–60.

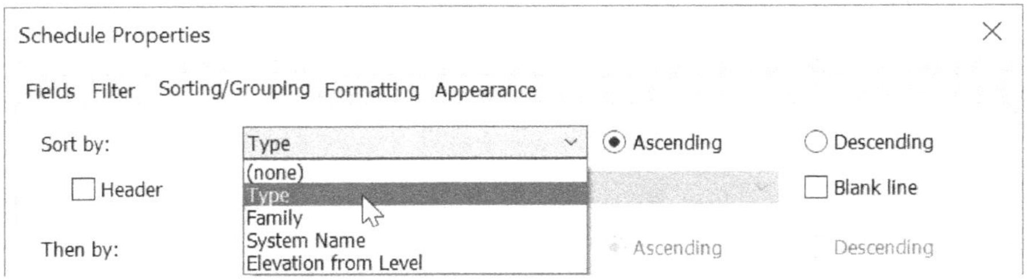

Figure 15–60

6. Select **Footer** and select **Title, count, and totals** from the drop-down list, as shown in Figure 15–61. Select the **Blank line** option and click **OK**.

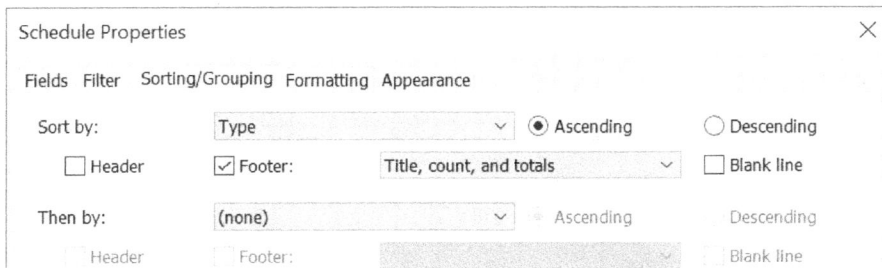

Figure 15–61

7. Scroll through the schedule and note how it has been divided by type (e.g., family size) with space between each family type.

Task 3: Add schedules to a sheet.

1. Open the **Duct Schedule**. Note that the different duct sizes show **<varies>** in some of the columns. This means that there are different values for these family types.

2. In the Project Browser, right-click on **Sheets (all)** and select **New Sheet**. Select the **ASCENT 30 x 42 Horizontal** title block and click **OK**.

3. In the Project Browser, right-click on the new sheet (which is bold) and select **Rename**. In the *Sheet Title* dialog box, set the *Number* to **M-003** and the *Name* to **Duct Schedule** and click **OK**.

4. Right-click on the Duct Schedule sheet and select **Duplicate Sheet>Duplicate Empty Sheet**, as shown in Figure 15–62. Rename it **M-004 Duct Schedule**.

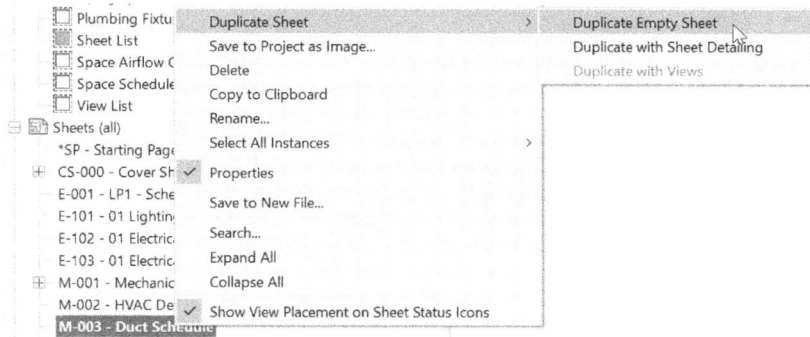

Figure 15-62

5. Return to the Duct Schedule.

6. In Properties, click **Edit...** next to *Sorting/Grouping*.

7. In the *Schedule Properties* dialog box, check the box for **Itemized every instance** and click **OK**.

8. This itemizes all the ducts and fittings in the model. Scroll down the schedule and note that this will not fit onto one sheet.

9. In the *Modify Schedule/Quantities* tab>*Split* panel, click ▦ (Split & Place).

10. In the *Split Schedule and Place on Sheets* dialog box, select the two Duct Schedule sheets, as shown in Figure 15-63.

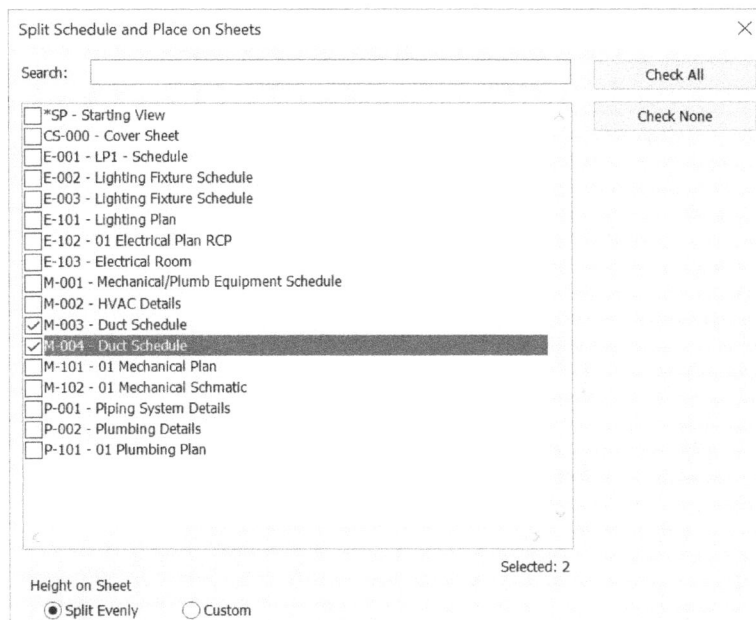

Figure 15-63

11. Click **Split & Place**.

12. The **M-003 - Duct Schedule** sheet automatically opens and the first segment of the split schedule is attached to your cursor. Use your mouse wheel to zoom out, if needed.

13. Place the Duct Schedule in the upper-left corner of the sheet.

14. From the Project Browser, open sheet **M-004**. Note that the other segment of the split schedule has automatically been added to the sheet in the same place as M-003. The schedule will be too long and needs to be split even more.

15. Click ⬚ (Modify).

16. Go back to sheet M-003. Click on the schedule and then click ⌄ (Split Schedule Table), as shown in Figure 15–64.

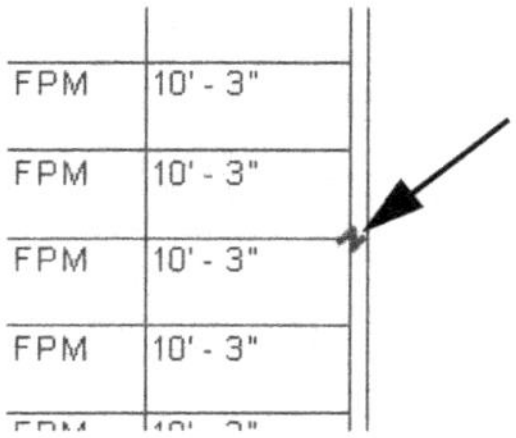

Figure 15–64

17. Select the first section of the schedule on the sheet and use the control grips at the bottom of the schedule to stretch it to fit the sheet. On the second section of the sheet, click

    ⌄ (Split Schedule Table), as shown in Figure 15–65, to split the schedule again and use the grips to stretch or shrink the schedule to fit.

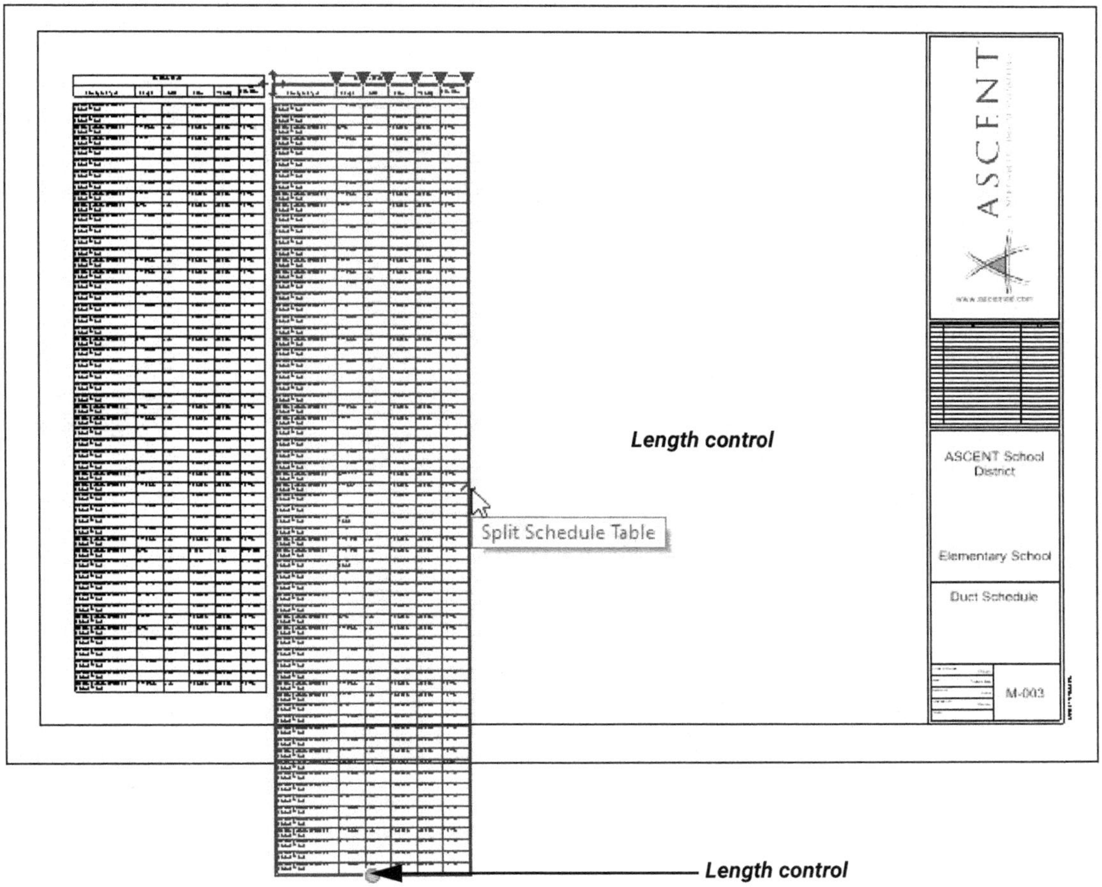

Figure 15–65

18. Open sheet **M-004** and adjust the schedule as needed.

19. Click in an empty space in the view to clear the selection.

20. Select the individual schedules and move them away from each other, as shown in Figure 15–66.

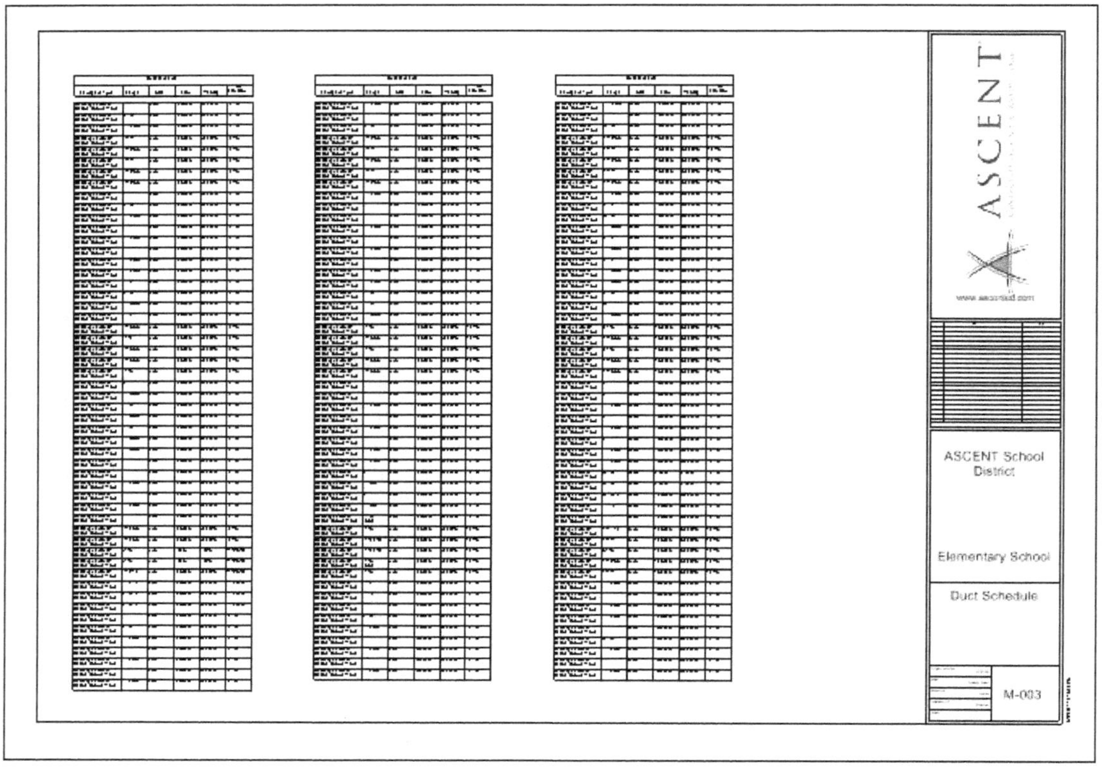

Figure 15–66

21. Save and close the project.

End of practice

Practice 15e
Work with Schedules – Electrical

Practice Objectives

- Update schedule information.
- Add a schedule to a sheet.

In this practice, you will update a schedule and place it on a sheet. The model used for this practice has been modified so you can see what happens when changing elements in the sheet as well as in the views.

Task 1: Fill in schedules.

1. In the practice files *Working Models>Electrical* folder, open **Elec-Schedules.rvt**.
2. In the Project Browser, expand *Schedules/Quantities*. Several schedules have been added to this project.
3. Double-click on **Lighting Fixture Schedule** to open it. The schedule is already populated with some of the basic information, as shown in part in Figure 15–67.

<Lighting Fixture Schedule>

A	B	C	D	E	F	G	H	I
					Lamp			
Type Mark	Description	Count	Manufacturer	Model	Lamp	Wattage	Illuminance	Electrical Data
	Emergency Recessed Lighting Fixture: 2x4 - 277	22				96 W	7 fc	Emergency 277 V/1-96 VA- 277 V/1-32
L1	Troffer Light - 2x4 Parabolic: 2'x4'(2 Lamp) - 277V	226			T-12	80 W	5 fc	277 V/1-80 VA
Grand total: 248								

Figure 15–67

4. Click in the empty *Type Mark* cell. In the *Modify Schedules/ Quantities* tab>*Element* panel, click (Highlight in Model).
5. In the dialog box that opens, stating there is no open view that shows any of the highlighted elements (as shown in Figure 15–68), click **OK** to search through closed views.

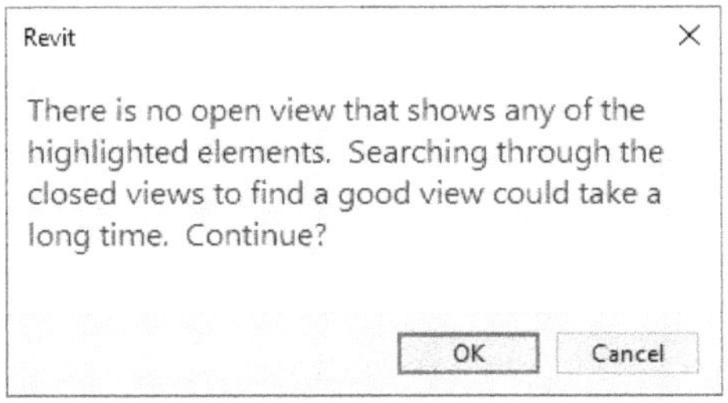
Revit
There is no open view that shows any of the highlighted elements. Searching through the closed views to find a good view could take a long time. Continue?
OK
Cancel

Figure 15–68

6. In the view that comes up, if it is not showing the element you need to see, click **Show**. If you can see the element that is highlighted in the view, click **Close** in the *Show Element(s) In View* dialog box (shown in Figure 15–69).

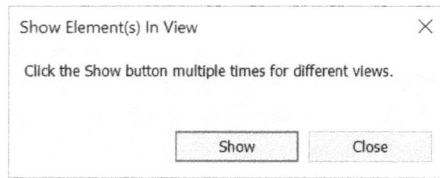

Figure 15–69

7. In Properties, you can see that multiple emergency light fixtures are selected but display **<varies>**, as shown in Figure 15–70. More than one light fixture is selected and you cannot edit values that are grayed out.

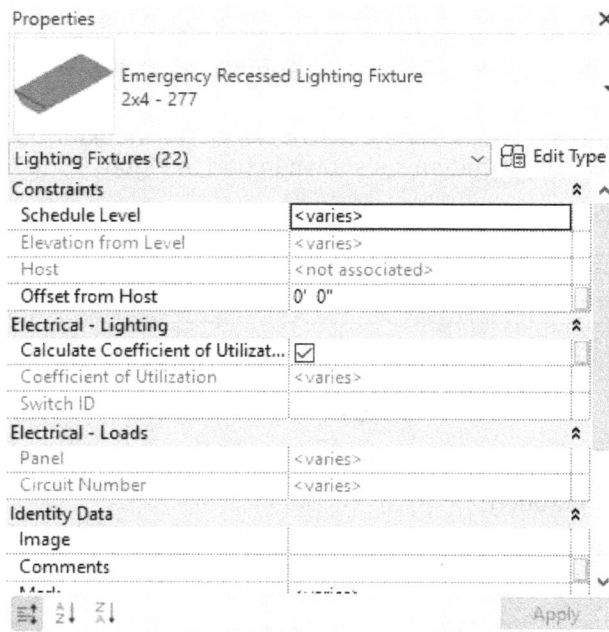

Figure 15–70

8. Click ⊞ (Edit Type).

9. In the *Type Properties* dialog box, in the *Identity Data* section, set the *Type Mark* to **EM-1**.

10. Click **OK** to finish.

11. Return to the Lighting Fixture Schedule (select the tab or press <Ctrl>+<Tab> to switch between open windows).

12. All the emergency light fixtures in the project now have a *Type Mark* set, as shown in Figure 15–71.

						Lamp			
A	B	C	D	E	F	G	H		I
Type Mark	Description	Count	Manufacturer	Model	Lamp	Wattage	Illuminance		Electrical Data
EM-1	Emergency Recessed Lighting Fixture: 2x4 - 277	22				96 W	7 fc		Emergency 277 V/1-96 VA- 277 V/1-32
L1	Troffer Light - 2x4 Parabolic: 2'x4'(2 Lamp) - 277V	226			T-12	80 W	5 fc		277 V/1-80 VA

Figure 15–71

13. For the L1 light fixtures, in the *Manufacturer* column, type **ME Unlimited**. A dialog box displays, as shown in Figure 15–72, letting you know all of the same elements will be changed. Click **OK**. The manufacturer is added to all of the Troffer light fixtures.

Type Mark	Description	Count	Manufacturer
EM-1	Emergency Recessed Lighting Fixture: 2x4 - 277	22	
L1	Troffer Light - 2x4 Parabolic: 2'x4'(2 Lamp) - 277V	226	ME Unlimited
Grand total: 248			

Revit ×

This change will be applied to all elements of type
Troffer Light - 2x4 Parabolic: 2'x4'(2 Lamp) -
277V.

OK   Cancel

Figure 15–72

14. Save the project.

Task 2: Add a schedule to a sheet.

1. In the Project Browser, right-click on **Sheets (all)** and select **New Sheet**. Select the **ASCENT 30 x 42 Horizontal** title block and click **OK**.

2. In the Project Browser, right-click on the new sheet (which is bold) and select **Rename**. In the *Sheet Title* dialog box, set the *Number* to **E-002** and the *Name* to **Lighting Fixture Schedule**, and click **OK**.

3. Create another sheet by right-clicking on the light fixture schedule sheet and selecting **Duplicate Sheet>Duplicate Empty Sheet**, as shown in Figure 15–73. Rename it **E-003 Lighting Fixture Schedule**.

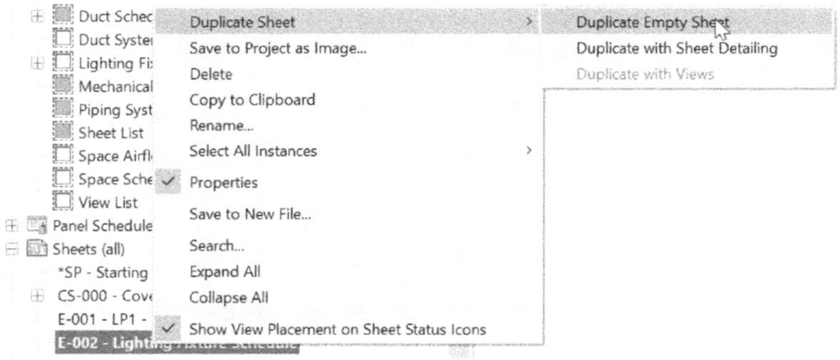

Figure 15–73

4. Open the Lighting Fixture Schedule.

5. In Properties, click **Edit...** next to *Sorting/Grouping*.

6. In the *Schedule Properties* dialog box, uncheck **Grand Totals** and check the box for **Itemized every instance** and click **OK**.

7. This itemizes all the light fixtures in the model. Scroll down the schedule and note that this will not fit onto one sheet.

8. In the *Modify Schedule/Quantities* tab>*Split* panel, click (Split & Place).

9. In the *Split Schedule and Place on Sheets* dialog box, select the two Lighting Fixture Schedule sheets, as shown in Figure 15–74.

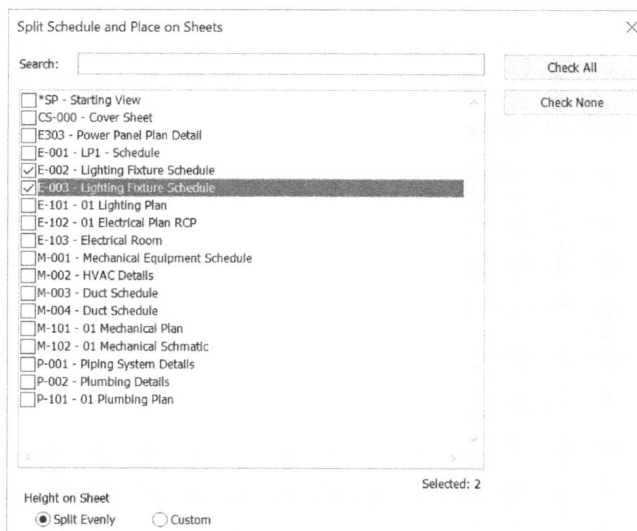

Figure 15–74

10. Click **Split & Place**.

11. The **E-002 - Lighting Fixture Schedule** sheet automatically opens and the first segment of the split schedule is attached to your cursor. Use your mouse wheel to zoom out, if needed.

12. Place the light fixture schedule in the upper-left corner of the sheet.

13. From the Project Browser, open sheet **E-003**. Note that the other segment of the split schedule has automatically been added to the sheet in the same place as E-002.

    - The schedule will be too long and needs to be split even more.

14. Click � (Modify).

15. Go back to sheet E-002. Click on the schedule and then click ☝ (Split Schedule Table), as shown in Figure 15–75.

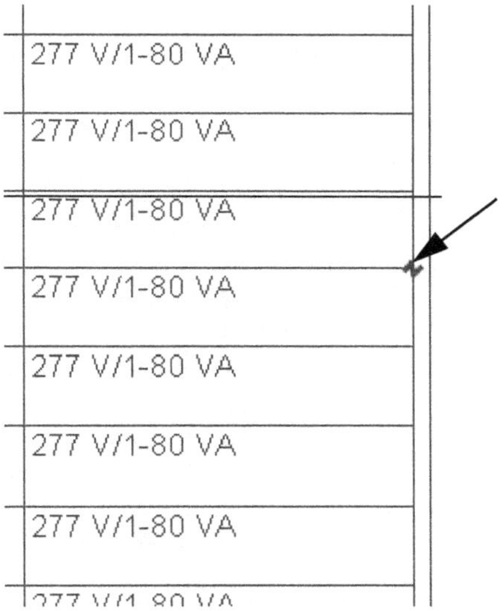

Figure 15–75

16. Select the first section of the schedule on the sheet and use the control grips at the bottom of the schedule to stretch it to fit the sheet. On the second section of the sheet, click ⤝ (Split Schedule Table), as shown in Figure 15–76, to split the schedule again and use the grips to stretch or shrink the schedule to fit.

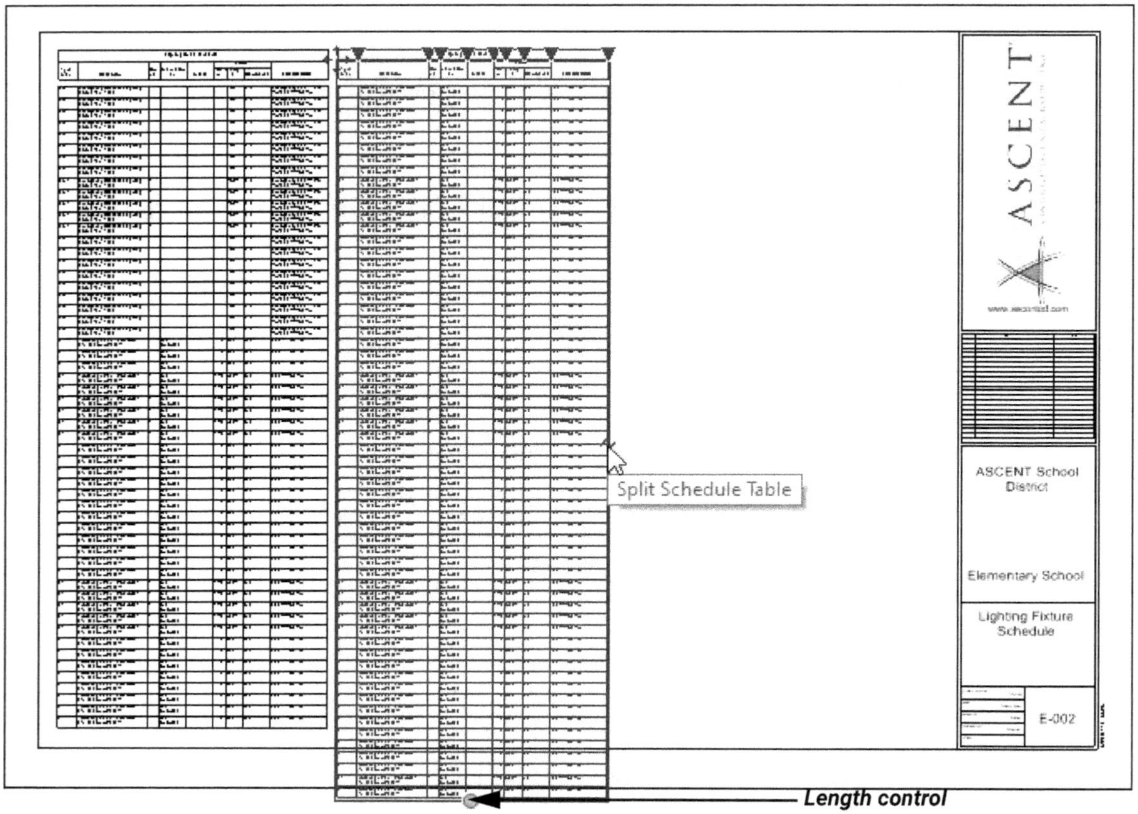

Figure 15–76

17. Click in an empty space in the view to clear the selection.

18. Select the individual schedules and move them away from each other, as shown in Figure 15–77.

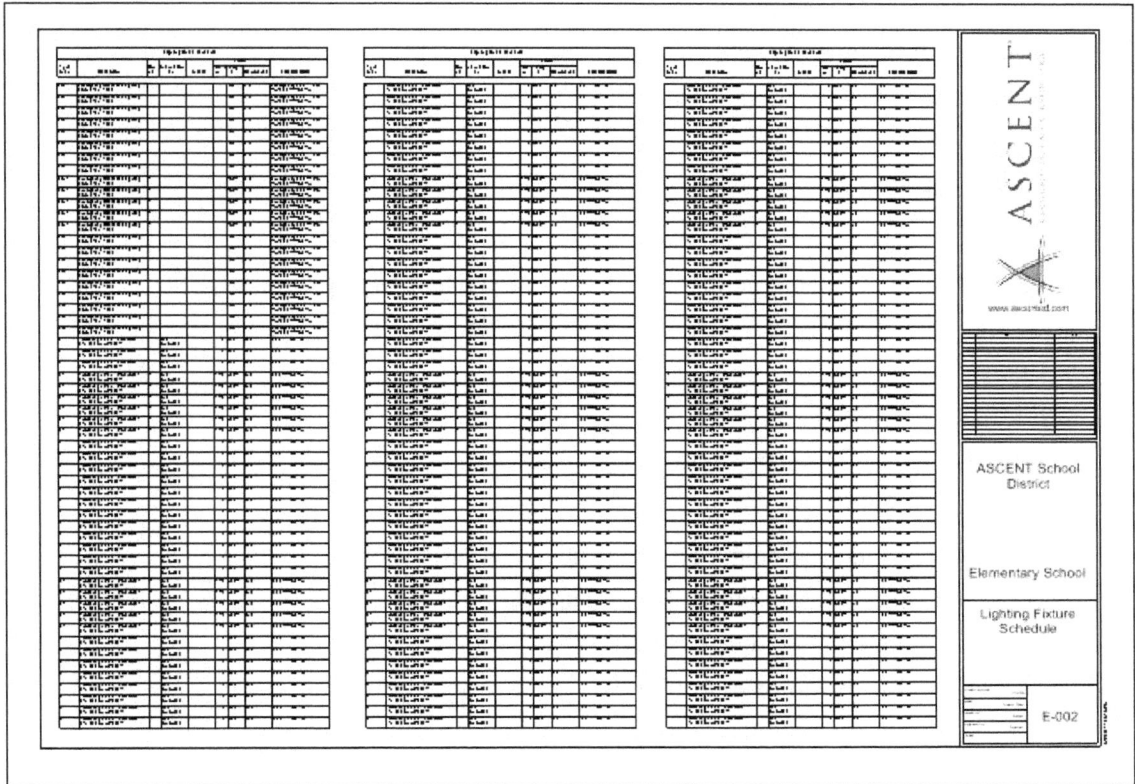

Figure 15–77

19. Open sheet **E-003** and adjust the schedule as needed.

20. Save and close the project.

End of practice

Chapter Review Questions

1. You can tag in a 3D view, but you first have to do what to the view?

   a. You cannot tag in a 3D view.

   b. Rename the view.

   c. Lock the view.

   d. Unlock the view.

2. Which of the following elements cannot be tagged using **Tag by Category**?

   a. Spaces

   b. Ducts

   c. Plumbing Fixtures

   d. Communication Devices

3. What happens when you delete an air terminal in a Revit model?

   a. You must delete the air terminal on the sheet.

   b. You must delete the air terminal from the schedule.

   c. The air terminal is removed from the model, but not from the schedule.

   d. The air terminal is removed from the model and the schedule.

4. In a schedule, if you change type information (such as a Type Mark), all instances of that type update with the new information.

   a. True

   b. False

5. You cannot remove split schedules once they have been created.

   a. True

   b. False

Command Summary

Button	Command	Location
	Freeze Header	• **Ribbon:** *Modify Schedule/Quantities* tab>*Titles & Header* panel
	Highlight in Model	• **Ribbon:** *Modify Schedule/Quantities* tab>*Element* panel
	Material Tag	• **Ribbon:** *Annotate* tab>*Tag* panel
	Multi-Category	• **Ribbon:** *Annotate* tab>*Tag* panel
	Schedule/Quantities	• **Ribbon:** *View* tab>*Create* panel, expand Schedules
	Split & Place	• **Ribbon:** *Modify Schedule/Quantities* tab>*Split* panel
	Stair Tread/Riser Number	• **Ribbon:** *Annotate* tab>*Tag* panel
	Tag All Not Tagged	• **Ribbon:** *Annotate* tab>*Tag* panel
	Tag by Category	• **Ribbon:** *Annotate* tab>*Tag* panel • **Shortcut: TG**

Creating Details

Creating details is a critical part of the design process, as it is the step where you specify the exact information that is required to build a construction project. The elements that you can add to a model include detail components, detail lines, text, tags, symbols, and filled regions. Details can be created from views in the model, but you can also add 2D details in separate views.

Learning Objectives

- Create drafting views where you can add 2D details.
- Add detail components that show the typical elements in a detail.
- Annotate details using detail lines, text, tags, symbols, and patterns that define materials.

16.1 Setting Up Detail Views

Most of the work you do in Revit is exclusively with *smart* elements that interconnect and work together in the model. However, the software does not automatically display how elements should be built to fit together. For this, you need to create detail drawings, as shown in Figure 16–1.

Note: Details are created either in 2D drafting views or in callouts from plan, elevation, or section views.

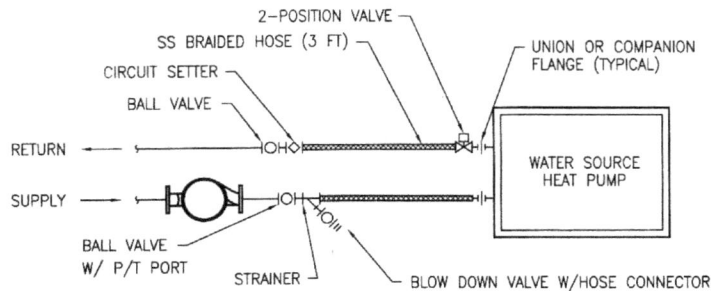

WATER SOURCE HEAT PUMP
PIPING DETAIL

Figure 16–1

How To: Create a Drafting View

1. In the *View* tab>*Create* panel, click ⬜ (Drafting View).

2. In the *New Drafting View* dialog box, enter a *Name* and set a *Scale*, as shown in Figure 16–2.

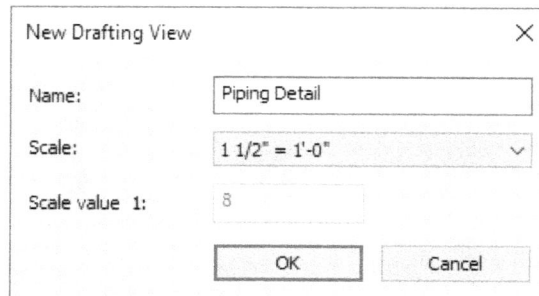

Figure 16–2

3. Click **OK**. A blank view is created with space in which you can sketch the detail.

    Note: Drafting views are listed in their own section in the Project Browser.

How To: Create a Detail View from Model Elements

1. Start the **Section** or **Callout** command.
2. In the Type Selector, select the **Detail View: Detail** type.
    *   The marker indicates that it is a detail, as shown for a section in Figure 16–3.

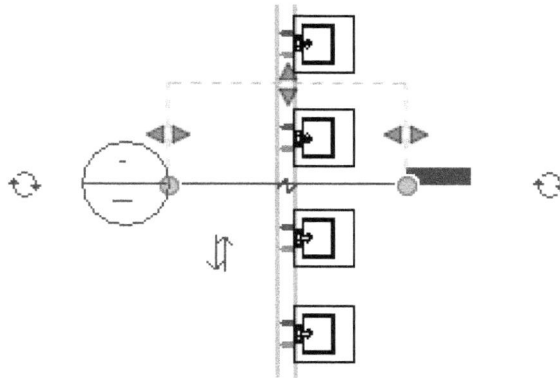

Figure 16–3

3. Place the section or a callout of the area you want to use for the detail.

    Note: Callouts also have a Detail View type that can be used in the same way.

4. Open the new detail.

*   Change the detail level to see more or less of the element materials.

*   Use the **Detail Line** tool to sketch on top of or add to the building elements.

*   Because you are working with smart elements, a detail of the model is a true representation. When the building elements change, the detail changes as well, as shown in Figure 16–4.

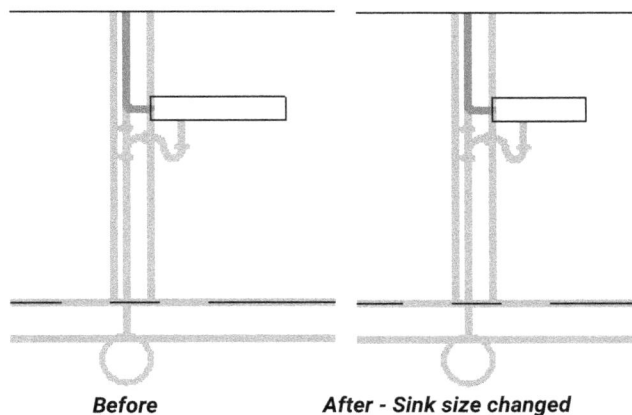

Before   *After - Sink size changed*

Figure 16–4

- You can create detail elements on top of the model and then toggle the model off so that it does not show in the detail view. In Properties, in the *Graphics* section, change *Display Model* to **Do not display**. You can also set the model to **Halftone**, as shown in Figure 16–5.

Figure 16–5

Referencing a Drafting View

Once you have created a drafting view, you can reference it in another view (such as a callout, elevation, or section view), as shown in Figure 16–6. For example, in a section view, you might want to reference an existing roof detail. You can reference drafting views, sections, elevations, and callouts.

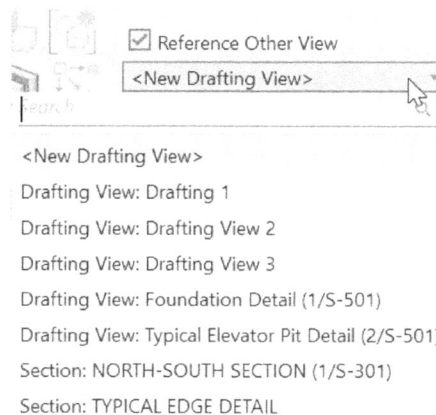

Figure 16–6

- You can use the search feature to limit the information displayed.

How To: Reference a Drafting View

1. Open the view in which you want to place the reference.
2. Start the **Section**, **Callout**, or **Elevation** command.
3. In the *Modify* contextual tab>*Reference* panel, select **Reference Other View**.
4. In the drop-down list, select **<New Drafting View>** or an existing drafting view.
5. Place the view marker.
6. When you place the associated drafting view on a sheet, the marker in this view updates with the appropriate information.

- If you select **<New Drafting View>** from the drop-down list, a new view is created in the *Drafting Views (Detail)* area in the Project Browser. You can rename it as needed. The new view does not include any model elements.
- When you create a detail based on a section, elevation, or callout, you do not need to link it to a drafting view.
- You can change a referenced view to a different view. Select the view marker and in the ribbon, select the new view from the list.

Saving Drafting Views

To create a library of standard details, save the non-model specific drafting views to your server. They can then be imported into a project and modified to suit. They are saved as .RVT files.

Drafting views can be saved in two ways:

- Save an individual drafting view to a new file.
- Save all of the drafting views as a group in one new file.

How To: Save One Drafting View to a File

1. In the Project Browser, right-click on the drafting view you want to save and select **Save to New File...**, as shown in Figure 16–7.

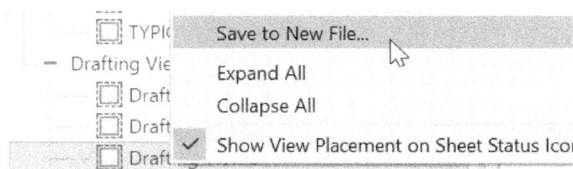

Figure 16–7

2. In the *Save As* dialog box, specify a name and location for the file and click **Save**.

How To: Save a Group of Drafting Views to a File

Note: You can save sheets, drafting views, model views (floor plans), schedules, and reports.

1. In the *File* tab, expand 💾 (Save As), expand 📖 (Library), and then click ⬚ (View).

2. In the *Save Views* dialog box, in the *Views:* area, expand the list and select **Show drafting views only**.

3. Select the drafting views that you want to save, as shown in Figure 16–8.

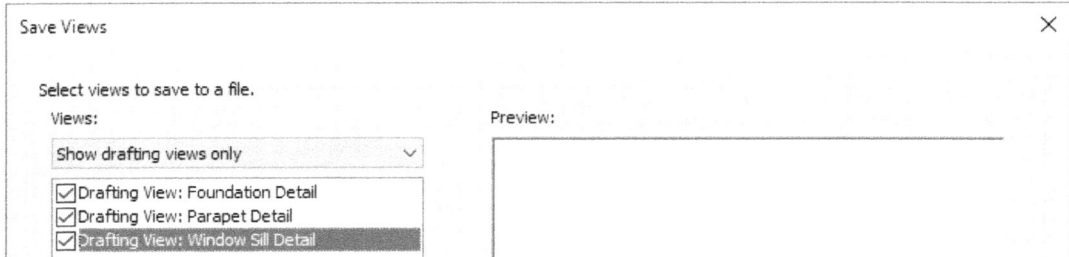

Save Views ✕

Select views to save to a file.

Views:

Show drafting views only ⌄

☑ Drafting View: Foundation Detail
☑ Drafting View: Parapet Detail
☑ Drafting View: Window Sill Detail

Preview:

Figure 16–8

4. Click **OK**.

5. In the *Save As* dialog box, specify a name and location for the file and click **Save**.

How To: Use a Saved Drafting View in Another Project

1. Open the project to which you want to add the drafting view.

2. In the *Insert* tab>*Load from Library* panel, expand 📄 (Insert from File) and click 📄 (Insert Views from File).

3. In the *Open* dialog box, select the project in which you saved the detail and click **Open**.

4. In the *Insert Views* dialog box, limit the types of views to **Show drafting views only**, as shown in Figure 16–9.

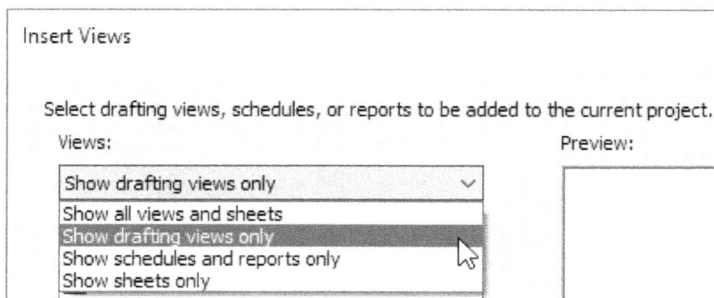

Insert Views

Select drafting views, schedules, or reports to be added to the current project.

Views:

Show drafting views only ⌄
Show all views and sheets
Show drafting views only
Show schedules and reports only
Show sheets only

Preview:

Figure 16–9

5. Select the view(s) that you want to insert and click **OK**.

Hint: Importing Details from Other CAD Software

You might already have a set of standard details created in a different CAD program, such as AutoCAD®. You can reuse the details in Revit by importing them into a temporary project. Once you have imported the detail, it helps to clean it up and save it as a view before bringing it into your active project.

1. In a new project, create a drafting view and make it active.

2. In the *Insert* tab>*Import* panel, click (Import CAD).

3. In the *Import CAD* dialog box, select the file to import. Most of the default values are what you need. You might want to change the *Layer/Level colors* to **Black and White**.

4. Click **Open**.

5. Use Revit detail lines and other tools to trace over the imported file.

6. Once finished, unpin the imported file and press <Delete>.

- If necessary, you can explode the imported file to modify it. This method is not recommended because it increases the file size and, depending on the importing objects, it could potentially take a long time to clean up and convert the objects and Revit-Specific elements and styles.

   - Select the imported data. In the *Modify | [filename]* tab>*Import Instance* panel, expand (Explode) and click (Partial Explode) or (Full Explode). Click (Delete Layers) before you explode the detail. A full explode greatly increases the file size.

   - Modify the detail using tools in the *Modify* panel. Change all the text and line styles to Revit-specific elements.

16.2 Adding Detail Components

Revit elements, typically require additional information to ensure that they are constructed correctly. To create details such as the one shown in Figure 16–10, you add detail components, detail lines, and various annotation elements.

- Detail elements are not directly connected to the model, even if model elements display in the view.

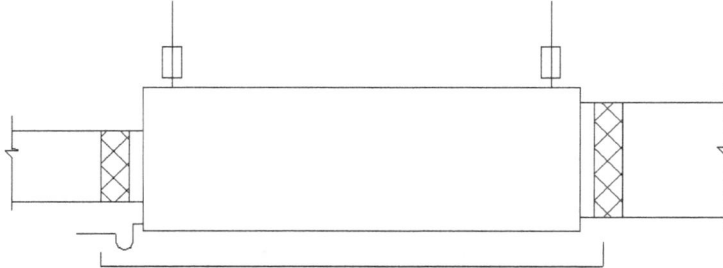

Figure 16–10

- If you want to draw detail lines in 3D, use the **Model Line** tool. Detail Line is grayed out when you are in a 3D view or perspective view.

Detail Components

Detail components are families made of 2D and annotation elements. Over 500 detail components organized by CSI format are found in the *Detail Items* folder of the Revit Library.

> **Note:** *For more information on how to load detail items using the Load Autodesk Family dialog box, see **4.2 Loading Components** in **Chapter 4 Revit Families**.*

How To: Add a Detail Component

1. In the *Annotate* tab>*Detail* panel, expand **Component** and click ▦ (Detail Component).
2. In the Type Selector, select the detail component type. You can load additional types from the Revit Library.
3. Many detail components can be rotated as you insert them by pressing <Spacebar>. Alternatively, select **Rotate after placement** in the Options Bar.
4. Place the component in the view.

Adding Break Lines

The break line is a detail component found in the Revit Library's *Detail Items\Div 01-General* folder. It consists of a rectangular area (shown highlighted in Figure 16–11) that is used to block out elements behind it. You can modify the size of the area that is covered and change the size of the cut line using the controls.

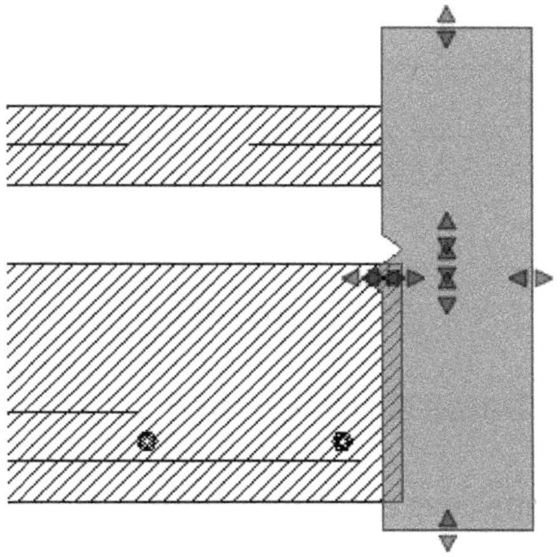

Figure 16–11

💡 Hint: Working with the Draw Order of Details

When you select detail elements in a view, you can change the draw order of the elements in the *Modify | Detail Items* tab>*Arrange* panel. You can bring elements in front of other elements or place them behind elements, as shown in Figure 16–12.

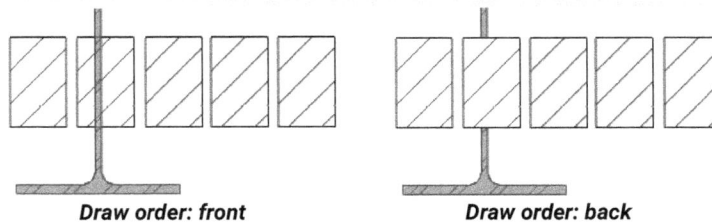

Draw order: front   Draw order: back

Figure 16–12

- 🔳 (Bring to Front): Places element in front of all other elements.

- 🔳 (Send to Back): Places element behind all other elements.

- 🔳 (Bring Forward): Moves element one step to the front.

- 🔳 (Send Backward): Moves element one step to the back.

You can select multiple detail elements and change the draw order of all of them in one step. They keep the relative order of the original selection.

Repeating Details

Instead of having to insert a component multiple times (such as brick or concrete block), you can use ▤ (Repeating Detail Component) and create a string of components, as shown in Figure 16–13.

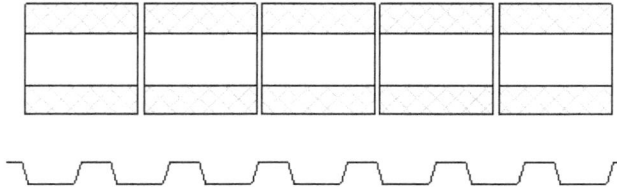

Figure 16–13

How To: Insert a Repeating Detail Component

1. In the *Annotate* tab>*Detail* panel, expand **Component** and click ▤ (Repeating Detail Component).
2. In the Type Selector, select the detail you want to use.
3. In the *Draw* panel, click ✎ (Line) or ▹ (Pick Lines).
4. In the Options Bar, type a value for the *Offset*, if needed.
5. The components repeat, as required, to fit the length of the sketched or selected line, as shown in Figure 16–14. You can lock the components to the line.

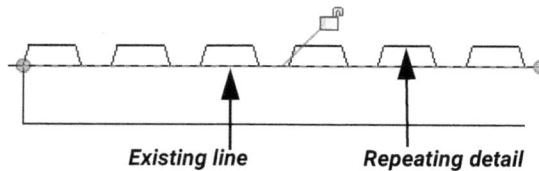

Existing line   Repeating detail

Figure 16–14

Hint: ⊠ **(Insulation)**

Adding batt insulation is similar to adding a repeating detail component, but instead of a series of bricks or other elements, it creates the linear batting pattern shown in Figure 16–15.

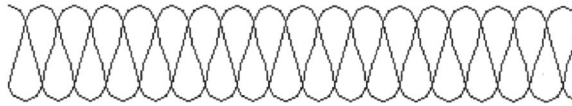

Figure 16–15

Before you place the insulation in the view, specify the *Offset* and other options in the Options Bar (as shown in Figure 16–16), as well as the *Width* in Properties.

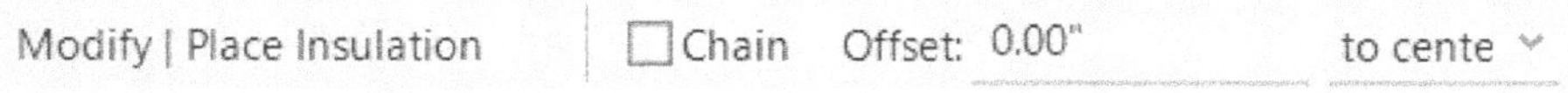

Modify | Place Insulation   ☐ Chain   Offset: 0.00"   to cente ⌄

Figure 16–16

16.3 Annotating Details

After you have added components and sketched detail lines, you need to add annotations to the detail view. You can place text notes and dimensions, as shown in Figure 16–17, as well as symbols and tags. Filled regions are used to add hatching.

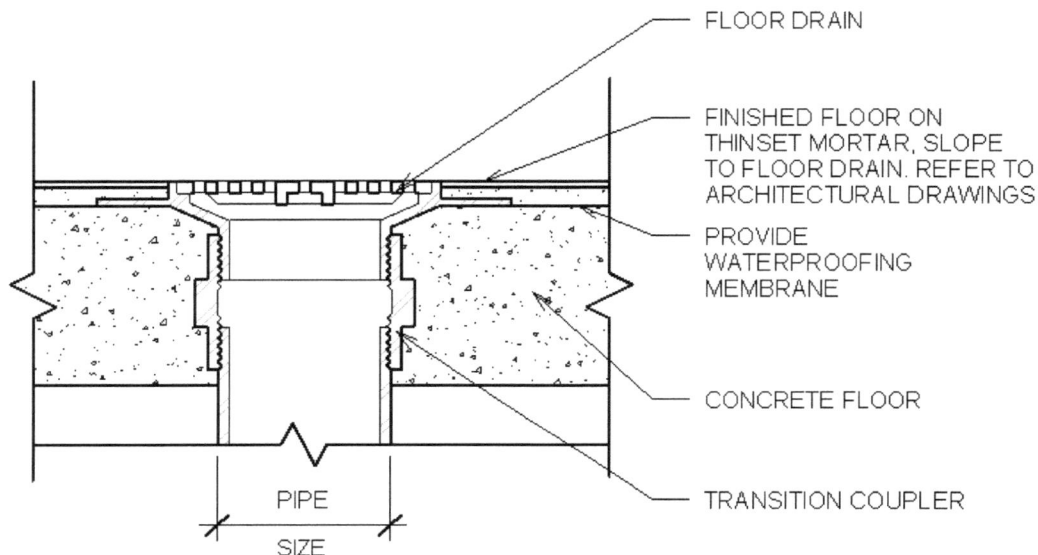

FLOOR DRAIN

FINISHED FLOOR ON THINSET MORTAR, SLOPE TO FLOOR DRAIN. REFER TO ARCHITECTURAL DRAWINGS

PROVIDE WATERPROOFING MEMBRANE

CONCRETE FLOOR

TRANSITION COUPLER

PIPE

SIZE

Figure 16–17

Filled Regions

Many elements include material information that displays in plan and section views, while other elements need more details to be added. For example, the concrete wall shown in Figure 16–18 includes material information, while the earth to the left of the wall needs to be added using the **Filled Region** command.

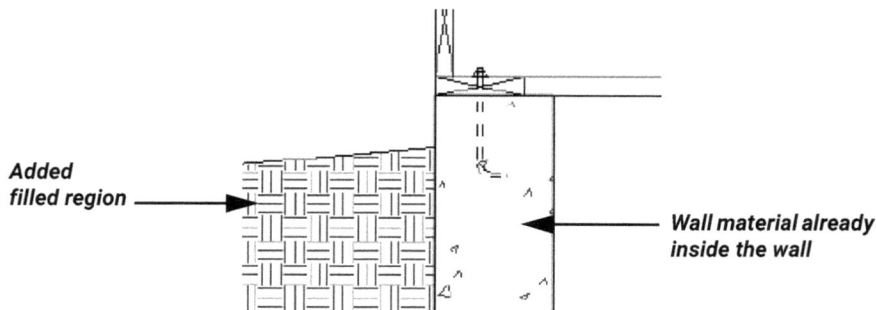

Added filled region ⟶

⟵ *Wall material already inside the wall*

Figure 16–18

The patterns used in details are *drafting patterns*. They are scaled to the view scale and update if you modify it. You can also add full-size *model patterns*, such as a Flemish Bond brick pattern, to the surface of some elements.

How To: Add a Filled Region

1. In the *Annotate* tab>*Detail* panel, expand ⊞ (Region) and click ⊞ (Filled Region).

2. Create a closed boundary using the Draw tools.

3. In the *Line Style* panel, select the line style for the outside edge of the boundary. If you do not want the boundary to display, select the **<Invisible lines>** style.

4. In the Type Selector, select the fill type, as shown in Figure 16–19.

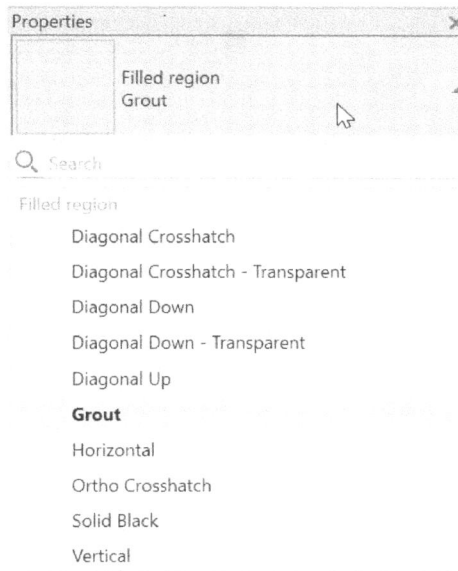

Figure 16–19

5. Click ✔ (Finish Edit Mode).

• You can modify a region by changing the fill type in the Type Selector or by editing the sketch.

• Double-click on the edge of the filled region to edit the sketch. If you have the Selection option set to ⬚ (Select elements by face), you can select the pattern.

💡 Hint: Creating a Filled Region Pattern Type

You can create a custom pattern by duplicating and editing an existing pattern type.

1. Select an existing region or create a boundary.

2. In Properties, click 🔲 (Edit Type).

3. In the *Type Properties* dialog box, click **Duplicate** and name the new pattern.

4. Select the *Foreground/Background Fill Pattern* and *Color* and specify the *Line Weight* and *Masking*, as shown in Figure 16–20.

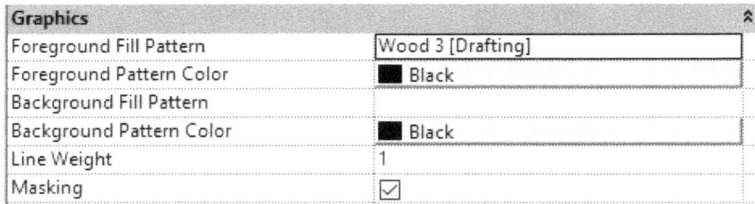

Graphics		⊗
Foreground Fill Pattern	Wood 3 [Drafting]	
Foreground Pattern Color	⬛ Black	
Background Fill Pattern		
Background Pattern Color	⬛ Black	
Line Weight	1	
Masking	☑	

Figure 16–20

5. Click **OK**.

- You can select from two types of fill patterns: **Drafting** (as shown in Figure 16–21) and **Model**. Drafting fill patterns scale to the view scale factor. Model fill patterns display full scale on the model.

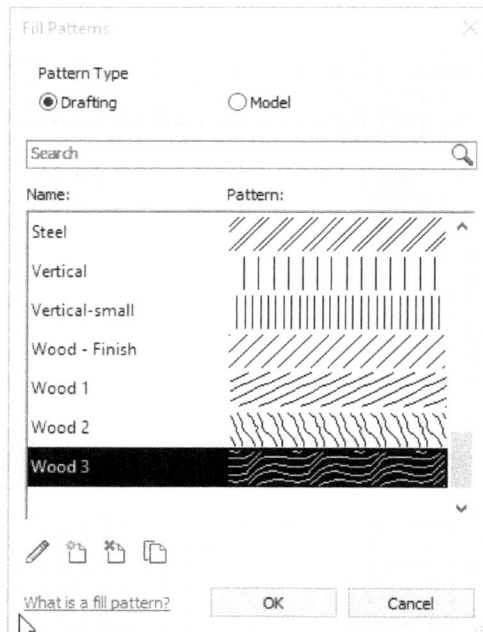

Figure 16–21

Adding Detail Tags

Besides adding text to a detail, you can tag detail components using ⌐① (Tag By Category). The tag name is set in the Type Parameters for that component, as shown in Figure 16–22. This means that if you have more than one copy of the component in your project, you do not have to rename it each time you place its tag.

*Note: The **Detail Item Tag.rfa** tag is located in the Annotations folder in the Revit Library.*

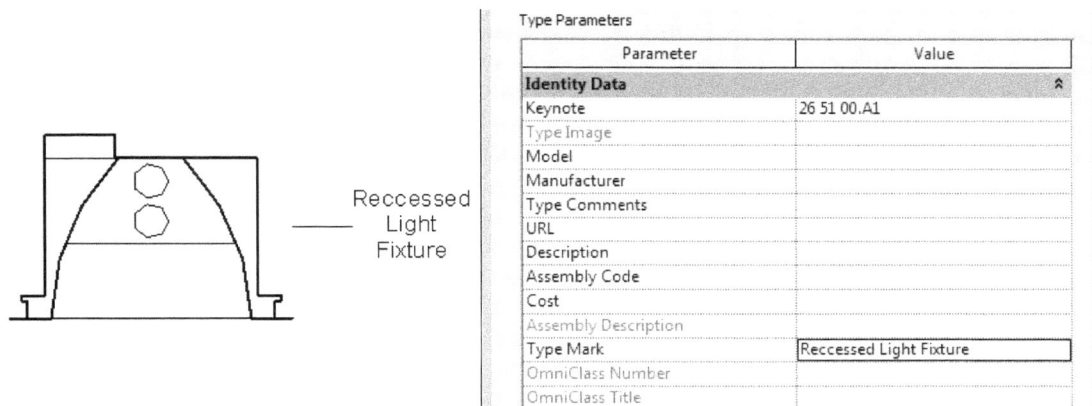

Type Parameters		
Parameter		Value
Identity Data		⌃
Keynote		26 51 00.A1
Type Image		
Model		
Manufacturer		
Type Comments		
URL		
Description		
Assembly Code		
Cost		
Assembly Description		
Type Mark		Reccessed Light Fixture
OmniClass Number		
OmniClass Title		

Figure 16–22

- For more information on annotating using keynotes see *B.6 Keynoting and Keynote Legends* in *Appendix B Additional Tools for Construction Documents*.

When you tag elements in a cropped view, the tag is placed at the default location of the element and might not display in the callout. In the View Control Bar, click ⌐ (Do not Crop). Tag the elements, and then move the new tags in the crop window. Click ⌐x (Crop View) to return to the area of the callout view.

Linework

To emphasize a particular line or change the look of a line in elevations and other views, modify the lines with the **Linework** command. Changes made to lines with the **Linework** command are view-specific, applying only to the view in which you make them.

- The **Linework** command can be used on project edges of model elements, cut edges of model elements, edges in imported CAD files, and edges in linked Revit models.

- You cannot use the **Linework** command to change the line style of annotation lines like a dimension line or leader line.

How To: Adjust Linework

1. In the *Modify* tab>*View* panel, click ⬇ (Linework), or type the shortcut **LW**.

2. In the *Modify | Linework* tab>*Line Style* panel, select the line style you want to use from the list.

3. Move the cursor and highlight the line you want to change. You can use <Tab> to toggle through the lines as needed.

4. Click on the line to change it to the new line style.

5. Click on other lines as needed or click ⬚ (Modify) to end the command

• If the line is too long or short, you can modify the length using the controls at the end of the line.

Practice 16a
Create a Fire Damper Detail – Mechanical

Practice Objectives

- Create a drafting view.
- Add filled regions, detail components, and annotations.

In this practice, you will create a drafting view. In the new view you will add detail lines of different weights, insulation, and filled regions. You will also add detail components, including break lines and text notes. Finally, you will place the detail view on a sheet (as shown in Figure 16–23) and place a reference section.

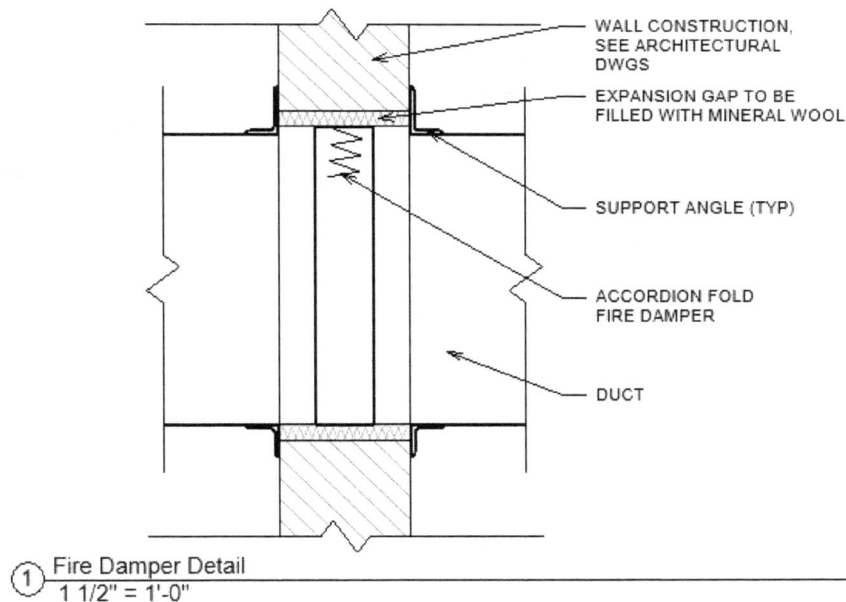

WALL CONSTRUCTION, SEE ARCHITECTURAL DWGS

EXPANSION GAP TO BE FILLED WITH MINERAL WOOL

SUPPORT ANGLE (TYP)

ACCORDION FOLD FIRE DAMPER

DUCT

① Fire Damper Detail
1 1/2" = 1'-0"

Figure 16–23

- It is recommended that you also complete the other Detail practices if time permits, even though they are not for your specific discipline.

Task 1: Create a drafting view.

1. In the practice files *Working Models>Mechanical* folder, open **Mech-Detailing.rvt**.

2. In the *View* tab>*Create* panel, click ⊟ (Drafting View).

3. In the *New Drafting View* dialog box, set the following:

    * *Name:* **Fire Damper Detail**

    * *Scale:* **1 1/2"=1'-0"**

4. In Properties, change *Discipline* to **Mechanical** and *Sub-Discipline* to **HVAC**. The new view moves to that node in the Project Browser.

Task 2: Draw detail lines.

1. In the *Annotate* tab>*Detail* panel, click ⍁ (Detail Line).

2. In the *Modify | Place Detail Lines* tab, set the *Line Style* to **Thin Lines** and make sure **Chain** is unchecked. Draw the two vertical lines shown in Figure 16–24.

3. Change the *Line Style* to **Wide Lines** and draw the two horizontal lines shown in Figure 16–24. These become the primary duct and wall lines.

    * If the difference in the line weights does not display clearly, zoom in and, in the Quick

      Access Toolbar, toggle off ⧼ (Thin Lines).

    Note: The dimensions are for information only.

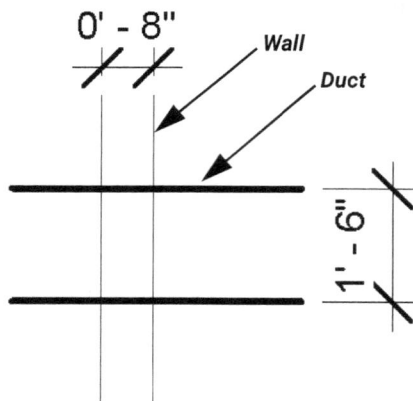

Figure 16–24

4. Continue adding and modifying detail lines to create the elements shown in Figure 16–25. Use modify commands (such as **Split** and **Offset**) and the draw tools.

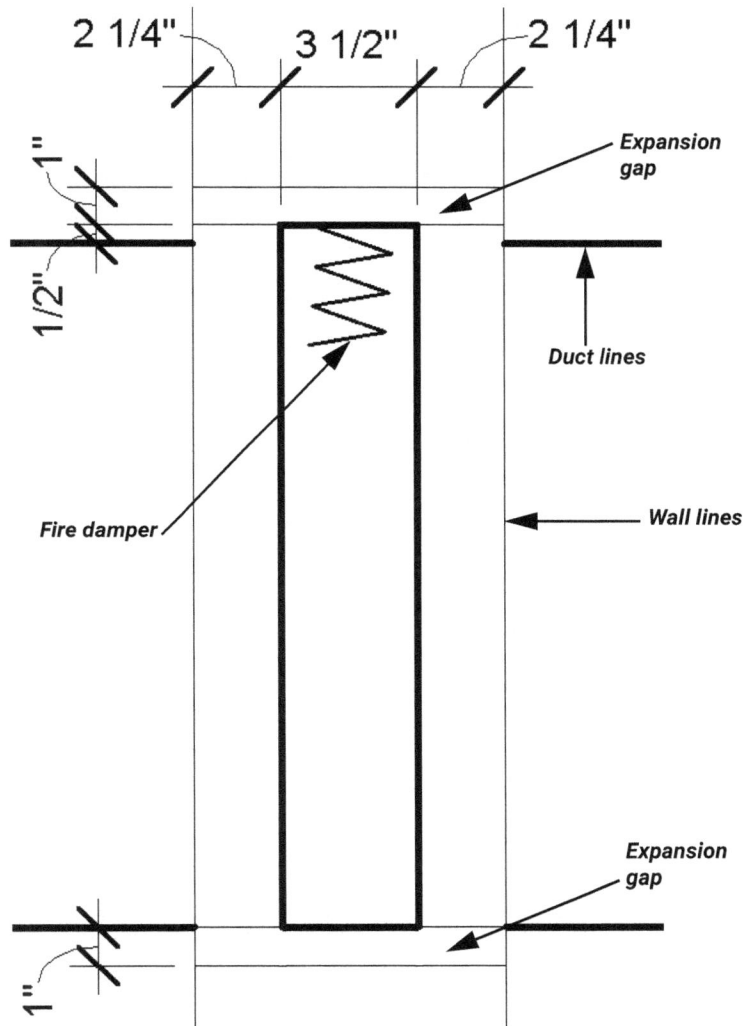

Figure 16–25

5. Save the project.

Task 3: Add detail components.

1. In the *Annotate* tab>*Detail* panel, expand **Component** and select ▨ (Detail Component).
2. In the Type Selector, select **AISC Angle Shapes - Section L3X2X1/4**.
3. Place the angle on the top left, as shown in Figure 16–26.

    • Press <Spacebar> to rotate the angle before placing it.

4. Change the type to **AISC Angle Shapes - Section L2X2X1/4** and place the angle on the bottom of the duct, as shown in Figure 16–26.
5. Select the two angle components and mirror them to the other side, as shown in Figure 16–26.

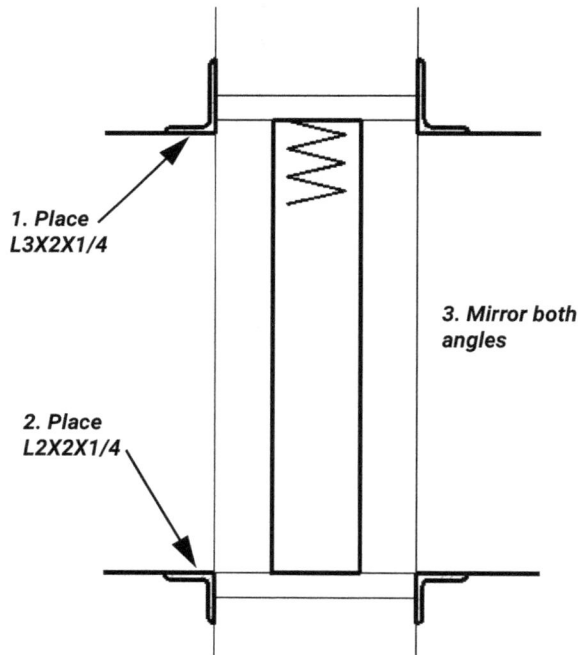

Figure 16–26

6. Add four break line components. Rotate and use the controls to modify the size until all of your excess lines are covered, as shown in Figure 16–27.

Note: The exact location and size of your break lines might vary.

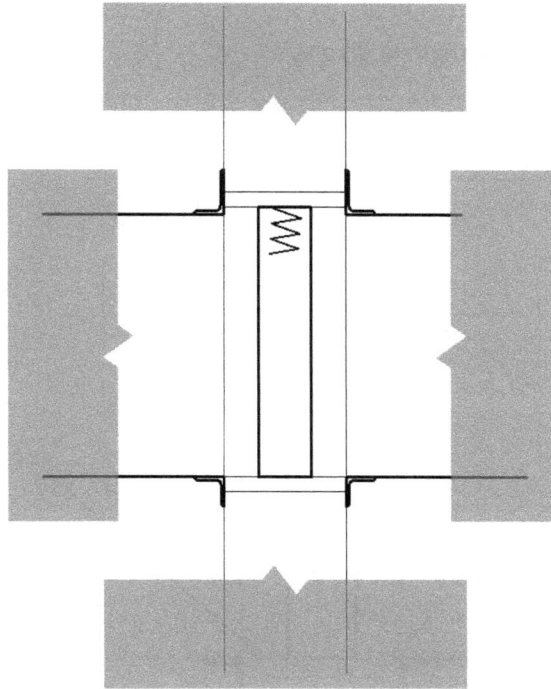

Figure 16–27

7. Save the project.

Task 4: Add insulation and filled regions.

1. In the *Annotate* tab>*Detail* panel, click ⌗ (Insulation).

2. In Properties, set the *Insulation Width* to **1"**.

3. Draw the insulation lines in the two expansion gaps, as shown in Figure 16–28.

4. In the *Annotate* tab>*Detail* panel, expand ▨ (Region) and click ▨ (Filled Region).

5. In the Type Selector, select **Filled region: Diagonal Down**.

6. Draw rectangles around the wall areas as shown in Figure 16–28.

7. Click ✔ (Finish). The filled regions display.

> *Note: The filled region pattern does not display until you finish the process.*

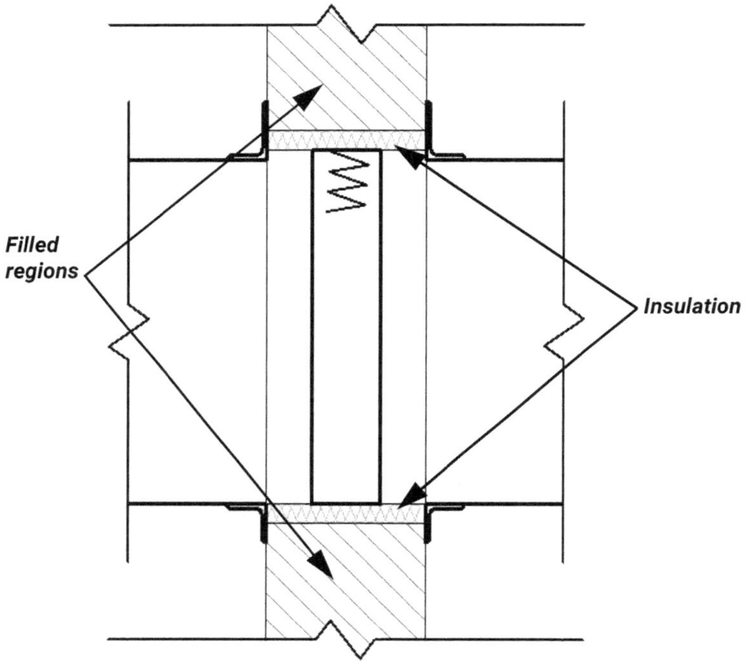

Figure 16–28

8. Save the project.

Task 5: Add text notes.

1. In the *Annotate* tab>*Text* panel, click **A** (Text).

2. In the *Modify | Place Text* tab>*Leader* panel, select ⌐A (Two Segments) as the leader style.

3. In the Type Selector, select **Text: Note 3/32"**.

4. Add text notes, as shown in Figure 16-29.

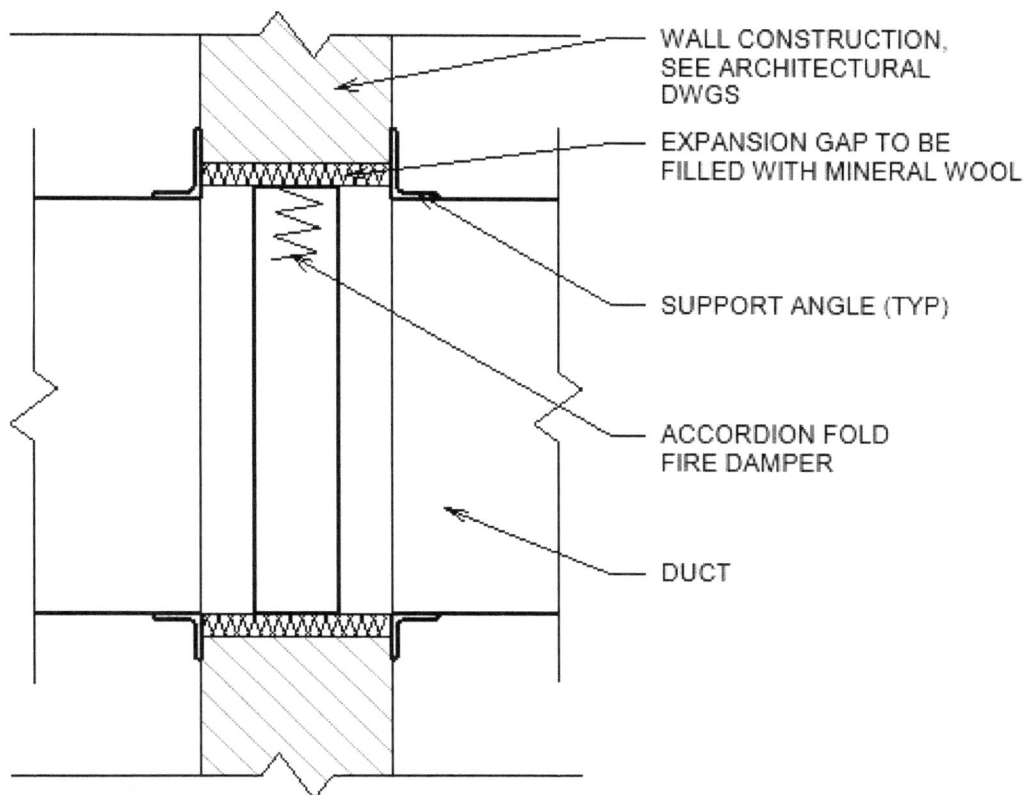

WALL CONSTRUCTION,
SEE ARCHITECTURAL
DWGS

EXPANSION GAP TO BE
FILLED WITH MINERAL WOOL

SUPPORT ANGLE (TYP)

ACCORDION FOLD
FIRE DAMPER

DUCT

Figure 16-29

5. Save the project.

Task 6: Place the detail on a sheet and reference it in the project.

1. In the Project Browser, open the sheet **M-002 - HVAC Details**.

2. In the Project Browser, drag the **Fire Damper Detail** view to the sheet.

3. Open the Mechanical>HVAC>**01 - Mechanical Plan** view.

4. Zoom in on one of the duct systems.

5. In the *View* tab>*Create* panel, click ⌀ (Callout).

6. In the *Modify | Callout* tab>*Reference* panel, select **Reference Other View**.

7. Expand the drop-down list and select the new **Fire Damper Detail**, as shown in Figure 16–30.
8. Place the callout at the intersection of a duct and the wall, as shown in Figure 16–30. The information is filled out based on the location of the detail view on the sheet.

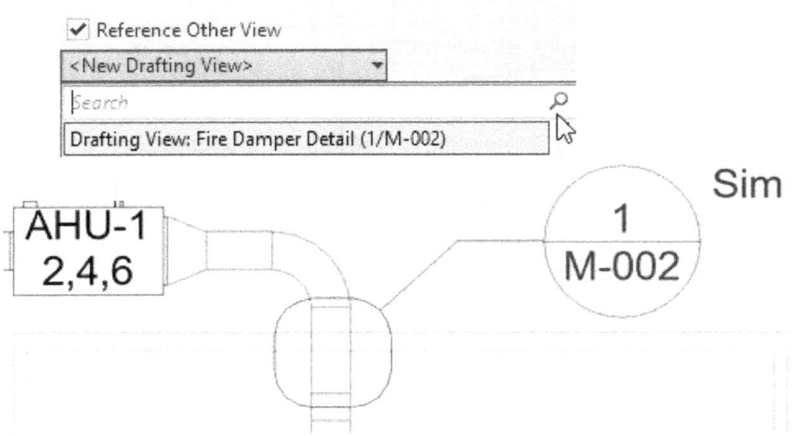

Figure 16–30

9. Click (Modify).
10. Double-click on the callout head, and note that the Fire Damper Detail drafting view becomes the active view. This is because the callout is now linked to this drafting view.
11. Save and close the project.

End of practice

Practice 16b
Create a Meter Pedestal Detail – Electrical

Practice Objective

* Create and annotate details.

In this practice, you will create a detail using detail lines and filled regions. You will then annotate the detail with text and dimensions, as shown in Figure 16–31.

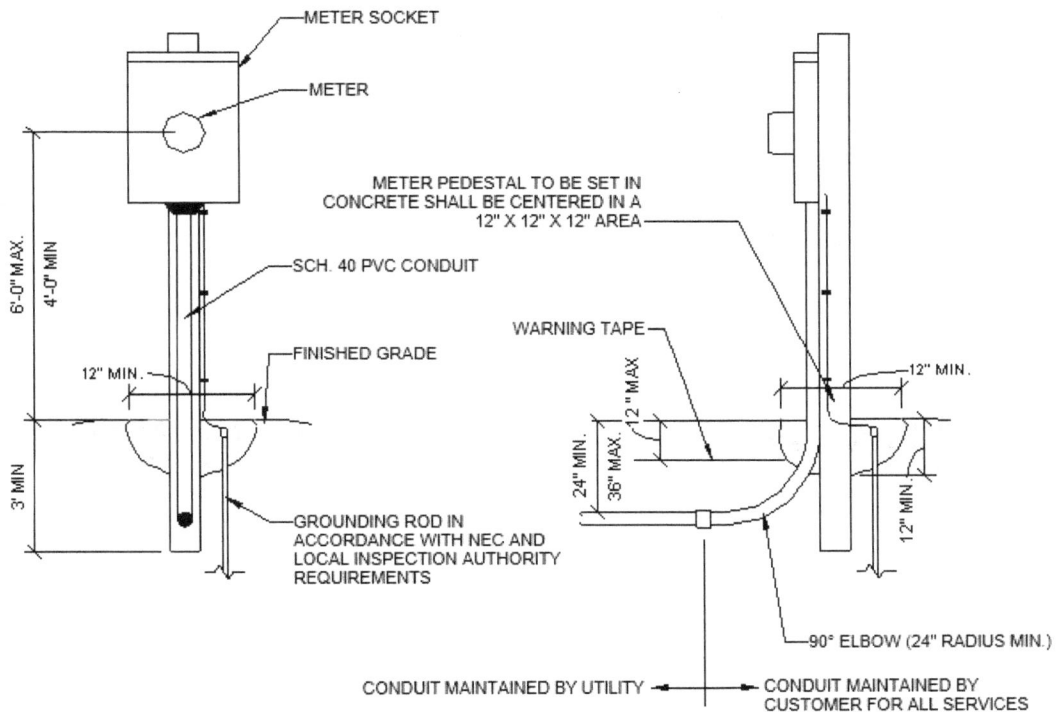

METER PEDESTAL - UG SERVICE
1 PHASE & 3 PHASE ALL VOLTAGES
SERVICE SIZE: 600 AMP MAXIMUM

Figure 16–31

* It is recommended that you also complete the other Detail practices if time permits, even though they are not for your specific discipline.

Task 1: Create a drafting view.

1. In the practice files *Working Models>Electrical* folder, open **Elec-Detailing.rvt**.

2. In the *View* tab>*Create* panel, click ⬚ (Drafting View).

3. In the *New Drafting View* dialog box, set the name and scale as follows:

    *   *Name:* **Electrical Meter Pedestal Detail**

    *   *Scale:* **1 1/2"=1'-0"**

4. In Properties, change *Discipline* to **Electrical** and *Sub-Discipline* to **Power**. The new view moves to that node in the Project Browser.

Task 2: Draw detail lines.

1. In the *Annotate* tab>*Detail* panel, click ⬚ (Detail Line).

2. In the *Modify | Place Detail Lines* tab, set the *Line Style* to **Wide Lines** and draw the meter box shown in Figure 16–32. As you draw, make sure **Chain** is checked or unchecked, as needed.

3. Change the *Line Style* to **Medium Lines** and draw the meter circle, as shown in Figure 16–32.

    *   If the difference in the line weights does not display clearly, zoom in and toggle off

        ⬚ (Thin Lines) in the Quick Access Toolbar.

The dimensions in the image are for information only.

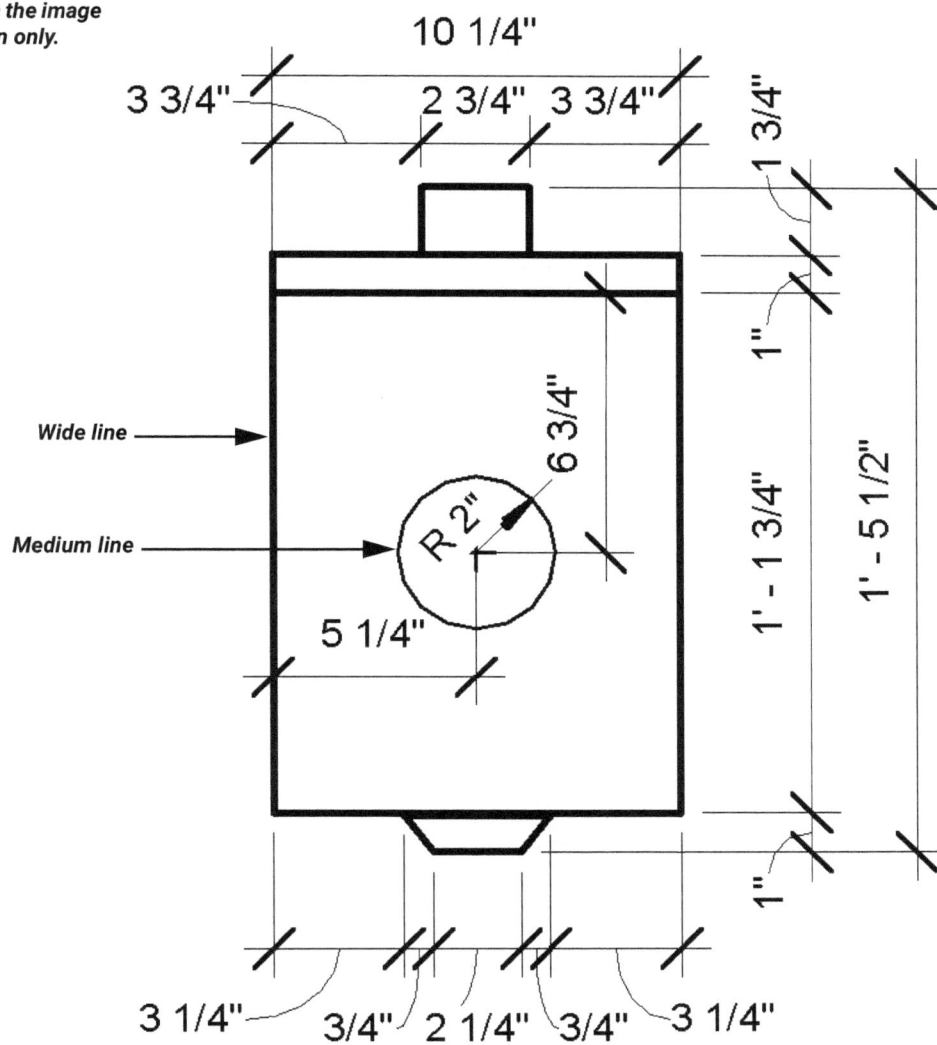

Figure 16–32

4. Continue adding and modifying detail lines to create the PVC conduit, meter pedestal, wire, wire clips, and grounding rod shown in Figure 16–33. Use Modify commands (such as **Copy** and **Offset**) and the draw tools.

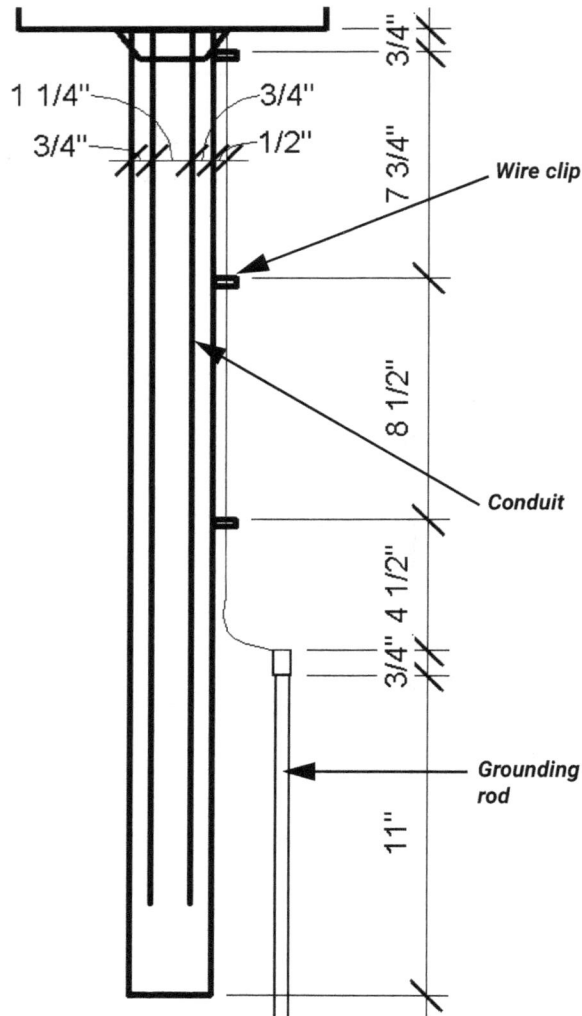

Figure 16–33

5. Create a side view of the meter using reference planes as your trajectory lines, as shown in Figure 16–34. When you are finished, you can delete the reference planes and select the elements and move them over so there is room for labels.

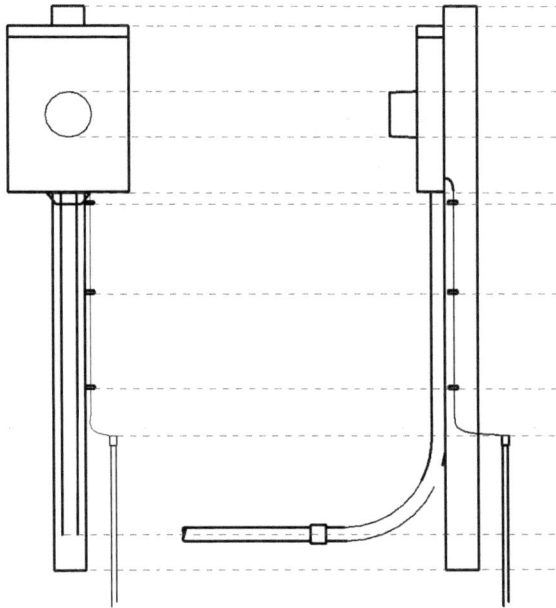

Figure 16–34

6. Save the project.

Task 3: Add detail components.

1. In the *Annotate* tab>*Detail* panel, expand **Component** and select ▦ (Detail Component).
2. In the Type Selector, select **Break Line**.

3. Add a break line to the bottom of both grounding rods. Rotate and use the controls to modify the size until all of your excess lines are covered, as shown in Figure 16–35.

   Note: The exact location and size of your break lines might vary.

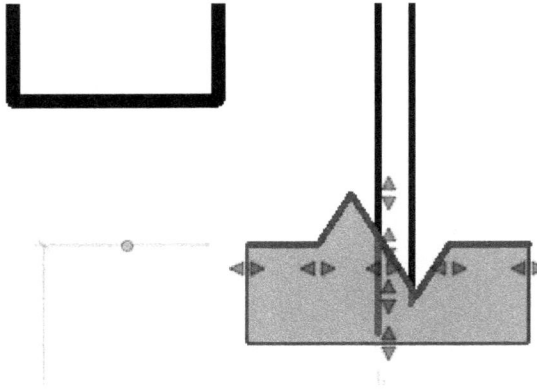

Figure 16–35

4. Save the project.

Task 4: Add filled regions.

1. Draw a reference plane **1'-0 3/4"** from the bottom of the post as shown in Figure 16–36 to help with drawing the finished grade.

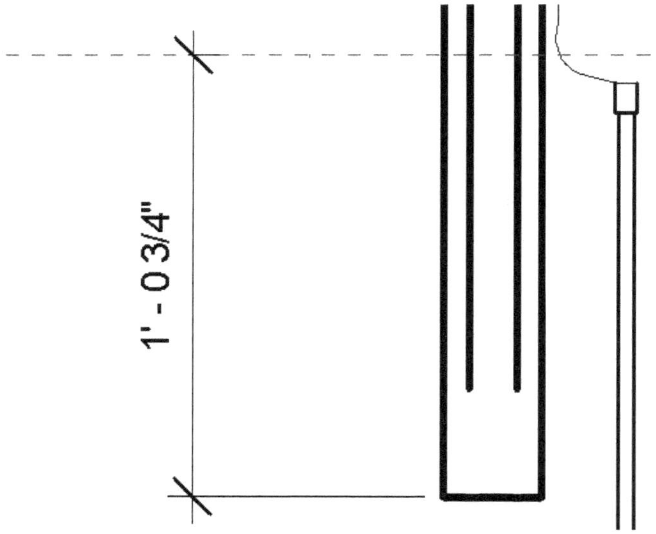

Figure 16–36

2. In the *Annotate* tab>*Detail* panel, expand ▦ (Region) and click ▦ (Filled Region).

3. In the Type Selector, select **Filled region: Earth**.

4. Set the *Line Style* to **Medium Lines**.

5. Use the different line tools to draw the finished grade areas, as shown in Figure 16–37.

6. Click ✔ (Finish). The filled regions display.

7. Start the **Filled Region** command again and draw areas for the concrete, as shown in Figure 16–37.

    Note: The filled region pattern does not display until you finish the process.

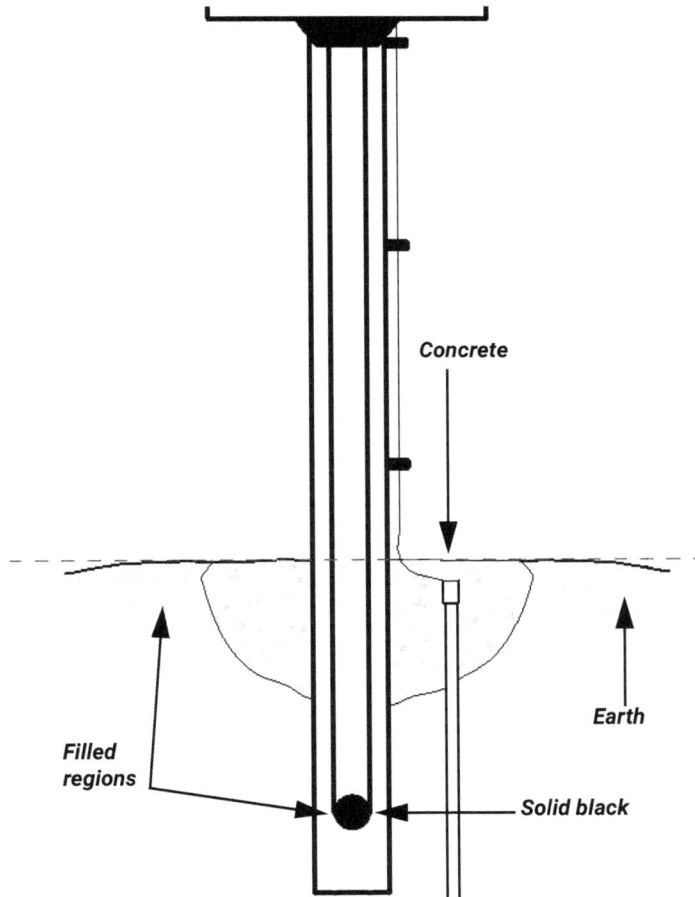

Figure 16–37

8. Save the project.

Task 5: Add text notes.

1. In the *Annotate* tab>*Text* panel, click **A** (Text).
2. In the *Modify | Place Text* tab>*Leader* panel, select **⤦A** (Two Segments) as the leader style.
3. In the Type Selector, select **Text: Note 3/32"**.
4. Add text notes, as shown in Figure 16–38.

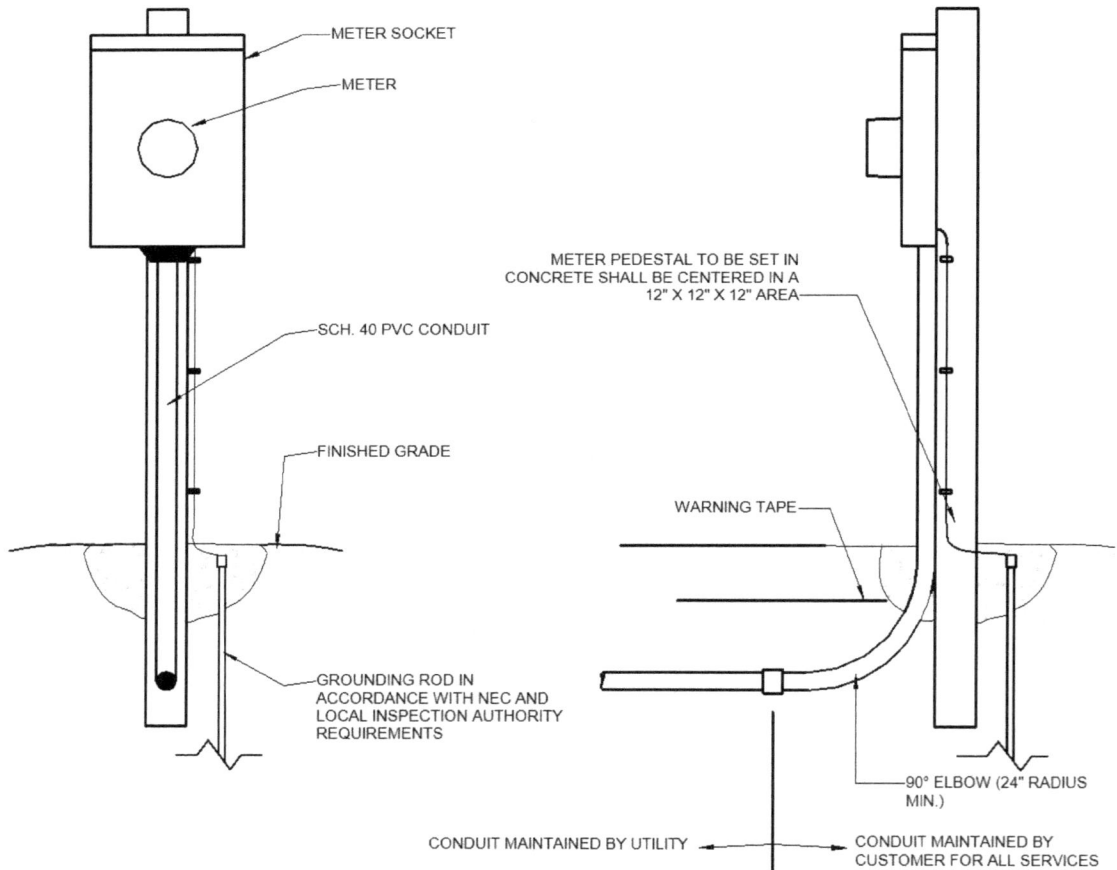

Figure 16–38

5. Save the project.

Task 6: Place the detail on a sheet and reference it in the project.

1. In the Project Browser, open the sheet **E-004 - Meter Details**.

2. In the Project Browser, drag the **Electrical Meter Pedestal Detail** view to the sheet.

3. Open the Electrical>Power>Floor Plans>**01- Power Plan** view.

4. Zoom in on the north wing above the electrical room.

5. In the *View* tab>*Create* panel, click ⌕ (Callout).

6. In the *Modify | Callout* tab>*Reference* panel, select **Reference Other View**.

7. Expand the drop-down list and select the new **Electrical Meter Pedestal Detail**, as shown in Figure 16–39.

8. Place the callout at the exterior wall, as shown in Figure 16–39. The information is filled out based on the location of the detail view on the sheet.

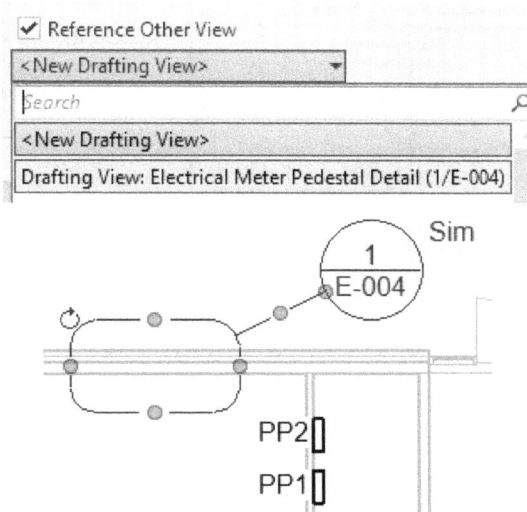

Figure 16–39

9. Click ⌕ (Modify).

10. Double-click on the callout head, and note that the Electrical Meter Pedestal Detail drafting view becomes the active view. This is because the callout is now linked to this drafting view.

11. Save and close the project.

End of practice

Practice 16c
Create a Floor Drain Detail – Plumbing

Practice Objective

- Create and annotate details.

In this practice, you will create a floor drain detail using detail components. You will then annotate the floor drain detail with text and a dimension, as shown in Figure 16–40.

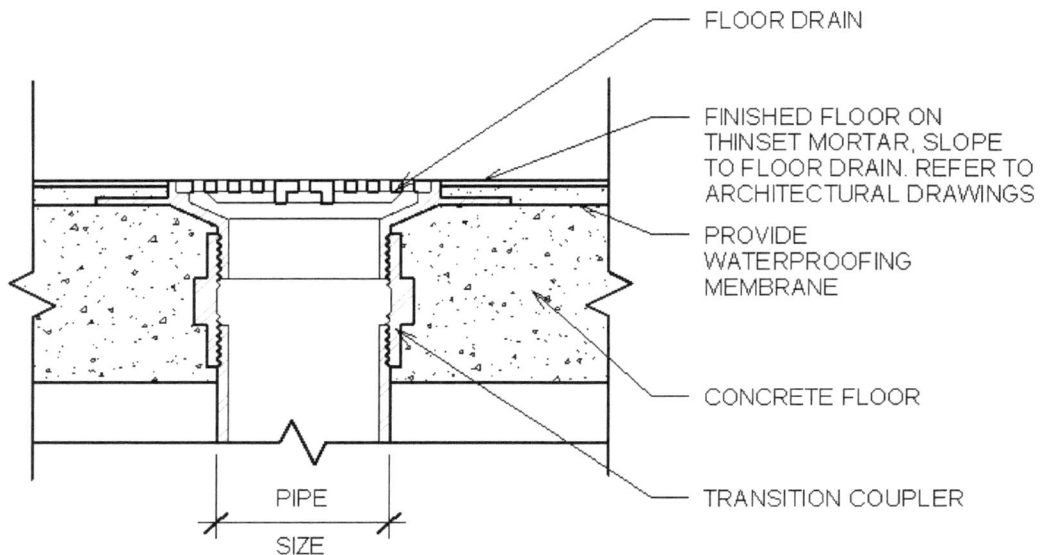

FLOOR DRAIN

FINISHED FLOOR ON THINSET MORTAR, SLOPE TO FLOOR DRAIN. REFER TO ARCHITECTURAL DRAWINGS

PROVIDE WATERPROOFING MEMBRANE

CONCRETE FLOOR

TRANSITION COUPLER

PIPE SIZE

Figure 16–40

- It is recommended that you also complete the other Detail practices if time permits, even though they are not for your specific discipline.

Task 1: Create a drafting view.

1. In the practice files *Working Models>Plumbing* folder, open **Plumb-Detailing.rvt**.

2. In the *View* tab>*Create* panel, click ⎘ (Drafting View).

3. In the *New Drafting View* dialog box, set the name and scale as follows:

   - *Name:* **Floor Drain Detail**
   - *Scale:* **3"=1'-0"**

4. In Properties, change *Discipline* to **Plumbing** and *Sub-Discipline* to **Plumbing**. The new view moves to that node in the Project Browser.

Task 2: Add detail components.

1. In the *Annotate* tab>*Detail* panel, expand ▦ (Component) and select ▦ (Detail Component).

2. In the Type Selector, select **Slab with Optional Haunch-Section 4"** and draw it so the length is **2'-3 1/4"**, as shown in Figure 16–41.

3. Start the **Detail Component** command again and add **Floor Drain - Section** at the center of the slab and **Resilient Flooring - Section** drawn on both sides of the drain out to the edge of the slab, as shown in Figure 16–41. (Dimension in figure is for reference only.)

Figure 16–41

4. Start the **Detail Component** command again and add three break line components. Rotate and use the controls to modify the size until all of your excess lines are covered, as shown in Figure 16–42. The break lines need to hide the portion of the detail components that you do not want shown.

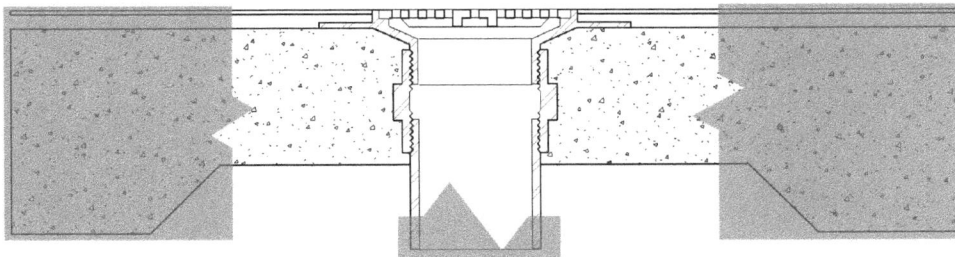

Figure 16–42

5. Save the project.

Task 3: Add grout and filled regions.

1. In the *Annotate* tab>*Detail* panel, expand 🔲 (Region) and click 🔲 (Filled Region).
2. In the Type Selector, select **Filled region: Grout**.
3. Draw lines around the areas between the drain and the floor, as shown in Figure 16–43.

   Note: The filled region pattern does not display until you finish the process.

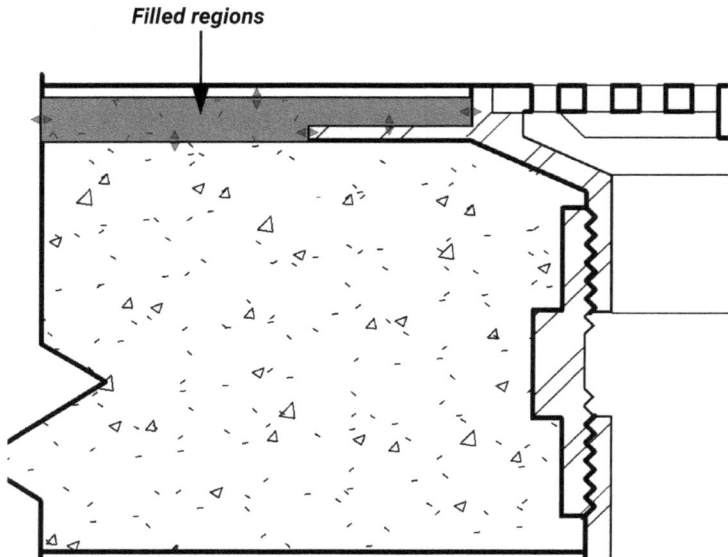

Figure 16–43

4. Click ✔ (Finish). The filled regions display.
5. Repeat the **Filled Region** command on the other side of the drain.
6. Save the project.

Task 4: Add text notes.

1. In the *Annotate* tab>*Text* panel, click **A** (Text).
2. In the *Modify | Place Text* tab>*Leader* panel, select ⤺**A** (Two Segments) as the leader style.
3. In the Type Selector, select **Text: Note 3/32"**.
4. Add text notes, as shown in Figure 16−44.

FLOOR DRAIN

FINISHED FLOOR ON THINSET
MORTAR, SLOPE TO FLOOR
DRAIN REFER TO
ARCHITECTURAL DRAWINGS

PROVIDE WATERPROOFING MEMBRANE

CONCRETE FLOOR

TRANSITION COUPLER

Figure 16−44

5. Save the project.

Task 5: Place the detail on a sheet and reference it in the project.

1. In the Project Browser, open the sheet **P-003 - Floor Drain Details**.
2. In the Project Browser, drag the **Floor Drain Detail** view to the sheet.
3. Open the Plumbing>Sanitary>**01- Sanitary Plan** view.
4. Zoom in on the kitchen in the upper-right side of the building.
5. In the *View* tab>*Create* panel, click ⬚ (Callout).
6. In the *Modify | Callout* tab>*Reference* panel, select **Reference Other View**.

7. Expand the drop-down list and select the new **Floor Drain Detail**, as shown in Figure 16–45.

8. Place the callout at the intersection of a duct and the wall, as shown in Figure 16–45. The information is filled out based on the location of the detail view on the sheet.

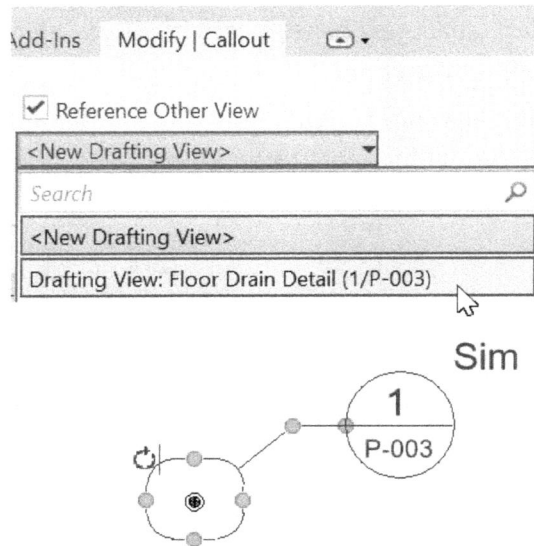

Figure 16–45

9. Click 🔓 (Modify).

10. Double-click on the callout head, and note that the Floor Drain Detail drafting view becomes the active view. This is because the callout is now linked to this drafting view.

11. Save and close the project.

End of practice

Chapter Review Questions

1. Which of the following are ways in which you can create a detail? (Select all that apply.)
   a. Make a callout of a section and sketch over it.
   b. Draw all of the elements from scratch.
   c. Import a CAD detail and modify or sketch over it.
   d. Insert an existing drafting view from another file.

2. How are detail components different from building components?
   a. There is no difference.
   b. Detail components are made of 2D lines and annotations only.
   c. Detail components are made of building elements, but only display in detail views.
   d. Detail components are made of 2D and 3D elements.

3. Which of the following statements is true when you sketch detail lines?
   a. Always the same width.
   b. Vary in width according to the view.
   c. Display in all views associated with the detail.
   d. Display only in the view in which they were created.

4. Which command do you use to add a pattern (such as concrete or earth, as shown in Figure 16–46) to part of a detail?

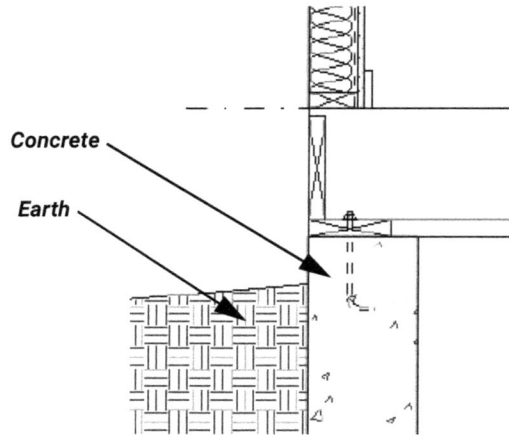

Concrete

Earth

Figure 16–46

a. Region

b. Filled Region

c. Masking Region

d. Pattern Region

Command Summary

Button	Command	Location
CAD Import Tools		
	Delete Layers	• **Ribbon:** *Modify | <imported filename> tab>Import Instance* panel
	Full Explode	• **Ribbon:** *Modify | <imported filename> tab>Import Instance* panel, expand Explode
	Import CAD	• **Ribbon:** *Insert* tab>Import panel
	Partial Explode	• **Ribbon:** *Modify | <imported filename> tab>Import Instance* panel, expand Explode
Detail Tools		
	Detail Component	• **Ribbon:** *Annotate* tab>*Detail* panel, expand Component
	Detail Line	• **Ribbon:** *Annotate* tab>*Detail* panel
	Insulation	• **Ribbon:** *Annotate* tab>*Detail* panel
	Filled Region	• **Ribbon:** *Annotate* tab>*Detail* panel
	Repeating Detail Component	• **Ribbon:** *Annotate* tab>*Detail* panel, expand Component
View Tools		
	Bring Forward	• **Ribbon:** *Modify | Detail Items* tab>*Arrange* panel
	Bring to Front	• **Ribbon:** *Modify | Detail Items* tab>*Arrange* panel
	Drafting View	• **Ribbon:** *View* tab>*Create* panel
	Insert from File: Insert Views from File	• **Ribbon:** *Insert* tab>*Load from Library* panel, expand Insert from File
	Send Backward	• **Ribbon:** *Modify | Detail Items* tab>*Arrange* panel
	Send to Back	• **Ribbon:** *Modify | Detail Items* tab>*Arrange* panel

Additional Tools for Design Development

There are many other tools available in Revit® that you can use when creating and working in models. This appendix provides details about several tools and commands that are related to those covered in the Design Development section of this guide.

Learning Objectives

- Change the display and organization of views in the Project Browser.
- Purge unused component elements to increase the processing speed of the model.
- Customize building type settings for heating and cooling loads.
- Define color schemes.
- Create custom ducts and piping types.
- Modify system graphics using filters and overrides.
- Understand worksharing and working with workset-related files.

A.1 Displaying Views in the Project Browser

You can customize how the views are displayed in the Project Browser by changing the Browser Organization for each of the tabs: *Views*, *Sheets* or *Schedules*, as shown in Figure A-1.

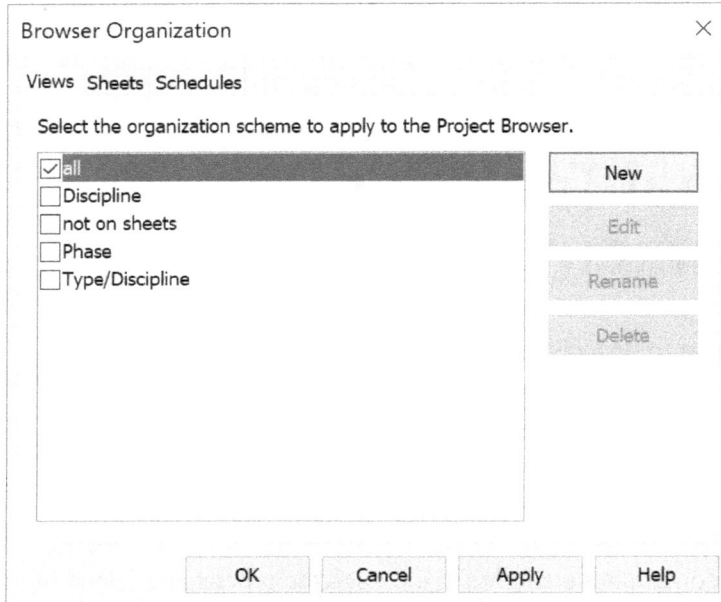

Figure A-1

How To: Change How the Project Browser Displays Views

1. In the Project Browser, right-click on **Views (all)** and select **Browser Organization...**, as shown in Figure A-2.

Figure A-2

2. In the *Browser Organization* dialog box, select **Type/Discipline**, as shown in Figure A–3.

Figure A–3

3. The Project Browser updates to sort by view type (e.g., Floor Plans, Ceiling Plans, etc.), then by discipline. Figure A–4 shows the difference between the two browser organization types.

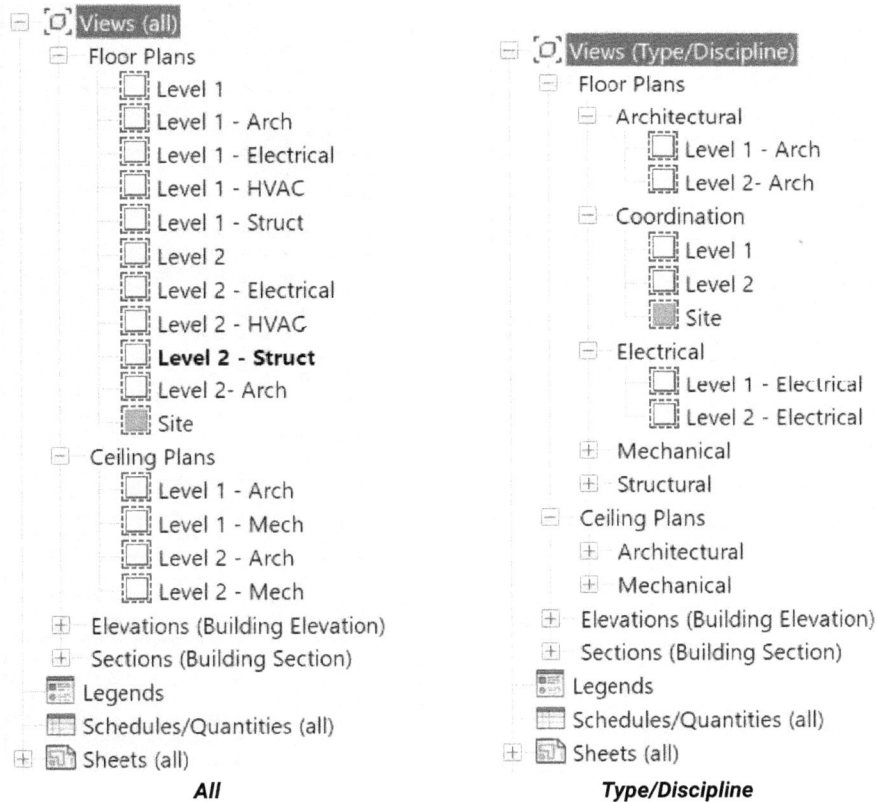

All   *Type/Discipline*

Figure A–4

Setting the Discipline of a View

You can utilize discipline in a view to display discipline-specific elements and to organize the Project Browser. When you duplicate or create a view, if it is not in the expected grouping in the Project Browser, you would need to set the *Discipline* in Properties. The view properties of *Discipline* (shown in Figure A–5) control the visibility of some elements and applies grouping in the Project Browser. For example, you can separate the coordination plans from the architectural plans, as shown in Figure A–6.

Figure A–5

Figure A–6

A.2 Purging Unused Elements

To reduce file size and remove unused elements from a project, including individual component types, you can purge the project, as shown in Figure A–7.

Figure A–7

- Some elements are nested in other elements and it might require several rounds of purging the project to remove them.

How To: Purge Unused Elements

1. In the *Manage* tab>*Settings* panel, click ▧ (Purge Unused).

2. In the *Purge unused* dialog box, click **Check None** and select the elements you want to purge.

3. Click **OK**.

- Purging unused components helps simplify the list of families loaded in a project.

A.3 Building Type Settings

For even more control over heating and cooling load analysis, you can customize the building types using the *Building/Space Type Settings* dialog box, as shown in Figure A–8.

- To open the dialog box, in the *Manage* tab>*Settings* panel, expand 🗒 (MEP Settings) and click 🔧 (Building/Space and Type Settings), or in the *Analyze* tab, click 🗒 in the *Reports & Schedules* panel title.

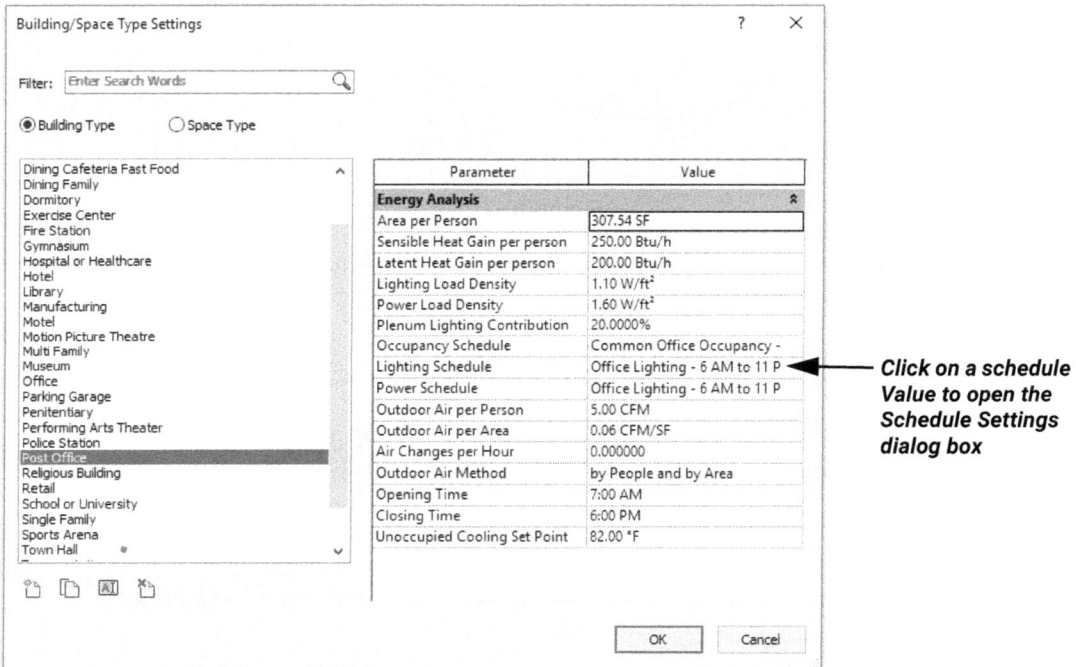

Figure A–8

- You can add, duplicate, rename and delete building and space types.

- For each type of building or space, you can specify energy analysis information, such as the number of people and expected heat gain per person, as well as the schedules of typical times that the building is occupied, as shown for a Warehouse in Figure A–9.

  - To get to the *Schedule Settings* dialog box, select a **Building Type** on the left, then on the right, click on *Occupancy*, *Lighting*, or *Power Schedule* and click within the *Value* name.

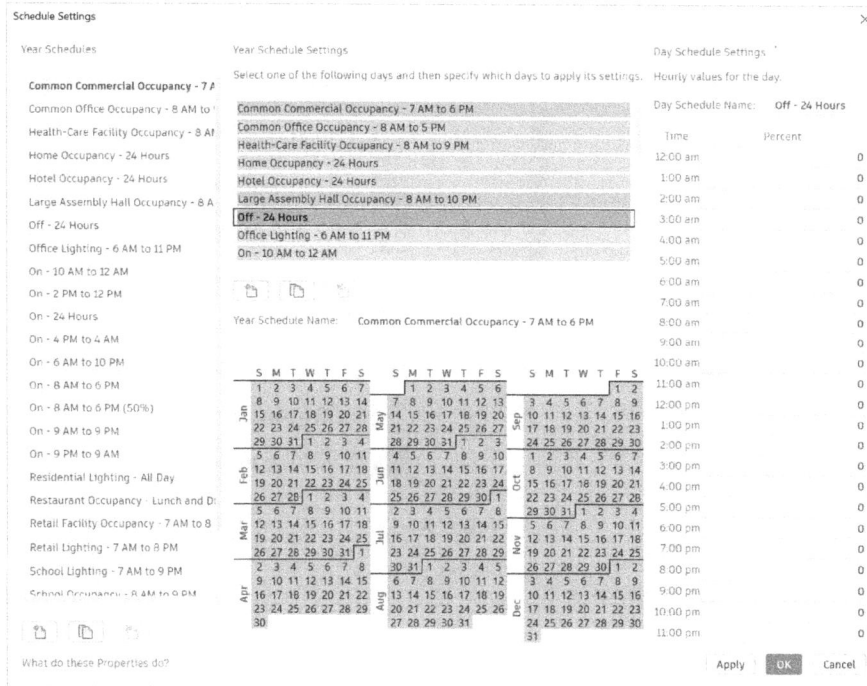

Figure A–9

- Building/space type names are exported when you export a project to gbXML for further processing in other energy analysis programs.

A.4 Defining Color Schemes

Color schemes are used with spaces, zones, ducts, and pipes. You can define colors using many of the properties connected to the elements such as the Duct Friction Color Fill, as shown in Figure A–10.

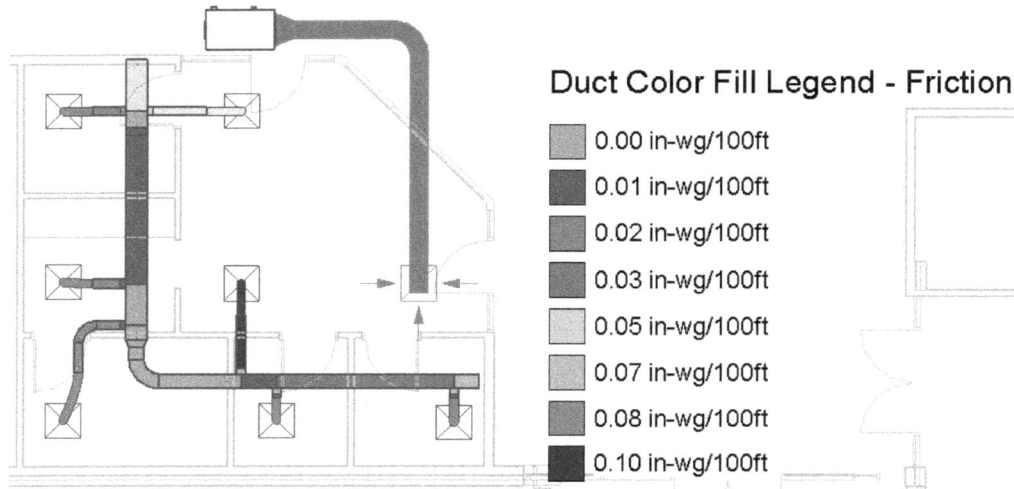

Duct Color Fill Legend - Friction

- 0.00 in-wg/100ft
- 0.01 in-wg/100ft
- 0.02 in-wg/100ft
- 0.03 in-wg/100ft
- 0.05 in-wg/100ft
- 0.07 in-wg/100ft
- 0.08 in-wg/100ft
- 0.10 in-wg/100ft

Figure A–10

How To: Define a Color Scheme

1. In Properties, click the button next to the **Color Scheme** (for spaces and HVAC zones) or **System Color Schemes** (for pipes and ducts) parameter.

   - **Color Schemes:** For spaces and HVAC zones, in the *Edit Color Scheme* dialog box, *Schemes* area, select a **Category**.

   - **System Color Scheme:** For pipes and ducts, in the *Color Schemes* dialog box, select the *Color scheme* for either the Pipes or Ducts category. Then, in the *Edit Color Scheme* dialog box, select a **Category** in the *Scheme* area.

2. Select an existing scheme and click ⬚ (Duplicate).

3. In the *New color scheme* dialog box, enter a new name and click **OK**. If the Colors Not Preserved warning displays, click **OK** again.

4. In the *Scheme Definition* area, type a name for the *Title* of the color scheme. This displays when the legend is placed in the view.

5. In the *Color:* drop-down list, select an option, as shown in Figure A-11. The available parameters depend on the type of scheme you are creating.

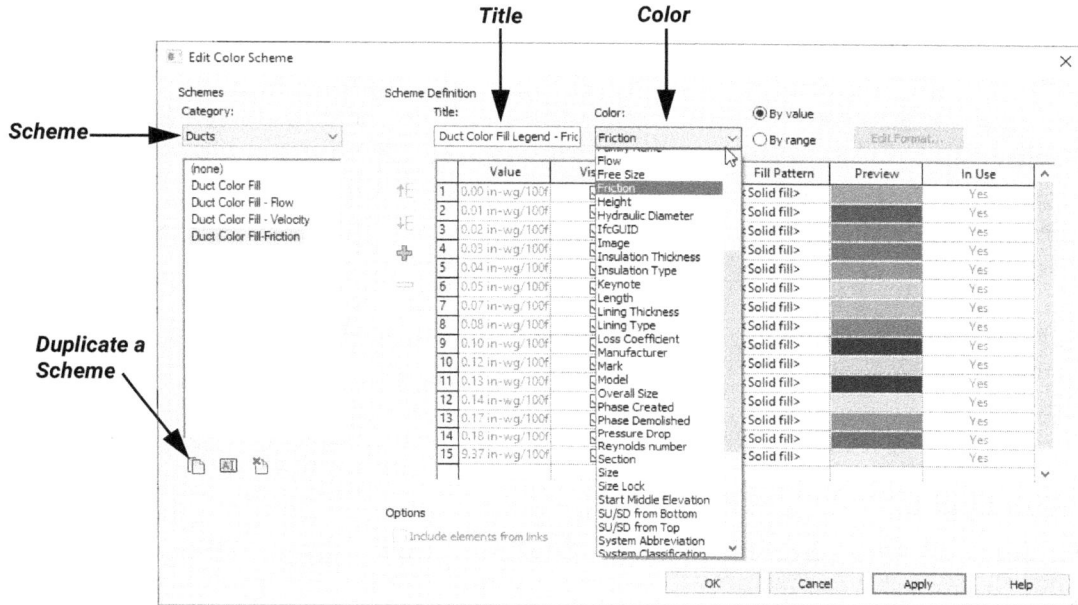

Figure A-11

6. Select the **By value** or **By range** options to set how the color scheme displays. Depending on the selection made in the *Color:* drop-down list, **By range** might not be available.

7. If required, click ✛ (Add Value) to add more rows to the scheme, as shown in Figure A-12. Modify the visibility (*Visible* column), *Color*, and *Fill Pattern* as needed.

Figure A-12

8. In the *Options* area, select **Include elements from linked files** if you are using linked models.

9. Click **OK** to end the command.

Color Schemes By Value

If you select the **By value** option, you can modify the visibility, color, and fill pattern of the scheme. The value is assigned by the parameter data in the room or area object.

- Values are automatically updated when you add data to the parameters used in the color scheme. For example, if you create a color by space name and then add another space name in the project, it is also added to the color scheme.

- Click ⬆E (Move Rows Up) and ⬇E (Move Rows Down) to change the order of rows in the list.

- To remove a row, select it and click ▭ (Remove Value). This is only available if the parameter data is not being used in the room or area elements in the project.

Color Schemes By Range

If you select the **By range** option, you can modify the *At Least* variable and the *Caption*, as well as the visibility, color, and fill pattern, as shown in Figure A–13.

Scheme Definition

Title: Space Area per Person   Color: Area per Person   ○ By value   ● By range   Edit Format...   1235 SF (Default)

At Least	Less Than	Caption	Visible	Color	Fill Pattern	Preview	In Use
	20.00 SF	Less than 20	☑	RGB 156-	Solid fill		Yes
20.00 SF	30.00 SF	20 SF - 30 SF	☑	PANTO	Solid fill		No
30.00 SF	40.00 SF	30 SF - 40 SF	☑	RGB 139-	Solid fill		No
40.00 SF	50.00 SF	40 SF - 50 SF	☑	PANTO	Solid fill		No
50.00 SF		50 SF or mor	☑	PANTO	Solid fill		Yes

Figure A–13

- Click **Edit Format...** to modify the units display format.

- To add rows, select the row above the new row and click

  ✚ (Add Value). The new row increments according to the previous distances set or by double the value of the first row.

A.5 Custom Duct and Piping Types

Duct/Pipe Types and Settings

The System and Mechanical default templates are pre-loaded with duct/pipe types and routing preferences set up. You can create additional duct/pipe types and modify the routing preferences. Ducts and pipes are system families; therefore, you need to duplicate an existing family in the *Type Properties* dialog box, as shown in Figure A–14.

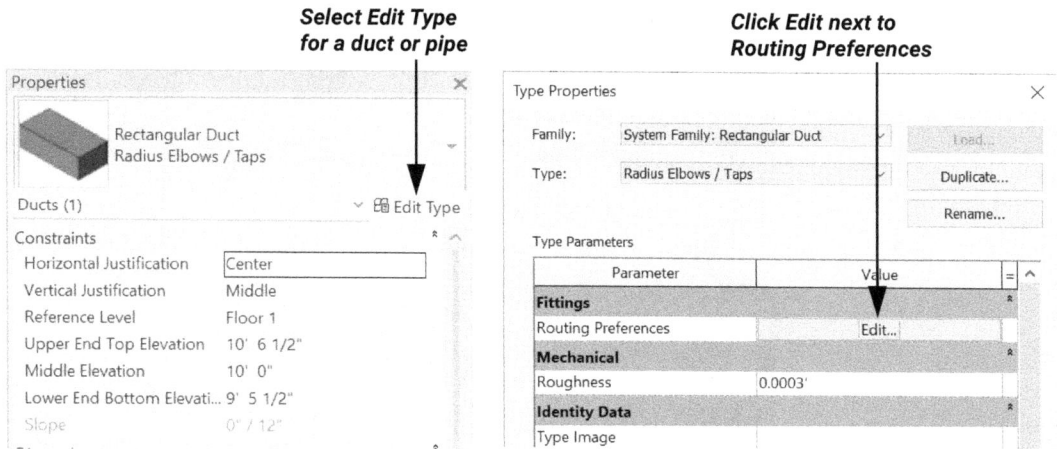

Figure A–14

Routing Preferences

The *Routing Preferences* dialog box enables you to specify the kind of pipe and pipe fittings to use. You can have a simple pipe type with one kind of pipe segment used for all sizes and one family for each kind of pipe fitting. Alternatively, you can set up the pipe type so that as the pipe size increases, different pipe and different fittings are used. Use ✚ (Add Row) and

▭ (Remove Row) to create or remove rows, and the arrows to re-order items.

- Duct routing preferences are similar.

The *Routing Preferences* dialog box is shown in Figure A–15.

Content	Min. Size	Max. Size
Pipe Segment		
Copper - K	1/4"	12"
Elbow		
Elbow - Generic: Standard	All	
Preferred Junction Type		
Tee	All	
Junction		
Tee - Generic: Standard	All	
Cross		
Cross - Generic: Standard	All	
Transition		
Transition - Generic: Standard	All	
Union		
Coupling - Generic: Standard	All	

Routing Preferences

Pipe Type: Standard

Segments and Sizes...   Load Family...

OK   Cancel

Figure A–15

- **Segments and Sizes...** enables you to create named segments with corresponding standard pipe sizes.

- **Load Family...** enables you to load additional pipe fittings if needed.

A.6 Work with System Graphics

Default system colors are set up by graphic overrides at the system family level. These can be modified to suit your company standards. Another useful graphic override is to create filters that display only the systems you want to see in a view. For example, use graphic override filters to display the sanitary piping only and not the hot and cold water piping, as shown in Figure A–16.

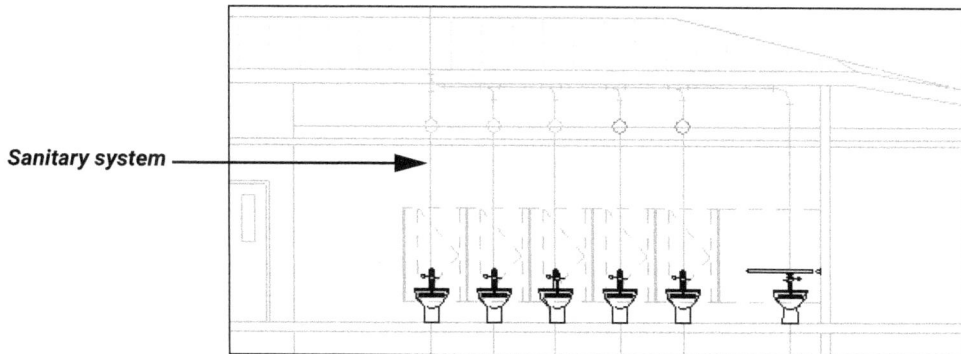

Figure A–16

System Graphic Overrides

By default, in the Autodesk Revit templates, the Return Air Systems are magenta and Supply Air Systems are blue. In Figure A–17, Hydronic Supply and Return Systems also have the colors specified. System colors display in all views including 3D views.

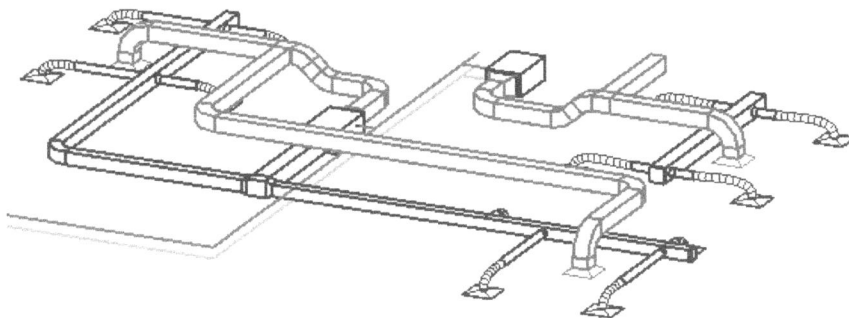

Figure A–17

*   System graphic overrides are consistent across the entire project. They are not view specific.

How To: Set Up System Graphic Overrides

1. In the Project Browser, expand **Families>Piping** (or **Duct**) **Systems>Piping** (or **Duct**) **System**.

   Note: To create a new system family, in the Project Browser, right-click on an existing type and duplicate it.

2. Double-click on the one that you want to modify or right-click and select **Type Properties**.

3. In the *Type Properties* dialog box, next to *Graphic Overrides*, click **Edit...**.

4. In the *Line Graphics* dialog box (shown in Figure A–18), make changes to the *Weight*, *Color*, and/or *Pattern*.

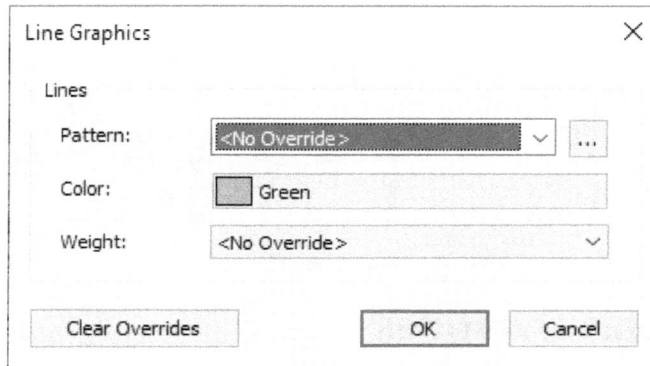

Figure A–18

5. Click **OK** twice to apply the changes.

Using Graphic Override Filters

Any view can be set to display specific systems by using filters. In the example in Figure A–19, the view on the left displays all of the systems along with extra elements such as data components. The view on the right has graphic overrides that toggle off extraneous elements and filter out all systems except duct and hydronic piping.

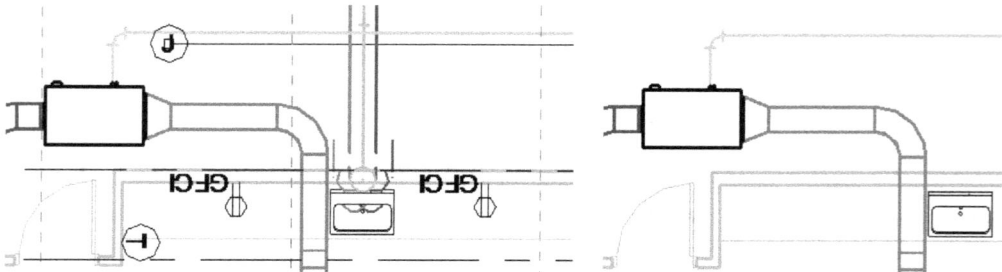

Figure A–19

How To: Apply a View Filter to Override a View

1. Open the *Visibility/Graphic Overrides* dialog box.

2. In the dialog box, select the *Filters* tab.

3. In the *Visibility* column, select the overrides you want to display. In Figure A–20, the Domestic and Sanitary categories have been toggled off while the Mechanical systems display.

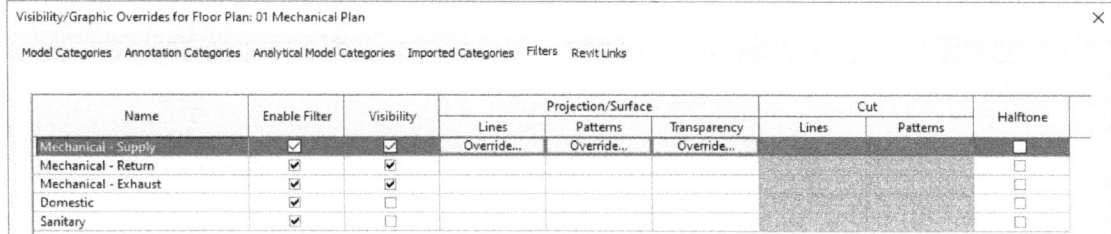

Name	Enable Filter	Visibility	Projection/Surface			Cut		Halftone
			Lines	Patterns	Transparency	Lines	Patterns	
Mechanical - Supply	☑	☑	Override...	Override...	Override...			☐
Mechanical - Return	☑	☑						☐
Mechanical - Exhaust	☑	☑						☐
Domestic	☑	☐						☐
Sanitary	☑	☐						☐

Visibility/Graphic Overrides for Floor Plan: 01 Mechanical Plan — Model Categories   Annotation Categories   Analytical Model Categories   Imported Categories   Filters   Revit Links

Figure A–20

4. To add a new filter to this view, click **Add**.

5. In the *Add Filters* dialog box (shown in Figure A–21), select the type of systems you want to modify and click **OK**.

    Note: *The list might vary depending on the filters set up in the project.*

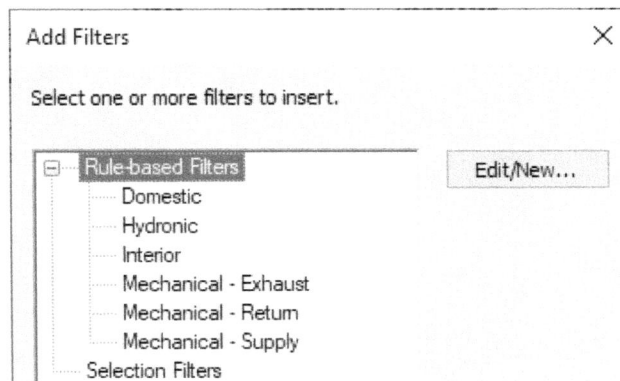

Add Filters

Select one or more filters to insert.

- Rule-based Filters
  - Domestic
  - Hydronic
  - Interior
  - Mechanical - Exhaust
  - Mechanical - Return
  - Mechanical - Supply
- Selection Filters

Edit/New...

Figure A–21

- View filters override system graphics so any colors you set in this dialog box supersede those specified in the system type.

- If you need to change information about the filter itself, click **Edit/New...** in the *Add Filters* or *Filters* dialog box. Then, modify the *Categories* or *Filter Rules*. For example, the **Mechanical - Exhaust** filter does not include **Air Terminals** by default so you need to select it, as shown in Figure A–22.

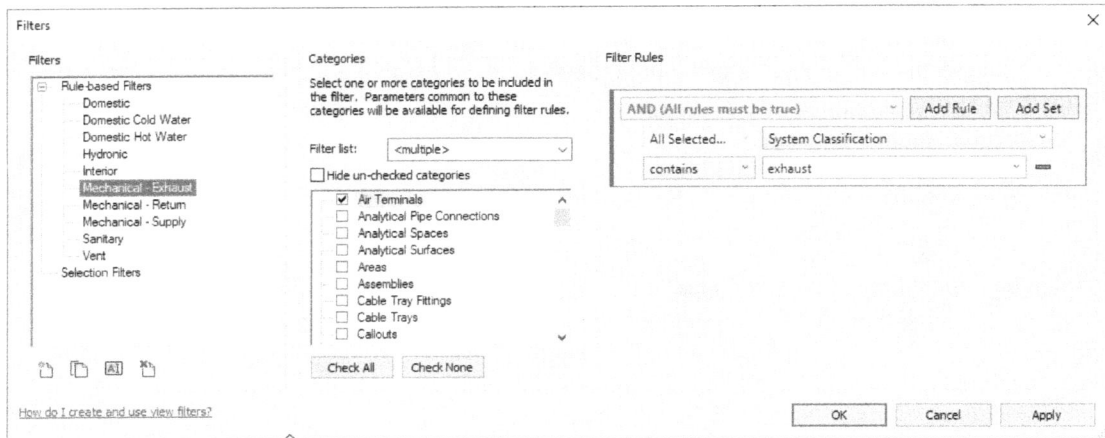

Figure A–22

A.7 Introduction to Revit Worksharing

When a project becomes too big for one person, it needs to be subdivided so that a team of people working on the same network can work on it. Since Revit projects include the entire building model in one file, the file needs to be separated into logical components, as shown in Figure A–23, without losing the connection to the whole. This process is called *worksharing* and the main components are worksets.

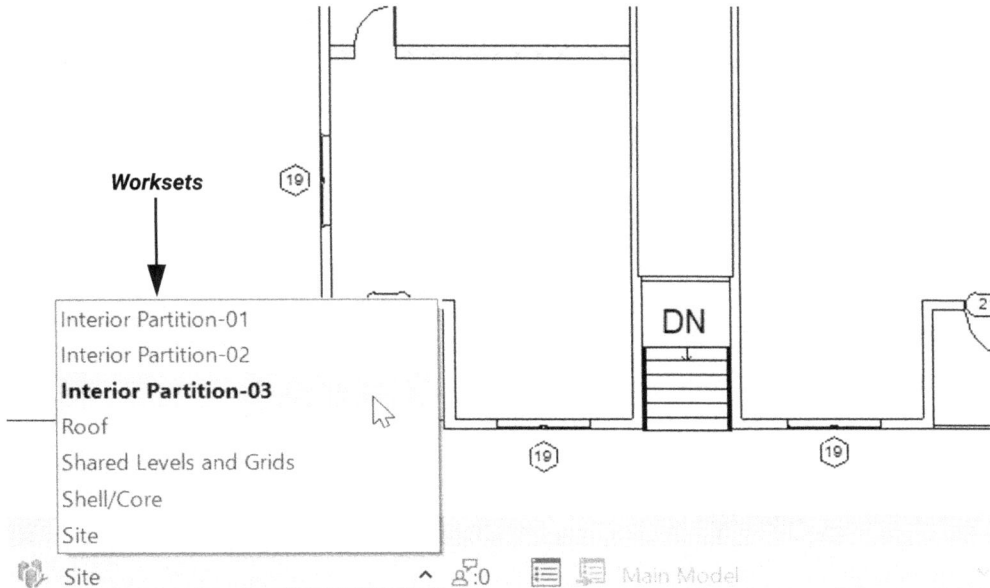

Figure A–23

Revit worksharing gives multiple team members connected on the same network the ability to co-author a single project model (one .RVT file). The appropriate team member creates a central model with multiple worksets (such as element interiors, building shell, and site) that are used by the project team members. Team members open and work in a local copy of the model that is linked back to the central model through saving and synchronizing. For more information about establishing and using worksets, refer to the ASCENT guide *Autodesk Revit: Collaboration Tools*.

A workshared project consists of one central model (also known as a central file) and individual models for each user known as local files, as shown in Figure A–24. Each team member will work in their local file and use a function called *synchronizing with central* to send and receive updates with the central model.

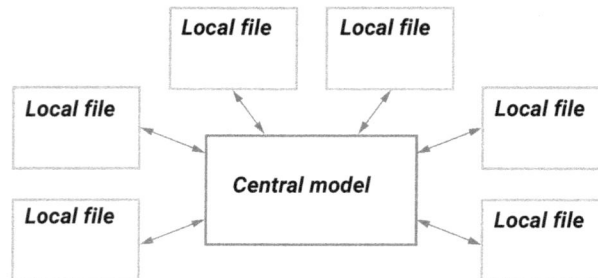

Figure A–24

- The **central model** is created by the BIM manager, project manager, or project lead and is stored on a server or in the cloud, enabling multiple users to access it.

- A **local file** is a copy of the central model that is stored on your computer.

- All local files are saved back to the central model, and updates to the central model are sent out to the local files. This way, all changes remain in one file, while the project, model, views, and sheets are automatically updated.

Worksharing Definitions

Worksharing: This is a functionality that, when enabled, allows multiple members of the team to access a project stored in one centralized location, which gives multiple users the ability to work on the same project simultaneously.

Workshared file: This is a project that has worksets enabled. If the project has no worksets enabled, it is called a *non-workshared file*.

Workset: This is a collection of elements that are related geometrically, parametrically, or by location within an overall project that are subdivided so they can be worked on while isolated from the rest of the model. When worksharing is enabled, worksets are automatically activated and the *Workset1* and *Shared Grids and Levels* worksets are added to the project by default.

Central model: Also called the central file, this is the main project file that is stored on a local network that all users can access. Using a central model is called *file-based worksharing*. The central model stores workset and element information in the project and is the file to which everyone saves and synchronizes their changes. The central model updates all the local files with the latest model information. This file should not be edited directly.

Local file: This is a copy of the central model that is saved to your local computer. This is the file that you modify and work in. As you work, you save the file locally and synchronize it with the central model.

Element borrowing: This refers to the process of modifying items in the project that are not part of the workset you have checked out. This either happens automatically (if no one else has checked out a workset) or specifically, when you request to have control of the elements (if someone else has a workset checked out).

Active workset: The workset that displays in the Status Bar is the active workset. Any new elements that are added will be placed on this workset. As you work, you will change the active workset accordingly.

Relinquish: This releases or returns a checked-out workset so that others can work on the elements within that workset. If you do not release or relinquish your checked-out worksets, other users will get a warning that they cannot edit the workset until you relinquish it, and they are given the option to request to borrow the workset. **Relinquish All Mine** allows you to relinquish worksets without synchronizing to the central model.

Reload Latest: This updates your local file without you needing to synchronize with the central model.

General Process of Using Worksets

1. Wait for the appropriate team member to enable worksharing, set up worksets, and create the central model.

2. Create a local file from the central model.

3. Work in your local file and select the worksets that you need to work on by verifying the active workset.

    - Work in your local model by adding, deleting, and modifying elements.

    - You may need to request to borrow elements in worksets that are currently checked out by other team members.

4. Save the local file as frequently as you would save any other project.

5. Synchronize the local file with the central model several times a day or as required by company policy or project status.

    - This reloads any changes from the central model to your local file and vice versa.

    - If the option to **Save Local File before and after synchronizing with central** is checked, your local file will be saved, but it is always recommended to save the local file yourself every time you synchronize to the central model.

Opening Workset-Related Files

When you open a workset-related file, it creates a new local file on your computer. Do not work in the main central model.

How To: Create a Local File

1. In the *File* tab or Quick Access Toolbar, click 🗁 (Open).

2. In the *Open* dialog box, navigate to the central model server location and select the central model. Do not work in this file. Select **Create New Local**, as shown in Figure A–25, and click **Open**.

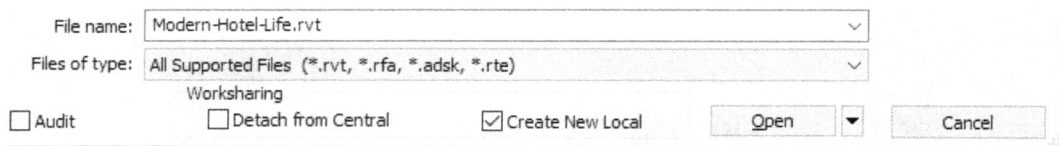

Figure A–25

3. A copy of the project is created. It will have the same name as the central model with your Autodesk Revit username added to the end.

*   If you are working with a recently used central model, it may display on the Home screen with the icon shown in Figure A–26. Clicking this file automatically creates a local copy of the model. The first time you use this option, a warning displays, as shown in Figure A–27.

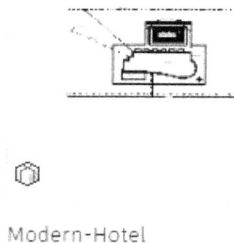

Modern-Hotel

Figure A–26

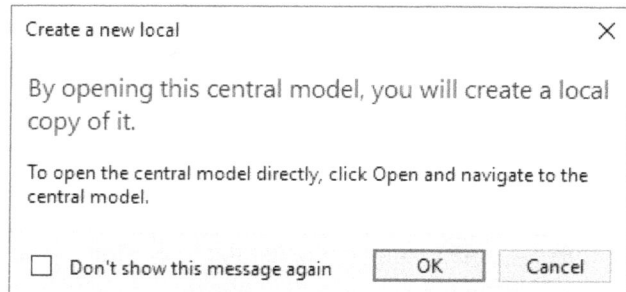

Figure A–27

4. You can save the file using the default name, or use 💾 (Save As) and name the file according to your office's standard. It should include *Local* in the name to indicate that it is saved on your local computer, or that you are the only one working with that version of the file.

*   Delete any old local files to ensure that you are working on the latest version.

How To: Work in a Workshared Project

1. Open your local file.

2. In the Status Bar, expand the *Active Workset* drop-down list and select a workset, as shown in Figure A–28. By setting the active workset, other people can work in the project but cannot edit elements that you add to the workset.

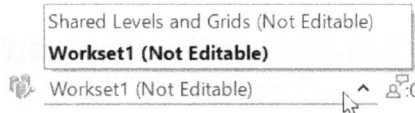

Shared Levels and Grids (Not Editable)
Workset1 (Not Editable)

Workset1 (Not Editable)

Figure A–28

3. Work on the project as needed.

Saving a Workshared Project

When you are working on a workshared project, you need to save the project locally and centrally.

* Save the local file frequently (every 15-30 minutes). In the Quick Access Toolbar, click

   (Save) to save the local file just as you would any other project.

* Synchronize the local file with the central model periodically (every hour or two) or after you have made major changes to the project.

Hint: Set Up Notifications to Save and Synchronize

You can set up reminders to save and synchronize files to the central model in the *Options* dialog box, on the *General* tab, as shown in Figure A–29.

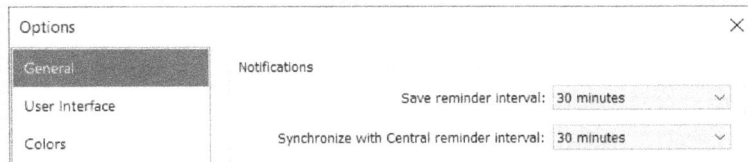

Options		×
General	Notifications	
User Interface	Save reminder interval: 30 minutes	
Colors	Synchronize with Central reminder interval: 30 minutes	

Figure A–29

Synchronizing to the Central Model

There are two methods for synchronizing to the central model. In the Quick Access Toolbar or

Collaborate tab>*Synchronize* panel, expand 🔲 (Synchronize with Central) and click

🔲 (Synchronize Now) or 🔲 (Synchronize and Modify Settings). The last-used command is active if you click the top-level icon.

- **Synchronize Now:** Updates the central model and then the local file with any changes to the central model since the last synchronization without prompting you for any settings. It automatically relinquishes elements borrowed from any workset but retains worksets used by the current user.

- **Synchronize and Modify Settings:** Opens the *Synchronize with Central* dialog box, shown in Figure A–30, so you can set the options for relinquishing worksets and elements, add comments, and specify to save the file locally before and after synchronization.

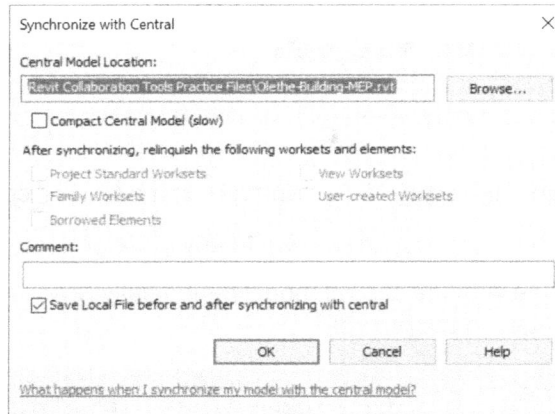

Figure A–30

- Always keep **Save Local File before and after synchronizing with central** checked to ensure your local copy is up to date with the latest changes from the central model.

- When you close a local file without saving to the central model, you are prompted to do so, as shown in Figure A–31.

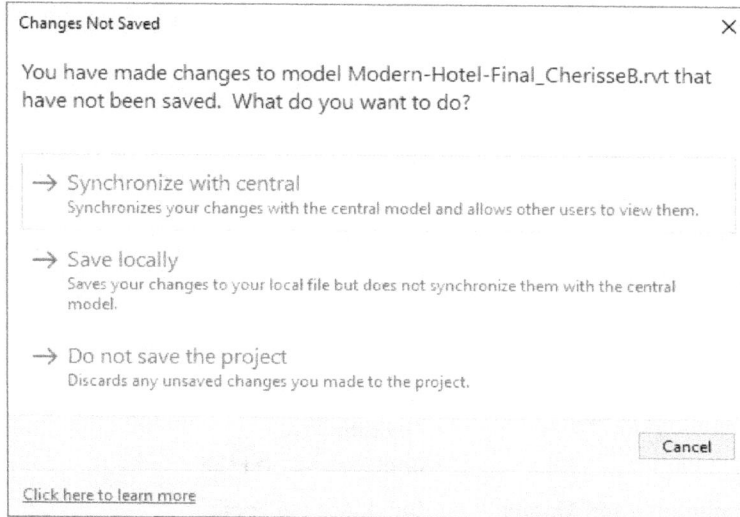

Changes Not Saved   ✕

You have made changes to model Modern-Hotel-Final_CherisseB.rvt that have not been saved. What do you want to do?

→ Synchronize with central
  Synchronizes your changes with the central model and allows other users to view them.

→ Save locally
  Saves your changes to your local file but does not synchronize them with the central model.

→ Do not save the project
  Discards any unsaved changes you made to the project.

                                                          Cancel

Click here to learn more

Figure A–31

- The maximum number of backups for workset-enabled files is set to 20 by default.

    Note: *Workshared files do not have the same backup files as non-workshared files.*

Command Summary

Button	Command	Location
MEP Tools		
	Building/Space and Type Settings	• **Ribbon:** *Manage* tab>*Settings* panel, expand MEP Settings • **Ribbon:** *Analyze* tab>*Reports & Schedules* panel title
Purge Elements		
	Purge Unused	• **Ribbon:** *Manage* tab>*Settings* panel
Worksharing		
	Save	• **Quick Access Toolbar** • *File* **tab:** Save • **Shortcut:** <Ctrl>+<S>
	Synchronize and Modify Settings	• **Quick Access Toolbar** • **Ribbon:** *Collaborate* tab>*Synchronize* panel, expand Synchronize with Central
	Synchronize Now	• **Quick Access Toolbar** • **Ribbon:** *Collaborate* tab>*Synchronize* panel, expand Synchronize with Central

Additional Tools for Construction Documents

There are many other tools available in Revit® that you can use when creating construction documents. This appendix provides details about several tools and commands that are related to those covered in the Construction Documentation section of this guide.

Learning Objectives

- Produce Pressure Loss reports.
- Use guide grids to help place views on sheets.
- Add revision clouds, tags, and information.
- Annotate dependent views with matchlines and view references.
- Import and export schedules.
- Place keynotes in a detail and add keynote legends that describe the full content of the keynotes.

B.1 Pressure Loss Reports

Pressure Loss reports are HTML files, as shown in Figure B-1, that include all of the data that can be viewed dynamically in the System Inspector. The reports can be set up to export exactly the information you need. They can be created for duct or pipe systems. The analysis for each system includes total pressure loss for the system and detailed information for various sections of duct or pipe.

System Classification	Return Air
System Type	Return Air
System Name	01 - RA01
Abbreviation	

Total Pressure Loss Calculations by Sections

Section	Element	Flow	Size	Velocity	Velocity Pressure	Length	Loss Co
	Duct	500 CFM	12"x12"	500 FPM	-	3' - 11 1/2"	-
1	Fittings	500 CFM	-	500 FPM	0.02 in-wg	-	0.17
	Air Terminal	500 CFM	-	-	-	-	-
2	Duct	1000 CFM	12"x12"	1000 FPM	-	12' - 4 15/16"	-
	Fittings	1000 CFM	-	1000 FPM	0.06 in-wg	-	0.81490!
3	Fittings	1000 CFM	-	409 FPM	0.01 in-wg	-	0
	Equipment	1000 CFM	-	-	-	-	-
	Duct	500 CFM	12"x12"	500 FPM	-	24' - 7 1/2"	-
4	Fittings	500 CFM	-	500 FPM	0.02 in-wg	-	0.34
	Air Terminal	500 CFM	-	-	-	-	-

Critical Path : 4-2-3 ; Total Pressure Loss : 0.14 in-wg

Detail Information of Straight Segment by Sections

Section	Element ID	Flow	Size	Velocity	Velocity Pressure
1	250437	500 CFM	12"x12"	500 FPM	0.02 in-wg
	250440	500 CFM	12"x12"	500 FPM	0.02 in-wg
2	250623	1000 CFM	12"x12"	1000 FPM	0.06 in-wg
	252421	1000 CFM	12"x12"	1000 FPM	0.06 in-wg
	252430	1000 CFM	12"x12"	1000 FPM	0.06 in-wg
4	250445	500 CFM	12"x12"	500 FPM	0.02 in-wg
	250446	500 CFM	12"x12"	500 FPM	0.02 in-wg
	250449	500 CFM	12"x12"	500 FPM	0.02 in-wg

Figure B-1

How To: Create a Duct/Pipe Pressure Loss Report

1. Select a system in a view. In the *Modify Duct (or Pipe) Systems* contextual tab>*Duct (or Pipe) System Report* panel, click 🖥 (Duct Pressure Loss Report) or 🖥 (Pipe Pressure Loss Report). If you have not preselected a system in the view, in the *Analyze* tab>*Reports & Schedules* panel, select **Duct Pressure Loss Report** or **Pipe Pressure Loss Report**. The *Pipe (or Duct) Pressure Loss Report - System Selector* dialog box (shown in Figure B–2) enables you to select the systems that you want to include in the report.

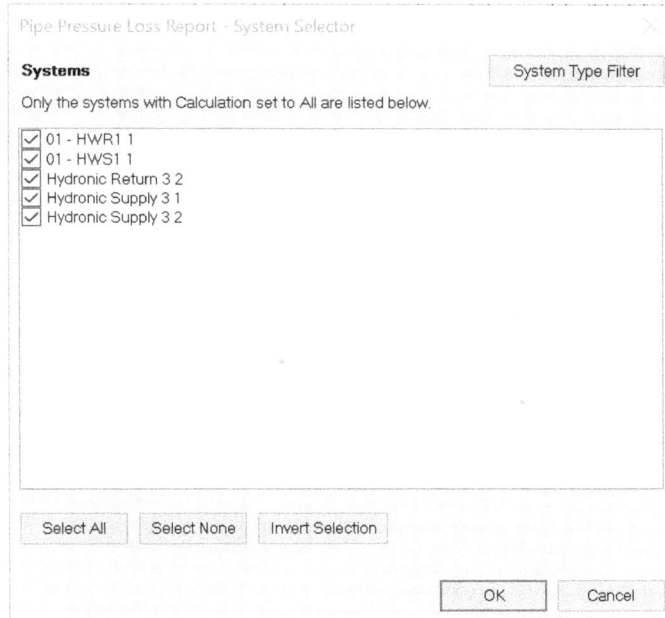

Figure B–2

- To limit the systems displayed in the System Selector, click **System Type Filter** to open the dialog box shown in Figure B–3. Select the types of systems you want to include in the report and click **OK** to return to the main dialog box.

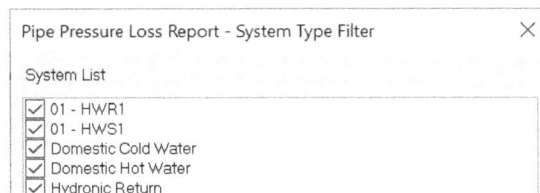

Figure B–3

- Use **Select All**, **Select None**, and **Invert Selection** to help with the selection.

2. When you have finished selecting the systems to include, click **OK**.

3. In the *Duct/Pipe Pressure Loss Report Settings* dialog box, specify the type of *Report Format* and the *Reports Fields*, and other information, as shown in Figure B–4.

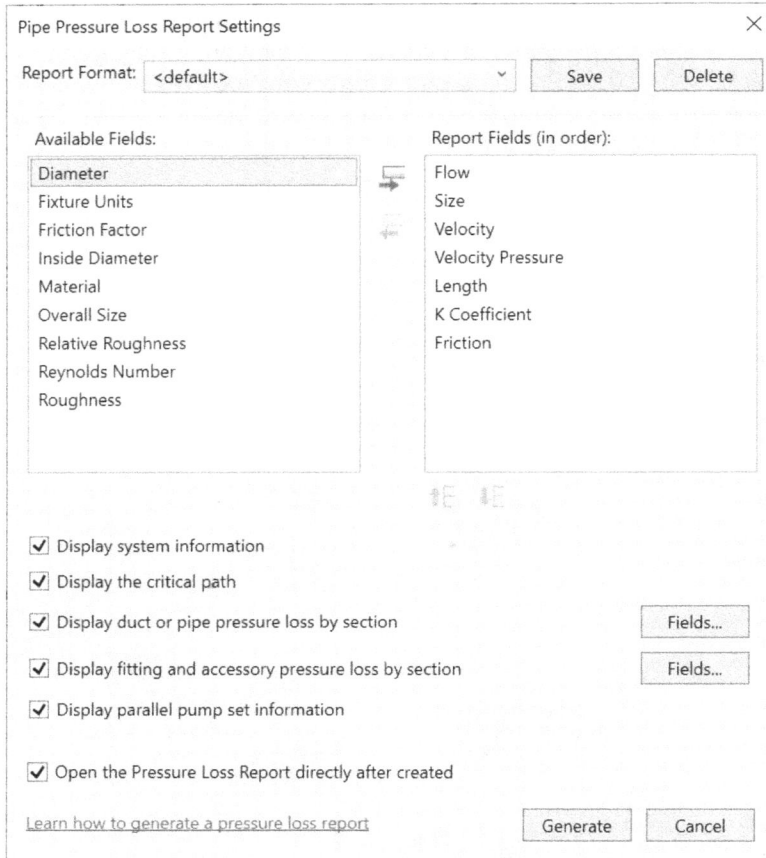

Figure B–4

4. Click **Generate**.

B.2 Working with Guide Grids on Sheets

You can use a guide grid to help you place views on a sheet, as shown in Figure B–5. Guide grids can be set up per sheet. You can also create different types with various grid spacings.

Figure B–5

- You can move guide grids and resize them using controls.

  Note: *When moving a view to a guide grid, only orthogonal datum elements (levels and grids) and reference planes snap to the guide grid.*

How To: Add a Guide Grid

1. When a sheet is open, in the *View* tab>*Sheet Composition* panel, click ⊞ (Guide Grid).

2. In the *Assign Guide Grid* dialog box, select from existing guide grids (as shown in Figure B–6), or create a new one and give it a name.

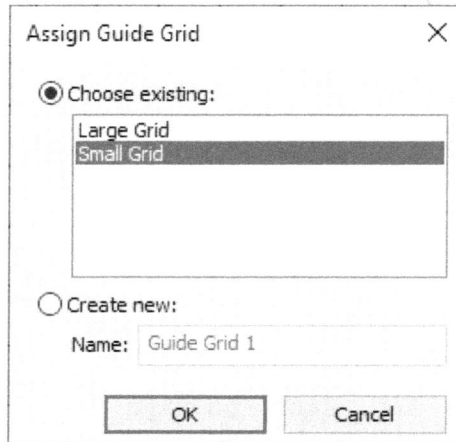

Figure B–6

3. The guide grid displays using the specified sizing.

How To: Modify Guide Grid Sizing

1. If you create a new guide grid you need to update it to the correct size in Properties. Select the edge of the guide grid.

2. In Properties, set the *Guide Spacing*, as shown in Figure B–7.

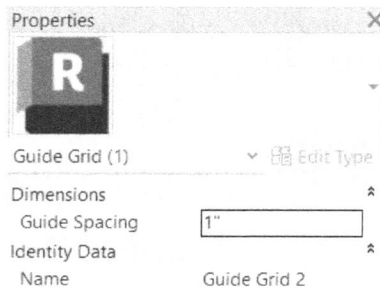

Figure B–7

B.3 Revision Tracking

When a set of working drawings has been put into production, you need to show where changes are made. Typically, these are shown on sheets using revision clouds and tags along with a revision schedule in the title block, as shown in Figure B–8. The revision information is set up in the *Sheet Issues/Revisions* dialog box.

No.	Description	Date
1	Changed drain pan size	5-30-12
2	Added sensor	5-30-12

Figure B–8

- More than one revision cloud can be associated with a revision number.

- The title blocks that come with Revit already have a revision schedule inserted into the title area. It is recommended that you also add a revision schedule to your company title block.

- You have the ability to create multiple revision numbering sequences and you can use **Transfer Project Standards** to transfer these custom revision settings and revision numbering sequences to other projects.

- You can create a revision cloud schedule that can include multiple revisions. In a sheet view, from Properties, you can click **Edit...** and specify which revision you want to display on the sheet even if the revision is not on the sheet.

How To: Add Revision Information to the Project

1. In the *View* tab>*Sheet Composition* panel, click ⟳ (Sheet Issues/Revisions).
2. In the *Sheet Issues/Revisions* dialog box, set the type of *Numbering* you want to use.
3. Click **Add** to add a new revision.
4. Specify the *Date* and *Description* for the revision, as shown in Figure B−9.

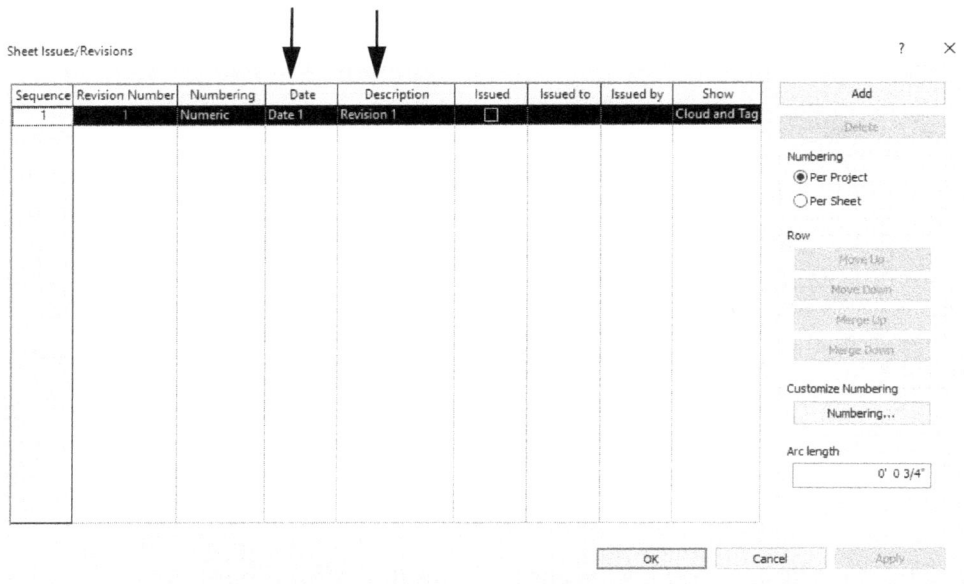

Figure B−9

*   Do not modify the *Issued*, *Issued by*, or *Issued to* columns. You should wait to issue revisions until you are ready to print the sheets.

5. Click **OK** when you have finished adding revisions.

*   To remove a revision, select its *Sequence* number and click **Delete**.

Revision Options

*   *Numbering:* Specify **Per Project** (the numbering sequence is used throughout the project) or **Per Sheet** (the number sequence is per sheet).

*   *Row*: To reorganize the revisions, select a row and click **Move Up** and **Move Down**, or use **Merge Up** and **Merge Down** to combine the revisions into one.

*   *Customize Numbering:* Click **Numbering...** to bring up the *Numbering* dialog box (shown in Figure B−10). You can edit the Alphanumeric or Numeric sequences or create custom sequences.

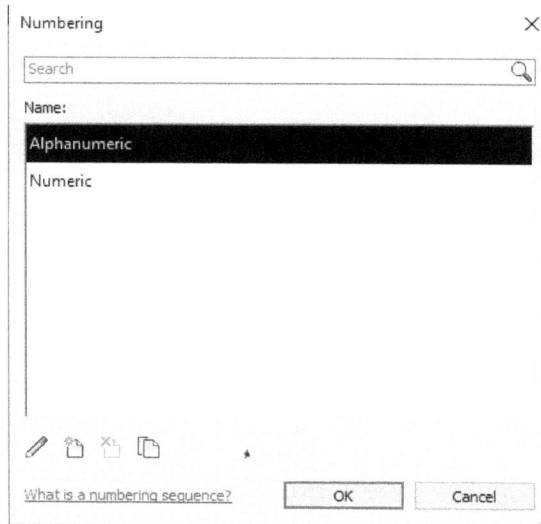

Figure B-10

- You can specify whether to create a new numbering sequence based off of **Numeric** or **Alphanumeric** as well as any prefix or suffix, as shown for the *New Numbering Sequence* dialog box in Figure B-11.

Figure B-11

- *Arc length:* Specify the length of the arcs that form the revision cloud. It is an annotation element and is scaled according to the view scale.

How To: Add Revision Clouds and Tags

1. In the *Annotate* tab>*Detail* panel, click ☁ (Revision Cloud).

2. In the *Modify | Create Revision Cloud Sketch* tab>*Draw* panel, use the draw tools to create the cloud.

3. In Properties, select which *Revision* type to use, as shown in Figure B–12.

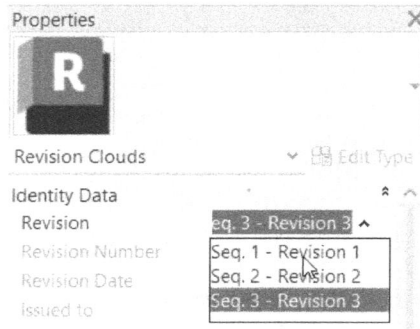

Figure B–12

4. Click ✔ (Finish Edit Mode).

•   To modify a revision cloud, select a revision cloud, then in the Options Bar or Properties, expand the *Revision:* drop-down list and select the revision, as shown in Figure B–13.

    Note: *If the revision table has not be set up, you can do this at a later date.*

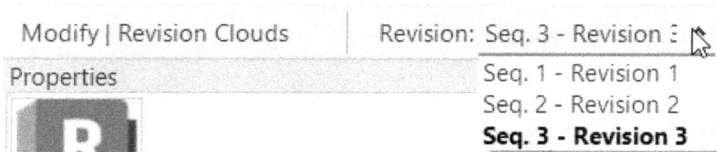

Figure B–13

5. In the *Annotate* tab>*Tag* panel, click 🏷 (Tag By Category).

6. Select the revision cloud to tag. A tooltip containing the revision number and revision from the cloud properties displays when you hover the cursor over the revision cloud, as shown in Figure B–14.

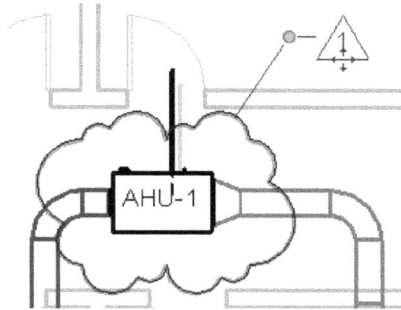

Figure B–14

- If the revision cloud tag is not loaded, load **Revision Tag.rfa** from the *Annotations* folder in the Revit Library.

- The *Revision Number* and *Date* are automatically assigned according to the specifications in the revision table.

- Double-click on the edge of revision cloud to switch to Edit Sketch mode and modify the size or location of the revision cloud arcs.

- You can create an open cloud (e.g., as a tree line), as shown in Figure B–15.

Figure B–15

Issuing Revisions

When you have completed the revisions and are ready to submit new documents to the field, you should first lock the revision for the record. This is called issuing the revision. An issued revision is noted in the tooltip of a revision cloud, as shown in Figure B–16.

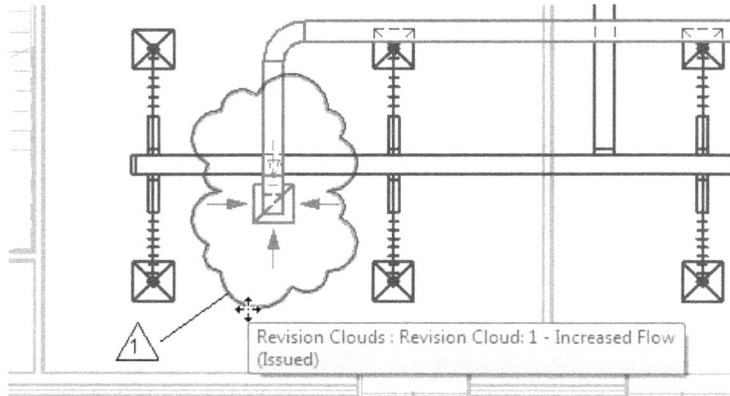

Revision Clouds : Revision Cloud: 1 - Increased Flow (Issued)

Figure B–16

How To: Issue Revisions

1. In the *View* tab>*Sheet Composition* panel, click ○ (Sheet Issues/Revisions).
2. In the *Sheet Issues/Revisions* dialog box, in the row for the revision that you are issuing, type a name in the *Issued to* and *Issued by* fields, as needed.
3. In the same row, select **Issued**.
4. Continue issuing any other revisions, as needed.
5. Click **OK** to finish.

• Once **Issued** is selected, you cannot modify that revision in the *Revisions* dialog box or by moving the revision cloud(s). The tooltip on the cloud(s) note that it is **Issued**.

• You can unlock the revision by clearing the **Issued** option. Unlocking enables you to modify the revision after it has been locked.

B.4 Annotating Dependent Views

The **Duplicate as a Dependent** command creates a copy of a primary view and links it to the selected view. Changes made to the original view are also made in the dependent view and vice-versa. Use dependent views when the building model is so large you need to split the building up on separate sheets, as shown in Figure B–17.

Figure B–17

- Using one overall view with several dependent views makes it easier to see changes, such as to the scale or detail level.

- Dependent views display in the Project Browser under the top-level view, as shown in Figure B–18.

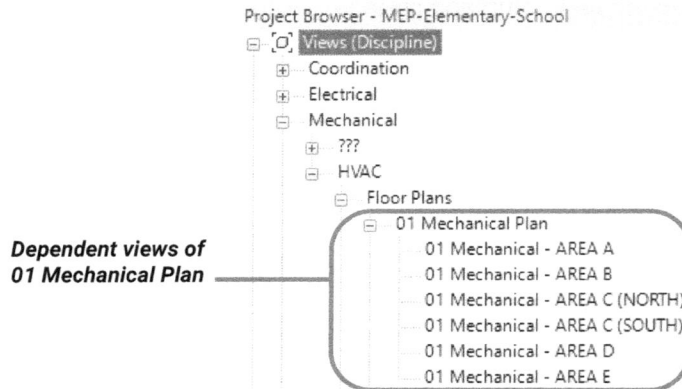

Figure B–18

How To: Duplicate Dependent Views

1. Select the view you want to use as the top-level view.
2. Right-click and select **Duplicate View>Duplicate as a Dependent**.
3. Rename the dependent views as needed.
4. Modify the crop region of the dependent view to show the specified portion of the model.

- If you want to separate a dependent view from the original view, right-click on the dependent view and select **Convert to independent view**.

Annotating Views

To clarify and annotate dependent views, use **Matchlines** and **View References**, as shown in Figure B–19.

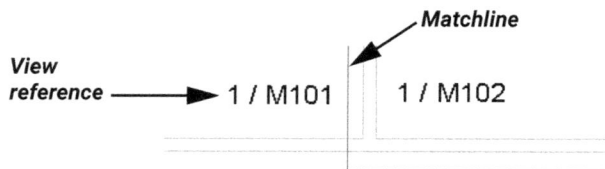

Figure B–19

- Sketch matchlines in the primary view to specify where dependent views separate. They display in all related views and extend through all levels of the project by default.

- View references are special tags that display the sheet location of the dependent views.

How To: Add Matchlines

1. In the *View* tab>*Sheet Composition* panel, click ⬚ (Matchline).

2. In the *Draw* panel, click ⁄ (Line) and sketch the location of the matchline.

3. In the *Matchline* panel, click ✔ (Finish Edit Mode) when you are finished.

• To modify an existing matchline, select it and click 🖉 (Edit Sketch) in the *Modify | Matchline* tab>*Mode* panel.

• To modify the color and line type of matchlines, in the *Manage* tab>*Settings* panel, click

⬚ (Object Styles). In the *Object Styles* dialog box that opens, in the *Annotation Objects* tab, you can make changes to Matchline properties.

How To: Add View References

1. In the *View* tab>*Sheet Composition* panel or *Annotate* tab>*Tag* panel, click 🏷 (View Reference).

2. In the *Modify | View Reference* tab>*View Reference* panel, search for or specify the *View Type* and *Target View*, as shown in Figure B–20.

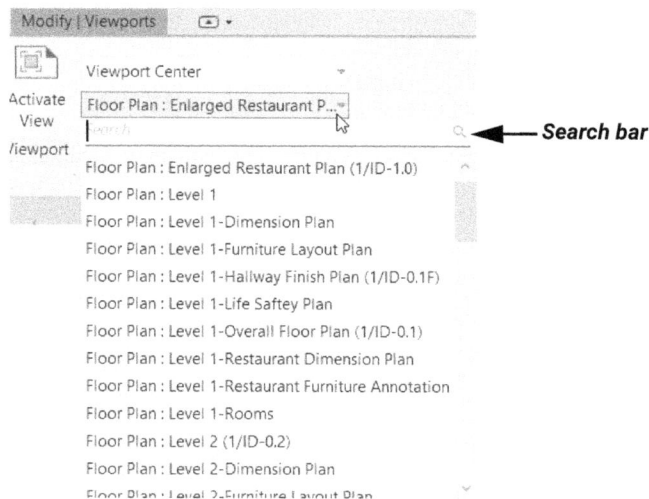

Figure B–20

3. Place the tag on the side of the matchline that corresponds to the target view.

4. Click ⬚ (Modify) to clear the selection.

5. Repeat the process and place the tag on the other side of the matchline.

6. The tags display as empty dashes until the views are placed onto sheets. They then update to include the detail and sheet number, as shown in Figure B–21.

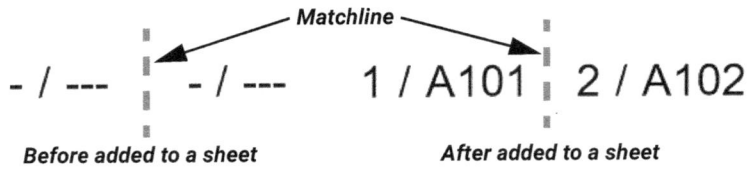

Before added to a sheet   *After added to a sheet*

Figure B–21

- Double-click on the view reference to open the associated view.

- If only a label named **REF** displays when you place a view reference, it means you need to load and update the tag. The **View Reference.rfa** tag is located in the *Annotations* folder in the Revit Library. Once you have the tag loaded, in the Type Selector, select one of the view references and, in Properties, click ⊞ (Edit Type). Select **View Reference** in the drop-down list, as shown in Figure B–22, and click **OK** to close the dialog box. The new tag displays.

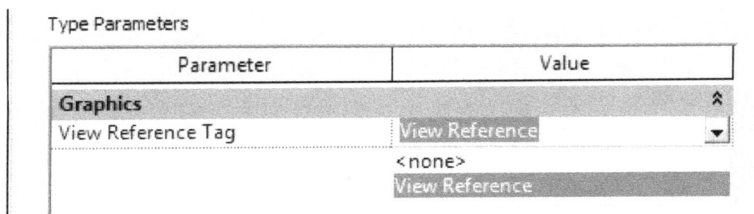

Figure B–22

B.5 Importing and Exporting Schedules

Schedules are views and can be copied into your project from other projects. Only the formatting information is copied; the information about individually scheduled items is not included. That information is automatically added by the project the schedule is copied into. You can also export the schedule information to be used in spreadsheets.

How To: Import Schedules

1. In the *Insert* tab>*Load from Library* panel, expand ⬚↓ (Insert from File) and click ⬚↓ (Insert Views from File).

2. In the *Open* dialog box, locate the project file containing the schedule you want to use.

3. Select the schedules you want to import, as shown in Figure B–23.

   Note: *If the referenced project contains many types of views, change Views: to **Show schedules and reports only***.

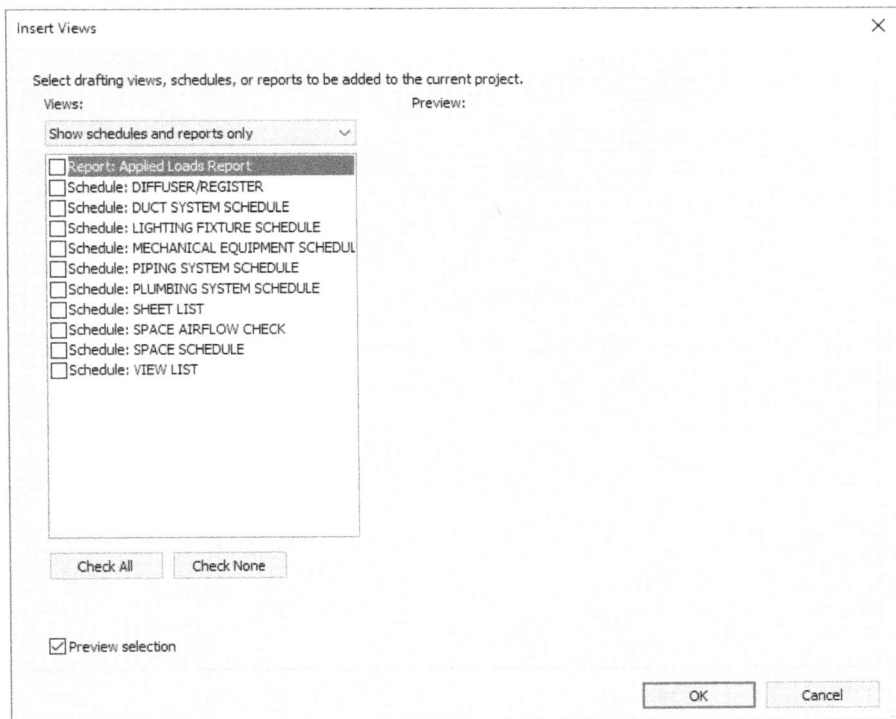

Figure B–23

4. Click **OK**.

How To: Export Schedule Information

1. Switch to the schedule view that you want to export.

2. In the *File* tab, click ⬆ (Export)> ▤ (Reports)> ▦ (Schedule).

3. Select a location and name for the text file in the *Export Schedule* dialog box and click **Save**.

4. In the *Export Schedule* dialog box, set the options in the *Schedule appearance* and *Output options* areas that best suit your spreadsheet software, as shown in Figure B–24.

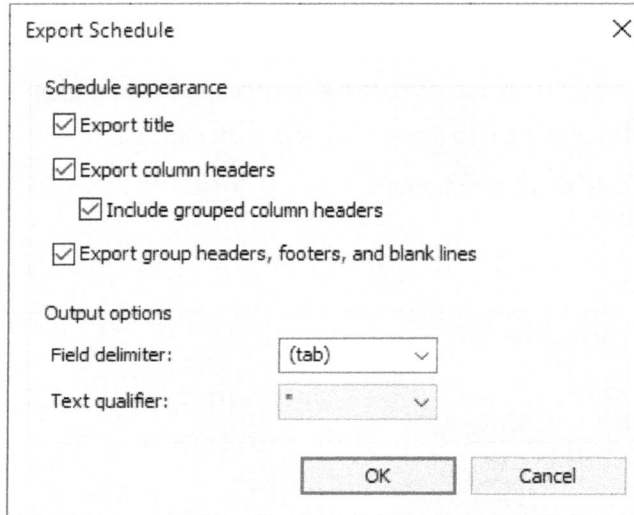

Figure B–24

5. Click **OK**. A new text file is created that you can open in a spreadsheet, as shown in Figure B–25.

	A	B	C	D	E
1	Duct System Schedule				
2	System Classification	System Name	Comments	Static Pressure	Flow
3					
4	Return Air	01 - RA01	RA	0.11 in-wg	1000 CFM
5	Return Air	01 - RA02	RA	0.11 in-wg	1000 CFM
6	Return Air	01 - RA03	RA	0.11 in-wg	1000 CFM
7	Return Air	01 - RA04	RA	0.11 in-wg	1000 CFM
8	Return Air	01 - RA05	RA	0.11 in-wg	1000 CFM
9	Return Air	01 - RA06	RA	0.11 in-wg	1000 CFM
10	Return Air	01 - RA08	RA	0.11 in-wg	1000 CFM
11	Return Air	01 - RA09	RA	0.11 in-wg	1000 CFM
12	Return Air	01 - RA10	RA	0.11 in-wg	1000 CFM
13	Return Air	01 - RA11	RA	0.11 in-wg	1000 CFM
14	Return Air	01 - RA12	RA	0.09 in-wg	500 CFM
15	Return Air	01 - RA13		0.11 in-wg	500 CFM

Figure B–25

B.6 Keynoting and Keynote Legends

A keynote is a special kind of tag that applies specific numbers to various elements in a detail. Keynotes can be used on all model and detail elements, as well as materials. Using keynotes requires less room on a view than standard text notes, as shown in Figure B–26. The full explanation of the note is shown in a corresponding *keynote legend* placed elsewhere in the sheet or sheet set.

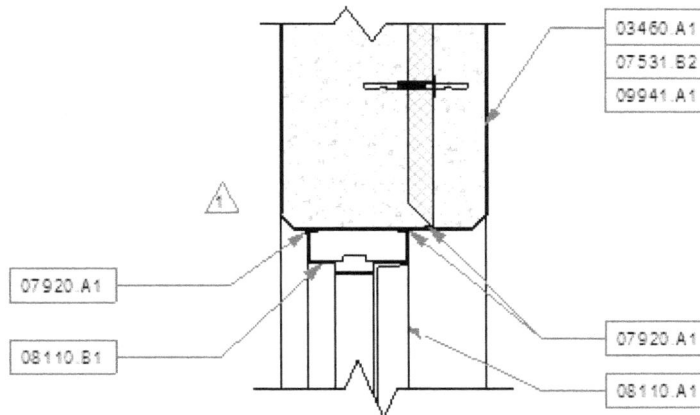

Figure B–26

- Keynote tags are found in the Revit Library in the *Annotations* folder and should be loaded into a project before you can apply them.

  Note: By default, Revit uses the CSI MasterFormat system of keynote designations.

There are three types of keynote tags:

- **Element:** Used to tag elements, such as a door, wall, or detail components.

- **Material:** Used for the material assigned to a component or applied onto a surface.

- **User:** A keynote that must first be developed in a keynote table.

How To: Place a Keynote

1. In the *Annotate* tab>*Tag* panel, expand (Keynote) and click (Element Keynote), (Material Keynote), or (User Keynote).

2. Move the cursor over the element you want to keynote and select it.

3. If an element has keynote information assigned to it, the keynote is automatically applied. If it is not assigned, the *Keynotes* dialog box opens, as shown in Figure B–27.

Figure B–27

4. Select the keynote you need from the list of divisions and click **OK**.

•   The options for keynotes are the same as for other tags, including orientation and leaders, as shown in Figure B–28.

    Note: The keynote remembers the leader settings from the last time it was used.

Figure B–28

💡 Hint: Setting the Keynote Numbering Method

Keynotes can be listed by the full keynote number or by sheet, as shown in Figure B–29. Only one method can be used at a time in a project, but you can change between the two methods at any time in the project.

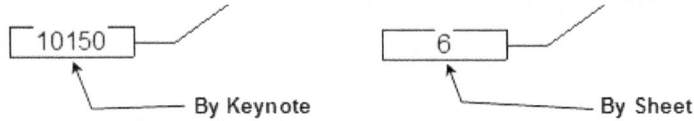

Figure B–29

1. In the *Annotate* tab>*Tag* panel, expand (Keynote) and click (Keynoting Settings).

2. In the *Keynoting Settings* dialog box, specify the *Keynote Table* information and the *Numbering Method*, as shown in Figure B–30.

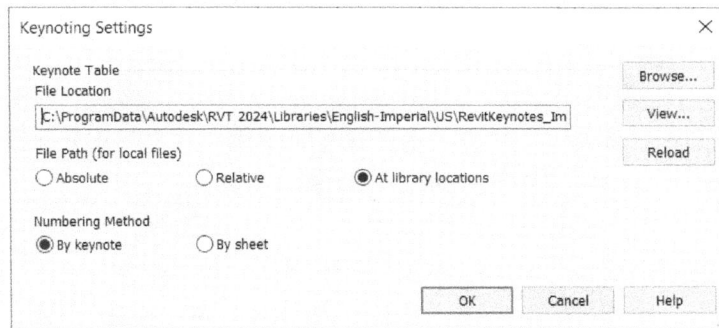

Figure B–30

- If you are using keynoting by sheet, create the Keynote Legend, and in the Keynote Legend Properties in the *Filter* tab, select **Filter by Sheet**.

- Keynotes are stored in a keynote table (a text file), as shown in Figure B–31. Any updates made to the keynote table are reflected in the project after it is closed and then re-opened.

RevitKeynotes_Imperial - Notepad

File   Edit   Format   View   Help

```
01000    Division 01 - General Requirements
02000    Division 02 - Sitework
03000    Division 03 - Concrete
04000    Division 04 - Masonry
05000    Division 05 - Metals
06000    Division 06 - Wood and Plastics
07000    Division 07 - Thermal and Moisture
08000    Division 08 - Doors and Windows
09000    Division 09 - Finishes
10000    Division 10 - Specialties
11000    Division 11 - Equipment
12000    Division 12 - Furnishings
13000    Division 13 - Special Construction
14000    Division 14 - Conveying
```

Figure B–31

Keynote Legends

A keynote legend is a table containing the information stored in the keynote that is placed on a sheet, as shown in Figure B–32. In Revit, it is created in a similar way to schedules.

Note: A keynote legend is different from a standard legend.

<Keynote Legend>	
A	**B**
Key Value	Keynote Text
11200	Water Supply and Treatment Equipment
15400	Plumbing Fixtures and Equipment
16200	Electrical Power

Figure B–32

How To: Create a Keynote Legend

1. In the *View* tab>*Create* panel, expand ⊞ (Legends) and click ⊞ (Keynote Legend).
2. Type a name in the *New Keynote Legend* dialog box and click **OK**.

3. The *Keynote Legend Properties* dialog box typically only displays two scheduled fields, which are already set up for you, as shown in Figure B–33.

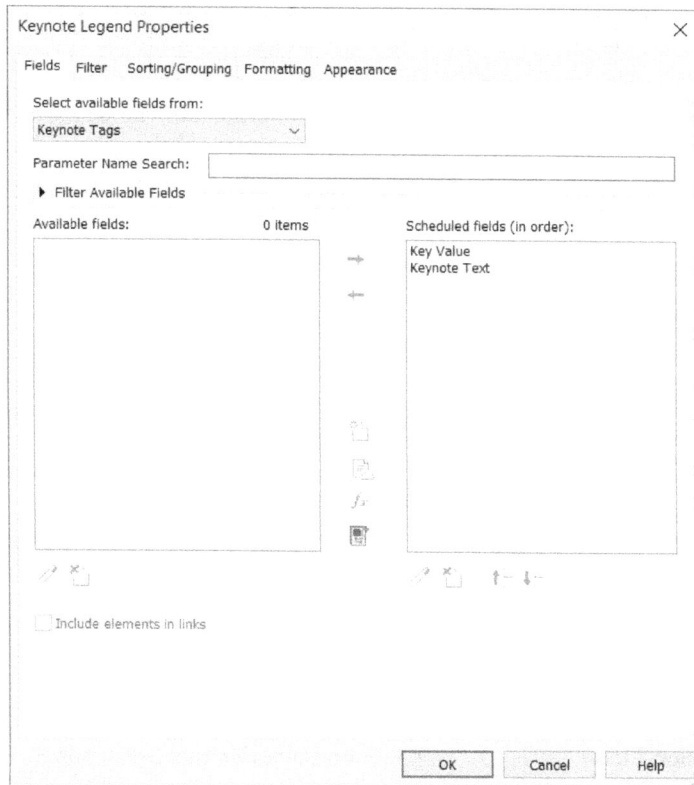

Figure B–33

4. In the other tabs, set up the format of the table as needed.

5. Click **OK** to create the keynote legend.

6. When you are ready to place a keynote legend, drag it from the Project Browser onto the sheet. You can manipulate it in the same way, similar to modifying other schedules.

- As you add keynotes to the project, they are added to the keynote legend.

- Use the *Multiple Align* tools to align your keynote tags.

Command Summary

Button	Command	Location
Annotations		
	Element Keynote	• **Ribbon:** *Annotate* tab>*Tag* panel, expand Keynote
	Material Keynote	• **Ribbon:** *Annotate* tab>*Tag* panel, expand Keynote
	User Keynote	• **Ribbon:** *Annotate* tab>*Tag* panel, expand Keynote
	Matchline	• **Ribbon:** *View* tab>*Sheet Composition* panel
	View Reference	• **Ribbon:** *View* tab>*Sheet Composition* panel or *Annotate* tab>*Tag* panel
MEP Tools		
	Duct Pressure Loss Report	• **Ribbon:** *Analyze* tab>*Reports & Schedules* panel
	Pipe Pressure Loss Report	• **Ribbon:** *Analyze* tab>*Reports & Schedules* panel
Revisions		
	Revision Cloud	• **Ribbon:** *Annotate* tab>*Detail* panel
	Sheet Issues/Revisions	• **Ribbon:** *Manage* tab>*Settings* panel, expand Additional Settings
Schedules		
	Insert Views from File	• **Ribbon**: *Insert* tab, expand Insert from File
N/A	**Schedule (Export)**	• *File* **tab:** expand Export>Reports>Schedule
	Schedule/Quantities	• **Ribbon:** *View* tab>*Create* panel, expand Schedules • **Project Browser:** right-click on Schedule/Quantities node>New Schedule/Quantities...

Zones

Preparing a project so that you can run a systems analysis involves grouping spaces into zones that are heated and cooled in the same manner. Creating color schemes that graphically indicate the various zones is helpful. Using the System Browser, you can review existing zones and any spaces that have yet to be assigned to a zone.

Learning Objectives

- Add zones to connect spaces for analysis.
- Use the System Browser with zones.
- Apply color schemes and color fill legends for spaces and zones.

C.1 Creating Zones

After creating spaces, the next step in preparing to compute Systems analysis is to divide the building into zones, as shown in Figure C-1. Each zone consists of similar spaces that would be heated and cooled in the same manner.

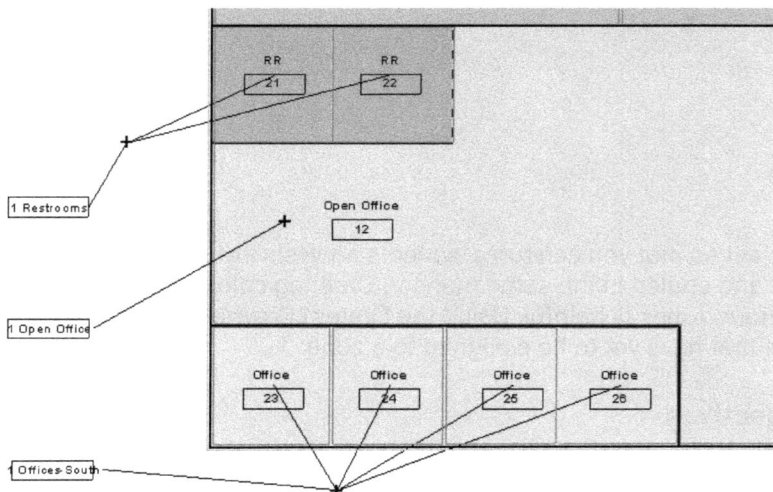

Figure C-1

- There is always one **Default** zone in a project. All spaces are automatically attached to that zone when they are created.

- While you can add zones into a template, you usually add spaces first, then create zones and add spaces to the zones.

- You can create zones in plan and section views.

How To: Add Zones

1. Open a plan view that contains the spaces you want to work with. If you have a zone that spans across two levels, open a section view as well.

   Note: You can set up a view template for zones in the same way as you set up one for spaces.

2. For each view, open the *Visibility/Graphic Overrides* dialog box and on the *Model Categories* tab, in the *Visibility* column, check the checkbox next to **HVAC Zones**, then expand it and select all of the options, as shown in Figure C−2.

Figure C−2

3. Click **OK**.

4. In the *Analyze* tab>*Spaces & Zones* panel, click ⊞ (Zone).

5. In Properties, under *Identity Data*, type a name for the Zone for the **Name** value. By default, the zones are numbered incrementally.

6. In the *Edit Zone* tab, ensure that ⊞ (Add Space) is automatically selected.

7. Select the spaces that you want to add to the zone.

8. Click ✔ (Finish Editing Zone).

• Another quick way to add a zone is to select the spaces first, then in the *Analyze* tab>*Spaces & Zones* panel, click ⊞ (Zone). The spaces are automatically added to the zone.

• To edit an existing zone, select one of the zone lines, as shown in Figure C−3, then in the *Modify | HVAC Zones* tab>*Zone* panel, click ⊞ (Edit Zone). The *Edit Zone* tab displays, which enables you to add more spaces.

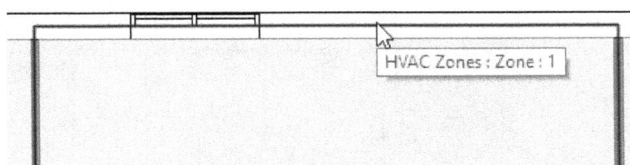

Figure C−3

• Click ⊞ (Remove Space) to remove a space from the zone or modify the zone properties.

- Zones do not automatically have a tag placed, but it is helpful to display these as you are working. In the *Annotate* tab>*Tag* panel, click ⌐① (Tag by Category) and select on the zone(s) that you want to tag, as shown in Figure C-4.

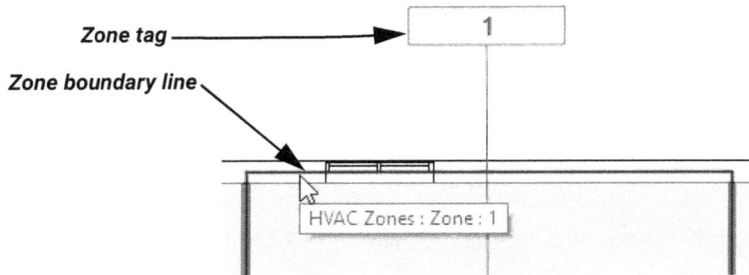

Zone tag ──────────────► [1]

Zone boundary line

HVAC Zones : Zone : 1

Figure C-4

- You can change the name of a zone by changing the tag or in Properties. Zone tags are found in the Revit Library in the *Annotations>Mechanical* folder.

Using the System Browser with Zones

The System Browser is a useful tool when working with systems, analytical systems, and zones. The System Browser is an effective tool that helps you in finding components that are or are not assigned to a system or zone. When you select a zone or space in the System Browser, it displays in the project, as shown in Figure C-5. The selected zone or space is automatically made active in the Properties. This enables you to modify names for spaces and zones and assign information, such as electrical loads and mechanical airflow.

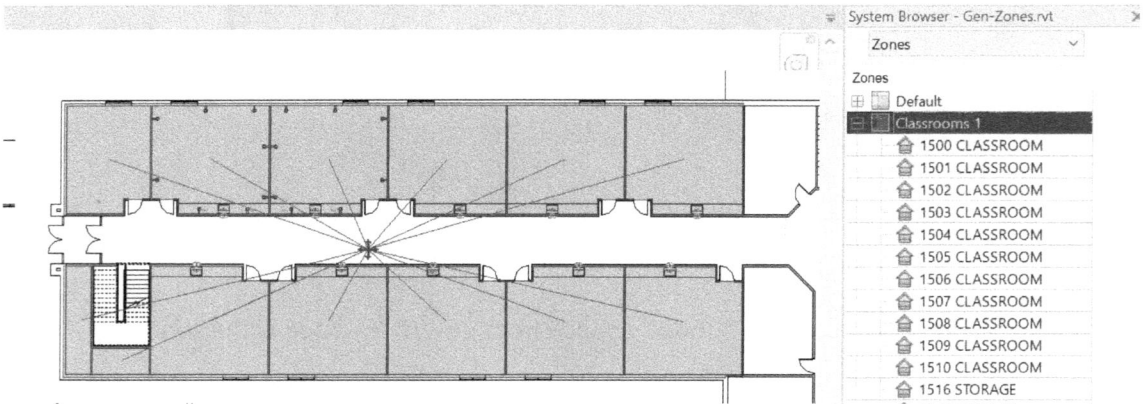

System Browser - Gen-Zones.rvt

Zones

Zones
- Default
- Classrooms 1
  - 1500 CLASSROOM
  - 1501 CLASSROOM
  - 1502 CLASSROOM
  - 1503 CLASSROOM
  - 1504 CLASSROOM
  - 1505 CLASSROOM
  - 1506 CLASSROOM
  - 1507 CLASSROOM
  - 1508 CLASSROOM
  - 1509 CLASSROOM
  - 1510 CLASSROOM
  - 1516 STORAGE

Figure C-5

- You can open the System Browser using any of the following methods:
  - Press <F9>.
  - In the view, right-click, expand **Browsers**, and select **System Browser**.
  - In the *View* tab>*Windows* panel, expand ⊞ (User Interface) and select **System Browser**, as shown in Figure C–6.

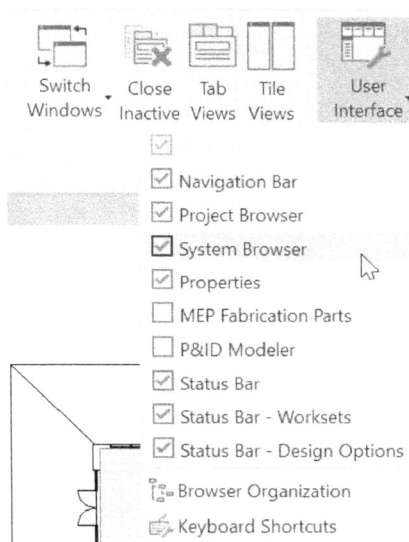

Figure C–6

- You can float or dock the System Browser to any side of the screen. You can also place it on a second monitor.
- The System Browser can be docked with Properties and the Project Browser to save screen space.

How To: Use the System Browser with Zones

1. Open the System Browser by pressing <F9>.
2. If the zones are not displayed, expand the *View* drop-down list and select **Zones**, as shown in Figure C–7.

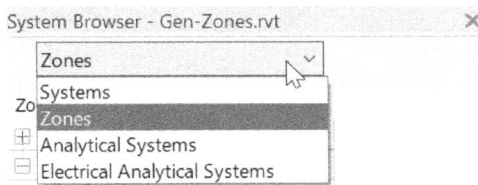

Figure C–7

3. All of the spaces are listed under the **Default** zone (as shown in Figure C–8) until they are added to a specific zone.

- Each space displays an icon showing its status: 🏠 (Occupiable), 🏠 (Not Occupiable), and 🏠 (Space not placed).

- As new zones are added, the spaces are moved into the new zones.

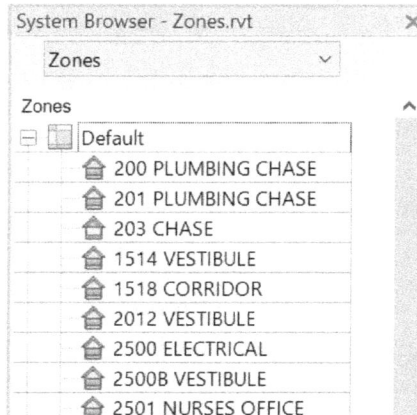

Figure C–8

4. Select a space or a zone. It is highlighted in the project and becomes active in the Properties.

- You can select more than one space or zone at a time using <Ctrl> and <Shift>.

- In the System Browser, if you right-click on a space or zone and select **Show**, you may get a message that says there are no open views that show any of the highlighted elements. Click **OK**. The software zooms in on the selected elements.

- If there is more than one view in which the space can be displayed, the *Show Element(s) in View* dialog box opens, as shown in Figure C–9.

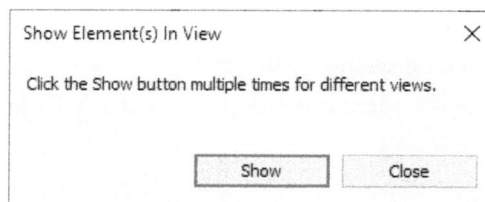

Figure C–9

- If you place spaces and then delete them, they remain in the project. To delete a space entirely, in the System Browser, right-click on the space name and select **Delete**.

- You can also delete spaces in a space schedule view.

C.2 Applying Color Schemes

When working with zones and spaces, it is useful to have a view that displays color coding for individual zones, spaces, or rooms, as shown in Figure C-10. You can include a color fill legend in the same view to clarify the use of the colors.

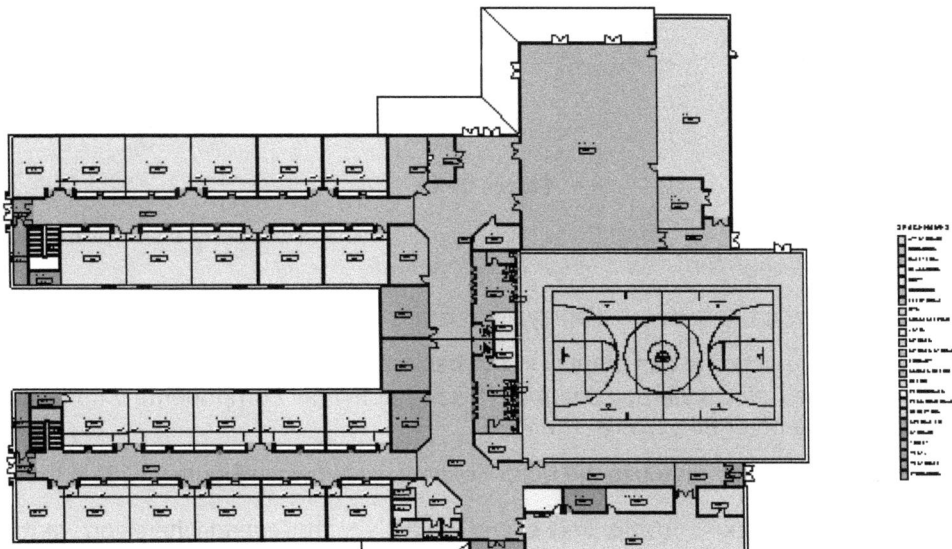

Figure C-10

- Color schemes are controlled by a view property. Therefore, you should create a view for each color diagram that you want to include.

How To: Set Up a Color Scheme in a View

1. Create or duplicate a view that you want to use for the color scheme.

2. In Properties, click the button next to the **Color Scheme** parameter, as shown in Figure C-11.

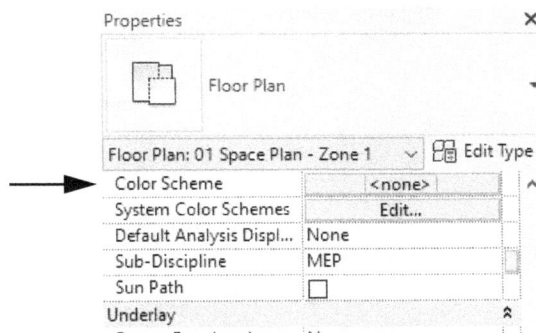

Figure C-11

3. In the *Edit Color Scheme* dialog box, in the *Schemes* area, select a **Category**.

4. Select a scheme in the list. In the example shown in Figure C–12, **Space Names** is selected.

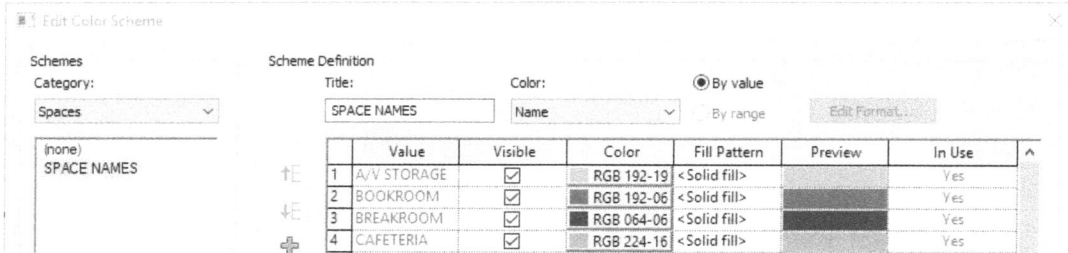

Figure C–12

*Note: For information about creating color schemes, see **A.4 Defining Color Schemes** in **Appendix A Additional Tools for Design Development**.*

5. Click **OK**. The new color scheme displays in the view.

• The color fill of the scheme can display in the background or foreground of the view. In Properties, set the *Color Scheme Location*. This impacts how components display and whether or not the color fill stops at the walls.

• You can add a legend that matches the Color Scheme, as shown in Figure C–13. In the *Analyze* tab>*Color Fill* panel, click ▤ (Color Fill Legend), and place the legend where you want it.

Note: The type properties for the Color Fill Legend control the appearance of the legend, including the swatch size and text styles.

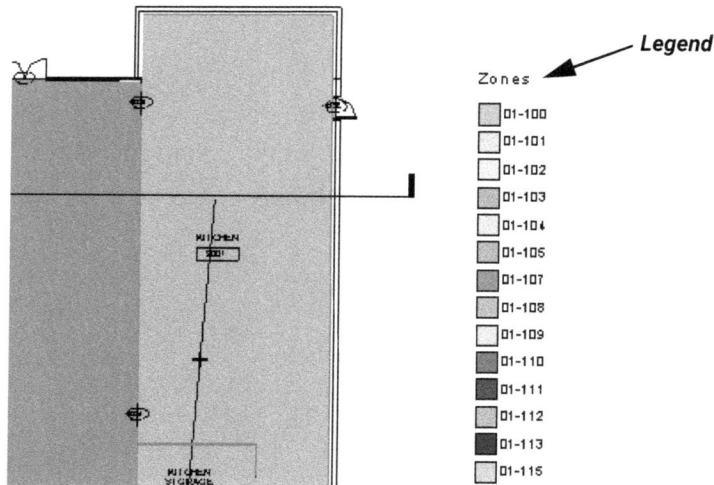

Figure C–13

• If you change the **Color Scheme** in the *View Properties* dialog box, it also updates in the associated legend.

Practice C1
Create Zones

Practice Objectives

- Add zones.
- Use the System Browser to identify and modify zone information.
- Create a color scheme showing the zones.

In this practice, you will add HVAC zones to the project. You will examine the zones and spaces in the System Browser and you set up a view that displays the zone names by color as shown in Figure C–14 with zone tags. Optionally, you can create additional zones.

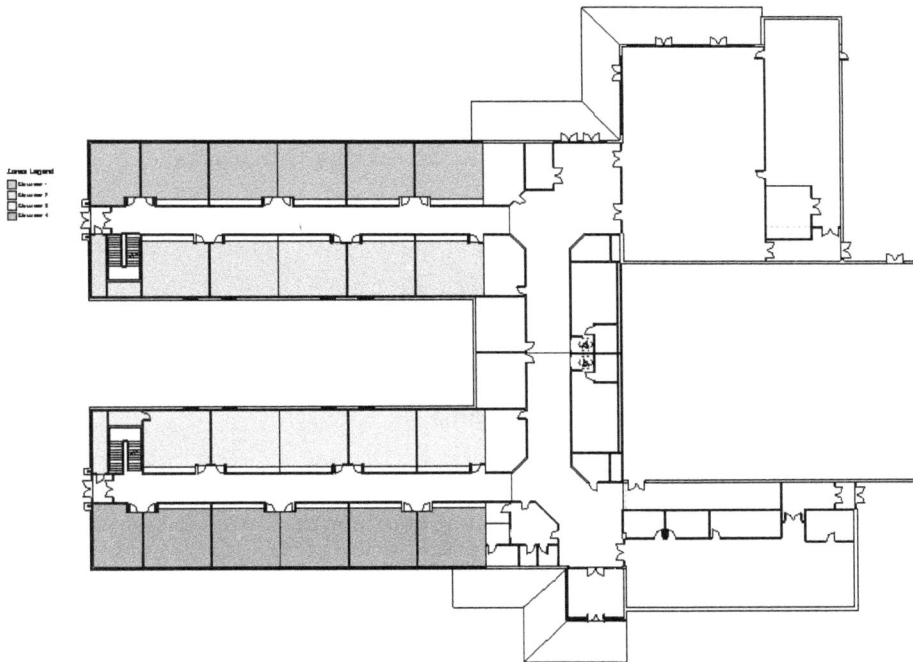

Figure C–14

Task 1: Add zones.

1. In the practice files *Working Models>General* folder, open **Gen-Zones.rvt**.
2. Duplicate the Coordination>MEP>Floor Plans>**01 Space Plan** view
3. Rename it **01 Zones Plan**.
4. Select one of the sections in the view and type **VH** to hide the category in the view.

5. Open the *Visibility/Graphic Overrides* dialog box, set the *Filter List* to **Mechanical**, and do the following in the *Visibility* column:

   - Select and expand the **HVAC Zones** node and check the checkboxes next to **Boundary, Interior Fill**, and **Reference Lines**.
   - Expand the **Spaces** node and clear the checkboxes for **Interior Fill** and **Color Fill**.

   Note: You can still select the spaces, but the interior fill does not display.

6. Click **OK**.

7. In the *Analyze* tab>*Spaces & Zones* panel, click ⬚ (Zone).

8. In the *Edit Zone* tab, verify that ⬚ (Add Space) is selected.

9. In the north wing, select the spaces across the top group of classrooms so the zone displays as shown in Figure C–15.

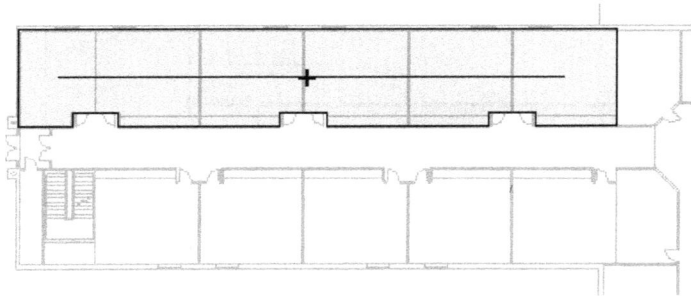

Figure C–15

10. In Properties, change the *Name* to **Classrooms 1**.

11. In the *Edit Zone* tab>*Edit Zone* panel, click ✔ (Finish Editing Zone).

12. Add another zone to the Classrooms and Storage Areas on the other side of the hall as shown in Figure C–16.

   Note: The name of the zone automatically increments as each zone is added.

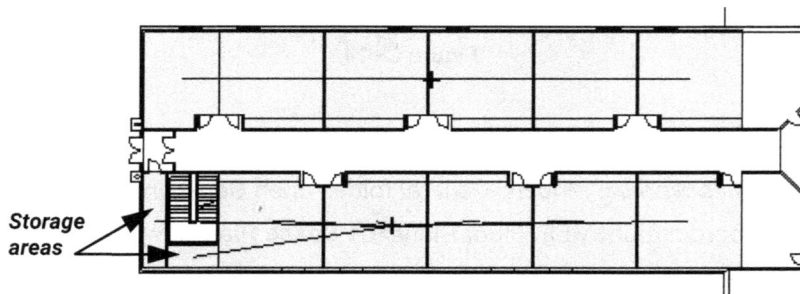

Storage areas

Figure C–16

13. Add zones to the two classroom groups in the south wing.

14. Save the project.

Task 2: Use the System Browser.

1. Press <F9> to open the System Browser, if it is not already open.

2. In the System Browser, verify that the view displays **Zones**, as shown in Figure C−17.

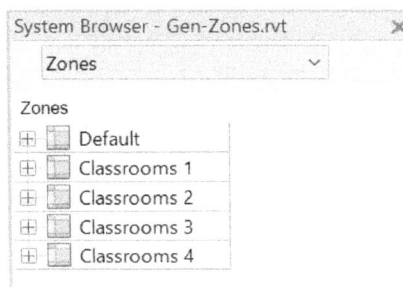

Figure C−17

3. Expand the **Default** zone. Note that there are a lot of spaces that are not placed in zones. There are also two different types of icons for spaces: occupied (green icon) and unoccupied (orange icon), as shown in Figure C−18.

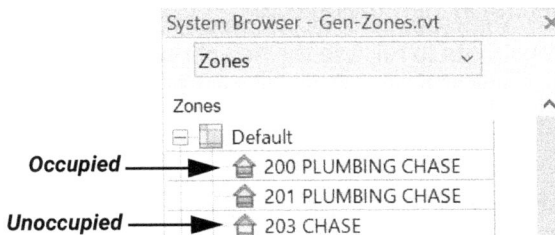

Figure C−18

4. Some of the spaces that should be unoccupied, such as the **200** and **201 Plumbing Chases** shown above in Figure C−18, are not set correctly. In the System Browser, hold <Ctrl> and select the two plumbing chases.

5. In Properties, scroll down to the *Energy Analysis* area and clear **Occupiable**.

6. In the System Browser, in the default zone, right-click on one of the plenums and select **Show** (open additional views as necessary). If necessary, click **OK** or **Show** in the dialog box that displays to search for the zone in the project's views. The view changes to display the location of the plenum, such as the one shown in Figure C–19.

    *   Note: The view that is shown may differ from the one in the image depending on which plenum zone you selected in the System Browser.

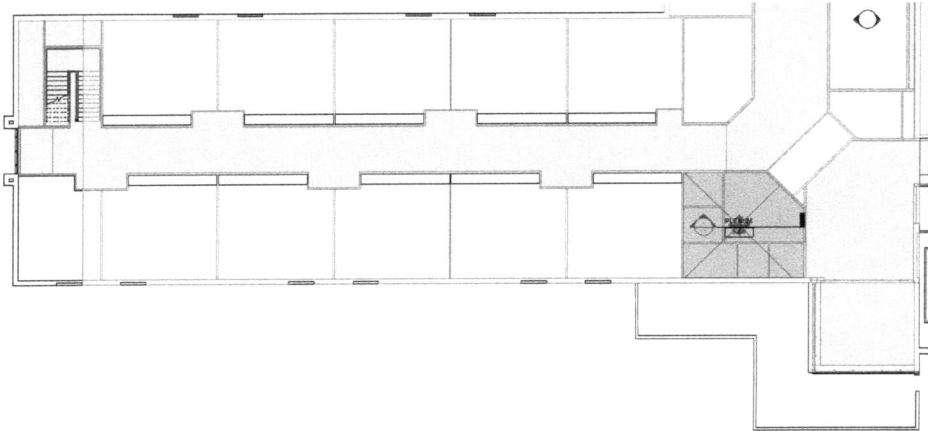

Figure C–19

7. Close the *Show Element(s) in View* dialog box.

8. Click away from any elements to release the selection.

9. Close the System Browser.

10. Save the project.

Task 3: Add a color scheme.

1. Ensure you are in the **01 Zones Plan** view. Zoom extents, if necessary, and close any extra view tabs.

    Note: *In the Quick Access Toolbar, you can click* *(Close Inactive Views).*

2. In Properties, in the *Graphics* section, click the button next to *Color Scheme*.

3. In the *Edit Color Scheme* dialog box, in the *Schemes* area, change the *Category* to **HVAC Zones**.

4. Select the default **Schema 1**. The Scheme Definition automatically populates by zone name as shown in Figure C–20.

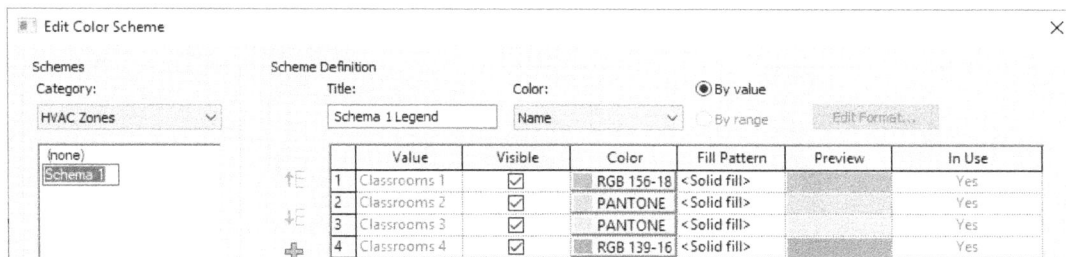

Figure C–20

5. In the *Schemes* area, rename *Schema 1* to **Zones**.

6. In the *Scheme Definition* area, in the *Title* field, type **Zones Legend**.

7. Click **OK**. The color scheme is applied to the view. The display will be similar to that shown in Figure C–21 (your zone colors may vary).

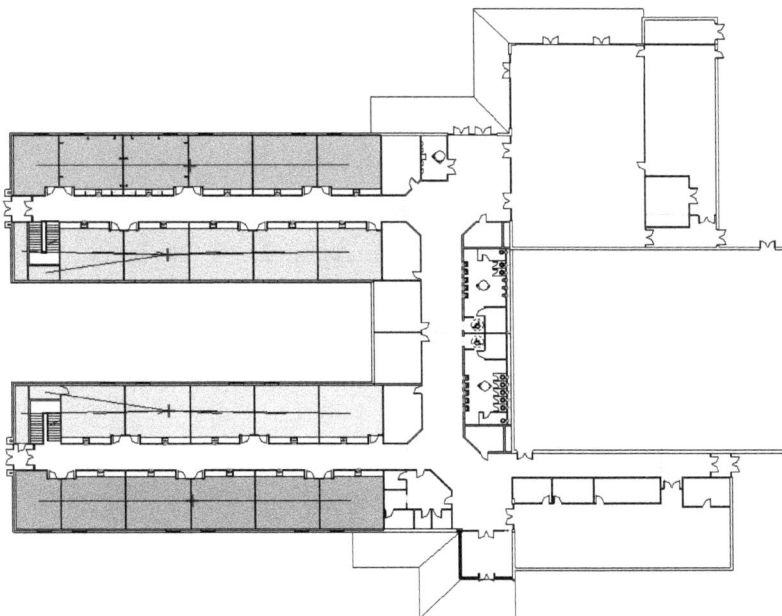

Figure C–21

- Open the *Visibility/Graphic Overrides* dialog box, expand **HVAC Zones**, and clear **Reference**.

   *Note: Refer to **A.4 Defining Color Schemes** in **Appendix A Additional Tools for Design Development** for more information on color schemes.*

8. In the *Analyze* tab>*Color Fill* panel, click ▦ (Color Fill Legend) and place the legend near the classrooms, as shown in Figure C–22.

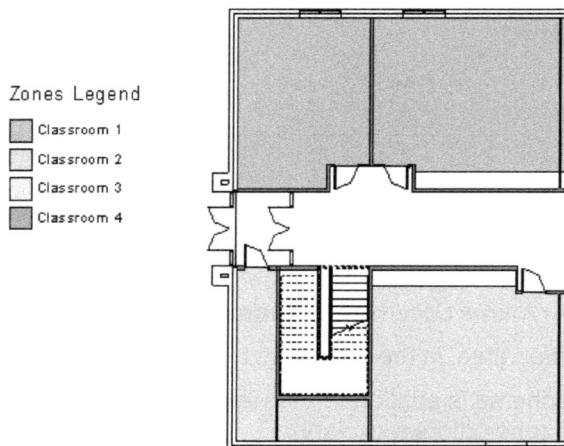

Figure C–22

9. Save the project.

Task 4: Add additional zones.

1. If time permits, add the zones listed below and shown in Figure C–23.

    *   (1) The classroom zones (created in previous steps)
    *   (2) All of the corridors plus the Electrical Room
    *   (3) All of the vestibules
    *   (4) Nurse's Office, Bookroom, Special Ed rooms, and Workroom
    *   (5) Reception, Offices, and Copy Room
    *   (6) Library and associated rooms
    *   (7) Gym
    *   (8) Cafeteria
    *   (9) Kitchen and Kitchen Storage
    *   (10) Restrooms
    *   (11) Housekeeping, Janitor, and associated chases

Note: This figure uses different shades for clarity.

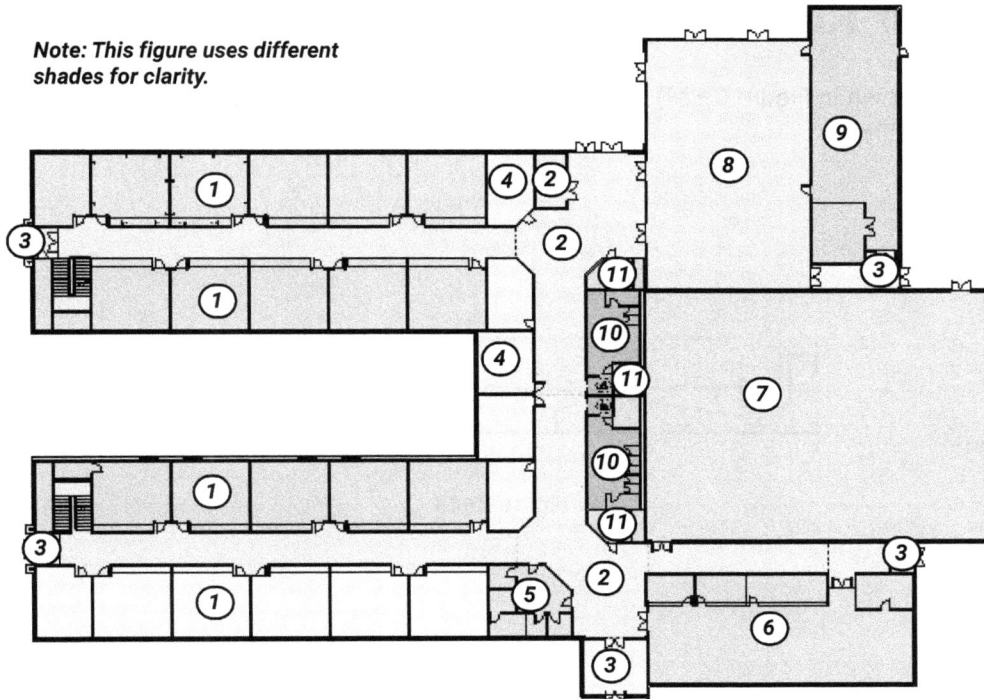

Figure C–23

2. Save and close the project.

End of practice

Chapter Review Questions

1. Zones (shown in Figure C–24) are formed of spaces that can be heated and cooled in the same manner.

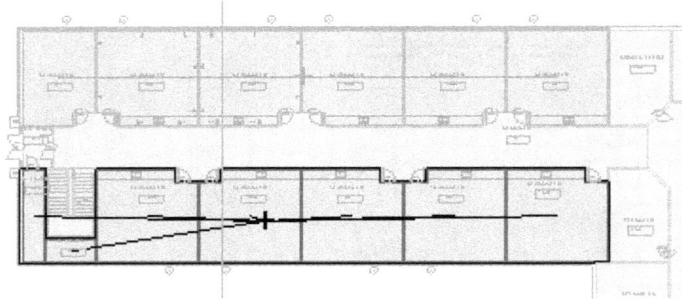

Figure C–24

   a. True

   b. False

2. In the System Browser, in the Zones view, 🏠 displays next to the name of the space. What does it indicate?

   a. The space occupancy has not been defined.

   b. The space does not have an upper boundary.

   c. The space has not been placed.

   d. The space is not part of a zone.

3. You want to modify a view so that colors for the various zones display as shown in Figure C–25. How do you apply the colors to the view?

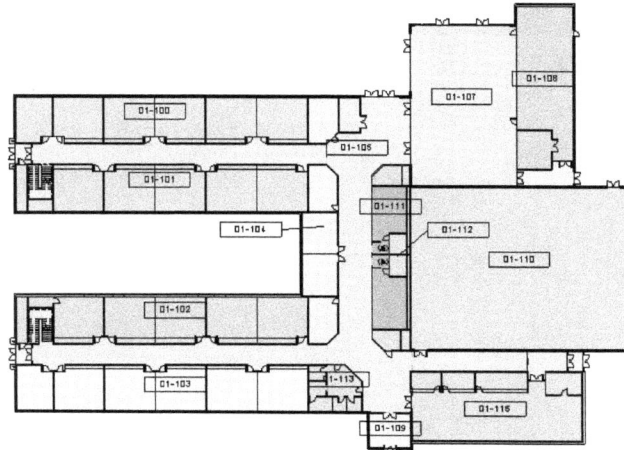

Figure C–25

a. Modify the color scheme in the *Visibility/Graphic Overrides* dialog box.

b. Assign a color scheme in Properties.

c. Toggle on **Color Schemes** in the View Control Bar.

d. Add a Color Fill Legend.

Command Summary

Button	Command	Location
	Color Fill Legend	• **Ribbon:** *Analyze* tab>*Color Fill* panel
	Zone	• **Ribbon:** *Analyze* tab>*Spaces & Zones* panel

Index
